Lecture Notes
in Business Information Processing   83

Series Editors

Wil van der Aalst
  Eindhoven Technical University, The Netherlands
John Mylopoulos
  University of Trento, Italy
Michael Rosemann
  Queensland University of Technology, Brisbane, Qld, Australia
Michael J. Shaw
  University of Illinois, Urbana-Champaign, IL, USA
Clemens Szyperski
  Microsoft Research, Redmond, WA, USA

Camille Salinesi
Oscar Pastor (Eds.)

Advanced Information Systems Engineering Workshops

CAiSE 2011 International Workshops
London, UK, June 20-24, 2011
Proceedings

 Springer

Volume Editors

Camille Salinesi
Université Paris 1 Panthéon - Sorbonne
75013 Paris, France
E-mail: camille.salinesi@univ-paris1.fr

Oscar Pastor
Universidad Politécnica de Valencia
46022 Valencia, Spain
E-mail: opastor@dsic.upv.es

ISSN 1865-1348 e-ISSN 1865-1356
ISBN 978-3-642-22055-5 e-ISBN 978-3-642-22056-2
DOI 10.1007/978-3-642-22056-2
Springer Heidelberg Dordrecht London New York

Library of Congress Control Number: 2011929928

ACM Computing Classification (1998): H.4, H.3.5, D.2, J.1, I.2

© Springer-Verlag Berlin Heidelberg 2011
This work is subject to copyright. All rights are reserved, whether the whole or part of the material is concerned, specifically the rights of translation, reprinting, re-use of illustrations, recitation, broadcasting, reproduction on microfilms or in any other way, and storage in data banks. Duplication of this publication or parts thereof is permitted only under the provisions of the German Copyright Law of September 9, 1965, in its current version, and permission for use must always be obtained from Springer. Violations are liable to prosecution under the German Copyright Law.
The use of general descriptive names, registered names, trademarks, etc. in this publication does not imply, even in the absence of a specific statement, that such names are exempt from the relevant protective laws and regulations and therefore free for general use.

Typesetting: Camera-ready by author, data conversion by Scientific Publishing Services, Chennai, India

Printed on acid-free paper

Springer is part of Springer Science+Business Media (www.springer.com)

Foreword

Information systems are worth billions! Our job, as scientists, academics, and engineers in this domain, is to help organizations understand how to make profits with information systems. In fact, there is more than money at stake. Social bounds, culture, rights, trust: there are diverse aspects of our daily life that can benefit from information systems. It is just a matter of innovation.

Innovation means invention and science. Both emerge from laboratories, but there is a time for communicating too. The series of workshops associated with the International Conference on Advanced Information Systems Engineering acts as a forum of discussion between all stakeholders in the domain of information systems engineering. It is the place where ground-breaking ideas about new methods, techniques and tools, or return on experience, can be shared between experts. Many of the mature research works published at the CAiSE conference were presented in CAiSE workshops when they were in their seminal phase.

This year, CAiSE had 2 associated working conferences and 10 workshops. Many more workshops were initially submitted, but we had to make choices, such as merging proposals or rejecting less mature proposals to comply with our usual quality and consistency standards. The themes of the 10 workshops this year are the following (in alphabetical order):

- BUSinness/IT ALignment and Interoperability (BUSITAL)
- Conceptualization of Modelling Methods (CMM)
- Domain Specific Engineering (DsE@CAiSE)
- Governance, Risk and Compliance: Applications in Information Systems (GRCIS)
- Information Systems Security Engineering (WISSE)
- Integration of IS Engineering Tools (INISET)
- Ontology-Driven Information Systems Engineering Workshop (ODISE)
- Ontology, Models, Conceptualization and Epistemology in Social, Artificial and Natural Systems Workshop (ONTOSE)
- Semantic Search (SSW)
- System/Software Architectures (IWSSA)

The variety of themes and quality publications at the workshops show that information systems engineering is a healthy research domain.

We, the CAiSE 2011 Workshops Chairs, would like to thank all the workshop organizers and all the referees and members of workshop Program Committees for their hard work in arranging the workshops and ensuring their high scientific quality.

We hope that you will enjoy the papers, and that this will encourage you to attend the CAiSE workshops and submit papers, or even organize workshops at CAiSE in forthcoming years.

May 2011

Oscar Pastor
Camille Salinesi

Table of Contents

6th International Workshop on BUSinness/IT ALignment and Interoperability (BUSITAL 2011)

Preface BUSITAL 2011 1
    Birger Andersson, Irina Rychkova, and Gianluigi Viscusi

Business IT Alignment from Business Model to Enterprise
Architecture 4
    Boris Fritscher and Yves Pigneur

Modeling Competition-Driven Business Strategy for Business IT
Alignment 16
    Constantinos Giannoulis, Michaël Petit, and Jelena Zdravkovic

The Quest for Know-How, Know-Why, Know-What and Know-Who:
Using KAOS for Enterprise Modelling 29
    Maxime Bernaert and Geert Poels

Value-Oriented Coordination Process Model Engineering 41
    Hassan Fatemi, Marten van Sinderen, and Roel Wieringa

The Business Behavior Model: A Revised Version 45
    Noelia Palomares and Birger Andersson

The Man Behind the Curtain. Exploring the Role of IS Strategic
Consultant 57
    Riccardo Bonazzi, Charlotte Ceccaroli, and Stéphanie Missonier

Enterprise Interoperability Maturity: A Model Using Fuzzy Metrics 69
    Wided Guédria, Yannick Naudet, and David Chen

Service Value Networks for Competency-Driven Educational Services:
A Case Study 81
    *Iván S. Razo-Zapata, Pieter De Leenheer, Jaap Gordijn, and
    Hans Akkermans*

Business/IT Alignment in Practice: Lessons Learned from a
Requirements Project at P & G 93
    *Gil Regev, Julien Favre, Erich Hayek, Paul Wilson, and
    Alain Wegmann*

First International Workshop on Conceptualization of ModellingMethods (CMM 2011)

Preface CMM 2011 102
  Dimitris Karagiannis and Xavier Franch

A Modelling Method for Consistent Physical Devices Management:
An ADOxx Case Study 104
  Srdjan Zivkovic, Krzysztof Miksa, and Harald Kühn

EIPW: A Knowledge-Based Database Modeling Tool 119
  Ornsiri Thonggoom, Il-Yeol Song, and Yuan An

On the Conceptualization of a Modeling Language for Semantic Model
Annotations 134
  Hans-Georg Fill

Modeling and Analyzing Non-Functional Properties to Support
Software Integration 149
  Henning Agt, Gregor Bauhoff, Ralf-D. Kutsche, and Nikola Milanovic

First International Workshop on Domain Specific Engineering (DsE@CAiSE 2011)

Preface DsE@CAiSE 2011 164
  Iris Reinhartz-Berger, Arnon Sturm, Yair Wand, Jorn Bettin, Tony Clark, and Sholom Cohen

Domain Specific Languages and Standardization: Friends or Foes? –
Invited Talk for DsE@CAiSE2011 166
  Øystein Haugen

Ontology Engineering Based on Domain Specific Languages and the
Application of Ontology Design Patterns 167
  Thomas Janke

A Domain Specific Metamodel for Semantic Web Enabled Multi-Agent
Systems 177
  Moharram Challenger, Sinem Getir, Sebla Demirkol, and Geylani Kardas

Reconstructing the Blade Technology Domain with Grounded
Theory 187
  André Zwanziger

Specification and Refinement of Domain-Specific ECA Policies 197
  Raphael Romeikat and Bernhard Bauer

4th International Workshop on Governance, Risk and Compliance: Applications in Information Systems (GRCIS 2011)

Preface GRCIS 2011 207
  Marta Indulska, Michael zur Muehlen, Shazia Sadiq, and Sietse Overbeek

Patterns for Understanding Control Requirements for Information Systems for Governance, Risk Management, and Compliance (GRC IS) 208
  Manuel Wiesche, Carolin Berwing, Michael Schermann, and Helmut Krcmar

Exploring Features of a Full-Coverage Integrated Solution for Business Process Compliance 218
  Cristina Cabanillas, Manuel Resinas, and Antonio Ruiz-Cortés

A Systematic Review of Compliance Measurement Based on Goals and Indicators 228
  Azalia Shamsaei, Daniel Amyot, and Alireza Pourshahid

Continuous Control Monitoring-Based Regulation: A Case in the Meat Processing Industry 238
  Joris Hulstijn, Rob Christiaanse, Nitesh Bharosa, Friso Schmid, Remco van Wijk, Marijn Janssen, and Yao-Hua Tan

Semantic Representation of Process and Service Compliance – A Case Study in Emergency Planning 249
  Aygul Gabdulkhakova, Birgitta König-Ries, and Norris Syed Abdullah

A Framework for Organizational Compliance Management Tactics 259
  Ralph Foorthuis and Rik Bos

First Workshop on Integration of IS Engineering Tools (INISET 2011)

Preface INISET 2011 269

Tool Integration beyond Wasserman 270
  Fredrik Asplund, Matthias Biehl, Jad El-Khoury, and Martin Törngren

Integrating Computer Log Files for Process Mining: A Genetic Algorithm Inspired Technique 282
  Jan Claes and Geert Poels

9th International Workshop on System/Software Architectures (IWSSA 2011)

Preface IWSSA 2011 294
    Lawrence Chung and Nary Subramanian

Ontology-Based Architectural Knowledge Representation: Structural
Elements Module 296
    David Ameller and Xavier Franch

The Overall Value of Architecture Review in a Large Scale Software
Organization 302
    Sofia Sherman, Irit Hadar, Ethan Hadar, and John J. Harrison Jr

Evaluating Complexity of Information System Architecture Using
Fractals... 308
    Nary Subramanian

Towards a Reconfigurable Middleware Architecture for Pervasive
Computing Systems 318
    Gustavo G. Pascual, Lidia Fuentes, and Mónica Pinto

A Reference Architecture for Building Semantic-Web Mediators 330
    *Carlos R. Rivero, Inma Hernández, David Ruiz, and
    Rafael Corchuelo*

F-STREAM: A Flexible Process for Deriving Architectures from
Requirements Models... 342
    *Jaelson Castro, João Pimentel, Márcia Lucena,
    Emanuel Santos, and Diego Dermeval*

Architecting Climate Change Data Infrastructure for Nevada 354
    *Michael J. McMahon Jr., Sergiu M. Dascalu,
    Frederick C. Harris Jr., Scotty Strachan, and Franco Biondi*

A Coordination Space Architecture for Service Collaboration and
Cooperation... 366
    *Claus Pahl, Veronica Gacitua-Decar, MingXue Wang, and
    Kosala Yapa Bandara*

A Framework to Support the Development of Collaborative
Components.. 378
    Hien Le and Surya Bahadur Kathayat

Resource Allocation, Trading and Adaptation in Self-managing
Systems 385
    Guglielmo Lulli, Pasqualina Potena, and Claudia Raibulet

Third International Workshop on Ontology-Driven Information Systems Engineering Workshop (ODISE 2011)

Preface ODISE 2011 397
Sergio de Cesare, Frederik Gailly, Grant Holland, Mark Lycett, and Chris Partridge

Ontology Mining versus Ontology Speculation 401
Chris Partridge

Design Patterns and Inductive Modeling Rules to Support the Construction of Ontologically Well-Founded Conceptual Models in OntoUML... 402
Giancarlo Guizzardi, Alex Pinheiro das Graças, and Renata S.S. Guizzardi

Semantic-Based Case Retrieval of Service Integration Models in Extensible Enterprise Systems Based on a Business Domain Ontology 414
Matthias Allgaier, Markus Heller, Sven Overhage, and Klaus Turowski

Sapphire: Generating Java Runtime Artefacts from OWL Ontologies ... 425
Graeme Stevenson and Simon Dobson

Mooop – A Hybrid Integration of OWL and Java 437
Christoph Frenzel, Bijan Parsia, Ulrike Sattler, and Bernhard Bauer

5th Ontology, Models, Conceptualization and Epistemology in Social, Artificial and Natural Systems Workshop (ONTOSE 2011)

Preface ONTOSE 2011 448

Improving the Effectiveness of Multimedia Summarization of Judicial Debates through Ontological Query Expansion........................ 450
E. Fersini and F. Sartori

Ontology-Based Composition and Matching for Dynamic Service Coordination 464
Claus Pahl, Veronica Gacitua-Decar, MingXue Wang, and Kosala Yapa Bandara

Detecting Antipatterns Using a Web-Based Collaborative Antipattern Ontology Knowledge Base.. 478
Dimitrios Settas, Georgios Meditskos, Nick Bassiliades, and Ioannis G. Stamelos

POWER - Politics Ontology for Web Entity Retrieval 489
  Silvio Moreira, David Batista, Paula Carvalho,
  Francisco M. Couto, and Mário J. Silva

An Error Correction Methodology for Time Dependent Ontologies 501
  Brett Drury, J.J. Almeida, and M.H.M. Morais

An Ontology-Based Integrated Approach to Situation Awareness for
High-Level Information Fusion in C4ISR 513
  María-Cruz Valiente, Rebeca Machín,
  Elena García-Barriocanal, and Miguel-Ángel Sicilia

Socio-technic Dependency and Rationale Models for the Enterprise
Architecture Management Function 528
  Sabine Buckl, Florian Matthes, and Christian M. Schweda

First International Workshop on Semantic Search (SSW 2011)

Preface SSW 2011 541
  Paolo Cappellari, Roberto De Virgilio, and Mark Roantree

Enhancing the Interface for Ontology-Supported Homonym Search 544
  Tian Tian, James Geller, and Soon Ae Chun

Combining Faceted Search and Query Languages for the Semantic
Web.. 554
  Sébastien Ferré, Alice Hermann, and Mireille Ducassé

Towards a Collaborative Framework for Image Annotation and
Search 564
  Yi Hong and Stephan Reiff-Marganiec

Semantic Reasoning with SPARQL in Heterogeneous Multi-context
Systems 575
  Peter Schüller and Antonius Weinzierl

Semantic Ontology-Based Strategy for Image Retrieval in Conceptual
Modelling 586
  Simon McGinnes

First International Workshop on Information Systems Security Engineering (WISSE 2011)

Preface WISSE 2011 590
  Nadira Lammari and David G. Rosado

Taking into Account Functional Models in the Validation of IS Security
Policies 592
    Yves Ledru, Akram Idani, Jérémy Milhau, Nafees Qamar,
    Régine Laleau, Jean-Luc Richier, and Mohamed-Amine Labiadh

Expressing Access Control Policies with an Event-Based Approach 607
    Pierre Konopacki, Marc Frappier, and Régine Laleau

An Extended Ontology for Security Requirements 622
    Fabio Massacci, John Mylopoulos, Federica Paci,
    Thein Thun Tun, and Yijun Yu

A Pattern Based Approach for Secure Database Design 637
    Jenny Abramov, Arnon Sturm, and Peretz Shoval

Analysis of Application of Security Patterns to Build Secure Systems ... 652
    Roberto Ortiz, Javier Garzás, and Eduardo Fernández-Medina

Modeling Support for Delegating Roles, Tasks, and Duties in a
Process-Related RBAC Context 660
    Sigrid Schefer and Mark Strembeck

Author Index 669

Preface BUSITAL 2011

1 Scope and Context

Continuous growth of Information and Communication Technologies (ICT) provide organizations with new efficient mechanisms for a sustainable competitive advantage and ICT-enabled innovations. Information systems have to support these evolutionary challenges while preserving the alignment between business strategies, business processes, and application portfolios. As taxonomy for strategic alignment, based on [1,2], we identify the following types of alignment essential for organization sustainability:

- Business strategy vs. IT Strategy;
- Business infrastructure and processes vs. IT infrastructure and processes;
- Business strategy vs. Business infrastructure and processes;
- IT Strategy vs. IT infrastructure and processes;
- Cross type alignment.

Multiple approaches to establish and validate alignment are discussed in the business and academic publications: the prevailing ones are top-down, they start from the business requirements of an organization and tend to define ideal business processes and the supporting application portfolio that would fully satisfy these requirements. Whereas, many practitioners acknowledge the need of alternative bottom-up or hybrid approaches for alignment, which would take into account the constraints related to the business processes and the ICT infrastructure on-place, by proposing realistic (budget-wise) solutions.

Nowadays, quite a few of the existing models of strategic alignment come from the management of Information systems (IS) research area. They help to study and model phenomena related to alignment (for example, the impact of alignment on the organizations performance), allowing for the elaboration of predictive models of the influence of alignment and misalignment. Whereas, these types of models do not provide the systemic view which is needed in IS engineering to support requirement analyses and elicitation. Enabling the exchange and the loosely integration of results and perspectives from both the IS and the engineering communities is a challenge but the results could be fruitful for both an academic and practitioner audience.

The objective of the 6th International Workshop on Business/IT-Alignment and Interoperability (BUSITAL 2011) is to build a repository of organizational alignment methodologies and approaches. The prospective contribution is a structured body of knowledge on the existing academic and industrial approaches to business-IT alignment that would help (a) the practitioners to better estimate their needs and, based on these needs, to select their own approach; (b) the researchers to get a better understanding of the problems encountered by practitioners and to improve their methodologies and approaches accordingly.

2 The BUSITAL 2011 Contributions

The above classification of alignment approaches and challenges related to them illustrates the overall context of the 6th International Workshop on Business/IT-Alignment and Interoperability (BUSITAL 2011). Furthermore, BUSITAL 2011 called explicitly for papers on the following topics:

- Methodologies, frameworks, and tools for modeling, validation, and support of Business/IT alignment;
- Qualitative and quantitative approaches for measuring Business/IT alignment;
- Taxonomies for Business/IT alignment classification;
- Business/IT alignment maturity models;
- Constraints and issues associated with Business/IT alignment (e.g. cultural, technical, economical, legal, political, etc.);
- Business/IT alignment in organizational networks, including private and public sector;
- Case studies, empirical reports, and industrial surveys illustrating success factors, challenges and failures of alignment.

Eighteen high quality submissions were received. From those nine papers – eight full papers and one short paper – were selected for presentation. All papers were reviewed by three reviewers.

3 Current and Future Trends

Until recently, the technical aspects of Business/IT alignment represented the main interest for the community. This BUSITAL edition focuses on managerial perspective of the problem and highlights the high importance of organizational aspect in business/IT-alignment.

As mentioned, the predominant view in the business/IT-alignment context is that IT should be aligned with business. Whenever the strategic concerns of the business change IT should change with it. In a recent talk at Stockholm University [3] Jerry Luftman also emphasized the importance of alignment in the other direction - to understand what IT resources and capabilities the business can utilize in order to change its strategies. Although not a new concept, alignment in this direction can be viewed as an important topic for future research. The general research question to be answered is *"what drives what?"*, and how can this be described.

Another direction for future research concerns the concept of *convergence*, a concept that is related to alignment as outlined above, but seems to be more general. In an analysis of literature, [4] notes that alignment is but an aspect of convergence and, hence, raises the question whether other aspects should be included in business/IT-alignment research as well. In the information systems field his analysis shown how the concept of convergence has been developed through different perspectives or views, such as e.g. convergence as alignment, convergence as correspondence, convergence as recombination, convergence as optimization, and convergence as interoperability. Furthermore [4] points out the multidisciplinary of the research topic, ranging from Computer Science, to Management of information systems and New media, where terms are often overlap with technological change and digitalization.

We, the workshop chairs, would like to thank all members of the program committee for their work on the reviews. We also thank the authors that submitted their research reports to BUSITAL 2011.

Birger Andersson, Irina Rychkova, and Gianluigi Viscusi

BUSITAL'11 Program Committee

E. Dubois	Public Research Centre Henri Tudor, Luxembourg
J. Gordijn	Vrije Universiteit, The Netherlands
K. Lyytinen	Case Western Reserve University, USA
M. Petit	University of Namur, Belgium
P. Johannesson	KTH Stockholm, Sweden
S. Nurcan	Université Paris 1 – Panthéon – Sorbonne
Y. Pigneur	University of Lausanne, Switzerland
R.J. Wieringa	University of Twente, Enschede, The Netherlands
H. Weigand	Tilburg University, The Netherlands
A. Wegmann	EPFL, Switzerland
J. vom Brocke	University of Liechtenstein, Lichtenstein
A. M. Braccini	CeRSI, LUISS Guido Carli University, Italy
A. Ravarini	Università Carlo Cattaneo – LIUC, Italy
A. L. Opdahl	University of Bergen, Norway
E Yu	University of Toronto, Canada
A Naumenko	Triune Continuum Enterprise, Switzerland
M. Themistocleous	University of Piraeus, Greece
J. Stirna	Stockholm University
J. Zdravkovic	KTH Stockholm
A. Edirisuriya	University of Colombo, Sri Lanka
J. Barjis	University of Delft, The Netherlands
J. Ralyte	University of Geneva, Switzerland
P. van Eck	University of Twente, The Netherlands
Tharaka Ilayperuma	University of Ruhuna, Sri Lanka
John Krogstie	NTNU Trondheim, Norway
Judith Barrios Albornoz	Universidad de Los Andes, Venezuela

References

1. Luftman, J.: Competing in the information age: Strategic alignment in practice. Oxford University Press, New York (1996)
2. Henderson, J., Venkatraman, N.: Strategic alignment: Leveraging information technology for transforming organizations. IBM Systems Journal 32 (1993)
3. Luftman, J.: Presentation held at Stockholm University 2011-03-21 on the topic of 'IT-Business Strategic Alignment Maturity' (2011), http://dash.dsv.su.se/files/2011/03/Luftman-SAM-MATURITY-Stockholm.pdf
4. Herzhoff, J.: The ICT convergence discourse in the information systems literature - a second-order observation. Paper Presented at the 17th European Conference on Information Systems, ECIS 2009 (2009)

Business IT Alignment from Business Model to Enterprise Architecture

Boris Fritscher[1] and Yves Pigneur

University of Lausanne, 1015 Lausanne, Switzerland,
boris.fritscher@unil.ch

Abstract. In this paper, we show how business model modelling can be connected to IT infrastructure, drawing parallels from enterprise architecture models such as ArchiMate. We then show how the proposed visualization based on enterprise architecture, with a strong focus on business model strategy, can help IT alignment, at both the business model and the IT infrastructure level.

Keywords: Business Model, IT Alignment, Enterprise Architecture, ArchiMate.

1 Introduction

Information Technology is becoming more and more ubiquitous, changing the way we exchange information and extending the realm of possibilities. This is true not only for Information Technology itself, but also for all domains interacting with it. Faster computation, increased storage and bandwidth, allow for new services, which in turn enable new business models, lower barrier of entry, more competition, but also possibilities for new innovation. The key, be it for the incumbent or the start-up, is to design and iterate around their business models. Furthermore, new services like cloud computing allow for experimenting with new business models without requiring huge investments in IT infrastructure. Nonetheless, a business model strategy still needs to be aligned with its processes and IT applications supporting them, regardless of the fact that IT infrastructure is virtual or physical.

As explained by Van Burren et al.[7] *'Enterprise architecture and business modeling methodologies meet in service offering and realization. In general, business models focus on the service value generated by a business, whereas enterprise architecture models show how a business realizes these services. Linking these approaches results in a powerful modeling tool that couples the value exchange between businesses and the costs that are required to realize these services'*

Beyond the possibility to link cost, we want to provide a way to identify key activities and key resources supporting the business models, as well as highlight underutilized assets. This in turn helps in recognizing new business model opportunities. The identification of key components can be helped by matching the modelled business model and infrastructure to patterns of known combination of components.

The objective of this paper is to propose a model construct that is similar to an enterprise architecture model, with the addition of a strong business model component, to allow for a better alignment of the value proposition with the IT infrastructure, which is require to realize this value.

2 Frameworks

In this section, we describe the different framework and models which individually address a part of the solution, before combining them into one model in the next section. The considered models are Enterprise Architecture frameworks, Business Models, as well as different classifications concerning IT Services.

2.1 Enterprise Architecture

Enterprise architecture describes components of an enterprise across domains and helps in communicating how they interact with each other. There are different frameworks supporting enterprise architecture such as The Zachman Framework[11], The Open Group Architecture Framework[8] and ArchiMate [3]. The later separates the domains into three layers: Business, Application, and Technology. Each layer has sub-layers splitting the internal representation from the external, by exposing its services as interfaces to the upper layer. The top most business layer exposes the enterprise services to an additional layer containing external roles and actors.

As can be seen in figure 1, what makes ArchiMate particularly attractive, is its focus on having a visual representation, and the fact that it encourages the use of visual cues such as colours to highlight the different modelling layers[4]. Moreover, ArchiMate also opts for one unique language (UML) to model every layer of the architecture, this eases the communication when teams responsible for the different layers need to collaborate.

Even thought, ArchiMate does go above the business processes layer and exposes external business services, there are still some limitations in order to be able to do a strategic analysis of the business model with only this framework. Furthermore, it is relevant to note that ArchiMate is infrastructure focused and has a bottom up construction. One model which can complement this lack in business model strategy is the Business Model Ontology presented in the next section.

2.2 Business Model Ontology

The Business Model Ontology is a representation of an enterprise's business model through nine building blocks. These elements were derived from an indepth literature review of a large number of previous conceptualizations of business models [5]. In this depiction, the business model of a company is a simplified

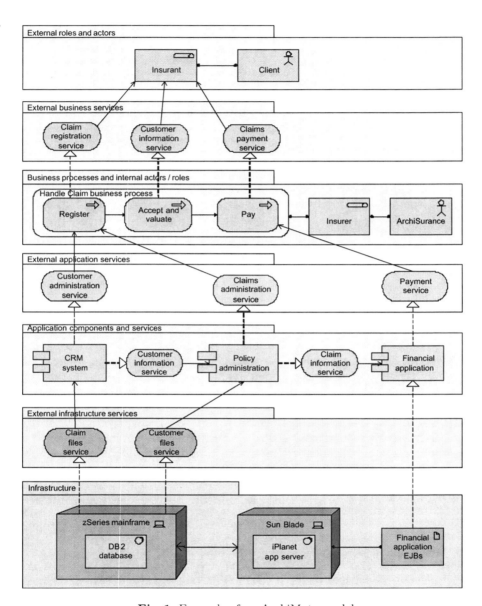

Fig. 1. Example of an ArchiMate model

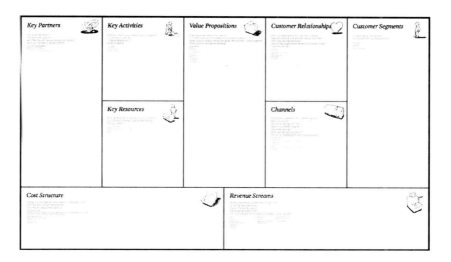

Fig. 2. Business Model Canvas

representation of its business logic viewed from a strategic standpoint (i.e. on top of Business Process Modeling), which can be seen in figure 2[1].

At the center there is the *Value Proposition*, it describes which customer's problems are solved and why the offer is more valuable than similar products from competitors (product, service). The customer themselves are analyzed in *Customer Segment*, separated into groups to help in identifying their needs, desires and ambitions (singles, families). *Distribution Channel* illustrates how the customer wants to be reached and by whom he is addressed (Internet, store).

In addition, *Customer Relationships* specifies what type of relationship the customer expects and how it is establish and maintained with him (promotion, support, individual or mass). To be able to deliverer the value proposition the business has to have *Resources* (staff, machines, secret knowledge). And transform theses resources through *Key Activities* into the final product or service (development, production, secret process). Most of the time a business depends also, either for resources or for activities, on an external *Partner Network* (logistics, financial), which can provide better quality or a lower price on non essential components. As any business model would not be complete without financial information the last two building blocks focus on cost and revenue: The *Cost Structure* which should be aligned to the core ideas of the business model (key resources, key activities) and *Revenue Streams* which mirrors the value the customers are willing to pay and how they will perform the transaction (one time fee, subscription).

---

[1] http://businessmodelgeneration.com/downloads/business_model_canvas_poster.pdf

2.3 IT Services

Approaching IT Services from a more managerial top down view, Weill et al.[9] [10] have defined two useful classifications.

First from a management perspective they defined four objectives for an IT application portfolio: Infrastructure, Transactional, Informational and Strategic.

Second, in order to better describe and compare IT resources, Weill and Vitale[10] provide a classification of IT capabilities: Application Infrastructure, Communication, Data Management, IT Management, Security, Architecture & Standards, Channel Management, IT Research & Development, IT Education. This list is based on a comprehensive survey they did and each item has a set of sub-items helping in assessing the importance of the capability. The next section describes how theses models can be put together as a business visualization of an enterprise architecture.

3 A Business Visualization of an Enterprise Architecture

3.1 Correspondence between Models

A comparison of the elements of models and framework described in the previous section can be seen in figure 3. The main objective is to have a visualization with a similar structure as the enterprise architecture framework ArchiMate, but to provide additional business model considerations. The matching of elements has been done at a high level using the general definition given to them in each theory.

3.2 Correspondence between BMO and ArchiMate

In ArchiMate the top most layers' concern is with external actors, which in the case of the BMO, are its customers segments and partners. ArchiMate does not have a distinct layer for financial considerations like cost and revenue. Evidently, since BMO describes business models, most of its elements can be compared to ArchiMate's business layer. The activity element can be consider to be similar to the external application services which the application layer exposes to the business layer, but does certainly not go into detail on how the activities are produced. Some of key resources of ArchiMate's Technical layer might emerge in BMO's resource element, but in general it is too high level to really identify technical components.

BMO's buildings blocks can also be grouped in three more general perspectives: a *financial perspective* including cost and revenue, which cannot be found in ArchiMate; a *customer perspective* including value proposition, channels, relationship and customers, which can be compared to the higher sub-layers of ArchiMate's business layer; and an *activity perspective* including partners, resources and activities, which are close to the business process layer.

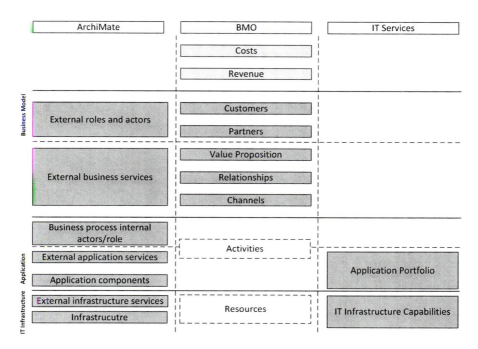

Fig. 3. Correspondence between ArchiMate's and models' elements

To complement the weak matching of BMO's activities and resources with the application and IT infrastructure layers, we propose to include the IT Services model in our construction.

3.3 IT Services

Instead of associating IT application directly to activities it is better to classify them by process type they support. One such classification is done in the internal perspective of Strategy Map[1][2]. Strategy Map is an evolution of the balanced scorecard from Kaplan-Norton, and provides an alternate, but very similar view to BMO's description of a business model. The four processes are Operations Management, Customer Management, Innovation and Regulatory & Social. This classification should fill the gap where BMO's activities not fully match ArchiMate's business processes.

In addition, to better classify the IT infrastructure, instead of addressing it as common resources of the BMO, a more detailed classification can be used as presented in the IT Services framework.

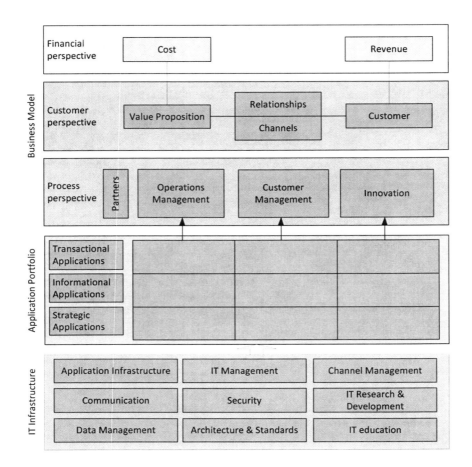

Fig. 4. Business visualization of an enterprise architecture inspired by [2][3][5][10]

3.4 Visualization of the Connected Models

Based on the described correspondence, figure 4 shows the proposed visualization integrating all the mentioned components. To further help connecting the components the IT services classification will be grouped into an application portfolio at the application level.

At the bottom, for the technology layer, the IT infrastructure is decomposed into the nine IT capabilities identified by Weill et al.[10]. Combination of these services enable different applications.

On the application layer, these applications make up the enterprise 'application portfolio. These can be organized into a three by three matrix: the rows of the portfolio distinguish transactional, informational and strategic applications;

the columns are given by the processes the application support in the business layer

The business layer has three sub layers: the process perspective which directly interfaces with the application layer, the customer perspective and the financial perspective, which represent the strategic business model.

The process perspective categorizes the process into three types: operations management, customer management and innovation.

In turn, these processes support different high level functions in the customer perspective layer.

The customer perspective can be detailed with the customer facing building block of BMO like Customer segments, through which channels they are reach and how the customer relationship is for each value proposition. In addition to the internal activities and resource which are described by the application and technical layers, there is also the need to identify partners involved in the realisation of some value propositions. The partners not being a customer, but deeply involved in the creation process of the value proposition, they are placed in the process perspective.

Finally, the financial layer takes into account the cost and revenue of the business model by basing itself on the functions used for each value proposition, which get their costs from the process they involve, which in turn can base their costs on the applications they involve, which themselves are based on IT services.

4 Instantiation Case: Switcher SA

The proposed visualization has been applied to illustrate the Business Model and Enterprise Architecture of a company called Switcher SA, which can be seen in figure 5. Switcher SA is a small private company engaged in the manufacture and distribution of garments with a particular focus on social responsibility throughout the whole value chain, from resource production to distribution of its products.

The way the diagram is structured, it is possible to see how the value proposition of responsibility produced garment (Ethics, Traceability) is delivered through the availability of tracing each step of the product. The traceability is made possible only by an innovative traceability management process, which heavily depends on a custom ERP application (Kookaburra), at the application portfolio level. To offer this application, at the IT Infrastructure level, there is a need for a custom ERP, which has to be developed in-house (IT research & development). Additionally, the channel which allows the customers to to consult tracking information, is made possible by a special website (respectcode.org).

Since the proposed visualization is inspired by ArchiMate's structure, it can be compared to it (figure 6). This allows for an even better alignment of the business components and the IT infrastructure exposed by ArchiMate.

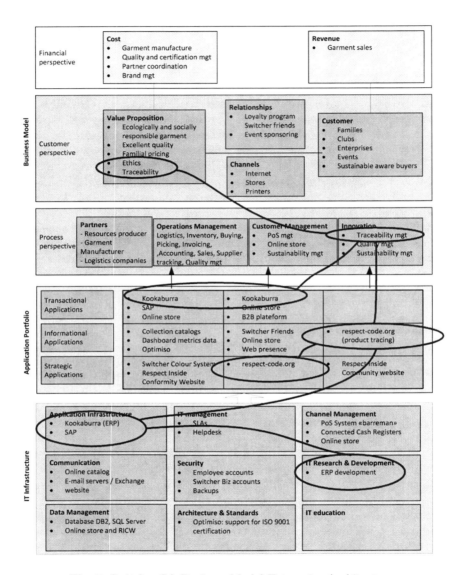

Fig. 5. Switcher SA Business Model Enterprise Architecture

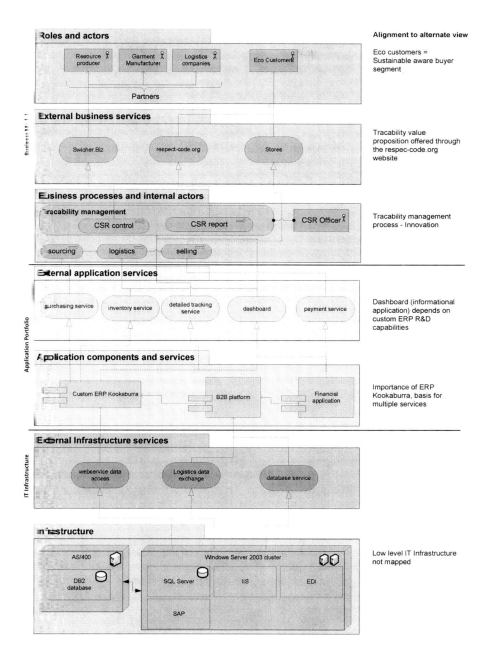

Fig. 6. Switcher SA ArchiMate for Tracability

5 Discussion and Future Works

Comparing IT services and Business model and seeing how they are connected, helps in aligning them and highlighting the interactions they have. This opens the road to enable cost assignment to each offered value proposition. And also, it could allow prioritizing the importance of the assets to allow for strategic outsourcing of none core services, or providing new value propositions involving underutilized services.

The proposed visualization provides a more business oriented view on enterprise architecture and has a model for each level: business, application, and infrastructure. This provides alignment between the strategic business vision and the strategic information system considerations. In addition, since the construction is based on the structure of ArchiMate, which aligns the three layers, there is also the possibility to align the strategic with the operational. This enables not only the possibility to have both a top-down and a bottom-up view of the enterprise architecture, but also a business focused and an IT focused view, thereby helping the alignment of business strategy and technical IT infrastructure.

ArchiMate provides a more IT centric view with technical details that have to be abstracted in order to transform it into business visualization. And the business visualization elements have to be extended with additional information in order to build an ArchiMate model from it. Therefore one business visualization might result in the possibility of creating multiple variants of the corresponding ArchiMate model.

Further use cases have to be tested to see how the method can help in identifying misalignments, as well as a more systematic way to transition between both models.

5.1 Applying Patterns

Beyond the possibility to visualize the business model on a one page canvas, the BMO provides the ability to highlight and compare business model patterns[6]. A business model pattern describes some components of a business model and their relationships, in manner they can be applied to similar situation. As with patterns in other fields, this allows to identify missing components once a certain situation is recognized (freemium, double-sided, unbundling, long tail).

In addition, Weill et al. [10] also use the notion of pattern to classify the importance of the IT capabilities they defined for each situation. Therefore, there is the possibility to compare implication of patterns at the IT infrastructure level as well as the strategic business model level to further help with alignment.

For example, Switcher SA is playing the role of a value net integrator, which according to the IT capabilities pattern requires important channel management systems. This is the case for Switcher SA, which has an important investment in Point of Sale system, and does align to the business model strategy of owning stores to reach niche customers interested in responsibly produced garments.

5.2 External Factors

In its current form, the proposed model focuses on the enterprises' internals. With the need for more collaboration and gaining importance of external factors, such as social and regulatory constraints, the model should be augmented with these concerns.

At the business layer, the environment map described for the BMO [6] could help in identifying external influences with its four components: key trends, market forces, industry forces and macro-economic forces. This in turn, as with the internal components, could be aligned to the fourth unused process category of strategy map: regulatory & social processes. Alignment with the lower layers might be more difficult because these concerns seem to impact every component of the schema and cannot be resolved by just adding one more column.

Nonetheless, the proposed model already provides good insights for a large part of internal considerations and should be further tested in use cases and tried in practice.

References

1. Kaplan, R.S., Norton, D.P.: Linking the balanced scorecard to strategy. California Management Review 39(1) (1996)
2. Kaplan, R.S., Norton, D.P.: Strategy maps, vol. 2. Harvard Business School Press, Boston (2004)
3. Lankhorst, M.: Enterprise architecture modelling the issue of integration. Advanced Engineering Informatics 18(4), 205–216 (2004)
4. Lankhorst, M.: Enterprise architecture at work: Modelling, communication and analysis (2005)
5. Osterwalder, A., Pigneur, Y.: An e-business model ontology for modeling e-business. In: 15th Bled Electronic Commerce Conference, Bled, Slovenia, pp. 17–19 (2002)
6. Osterwalder, A., Pigneur, Y.: Business model generation: a handbook for visionaries, game changers, and challengers. Wiley, Hoboken (2010)
7. van Buuren, R., Gordijn, J., Janssen, W.: Business Case Modelling for E-Services. In: Proceedings of BLED 2005, vol. 8 (2005)
8. VHP. TOGAF Version 9 (TOGAF Series). VAN HAREN PUBLISHING, 2009.
9. Weill, P., Broadbent, M.: Leveraging the new infrastructure: how market leaders capitalize on information technology. Harvard Business Press, Boston (1998)
10. Weill, P., Vitale, M.: What IT infrastructure capabilities are needed to implement e-business models, vol. 1(1), pp. 17–34 (2002)
11. Zachman, J.A.: A framework for information systems architecture. IBM Syst. J. 26, 276–292 (1987)

Modeling Competition-Driven Business Strategy for Business IT Alignment

Constantinos Giannoulis[1], Michaël Petit[2], and Jelena Zdravkovic[1]

[1] Department of Computer and Systems Sciences, Stockholm University
Forum 100, SE-164-40 Kista, Sweden
`constantinos, jelenaz@dsv.su.se`
[2] PReCISE Research Center, Computer Science Department, University of Namur
Rue Grandgagnage 21, B-5000 Namur, Belgium
`mpe@info.fundp.ac.be`

Abstract. Business strategy aims at supporting the vision of an enterprise, by paving the way to achieve it through goals that direct the strategy's execution. Aligning business strategy to system requirements requires explicit models from both business strategy and requirements engineering. However, existing business strategy definition approaches are informal and their syntax is based on natural language, therefore, they cannot be used in model-driven alignment. An objective of our research is to define a well-structured business strategy modeling language. In this paper, we propose a business strategy meta-model based on Porter's work on competition driven strategy and its extension by Stabell and Fjeldstad. Our UML meta-model is formalized in Telos and OWL. An initial validation is performed by instantiating the meta-model using a case scenario.

Keywords: business strategy, alignment, meta-modeling, Telos, OWL.

1 Introduction

Enterprises constantly aim at enabling the communication of business strategy, typically by linking decision makers and executives with practitioners and employees, and product and service offers with concrete tasks [1]. Such links are necessary to align people, products and services with long-term visions, and further, to help in ensuring that IT systems are defined and designed in accordance to business strategy, thereby contributing to solve the always-present problem of business-IT alignment [2].

Within the Information Systems modeling community, business intentions and following strategies are typically conceptualized using goal-based modeling approaches, such as in Goal-Oriented Requirements Engineering (GORE) [3]. The capabilities of the those approaches are challenged when capturing and expressing abstract business notions and interrelations such as the ones defined by business strategy. On the other side, the generality of these notions, constitutes a challenge for their representational capabilities at a conceptual level; existing business strategy frameworks provide rich expressiveness but are not formal and precise In [4] we have elicited the gap between business strategy and requirements for system development. Additionally, we argued that a formal conceptualization of business strategy becoming the interface to GORE contributes towards the improvement of business-IT alignment.

In our research, we aim at unifying rigorously business strategy concepts proposed by approaches rooted in Strategic Management (e.g. (Mintzberg's ten schools of thought on strategy [5]), into an ontology. Gradually, we aim to examine noteworthy business strategy definition approaches and create their representations in an ontology to provide a unified business strategy meta-model (UBSMM) with applicability for practice. Our mode of work was inspired by the Unified Enterprise Modeling Language (UEML) approach aiming at a framework for interoperability of enterprise modeling languages by defining a core language for enterprise and IS modeling [6]. In previous work [4,7], we have conceptualized Strategy Maps [8,1] and Balanced Scorecards (BSC) [9] by the means of a meta-model and we have also formalized the ontological base using OWL [10] and Telos [11].

In this study, we extend our modeling efforts towards competition driven strategy approaches, as proposed by the work of Porter named Value Chain [12,13,14], further extended by Stabell and Fjeldstad with the Value Shop and the Value Network configurations [15]. To the best of our knowledge no similar effort exists, including both modeling and formalizing the Value Chain, Shop and Network. Following a similar methodological path as in [7], in this study, we have first conceptualized a meta-model to capture business strategy defined using the aforementioned value configurations. Then we have formalized the meta-model to the ontology level, to improve both its quality (such as unambiguity and model-consistency checking) and usability in the model-driven development context (automatic process-ability). We chose to formalize the strategy meta-model in two complementary ontology languages, Telos [11] and OWL [10], having different expressiveness, tool support and capabilities. To demonstrate the applicability and validity of the modeled value-based business strategy, we have considered a real case scenario, which captures an experience report from the application of the Value Shop at the Norwegian Police [16].

The paper is structured as follows: Section 2 presents Porter's positioning strategy approach extended beyond the Value Chain to include the Value Shop and the Value Network as well as the Norwegian Police case scenario [16] used later to validate our contribution. Section 3 motivates modeling business strategy from an RE perspective and presents our contribution: an extended conceptualization of the value configuration (Porter, Stabell and Fjeldstad), as well as its ontological definition with OWL and Telos. Section 4 illustrates the validation of the meta-model using the Norwegian Police case scenario by prototype implementation using Telos and OWL support tools. Section 5 provides our conclusions and directions for further work.

2 Business Strategy

Strategic planning is the process during which a strategy is defined by analyzing the current status of the enterprise and the competitive environment in which it resides. Within the premises of this generic definition of strategic planning, prevalent approaches defining business strategy include; Miles et al. [17], Desarbo et al [18], Blue Ocean Strategies [19], Strategy Maps [20] & Balanced Scorecards [9] and the Value Chain [12] extended by Stabell and Fjeldstad [15]. In [4,7], as part of our incremental effort, we have conceptualized Strategy Maps & Balanced Scorecards which utilize the three views identified by Barney's grouping of strategic planning approaches [21]: *resource-based view, Schumpeterian view, industrial organization*. In the remaining of this section we present the Value Chain, and its extensions of Stabell and Fjeldstad, which are conceptualized in section 3.

2.1 Porter vs Stabell and Fjeldstad

According to Porter: *"Strategy is the creation of a unique and valuable position involving a different set of activities."* [12,14]. Strategic positioning requires establishing and maintaining six essential principles: *the right goal, a value proposition, a distinctive value chain, trade-offs, fit and continuity* [14]. The value chain [12] (figure 1(a)) reflects how an organization structures its activities to offer the unique value differently from any competitor and highlights a company's strategy and strategy implementation depending on how activities for production are carried out. It consists of value activities and margin. Value activities capture everything an organization does to create value for its buyers, divided into primary and support, while margin is the difference between the total value and the total cost of performing the value activities. Primary activities are the ones involved in a product's creation, sale, and transfer and post-sale assistance. Support activities provide procured inputs, technology, human resources, and general company support across the organization.

Each activity is classified based on its contribution to a firm's competitive advantage, primarily from an economic view; those that have high impact of differentiation and those that have a considerable proportion of cost. Porter identifies ten generic *drivers* for cost and value [12], which shape the competitive position of the firm: scale, capacity utilization, linkages, interrelationships, vertical integration, location, timing, learning, policy decisions and government regulations. Value activities interact with each other within the value chain via *linkages*, which are relationships between the way a value activity is performed and the cost of another (e.g. the dotted lines in figure 1(a)). They support optimization and coordination among value activities, thus competitive advantage. Linkages may exist between multiple value chains (e.g. firm and suppliers). All support activities except from firm infrastructure can directly be linked to specific primary activities as well as support the whole value chain, whereas firm infrastructure cannot but only support the value chain in its totality. According to Porter, success in a competitive environment accompanied with an enterprise's desired

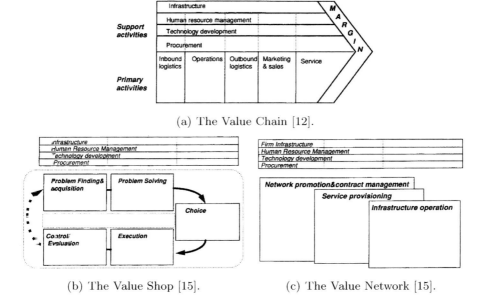

Fig. 1. The Value Configurations (a), (b) and (c)

targeted market segment results into three generic strategies; cost leadership, differentiation and focus [12].

Stabell and Fjeldstad [15] introduced the choice of value configuration to move beyond production and extend the value chain to the value shop, where value is created by using resources and activities to resolve a customer problem as well as to the value network, where value is created by facilitating relationships among a network of enterprises and their customers via a mediating technology. In a value shop the primary value activities include; problem finding and acquisition, problem solving, choice, execution, control and evaluation (figure 1(b)). In a value network the primary value activities include; network promotion and contract management, service provisioning and infrastructure operation (figure 1(c)).

A fundamental difference among the value configurations lies on the value creation logic; the value chain focuses on transforming inputs into outputs, the value shop focuses on resolving customer problems and the value network focuses on linking customers. Additionally, value activities within a value chain are linked sequentially (suppliers, producers, and distributors) by adding value to what the preceding activity has produced, within a value shop value activities are linked spirally interchanging problem-solving and implementation activities, and finally, within a value network value activities are linked simultaneously and in parallel forming horizontally interconnected activities. For the remaining of the paper, we will be referring to the value chain, the value shop and the value network as value configuration.

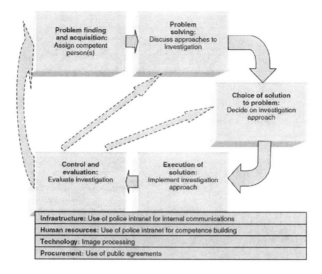

Fig. 2. Police investigation unit as value shop with activity examples [16]

2.2 Case Scenario: A Value Shop for police investigation

Gottschalk and Berg [16] have applied the value configuration of the value shop to evaluate police investigation performance for investigations that use information systems. The case scenario does not capture the strategy of the whole organization, it rather captures the strategic intent of a unit, investigation, where value is created by solving unique problems. Figure 2 illustrates the example of a police investigation unit as a value shop with concrete activities introduced. Solid arrows represent the sequential execution of activities while dotted arrows represent the cyclical execution.

3 Modeling Competition-Driven Business Strategy

This section presents our contribution, a conceptualization of value configurations into a well defined meta-model. The first part motivates how modeling business strategy contributes to business-IT alignment, the second part presents our meta-model, the third part presents the formalization using Telos and OWL.

3.1 Modeling of Business Strategy for Alignment

The increased availability of IT means for facilitating the businesses of enterprises, requires their alignment with business strategy to make them operational and also justify investments on IT[1]. A common approach is to map business

---
[1] This paper addresses business strategy from the scope of Strategic Management independent of business-IT alignment approaches.

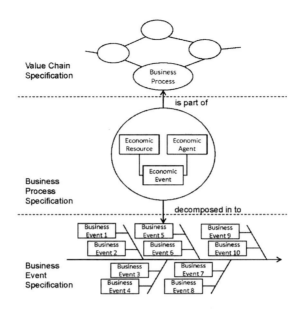

Fig. 3. Value driven alignment [27]

strategy to enterprise models and then further to system requirements. Goal-oriented enterprise models are often used in this context [22,23]. Obtained goal models are then, using GORE, transformed to requirements for systems.

A fundamental notion for value configurations is that a product or a service gains a value as it passes through a stream of business activities of an enterprise. Thereby, it seems reasonable to refine a strategy defined using a value configuration approach, by exploring it using value-centric enterprise models such as business value models. Notable examples of business-value frameworks are FEA [24], BMO [25] and e^3value [26].

In [27], the REA framework has been extended to capture value analysis starting from Porter's value chain (figure 3). At the top, an enterprise value chain is defined as a series of connected business processes, where each process is adding value towards customers and corresponds to value activities. For example in the "Find competent persons" value process shown in figure 3, the inputs will be the people and means responsible for finding the persons competent for investigations, and the output, the commitment of the persons found towards the investigations of interest. Each process in an enterprise value chain is decomposed to the next level (Business Process Specification) by exploring at least two economic events related to the process: a decrement event that consumes the input resource and an increment event that acquires the output resource. "Find competent persons" process includes a "recruit" decrement event and a "contract obtainment" increment event. Once all economic events issuing the exchange of economic resources are elicited, they may be decomposed into workflows of low-level tasks, i.e. business events. These workflows correspond to business processes, which involve the tasks that operationalize consumption and acquisition of resources, such as announcing the positions for investigators, contacting candidates, analyzing obtained applications, and so forth. A value configuration strategy decomposed in the described way typically results in a large number of operational business processes. The models obtained can be further transformed to high-level system requirements, which may facilitate goals of individual process tasks or a group of tasks using IT means.

In [28], the described REA framework is considered as the starting model in an MDA-like approach for designing e-services and further Web services. In [29], the authors elaborate an approach, based on requirements engineering techniques, to design e-services from e^{3}value business models. The approach is model-driven and considers three vertical/successive perspectives in design: value perspective (from the business model), process perspective (primary, management and support business processes are captured) and information systems perspective (Web services, BPEL orchestrations). Since any of these approaches rely on a value analysis using business models, adding the strategy analysis dimension on top of the business modeling is of an important benefit; additionally, having this dimension modeled in a formal and precise way as we propose in this paper, contributes to some of the major principles of model-driven development, as advocated in [30].

3.2 The Value Configuration Meta-model

A meta-model defines the conceptual elements of a language, their possible interrelations and constraints on possible syntactically correct combinations of these elements and relations [31] (also echoed by [32]). We have defined our meta-model through inference from the value chain, value shop and value network found in the studied literature [12,13,14,15]. Our meta-model, formalized in UML, is presented in figure 4. Constraints define the allowed interrelations and imposed restrictions for each construct. Some constraints are represented as cardinalities on relationships and others captured in natural language are presented later in this section. Given the ambiguity of value configurations and textual descriptions, we have considered and analyzed them all, to obtain a precise and complete formalization. Due to space limitations some generalizations are not shown in figure 4. A complete version of the value configuration meta-model including all specializations can be found on the authors' web-page [2].

Classes, relationships and cardinalities: *Strategy* captures the desired strategic positioning of an organization and according to [14] should include a long term goal, the value proposition, which appear as attributes.

Value Configuration captures the value configuration of an organization that supports the strategy and can be either a value chain or a value shop or a value network. It includes a description and a margin.

---

[2] http://www.info.fundp.ac.be/~mpe/BUSITAL2011

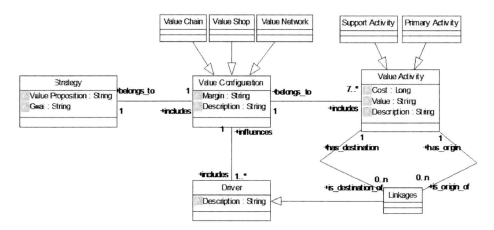

Fig. 4. The Value Configuration Meta-model

Driver captures all parameters influencing cost and value in a value configuration and includes a description as attribute but also 10 specializations (scale, capacity, utilization, linkages, interrelationships, vertical integration, location timing, learning, policy decisions and government regulations). Due to space limitations only *linkages* are shown in figure 4 as they are of significant importance, which represent the links between *Value Activities*.

Value Activity captures the activities that constitute a value configuration of an organization and is specialized into *Primary Activity* and *Support Activity* while it includes cost, value and description as attributes. Support Activity is further specialized into four common classes to all value configurations: infrastructure management, HR management, procurement, technology development. Primary Activity is also further specialized into: (i) Value Chain Primary Activity, further specialized to all value chain primary activities: Inbound Logistics, Operations, Service, Marketing & Sales, Outbound Logistics. (ii) Value Shop Primary Activity, specialized to all value shop primary activities: Problem Solving, Choice, Execution, Problem finding & Acquisition, Control & Evaluation and Value Network Primary Activity. (iii) Value Network Primary Activity, specialized to all value network primary activities: Infrastructure Operation, Service Provisioning, Network Promotion & Contract Management.

Constraints: Specialization hierarchies are modeled as partitions; an instance of a parent class must be an instance of exactly one child class. Value configurations include at least one instance of each type of support activity. Primary activities must be of the appropriate type (e.g. primary activities in a Value Network are all belonging to the class of value network primary activities). A value configuration of a particular type includes at least one primary activity of each relevant type (e.g. a value network includes at least one activity of network promotion, one activity of service provisioning and one of infrastructure operation. Each *SupportActivity* is origin of at least one Linkage. Each *PrimaryActivity* is destination of at least one Linkage whose origin is a *SupportActivity*. A Linkage links two different value activities.

3.3 Formalization

The meta-model presented in the previous section is meant to be input for a unified business strategy meta-model (UBSMM), integrated with our Strategy Map and Balanced Score Card meta-model [7]. Therefore, the meta-model should be as precise and validated as possible. In this direction, we have formalized our meta-model because (i) the process of formalizing the meta-model itself helps to improve its quality because it raises questions that would not otherwise be asked; (ii) formal semantics of the languages used for formalization allow to discover properties of the meta-model (consistency, un-anticipated properties, etc.); (iii) the non-ambiguity of formalisms results in a clear and unambiguous abstract syntax for our UBSMM; (iv) formal languages are often equipped with tools that support the expression and analysis of the meta-model, as well as other operations on meta-models helpful in future steps of our research (particularly in integration); (v) using standard languages for formalization can help both in diffusion and re-usability of our UBSMM.

Considering the aforementioned benefits, we chose to formalize our meta-model in two complementary languages with different expressiveness, tool support and capabilities, Telos and OWL. The complete Telos and OWL models, as well as the relevant code, can be downloaded from the authors' web-page [3].O-Telos, a dialect of Telos, is a classical object-oriented deductive knowledge representation language, particularly suited for meta-modeling, supported by the Conceptbase [33]. We have used the language's expressive and simple syntax to formalize the advanced constraints that apply to our meta-model. We have used Conceptbase to check the consistency of the set of constraints by instantiating the meta-model with particular elements from our case scenario. However, Conceptbase and Telos do not provide elaborate built-in capabilities to reason about the meta-model as well as integrate several meta-models. The formalization in OWL, using Protégé [34], serves as a basis for future more thorough analysis and integration of meta-models. We have transformed our UML class diagram into an OWL implementation based on the rules found in [35].Constraints, are captured through OWL restrictions within the documented limitations of the language (e.g. derivation is not directly supported by OWL [35]). OWL allows for more advanced reasoning by checking that the ontology makes sense (satisfiability), finding implicit terminology (e.g. subsumption) and finding implicit facts, etc. [36]. Additionally, OWL has the advantage of being more widely accepted and used, and supported by numerous freely available tools.

4 Validation

In this section we illustrate the applicability and validity of our meta-model using Telos and OWL for the application of the Value Shop at a police investigation

---
[3] http://www.info.fundp.ac.be/~mpe/BUSITAL2011

Modeling Competition-Driven Business Strategy for Business IT Alignment

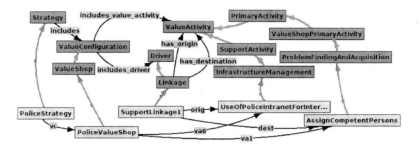

Fig. 5. The Value Shop in Telos: the Police Investigation Unit

unit (figure 2, section 2.2) and due to space limitations we present an extract from Telos (complete Telos and OWL instantiation models, can be downloaded from the authors' web-page [3]).

The model was produced using mapping rules from UML, similar to the ones used in [7]. Constraints described in section 3.2 were formalized and attached to the relevant classes. Figure 5 shows an extract of the Telos meta-model for the case. Boxes on top represent classes of the meta-model and boxes on the bottom instances from the case, which are related through Telos attributes classes corresponding to the UML associations, specialization links and instantiation relationships (arrows). The figure shows that the *PoliceValueShop* includes amongst others two value activities, namely *AssignCompetentPersons*, an instance of *ProblemFindingAndAcquisition*, itself a subclass of *PrimaryActivity*. This activity is supported through a linkage by the *UseOfPoliceIntranetForInternalCommunications* activity which is an instance of *InfrastructureManagement*, a subclass of *SupportActivity*. We formalized all constraints and instantiated the constructs one by one (e.g. starting from the concept of Strategy). When the instantiation did not result into any violation of any constraint, then we checked if it was intuitively correct (according to our understanding of the literature). If correct, we proceeded with the creation of more instances of the case. If incorrect, we refined the model, possibly by adding a missing constraint. When the instantiation resulted into the violation of a constraint, we checked if it was intuitively correct (according to our understanding of the literature). If correct, we completed the model with additional instances required to avoid the constraint violation and then tried again. We continued until all constructs of the case were instantiated. Additionally, we tested some cases that would intuitively violate the constraints and we checked whether they were not accepted. If they were, we corrected the constraints accordingly.

Finally, it should be noted that this process does not guarantee the meta-model is error free, as more test cases would be required to improve the coverage of the tests. Nevertheless, it indicates a real case can be instantiated illustrating the model is consistent and accepts at least one model, which is applicable to reality.

5 Conclusions and Future Work

In this paper, we presented a step towards our objective of creation of a well-defined meta-model for modeling business strategy. We reported on the formalization of the specific set of concepts proposed by a well-know approach for strategy definition, namely the Value Chain concept proposed by Porter and its extensions by Stabell and Fjelstad. The meta-model is defined in terms of a UML class diagram but is also formalized in Telos and OWL that allow a rigorous expression of constraints. Furthermore, we used supporting tools associated with these languages to perform an initial validation of the meta-model and its constraints by showing that it can be instantiated, respecting the constraints, for a case from the literature, thus demonstrating applicability in practice.

Despite the fact we have systematically elicited the concepts from the input texts, some more fuzzy concepts have not yet been integrated. We intend to further analyze these concepts in the future and evaluate the benefits of integrating them in the meta-model. Further validation of the meta-model is obviously needed by testing it on more cases. The next steps of our research, consist of integrating our meta-model to more business strategy modeling approaches , such as [7] and start mapping them to GORE.

References

1. Kaplan, R.S., Norton, D.P.: Mastering the Management System. J. Harvard Business Review 86, 63–77 (2008)
2. Chan, Y.E., Horner, R.B.: IT alignment: what have we learned? J. Journal of Information Technology 22(4), 297 (2007)
3. van Lamsweerde, A.: Requirements Engineering: From System Goals to UML Models to Software Specifications. Wiley, West Sussex (2009)
4. Giannoulis, C., Petit, M., Zdravkovic, J.: Towards a Unified Business Strategy Language: A Meta-model of Strategy Maps. In: van Bommel, P., Hoppenbrouwers, S., Overbeek, S., Proper, E., Barjis, J. (eds.) PoEM 2010. Lecture Notes in Business Information Processing, vol. 68, pp. 205–216. Springer, Heidelberg (2010)
5. Mintzberg, H., Ahlstrand, B., Lampel, J.: Strategy Safari: The complete guide through the wilds of strategic management. Prentice Hall, London (1998)
6. Anaya, V., Berio, G., Harzallah, M., Heymans, P., Matulevicius, R., Opdahl, A., Panetto, H., Verdecho, M.J.: The Unified Enterprise Modeling Language – Overview and further work. J. Computers in Industry 61 (2009)
7. Giannoulis, C., Petit, M., Zdravkovic, J.: Modeling Business Strategy: A Meta-model of Strategy Maps and Balance Scorecards. In: 5th IEEE International Conference on Research Challenges in Information Science (RCIS 2011). IEEE, New York (2011) (accepted)
8. Kaplan, R.S., Norton, D.P.: Having trouble with your strategy? Then map it. J. Harvard Business Review 78(5), 167–176 (2000)
9. Kaplan, R.S., Norton, D.P.: The Balanced Scorecard: translating Strategy into Action. Harvard Business School Press, Boston (1996)
10. Smith, M., Welty, C., McGuinness, D.: OWL Web Ontology Language Guide, http://www.w3.org/TR/2003/WD-owl-guide-20030331

11. Mylopoulos, J., Borgida, A., Jarke, M., Koubarakis, M.: Telos: A Language for Representing Knowledge About Information Systems. J. ACM Transaction on Information Systems 8(4), 325–362 (1990)
12. Porter, M.E.: Competitive Advantage: Creating and Sustaining Superior Performance. Free Press, New York (1985)
13. Porter, M.E.: Competitive Strategy: Techniques for Analyzing Industries and Competitors. Free Press, New York (1998)
14. Porter, M.E.: On Competition. Harvard Business School Publishing, Boston (2008)
15. Stabell, C.B., Fjeldstad, Ø.D.: Configuring Value for Competitive Advantage: On Chais, Shops, and Networks. J. Strategic Management 19(5), 413–437 (1998)
16. Gottschalk, P., Holgersson, S.: Stages of Knowledge management technology in the value shop: the case of police investigation performance. J. Expert Systems 23(4), 183-193 (2006)
17. Miles, R.E., Snow, C.C., Meyer, A.D., Coleman, H.J.: Organizational strategy, structure, and process. J. Academy of Management Review 3(3), 546–562 (1978)
18. DeSarbo, W.S., Benedetto, C.A., Sinha, I.: Revisiting the Miles and Snow strategic framework: uncovering interrelationships between strategic types, capabilities, environmental uncertainty, and firm performance. J. Strategic Management 26(1), 47–74 (2005)
19. Mauborgne, R., Kim, W.C.: Blue Ocean Strategy: From Theory to Practice. J. California Management Review 47(3), 105–122 (2005)
20. Kaplan, R.S., Norton, D.P.: The strategy map: guide to aligning intangible assets. J. Strategy & Leadership 32(5), 10–17 (2004)
21. Barney, J.: Types of Competition and the Theory of Strategy: Toward an Integrative Framework. J. Academy of Management Review 32(11), 1231–1241 (1986)
22. Bleistein, S.J., Cox, K., Verner, J.: Validating strategic alignment of organizational IT requirements using goal modeling and problem diagrams. J. Systems and Software 79, 362–378 (2006)
23. Babar, A., Zowghi, D., Chew, E.: Using Goals to Model Strategy Map for Business IT Alignment. In: 5th International Workshop on Business/IT Alignment and Interoperability (BUSITAL 2010), pp. 16–30 (2010)
24. McCarthy, W.E.: REA Accounting Model: A Generalized Framework for Accounting Systems in a Shared Data Environment. J. The Accounting Review 57(3), 554–578 (1982)
25. Osterwalder, A. (2004). The Business Model Ontology. Doctoral thesis, HEC Lausanne (2004), http://www.hec.unil.ch/aosterwa/ (retrieved May 02, 2009)
26. Gordijn, J.: E-Business Modeling Using the e3 Value Ontology. In: Curry, W. (ed.) E-Business Model Ontologies, pp. 98–128. Elsevier, Butterworth-Heinemann, UK (2004)
27. Geerts, G., McCarthy, W.E.: An Ontological Analysis of the Primitives of the Extended-REA Enterprise Information Architecture. The International Journal of Accounting Information Systems 3, 1–16 (2002)
28. Gordijn, J., van Eck, P., Wieringa, R.: Requirements Engineering Techniques for e-Services. In: Georgakopoulos, D., Papazoglou, M.P. (eds.) Service-Oriented Computing: Cooperative Information Systems Series, pp. 331–352. The MIT Press, Cambridge (2008)
29. Zdravkovic, J., Ilayperuma, T.: A Model-driven Approach for Designing E-Services Using Business Ontological Frameworks. In: 14th IEEE International EDOC Conference, pp. 121–130. IEEE Computer Society, Los Alamitos (2010)
30. Selic, B.: The pragmatics of model-driven development. IEEE Software 20, 19–25 (2003)

31. Harel, D., Rumpe, B.: Meaningful Modeling: What's the Semantics of "semantics"? J. Computer 37, 64–72 (2004)
32. Lucena, M., Santos, E., Silva, C., Alencar, F., Silva, M.J., Castro, J.: Towards a unified metamodel for i*. In: 2nd International Conference on Research Challenges in Information Science (RCIS 2008), pp. 237–246. IEEE Press, New York (2008)
33. Conceptbase: A Database System for Meta-modeling and Method Engineering (tool), http://conceptbase.sourceforge.net/ (last accessed 2010-11-20)
34. Protégé Ontology Editor. Open source tool, http://protege.stanford.edu/ (last accessed 2010-11-20)
35. Ontology Definition Meta-model (ODM): Object Management Group (2009)
36. Calvanese, D., Giacomo, G.D., Horridge, M., Möller, R., Turhan, A.Y.: Reasoning for Ontology Engineering and Usage. In: Tutorial at ISWC 2008 (2008), http://owl.cs.manchester.ac.uk/2008/iswc-tones/

The Quest for Know-How, Know-Why, Know-What and Know-Who: Using KAOS for Enterprise Modelling

Maxime Bernaert and Geert Poels

Department of Management Information Systems and Operations Management
Faculty of Economics and Business Administration,
Ghent University, Tweekerkenstraat 2, B-9000 Ghent, Belgium
{Maxime.Bernaert,Geert.Poels}@UGent.be

Abstract. While the field of information systems engineering is largely focussed on developing methods for complex problems and larger enterprises, less is done to specifically address the needs of smaller organizations like small and medium sized enterprises (SMEs), although they are important drivers of economy. These needs include a better understanding of the processes (know-how), why things are done (know-why), what concepts are used (know-what) and who is responsible (know-who). In this paper, the KAOS approach is evaluated as not only useful for developing software projects, but with the potential to be used for developing a business architecture or enterprise model. An example of KAOS is given, by way of illustration, and KAOS was applied by an SME's CEO, which resulted in a set of questions for further research.

Keywords: Requirements Engineering, Business Process Management, Small and Medium Sized Enterprises, Goal Modelling, KAOS, Business Architecture, Enterprise Architecture, Enterprise Modelling.

1 Introduction

In the state-of-the-art of the field of information systems engineering, a lot of emphasis is placed on automation through software systems. However, information systems can exist without much or even any support of software.

Smaller organizations, like small and medium sized enterprises (SMEs), do require proper systems to fulfil their information and automation needs, but their first concerns are organizational issues, with IT as a means for achieving business objectives [1]. While most of the effort in the field of information systems engineering is focused towards complex problems and large enterprises, the specific needs and problems of smaller enterprises are often forgotten [2].

An enterprise can be interpreted in a very wide sense. It could mean the whole enterprise, a smaller part of it (e.g., a business unit), or an area of activity of the enterprise (e.g., the purchasing). This research limits itself to SMEs, although the problems addressed could be the same in larger organizations as well. The purpose of our research is to investigate the problems that SMEs are facing today and if methods or techniques that are used in requirements engineering can provide an adequate solution to those problems. The problems we will specifically look at are the need for a better documentation, understanding, and analysis of the processes (know-how), why things are done (know-why), what concepts are used (know-what) and who is responsible (know-who), taking into account the specific characteristics of SMEs that may impose constraints on potential solutions.

In this paper, KAOS is proposed as a solution to document SMEs' know-how in process models, know-why in goal models, know-what in object models and know-who in responsibility models, and to make sure these models are aligned to achieve internal consistency and traceability.

This work extends that of others in several ways. Kamsties et al. [3] investigated the use of requirements engineering for developing software products by SMEs in the software and embedded systems industry. A more recent paper of Zickert and Beck [4] extends the work of Kamsties et al. This paper evaluated whether KAOS addresses the characteristics of complex tasks in software engineering. They conducted a literature analysis and applied KAOS to two software development projects. In our paper, however, requirements engineering is used to explicate how an SME's activities relate to its goals, without necessarily thinking about how the resulting requirements models could be used for systems development.

The people working on enterprise modelling [5, 6] have already put a lot of effort in developing the enterprise model, in which different submodels are interrelated and describe these four dimensions [5]. More recent work on the Enterprise Knowledge Development (EKD) method for enterprise modelling defines six submodels, but agrees that its Goals Model (Why), Business Process Model (How), Concepts Model (What), and Actors and Resources Model (Who) tend to dominate EKD usage ([6], p. 7). We consider this work to be very useful and see KAOS as a feasible language for describing these submodels. In addition, KAOS already has tool support, which the authors of [6] considered to be the main weak point of the EKD method ([6], p. 9).

This work can also be situated in the research on enterprise architecture. In The Open Group Architecture Framework (TOGAF) [7], this work can be seen as creating a business architecture, after which the information systems architectures and technology architecture can be developed. According to the Zachman Framework [8], this work covers four focuses (what, how, who, why) across two views (contextual, conceptual). Finally, KAOS' responsibility, operation, and object model respectively correspond to ArchiMate's [9] active structure, behaviour, and passive structure.

This paper is structured as follows. Section 2 starts with describing the relevant characteristics of SMEs and their CEOs. Section 3 evaluates KAOS in terms of how well it addresses the specific characteristics and needs of SMEs. Section 4 illustrates how KAOS can be used in an SME. An example of each of the four core models of KAOS is given for an existing Belgian company that sells tyres for passenger cars. The questions of this SME's CEO regarding KAOS and Objectiver while building his own models are presented in Section 5. The paper ends with a discussion and guidelines for future research in Section 6.

2 Small and Medium Sized Enterprises (SMEs)

SMEs have very specific problems [3]:

1. Employees and management are typically overwhelmed with day-to-day business, leaving **little space for strategic issues** and other issues, such as process management, not to mention quality and process improvement.
2. There is a **large demand within the enterprise for know-how transfer** with respect to basic issues and 'how to do it'.

Besides the problems SMEs are facing, they also have some specific characteristics which are defining for their business [10]:

3. Small businesses have significantly fewer resources than large companies. This **resource poverty** is a result of their highly competitive environment, financial constraints, lack of professional expertise, and their sensitivity to external forces [11]. The smaller the business, the less able it is to hire people with specialized skills, like for example IT skills [12].
4. SMEs are **lacking in specialized IT knowledge and technical skills** [13-16]. The main reason why European SMEs fail in utilizing IT is their lack of IT knowledge [17]. This advocates for the offering of easy-to-use and easy-to-learn tools to SMEs.

By definition, SMEs are organizations with fewer employees than large companies. The manager or CEO, who is often the company's owner, is commonly the single person who decides on strategic issues. CEOs of an SME also tend to share some characteristics [10]:

5. The **CEO is the central figure** who determines the direction of an SME [18]. The CEO's abilities and inclinations are, next to other factors like business size or market forces, important determinants for the rate at which an SME changes [19].
6. In SMEs, the **CEO makes the decision whether to adopt a new method or not**. Rogers' model of an individual's innovation-adoption process [20] reveals that before such a decision is made, a positive or negative attitude towards the innovation is formed. With each innovation, a degree of uncertainty is present, so the perceived benefits of the proposed method have to outweigh the risks and costs (time, money, effort) associated with it, in order to be adopted by the SME.

Table 1. Characteristics of SMEs and their CEOs

Characteristics of SMEs and their CEOs
1. Little space for strategic issues
2. Large demand within the enterprise for know-how transfer
3. Resource poverty
4. Lack of specialized IT knowledge and technical skills
5. CEO is the central figure
6. CEO makes the decision whether to adopt a new method or not

The previous six problems and characteristics (summarized in Table 1) clearly define SMEs and will be the main criteria for evaluating the possible solutions with respect to the context in which they are used.

3 KAOS

Goal-oriented requirements engineering (GORE) can help SMEs to discover and define their strategic issues (i.e. problem domain) by developing and elaborating goal models. GORE is used nowadays as a means for information systems engineering, more particularly as a basis for the development of software systems, while it could also be of great help as a basis for the development of the internal processes of an enterprise. SMEs could benefit from a number of important advantages of modelling, refining, and analysing goals [21]:

- The system environment is included in the modelling.
- Goals provide a rationale for requirements that operationalize these goals.
- A goal refinement tree provides traceability between high-level strategic objectives and low-level requirements.
- Goals can be used to provide the basis for the detection and management of conflicts among requirements [22, 23].
- A goal model can capture variability in the problem domain by using alternative goal refinements. Goal models provide the opportunity to communicate about requirements.
- Goals are much more stable than lower-level concepts like requirements or operations. The higher level the goal is, the more stable it is. [21, 24]

As these advantages illustrate, when using goal models, an enterprise could elevate its knowledge from know-how to know-why. As Dougherty demonstrated in her study [25], successful enterprises are able to bring these different knowledge components together. Other distinctions between these two components of knowledge can be found in [26].

When considering the six characteristics of SMEs and their CEOs (Table 1), KAOS [27] is according to our analysis a suitable approach (Table 2). First, KAOS provides SMEs with a means to think about strategic issues and process management. Moreover, KAOS' goal model and operation model (see Section 4.1) link the problem domain (i.e. strategic issues, goal model, know-why) with the solution domain (i.e. process management, operation model, know-how). Furthermore, Objectiver [28], a tool support for KAOS created by Respect-IT [29], provides SMEs with an easy-to-use environment in which they can create, enlarge, and adapt the KAOS model whenever they have time for it. This tool can help the EKD method in providing integrated tool support. Second, SMEs can document their processes (know-how) in Objectiver and even the rationale behind the processes (know-why). Third, an easy-to-learn approach (KAOS) with an easy-to-use tool (Objectiver), replaces the need to hire analysts and people with specialized IT skills. Fourth, KAOS in combination with its tool reduces the need to have specialists in-house. Fifth, this also means that the CEO, as the central figure responsible for the strategy, has to be involved in the development of the KAOS model. At every possible moment, he can adjust the KAOS model and even look at the impact that changes in the goal model could have on operations (operation model) and the agents responsible for the operations (responsibility model). Sixth, KAOS has the advantage to be an easy-to-learn approach and to have Objectiver as an easy-to-use tool. Of course these advantages have to be compared to the total cost of time, money, and effort to implement the KAOS approach. If the benefits outweigh the costs, the CEO could be convinced to adopt this method in his SME.

Table 2. KAOS in accordance to the characteristics of SMEs and their CEOs

KAOS in accordance to the characteristics of SMEs and their CEOs
1. Problem domain linked with solution domain
2. Objectiver as a means to document know-how and know-why
3. An easy-to-learn approach and easy-to-use tool
4. An easy-to-learn approach and easy-to-use tool
5. CEO involved in developing the KAOS model
6. An easy-to-learn approach with an affordable and easy-to-use tool

4 Modelling an SME with KAOS

The KAOS approach consists of a modelling language, a method and tool support (Objectiver). It was developed by Axel van Lamsweerde in the early 90s [27]. In this work we are using KAOS as defined in [30].

To understand the full potential of the KAOS approach, a short overview will be given in the next section, including the benefits SMEs could get from using KAOS.

4.1 Overview

KAOS is composed of four core models, which are closely related:

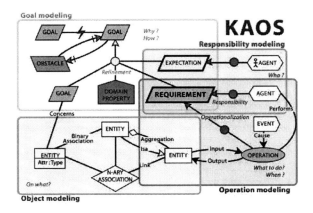

Fig. 1. Four core models in KAOS [31]

- A **goal model (why?)**, where goals are refined and justified until a set of interrelated goal diagrams have been put together for tackling a particular problem.

- A **responsibility model (who?)**, in which agents are assigned to the goals they are responsible for.
- An **object model (what?)**, which is used to define and document the objects (entities, agents, and associations).
- An **operation model (how?)**, which defines various behaviours that the agents need to fulfil their requirements.

Fig. 1 shows these four core models and how they are related to each other. The rest of this section will elaborate these four models in an example of a Belgian SME that sells tyres for passenger cars. In Section 5, the CEO of the same SME has used KAOS and Objectiver himself and his questions are listed in that section.

4.1.1 Goal Model (WHY?)

Goals are desired system properties that have been expressed by system stakeholders. An example of a goal could be:

'The cars of the customers are provided with the recommended tyre pressure'

KAOS makes it possible to discover the goals by interviewing the stakeholders and by analysing the already existing systems. The goals can be structured in a goal model and:

- Each goal in the model (except the goals at the top of the diagram) can be **justified** by at least one higher level goal that explains **why** the goal exists.
- Each goal in the model (except the goals at the bottom of the diagram) can be **refined** in one or more subgoals describing **how** this refined goal can be reached.

In the example, a justification for the example goal could be:
'Vehicle safety improved'
The example goal can be refined into two subgoals:
'Tyre pressure checked before the vehicle leaves the company'
'Car tyres inflated with nitrogen instead of oxygen'

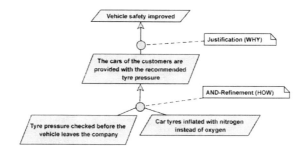

Fig. 2. An example of justification and refinement of a goal

Our example in Fig. 2 shows that a goal can be justified (why-question, linking to a higher level goal) and refined (how-question, refine in one or more lower level goals), which is the beginning of the development of the goal model. In our example, the AND-refinement is used (all subgoals must be satisfied to satisfy the parent goal).

OR-refinements (one subgoal must be satisfied to satisfy the parent goal) can also be used in KAOS.

At the top of the goal model, goals are more strategic, whereas at the bottom, the goals are more operational. Identifying goals is a combination between a top-down and a bottom-up approach.

Goals can be **conflicting** if the SME can reach a state in which it is not possible to satisfy both goals simultaneously. In our example, inflating car tyres with nitrogen is not one of the cheapest solutions for the customers (Fig. 3).

Fig. 3. An example of two conflicting goals

4.1.2 Responsibility Model (WHO?)

A goal is called a requirement or an expectation from the moment an agent can be made responsible for it. This **agent** can be either a human or an automated component. The difference between a **requirement** and an **expectation** is that the former is a low-level type of goal to be achieved by an agent which is part of the SME, while the latter is to be achieved by an agent which is part of the SME's environment.

Suppose in our example that it is possible to install a device that automatically reads tyre pressure (requirement) and tread depth as a vehicle rolls over it at a steady pace (expectation) and that this device has to be installed at the entrance of the workplace (Fig. 4).

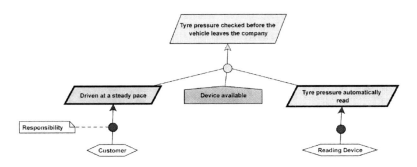

Fig. 4. An example of responsibilities

4.1.3 Obstacle Analysis (Part of the Goal Model)

If the SME believes that not all customers will drive over the device at a steady pace, then the expectation '*Driven at a steady pace*' is violated and an obstacle has to be added to the diagram. An obstacle obstructs a goal, requirement or expectation. Obstacles can be resolved in four ways.

First, new requirements can be defined that prevent the obstacle from occurring (for example in Fig. 5, a requirement can be added to warn the customers to drive at a steady pace). Second, the obstructed goal can be restored once the obstacle occurs (for example, if the device could not read the tyre pressure, the customer is asked to drive over it again). Third, an obstacle can be fixed by minimizing its effects (for example, the tyre pressure is checked both automatically and manually). Fourth, instead of adding new requirements in the first three solutions, the KAOS model can be modified in different ways to minimize or prevent the obstacle (for example in Fig. 6, one of the employees can be made responsible for driving the customers' vehicle over the device).

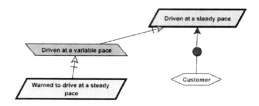

Fig. 5. Obstacle resolved by adding a new requirement

Fig. 6. Obstacle resolved by modifying the KAOS model

4.1.4 Object Model (WHAT?)

A KAOS object model is a glossary of all the specific terms used. It includes agents, entities and associations among them:

- **Agents** represent independent, active objects. Independent means that their description need not refer to other objects in the model. Active means they can perform operations. Examples of agents are '*Customer*' and '*Employee 1*'.
- **Entities** represent independent, passive objects. Independent means that their description need not refer to other objects in the model. Passive means they cannot perform operations. Examples of entities are '*Vehicle*', '*Tyre*' and '*Brand*'.
- **Associations** are dependent, passive objects. Dependent means that their description needs to refer to other objects in the model. Passive means they cannot perform operations. An example of an association is '*Read tyre pressure (a,t)*' if agent '*a*' is reading the tyre pressure of tyre '*t*'.

Object identification is driven by the goal definition process and stakeholders will have to agree on this common vocabulary of different objects identified while browsing through the goal model. Fig. 7 shows an example of an object diagram in which the requirement '*Tyre pressure automatically read*' concerns the object '*Tyre*', with the attribute '*Tyre pressure*'. A '*Tyre*' is of a particular '*Type of Tyre*' and

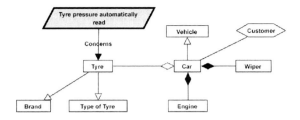

Fig. 7. An example of an object diagram

'*Brand*' and is part of '*Car*', which is (a specialization of) a '*Vehicle*' and is composed out of other parts which could be of importance to the company, like '*Wiper*' and '*Engine*'. A '*Car*' is linked to a '*Customer*', who is the owner of this car.

4.1.5 Operation Model (HOW?)

The KAOS operation model describes the solution space, which means that it is a collection of all the behaviours necessary for the agents to fulfil their requirements. Operations either work on the objects defined in the object model, by creating objects or triggering object state transitions, or activate other operations by sending an event.

Operationalization can happen in three ways. First, requirements that describe static properties are operationalized by objects. Second, requirements focussing on dynamic properties are operationalized by operations via operationalization links. Third, requirements with a focus on both static and dynamic aspects are operationalized by a combination of objects and operations. If we consider Fig. 6, we can operationalize this requirement by adding both objects and operations (Fig. 8).

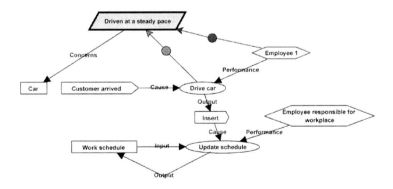

Fig. 8. Example of an operationalization

In this example, to drive at a steady pace, a car is needed and when the customer arrives, this causes the employee to drive the car over the tyre pressure reading device into the workplace. When the car is driven into the workplace, the employee responsible for the workplace has to update the work schedule of that day by inserting the handling of this car into the schedule.

5 Evaluation

This company's CEO got a half day training, looked at our example from Section 4, and worked in his spare time for one week on the model of his company (which is not included). This yielded some questions which could be the basis for future work:

- Good guidelines should be provided on how to start building these models. EKD already provides a way of working, which could possibly be used.
- It has to be possible to distinguish between goals that are already fulfilled and non-fulfilled goals. The measurement of goal-fulfilment could be done by linking them to key performance indicators (KPIs).
- Some constraints have to be respected, like a total budget, a maximum amount of working hours, and other restrictions. Non-functional requirements could provide a possible solution for this remark.
- It has to be possible to fill in some characteristics of goals, like the cost and time needed. In this way, trade-offs can be made.
- The alternative of doing things in-house or outsourcing has to be visible.
- Goals can change over time (e.g., seasonal goals), so the model has to be able to show the critical goals according to the period.
- If the model is not kept up-to-date, the approach does not work.
- Objectiver does not provide a way to link two or more resolving goals to an obstacle.
- Objectiver should have an easy way to search through elements, like Google.
- It is difficult to adjust the model once it contains many elements.
- Domain properties are hard to understand and distinguish from regular goals.
- An overview of the overall goal model should be provided in which the different parts (goal models in separate packages according to different topics) are highlighted in a different colour. This overview should be easily folded and unfolded according to different packages and goal levels.
- It should be possible to easily insert a goal between higher and lower level goals.
- A project planning module or exporting function to Microsoft Outlook could be useful. The workload per agent should be visible.

6 Discussion and Future Research

In this paper we investigated how KAOS can help SMEs in documenting their know-why, know-who, know-what, and know-how by respectively using its four core models: the goal model, the responsibility model, the object model and the operation model. The KAOS approach, with its Objectiver tool, is a suitable approach to implement in an SME, keeping in mind the specific characteristics of SMEs and their CEO which are mentioned in this paper. Objectiver can be the basis for an integrated tool support for the EKD method, in addition to the 'plastic wall' which is extensively used in that method [32].

An example was given for an existing SME, which delivered some insights. First, the KAOS goal model enables SMEs to document their know-why by asking why-questions (justification) and how-questions (refinement). Alternatives can be expressed by OR-refinements, conflicts by conflicting goals, and obstacles can be analysed and resolved to make the goal model more robust. Second, SMEs' know-how can be expressed by means of a KAOS operation model, which has the extra advantage that the rationale behind the processes can be expressed by linking the operation model with the goal model via operationalization links. In this way, bi-directional traceability between problem and solution spaces is being assured. Third, an SME can make an internal or external agent responsible for goals and for performing operations. Fourth, the KAOS object model provides a common glossary.

This example showed that KAOS, as it was originally developed to be used in software system development projects, has the ability to document and analyse an SME. The SME's CEO was very satisfied with the way in which KAOS and Objectiver enabled him to analyse his enterprise and to document both know-how and know-why. However, when building his model, he had some questions which provide us with material to work on in future research. Although this study does not offer an exhaustive look at the use of KAOS in all SMEs and while the study has been primarily descriptive, this study does serve to highlight the potential benefits that KAOS could provide to SMEs in particular, and other enterprises in general. Our future work includes implementing KAOS in multiple enterprises and derive both quantitative and qualitative data from predefined criteria, estimating the return on investment for particular enterprises (as in [33] for software projects), looking at the difference between using KAOS in an existing enterprise and in a new enterprise, and improving the visual effectiveness of KAOS according to [34]. The KAOS approach can also be combined with EKD and other methods to gain a better understanding of the existing material in business architecture and enterprise modelling. At last, more rigorous study is required in which KAOS is compared with other modelling methods and frameworks to evaluate its effectiveness and user-friendliness.

References

1. Levy, M., Powell, P.: Information Systems Strategy for Small and Medium Sized Enterprises: An Organisational Perspective. The Journal of Strategic Information Systems 9, 63–84 (2000)
2. Huang, R., Zmud, R.W., Price, R.L.: IT Governance Practices in Small and Medium-Sized Enterprises: Recommendations from an Empirical Study. Information Systems – Creativity and Innovation in Small and Medium-Sized Enterprises 301, 158–179 (2009)
3. Kamsties, E., Hörmann, K., Schlich, M.: Requirements Engineering in Small and Medium Enterprises. Requirements Engineering 3, 84–90 (1998)
4. Zickert, F., Beck, R.: Evaluation of the Goal-Oriented Requirements Engineering Method KAOS. In: AMCIS 2010 Proceedings, Lima, Peru (2010)
5. Bubenko, J.: Extending the Scope of Information Modelling. In: International Workshop on the Deductive Approach to Information Systems and Databases, Lloret, Costa Brava (1993)
6. Stirna, J., Persson, A.: Ten Years Plus with EKD: Reflections from Using an Enterprise Modeling Method in Practice. In: Pernici, B., Gulla, J.A. (eds.) EMMSAD, Trondheim, Norway, pp. 99–108 (2007)
7. TOGAF Version 9, Vol. 2011. The Open Group (2009), http://www.opengroup.org/architecture/togaf9-doc/arch/
8. Zachman, J.A.: A Framework for Information Systems Architecture. IBM Systems Journal 26, 276–292 (2010)

9. Lankhorst, M.: Enterprise Architecture at Work: Modelling, Communication and Analysis. Springer, Heidelberg (2009)
10. Thong, J., Yap, C.: CEO Characteristics, Organizational Characteristics and Information Technology Adoption in Small Businesses. Omega, International Journal of Management Science 23, 429–442 (1995)
11. Welsh, J., White, J.: A Small Business is Not a Little Big Business. Harvard Business Review 59, 18–32 (1981)
12. Alpar, P., Reeves, S.: Predictors of MS/OR Application in Small Businesses. Interfaces 20, 2–11 (1990)
13. DeLone, W.: Firm Size and the Characteristics of Computer Use. MIS Quarterly 5, 65–77 (1981)
14. DeLone, W.: Determinants of Success for Computer Usage in Small Business. MIS Quarterly 12, 51–61 (1988)
15. Gable, G.: Consultant Engagement for First Time Computerization: A Pro-Active Client Role in Small Businesses. Information & Management 20, 83–93 (1991)
16. Arlbjørn, J.S., Haug, A.: Identifying the IT Readiness of Small and Medium Sized Enterprises. In: AMCIS, Lima, Peru, p. 56 (2010)
17. Neidleman, L.: Computer Usage by Small and Medium Sized European Firms: An Empirical Study. Information & Management 2, 67–77 (1979)
18. Rizzoni, A.: Technological Innovation and Small Firms: A Taxonomy. International Small Business Journal 9, 31 (1991)
19. Birley, S.: Corporate Strategy and the Small Firm. Journal of General Management 8, 82–86 (1982)
20. Rogers, E.: Diffusion of Innovations. Free Press, New York (1983)
21. van Lamsweerde, A.: Goal-Oriented Requirements Engineering: A Guided Tour. In: 5th IEEE International Symposium on Requirements Engineering. IEEE Computer Society, Los Alamitos (2001)
22. van Lamsweerde, A., Darimont, R., Letier, E.: Managing Conflicts in Goal-Driven Requirements Engineering. IEEE Transactions on Software Engineering 24, 908–926 (2002)
23. Robinson, W.N.: Integrating Multiple Specifications Using Domain Goals. SIGSOFT Software Engineering Notes 14, 219–226 (1989)
24. Anton, A., McCracken, W., Potts, C.: Goal Decomposition and Scenario Analysis in Business Process Reengineering. In: CAiSE, Utrecht, Holland, pp. 94–104 (1994)
25. Dougherty, D.: A Practice-Centered Model of Organizational Renewal through Product Innovation. Strategic Management Journal 13, 77–92 (1992)
26. Garud, R.: On the Distinction between Know-How, Know-Why, and Know-What. Advances in Strategic Management 14, 81–101 (1997)
27. van Lamsweerde, A., Dardenne, A., Delcourt, B., Dubisy, F.: The KAOS Project: Knowledge Acquisition in Automated Specification of Software. In: Proceedings AAAI Spring Symposium Series, pp. 59–62. Stanford University, Menlo Park (1991)
28. Respect-IT: Objectiver, Vol. 2011 (2010), http://www.objectiver.com/
29. Respect-IT: Respect-IT, Vol. 2011 (2010), http://www.respect-it.be/
30. van Lamsweerde, A.: The KAOS Meta-Model: Ten Years After. Université Catholique de Louvain (2003)
31. Respect-it: KAOS Meta-model, Vol. 2011 (2007), http://www.respect-it.be/
32. Bubenko Jr., J., Persson, A., Stirna, J.: An Intentional Perspective on Enterprise Modeling. Intentional Perspectives on Information Systems Engineering, 215–237 (2010)
33. Objectiver: A KAOS Tutorial, Vol. 2011 (2007), http://www.objectiver.com/
34. Matulevicius, R., Heymans, P.: Visually Effective Goal Models Using KAOS. In: Conference on Advances in Conceptual Modeling: Foundations and Applications, Auckland, New Zealand (2007)

Value-Oriented Coordination Process Model Engineering

Hassan Fatemi, Marten van Sinderen, and Roel Wieringa

Information Systems (IS) Research Group,
Electrical Engineering, Mathematics and Computer Science (EEMCS) Department,
University of Twente, Enschede, The Netherlands
h.fatemi@utwente.nl, m.j.vansinderen@ewi.utwente.nl, roelw@cs.utwente.nl

Abstract. One of the most important aspects of a business collaboration is the value aspect. Analyzing a business collaboration form the value point of view enables us to understand the value-creation and sustainability of the collaboration. Therefore, having a business collaboration up and running for some time, the stakeholders involved in the collaboration can asses its performance by designing a value model of the collaboration and analyzing it. A value model is an abstract and easy to understand image of the collaboration from the value point of view. In this paper we elaborate on producing a business value model from a coordination process model.

1 Introduction

There are a lot of collaborations in business running for a long time without being really analyzed to see if they still are performing optimally from the business value point of view. Therefore, after using a business process for some time, it may be worthwhile we need to revaluate the business collaboration and reengineer it if necessary. Value productivity and sustainability are the most important aspects of a business collaboration. A value model of a business collaboration, enables the stakeholders to develop a better understanding of the performance of the collaboration from a value productivity and sustainability point of view.

For value modeling, we use the e^3value methodology [1]. e^3value is a notation to show the creation, distribution, and consumption of goods or services of economic value in a business collaboration. The main goal of value modeling is to reach agreement amongst profit-and-loss responsible stakeholders regarding the question "Who is offering what of value to whom and expects what of value in return?" Besides a graphical model, the e^3value methodology includes a computational model which enables the stakeholders to assess their potential profitability in the business collaboration over a specific period. For the sake of space we exclude the computational part of value modeling.

In [2] we have proposed a stepwise and pattern-based method for generating a coordination model from a value model. In our transformation method, we start by finding value patterns in the value model and add their counterpart coordination patterns to the coordination model. In this paper, we introduce the reverse transformation.

2 From Coordination Model to Value Model

A business value model is not a process model [3], they have different goals and concepts. Nevertheless they should be consistent with each other because they both refer to the same system. A lot of research have been done to check the consistency between these two types of models [4,5] and generating one based on the other [6,7,2]. Here we aim at developing a value model from a coordination model. A value model shows the stakeholders involved and the value objects which the stakeholders exchange between each other. Hence, the first step is identifying the stakeholders. We assume that the stakeholders are the same in both value model and coordination model. The next step is identifying the value exchanges between the stakeholders.

Exchanged messages between stakeholders are either value or non-value messages. Value messages are messages that indicate the transfer of value from one stakeholders to an. All other messages are non-value messages; they are used to coordinate the actions of the stakeholders. We exclude internal activities of actors, because from the value modeling point of view, exchanged messages between stakeholders is the only thing that matters.

Consider the business case shown in Figure 1, taken from [8], which consists of a copier company that sells and leases copiers to customer companies. When leasing a copier, it is mandatory to purchase maintenance on a yearly basis. Figure 1(a) is an *inter-organizational* process model of this business case that shows which messages and in which order are to be exchanged between stakeholders.

Having such a coordination model, we need to identify the value messages and the relation between them to design the value model. In this case messages indicating value transfer are those labelled by *service €+ lease €*, *copier l*, *purchase €*, and *copier p*. Figure 1(b) shows the value model of this simple case.

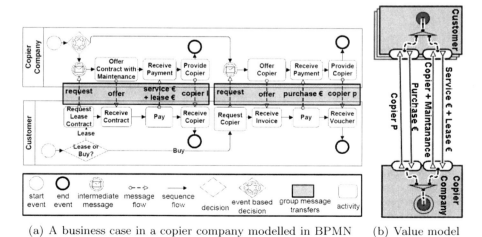

(a) A business case in a copier company modelled in BPMN (b) Value model

Fig. 1. From Coordination Process model to Business Value model

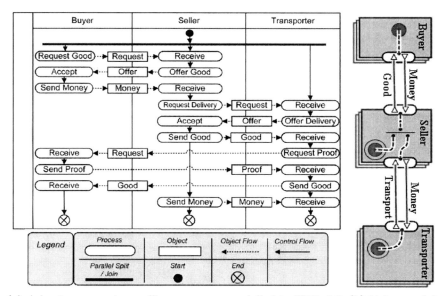

(a) A business case in a selling company modelled in UML 2.0 (b) Value model

Fig. 2. From Coordination Process model to Business Value model

As another example consider the business case shown in Figure 2, taken from [9]. For generality of our discussion, it is modelled in UML 2.0 activity diagrams (see www.uml.org). Here, identifying the value-related messages (those labelled with Money and Good) is simple, but there is a complication regarding the order and direction of the value exchanges. The two messages labelled with Money are obvious. However, there are two messages labelled with Good, one form the Seller to the Transporter and the other from the Transporter to the Buyer, which both indicate the same value object. Here, the Transporter plays a mediator role. Therefore in the value model we would have a value transfer labelled with Good from the Seller (the originating stakeholder of the value object) to the Buyer (the final destination of the value object). In value modeling, we model the transfer of value objects between the real owner and the final receiver. We add a value object transfer labelled with Transporter from the Transporter to the Seller because the Transporter does the transportation service for the Seller (the Transporter is being paid by the Seller). This way we see the duality and reciprocity of the value objects as well. Value reciprocity basically means every value transfer should have a corresponding reverse value transfer; i.e., they always come in pairs. The value model of this case is shown in Figure 2(b).

3 Discussion and Conclusion

Once business stakeholders come together and start a business collaboration, any of those stakeholders may want to investigate the productivity of the collaboration and make a change to it if and when needed. This requires knowledge on how good the performance of the business collaboration is from the value point of view. Here is where value modeling comes into play. Value modeling enables the stakeholders to run some value analysis of the collaboration and this helps the stakeholders to develop a shared understanding regarding the collaboration. Here, for the sake of brevity, we abstracted from the computational part of the value modeling. After developing a value model based on an existing coordination model, we can run a value analysis on the model and based on the analysis outcome either regenerate a refined or modified version of the process model from the value model [7,2], or breaking the whole business collaboration and make a new collaboration from the scratch.

References

1. Gordijn, J., Akkermans, H.: Value Based Requirements Engineering: Exploring Innovative e-Commerce Ideas. Requirements Engineering Journal 8, 114–134 (2002)
2. Fatemi, H., van Sinderen, M., Wieringa, R.J.: Value-oriented coordination process modeling (Lecture Notes in Computer Science). In: Hull, R., Mendling, J., Tai, S. (eds.) BPM 2010. LNCS, vol. 6336, pp. 162–177. Springer, Heidelberg (2010)
3. Gordijn, J., Akkermans, H., van Vliet, H.: Business modelling is not process modelling. In: Mayr, H.C., Liddle, S.W., Thalheim, B. (eds.) ER Workshops 2000. LNCS, vol. 1921, p. 40. Springer, Heidelberg (2000)
4. Zlatev, Z., Wombacher, A.: Consistency between e3-value models and activity diagrams in a multi-perspective development method. In: Chung, S. (ed.) OTM 2005. LNCS, vol. 3760, pp. 520–538. Springer, Heidelberg (2005)
5. Zarvić, N., Wieringa, R., van Eck, P.: Checking the alignment of value-based business models and it functionality. In: SAC 2008: Proceedings of the 2008 ACM Symposium on Applied Computing, pp. 607–613. ACM, New York (2008)
6. Andersson, B., Bergholtz, M., Grégoire, B., Johannesson, P., Schmitt, M., Zdravkovic, J.: From business to process models - a chaining methodology. In: Proceedings of the 8th International Conference on the Advanced Information Systems and Engineering, CAiSE 2006 (2006)
7. Fatemi, H., van Sinderen, M.J., Wieringa, R.J.: From business value model to coordination process model. In: Poler, R., van Sinderen, M., Sanchis, R. (eds.) IWEI 2009. Lecture Notes in Business Information Processing, vol. 38, pp. 94–106. Springer, Heidelberg (2009)
8. Bodenstaff, L., Wombacher, A., Wieringa, R., Reichert, M.: An approach for maintaining models of an e-commerce collaboration, pp. 239–246 (July 2008)
9. Vincent, P., Jaap, G.: Bridging business value models and process models in aviation value webs via possession rights. In: HICSS 2007: Proceedings of the 40th Annual Hawaii International Conference on System Sciences, p. 175a. IEEE Computer Society, Washington, DC, USA (2007)

The Business Behavior Model: A Revised Version

Noelia Palomares[1] and Birger Andersson[2]

[1] Valencia University of Technology, Department of Information Systems and Computation
Camí de Vera s/n, 46071 Valencia, Spain
noepabo@posgrado.upv.es
[2] Stockholm University, Department of Computer and System Sciences
SE-164 40 Kista, Sweden
ba@dsv.su.se

Abstract. The problem of aligning the strategy of an enterprise and supporting IT resources has been recognized since decades. In this paper we revise a model – The Business Behavior Model (BBM) – which is envisioned to help in the alignment between the goal layer and the business layer of an enterprise. A number of problems are identified in the original BBM and solutions for those problems are proposed. A short illustrative case is provided that shows the applicability of the revised BBM.

1 Introduction

The problem of aligning the strategy of an enterprise and supporting IT resources has been recognized since decades [1]. The common understanding is that once a strategy is made explicit then, somehow, available IT resources should be configured to provide maximum support for the strategy [2]. Instrumental for this work has been the use of models. Strategy has been captured or made explicit in Goal models [3, 4, 5] and IT resources have been captured through Data or Process models [6, 7, 8] in an operational layer.

One way to achieve alignment then has been through the application of rules and use of patterns [9, 10]. The introduction of a new strategy in a goal model results in a selection of a pattern that when applied changes e.g. a process model in a well defined way. For example, the formulation of the goal "I need to increase production 10% the coming six months" can result in introduction of new actors and support systems in a process model.

It has been argued that the gap between the strategy level and the operational level is too large to effectively achieve business and IT alignment as alluded to above [11]. To decrease this gap a business layer was introduced between them. The layers reflect a separation of concerns:

- Goal layer. The goal layer is described by means of goal models. Goal models are used in the earliest phases of business and information systems design, where they help in clarifying interests, intentions, and strategies of different stakeholders answering to the "why" of the business;
- Business layer. The business layer is described by means of business models [12, 13, 14]. Business models give a high level view of the activities taking place in and

between organizations by identifying agents, resources, and the exchange of resources between the agents. So, a business model focuses on the "what" of a business;
- Process layer. The process layer is described by means of data and process models. Process models focus on the "how" of a business, as they deal with operational and procedural aspects of business communication, including control flow, data flow and message passing.

The focus of this paper is on the alignment between the goal layer and the business layer. In particular, we want to investigate the Business Behavior Model (BBM) [15, 16] that was conceived as a model that complements traditional models and methods for alignment, e.g. [1, 17, 18]. The main feature of the BBM is that it is deliberately designed to contain concepts that is normally thought of as belonging to different modeling layers (in the case of BBM both the goal layer and business layer). As far as we are aware there has been no attempt at this approach when trying to align goal and business layers. The design was motivated by the sometimes poor results achieved when working in the traditional ways [16]. While investigating the BBM a number of unclear or problematic points were discovered. The purpose of this paper is to point at those problems and discuss some solutions. By strengthening the BBM it is envisioned that it will become a useful and valuable tool for business/IT-alignment.

The rest of the paper is structured as follows: in section 2 we describe the original BBM and its theoretical foundations. Section 3 defines and explains important modifications done to the original BBM. Section 4 contains an illustrative example to show how to use the model; and finally, section 5 contains a concluding discussion and directions for future research.

2 Theoretical Backgrounds for the BBM

In this section we briefly overview the theoretical foundations for the Business Behaviour Model.

The Rational Agent Theory [19] describes how agents can reach their intentions by means of decisions. Agents are considered rational and are represented as having mental attitudes like beliefs, desires, and intentions (BDI). Based on its beliefs the agent constructs a set of desires from which it deliberately and rationally selects one. The selected one becomes its intention. This way of describing an agent lies at the heart of the BBM.

The Resource-Based View (RBV) [20] is a business management tool able to determine what resources are strategic for an organization. A resource is strategic when it fulfills a set of criteria. The VRIN (Value, Rareness, Inimitability, and Non-substitutability) framework is a commonly used set of criteria proposed by Barney [21]. In the BBM the way for a rational agent to fulfill its intentions is through exchange of resources with its environment.

The Business Model Ontology (BMO) [12, 22] describes the business model of a firm. As a minimum a business model has to address the following four perspectives: Product and Service: what an agent offers; Client: who the agent's envisioned customers are; Activity: who the agent's envisioned partners are; Financial: the costs and revenues associated with the offering. The perspectives proposed in BMO are reflected in the way resources are analysed in BBM.

Causal graphs [23] are directed acyclic graphs, in which nodes denote variables features of a system and arcs denote direct causal relations between these features. The Causal graph constitutes the basis for the syntax of the BBM. The basic concepts of the causal graph are summarized in table 1:

Table 1. Basic concepts of causal graph [15, 23]

Nodes	Arcs
Chance: A variable that could conditionally be influenced by other nodes.	Informational: The out-node is considered before the in-node is analyzed.
Utility: The expected utility of the outcome from decisions nodes.	Causal: The in-node has conditional probability to take a certain value considering a previous out-node.
Decision: The alternatives that are possible considering the studied domain.	Definitional: The in-node is composed of the all nodes linked to it.

2.1 The Original BBM

The BBM is a model which describes the impact of the participation of agents in a business by integrating their resources in a causal graph. The participation is realized through decisions and driven by motivations [15]. Figure 1 shows the initial proposal.

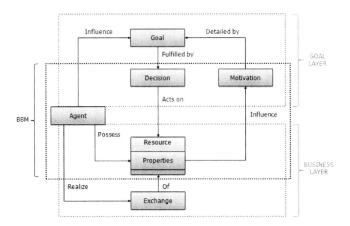

Fig. 1. The main concepts and position of the BBM [15]

According to figure 1, the BBM was developed as an intermediate model between the strategic layer and the business layer by simultaneously incorporating notions of goal models and value models.

The BBM has two parts – the modeling formalism and a methodology for applying it. Firstly, the modeling formalism contains agents, decisions, motivations, resources (with properties), and relations between those concepts. Secondly, using the BBM for alignment work means to use it systematically. This is done either by constructing a BBM on the basis existing goal or business models, or vice versa (i.e., constructing goal or business models based on an existing BBM). In order to do this a modeler must find correspondences between the notions of those models and the concepts of the BBM. As a result of semantic analyses correspondences between concepts of the BBM and several goal and business models are presented in table 2. Table 2 contains in part results of previous work presented in [15].

2.2 Problems in the Original BBM

We have found several problems related to the layer positioning of the concepts, syntax, semantics, and methodology in the original BBM proposal.

For the positioning of the concepts (according to figure 1); on one hand, the strategic layer contains goals, decisions and motivations. On the other hand, the business layer contains resources (with properties) and exchanges of resources. The original positioning of decisions in the goal layer is problematic. To ease the analysis we now position decision between the goal layer and the business layer together with agent. Based on what goals exist in the goal layer an agent takes a decision that affects the resource exchanges in the business layer. In other words, an agent that takes decisions conceptually becomes the "bridge" between the layers. An added benefit is that the separation of concerns between the layers is mostly maintained.

For the syntax, the original version presented graphical notation just for the following nodes: economic resources, economic resources properties, non-economic resources, and decisions. However, agents were not explicitly included and motivations were not precisely observable in the language – a motivation was modeled trough the improvement (increase or decrease) of non-economic resources by means of value indicators on causal links. Agents are now included giving the possibility to model external agents with whom the principal agent exchange resources with. In the original BBM motivations were treated as synonyms of non-economic resources. This was problematic as one can argue that an agent can have as a motivation to create a non-economic resource (e.g., some skill). Added symbols for motivations have been added to capture this.

Regarding links, the original version included informational links, causal links (using value indicators), definitional links, creational links, XOR-relation, and AND-relation. We found it problematic to handle value indicators of the causal links which could take two values indicating strong or light impact (++, +, -, --). But it is quite hard to discern between strong or light so we now use a one level scale – positive or negative impact. We have also added a new type of link which we call a suppressing link. It is represented using the same symbol that it is used to represent creational links. The reason for adding it is to be able to capture that a motivation can result in a decision to delete a resource in a business model. This was not possible to express in the original BBM.

For the semantics, we added definitions for new concepts (agent and motivation) and clarified other definitions. The first point is about resources. In the original BBM, there were different types of resources: economic and non-economic ones. Economic resources were defined by at least one property. A property was composed of a name, a scale, and a value where properties always had a positive value on their scales. We specify the differences between both types of resources – above all the operations that are permitted depending on the type. For example, economic resources can be exchanged but non-economic resources cannot. We establish a criterion to be able to tell the difference between an economic resource and a property, and include negative value on the property scales. The other points relates to decisions and motivations.

Finally, it was necessary to change the original methodology because of inclusion of new elements and altered definitions.

3 Improvement of the Business Behavior Model

Meta-model, Syntax, and Semantics. The meta-model for the original BBM is changed and figure 2 shows the new proposal. A model is built from one agent's (called 'the principal agent') point of view. The model is a scenario where an agent's motivations are represented. Motivations can be fulfilled in several ways; by obtaining a certain resource, either economic resources (new ones can be introduced or deleted by taking decisions), or non-economic resources (which are created, e.g. a 'skill'). Economic resources are defined by their properties. A value of a property can positively or negatively affect other properties. The ways by which motivations are fulfilled are represented as hierarchies or sequences of decisions.

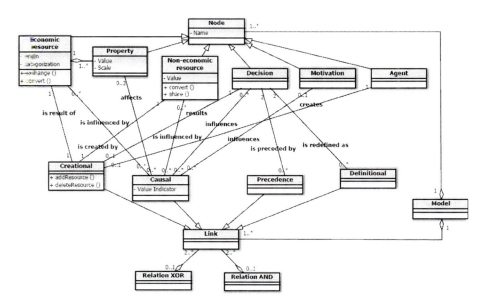

Fig. 2. The BBM meta-model

Table 2 presents the syntactically and semantically modified BBM. A number of changes from the original were done in order to improve it. In particular, the following items are of interest: new nodes for agent and motivation are introduced;

Table 2. Syntax and semantics of BBM

BBM Concept	Syntax	Semantic
Agent	Circle	Rational entity capable to achieve goals (resources) by taking decisions based on motivations.
Economic resource (noun)	Dotted square box	Resources which are transferable (or convertible) and valuable. They are described by a set of properties (at least one). There are subcategories: goods, information, services or money.
Economic resource property (adjective)	Rounded box	Property of a resource evaluated on a qualitative or quantitative scale (either positive or negative value). Property concerns inner characteristics but also customer, financial and infrastructural aspects.
Categorization	Rectangle box	Classification of the properties of an economic resource in four perspectives: Customer, Financial, Infrastructure and Value proposition.
Non-economic resource	Diamond box	Resources which are not transferable. They are convertible or shared. They are concerning inner value for the studied agent.
Motivation	Parallelogram box	Real reasons (either positive or negative) that the agent possesses to achieve goals and means (either economic or non-economic resources).
Decision	Square box	Decision nodes represent ways to achieve goals and means.
Precedence link	Arrow	The information from the out-node decision is available at the time the in-node decision is taken. It expresses temporality: the change from one state to other state depending on decisions that have been taken.
Causal link	Arrow with value indicator	Out-node has an impact in the in-node depending on the value indicator.
Definitional link	Empty arrow	The connected nodes are decision nodes. The purpose is to improve the definition of a decision by using sub-decisions (which are more detailed).
Creational link	Dotted links	Both links are used to trace the reason why resources are added or deleted. The reason is linked to a specific decision.
XOR-relation	Bounded connector	A connector between links of same type. Those connectors act as constraint on the nodes attached to the links; at least one out-node have to be considered to grant the consideration of the in-node but not all of them.
AND-relation	Double bounded connector	A connector between links of same type. Those connectors act as constraint on the nodes attached to the links; all out-nodes have to be considered to grant the consideration of the in-node.
Value indicator		
Positive	+	Positive influence.
Negative	-	Negative influence.

definitions for economic resource, economic resource properties, non-economic resource and decision are updated; and modifications in value indicator and creational link are introduced. For space reasons we did not include the graphical representations of the concepts; however, a sub set of them are used in figure 5.

Table 3. Translation table between goal models (i*, BMM, KAOS), value models (e³value, BMO, REA), and the BBM

BBM	i*	BMM	KAOS	e³value	BMO	REA
NODES						
Agent	Actor	External influencer	Agent	Actor	Main actor Partners Customers	Economic agent
Economic resource	Resource	Internal influencer	Entity	Value object	Resources Costs Revenues	Economic resource
Origin	Dependency link	External influencer		Value exchange		
Property	Goal Soft-goal	End: goal	Goal			
Categorization						
Non-economic resource	Soft-goal					
Motivation	Goal	Ends	Expectation Goal			
Decision	Task	Means	Requirement Operation Event	Value activity Start stimulus	Activity	Economic event
LINKS						
Causal	Contribution link Dependency link	Links among nodes		Value exchange	Links among nodes	Links among nodes
Value Indicator	Contribution indicator	Assessment	Obstacle			
Precedence						
Definitional	Decomposition		Refinement			
Creational						
Suppressing						

Methodology. The purpose of the methodology is to construct the BBM on the basis of other models, or vice versa. The methodology is composed of several methods. The modeler can commence work by eliciting motivations, decisions, or resources. Depending on the starting point and what the modeler wants to achieve, the methods differ.

Firstly, a translation table (table 3) provides the mapping of related concepts to clarify them to the modeler. The goal modeling languages considered are i*, BMM, and KAOS. The business modeling languages are e³value, BMO, and REA. Note that the mapping table does not imply that we use a straight mapping between the goal layer and the business layer. The gaps in the table (empty cells) shows that we need another tool – the BBM model – to fix them and provide a consistent flow of information for the alignment work.

Secondly, the methods of the methodology are altered. Here we illustrate one method ('start with a goal model, create a BBM, and end with an aligned value model') that is re-defined with the 'create the BBM' part outlined as follows:

- The first step is to identify the involved agents.
- For each agent, it is relevant to collect motivations, decisions and resources. The modeler can establish the relation between these concepts in several ways but we focus on a reformulated core idea from the Rational Agent theory: based on a motivation an agent takes a decision to exchange resource(s) with other agents in order to fulfill its intentions (Motivation – Decision – Resource).
- In the next step, the modeler defines the economic resources by means of their properties. It is optional to use the categorization element for further details.
- Afterward, the modeler starts to relate nodes using causal links. The value indicators on the causal links are added by a simple criterion: it helps, the modeler adds '+'; or it hurts, the modeler adds '-'. Note that, depending on the purpose of the model, there can be no '+' and '-'simultaneously. The modeler must fix the analysis context and decide according to her/his understanding.
- Finally, the modeler refines the model by using creational, definitional or precedence links.

4 Illustrative Case Study

To illustrate the use of the BBM we include a (very) short case. It is a fraction of a case that we currently study. The case is based on [9] and revolves around the organization of a scientific conference.

"The Scientific Conference scenario (SC) is about organizing a scientific conference. For this purpose a set of activities have been arranged to acquire submissions, assign reviewers, decide on papers and organization of the conference. The business scenario involves four agents: program committee, steering committee, author and reviewer. The task of the program committee is to organize the conference. The authors send submissions to the program committee. The program committee assigns reviewers to each paper and sends papers for reviewing. The reviewers submit their review reports to the program committee. Upon receiving the review reports the program committee decides on acceptance of papers. The decision is sent to the authors together with evaluations. The program committee is responsible for providing the conference program. The steering committee is responsible for funding the conference."

The objective is to construct the BBM model from an instance of i^* goal model and derive an instance of e^3value business model from the BBM. After this, we reflect on the quality of the result.

Figure 3 shows an overview of the text description using the i^* notation. It presents the boundary of each agent and the elements (goals, soft-goals, tasks and resources) that belong to each one. As prescribed the BBM the modeler has to develop one model for each agent's point of view. In this case, we focus on the program committee's. Figure 4 shows the scenario for the program committee. We observe that the main goal is 'Organize a quality SC', that is, a popular conference. It means to attain

The Business Behavior Model: A Revised Version 53

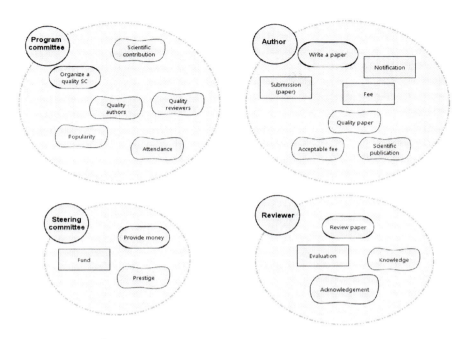

Fig. 3. i* model (strategic dependency) for the case (general overview)

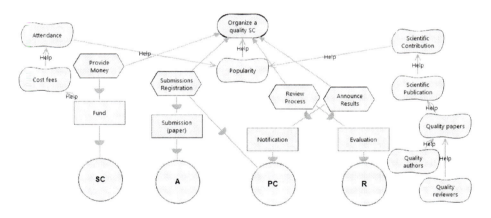

Fig. 4. i* model (rationale dependency) for the case (program committee's view)

high popularity by means of high attendance and significant scientific contributions. The attendance depends on the costs of the fees and the scientific contributions on the quality of the papers that have been submitted.

According to figures 3 and 4, we follow the described method and obtain the BBM model shown in figure 5.

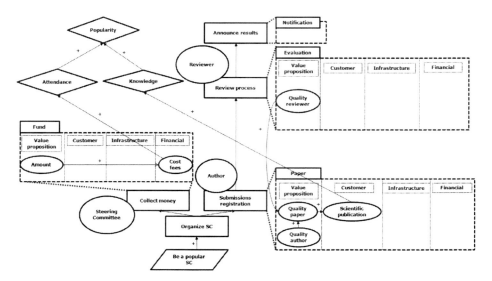

Fig. 5. BBM model for the case by using the new approach (program committee's view)

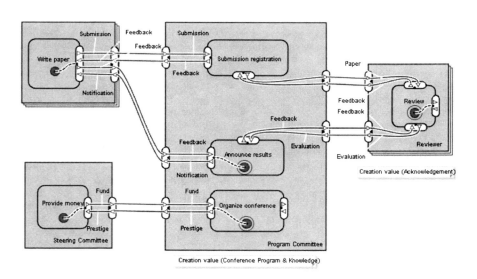

Fig. 6. e³value model for the case (program committee's view)

Figure 5 starts from the motivation of 'Be a popular SC'. To obtain popularity, it drives to take the decision of organizing a scientific conference. This decision splits into two sub-decisions: 'Collect money' (interacting with Steering Committee) and 'Submissions registration' (interacting with Author). A submission registration creates a resource 'Paper' that has some properties. Reviewers should review papers and select the better ones. Finally, the program committee announces the results to the authors. Note that one property can affect (positive or negative) another property. In this example, attendance is influenced by the costs of the fees and knowledge (scientific contribution) by the quality of the papers. Both attendance and knowledge affect to the popularity. It is important to notice that decisions can include a communication with external agents by adding a circle beside the decision. These communications are translated in exchanges of resources between agents in value models. Figure 6 shows an example using e^3value notation.

Compared to the original version of the BBM presented in [16] we are now in the position to make a better alignment work. I.e., we claim that the e^3value model in figure 6 is of higher quality than what it would have been should we have used the original BBM. As we now have a better understanding of agent motivations, we clearly can describe the goals of the PC and understand what resources it will exchange with other agents in order to attain those goals. In particular, we are able to describe how properties of resources help or hinder in goal attainment. Another improvement is that, by incorporating the agent construct in the BBM, this information can be used directly when constructing the business model.

5 Concluding Discussion and Future Work

In this paper we have revised the initial proposal of the BBM for the purpose of making it more useful in the business/IT-alignment context. While the main ideas remain, we have introduced new features in its meta-model, syntax, semantics, and methodology. The most important contribution is that we have considered the concepts of agent and motivation. This way managers can make more supported decisions by means of being able to model the whole business collaboration, that is, why are they taking these decisions (both internal and external reasons), who is participating in it (competitors and partners), and what is the benefit of it (strategic resources). So, we provide a tool to help the decision making process and, in consequence, align the goal and business layers.

Future research directions include more validations. This means testing it on real cases and more deeply in each case. Another research direction, which will be worked on, is the methodology. In this paper we report on a method that starts with goals and arrives at resource exchanges (via decisions). Another method approach is to start by looking at what resources are available for an agent and formulate goals based on this availability. For this, the meta-model and the methodology need to be complemented in several ways.

References

1. Chan, Y.E., Reich, B.H.: IT alignment: what have we learned? Journal of Information Technology 22, 297–315 (2007)
2. Luftman, J., Kempaiah, R.: An Update on Business-IT Alignment: "A Line" Has Been Drawn. MIS Quarterly Executive 6(3), 165–177 (2007)
3. van Lamsweerde, A.: Goal-oriented requirements engineering: A guided tour. In: Proc. International Joint Conference on Requirements Engineering (RE 2001), pp. 249–263. IEEE, Los Alamitos (2001)

4. Business Motivation Model (BMM), v.1.1. Object Management Group (OMG), http://www.omg.org/spec/BMM/1.1/
5. Yu, E.: Modelling Strategic Relationships for Process Reengineering, PhD thesis, University of Toronto, Department of Computer Science (1995)
6. Van der Aalst, W.: Formalization and Verification of Event-driven Process Chains. Information and Software Technology 41(10), 639–650 (1999)
7. Van der Aalst, W.: Petri Nets. Encyclopedia of Database Systems Part 16, 2103–2108 (2009)
8. BPMN Information Home Page, http://www.bpmn.org/
9. Edirisuriya, A.: Design Support for e-Commerce Information Systems using Goal, Business and Process Modelling. Doctoral Thesis, Stockholm University (2009)
10. Ilayperuma, T.: Improving E-business Design through Business Model Analysis. Doctoral Thesis, Stockholm University (2010)
11. Andersson, B., et al.: Enterprise Sustainability through the Alignment of Goal Models and Business Models. In: Proc. BUSITAL 2008, Montpellier, France (2008)
12. Osterwalder, A., Pigneur, Y.: An e-Business Model Ontology for Modeling e-Business. In: 15th Bled Electronic Commerce Conference e-Reality: Constructing the e-Economy (2002)
13. Gordijn, J., Yu, E., Van der Bas, R.: E-Service Design Using i* and e3value Modeling. IEEE Software 23(3), 26–33 (2006)
14. McCarthy, W.E.: The REA Accounting Model: A Generalized Framework for Accounting Systems in a Shared Data Environment. The Accounting Review (1982)
15. Lemaire, D., Andersson, B.: The Business Behavior Model. In: 5th International Workshop on Business/IT Alignment and Interoperability (BUSITAL 2010), Tunisia (2010)
16. Lemaire, D.: The Business Behavior Model: Concepts and Usages. Master's Thesis in Computer and Systems Sciences at Stockholm University (2010)
17. Bleistein, S.J., et al.: Validating strategic alignment of organizational IT using goal modeling and problem diagrams. Journal of Systems and Software 79, 362–378 (2006)
18. Nurcan, S., Rolland, C.: A multi-method for defining the organizational change. Information and Software Technology 45(2), 61–82 (2003)
19. Rao, A.S., Georgeff, M.P.: BDI-Agents: From Theory to Practice. In: 1st International Conference on Multiagent Systems, ICMAS 1995, San francisco (1995)
20. Wernerfelt, B.: The Resource-Based View of the Firm. Strategic Management Journal 5(2), 171–180 (1984)
21. Barney, J.: Firm Resources and Sustained Competitive Advantage. Journal of Management 17(1), 99–120 (1991)
22. Osterwalder, A.: The Business Model Ontology: A Proposition in a Design Science Approach. HEC de l'Université de Lausanne (2004)
23. Gammelgård, M., et al.: Business Value Evaluation of IT Systems: Developing a Functional Reference Model. In: Conference on Systems Engineering Research, Los Angeles (2006)

The Man behind the Curtain: Exploring the Role of IS Strategic Consultant

Riccardo Bonazzi, Charlotte Ceccaroli, and Stéphanie Missonier

University of Lausanne, Information Systems Institute, UNIL-Dorigny,
1015 Lausanne, Switzerland
{riccardo.bonazzi,charlotte.ceccaroli,
stephanie.missonier}@unil.ch

Abstract. Most organizations encounter business-IT alignment problems because they fail to properly understand how well an enterprise software package aligns with or fits their needs. Strategic consultants make a profit by reducing such external manifestations of the differences between the organization's needs and the system's capabilities. Therefore it appears relevant to understand how consultants behave.

Our theoretical model shows how a consultancy can assess the way to extract and to generalize knowledge from its clients. The share of a consulting firm's global knowledge is compensated with new local knowledge obtained from the client. Hence we underline a way to assess the quality of that contribution and the mutual knowledge exchange.

Keywords: IS Strategy, Strategic consultant, Business-IT alignment, ontological distance, design science, business model, knowledge-based theory, Organizational Knowledge Creation theory.

1 Introduction

The development, implementation, operation, support, maintenance, and upgrade of enterprise systems (ES) have given rise to a multibillion dollar industry. Nonetheless organizations encounter difficulties in achieving an adequate return on investment since they fail to properly assess the ontological distance between software capabilities and their organizational needs. (Rosemann et al. 2004)

Consultants are often used to reduce the differences between the organization's needs and the system's capabilities. Yet their strategic role in this domain has often been neglected by scholars (Pozzebon and Pinsonneault, 2005; Swanson, 2010). Over a period of more than twenty-six years, the Strategic Management Journal has given large attention to top management teams, and increasingly to middle managers, but has not published a single article on strategy consultants (Whittington 2007). Strategic consultants are sometimes considered magic wizards with unknown power. But the title of this article recalls that even the wizard of Oz was just a man with a fancy machine behind a curtain. The purpose of this article is to study that fancy machine, and how it can be used to produce magic.

In the rest of the paper we take a look at IS Strategy, defined as 'the organizational perspective on the investment in, deployment, use, and management of information systems' (Chen et al. 2010, p.237). The aim of this paper is to model IS "strategy as a profession". In doing so we respond to the call by Whittington (2007), and we are interested in the risk reduction by minimization of the ontological distance between software capabilities and their organizational needs identified by Rosemann et al. (2004). The work of a consultant is an example of "strategy as a profession" and it is an archetype of a knowledge intensive firm. The most important assets (key resources) and actions (key activities) that a consultancy must use to make its business model work are worth investigating in detail. In this study we consider Small and Medium Enterprises (SME) offering IS strategic consulting. We ground our theory into practice by presenting the outcomes of a six-month internship in a strategic consulting firm which moved from its start-up status toward SME status by means of a shift toward business process management. Our research question is obtained accordingly:

RQ: How a small/medium strategic consultancy can positively use its expertise to gain a sustainable competitive advantage?

The main audience for this paper is composed of IS strategic consulting firms, which seek a sustainable advantage based on their core competences. We also hope to raise the interest of Chief Information Officers of companies which are clients of IS strategic consulting firms and which are interested in understanding how IS strategic consulting firms work. Finally we address IS strategy scholars interested in business-IT alignment, hoping to open a set of new directions to be explored. From a theoretical perspective, our model shows part of the elaboration of an IS "strategy as profession" and more precisely how to assess quality. From a practical perspective, our research helps both consultancies and CIOs to understand their work and improve the implementation of a configurable IT. The rest of the paper proceeds as follows. We start by reviewing the existing literature on IS strategic consultancies and identify the gaps to address through a set of research sub-questions. Then we introduce our theoretical model and suggest a set of testable propositions. For the sake of clarity, we address IS scholars and present the instantiation which we intend to use to test our proposition. Then we address to practitioners and describe how our theoretical model can be used in a business model. We conclude with a set of discussions and directions for further research.

2 Literature Review

In this section, we present previous works on IS strategic consultancies and assess the gaps in the existing literature to refine our research question into a set of research sub-questions. According to Swanson (2010) "while they often appear as players, even major ones, in the IS field's many case studies, consultancies are rarely the focus of the research questions addressed" (p.18). Since this topic is at the cross-road of different disciplines, we present four articles representing the contributions of four research domains.

Table 1. The constructs of our model

Article	Research Domain	Key activities	Key resources
Pozzebon, M., & Pinsonneault, A. (2005)	Resource-Based View	From global to local	Global Vs Local Knowledge
Werr and Stjnberg (2003)	Organizational Knowledge Creation Theory	From case to methods and tools	Global Vs Local; Tacit Vs Explicit Knowledge
Swanson (2010)	IS Strategy	---	5 deliverables
Rosemann et al. (2004)	Requirement Engineering	5 steps	Organizational needs Vs Software Capabilities

According to Pozzebon and Pinsonneault (2005) the role of a consultancy is to translate global knowledge, defined as "generalizable features that may be divorced from particular settings and applied more widely" (p.122) into local knowledge, i.e. practical knowledge that is "highly specific to each particular firm and depends on the firm's employees" (p.122). This approach grounded in the resource-based view (Barney, 1991) fails to detail the key activities required to pass from global to local and vice-versa. Werr and Stjnberg (2003) focus on the importance of translating the experience of a consultant into a set of cases, which are local and explicit knowledge that contributes to the creation of global and explicit knowledge in the form of methods and tools. Such methods and tools are then converted into other cases and improved. This approach follows the stream of organizational knowledge creation theory summarized in Nonaka & Von Krogh (2009), which focuses more on the dynamic creation of knowledge rather than the type of knowledge created. Swanson (2010) extends the work of Werr and Stjnberg (2003) by identifying five consultancy roles (Business strategy, IT research and analysis, Business process improvement, Systems integration and Business services). Each role is associated to a set of deliverables (in this paper we focus on the deliverables of the Business strategy role, which are a valuable input to this first stage of innovation, by creating a strategic framework for change). This approach, belonging to the field of IS strategy and innovation management, recognizes the role of the consultancy as an IT-broker but fails to explain in detail the process of requirement elicitation. Rosemann et al. (2004) do not address the role of consultancies, but identify two ontologies to be aligned: organizational needs and software capabilities, which we claim to correspond to local and global knowledge. This work, which comes from the literature in requirement engineering, drafts a five step process to align the two ontologies, but it is not concerned about how a consultancy could make a profit from this activity.

In conclusion, the existing research has not yet analyzed how to assess the quality of the global-local translation by a consultancy, how a consultancy can make a profit out of such translation, and what is the role of the customer in such translation. Hence, we derive the following research sub-questions:

R-SQ1: How can the quality of the global-local knowledge translation process carried out by a IS strategic consultancy be increased.
R-SQ2: How can an IS strategic consultancy gain a sustainable competitive advantage from a high-quality global-local knowledge translation.
R-SQ3: What is the role of the customer in the global-local translation process?

From the literature review we also derive that there is no definitive formulation of the key activities and resources to be profitably used by a IS strategic consultancy, and that the existence of a discrepancy representing this issue can be explained in numerous ways. The choice of explanation determines the nature of the problem resolution. Thus the problem we address could be defined as "wicked" and best to be addressed using a design research methodology, as explained in the next section.

3 Methodology

In this section we briefly describe the methodology we used. Based on the relevant literatures, we create an artifact in the form of a model to express the relationship between local and global knowledge. We adopt a design science research methodology and refer to existing guidelines for design theories (Gregor and Jones, 2007), which "give explicit prescriptions on how to design and develop an artifact, whether it is a technological product or a managerial intervention" (p. 312). Therefore we advance in three steps as illustrated in the figure below.

| Description of the theoretical model (Section 4) | Illustratory instantiation (Section 5) | Example of a business model (Section 6) |

Fig. 1. Following sections

An information system design theory (ISDT) should define its purpose and scope, i.e. the boundaries of a theory. In our case, the theory relates to knowledge management to support customer retention. In this sense we introduce the representations of the entities of interest in the theory, i.e. constructs. The principles of form and function define the structure, organization, and functioning of the design product or design method. The justificatory knowledge provides an explanation as to why an artifact is constructed as it is and why it works. Accordingly in section 4 we introduce a model indicating how to assess the quality of the local-global knowledge translation. In doing so we ground our claims on existing theories of knowledge management, as well as principles of theory building. In section 5 we illustrate how to derive software requirements from our theoretical model by means of an example derived from the six-month internship in a strategic consultancy and we briefly illustrate our on-going evaluation strategy of testable propositions. In section 6 we present a possible use of our theoretical model by presenting a set of business model components for a consultancy.

4 The Theoretical Model

In this section we present a model that addresses our research question. We wish to extend the previous literature trying to explain how to best pass from local knowledge to global knowledge. In order to do so, we introduce the notion of quality of the output in the translation process.

Our definition of **consultancy benchmarks** extends the definition of Werr and Stjnberg (2003) for "cases" i.e. "documents produced in projects, e.g. maps, process and proposals" (p.889). Indeed we identify our benchmarks as ideal types of a typology and we measure them collecting the number of templates used by the consultancy. The benchmarks are collected within a framework, which in the words of Weber (2010) to define a theory, is. "a particular kind of model that is intended to account for some subset of phenomena in the world" (p.3). The concept of theory recalls Pozzebon and Pinsonneault's (2005) idea of global knowledge. According to Weber (2010) the quality of a theory can be evaluated in part and in whole. The **quality of the whole framework** can be assessed using five criteria: importance, novelty, parsimony, level, falsifiability. The *importance* of the framework can be measured by the number of clients using it. The *novelty* of the framework depends on the level of innovation requested by the customer and could have two values. Swanson (2010) claims that customers use consultancies to be at the same level as their competitors, rather than to discover disruptive uses of a new technology. A framework is *parsimonious* when "it achieves good levels of predictive and explanatory power in relation to its focal phenomena using a small number of constructs, associations, and boundary conditions" (Weber 2010, p.8). The guidelines to create a typology-inspired framework allow for *meso-levels* of precision. i.e. a good balance between too much precision and too much abstraction. The level of the framework can be measured using the types of IS consulting (Swanson, 2010): business strategy, technology assessment, business process improvement, systems integration, business process support. The *falsifiability* can be associated to the number of key performance indicators used in the framework. The table for the operationalization of our constructs can now be derived.

Table 2. The constructs of our model

Construct	Definition	Source
Consultancy benchmarks	Complex constructs that can be used to represent holistic configurations of multiple unidimensional constructs	Doty and Glick (1994, p.233)
Framework Quality	The value of *emergent* attributes of the framework	Adapted from Weber (2010)

Table 3. Operationalization of constructs

Thing: attribute	Variable	Values
Consultancy benchmarks	Number of templates	Integer [0:n]
Framework Quality: importance	Number of clients	Integer [0:n]
Framework Quality: novelty	Disruptive innovation	Boolean [true:false]
Framework Quality: parsimony	Framework dimensions	Integer [0:n]
Framework Quality: level of interest	IS Levels covered	Integer [0:5]
Framework Quality: falsifiability	Key performance indicators	Integer [0:n]

Once the constructs are operationalized we state our null hypothesis, which concerns a non-linear relationship between the quality of the framework and the number of consultancy benchmarks. The role of an IT-broker in the IS strategic consultancy is to align two customer's organizational needs and software capabilities. Since those two ontologies are finite sets, the marginal contribution of a new best practice will eventually have to go to zero, since it adds no knowledge.

H0: The positive relationship between number of benchmarks and quality of the consultancy framework is not linear.

One possible trend of such a non-linear function can be derived by considering the framework as a sort of theory. Weber (2010) explains that "as the number of constructs, associations, and boundary conditions in a theory increases, the theory might be better able to predict and explain the focal phenomena. As some point, however, users of the theory will deem it to be too complex. The goal is to achieve high levels of prediction and explanation with a small number of theoretical components (Ockham's Razor)"(p.8). Accordingly one could expect the framework parsimony to follow an inverted quadratic function as illustrated in the figure below.

H1: The positive relationship between number of benchmarks and parsimony of the consultancy framework follows an inverted u-shaped function.

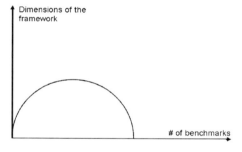

Fig. 2. Example of an inverted U-shape curve

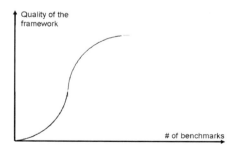

Fig. 3. Example of an S-shaped curve

Another trend is suggested by the literature on innovation, which leads us to believe that the relationship between number of benchmarks and framework quality should follow an S-shaped curve.

H2: The positive relationship between number of benchmarks and quality of the consultancy framework follows a logistic function.

Given this theoretical model in the following sections we wish to illustrate the guidelines to test its validity.

5 Illustratory Instantiation

In this section we present how we intend to test our theoretical model using a repository for consultancy benchmarks. The figures used for illustrative purpose have been changed from the original images developed during the six-month internship at the consultancy to respect its confidentiality requirements.

Components: Goal oriented requirement engineering allows to express goals, tasks required to achieve the goals, and indicators to measure the task performance. A large amount of work already exists, the most cited being Van Lamsweerde (2002). Therefore we limit ourselves to claim that the first-order constructs of the consultancy framework can be represented using the goal oriented language (GRL) as goals and soft-goals, whereas the best-practices can be modelled as task, as shown in the figure below. To present the tasks in detail we have chosen to use the Use Case Maps (UCM) approach described in Buhr (2002). As illustrated in the figure below a process is composed of various tasks and sub-processes affected to various actors. The elements presented in this figure come from results of a six-month internship in a strategic consulting firm. According to figure 4 the "Earning before Interest and Taxes" is an indicator of the "Profit increase". "Cost reduction" (measured by "Yearly cost") and "Revenue increase" (measured by "Yearly revenues") have a positive effect on "Profit increase". On the cost side the action "Knowledge management" has a positive effect on the element "Best practices", which lowers the "Yearly cost". On the revenue side the action "Customer relationship management" has a positive effect on the soft-goal "Trusted relationship", which increases the yearly revenues. The main reason behind the choice of UCM is the possibility to combine GRL and UCM by means of the Unified Requirements Notation (URN) described in Amyot (2003).

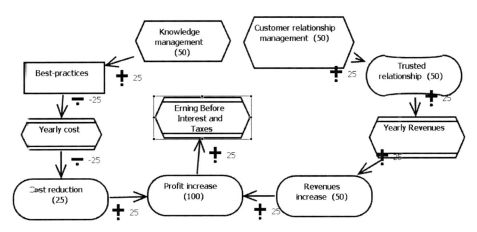

Fig. 4. Example of GRL use to represent profit increase

Architecture: We use the Eclipse plug-in called jUCMNav to implement our repository. For the moment we limit ourselves to the supporting processes of the strategic consultancy. Use case map (UCM) allows representing the 73 supporting processes in a consistent way, whereas the goal requirement language (GRL) is used to express the goals and soft-goals of the consultancy.

System mutability: The goals in GRL and the tasks in UCM are connected in URN. Once a new task is introduced it has to be linked to a goal to assess its contribution. In the same way, once a new goal is added it has to be linked to the existing set of tasks to assess its feasibility. This phase of the implementation has not been completed yet and will be used to verify our model.

Evaluation strategy: the evaluation of our instantiation is currently ongoing. During the six-month internship a set of iterations was set to formalize the processes of the consultancy. At the end of each iteration an expert from the firm and researchers gathered to assess the quality of the work-in-progress. The first prototype for the processes was created using Visio to respect the existing software approach of the consultancy. Visio's prototype usability was tested through a survey. The second prototype using URN was created in the lab, leaving only the task-goal linking process left to be done by the consultancy. We expect that once we link goals to processes (considered here as benchmarks for consultants) the amount of soft-goals (dimensions of the framework) will follow an inverted u-shape, whereas the KPI, the number of soft-goals and the number of clients using the framework will increase following an S-shape.

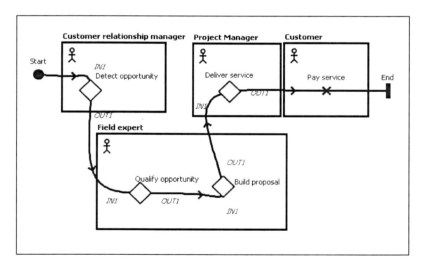

Fig. 5. Example of use case map for contract management

6 Implementation of Our Model

In the previous section we illustrated how a consultancy can use its key resources to pass from client's local knowledge in its tacit form to global knowledge under the shape URN diagrams. We conclude now by suggesting how this could be profitable for the consultancy. In doing so we consider the consultancy as an example of strategy as a profession associated to a particular business model. The figure below shows that the business model ontology of Osterwalder and Pigneur (2010) states that a company can offer a specific value proposition (VP) by combining key activities (KA), key resources (KR) and key partnership(KP). Such a value proposition is delivered through a channel (CH) to a customer segment (CS), with whom the company establishes a relationship (CR). The difference between the revenue flows (R$) and the cost structure (C$) is the profit for the company. In our case the **main customer segment** (CS) of the consulting firm is composed of the companies using its strategic advice. The **value proposition** (VP) offered to this customer falls into five types of contributions to innovation with IT identified by Swatson (2010): Business strategy, Technology assessment, Business process improvement, Systems integration and Business support services. According to our research question we focus on the first type of contribution, and we are interested in the risk reduction by minimization of the ontological distance between organizational needs and software capabilities (Rosemann et al. 2004). The consulting provider delivers the **channel** (CH) services as a project. Each project has to respect a set of quality guidelines defined in accordance with the customer. One could consider the exchanges among the consulting firm and the customer as information economics. Therefore each project requires the consulting provider and the customer to manage a contract under asymmetry of information (Akerlof, 1970). Accordingly, the process is composed of four steps. At t=1 the consulting provider knows the quality of the service offered. At t=2 the customer offers a price in exchange for service quality, which can be accepted or refused by the consulting provider. At t=3 the consulting provider delivers the service. At t=4 the customer assesses the quality of the service against the agreement made at t=2. If the service quality complies with the agreement, the customer is satisfied and the consulting provider is paid. Regarding the **customer relationship** (CR) Rhenman (1973) acknowledges that "there is in the consultant-client relationship an element of conflict.[…] Whether he realizes it or not, the consultant will become a pawn in the political game: his presence will always have some effect on the balance of power, sometimes perhaps a good deal." (pp. 160-171). Hence the customer agreement to pay might not be a good proxy for the quality of the service delivery. To address this issue we assume that the customer finds hidden costs after the payment, derived from a shading attitude of the consultant. But in this case the consulting provider is likely to not be hired again. Therefore we focus on project contracts that are managed among consulting firms and customers that have previously worked together, and we intend customer retention as a proxy of trusted relationship among a consultancy and its customers.

Among the **key partnerships** (KP) of the consulting firm are its customers since they are the source of local knowledge. On the one hand, in the role of information broker the consultancy delivers global knowledge and obtains local knowledge from each customer. On the other hand each customer can decide to hire one consultant. Therefore we identify these as "co-opetition" (Nalebluff and Brandenburger, 1997) relationships among the consultancy and its customers. In this type of this strategic alliance each strategic partners can decided to follow one of the four strategies suggested by Noteboom (2003). Since we limit ourselves to recurrent interactions among a consultancy and a firm, we focus on the so-called "making attractive" strategy, which is cooperative and fastening and which depends on mutual trust. The **critical resource** (KR) is the consultancy framework previously described. The **critical activity** (KA) is the global-local knowledge translation previously described. The **revenue flow** (R$) emerges from the satisfaction of the customer relative to the quality of the service provided and then the payment of the agreement. As previously mentioned in this paper, we focus on consultant contribution in Business strategy. The **costs structure** (C$) mainly emerges from the dynamic transaction cost and human resources. Dynamic transaction cost derives from the inability of the customer to internally create these capabilities (Langlois, 1992). Therefore consultants are more likely to contribute more to the processes by which firms imitate each other, than to those by which firms differentiate themselves (Swanson, 2010).

Table 4. Consultancy as innovation broker

KR	KA	VP	CR	CS
Customer's local knowledge	Consultancy/ customer social exchange	Relational risk perceived by the customer	Consultancy/ customer relationship recurrence	
	KR Consultancy benchmarks	Performance risk reduction perceived by the customer	CH Quality the consultancy framework	
C$; R$ Customer's dynamic transaction costs – Consultancy dynamic transaction costs				

7 Discussions and Conclusions

In this section we conclude addressing our research sub-questions:

R-SQ1: How is it possible to increase the quality of the global-local translation process which an IS strategic consultancy goes through? In table 3 of section 4 we present a set of five criteria to assess the quality of the consultancy framework and suggest the correlations among customer cases and consultancy framework quality. The idea of framework quality allows a consultancy to find the proper trade-off between the effort required to do the local-global translation and the creation of a competitive advantage.

R-SQ2: How an IS strategic consultancy can gain a sustainable competitive advantage from a high-quality global-local knowledge translation? Section 5 briefly introduces an instantiation of the framework using URN, illustrating how to convert our model into software specifications. Section 6 illustrates how to create a business model using of the consultancy framework.

R-SQ3: What is the role of the customer in the global-local translation process? Section 5 underlines how the customer is also the supplier of new cases. We identify a particular relationship between a consultancy and its customers. Both of them aim to access new global/local knowledge. In this co-opetition situation, customer trust is important in the consultancy and is the key for relationship success.

In conclusion we would like to recall our Wizard of Oz metaphor and the man behind the curtain. Trying to understand in which ways and under which conditions consultants contribute to their clients' learning and knowledge development (and vice versa), we have underlined one way to assess the quality of that contribution and the important role of mutual knowledge exchange to make it sustainable. At times, a consultant is like the Wizard of Oz, whose critical role is to lead the customer towards various quests to make him understand, at the end, that most of what he needs was already in his shoes.

Acknowledgements. The work presented in this paper was supported by the Swiss National Science Foundation (NSF) under grant number 205121-120534.

References

1. Akerlof, G.A.: The market for "lemons". The Quarterly Journal of Economics 84, 488–500 (1970)
2. Barney, J.B.: Firm resources and sustained competitive advantage. Journal of Management 17, 99–120 (1991)
3. Chen, D.Q.: Information Systems Strategy: Reconceptualization, Measurement, and Implications. MIS Quarterly 34, 233–259 (2010)
4. Doty, D.H., Glick, W.H.: Typologies as a unique form of theory building: Toward improved understanding and modeling. Academy of Management Review 19, 230–251 (1994)
5. Gregor, S., Jones, D.: The Anatomy of a Design Theory. Journal of the Association for Information Systems 8, 312 (2007)
6. Langlois, R.N.: Transaction-cost economics in real time. Industrial and Corporate Change 1, 99–127 (1992)
7. Nalebuff, B., Brandenburger, A.: Co-opetition: Competitive and cooperative business strategies for the digital economy. Strategy & Leadership 25, 28–35 (1997)
8. Nonaka, I., Von Krogh, G.: Tacit Knowledge and Knowledge Conversion: Controversy and Advancement in Organizational Knowledge Creation Theory. Organization Science 20, 635–652 (2009)
9. Osterwalder, A., Pigneur, Y.: Business Model Generation: A Handbook for Visionaries, Game Changers, and Challengers. Wiley, Chichester (2010)
10. Pozzebon, M., Pinsonneault, A.: Global-local negotiations for implementing configurable packages: The power of initial organizational decisions. The Journal of Strategic Information Systems 14, 121–145 (2005)
11. Rhenman, E., Adler, N.: Organization theory for long-range planning. Wiley, Chichester (1973)
12. Rosemann, M., Vessey, I., Weber, R.: Alignment in enterprise systems implementations: the role of ontological distance. In: Proceedings of the International Conference on Information Systems, Washington, DC, pp. 439–447 (2004)
13. Swanson, E.B.: Consultancies and capabilities in innovating with IT. The Journal of Strategic Information Systems 19, 17–27 (2010)

14. Weber, R.: Theory Building in the Information Systems Discipline: Some Critical Reflections. In: Presented at the Information Systems Foundations: Theory Building in Information Systems, Canberra, Australia, (September 30, 2010)
15. Werr, A., Stjernberg, T.: Exploring Management Consulting Firms as Knowledge Systems. Organization Studies 24, 881–908 (2003)
16. Whittington, R.: Strategy practice and strategy process: family differences and the sociological eye. Organization Studies 28, 1575 (2007)

Enterprise Interoperability Maturity: A Model Using Fuzzy Metrics

Wided Guédria[1,2], Yannick Naudet[1], and David Chen[2]

[1] CITI, Henri Tudor Public Research Center
29, Avenue J.F. Kennedy, L-1855 Luxembourg-kirchberg
`prenom.nom@tudor.lu`,
[2] IMS/LAPS,Université Bordeaux 1,
351, cours de la libération, 33405 Talence cedex
`prenom.nom@ims-bordeaux.fr`

Abstract. Measuring interoperability maturity allows a company to know its strengths and weaknesses in terms of interoperability with its current and potential partners, and to prioritize improvement actions. Existing maturity models however cover only few aspects of interoperability. This paper aims at presenting a Maturity Model for Enterprise Interoperability (MMEI) based on the Framework for Enterprise Interoperability currently under CEN/ISO standardization process. The proposed model takes into account the existing relevant maturity models and goes beyond, extending the coverage of the interoperability domain. Together with the MMEI, we provide an assessment framework which has the particularity to be based on Fuzzy sets theory. Both are demonstrated with an illustrative case study.

Keywords: Interoperability, Framework of Enterprise Interoperability, maturity model, maturity level, linguistic variable.

1 Introduction

In order to support enterprises to better interoperate with their partners, clients, providers, etc; enterprise interoperability requires to be assessed and continuously improved. Enterprise interoperability can be measured in two ways : *a priori* where the measure relates to the potentiality of a system to be interoperable with a possible future partner whose identity is not known at the moment of evaluation; *a posteriori* where the measure relates to the compatibility measure between two (or more) known systems willing to interoperate. Today there exist many maturity models. Few were developed for interoperability assessment. The most known existing interoperability maturity models are: LISI (Levels of Information System Interoperability) [1], OIM (Organizational Interoperability Model) [2], LCIM (Levels of Conceptual Interoperability Model) [3], and EIMM (Enterprise Interoperability Maturity Model) [4]. In most of cases, these models focus on one simple facet of interoperability (data, technology, conceptual, Enterprise modeling, etc.),while sometimes also developing in a superficial manner other facets [10]. Measuring more than one facet of interoperability implies using multiple maturity models. This creates redundancies and incompatibilities and makes the aggregation process more difficult. The objective of this paper is to present the Maturity Model for Enterprise Interopeability (MMEI) and its methodologies. MMEI is based on existing relevant maturity models and it extends existing works to cover all main aspects and dimensions of enterprise interoperability. In particular MMEI focus on the a priori interoperability measurement and is built using the Framework for Enterprise Interoperability (FEI) [7]. As part of the MMEI assessment process, allowing to determine the maturity of an enterprise in terms of interoperability, we introduce an innovative method which relies on the Fuzzy Sets theory [5]. In fuzzy logic applications, non-numerical linguistic variables are often used to facilitate the expression of rules and facts. Traditional methods of assessment are based on assessor's judgment which is subjective and can be source of incomplete information, interpersonal contradictions, etc. Moreover employees of the evaluated enterprise reply to questions using their own words and interpretations. To facilitate the use of the collected information from human sources and to lower biases due to human judgment, we propose the use of linguistic variables. The maturity level is then obtained by aggregating the assessment results according to a suitable operator. In our case, we use the Ordered Weighted Average (OWA) operator [14]. The paper is structured as follows. In section 2, the FEI is briefly presented. Then, MMEI is outlined in section 3. In section 4, the basis of the assessment framework and associated metrics are exposed and an illustrative example is presented. Finally section 5 concludes the paper and proposes future work.

2 Preliminaries

Generally speaking, interoperability is the ability of two or more systems or components to exchange information and to use the information that has been exchanged [6]. When this ability is not achieved, interoperability becomes a problem that must be solved.

Solutions to interoperability problems can be characterized according to interoperability approaches defined in [11] and both solutions and problems can be localized into enterprises levels and characterized by interoperability levels, as defined in the Framework for Enterprise Interoperability (FEI). FEI has been initially elaborated in INTEROP NoE [7] and is now under development within the CEN/ISO standardization process (CEN/ISO 11354). It defines a classification scheme for interoperability knowledge according to three dimensions:

- Interoperability concerns, defining the content of interoperation that may take place at various levels of the enterprise (data, service, process, business).
- Interoperability barriers, identifying various obstacles to interoperability in three categories (conceptual, technological, and organizational)
- Interoperability approaches, representing the different ways in which barriers can be removed (integrated, unified, and federated)

The first two dimensions, interoperability concerns and barriers, constitute the problem space of enterprise interoperability. The intersection of a barrier and a concern is the set of interoperability problems having the same barrier and concern. The three dimensions together constitute the solution space of enterprise interoperability. FEI is used as a basis to build MMEI, but has been slightly changed. We use the term *"interoperability level"* instead of *"interoperability barrier"*. Indeed, by having an *a priori* approach of interoperability measurement, MMEI does not deal with removing barriers but it allows an enterprise to be prepared to interoperability through the respect of defined practices. Moreover the cited dimensions (conceptual, technological and organizational) can also be used to characterize interoperability solutions. They are, obviously, specific for interoperability domain and related to aspects or facets of interoperability [12]. Furthermore, Interoperability concerns is specific to the enterprise domain so we should use the term *"enterprise interoperability concern"*. However, for a matter of simplicity, we use the term *"enterprise concerns"*. The development of the MMEI is a long and iterative process which needs significant industrial applications and case-studies for its improvement and validation. The model presented here is an evolution of a preliminary version presented in [10], [9] and it is currently being discussed in the ISO TC184 SC5 Working Group.

3 MMEI Model

When an enterprise wants or needs to work or collaborate with other enterprises, different tools such as guidelines or metrics might be useful in order to ensure proper interoperation at all levels of the enterprise system. The idea of our research is to propose a Maturity Model for Enterprise Interoperability (MMEI) allowing companies to evaluate their interoperability potentiality in order to know the probability that they have to support efficient interoperation and to detect precisely the weaknesses that are sources of interoperability problems. In this section we present an overview of the MMEI model with a brief description of its levels. The complete description of the model can be found in [9].

The proposed model differs from all other maturity models dedicated to interoperability so far. It is intended to cover the three interoperability levels (conceptual, technological, organizational) which are used to classify the barriers in FEI, at each of the enterprise interoperability concerns (business, process, service, data). MMEI defines five levels of interoperability maturity as presented in table 1.

Each one of the cited levels is described based on a simplified version of the interoperability framework that contains only two basic dimensions "interoperability levels" and "enterprise concerns" as shown in figure 1.

The intersection between the two dimensions is described as states or qualities that should have the assessed enterprise and best practices to be considered at each level. Best practices are tasks and activities that when put in place, allow reaching a targeted level of interoperability maturity. In order to have a

Table 1. Overview of MMEI levels

Maturity Level	Maturity Capability
Level 4 - Adapted	Capable of negotiating and dynamically accommodating with any heterogeneous partner
Level 3 - Organized	Capable of meta modeling to achieve the mappings needed to interoperate with multiple heterogeneous partners
Level 2 - Aligned	Capable of making necessary changes to align to common formats or standards
Level 1 - Defined	Capability of properly modeling and describing systems to prepare interoperability
Level 0 - Isolated	Not relevant: there is no capability for interoperation

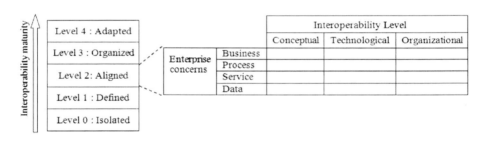

Fig. 1. Zoom on MMEI level

clearer idea of the description of a maturity level and the way that best practices are presented, we provide in Table 2 the description of the MMEI level 2.

A possible graphical representation of interoperability maturity using MMEI is a camembert form divided into three parts (see Figure 2). Each part stands for an assessed interoperability level: conceptual, technological or organizational. In each part, arrows represent enterprise concerns : business, process, data and service. The arrows are graduated to present the maturity level: 1, 2, 3 or 4. Figure 2 illustrates a case where the assessed enterprise is at the level 3 regarding the conceptual interoperability, level 2 regarding technological interoperability and the level 4 regarding organizational interoperability.

4 MMEI Assessment

The assessment is an activity that can be performed either as part of an improvement initiative or as part of a maturity determination approach. In this

Enterprise Interoperability Maturity: A Model Using Fuzzy Metrics   73

Table 2. Description of the MMEI level 2

	Conceptual	Technological	Organizational
Business	Use of standards to facilitate the alignment with other Business models	Use of standards to facilitate the alignment with other IT infrastructures / platforms	Adjustable business rules
Process	Use of standards to facilitate the alignment with other process models	Platform process execution tools using standards	Procedures of work defined and adjustable
Service	Use of standards to facilitate the alignment with other service models	Use of standards to facilitate the alignment with other platforms Service execution	Guidelines for service exchanges in place and can be adjusted
Data	Use of standards to facilitate the alignment with other data models	Data bases connectable, remote access to data base possible	Rules and methods for data interoperability management in place and can be adjusted

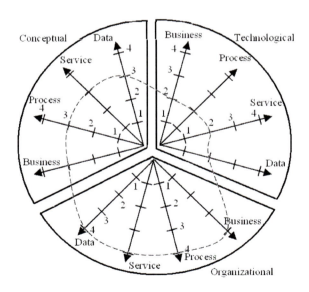

Fig. 2. Graphical representation of an MMEI application example

part, we present the different stages of the assessment process and the associated methodologies to determine the enterprise interoperability maturity level.

4.1 MMEI Assessment Stages

The first step when conducting an assessment process is to define the purpose of the assessment, its scope, under which constraints it is done (i.e., the context) and any additional information that needs to be gathered. Assessors may originate from the organization, be external to the organization or a combination of both.

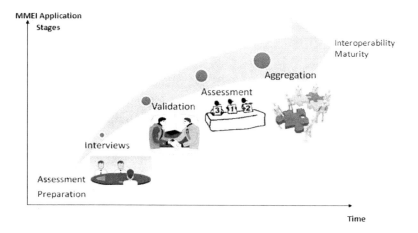

Fig. 3. Membership diagrams of the linguistic variables

They need to collect information through a series of interviews. The content of the assessment interview depends on the assessment scope and the enterprise needs. From the interviews, a rating shall be assigned based on validated data. Actions are taken to ensure that the data is accurate and sufficiently covers the assessment scope, including seeking information from independent sources; using past assessment results; and holding feedback sessions to validate the information collected. A quick synthesis on the interview and conclusion is finally performed by the assessor team. A value is associated to each practice, based on what should be done according to the maturity model. It is assigned based on assessors' judgment about the achievement degree of considered practices. Such judgment is subjective and can be source of incomplete information, interpersonal contradictions, etc. Moreover employees of the evaluated enterprise will reply to questions using their own words and not with numerical degrees to quantify a task achievement. To facilitate the mapping between collected information from human sources and the global evaluation of a maturity level, we propose to use linguistic values (like e.g. "achieved" practice, "partially achieved" practice), etc.) and to exploit the Fuzzy sets theory. The obtained values are then aggregated allowing to determine the interoperabiliy maturity level of the enterprise under assessment. An overview of the assessment process is given by the figure 3.

4.2 Linguistic Variable

Definition 1. *A linguistic variable is a variable whose associated values are linguistic rather than numerical. Each linguistic variable is characterized by the set:*
$(x, T(x), U, G, M)$, *where: x is the variable name, $T(x)$ is the set of linguistic values that may take x, U is the universe of discourse representing the whole repository that contains all the elements linked to the given context, G is the syntactic rule to generate linguistic values of x, M is the semantic rule for associating a meaning to each linguistic value [5].*

Consider the linguistic variable x = "state of the best practice"; x can be defined with the set of terms: $T(x)$ = (Not Achieved (NA), Partially Achieved (PA), Achieved (A), Fully Achieved (FA)), which form the universe of discourse X = [0%, 100%]. We characterize both levels of maturity and practices achievements using variables associated to $T(x)$. Each one is respectively represented by a membership function (c.f. figure 4).

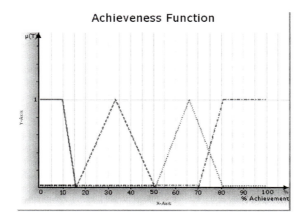

Fig. 4. Membership diagrams of the linguistic variables

In the enterprise context, multiple information sources having different knowledge level can be exploited during an evaluation. Assessors need to aggregate linguistic values issued from these sources in order to determine the achievement degree of needed practices and thus the enterprise level. To obtain directly an aggregated value, we use the Ordered Weighted Average (OWA) operator [14]. In addition to systematize the aggregation process, it has the main advantage to allow obtaining a value that reflects the opinion of the assessors taking into account all the scores affected to the evaluated practices. From the obtained aggregation, we can determine if a level is fulfilled or not. A level is reached if it is at least A and the preceding level is reached with FA.

4.3 Linguistic Variable and OWA Operators

The OWA operator was introduced in [13]. It is an aggregation technique based on the ordered weighted averaging operator.

Definition 2. *An OWA operator of dimension n is a mapping $OWA : R^n \rightarrow R$ that has an associated n vector : $w = (w_1, w_2, ... w_n)$ such as $w_j \in [0,1]$, $1 \leq j \leq n$ and $\sum_{j=1}^{n} w_j = w_1 + w_2 + ... + w_n = 1$ furthermore*

$$OWA(a_1, a_2, ...a_n) = \sum_{j=1}^{n} w_j b_j = w_1 b_1 + ... + w_n b_n \quad (1)$$

where b_j is the $j-th$ largest element of the bag $(a_1, ...a_n)$.

Definition 3. *Let a_1, a_2, ..., a_n be a collection of arguments, and let A be the average value of these arguments: $A = \frac{1}{n} \sum_{j=1}^{n} a_j$, then :*

$$s(b_j, A) = 1 - \frac{|b_j - A|}{\sum_{j=1}^{n} |a_j - A|}, j = 1, 2, ..., n \quad (2)$$

is called the similarity degree of the j-th largest argument b_j and the average value A.

Definition 4. *Let the $w = (w_1, w_2, ..., w_n)$ be the weight vector of the OWA operator, then we define the following:*

$$w_j = \frac{s(b_j, A)}{\sum_{j=1}^{n} s(b_j, A)}; j = 1, 2, ..., n, \quad (3)$$

4.4 Illustrative Example

To illustrate the use of the maturity model and its metrics, we present in this section an illustrative example that is inspired from a case study proposed by the Network of Excellence INTEROP [8]. The company modeled is part of a group of companies, which is specialized in telecommunications, production and distribution of batteries, as well as mobile phones.

To distribute its products and services, the company retail sales to two kinds of distributors: franchisees, who are distributors in exclusive contract with the company and may only offer its products and services; and independent dealers, who may have contracts with other companies. A franchisee must use the same tools as the company; therefore, interoperability issues in this case are irrelevant for our study. However, with independent dealers, the interoperability subject can be tackled.

There are 5 main departments in the company: Commercial, Sales, Financial, Logistics and IT. IT department is responsible for system administration, imports and exports of data in different databases and creating specific reports needed by the other departments. The products distribution is based on the rule of proportionality: If the total quantity of ordered products is available, all orders are fulfilled. Otherwise, the company decides what quantities to be allocated based on the proportionality between the quantity of products available and the quantity ordered by retailers. According to this rule, it adjusts its orders and publishes the bills that are sent to corresponding retailers for payment. Upon receipt of invoice, retailers emit a debit authorization for the sales department. This work procedure is well known by the company staff, it is successful and the Enterprise is able to adjust it when needed. Exchanged data between partners are of three types. (1) Orders from the retailer to the company (2) Invoices from the company to its retailer and, (3) Levy authorization from the retailer to the company.

Currently the company headquarters and branches work with a decentralized database and there is a daily transfer of information from the shops to the headquarters and back. The goal of the enterprise is to investigate its interoperability potential in order to anticipate future interoperability operations. According to the preparations made, the company aims to reach Level 2 of potential interoperability. According to the given information, we make an assessment of the Organizational Interoperability. After a series of interviews, the assessors provide the evaluation sheet shown by table 3 where B stands for Business, P stands for Process, S stands for Service and D stands for Data.

This evaluation consists in combining the assessors ratings for each practice in order to determine the interoperability maturity level. Using the achieve-

Table 3. Evaluation sheet for potential interoperability

	Practices to Evaluate	Findings	Team Rating
Business	Adjust business rules	Business is adjusted according to the proportionality rule	90%
Process	Procedures of work and guidelines are defined	yes	85%
Service	Adjustable procedures of work	Procedures can be adjusted if needed	80%
Data	Rules for data interoperability are in place	Daily transfer of data	70%

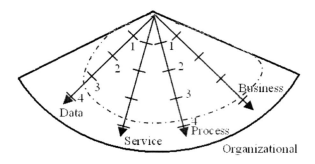

Fig. 5. Zoom on the MMEI organizational interoperability maturity of the use case

ment functions (see fig.4), assessors can provide either a linguistic variable or a percentage value corresponding to the practice achievement. For the sake of simplicity, we use the percentage rating. According to table 3, we have the following ratings : $a_1 = 90$, $a_2 = 85$, $a_3 = 80$, $a_4 = 70$.

Therefore, the re-ordered arguments a_j: $j = 1, 2, 3, 4$ in descending order are: $b_1 = 90$, $b_2 = 85$, $b_3 = 80$, $b_4 = 70$.
Using eq.(2) and eq. (3), we find : $w_1 = 0.35$, $w_2 = 0.15$, $w_3 = 0.05$, $w_4 = 0.45$.
By eq. (1), the aggregated rating argument is computed as:
OWA $(a_1, a_2, a_3, a_4) = 79.75$

Using the membership functions we have defined for our variables (here maturity level),(see fig.4), we find that,all practices are "Fully Achieved" and the level 2 of organizational interoperability level is fully reached. Figure 5 shows a graphical representation of this example.

4.5 Discussion

MMEI proposes an innovative approach for interoperability assessment. It allows to have an automatic aggregation of the affected scores. Here, we haven't presented the aggregation of the individual assessors allowing to have the global evaluation sheet. This step is done by an iterative application of the OWA operator. Semantically, OWA allows to relieve the influence of unfair arguments on the aggregated results. It assigns low weights to the extreme scores which are considered as "false" or "biased" ones, that is to say, the closer a value to the average value A, the more the weight is. This method has advantages and drawbacks. In fact, it allows to take into account the most of the assessors opinions and to find a consensus. However, we have no idea about the characteristics and expertise of the evaluators which can be the cause of biased results. A possible solution is to give more importance to the evaluations of true experts and to multiply the OWA weights with a confidence coefficient based on a self-evaluation of the assessors and the history of their assessment qualities.

5 Conclusion

In this paper, we have presented a maturity model for enterprise interoperability (MMEI). MMEI proposes an innovative approach for interoperability assessment which uses the OWA aggregation operator. The latter allows a positive compensation between the assigned ratings, in order to find a trade-off between the enterprise assessors. The idea behind this is to find the global evaluation between the worst and the best ratings. MMEI covers other approaches in terms of measurement and deals with the potential interoperability assessment which is not addressed by existing ones. Future work is planned to refine the proposed model and metrics in order to take into account the individual expertise of the assessors in the aggregated ratings, and to perform some more detailed case studies in enterprises. A detailed questionnaire associated with a structured methodology will also be elaborated to support the use of MMEI in industry.

Acknowledgment

This work has been performed under the PhD grant TR-PhD-BFR07 funded by the Luxembourg National Research Fund (FNR).

References

1. C4ISR Interoperability Working Group.: Levels of Information Systems Interoperability (LISI). US Department of Defense (1998)
2. Clark, T., Jones, R.: Organizational interoperability maturity model for c2. In: Command and Control Research and Technology Symposium, Washington (1999)
3. Tolk, A., Muguira, J.: The levels of conceptual interoperability model. In: Fall Simulation Interoperability Workshop (2003)
4. ATHENA.: Advanced Technologies for Interoperability of Heterogeneous Enterprise Networks and their Applications, FP6-2002-IST1, Integrated Project Proposal (2003)
5. Zadeh, L.A.: Soft computing and Fuzzy logic. IEEE Software (1994)
6. IEEE (Institute of Electrical and Electronics Engineers).: Standard computer dictionary: A compilation of IEEE standard computer glossaries (1990)
7. Chen, D., Dassisti, M., Elvester, B.: Deliverable Interop DI.2. Enterprise Interoperability-Framework and knowledge corpus-Advanced report (2006)
8. Chen, D., Dassisti, M., Elvester, B.: Interop NOE deliverable di.3: Enterprise interoperability framework and knowledge corpus - final report. Technical report, Interoperability Research for Networked Enterprises Applications and Software (INTEROPNetwork of Excellence), IST - Contract no. IST-508 011 (2007)
9. Guédria, W., Chen, D., Naudet, Y.: A Maturity Model for Enterprise Interoperability. In: On the Move to Meaningful Internet Systems: OTM Workshops (2009)
10. Guédria, W., Naudet, Y., Chen, D.: Interoperability Maturity Models - Survey and Comparison. In: On the Move to Meaningful Internet Systems: OTM Workshops (2008)

11. ISO 14258.: Industrial Atomation Systems - Concepts and Rules for Enterprise Models, ISO TC184/SC5/WG1 (1999)
12. Naudet, N., Latour, T., Guédria, W., Chen, D.: Towards a Systemic Formalisation of Interoperability. Computers in Industry, Special Issue on Integration and Information in Networked Enterprises (61/2) (2010)
13. Yager, R.R.: On ordered weighted averaging aggregation operators in multi-criteria decision making. IEEE Transactions on Systems, Man and Cybernetics 18, 183–190 (1988)
14. Yager, R.R.: Families of OWA operators. Fuzzy Sets and Systems 59, 125–148 (1993)
15. Yager, R.R.: Aggregation operators and fuzzy systems modeling. Fuzzy Sets and Systems 67, 129–145 (1994)

Service Value Networks for Competency-Driven Educational Services: A Case Study

Iván S. Razo-Zapata, Pieter De Leenheer, Jaap Gordijn, and Hans Akkermans

VU University, Amsterdam, The Netherlands
{i.s.razozapata,p.g.m.de.leenheer,j.gordijn}@vu.nl

Abstract. Service networks represent a flexible way for delivering services to customers. In earlier work, we have applied the e^3-*value* methodology to conceptually model such networks. This paper, however, presents an approach for composing Service Value Networks (SVNs) based on customer and supplier perspectives. A broker is in charge of composing a SVN that reflects not only customer desires but also supplier offerings. Moreover, the application of using real-world services is shown by means of a case study. Finally, we provide some reflections as well as future lines of research.

1 Introduction

Service industry has been experiencing an enormous growing in the last years, it encapsulates over 70% of USA and Europe economies. Although the evident potential of this sector is clear, there are still some misunderstandings in areas like service composition, customer targeting and service provision [14]. Service composition briefly states that, given a specific customer need, at least one arrangement of service suppliers must be automatically composed to cope with such a need [9]. The assumption here is that due to the wideness of customer needs, it is necessary to combine the functionality of several services to cope with such needs. Even though service networks represent a flexible and dynamic way for service delivering, yet some knowledge gaps exist, specially regarding strategic bundling of services and value (co)creation within the network.

In this paper we aim at a framework for SVN composition from a business-oriented perspective. By business orientation we mean that the framework must take into account economic relationships rather than work flow properties. Business models are centred around the notion of value, therefore it is relevant to determine who is offering what of value to whom and what expects of value in return [10].

We propose an interactive dialogue to express customer needs based on marketing theory [15]. In addition, we also provide capabilities to publish service offerings by means of an ontology-based catalogue. Moreover, since mass configuration of products is playing an important role, dynamic composition of SVNs has been also supported. Finally, our long-term ultimate goal is to automatically compose a SVN, including the required business processes and Information Technology (IT) support in the form of web services. Such IT is then aligned with the business, since both are designed in an integrated way.

The rest of the paper is organized as follows. Sect. 2 introduces a set of basic concepts. In Sect. 3 we describe some related work. Afterwards, Sect. 4 provides the description of our case study. Later on, Sect. 5 presents our approach for SVN composition while Sect. 6 shows the performance of such approach in our case study. Finally, conclusions and future work are described in Sect. 7.

2 Basic Concepts

Service has become a term loaded with different meanings in different circumstances, mostly depending on who uses it [4,8]. In this paper, we focus only on a set of features that are relevant for our research. We refer to a service as follows.

Definition 1. *A service is an economic activity possessing intangible nature and offering consequences for which customers are willing to sacrifice [4,8]*[1].

Moreover, we are interested in services that can be provided through IT infrastructures, e.g. internet connectivity, network hosting amongst others. Such services are commonly offered by alternative suppliers which can publish their offerings with different consequences. In addition, sometimes customer requirements can not be covered by a single service but by a combination of them, which can involve one or more suppliers *i.e.* a *service bundle*.

Definition 2. *A service bundle is a package of one or more services, these services can be provided by a single entity or by different enterprises, who each focus on their core competency [8]*.

When bundles or single services are offered to final customers we say that there is a business to customer (B2C) relationship, otherwise, if offered to another service supplier we have a business to business (B2B) relationship. Furthermore, when suppliers work together to cover a specific customer need, they compose a *service network*. The creation of such networks is, most of the time, driven by the *value* they provide to customers. Value networks have been broadly defined by several authors, some of them use terms such as economic web, business web, value web or value constellation [1,5]. From these definitions we can abstract basic denominators. First of all, value networks are composed of economic entities. These entities work together to achieve some objective. In this way, we can consider that those entities can be represented by services.

Definition 3. *A service value network is a flexible and dynamic delivery of services, such that a value-adding specific solution is delivered to the individual customer*[2].

By means of SVNs it is possible to model not only the structure and dynamics of service networks but also customer expectations and their influence in these networks [5]. Fig. 1 depicts the three types of actors participating in a SVN, as well as the interactions among them. On the one hand, a customer interacts with service suppliers by means of B2C relationships. On the other hand, through B2B relationships, service suppliers not only interact with other service suppliers but also with service enablers.

---
[1] The sacrifice is usually expressed in terms of money exchange.
[2] Adapted from Hamilton, 2004 [14].

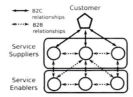

Fig. 1. Service Value Network

Customers are considered the starting point and the reason why a SVN must be generated. Briefly, according to their needs, customers send requests to the service network. *Service suppliers* provide resources that match customers requests. To foresee customer needs and adapt to changes in the network, they perform B2C and B2B relationships. *Service enablers* support the operation of service suppliers. In this sense, service enablers also establish B2B relationships with service suppliers.

Furthermore, there are at least two aspects pushing up the need for service value networks: *1) policy issues:* due to market liberalization, many services that were traditionally provided by monopolies can be now offered by alternative suppliers. *2) rapid technological change:* many sectors, like the music industry, are experimenting revolutionary changes in their traditional business models, mainly because of the emergence of new ways of delivering services [19].

In the end, we aim at a runtime composition framework where customers and suppliers dynamically establish relationships with each other. To achieve this goal, we propose the use of customer and supplier ontologies where concepts at both sides can be automatically matched allowing for the establishment of B2C and B2B relationships. Moreover, we are interested in modelling business-oriented aspects such as value exchanges.

3 Related Work

Since service network composition must deal with issues related to establishing B2C and B2B relationships, we have analyzed related work about service composition and service network modelling. Moreover, we have also made a distinction between e^3-*value* based and service science approaches.

Although many e^3-*value* inspired approaches focus on business aspects, they have a static flavor. According to Dustdar *et al.*, [9], static approaches perform several step during design-time which make them unsuitable for dynamic composition. Zlatev, [24], proposes a framework for service composition based on value, process and goal models, however the transformations among these three representations require a lot of manual steps, which is not appropriate for automation. VBC, [18], aims at an automatic framework. Although the idea about using a value meta-model to compose service networks is well supported, the lack of results brings about some doubts over its applicability. e^3*service* , [8], is one of the latest efforts in the field of value modelling. De Kinderen *et al.*, propose a framework for matching customer and supplier views. Even though, e^3*service* allows B2C interaction for service bundling, the main drawback is that the service bundles have been generated at design time. Serviguration [4] presents a more dynamic strategy for service bundling, nevertheless, the generated bundles do not always depict the concept of economic reciprocity, *i.e.* what they expect in return for an object of value delivered, which is important to understand the value exchanges within a SVN.

Traverso and Pistore, [23], have proposed a framework which makes use of a Model Based Planner (MBP). Because the MBP module generates work-flow-based plans, this approach is not business oriented and does not support any visualization for the generated plans. OntoMat-Service, [2], offers a dynamic approach for service composition. Although the approach allows basic modelling and visualization of service networks, it is focused on process-oriented issues. METEOR-S, [22], provides Semantic Process Templates (SPTs) to discover and add services. Because SPTs model the required activities to be performed, they give a basic notion of how a service network can be described. However, because of SPTs construction is performed at design-time, METEOR-S is an static approach. Moreover, it is also process-oriented. DynamiCoS, [21], supports run-time discover and composition of services. Nevertheless, it does not offer any formal definition to represent service networks in terms of economical exchanges. Finally, Danylevych *et al.*, [6], present a framework for modelling service networks. Even though it gives formal backgrounds, some manual steps are required to build the service network and to transform it into BPMN.

As can be observed, many service science approaches focus on process-oriented issues, that is why the composition process is usually modelled as a planning problem. However, as we describe in Sect. 5, a business-oriented approach might rely on other strategies. Finally, we emphasize our interest in dynamic and business-oriented approaches allowing for customers and suppliers to co-create service value networks as well as providing visual representation of economic relationships among them.

4 Case Study

The European employment market is characterized by a contradictory situation: a very large number of candidates fail to find a job; and many employers are unsuccessful in locating appropriate candidates for their vocations. Given a Vocational Competency Ontology (VCO) (collaboratively developed in previous work [7]), skill gap analysis can overcome the semantic mismatch between candidate and market profiles, and capture a candidate's missing competencies. Stakeholders include educational institutes, public employment organizations, and industry partners from different European countries.

Central actor driving the evolution of the Educational Service Web are the enterprise ecosystems. Once set out the goals and strategy of the company, different supporting business processes are lined out, involving the creation of (new) functions and tasks. Each of them require human performance, which in turn require certain competencies. From this feedback loop, relations between Functions and Competencies emerge. To describe competencies, there is a widely used HR-XML-standard called reusable competency definitions (RCDs). RCDs are yet underspecified so they retain their generative character. To describe the relationship between functions and competencies enterprises define function profiles, which usually contain a competency map, RCDs and

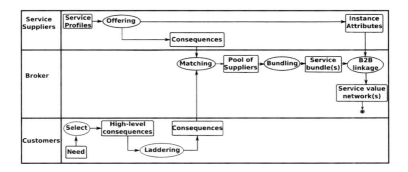

Fig. 2. Service Value Network composition

proficiency levels for Competencies (default +1) (IEEE score or SCORM uses an interval of -1 to +1).

E.g., in the automotive industry functions are categorized along the car manufacturing process: going from press shop, to the body shop, to finally end at the assembly shop[3]. In order to perform each of those functions, human operators with specialized competencies are required.

The candidate's search is equally driven by populating its CV by RCDs he collects through experience and education. If its current CV shows gaps to fulfil a certain function profile, a need emerges that has to be answered by the Service Web. The final stakeholder's cycle are the educational service suppliers. They monitor needs and function profiles and define services accordingly.

Currently the stakeholder community is simplified for the sake of illustration. In reality there are additional parties that are responsible for identifying large gaps in the candidate pools and predicting future needs in education, and finally organize this education. The main point we want to make here is that all these parties can act independently and by doing so converge towards each other as long as their information (about functions, competencies and education service offerings) is published using (as shown below) open (IEEE and HR-XML) standards like RCD, SCORM, and LOM.

5 SVNs Composition

In order to deal with composition of SVNs a novel approach based on several steps is proposed in Figure 2. The idea is to provide a framework for achieving automatic composition of SVNs. Such framework relies on two perspectives, one for customer and the other one for suppliers. Initially, by means of a laddering process, a customer express its need in terms of consequences. Later on, a broker starts an automatic composition for matching, bundling and linking services. At the end of the process, a SVN with detailed information about specific suppliers and value exchanges must be generated. Subsections 5.1- 5.3 give a deeper explanation of each step.

---

[3] cf. http://www.nedcar.nl/content/view/44/49/lang,en/

5.1 Supplier Perspective

To publish service offerings we promote the use of an ontology. Fig. 3 depicts an ontology, which is the result of aligning the $e^3service$ [8] supplier ontology with the e^3-*value* [11] ontology. We only describe what is relevant for defining supplier profiles. Service suppliers are *actors* performing activities (*value activities*) to produce resources (*value objects*) which can be offered to customers. In addition, as a result of its use or consumption, a value object has *functional consequences* and *quality consequences*. Finally, a *service bundle* consists of *service elements* which are special types of value activities. For a full elaboration of these concepts we refer to [11] and [8].

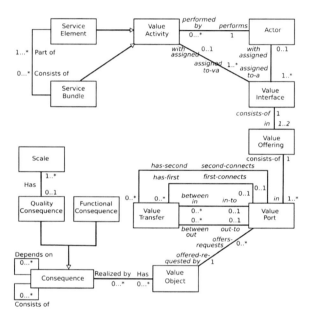

Fig. 3. The $e^3service$ [8] supplier perspective ontology aligned to the e^3-*value* [11] ontology

5.2 Customer perspective

In the same way, customers can express their needs by using another ontology. Figure 4 shows a UML rendering of the customer perspective. It is based on concepts from established customer needs literature [8,15].

- A Need represents a problem statement or goal (see[3,15,8])[4]. *E.g.*, a job candidate has a need to fulfil a certain Function profile.
- A Consequence is anything that results from consuming (a combination of) valuable service properties [13,8]. We distinguish between two types.

---

[4] Needs are the basic human requirements. Wants are specific objects that might satisfy the need.

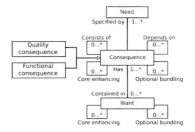

Fig. 4. The $e^3service$ customer perspective ontology, based on [8]

- Functional Consequence [8] represents the functional goal that can be achieved through consumption of a service that has a certain valuable property. E.g., a Functional Consequence from the need to fulfil a certain Function profile are all the involved Competencies[5]. E.g., the consequence "read and write" consists of the consequences "read" and "write"; or the consequence "writing english" is core-enhancing for "programming", etc..
- Quality Consequence [8] A quality consequence expresses qualitative properties of other. Because it expresses the qualitative properties of another Consequence, a Quality Consequence cannot be acquired separately: It always depends on (a relation between Consequences) another type of Consequence . E.g., Writing English has a required proficiency as a Quality Consequence.
- A Want [8] is a solution that is commercially feasible to be provisioned on its own. As a Want indicates a solution available in the market, at least one supplier should be willing to provide the solution. An example of a Want could be learning objects for which multiple institutes are accredited to deliver them.
- A Scale [8] groups Quality Consequences of the same type. E.g., a proficiency level according to IEEE or SCORM is defined by a number in an interval between -1 and +1.

5.3 Combining Perspectives

To compose a SVN according to customer-expressed needs, some steps must be performed: offering, laddering, matching, bundling, and B2B linkage.

Offering suppliers publish their resources by using service profiles, which are designed according to the ontology in Fig. 3. Moreover, these profiles also enable interaction not only with customers but also with other suppliers and enablers.

Laddering is a marketing practice which uses a conceptual map to represent how a customer links specific product attributes to high-level values [8]. In our case we apply it to link service consequences to customer needs via high-level consequences (Fig. 4).

---

[5] The structure of the tree in between function and competencies may be defined by the RCM as described above.

Matching determines a *pool* of service suppliers that plausibly provide part of the required consequences. Due to the variability of customer needs, single suppliers rarely provide all the required consequences on their own. Consequences are the key components for matching the two perspectives. For each functional consequence at the customer side, this matching process performs a (semantic) comparison with all the functional consequences expressed at the supplier side and retrieves the service that offers the required consequences.

Bundling takes as input the pool of suppliers and finds combinations of suppliers that collectively cover the required consequences. At this stage, we have applied a modified version of Baida's algorithm [4]. Whereas the original Baida's algorithm bundles services according to the value objects they offer, we bundle services depending on the consequences they provide. Moreover, our algorithm generates bundles depicting the concept of economic reciprocity by means of e^3-*value* interfaces and ports. A deep explanation of such algorithm is out of the scope.

B2B Linkage is applied to those bundles requiring to exchange resources with service enablers. For instance, for educational services such as On-line IT Training, enabler services like Black Board or Simulation platforms might be needed. Therefore, those additional services must be obtained by exchanging resources between service suppliers and service enablers. Moreover, at this stage, instance attributes of services are used to perform the linkage[6]. In previous work, [12], we have defined a methodology for achieving B2B linking. Such methodology involves a searching process based on the value objects a service supplier requires.

As can be observed in Fig. 2, once the pool of suppliers has been found, the composition of the SVN involves bundling and B2B Linkage. We claim that by firstly generating service bundles, the broker can focus on the main services to fulfil the customer need. At this point strategic decisions might take place. On the contrary, B2B linkage requires less strategic consideration and constraints might be relaxed. However this step is also important to have a complete SVN and compute the total cost of what is offered to the customer.

6 Running Example

In order to show the applicability of our composition approach, we have developed a Java-and-Jena-based[7] prototype which automates the composition of a SVN to fulfill a candidate's need[8]. The educational e-service Web acts on publicly available instance data about related needs and services we found on the Web.

Offering. For modelling service suppliers and enablers, we surveyed a number of publicly available competency databases and harvested the National Database of Accredited Qualifications[9] (NDAQ). Fig. 5 depicts a sample of the service catalogue for educational

---

[6] Instance attributes are details about resources such as price or resource's ids.
[7] http://jena.sourceforge.net/
[8] We assume that such need was already identified during skill gap analysis.
[9] http://www.accreditedqualifications.org.uk

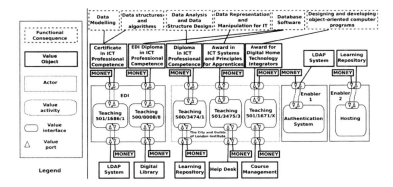

Fig. 5. Service catalogue generated from Web data in NDAQ

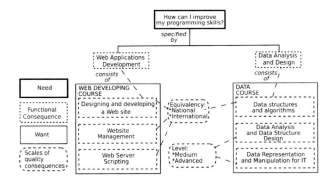

Fig. 6. Customer catalogue

services. These service profiles were designed based on the ontology depicted in Fig. 3. Service suppliers are represented by actors providing educational services (value activities) which in turn offer several resources (value objects) that have different functional consequences (Competencies). Service enablers are represented by actors providing or by supporting services.

Laddering. At this step customers express their needs using an interactive dialogue in which they can refine vague needs in terms of functional consequences. To illustrate the laddering, we have designed a customer catalogue (Fig. 6) based on the NDAQ database, by using the ontology in Fig. 4 and grouping consequences according to possible courses in which they can be offered. Later on, these consequences are linked to customer needs via high-level consequences. The high-level customer need How can I improve my programming skills? is refined by two optional consequences: Web Applications Development and Data Analysis and Design. These consequences are recursively refined further. E.g., if the consequence Data Analysis and Design is selected to cover the customer need, the laddering will determine that

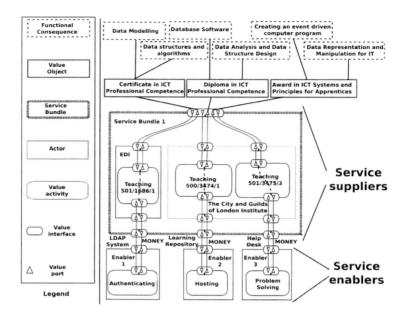

Fig. 7. Service Value Network to be offered at the Customer

the functional consequence Data structures and algorithms is more concrete to fulfil such need, since the first one *consists of* the second one.

The next step involves discovering more consequences through the notion of wants. In Fig. 6 the functional consequence Data structures and algorithms is contained in the Data Course want. By exploring this want, the functional consequences Data Analysis and Data Structure Design and Data Representation and Manipulation for IT are discovered. Finally, as part of the interactive dialog, customers are asked to evaluate functional consequences by scoring their quality consequences. *E.g.*, for the functional consequence Data Representation and Manipulation for IT, a customer is requested to score the relevance of the functional qualities Medium and Advanced. In this way, unimportant functional consequences can be depreciated while preference for relevant functional consequences can be highlighted.

Matching. Once the required consequences have been specified, the matching process retrieves all the possible service suppliers that offer the required consequences. As already explained, the core of this process is a (semantic) comparison between concepts at both catalogues (supplier and customer).

Bundling. Fig. 7 depicts one of the alternative service bundles providing the required functional consequences for the customer need How can I improve my programming skills?. Since our algorithm generates several bundles, the depicted bundle was selected by hand. As can be observed, the bundle includes different suppliers which offer different services through a common interface that can be later offered to the final customer. Moreover, our bundle is visualized according to the e^3-*value* ontology.

B2B Linkage. Finally, once the bundles are generated, the last step is to solve the dependencies of the service suppliers. By dependencies we mean the extra resources that are needed by the service suppliers. Usually those extra resources might be obtained via other suppliers or enablers. In our case, as depicted in Fig. 7, the service bundle gets the extra resources from a pool of service enablers. For instance, the service Teaching 500/3474/1 requires a *Learning Repository* which is obtained from the Hosting service that is provided by **Enabler 2**.

7 Conclusions and Future Work

In this paper we have presented a novel approach for automatically composing SVNs, which takes into account service suppliers and customers. On the one hand, our approach provides mechanisms for publishing supplier's offerings that can be later used to cover customer needs. On the other hand, it also provides a reasoning process, called laddering, that allows customer to represent vague needs in terms of specific consequences, which can be later matched with supplier's offerings. Since it is not only aligned with marketing theory concepts but also provides a better understanding about customer needs, the laddering is one of the benefits of this approach.

Once the matching is done, a bundling process generates all the possible bundles that can cover the given customer need. The last step is to solve all the bundle's dependencies, *i.e.* getting the extra resources that are required by each bundle (B2B Linkage). As a matter of fact, this dynamic on-the-fly composition of SVNs based on service bundling and B2B Linkage is other benefit of the approach. Moreover, by allowing to customers interacting with suppliers, we are not only providing a mechanism for co-creating new SVNs, but we are also increasing the perceived value of the SVN, since it fits better the customer need.

Although SVN composition is driven by a specific customer need, our approach offers a wide pool of SVNs to cover with such need. Consequently, the next steps in our research are focused on issues such as improvement of the bundling process, including business rules and selection of SVNs by customers.

To deal with the first issue we might explore combinatorial optimization strategies or even evolution-based methods. About business rules inclusion, we plan to apply them in both steps: in the bundling process and in the B2B linkage. Afterwards, to allow se ection among alternative SVNs we will provide a mechanism to customers so they can explore all the SVNs and pick one according to her/his desires.

References

1. Allee, V.: A value network approach for modeling and measuring intangibles. In: Transparent Enterprise Conference (2002)
2. Agarwal, S., Handschuh, S., Staab, S.: Annotation, composition and invocation of semantic web services. Journal of Web Semantics 33(1), 1–24 (2004)

3. Arndt, J.: How broad should the marketing concept be? Journal of Marketing 42(1), 101–103 (1978)
4. Baida, Z.: Software-aided service bundling. PhD thesis, Free University Amsterdam (2006)
5. Basole, R.C., Rouse, W.B.: Complexity of service value networks: conceptualization and empirical investigation. IBM Syst. J. 47, 53–70 (2008)
6. Danylevych, O., Karastoyanova, D., Leymann, F.: Service Networks Modelling: An SOA & BPM Standpoint. J. UCS 38(5), 1668–1693 (2010)
7. De Leenheer, P., Christiaens, S., Meersman, R.: Business semantics management: a case study for competency-centric HRM. Computers In Industry 61(8), 760–775 (2010)
8. de Kinderen, S.: Needs-driven service bundling in a multi-supplier setting: The computational e3service approach. PhD Thesis, Free University Amsterdam (2010)
9. Dustdar, S., Schreiner, W.: A survey on web services composition. Int. J. Web Grid Serv. 1(1), 1–30 (2005)
10. Gordijn, J., Akkermans, H., van Vliet, H.: Business Modelling Is Not Process Modelling. In: Mayr, H.C., Liddle, S.W., Thalheim, B. (eds.) ER Workshops 2000. LNCS, vol. 1921, pp. 40–51. Springer, Heidelberg (2000)
11. Gordijn, J., Akkermans, J.M.: e3-value: Design and evaluation of e-business models. IEEE Intelligent Systems, 11–17 (2001)
12. Gordijn, J., De, P.L., Razo-Zapata, I.S.: Generating service valuewebs by hierarchical configuration: An IPR case. In: HICSS 44 (2011)
13. Gutman, J., Reynolds, T.J.: Laddering theory-analysis and interpretation. Journal of Advertising Research 28(1), 11 (1988)
14. Hamilton, J.: Service value networks: Value, performance and strategy for the services industry. Journal of Systems Science and Systems Engineering 13(4), 469–489 (2004)
15. Kotler, P., Keller, K.: Marketing Management. Prentice Hall, Englewood Cliffs (2006)
16. Lam, S.Y., Shankar, V., Erramilli, M.K., Murthy, B.: Customer value, satisfaction, loyalty, and switching costs: An illustration from a business-to-business service context. Academy of Marketing Science 32, 293–311 (2004)
17. Legarreta, J.M.B., Miguel, C.E.: Collaborative relationship bundling: a new angle on services marketing. International Journal of Service Industry Management 15, 264–283 (2004)
18. Nakamura, K., Aoyama, M.: Value-Based Dynamic Composition of Web Services. In: Asia-Pacific Software Engineering Conference (2006)
19. Premkumar, G.: Alternate distribution strategies for digital music. Communications of the ACM 46, 89–95 (2003)
20. Razo-Zapata, I.S., Chmielowiec, A., Gordijn, J., Van Steen, M., De Leenheer, P.: Generating value models using skeletal design techniques. In: 5th International BUSITAL Workshop (2010)
21. da Silva, G.E., Pires, L.F., van Sinderen, M.: Towards runtime discovery, selection and composition of semantic services. Comput. Commun. 34(2), 159–168 (2011)
22. Sivashanmugam, K., Miller, J.A., Sheth, A.P., Verma, K.: Framework for Semantic Web Process Composition. Int. J. Electron. Commerce 9(2), 71–106 (2005)
23. Traverso, P., Pistore, M.: Automated Composition of Semantic Web Services into Executable Processes, pp. 380–394. Springer, Heidelberg (2004)
24. Zlatev, Z.: Goal-oriented design of value and process models from patterns. PhD thesis, Twente University (2007)

Business/IT Alignment in Practice: Lessons Learned from a Requirements Project at P&G

Gil Regev[1], Julien Favre[2], Erich Hayek[2], Paul Wilson[2], and Alain Wegmann[1]

[1] Ecole Polytechnique Fédérale de Lausanne (EPFL),
School of Computer and Communication Sciences
CH-1015 Lausanne, Switzerland
{gil.regev,alain.wegmann}@epfl.ch
[2] Procter and Gamble Information Technology (Information and Decision Solutions, IDS)
{favre.j,hayek.e,wilson.pa}@pg.com

Abstract. One of the main objectives of the alignment of Business and IT in both small and large organizations is to improve the chances for an IT department to provide services that result in business success. An essential phase for this alignment is the definition of business requirements. In this paper we describe the successful use of a blend of industrial and academic requirements methods for an IT system development at Procter and Gamble, (P&G), UK. We identify two main elements for the success of this phase: (1) the combination of methods from P&G and academia, (2) the focus of P&G's IT department on providing business solutions. This shift is accompanied by a move from writing specifications of IT systems towards defining business requirements. We discuss how these elements explain the success of this phase and propose research directions that may ease the introduction and use of requirements definition methods in organizations.

1 Introduction

Business and IT alignment is often considered to be a necessary ingredient for improving the chances of success in small and large organizations [2, 3], even those that do not produce IT products or services. In a recent study about enablers and inhibitors of business and IT Alignment [5], the following aspects were reported as the two main enablers: "IT understanding of the firm's business environment" and "Close partnership between IT and business." The "Lack of effective business communication with IT" scored third in the list of inhibitors, just after "Lack of senior executive support for IT" and "Lack of influence of headquarters' leadership." These enablers and inhibitors are addressed in a large part during the definition of business requirements. Furthermore, IT people need to improve their understanding of the business [3]. The question of business and IT collaboration through Requirements Engineering is therefore becoming an important element in Business and IT alignment. In this paper we describe the successful use of a blend of industrial and academic requirements methods for an IT system development at Procter & Gamble (P&G). The project resulted in improvements in both P&G and academia[1].

---

[1] A shorter version of this paper was published as a technical report, see [9].

The project was performed as a 6 months long Master's project by Julien Favre in 2005. It was deemed a success by P&G as well as from the academic standpoint. For P&G, the project established a firm set of requirements and prototypes that is now being used by the development team.

For the academic side, the adoption process described by Moore [7] was used to improve the SEAM Enterprise Architecture method [11, 12], and integrated in an Enterprise Architecture course given at EPFL [10].

The paper is an experience report and only relates the opinions of its authors. No systematic research or formal validation has been carried out.

In Section 2 we present the project on which this paper is based. In Section 3 we present the RE methods that were used in this project. In Section 4 we explain the influence that this project had on academia. In Section 5 we discuss the key learning points we draw from this project before concluding in Section 6.

2 The Project

Procter & Gamble (P&G) is one of the leading global manufacturers of branded consumer goods. P&G's IT department has changed its mission some years ago from developing IT systems to providing business solutions. This shift is reflected in the name change from IT to IDS (Information and Decision Solutions). IDS is part of the internal business unit Global Business Services (GBS). GBS provides business process services and business process transformation to all other business units. IDS focuses on service creation and service management while operations and transactional processes are mostly outsourced. IDS acts as mediator between the business-related organizational units and the service vendors (see Figure 1). Business transformation is enabled by IDS in three main ways: (i) analysis of the needs (i.e. the requirements) expressed by the business organizational units, (ii) the technology and vendor selection, (iii) set up of end-to-end services. The IDS contribution is evaluated in terms of its impact on the P&G Brand's "in-market" performance.

P&G worked hard on managing the innovation and growth process, while remaining focused on keeping financial performance in the top third of the industry peer group every year. This is done via very vigorous tracking of how many of P&Gs ideas get prototyped, how many of the prototypes get developed and qualified, and how many of those get test marketed and then successfully commercialized. Procter & Gamble has taken its success rate, which in 1999 was about 15 percent or 20 percent to above 60 percent today.

P&G uses the concept of "initiative" for the development of any new product, a change of an existing product or in general any project that implies involvement of resources or capital across the organization.

Consequently, the initiative Tracking and initiative Management Optimization has become one of the key focus areas of IDS. The opportunity and goal is to create high value for P&G by improving initiative success and reducing initiative development costs and time.

The management of initiatives today is a complex task due to the large number of organizational units, functions and IT systems involved (e.g. R&D, Supply Chain, Sales and Marketing Analysis) and the difficulty to obtain the necessary data to monitor an initiative's progress.

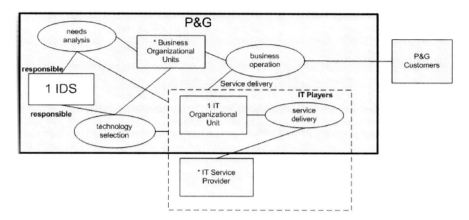

Fig. 1. P&G IT project organization

The project on which this paper is based was aimed at defining the requirements for an integrated IT solution for the part of the initiative that monitors the success of the initiative once it was launched.

3 The RE Methods Used

At the initial stage of the project, it was decided to use Adoption Methodology because it is the recommended approach inside P&G. The use of Adoption Methodology was supplemented by the use of Contextual Inquiry [1, 4] and SEAM goal and belief models [8]. Contextual Inquiry improved the collection of information. SEAM goal and belief models provided an early requirements method, increased the focus on certain elements such as relationships between stakeholders and improved some aspects of Adoption Methodology.

3.1 Adoption Methodology

The goal of Adoption Methodology is to improve technology adoption, and hence project success rates. It has the secondary benefit of ensuring IT project leaders understand the business implications of their technology.

The need for focusing on adoption came with the change of the definition of success for an IT project. The definition of success evolved from the roll out of a product to the actual adoption of the product by its intended users. This change triggered the need for developing a standard approach, that is, Adoption Methodology. Technology adoption is a term now used broadly within IDS. It is widely understood that adoption should be the end goal of any IT project. By leveraging Adoption Methodology, IT project managers can now set realistic technology adoption measures, and take specific steps to deliver on them.

Adoption Methodology is based on Moore's method for marketing high-tech products to mainstream customers [7]. It was initially developed in 2002 to increase adoption rates of Procter & Gamble IT projects in North America. Instead of targeting customers in a market segment, as is the case in Moore's method, Adoption methodology targets Procter & Gamble employees who are users of the IT systems developed by IDS (IDS customers). Hence, when we refer to users in the rest of the paper, we mean IT system users, not users of Procter & Gamble products.

Adoption Methodology blends IT industry best practices, user psychology, macroeconomics, specific training techniques, market segmentation methods, and business understanding to create an optimal training and deployment plan for any IT project. Adoption Methodology provides a way to translate the business understanding into a business validated IDS solution. Adoption Methodology uses the concepts of segmentation, scenarios and whole product.

The segmentation is the grouping the potential users of the system by their way of using it. For example, if some users will use a subset of the capabilities of the system and other users will use another distinct subset, they will form two segments. A segment is a group of potential users that will benefit from the same set of opportunities.

Scenarios represent a way of communicating an IT system functionality to a particular segment of users. There is one scenario for each opportunity and segment. The scenarios are also used to assess their value and probability of being adopted.

A whole product is the combination all the aspects that users expect, mostly implicitly from a new IT system. It includes among other things the IT system itself, the IT service associated with the system and the training.

Adoption Methodology is strongly "value focused" and helps to understand where the value of a product comes from. It gives a very realistic view on which functionality provides which value to which user. For example, the value and users' benefits can be detailed by segment and consequently can be more accurate than if all users are treated in the same way. In effect, an overall value or overall benefit is not very useful since it is unlikely that it will be valid for all users.

Adoption Methodology addresses several steps in an IT project: the business understanding, the complete requirements (including changes to the business processes), the system rollout, the users training and the marketing of the solution. The concrete adaptation of Adoption Methodology to this project involved the following steps:

1. Early requirements – business understanding
2. Initial users involvement
3. 1st round of interviews – business understanding
4. Scenarios development
5. 2nd round of interviews – scenario assessment

The first round of interviews is structured so as to uncover users' pain areas that are then converted into opportunities through the use of scenarios.

In its simplest form, the Adoption Methodology addresses nine core questions:

1. Who is the target customer?
2. What is this customer's compelling reason to use the envisioned solution?
3. What is the whole product solution that fulfills this reason?
4. Who are the key partners and allies who might be part of this whole product?
5. What is the optimal deployment method or scheme (e.g. online, face to face)?
6. What is the customers' cost of using the envisioned solution?
7. Who, what, and where are there competing solutions?
8. What is the optimal positioning of the envisioned solution?
9. Who is the next target?

These questions are asked for each functionality. Going through these questions leads to:

- A clear vision, or goal, articulating the project's desired end state (what work will be done differently, and by whom).
- A clear action plan that optimizes available resources and delivers on the vision or goal.

In the second round of interviews, we made several iterations. We started with a very simple set of requirements and a very simple mock-up.

Then, during each interview we improved the mock-up and got more and more details about the requirements. In order to validate the addition of the requirements, we systematically asked two questions:

- Why do you need this requirement?
- Which precise actions can you take with this functionality?

The 9 questions of the adoption methodology and these 2 questions have two distinct uses. The two questions provided us a good and rigorous way of selecting the more interesting functionalities. To assess the value of those selected functionalities and their chances of being adopted, we used the 9 questions listed above.

They were also the base for defining the compelling reasons to buy and the value of a given functionality.

3.2 Contextual Inquiry

Contextual Inquiry [1, 4] is an interviewing technique where interviewers establish an apprentice-master relationship with the interviewees. The interviewer plays the apprentice role and the interviewee the master role. The interview is done on the working premises of the interviewee and while the interviewee accomplishes the normal tasks that the interviewer wants to learn about. Contextual Inquiry is based on the assumption that during normal interviews interviewees talk in generalities and have difficulties in remembering and expressing the details that the interviewer needs in order to define accurate requirements. It is often difficult to introduce Contextual Inquiry in practice because it takes more time than traditional interviews and because of the interference with normal operations.

For the interviews, we used some of the guidelines from Contextual Inquiry. The main constraint was the time in our case; consequently, we haven't been able to use every aspect of this method.

As a general principle, we tried to optimize the time we spent with system's users and sometimes this optimization was not compatible with the contextual inquiry principles.

On the other hand, we maximized the time we spent with the users by attending various meetings as observers. We also simply spent time in one of the users' areas to observe the relationships between the individuals.

3.3 SEAM

SEAM [11, 12], is an Enterprise Architecture method. It is mainly used for business and IT alignment projects. One of the SEAM modules enables to create models of networks of stakeholders and their motivations in terms of goals and beliefs [8]. These models are used for the definition of early (or business) requirements. During the project we used only this goal-belief module.

The first contribution of the goal-belief models was to analyse the stakeholders' relationships. We oriented the first round of interviews so that we could clearly understand the relationships between the different actors.

The analysis was then modified to be more goal-oriented. In effect, Adoption Methodology doesn't really emphasize this aspect. The goal-belief models and goal oriented requirements engineering in general influenced this aspect of our approach.

To be precise, we used a hybrid version of the goal-belief discovery process. Instead of identifying the maintenance goals of the organisation and individuals at the beginning of the analysis, we first considered the performance goals of individuals. The performance goals of an individual are all the elements on which the individuals are evaluated. The salary and the career of the individual will depend on achieving those goals. The approach was a bottom-up individual to organisation analysis.

Concretely, we focused the interviews on the goals, belief and interests of the users. In order to optimise the limited time we had, we took into account for the first round of interviews the double challenge of asking enough why questions but not too many. It helped us to improve our analysis and understanding of the business processes and current practices.

The performance goals of every individual are influenced by the maintenance goals of the organisation. However, in the case of this project, it was more realistic to identify the performance goals of each individual and then understand which maintenance goal was influencing them rather than the other way around.

In conclusion, the two approaches have the same objective. The bottom-up is more realistic in a Procter & Gamble context and has the important advantage that it allows focusing directly on the target

The goal-belief analysis helped us to narrow our focus on the motivations of the users. For example, it raised the importance of understanding the external factors that impact the work of the users. The organisation we considered in the analysis is not directly connected to the external world, but the external influences are represented via different ways. We modified our approach to identify those factors and tried to understand their impact on the users' goals.

4 Academic Results of the Project

Even though this was an industrial project, the relationship between academia and industry (i.e. between P&G and EPFL) resulted in cross-pollination of methods. P&G's Adoption Methodology reminded us of Moore's Chasm theory [7] on which it is based. Moore's theory is based on the well-known technology adoption lifecycle but argues that there is a chasm between the different segments represented in this cycle, i.e. innovators, early adopters, early majority, late majority and laggards.

We integrated Moore's Chasm theory into our experiential Enterprise Service Oriented Architecture (ESOA) course [10]. The course's main goals are to give undergraduate students a sense of the real problems faced by organizations and to provide them with conceptual tools to provide solutions to these problems. To make the course as real as possible we use an experiential pedagogy [6].

The course illustrates Business/IT alignment by showing the direct relationship between marketing and sales issues on the one hand and IT solutions on the other hand. SEAM is used throughout the course for helping with business/IT alignment.

We place the students in a situation where they must identify the problems a commercial company has in selling a revolutionary product in a conservative market. Following the P&G project we integrated Moore's Chasm theory into the course to show the students how difficult it is to prevail over the long term in a conservative market when introducing a disruptive technology.

Just like the P&G project, the ESOA course shows students the importance of Contextual Inquiry by placing them in a situation where traditional interviews do not permit to identify the whole set of problems faced by the stakeholders. The results of the interviews and contextual inquiry are formalized in SEAM goal-belief models.

5 Key Learning Points

In this section we describe the main points that we believe made this project successful and that can serve other Business/IT projects in industry.

Business/IT Alignment Enables IT to Understand the Business
On of the main principles of the project was for IDS to understand the business rather than requiring the business to understand IDS. The tools used, Adoption Methodology, Contextual Inquiry and SEAM were used for and to the extent that they helped with this principle.

The Emergence of Units Such as IDS Makes RE Visible in Large Corporations
The shift in the mission of IDS from the specification of IT systems to a focus on providing value to its (internal) clients meant that IDS had to implement RE methods. This in turn made RE visible to both clients and management. Note that we have seen this trend in another large corporation as well.

The Adoption of RE Methods in Industry Requires Industry Tuned Methods
The first element to recall and it was the main driver of our methodology choices is that the Adoption Methodology is a recommended standard by Procter & Gamble.

The employees of a company are used to principles and not theory. They don't have enough time to understand a theory, but they can apply principles. To be used in industry, RE methods need to be tailored to the specific needs of each organization so that clear principles can be given. The key benefits of principles are that they are easy to communicate and implement.

Combining Industrial and Academic Methods
The combination of Adoption Methodology with Contextual Inquiry and SEAM is an illustration of collaboration between industry and academy. Adoption Methodology captures requirements from a management standpoint.

Adoption methodology addresses business and user benefits (strategic and operational issues). SEAM was used to analyze relationships and goals. Contextual inquiry was used to understand current practice.

Adoption Methodology specifies concrete principles such as the use of segmentation and scenarios. It doesn't provide a theoretical basis. Conversely, SEAM is grounded in theory but provides guidelines that are more difficult to apply. By using the principles of Adoption Methodology with a mindset inspired by SEAM we were able to define better requirements than was possible with the use of just one of these methods.

Requirements Engineering can become a Strategic Tool for Enterprises
This is very important for the requirements gathering area and for the IT system development in general, because sometimes those domains lack senior management support. This approach can really stimulate their interest and make them realise the potential impact of an IT system.

It is important to approach senior management with concrete proposals of requirements that can have a strategic impact rather than waiting for them to identify those opportunities.

At the end of the project, senior management was interacting proactively with IDS to discuss those aspects. Their interest and involvement changed dramatically between the start and the end of the discovery phase. This is mainly due to the fact that they realised the possibilities of influencing employees' current practices.

Internships are a Good way to Cross Pollinate between Industry and Academia
Internships represent a lightweight collaboration between industry and academia. When a student works as an intern for a Master's project, he or she has two clients to satisfy (the industrial supervisor and the professor). The academic requirements on a Master's thesis result in methods coming from research being applied to the industrial case. The industrial case, in turn, serves as a validation for the methods coming from research. This is a good way for industry and research to learn from each other and innovate, each one in its own field. In the case of the P&G project, P&G was able to apply new requirements techniques in concert with Adoption Methodology whereas EPFL was able to improve SEAM.

6 Conclusions

We believe there will be a steadily growing need for Business/IT alignment methods in the industry as IT departments of large organizations are shifting their focus away from technology and operations towards tangible business impact, in essence striving to improve their business/IT alignment. Business/IT alignment methods in general and RE methods in particular represent, in theory, a perfect fit for this new kind of industrial IT.

Today's research based methods seem difficult to implement in business organizations due to their high level of abstract complexity and the in-depth knowledge required for their implementation. Both elements do not support industrial IT departments in their key task, namely to interface with the business users in the users own "language." Hence, the industry is forced to create a set of different methods with clear and simple guidelines and easy end user communication tools. To address this need for Business/IT methods in industry, we recommend specific research geared towards the creation of industry-oriented methods. In this research we need to analyze the strengths and weaknesses of industry developed methods. This will enable blending existing research methods with industry methods so that the products are simple and quickly usable by the industry.

References

1. Beyer, H., Holtzblatt, K.: Contextual Design: A Customer-Centered Approach to System Designs. Morgan Kaufmann, San Francisco (1997)
2. Chan, Y.E.: Why Haven't We Mastered Alignment? The Importance of the Informal Organization Structure. MIS Quarterly Executive 1(2) (2002)
3. Chan, Y.E., Reich, B.H.: IT alignment: what have we learned? Information Technology 22, 297–315 (2007)
4. Holtzblatt, K., Jones, S.: Contextual Inquiry: A ParticipativeTechnique for System Design. In: Schuler, D., Namioka, A. (eds.) Participatory Design: Principles and Practices. Lawrence Erlbaum, Mahwah (1993)
5. Luftman, J.: Key Issues for IT Executives. MIS Quarterly Executive 3(2) (2004)
6. Kolb, D.A.: Experiential learning: experience as the sourceof learning and development. Prentice Hall, Englewood Cliffs (1984)
7. Moore, G.A.: Crossing the Chasm: Marketing and Selling High-Tech Products to Mainstream Customers. Harper Business, NY (1999)
8. Regev, G., Wegmann, A.: Defining Early IT System Requirements with Regulation Principles: The Lightswitch Approach. In: 12th IEEE International Requirements Engineering Conference (RE 2004), Kyoto, Japan (2004)
9. Regev, G., Favre, J., Hayek, E., Wilson, P., Wegmann, A.: Emergence of RE in Large Corporations: Lessons Learned From an RE Project at P&G. Technical Report, EPFL (2006)
10. Regev, G., Gause, D.C., Wegmann, A.: Experiential learning approach for requirements engineering education. Requirements Engineering 14(4), 269–287 (2009)
11. Wegmann, A.: On the Systemic Enterprise Architecture Methodology (SEAM). In: International Conference on Enterprise Information Systems (ICEIS), Angers, France (2003)
12. Wegmann, A., Regev, G., Rychkova, I., Lê, L.-S., De La Cruz, J.D., Julia, P.: Business-IT Alignment with SEAM for Enterprise Architecture. In: 11th IEEE International EDOC Conference. IEEE Press, Los Alamitos (2007)

Preface CCM 2011

A growing number of groups around the world design their individual modelling methods, in addition to existing standard ones for a variety of application domains. Modelling methods provide the necessary concepts capable to capture domain knowledge in terms of models that describe relevant aspects of an application domain. The construction of useful modelling methods is a complex task and requires high effort particularly when the entire spectrum of a method, ranging from language artefacts and a dedicated process, to functionality in terms of platform mechanisms (e.g., comparison, composition, translation, etc.) is addressed during the development.

Today, different approaches, guidelines and practices for the development of modelling methods are available and promoted by different communities in research as well as practice. The workshop on Conceptualization of Modelling Methods (CMM) is dedicated to the conceptualization, i.e., early development phases down to the actual implementation of modelling methods and how contemporary meta-modelling concepts and modern platforms address challenges that arise during a holistic modelling method life cycle. In this way, the aim of this workshop is to bring together researchers and practitioners mainly interested in applying modelling methods in arbitrary application domains, engineering methods based on meta-modelling platforms or developing platform functionality. These primary topics should provide the grounding for controversial opinions and intensive debates as well as a unique opportunity for discussing new ideas and forging new paths of collaboration.

The first edition of the CMM workshop is co-located with the 23rd International Conference on Advanced Information Systems Engineering (CAiSE 2011), London, United Kingdom, June 20-24, 2011, benefiting from the common interests shared by both the workshop and the conference. 13 papers were submitted to the workshop, which were peer-reviewed by three different referees. From them, 4 papers were finally selected for presentation in the workshop, yielding thus to a 30.7% acceptance rate. Revised versions of these accepted papers are included in these proceedings. The workshop program included also a keynote talk by Prof. John Mylopoulos (University of Trento, Italy), entitled *'Everything you wanted to know about conceptual modelling languages (... and were afraid to ask)'*. We thank the organizers of the CAiSE 2011 conference for their support and in particular the authors as well as the reviewers for their contribution to the CMM workshop!

Dimitris Karagiannis, University of Vienna, Austria
Xavier Franch, Universitat Politècnica de Catalunya, Spain

Program Committee

Alexander Bergmayr	University of Vienna, Austria
Carlos Cares	Universidad de la Frontera, Chile
Tony Clark	Middlesex University, United Kingdom
Rébecca Deneckère	Université Paris, France
Gregor Engels	University of Paderborn, Germany
Ulrich Frank	University of Duisburg-Essen, Germany
Roxana Giandini	National University of La Plata, Argentina
Esther Guerra	Universidad Autónoma de Madrid, Spain
Renata S. S. Guizzardi	Federal University of Esprito Santo, Brazil
Yoshinori Hara	Kyoto University, Japan
Igor Hawryszkiewycz	University of Technology Sydney, Australia
Lin Liu	Tsinghua University, China
Lidia López	Universitat Politècnica de Catalunya, Spain
Heinrich Mayr	Alpen-Adria University Klagenfurt, Austria
Ana Moreira	Universidade Nova de Lisboa, Portugal
Razvan Petrusel	Babes-Bolyai University of Cluj-Napoca, Romania
Alfonso Pierantonio	Università degli Studi dell` Aquila, Italy
Dimitris Plexousakis	University of Crete, Greece
Gianna Reggio	Università di Genova, Italy
Peter Reimann	University of Sydney, Australia
Werner Retschitzegger	Johannes Kepler University Linz, Austria
Michal Smialek	Warsaw Univeristy of Technology, Poland
Arnor Solberg	SINTEF, Norway
Katsumi Tanaka	Kyoto University, Japan
Antonio Vallecillo	Universidad de Málaga, Spain
Robert Winter	University of St. Gallen, Switzerland
Eric Yu	University of Toronto, Canada

Workshop Organization

Alexander Bergmayr	University of Vienna, Austria
Elena-Teodora Miron	University of Vienna, Austria
Lidia López	Universitat Politècnica de Catalunya, Spain

A Modelling Method for Consistent Physical Devices Management: An ADOxx Case Study

Srdjan Zivkovic[1,3], Krzysztof Miksa[2], and Harald Kühn[3]

[1] DKE, Faculty of Computer Science, University of Vienna
Brünnerstrasse 72, 1210 Vienna, Austria
srdjan.zivkovic@dke.univie.ac.at
[2] Comarch SA Al. Jana Pawla II 39A, Krakow, Poland
krzysztof.miksa@comarch.com
[3] Core Development, BOC Information Systems GmbH
Wipplingerstrasse 1, Vienna, Austria
{srdjan.zivkovic,harald.kuehn}@boc-eu.com

Abstract. In the domain of network management and operation support systems (OSS), maintainance of thousands of physical network devices is a complex, error-prone and time-consuming task. Consistent device configuration and error identification among plethora of network device types is impossible without tool support. Domain-specific modelling (DSM) methods promise to deal with system complexity by raising the level of abstraction to models. In this paper, we report about conceptualization of a DSM method for physical devices management, that is implemented based on the ADOxx metamodelling platform. The method introduces a hybrid modelling approach. A dedicated DSML is used to model the structure of physical devices, whereas the ontology language OWL2 is used to specify configuration-related constraints. The work resulted in a novel semantic modelling tool prototype that leverage ontology reasoning technology to enhance the modelling.

Keywords: Modelling Methods, Domain-specific Modelling, Metamodelling Platforms, Modelling Tools, Semantic Technology, Case Study.

1 Introduction

One of the challenges faced by OSS [3] is the increasing need for consistent management of physical network equipment. In large companies, maintainance of thousands of devices is a complex, error-prone and time-consuming task. Proper device configuration and identification of errors among myriads of network device types cannot be done without tool support. State-of-the-art technologies enable vendor independent equipment type identification and access to the attributes of the component types. However, they fail at providing the consistent support to the user by answering questions that involve sophisticated, configuration related constraints.

Model-based approaches such as MDA [11] and DSM [4] deal with the increased system and software complexity by raising the level of abstraction to models. Modelling methods provide necessary concepts to systematically capture relevant domain knowledge in terms of models. A modelling method usually contains 1) a modelling language (ML) used to describe the domain in terms of models, 2) mechanisms and algorithms (M&A) which in general process the knowledge in models and 3) a modelling procedure (MP) defining the steps, results and roles for modelling [9]. Metamodelling platforms provide flexible means for the realization of the modelling methods for arbitrary domains, producing a modelling tool tailored to a specific domain.

The system complexity in the domain of network physical devices management can be greatly reduced by capturing the semantics of physical devices and their specific configurations in models using DSLs and visual modelling tools. Whereas the adequate definition of a domain-specific ML is important for succesful capturing of network equipment information structures, it is equally important to define domain-specific M&As to check and ensure consistency of models, considering the specific semantics of the domain. In addition, a MP should guide the users through the network management configuration process by pointing out possible and allowed next steps by considering the given specifics of ML and M&A.

In this paper, we report on the conceptualization of such modelling method, and its implementation using the ADOxx metamodelling platform. The method has been constructed within the MOST project[1] in order to build a novel modelling tool that leverage ontology technology to enhance the modelling.

Following this introduction, Sect. 2 provides an overview of the case study. Sect. 3 explains the main concepts of the PDDSL method. Sect. 4 shows how the conceptualized method is implemented using the ADOxx metamodelling platform. In Sect. 5, we discuss the lessons learned, both from the conceptualization as well as from the implementaiton viewpoint. This is followed by a brief overview of the related work in Sect. 6. Finally, Sect. 7 concludes this paper and offers an outlook on future work.

2 Case Study: Consistent Physical Devices Management

The consistent management of the repository of physical network equipment is important prerequisite for efficient network management. Let us take an example of a usual situation in the telecommunication companies when one of the physical device cards is broken and requires replacement. Fig. 1a represents a particular configuration of the `Cisco 7603`. It contains two cards. The card in `slot 1` is a `supervisor2` of type `Supervisor Engine 2`, required by the device to work properly. In `slot 2`, two additional cards `hotswap` and `supervisor720` are inserted.

Let's suppose that the main supervisor card is broken and requires replacement. The person responsible for this device receives a notification about the problem and begins to resolve it. The process of finding a valid replacement requires deep knowledge about every sub-component of the physical device (what

---

[1] http://www.most-project.eu

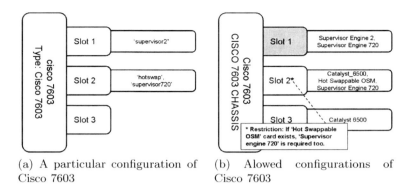

Fig. 1. Configuration of Cisco 7603

kind of cards can be used as a replacement for a broken card, what kind of constraints a particular card has, etc.). As shown in Fig. 1b, the device type Cisco 7603 requires at least one card in Slot 1 either of type Supervisor Engine 2 or Supervisor Engine 720. Furthermore, Slot 2 allows three types of cards to be inserted: Catalyst6500, Hot Swappable OSM or Supervisor Engine 720. However, there is an additional restriction that if a card of type Hot Swappable OSM is inserted, a Supervisor Engine 720 card is needed as well.

As shown, there is clearly a need for tools that provide not only the modelling capabilities to capture the knowledge about various device configurations, but also an advanced set of mechnanisms that should identify inconsistencies in configurations, pin-point invalid cards and, in general, help users to make correct decisions. The problems to address can be summarized as follows:

1. Network planning - what components can I use with a given configuration of a device to build my service?
2. Consistency checks - is my configuration valid?
3. Data quality - what is the exact type of device, given it's configuration?
4. Explanations and guidance: Why is my configuration invalid? How can I fix it?

Such tools, guiding and supporting users through tedious tasks by answering the questions mentioned, would generate substantial profit, and reduce the number of potential errors in the device configurations. It would also improve productivity, and mitigate the time consumed studying the technical details of a device's documentation.

3 Method Design

The modelling method for physical devices management (PDDSL method) has been conceptualized within the MOST project as a result of the case study of Comarch[2], with the goal to investigate the possibilities of semantic technolo-

---

[2] http://www.comarch.com

gies in model-based software engineering approaches. MOST offers, to our best knowledge, the first systematic approach of bridging the model and ontology technical spaces [18]. In the case study the approach is instantiated in the domain of physical devices management. Formal ontology languages bring more modelling power for defining precise constraints on models through formal semantics. Models translated to ontologies and integrated with constraints enable the usage of reasoning mechanisms such as consistency and subsumption checking, classification, explanation and justification. In the following, we explicate the design of each of the method elements: the *PDDSL modelling language*, a hybrid language for semantically rich modelling of physical devices (Sect. 3.1), the *PDDSL mechanisms* needed for checking consistency of physical device models (Sect. 3.2) and the *PDDSL modelling procedure* to guide users through the network configuration process (Sect. 3.3).

3.1 PDDSL: A Hybrid Modelling Language

The modelling of physical devices as introduced in case study (Sect. 2) poses two major requirements on the underlying modelling language 1) support for both *linguistic* and *ontological* instantation 2) support for semantically-rich constraints definition. On the one side, the pure PDDSL needs to support modelling of both network device types (Fig. 1b) and concrete device instances (Fig. 1a) at the same modelling level. Therefore, PDDSL is designed according to the *two-dimensional metamodelling architecture* [2], with both *linguistic* and *ontological* instantiation. On the other side, the language has to be expressive enough, to enable definition of additional constraints on device type structure, that should hold for all device instances. To approach this challenge, PDDSL is integrated with the formal knowledge representation language OWL2 [14], thus providing a *hybrid language* for modelling both structure and semantics of the domain.

Abstract Syntax. As pivotal element in the language definition, we define the abstract syntax using metamodels. The hybrid language consists of metamodels of PDDSL and OWL2, both integrated using well-defined integration points.

PDDSL Metamodel. Fig. 2 illustrates the excerpt of the PDDSL metamodel enabled for the ontological instantiation. It consists of constructs for the modelling of device types (LHS) and device instances (RHS). The fundamental element of the PDDSL metamodel is the relationship `hasType` between `Artefact` and `ArtefactType`, which enables instantiation of all concrete artefact instances based on their artefact types on the same modelling level. (e.g. the `supervisor2` is a particular inventory instance of card type `Supervisor Engine` 2).

OWL2 Metamodel. The OWL2 metamodel is based on the abstract syntax metamodel of the *OWL2 Manchester Syntax* [7]. The syntax is object-centered and *frame-based*, unlike other OWL2 syntaxes which are axiom-based. Fig. 3 illustrates a small, but relevant subset of rather complex OWL2 metamodel.

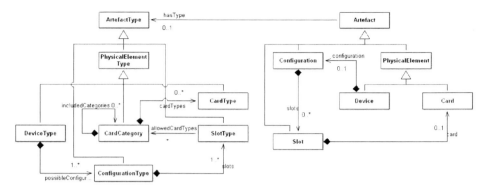

Fig. 2. Excerpt of the PDDSL metamodel

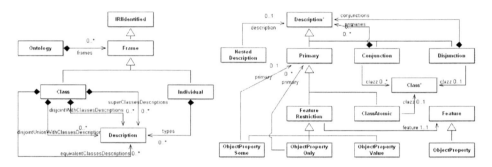

Fig. 3. Excerpt of the OWL2 metamodel (based on Manchester Syntax)

Entities such as **Class** and **Individual** can be defined as **Frame**. A class can contain **Descriptions**, which in turn may form simple or complex class expressions using logical operators such as **Conjuction** and **Disjunction** or existential and universal quantification operators. For example, through **equivalentClassesDescriptions** it is possible to define equivalent classes. Similarly, an individual can be related to the class description representing its type, through **types** reference.

Metamodel Integration. The metamodels of PDDSL and OWL2 have been integrated according to the well-defined integration points for bridging the structural languages with ontology languages [18] and following the basic metamodel integration rules [22]. The integration is fairly simple, but powerful, considering the outcome (see Fig. 4). The PDDSL metamodel element **ArtefactType** becomes the subclass of OWL2 **Class**, thus inheriting the rich OWL2 class expressiveness. Similar is done between **Artefact** and **Individual**. The integration is invasive from the viewpoint of PDDSL, since PDDSL classes are extended by the inherited attributes of the OWL2 super classes.

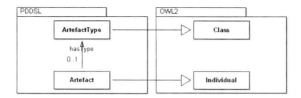

Fig. 4. Metamodel Integration of PDDSL and OWL2

Semantics. Semantics of the language assigns meaning to the abstract syntax constructs and it may be specified by a natural language specification or formalized (partially) by logics. The semantics of our language contains several aspects such as PDDSL semantics, OWL2 semantics, integration semantics and operational semantics of the integrated language. PDDSL semantics and the integration with OWL2 is formalized in Description Logics (DL). The semantics of OWL2 is formally defined using DL, too [13]. The operational semantics defines how hybrid PDDSL-OWL2 models should be interpreted/transformed into pure OWL2 ontology, considering the open-world (OWA) and close-world assumptions (CWA) [12].

Concrete Syntax (Notation). A language can have one or more concrete (graphical, textual) syntaxes. We defined a graphical notation both for PDDSL and OWL2 by mapping the abstract syntax elements to concrete syntax symbols. Table 1 provides an extract of the graphical syntax specification.

Table 1. Example of graphical syntax specification for PDSL and OWL2

PDDSL

Symbol	Device	Config	Slot	o—o
Element	Device	Config.	Slot	slots

OWL2

Symbol	C	P	[ ]	AND
Element	Class	Obj.Property	Nested Descr	Conjuction

3.2 PDDSL Mechanisms: Services for Consistency Guidance

PDDSL method introduces a set of metamodel-specific M&As as services for consistent modelling of physical devices. Considering domain-specific semantics of PDDSL, these services check both device type models and device instance models for validity. We specify some of the consistency services using a high-level specification pattern, that considers the following characteristics of M&As: *Name, Signature, Description, Trigger, Input, Output* (see Table 2).

Table 2. Services for consistency guidance

	Service: Device types consistency checking
Name	*Consistency checking of device types*
Signature	`bool check (in PDDSL.DeviceType deviceType, out List<CheckResult> results))`
Trigger	System Event: `pddsl.device.type.before.save`, User Event: validation service invoked.
Description	Given a device type and a set of constraints defined for device type, the consistency of the definition is checked.
Input	`deviceType` - a device type definition.
Output	`boolean` - device type consistency state. `results` - a list of result messages of type: error, warning, information.
	Service: Device instances consistency checking
Name	*Consistency checking of device instances*
Signature	`bool check (in PDDSL.Device device, in PDDSL.DeviceType deviceType, out List<CheckResult> results)`
Trigger	System Event: `pddsl.device.instance.before.save`, User Event: validation service invoked.
Description	Given a device instance and its corresponding device type (incl. constraints), the consistency of the device configuration is checked.
Input	`device` - a device istance. `deviceType` a device type, against which the device istance is checked.
Output	`boolean` - device consistency state. `results` - a set of result messages of type: error, warning, information.

3.3 PDDSL Modelling Procedure

The PDDSL method introduces a modelling procedure to guide users through consistent network configuration process. PDDSL MP considers two roles: *Domain Expert* which specifies possible device type structures, and *Domain User* which configures devices according to device types. Activities in the MP prescribe modelling tasks, that can be performed towards consistent network devices modelling. For example, the activity `Fix Device` must be performed for each device that has been found to be invalid (see Table 3). For the specification, we consider the following activity characteristics: *Role*, *Modelling Language(ML) Element*, and *Pre- and Postconditions*.

4 Method Implementation based on ADOxx

The PDDSL modelling prototype has been implemented based on the ADOxx metamodelling platform and by integrating the set of ontology-based components developed within the MOST project. It represents one of the two proof-of-concept demostrators developed using a feature-based product-line development approach [21]. The prototype features hybrid visual modelling of physical devices and OWL2 constraints, semantic validation of models and modelling guidance

A Modelling Method for Consistent Physical Devices Management   111

Table 3. Activity: Fix device

Name	Fix Device
Description	An activity that should be performed if the validation service detects an invalid device.
Role	Domain User
ML Element	PDDSL.Device
Precondition	An instance of device which is marked invalid.
Postcondition	A valid instance of device.

(cf. Fig.7)[3]. In the following, we first introduce the ADOxx metamodelling platform as a basis for the implementation of the PDDSL method. Then, we provide an overview of the prototype architecture, followed by the implementation details for each of the PDDSL method elements.

4.1 ADOxx: A Platform for Developing Modelling Environments

ADOxx is an extensible, repository-based metamodelling platform developed by the BOC Group[4]. ADOxx can be customized using metamodelling techniques and extended with custom components to build a modelling environment for a particular application domain. ADONIS [8] is a modelling tool based on ADOxx for the domain of business process management. The ADOxx platform kernel provides basic modules for managing models and metamodels. In addition, the ADOxx generic components for graphical and tabular model editing, for model analysis, for simulation, or for model comparison can be reused and customised in all products derived from ADOxx. Each ADOxx-based product contains a product-specific modelling language and may have additional set of product-specific components.

4.2 PDDSL Prototype Architecture

The PDSSL modelling tool has been developed as a product instance of ADOxx, according to the architecural blueprint for ontology-based modelling environments [21]. Fig. 5 illustrates the instantation of the architecture for the PDDSL tool. The uppermost layer contributes various Editors to create and edit models and metamodels. Views provide modellers information about the current development status. Further below, we find various components that contribute Ontology-based Services for modelling process guidance, consistency guidance and querying. These services are enabled by the subjacent Integration Infrastructure that provide bridges between the Modelling Infrastructure and the Ontology Infrastructure. In addition, the generic architecture contains Vertical Services like user and rights management or import/export and Persistency Services. Note that components in grey colour rely on

---
[3] The prototype is available at Open Models Initiative: http://www.openmethods.at
[4] http://www.boc-group.com/

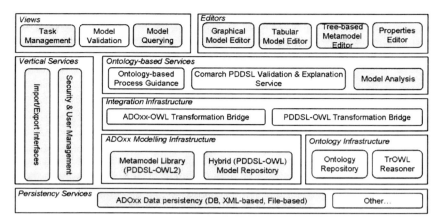

Fig. 5. Ontology-based Modelling Tool Architecture based on ADOxx

ADOxx generic platform components, whereas other components are product-specific, i.e. implemented and/or integrated specific for the PDDSL tool.

4.3 PDDSL Modelling Language Implementation

Abstract Syntax ADOxx supports three-layered metamodelling architecture. The abstract syntax of our hybrid language has been implemented on the M2 level using the constructs of the ADOxx Meta^2–Model positioned at M3 level. ADOxx Meta^2–Model (see Fig. 6a) organizes metamodel elements such as Classes and Relation Classes into Model Types i.e. diagram types. A model type may have different modes, that filter a model type only for a specific subset of contained elements. In our language, we defined three model types: Device types, Devices and OWL2. OWL2 was splitted in two modes: OWL2 Frames and OWL2 Descriptions (see Fig. 6b). Further, ADOxx features a special kind of relation class called *Interref* that enables to connect elements crossing the model border. This feature helped us to implement the *ontological-instantiation* relation between model types by defining interref-relationship hasType between Artefact and ArtefactType. Similarly, the *metamodel integration* with OWL2 has been achieved by specifying the generalization relationships between both ArtefactType and Class, and Artefact and Individual.

Semantics. ADOxx doesn't provide a declarative formalism to define metamodel semantics. However, operational metamodel semantics in ADOxx can be defined in a imperative way using a scripting language or by integrating external components. For our hybrid language, the semantics is implemented by a Comarch PDDSL-OWL Transformation Bridge. The component considers both the *ontological instantation* and the *metamodel integration* semantics of the language and translates the models into a set of description logic axioms. The transformation was implemented using QVT Operational [15] and Java. For example, the

A Modelling Method for Consistent Physical Devices Management   113

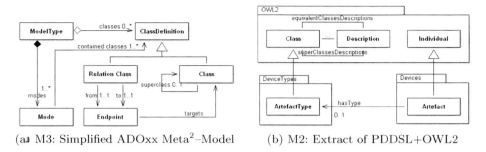

(a) M3: Simplified ADOxx Meta^2–Model   (b) M2: Extract of PDDSL+OWL2

Fig. 6. Integrated metamodel based on ADOxx Meta^2–Model

semantics of the ontological instantiation relationship `hasType` can be defined by transforming each occurence of it to an appropriate class assertion axiom in OWL2. On the other side, the direct semantics of OWL2 is directly implemented in the semantic reasoner (in our case the `TrOWL`[5] `Reasoner`).

Concrete Syntax (Notation). ADOxx supports the definition of the graphical concrete syntax. To define the graphical representation (GraphRep) of a metamodel element, the platform provides a set of dedicated APIs that can be accessed via JavaScript. This allows to define not only statical elements of the GraphRep (curves, lines etc.), but also to add dynamical aspects by considering the changes in element property values. For example, the GraphRep of the `Slot` may change the color to red if the slot property `required` is true (see List. 1.1).

```
if (graphRep.getAttr ("cardRequired"))
{
    graphRep.fillColor.setColorByName (graphRep.fillColor.red);
}
graphRep.fillRoundRect (...);
```

Listing 1.1. A code snippet for the graphical representation of `Slot`

4.4 PDDSL M&As: Ontology-Based Consistency Services

PDDSL M&As (cf. Sect. 3.2) are implemented based on ontology reasoning services and additional post-processing. The service `Consistency checking of device instances` relies on pure *satisfiability checking* to compute unsatisfiable set of classes. On the other side, the service `Consistency checking of device instances` uses *consistency checking* in combination with *explanation services* (known as justifications for inconsistency [6]). Reasoning explanations are additionally post-processed and interpreted in the domain specific manner. We rely on OWL2 annotations to report users inconsistency reasons. Each axiom

---
[5] http://trowl.eu

meaningful to the user is annotated with user-friendly error description. Consistency guidance services are part of the product-specific component `Comarch Consistency Guidance` (cf. Fig. 5) [12].

4.5 PDDSL MP: Ontology-Based Process Guidance Engine

In order to provide a tool support for PDDSL modelling procedure, the `ontology-based process guidance engine`(cf. Fig. 5) developed by BOC is used [23]. The guidance engine relies on the ontology reasoning services such as *classification* and *query answering* to infer availability of the next possible tasks [16]. The activities, its pre- and postconditions, the affected metamodel elements and user roles are part of the modelling procedure definition and are specified in OWL2 as an ontology `TBox`. List. 1.2 provides a simplified example of `Fix Device` (cf. Tab. 3) activity definition. First, the artifact `IncorrectDevice` is defined to describe the invalid state of a `Device`. Then, the activity `FixDeviceTask` is said to be performed by the role `DomainUser`. Finally, the object property `fixDevice` states that `IncorrectDevice` is a precondition for `FixDeviceTask` activity.

```
Class: IncorrectDevice
    EquivalentTo: Device and Incorrect

Class: FixDeviceTask
    SubClassOf: TaskType, performedBy some DomainUser

ObjectProperty: fixDevice
    Domain: IncorrectDevice Range: FixDeviceTask
```

Listing 1.2. Excerpt of the modelling procedure definition using OWL2

5 Lessons Learned

In the following, we discuss the lessons learned during the PDDSL method design (Sec. 5.1) and implementation (Sec. 5.1).

5.1 Experiences from Method Design

Metamodel integration. Metamodel integration of PDDSL and OWL2 is a cornerstone of our prototype. However, it solves only part of the issues. Most notably, we were unable to simply express the equality of attributes of metamodel elements. For example, after integrating `PDDSL.PhysicalElementType` and `OWL2.Class` by generalization, it was not possible to define that attribute `name` of PhysicalElementType is the same as attribute `iri` of Class. Thus, we were forced to change the PDDSL metamodel and use `iri` attribute instead of `name`. As a consequence, we had to adapt all metamodel-specific mechanisms working on the PDDSL part of the language. Therefore, we see a need for *non-invasive metamodel composition techniques*.

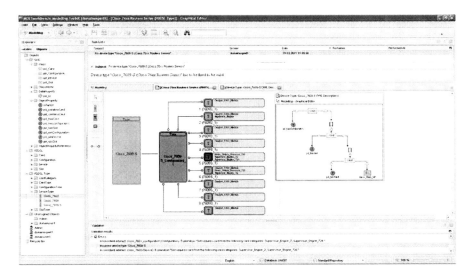

Fig. 7. The PDDSL modelling tool prototype based on ADOxx

Language and ontological instantation. We found that language and ontological instantation approach perfectly solved the problem of modelling device types and device instances. Futhermore, cases where two-dimensional modelling could be useful are quite frequent in OSS domain such as service management or connectivity modelling.

5.2 Experiences from Method Implementation

Reusability of platform components. ADOxx was previously applied in various modelling domains, offering a plethora of ready-to-use generic (metamodel-independent) components such as graphical editor, generic model repository or analysis component. Thus, we had to develop and integrate comparatively small number of new components for the PDDSL tool prototype, that were needed only due to the explorative and research-oriented product requirements.

Platform extensibility and interoperability. The extensibility of ADOxx made it easy to integrate new components into the final product. Using dedicated bridges, it was possible to integrate Comarch guidance services that are based on Eclipse EMF technology. Furthermore, the interoperatiblity with ontology editors (Protege) and reasoners (TrOWL, Pellet) has been established over the ADOxx2OWL Bridge based on OWL API.

Ontology-based validation mechanisms. The reasoning services provided by the semantic reasoner are crucial for the implementation of consistency mechanisms in our prototype. However, to provide the meaningful answers to the users of PDDSL method, it is also necessary to translate the results from ontology technical space back to the domain of PDDSL. For instance, we post-process the justifications of the inconsistency of the ontology in order to retrieve the set of incorrect model elements. Additionally, it is also necessary to pre-process the ontology prior to invoking the reasoning service. For example, before checking the consistency of the devices we need to close certain aspect of the ontology, while in order to properly compute the card suggestions for the slots, the same aspects of the domain have to remain open.

Support for two-dimensional metamodelling. We implemented the semantics of ontological-instantiation (hasType) directly in our language on M2 level. We found that this feature could be implemented in metamodelling platforms on M3 level, to be used for arbitrary metamodels on M2 level.

6 Related Work

Consistency checking of UML models may be performed by transforming UML and OCL to a more formal language such as Alloy [1]. Different works (e.g. [19,5]) have explored the usage of logic-based language F-Logic to describe configurations of devices or the semantics of MOF models. The mentioned approaches rely on pure transformation of models to languages with more formal semantics for consistency checking. Besides the transformation of PDDSL to OWL2, our approach provides the possibility to define additional constraints in OWL2 based on metamodel integration. This basic idea has been applied in [17], to integrate UML and OWL for consistent class-based modelling. An alternative implementation of our approach called OntoDSL [20] combines EMOF and OWL at the metametamodel level to take profit from OWL expressivity and reasoning services to help DSL engineers and DSL users through the development and usage of DSLs. In [10] a metamodel-based approach is proposed that bridges the business process and knowledge engineering spaces, to support knowledge-intensive business process modelling actions by semantic technology.

7 Conclusion and Outlook

In this paper, we reported on the design of the DSM method for the consistent management of physical network equipment, and its implementation based on the ADOxx metamodelling platform and the set of ontology-based components developed within the MOST project. The method conceptualization resulted in a prototype featuring a hybrid DSML for semantically rich modelling of physical devices, a set of mechanisms for consistency checking of models, a modelling procedure to guide users through the network configuration process. We discussed lessons learned both in method design and method implementation. Hence, we hope that our paper helps method developers to experience the potential and challenges of domain-specific method design and realization based on metamodelling platforms and ontology technology. Our future work will be concentrated on several topics derived from lessons learned. Concepts and techniques for non-invasive metamodel composition integration could bring benefits to metamodelling platforms while fostering metamodel reuse and compatibility of mechanisms. Furthermore, we want to generalize the ontological approach for two-dimensional modelling to be applicable for various methods having two-dimensional charactestics. Finally, we will investigate the possibilities of integrating the semantic technology on the metamodelling language level as well. This would allow us to provide better support for metamodelling by relying on formal, declarative languages for knowledge representation and on reasoning mechanisms.

Acknowledgment

This research has been co-funded by the European Commission and by the Swiss Federal Office for Education and Science within the 7th FP project MOST # 216691.

References

1. Anastasakis, K., Bordbar, B., Georg, G., Ray, I.: UML2Alloy: A challenging model transformation. In: Engels, G., Opdyke, B., Schmidt, D.C., Weil, F. (eds.) MODELS 2007. LNCS, vol. 4735, pp. 436–450. Springer, Heidelberg (2007)
2. Atkinson, C., Kuehne, T.: Model-driven development: a metamodeling foundation. IEEE Software 20(5), 36–41 (2003)
3. Fleck, J.: Overview of the Structure of the NGOSS Architecture (2003)
4. France, R., Rumpe, B.: Domain specific modeling. Software and Systems Modeling 4, 1–3 (2005) 10.1007/s10270-005-0078-1
5. Gerber, A., Lawley, M., Raymond, K., Steel, J., Wood, A.: Transformation: The Missing Link of MDA. In: Corradini, A., Ehrig, H., Kreowski, H.-J., Rozenberg, G. (eds.) ICGT 2002. LNCS, vol. 2505, pp. 90–105. Springer, Heidelberg (2002)
6. Haase, P., Qi, G.: An analysis of approaches to resolving inconsistencies in dl-based ontologies (2007), http://kmi.open.ac.uk/events/iwod/papers/paper-13.pdf
7. Horridge, M., Patel-Schneider, P.F.: OWL 2 Web Ontology Language Manchester Syntax (2009), http://www.w3.org/TR/owl2-manchester-syntax/
8. Junginger, S., Kühn, H., Strobl, R., Karagiannis, D.: Ein Geschäftsprozessmanagement-Werkzeug der nächsten Generation. Wirtschaftsinformatik 42(5), 392–401 (2000)
9. Karagiannis, D., Kühn, H.: Metamodelling platforms. In: Bauknecht, K., Tjoa, A.M., Quirchmayr, G. (eds.) EC-Web 2002. LNCS, vol. 2455, p. 182. Springer, Heidelberg (2002)
10. Karagiannis, D., Woitsch, R.: Knowledge engineering in business process management. In: Handbook on Business Process Management. International Handbooks on Information Systems, vol. 2, pp. 463–485. Springer, Heidelberg (2010)
11. Kleppe, A., Warmer, J., Bast, W.: MDA Explained: The Model Driven Architecture: Practice and Promise. Addison-Wesley, Reading (2003)

12. Miksa, K., Sabina, P., Kasztelnik, M.: Combining ontologies with domain specific languages: A case study from network configuration software. In: Aßmann, U., Bartho, A., Wende, C. (eds.) Reasoning Web. LNCS, vol. 6325, pp. 99–118. Springer, Heidelberg (2010)
13. Motik, B., Patel-Schneider, P.F., Grau, B.C.: OWL 2 Web Ontology Language Direct Semantics (2009),
    http://www.w3.org/TR/2009/REC-owl2-direct-semantics-20091027/
14. Motik, B., Patel-Schneider, P.F., Parcia, B.: OWL 2 Web Ontology Language Structural Specification and Functional-Style Syntax (2009),
    http://www.w3.org/TR/2009/REC-owl2-syntax-20091027//
15. OMG: MOF QVT Final Adopted Specification (2005),
    http://www.omg.org/docs/ptc/05-11-01.pdf
16. Ren, Y., Lemcke, J., Friesen, A., Rahmani, T., Zivkovic, S., Gregorcic, B., Bartho, A., Zhao, Y., Pan, J.Z.: Task representation and retrieval in an ontology-guided modelling system. In: OWLED (2009)
17. Silva Parreiras, F., Staab, S., Winter, A.: TwoUse: Integrating UML Models and OWL Ontologies. Tech. Rep. 16/2007, Universität Koblenz-Landau (2007)
18. Staab, S., Walter, T., Gröner, G., Parreiras, F.S.: Model driven engineering with ontology technologies. In: Aßmann, U., Bartho, A., Wende, C. (eds.) Reasoning Web. LNCS, vol. 6325, pp. 62–98. Springer, Heidelberg (2010)
19. Sure, Y., Angele, J., Staab, S.: OntoEdit: Guiding ontology development by methodology and inferencing. LNCS, pp. 1205–1222.
20. Walter, T., Silva Parreiras, F., Staab, S.: *ontoDSL*: An ontology-based framework for domain-specific languages. In: Schürr, A., Selic, B. (eds.) MODELS 2009. LNCS, vol. 5795, pp. 408–422. Springer, Heidelberg (2009)
21. Wende, C., Zivkovic, S., Aßmann, U., Kühn, H.: Feature-based Customisation of MDSD Tool Environments. Tech. Rep. TUD-FI10-05-Juli 2010, Technische Universität Dresden (July 2010),
    http://ftp.inf.tu-dresden.de/berichte/tud10-05.pdf
22. Zivkovic, S., Kühn, H., Karagiannis, D.: Facilitate modelling using method integration: An approach using mappings and integration rules. In: ECIS 2007, University of St. Gallen, Switzerland (2007),
    http://is2.lse.ac.uk/asp/aspecis/20070196.pdf
23. Zivkovic, S., Wende, C., Bartho, A., Gregorcic, B.: D2.3 - Initial Prototype of Ontology-driven Software Process Guidance System (2009),
    http://most-project.eu/documents.php

EIPW: A Knowledge-Based Database Modeling Tool

Ornsiri Thonggoom, Il-Yeol Song, and Yuan An

The iSchool at Drexel University, Philadelphia, USA
{ot62,songiy,yuan.an}@drexel.edu

Abstract. Reuse of already existing resources and solutions has become a strategy for cost reduction and efficient improvement in the information system development process. Currently, building a repository of reusable artifacts involves explication of human developer's knowledge, which is a major obstacle in facilitating reuse of knowledge. In this research, we explore knowledge-based and pattern-based approaches that help database designers develop quality conceptual data models based on reusable patterns. Our methodology includes database reverse engineering concepts. We propose new types of reusable instance patterns containing knowledge about an application domain, called entity instance repository (EIR) and relationship instance repository (RIR), which can be automatically generated from prior designs. The knowledge-based system (KBS) with EIR, RIR, and WordNet called EIPW (Entity Instance Pattern WordNet) is developed. The empirical study was conducted to test the efficiency of the KBS and indicated the significant improvement in novice designer performance.

Keywords: automate database design, reusable artifacts, patterns, conceptual modeling, entity-relationship modeling, ER diagram.

1 Introduction

The Entity-Relationship (ER) model [1] is one of the most well-known conceptual modeling formalisms. It is easy to understand, powerful to model real-world problems, and readily translated into a database schema. The ER model consists of a collection of entities, relationships between entities and attributes describing entities and relationships. Many studies [2, 3] have shown that conceptual modeling designs, especially developed by novice designers, may lead to inaccurate models.

Available commercial graphical CASE tools can be useful in documenting the output of analysis and design. However, they do not provide any supports in conceptual data modeling- especially during a stage of identifying the entities, attributes, and relationships, which represent the problem domain. Therefore, many researchers have proposed knowledge-based systems (KBSs) or tools to support the designers in developing conceptual models. One of the limitations of proposed tools or KBSs is that such tools have no domain knowledge or semantic analysis capacity incorporated into them. Therefore, these tools cannot solve the incomplete knowledge of designers [4] and semantic mismatch [5].

Most conceptual designs are usually created from scratch, although similar design might have previously been created. And in many organizations there are a large number of database designs that have been already developed over many years. Reuse of already existing resources and solutions has become a strategy for cost reduction and efficient improvement in the information systems development process. Currently, building a repository of reusable artifacts involves explication of human developers' knowledge, which is a major obstacle in facilitating reuse of knowledge [6]. It requires efforts from experts to identify elements with potential reuse, and then convert these into reuse elements. One solution to reduce the efforts and time of human experts comes from extracting the artifacts from the prior designs. If this could be conducted for various application domains, then it would assist in creating the practically reusable artifacts.

In this research, we explore knowledge-based and pattern-based approaches that help database designers develop quality conceptual data models. Our methodology includes database reverse engineering concepts. We propose new types of reusable artifacts that contain knowledge about an application domain, called the entity instance repository (EIR) and the relationship instance repository (RIR), which are repositories of entity instance patterns (EIPs) and relationship instance patterns (RIPs), respectively. An EIP is a pattern of a single entity and its properties. An RIP is a binary relationship with cardinality constraints between two entities. The EIP and RIP can be automatically extracted from prior relational database schemas. The patterns in EIR and RIR are also extended with the case studies. Our proposed artifacts are useful for conceptual designs in the following aspects: (1) they contains knowledge about an application domain; (2) automatic generation of EIR and RIR overcame a major problem of inefficient manual approaches that depend mainly on experienced and scarce modeling designers and domain experts; and (3) they are domain-specific and therefore easier to understand and reuse.

This paper aims at (1) proposing an automated methodology for creating the EIR and RIR as new types of reusable artifacts for conceptual modeling design which contain knowledge about an application domain; (2) developing an effective knowledge-based system with EIR and RIR called EIPW (Entity Instance Pattern WordNet), by integrating pattern-based technique and various modeling techniques; and (3) evaluating the usefulness of the KBS by human subject experiments.

The remainder of this paper is organized as follows. Section 2 summarizes the work on reusable artifacts related to our work, including the tools that incorporate with the reuse patterns. Section 3 presents the architecture of EIPW. Section 4 provides a methodology to create EIR and RIR. Section 5 describes the implementations of EIPW. Section 6 presents results from empirical testing of the EIPW. Finally, Section 7 concludes the paper and gives directions for future work.

2 Prior Research

This section presents the research on reusable artifacts related to our work, including the tools that incorporate with the reuse patterns.

2.1 Reusable Artifacts

To date, patterns have been well established as a technique for reusing solutions of recurrent problems in the software development process. Integrating patterns into conceptual design is challenging. The recognition of patterns in conceptual data modeling field is based on works by Coad et al. [7], Hay [8], and Fowler [9]. Several authors have proposed various kinds of patterns [6-13]. However, their utility to conceptual modeling varies greatly. For the latest one, Blaha [3] proposes several types of data modeling patterns: Universal antipatterns are the patterns that we should avoid for all applications; Archetypes are the common modeling patterns occurring across different applications; and canonical patterns are corresponding to meta models of modeling formalisms. Finally, he presents how to map his patterns to relational schema for database design.

There are the packaged data models (or model components) available, which can be purchased and after suitable customization, assembled into full-scale data models. These generic data models are designed to be used by organizations within specific industries. Well-known examples of packaged data models are provided by [14] and [15]. However, packaged data models cannot replace the sound database analysis and design. Skilled designers are still needed to determine requirements and select, modify, and integrate any packaged models that are used. And no packaged data models provide any automated support for extracting the most suitable pattern for a particular situation. In this research, we created a library of patterns based on the package data models [14] and automated finding the most appropriate one for a certain situation, in which the reuse of the huge amount of knowledge saved in the patterns. As a first step, a pattern library included patterns from one domain only.

2.2 Tools and Systems Using Pattern Techniques

Analysis pattern repository has been the most popular and used in conceptual modeling tools or systems. To make use of patterns from a repository, the designer must be able to match a task description with a candidate pattern. Purao et al. [16] develop a KBS called APSARA, which automates analysis patterns to create object-oriented conceptual design. In his method, he first uses natural language processing (NLP) to parse the problem statement into significant keywords, and eventually objects. Based on object identification, analysis patterns are retrieved from the pattern base, then instantiated and synthesized into a conceptual model. In his pattern base, analysis patterns by Coad are used. Later, he augments his approach with a supervised learning concept [17]. The limitation of this KBS is that analysis patterns are so abstract that mismatches to patterns are fairly common. Wohed [18] proposes a Modeling Wizard Tool, which is a dialogue tool for selecting the appropriate patterns. Booking domain patterns are stored in the system. The appropriate pattern is selected step by step according to the answers given to the questions. However, this tool requires much more on user's interventions and it is hard to use it for large scale batch processing.

3 Overview of EIPW Architecture

The system modules and data flow of EIPW are shown in Figure 1. A prototype of EIPW has been developed by using Java Applet. Firstly, the system passes a NL requirement specification as an input to a preprocessing module. The main functionality of the preprocessing module is to do the part of speech tagging (POS) in order to list all of the possible candidate entities. Then, The EIR and the hypernym chains in

WordNet [19], and entity categories which are knowledge repositories in an application domain are used for the entity identification. Our entity categories in business domain are adopted from the class categories developed by Song et al. [20]. WordNet is also used to ensure that the synonyms of EIR's entities are not missed out while preparing the list of candidate entities. After, getting the entity list from Entity Identification Module, relationships between entity list are generated by considering the application domain semantics inherent in the RIR. The modeling rules are used to ensure that all of the relationships are identified. The lists of EIR and RIR are extended by case studies.

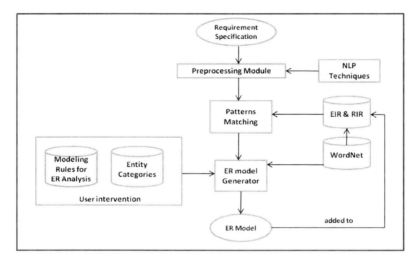

Fig. 1. The EIPW Architecture

4 Methodology for Creating EIR and RIR

This section presents the automatic methodology for creating EIR and RIR, which are the repositories of EIPs and RIPs, respectively. These repositories contain ER modeling patterns from prior designs and serve as knowledge-based repositories for conceptual modeling. An EIP is a pattern of a single entity and its properties. An RIP is a binary relationship with cardinality constraints between two entities. We propose a method based on a database reverse engineering concept and were inspired by Chaing et al. [21] to automatically extract EIPs and RIPs from relational schemas. In this paper, we use UML class diagram notation representing the ER models. This methodology employed three assumptions involving the characteristics of the input schemas for database reverse engineering process:

1) Relational schemas: An input is a DDL (Data Definition Language) schema that contains data instances of an application domain.
2) 3NF relations: There are no non-3NF relations in the input relational schemas. It would simplify the extraction process.

3) Proper primary keys (PK) and foreign keys (FK): PKs or FKs are specified for every relation of the input DDL schemas.

An example of an EIP and an RIP is shown in Figure 2.

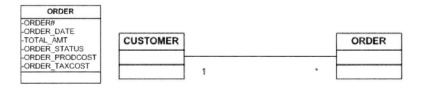

Fig. 2. An example of an EIP and an RIP, respectively

The method for creating EIR and RIR consists of the following three main steps:

INPUT: DDL schemas
OUTPUT: EIR and RIR

(1) Obtaining information about the executable schemas (DDL schemas)
In order to reverse engineer existing database schemas, the information about the executable schemas must be available. These executable schemas have to provide at least relation names, attribute names, and PKs. In our paper, we use the library of DDL schemas created by Silverston [14] containing 464 entities and 1859 attributes as our first input. Later the lists of EIR and RIR are extended by case studies.

(2) Extracting EIP's elements
We extracted the EIP's elements from the input DDL schemas by storing a relation name as an entity_name and an attribute as an attribute_name in EIR. The metadata model of EIP and RIP is shown in Figure 3.

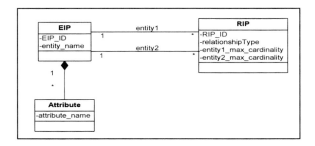

Fig. 3. The Meta-Model of EIP and RIP

(3) Extracting RIP's elements
We extracted the RIP's elements by identifying relationships between extracted entities from Step (2) above. In this research, we only specified the default cardinality ratios for binary models. Most of the ER methods used in textbooks or CASE tools

can be classified as either binary models or n-ary models [22]. Because of the limited semantic expressiveness of DDL schemas, the minimum cardinality cannot be automatically identified. For totally automatic process, we can identify five binary relationship types:

    3.1   1:N for relationships identified by FK
    3.2   1:N for relationships identified by partial keys
    3.3   N:M for relationships identified by relationship relations
    3.4   Is-a relationships
    3.5   Recursive relationships

Then, these binary relationships are stored in RIR. The reverse engineering schema transformation rules used in this step were created by inverting the traditional concepts of database design based on EER approach [23]. These transformation rules are described as following:

3.1 1: N for relationships identified by FK
IF: the PK of a relation T_1 is shown as a FK of another relation T_2,
THEN: there is a 1: N relationship between T_1 and T_2.
Consider these two relations:

    $T_1 (\underline{K_1}, a_{11}, a_{12}, a_{13}, …, a_{1i})$
    $T_2 (\underline{K_2}, a_{21}, a_{22}, a_{23}, …, a_{2i}, K_1^*)$

where T_i represents a relation, a_{ij} represents an attribute in a relation, PK is underlined, and FK is followed by a star symbol.
    If $T_2.K_1^*$ is a FK coming from T_1, then there is a 1: N relationship between T_1 and T_2.

3.2 1: N for relationships identified by partial keys
IF: the PK of a relation T_1 appears as a composite PK of another relation T_2 and the PK of relation T_1 is the FK of table T_2 as well,
THEN: T_1 is a strong entity.

    T_2 is a weak entity.
    And there is a 1: N relationship between T_1 and T_2.

Consider these two relations:

    $T_1 (\underline{K_1}, a_{11}, a_{12}, a_{13}, …, a_{1i})$
    $T_2 (\underline{K_1^* \ K_2}, a_{21}, a_{22}, a_{23}, …, a_{2i})$

T_2 has a composite PK of (K_1, K_2) and only K_1 is a FK of table T_2, and K_1 is a PK of T_1. So, T1 is a strong entity, T_2 is a weak entity, and there is a 1: N relationship between T_1 and T_2.

3.3 N: M for relationships identified by relationship relations
Consider these two relations:

    $T_1 (\underline{K_1}, a_{11}, a_{12}, a_{13}, …, a_{1i})$
    $T_2 (\underline{K_2}, a_{21}, a_{22}, a_{23}, …, a_{2i})$
    $T_3 (\underline{K_2^*, K_1^*}, a_k)$

IF: T_3 has a composite primary key of (K_2, K_1), when consisting of FKs from the other two different tables T_1 and T_2,
THEN: there is a M : N relationship between T_1 and T_2.

3.4 Is-a Relationship
IF: two strong entities, T_1 and T_2, have the same PK and T_2 has a key being both PK and FK,
THEN: T_2 has "Is-a" relationship with T_1 (T_2 Is-a T_1).

Consider these two relations:
T_1 ($\underline{K_1}$, a_{11}, a_{12}, a_{13}, ..., a_{1i})
T_2 ($\underline{K_1}^*$, a_{21}, a_{22}, a_{23}, ..., a_{2i})

3.5 Recursive Relationship
IF: T1 has a FK that references its own table (T),
THEN: T has recursive relationship.
Consider this relation:

T($\underline{K_1}$, a_{11}, a_{12*}, a_{13*}, ..., a_{1i})

Ex. EMPLOYEE (FNAME, LNAME, <u>SSN</u>, ADDRESS, SALARY, SUPERSSN*, DNO*)

In this case, each Employee occurrence contains two social security numbers (SSN), one identifying the employee, the other being the SSN of the employee's supervisor.

5 The EIPW

This section shows the workflow of EIPW and its use for generating an ER model. In the previous section, EIR and RIR have been created as the reusable pattern repositories. This section discusses how these patterns will be implemented. EIPW can be divided into two subtasks: entity identification and relationship identification.

1. Entity Identification
The actual step-by-step activities of our methodology outlined in Figure 4 are in the form of an activity diagram in the UML.
In Figure 4, the three swimlanes perform the following activities:

- The middle swimlane: The aim of these swimlane activities is to identify the entities based on EIR.
- The rightmost swimlane: The aim of these swimlane activities is to identify the entities that are not detected by EIR by applying the hypernym chains in WordNet.
- The leftmost swimlane: The aim of these swimlane activities is to identify hidden entities that are not explicitly stated in the requirements but are necessary for the conceptual modeling by applying entity categories. Our entity categories in business applications adopt the class categories created by Song et al. [20]. Entities categories are used as a tip for identifying entities.

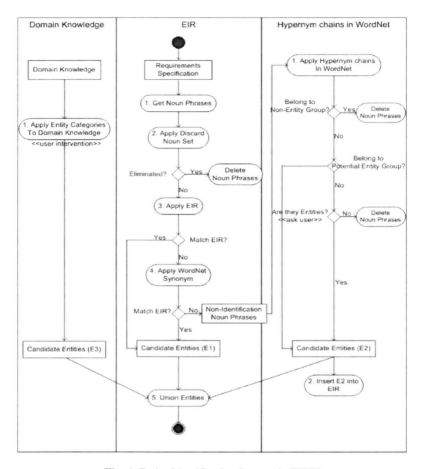

Fig. 4. Entity Identification Process in EIPW

The details of the activities in Figure 4 are presented below.

Activities of Middle Swimlane of Figure 4

- Begin with a requirement and remove the partial explanation statements

Explanation statements in a requirement specification aim to help human to understand the requirement better but they are harmful for automated requirement analysis [8]. Heuristics based on parenthesis and some words (e.g. such as) were used to remove the explanation statement.

- Step 1: Get noun phrases.

The Part of speech (POS) tags provide the word's syntactic categories of words whereby candidate entities can be identified from either noun phrases [5] or verb phrases [22]. In this research, we used a well-known open source called LingPipe (http://alias-i.com/lingpipe) for POS tagging to get all the noun phrases from requirement specification. Figure 5 shows the user interface of Step 1 that lists all the noun phrases appearing in the requirement specification.

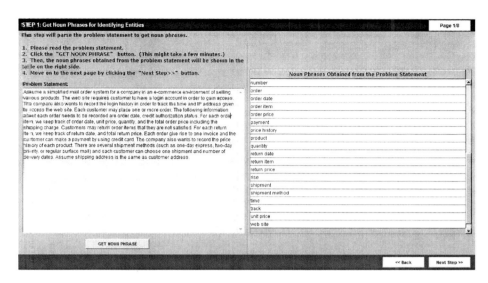

Fig. 5. The user interface of Step 1 listing all noun phrases appearing in the requirement

- Step 2: Test the discard noun set.

To facilitate the post-parsing analysis, noun phrases belonging to any of the discard noun set will be deleted. The discard noun set was created based on the history of words discarded by designers and the class elimination Rule [22]. The discard noun set is domain independent. The examples of nouns in discard noun set are number, ID, information, database, track, record, and system.

- Step 3: Identify entities based on EIR

Each noun phrase gotten from Step 2 was compared to entity names in the EIR. If a noun phrase matches an entity name in EIR, then the noun phrase becomes a candidate entity (E1).

- Step 4: Apply WordNet Synonym.

Out of these entity names, identify synonyms of a noun phrase from WordNet. If the synonyms of the noun phrase match an entity name in EIR, then the noun phrase becomes a candidate entity (E1).

Activities of RightMost Swimlane of Figure 4

- Step 1: Apply hypernym chains in WordNet

They are used to perform entity categorizations. The entity categories can help identifying entities from non-identifiable noun phrases from the MiddleMost Swimlane. These entity categories can be divided into two groups and defined as follows:

  - Potential-Entity Group: group, physical object, physical entity, thing, transaction.
  - Non-Entity Group: cognition, attribute, value, measure, constituent, language_unit, feeling.

If the hypernym chain of a noun phrase reaches to one of the categories in the "Potential-Entity" group, the system will label this term as a candidate entity (E2) and insert it to the EIR to expand the list of EIP. On the other hand, if the hypernym chain of a term reaches to one of the categories in the "Non-Entity" group, the system will delete this noun phrase.

If the hypernym chain of a term does not belong to any groups, the system will ask the user to make judgments regarding this term. If the user labels it as a candidate entity (E2), then insert it to the EIR, else delete this noun phrase.

Activities of LeftMost Swimlane of Figure 4
In this swimlane, the system asks the users to identify the hidden entities by applying domain knowledge to entity categories. In this process, we adopted the class categories created by Song et al. [22] as the entity categories.

- Step 1: Apply domain knowledge to entity categories (user intervention)

For each entity category, check whether all the entities representing the entity categories are already captured. Otherwise create a new entity (E3) based on the entity categories.

A set of entities identified from our methodology is a union of the entities identified from the three swimlanes. That is: $\{E\} = \{E1\} \cup \{E2\} \cup \{E3\}$

2. Relationship Identification
After the entity list has been identified in the entity identification process, relationships between entity list are generated by considering the application domain semantics inherent in the RIR. This repository is used to identify occurring relationships within an application domain and to generate the relationship between entities. The flowcharts for the relationship identification are shown in Figure 6. In Figure 6, there are two swimlanes performing the following activities.

- The left swimlane: The goal of these swimlane activities is to identify relationships (r) between candidate entities based on RIR.
- The right swimlane: The goal of these swimlane activities is to ask the user to identify the relationships, which are not detected by the RIR, by applying Need-to-Remember Rule [20].

The details of the activities in Figure 6 are discussed below.
Activities of left swimlane of Figure 6

- Begin with the candidate entity list gotten from entity identification process.
- Step 1: Delete duplicate entities.
  This will be conducted through WordNet synonyms.
- Step 2: Assign all the possible relationships (r_{ij}) between the candidate entities.
- Step 3: Match the possible relationships (r_{ij}) with RIR.
  If r_{ij} match the relationships in RIR, add r_{ij} into Relationship set (R).
- Step 4: Apply WordNet Synonym
  Out of the matching, identify synonyms of entity names from WordNet. If the synonyms of r_{ij} match the relationship in RIR, add r_{ij} in R.

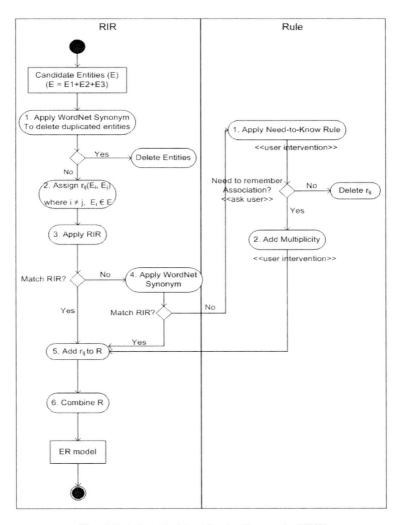

Fig. 6. Relationship Identification Process in EIPW

Activities of right swimlane of Figure 6

- Begin with the possible relationships that are not detected by the RIR from left swimlane.
- Step 1: Apply Need-to-Know rule (user intervention)
  If a relationship represents an association that does not have to be remembered between two entities, then eliminate this relationship.
- Step 2: Assign the multiplicity (user intervention)
  Assign the multiplicity to each relationship obtained from Step 5.

The ER model is created by combining a set of relationships (R) identified from the two swimlanes. Figure 7 shows the output of EIPW.

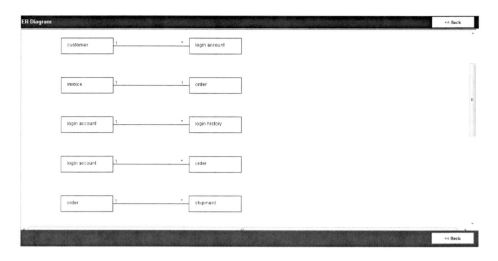

Fig. 7. The Output of EIPW

6 Empirical Evaluation

In this section, we evaluate the quality of output generated by EIPW by using an ANOVA technique. The resulting ER model created with our EIPW would be of higher quality than the one created with no tool. Since the quality of the ER models is of interest, the following hypothesis is tested:

H1: Novice Designers using EIPW will create ER models with better quality compared to the models generated by designers without the use of the system.

6.1 Experiment Design

We used an ANOVA technique called *2x2 within-subjects (repeated-measures) design*. The two independent variables are the system (with the aid of EIPW and no tool) and the task size (medium, moderate). Based on the combinatorial complexity [5], as the task size increases, so do the numbers of decisions required in the modeling process. Therefore, our experiment design incorporated two levels of the task size to provide some sensitivity for this factor. The medium task size has 9 entities and 9 relationships, while the moderate task size has 14 entities and 14 relationships. The dependent variable is the quality scores of the ERD. The accuracy of an ER model is evaluated by a scoring schema. In this research we adopted the grading scheme proposed by Du [19]. It focuses on the correct identification of appropriate entities and relationships based on the given problem statements. The ER models created by the subjects were judged by a third party (not the authors of this paper).

6.1.1 Subjects and Tasks
There were 20 subjects. All of the subjects were students in the iSchool at Drexel University and did not work in database design field before. Therefore, we concluded that

all of our subjects were novice designers. Eight are undergraduates and twelve are graduate students. Twenty subjects were divided into two groups as shown in Table 1. Each subject worked on four problem statements: one medium size and one moderate size problem statements with the aid of EIPW and one medium size and one large moderate problem statements with no tool. The problem statements were in an e-commerce domain. This domain was not too familiar to the students (unlike e.g. university management and library domains), and thus there was no concern that students would answer the questions due to their background experiences. The subjects can take time as long as they wanted to create ER models based on the given problems.

Table 1. The Experiment Design

Group	Num of subject	Problem1	Problem2	Problem3	Problem4
Group 1	10	No tool	No tool	Using EIPW	Using EIPW
Group 2	10	Using EIPW	Using EIPW	No tool	No tool

6.2 Results

A 2x2 within-subjects analysis of variance was performed on ERD quality scores as a function of EIPW (with, no tool) and task sizes (medium, moderate) as shown in Table 2. Considering the differences between the task sizes, the quality scores obtained for each design were calculated in percentage.

Table 2. Test of between subjects with dependent variable QUALITY SCORE

	QUALITY SCORE
System (EIPW, no tool)	$F(1,19) = 96.01$, $p < 0.000$
Task Size (medium, moderate)	$F(1,19) = 33.01$, $p < 0.094$
System x Task Size	$F(1,19) = 1.06$, $p < 0.317$

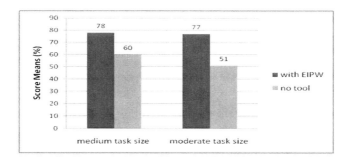

Fig. 8. The plot of the mean quality scores

From the calculated means shown in Figure 8, the ER models created by the EIPW are better than those created by no tool for each task size. From Table 3, the result shows that the main effect of system (with EIPW, no tool) was significant

($p < 0.00$). Therefore, this result supported our hypothesis (H1) that the EIPW helped subjects create better ER models than they do without it. There was no significant main effect for task size ($p < 0.094$). There was no significant system by task size ($p < 0.317$). It suggested that the main effect of the system (with EIPW, no tool) was not significantly different at the two levels of task size.

7 Conclusions and Future Research

In this paper, we have proposed a method for improving the process of conceptual modeling design. This research is an initial step to show how domain knowledge stored in the instance patterns can be reused for the conceptual modeling design. The EIPW, which integrated pattern-based technique and various modeling techniques, clearly helped the designers in creating better quality ER models. The empirical results indicated the significant improvement in novice designer performance when using the tool. The tool can help novice designers who are less experienced and who have incomplete knowledge in an application domain. The initial results suggested that our instance patterns can indeed be an asset in supporting conceptual modeling process because they minimize the cognitive load on the designers and ensure that the ER models are correct. In the educational context, our KBS can serve as the learning tool. It simplifies the work of experienced designers and provides a smooth head start to novice. However, the study has, so far, been carried out on one domain only, but it provides a theoretical background for research on other domains as well. For the future work, we want to test the usability of the KBS for different categories. For example, we want to repeat the experiment using the expert designers as the subjects. And we plan to make our EIPW interface module to import the output schema into an ER diagram or a class diagram in commercial graphical CASE tools.

References

1. Chen, P.: The Entity-Relationship Model: Toward A Unified View of Data. ACM Transactions on Database Systems 1(1), 9–36 (1976)
2. Moody, D.: Theoretical and Practical Issues in Evaluating the quality of conceptual models: Current State and Future Directions. Data & Knowledge Engineering 55, 243–276 (2005)
3. Simsion, G.: Data Modeling Theory and Practice. Technics Publications, LLC (2007)
4. Kim, N., Lee, S., Moon, S.: Formalized Entity Extraction Methodology for Changeable Business Requirements. Journal of Information Science and Engineering 24, 649–671 (2008)
5. Batra, D.: Cognitive complexity in data modeling: causes and recommendations. Requir. Eng. 12(4), 231–244 (2007)
6. Han, T., Purao, S., Storey, V.: Generating large-scale repositories of reusable artifacts for conceptual design of information systems. Decision Support Systems 45, 665–680 (2008)
7. Coad, P., North, D., Mayfield, M.: Object Models – Strategies, Pattern, & Applications. Yourdon Press, Englewood Cliffs (1995)
8. Hay, D.C.: Data model patterns: Conventions of Thought. Dorset House Publishing, New York (1996)

9. Fowler, M.: Analysis Patterns: Reusable Object Models. Addison Wesley, Menlo Park (1997)
10. Batra, D.: Conceptual Data Modeling Patterns: Representation and Validation. J. Database Manag. 16(2), 84–106 (2005)
11. Blaha, M.: Patterns of Data Modeling. CRC Press, Boca Raton (2010)
12. Fayad, M., Schmidt, D., Johnson, R.: Object-oriented Application Frameworks: Problem and Perspectives. Willy, NY (1997)
13. Szyperski, C.: Component Software: Beyond Object-Oriented Programming. Addison-Wesley, Reading (1998)
14. Silverston, L.: The Data Model Resource Book Revised Edition, vol. 2. John Willey & Sons Inc., New York (2001)
15. Kimball, R., Ross, M.: The Data Warehouse Toolkit: The Complete Guide to Dimensional Data Modeling. John Wiley & Sons, Inc., New York (2002)
16. Purao, S.: APSARA: A tool to automate system design via intelligent pattern retrieval and synthesis. Database Advance Information Systems 29(4), 45–57 (1998)
17. Purao, S., Storey, V., Han, T.: Improving Analysis Pattern Reuse in Conceptual Design: Augmenting Automated Processes with Supervised Learning. Information Systems Research 14(3), 269–290 (2003)
18. Wohed, P.: Tool Support for Reuse of Analysis Patterns - A Case Study. In: The 19th Int. Conf. on Conceptual Modeling (2000)
19. Du, S.: On the Use of Natural Language Processing for Automated Conceptual Data Modeling. Ph.D Dissertation, University of Pittsburgh (2008)
20. Song, I.-Y., Yano, K., Trujillo, J., Lujan-Mora, S.: A Taxonomic Class Modeling Methodology for Object-Oriented Analysis. In: Krostige, T.H.J., Siau, K. (eds.) Information Modeling Methods and Methodologies. Advanced Topics in Databases Series, pp. 216–240. Idea Group Publishing (2004)
21. Chiang, R., Barron, T., Storey, V.: Reverse engineering of relational databases: Extraction of an EER model from a relational database. Data & Knowledge Engineering 12, 107–142 (1994)
22. Song, I.-Y., Evans, M., Park, E.: A Comparative Analysis of Entity-Relationship Diagrams. Journal of Computer and Software Engineering 3(4), 427–459 (1995)
23. Elmasri, R., Nevathe, S.: Fundamentals of Database Systems. The Benjamin/Cummings Publishing Co., Inc., Redwood City,CA (2004)

On the Conceptualization of a Modeling Language for Semantic Model Annotations

Hans-Georg Fill

Stanford University BMIR / University of Vienna DKE,
251 Campus Drive, Stanford CA 94305, USA
fill@stanford.edu

Abstract. In this paper we describe the theoretical foundations, formal considerations, and technical characteristics that were taken into account for the conceptualization of a modeling language for the semantic annotation of visual models. Thereby it is envisaged to give insights into the underlying processes for the development of new visual modeling languages and thus provide input for a future model of the conceptualization process. To illustrate the realization of the approach we revert to the semantic annotation of a business process model using concepts from the web ontology language OWL, which allows us to show the iterations that were conducted to develop the approach. As a first evaluation the approach has been implemented on a meta modeling platform and will be made freely available to the interested community in the course of the SeMFIS project on www.openmodels.at.

Keywords: Conceptualization, Design, Semantic Annotation, Conceptual Models, Ontologies.

1 Motivation

When a new modeling language is being defined, it is mostly not made explicit how the designers of the modeling language derived the particular elements, relations, attributes, visual representations and model types from the underlying theoretical bodies. Rather, it is often referred to previously existing, similar languages and the incorporation of best practice examples, as e.g. stated in the UML and BPMN specifications [1,2]: "...UML originated with three leading object-oriented methods (Booch, OMT, and OOSE), and incorporated a number of best practices from modeling language design, object-oriented programming, and architectural description languages." [1][p.1] and "This specification represents the amalgamation of best practices within the business modeling community..." [2][p.1]. It is thus not clear whether the creators of the language applied some kind of structured, reproducable process, whether a formal, mathematical approach has been used, or whether the outcome is the result of a serendipitous inspiration of one or several persons. From a scientific point of view it seems however necessary to investigate this process in more detail in order to make the used techniques learnable and thus usable by a wider audience. In order to gain insight into such a process we will describe in the following the underlying theoretical foundations, formal considerations, and technical characteristics that have led to the development of a modeling language for the semantic annotation of conceptual visual models.

2 Background: Semantic Annotation of Models

Several areas in information systems make use of conceptual visual modeling methods today. They are used to represent both static and dynamic phenomena and thus support human communication and understanding [3,4]. Their usage spans from business oriented applications such as for strategic and business process management to the technical realization of information systems in software engineering and IT infrastructure management, c.f. [5]. In recent years, several approaches have been elaborated that focus on the processing of unstructured semantic information that is contained in these models. Similarly to the idea of a semantic web where unstructured textual information is enhanced by using references to ontologies, the unstructured information that is expressed in the models using natural language is made machine processable by defining mappings to semantic schemata. In contrast to approaches that aim for a complete, a-priori formal definition of all model content, e.g. [6,7], the use of semantic annotations gives way to a flexible, stepwise semantic enrichment. Thus, a domain expert can easily choose which parts of the contained semantic information shall be expressed in a formal way and which parts can be left in the traditional natural language format. At the same time, the traditional way of using the modeling language is not changed.

Especially in the area of business process modeling a range of benefits have been described that are based on the processing of such semantic annotations. Examples include the measuring of the similarity of models [8], the automatic execution of process instances using web services [9] or the detection of regulatory compliance [10]. However, the approaches that have been described in the past are usually targeted towards a specific business process modeling language. It therefore seemed worthwhile to develop an approach that can be applied to arbitrary conceptual modeling languages and thus reap the benefits of semantic annotations also for other knowledge areas and according modeling languages.

For this purpose we will first describe the foundations and concepts our approach is based on and then discuss the process of how a modeling language has been conceived that permits to annotate arbitrary conceptual models with concepts from ontologies.

3 Fundamental Concepts

For describing our approach we will refer to a number of specific terms in regard to modeling methods and modeling languages. Therefore, we will briefly define some fundamental concepts and thus clarify their meaning in our context.

3.1 Components of Modeling Methods

To define the components of modeling methods we refer to the generic framework developed in [11] - see also figure 1. A modeling method is thereby composed of a modeling technique and mechanisms and algorithms. The modeling technique contains a modeling language, which is specified by a syntax, semantics, and visual notation, and a modeling procedure that defines the steps and results for applying the modeling language. The semantics of the modeling language defines the meaning of the syntactic elements by establishing a mapping to a semantic schema. The mechanisms and algorithms are used in the modeling procedure and can either be generic, i.e. applicable to arbitrary modeling languages, specific, i.e. applicable only to a particular set of modeling languages or hybrid, i.e. they can be parameterized for a specific modeling language.

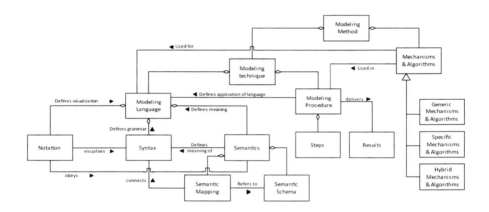

Fig. 1. Components of Modeling Methods [11]

For the conceptualization of a modeling method at least some of these generic concepts need to be specified. To do so it can be chosen from several entry points: One would be to start with the definition of the syntax of the modeling language and its semantics. Then assign an appropriate visual notation to the syntactic elements based on the semantics and finally specify the details of the modeling procedure and the corresponding mechanisms and algorithms. Another direction would be to focus on the modeling procedure and its results and then derive the according modeling language and the mechanisms and algorithms. Similarly, if one wants to focus on particular mechanisms and algorithms, e.g. for conducting mainly machine based processing, it is also an option to start from there and then develop the modeling language and the modeling procedure. However, a modeling method does not necessarily need to contain all the elements shown in the framework and not all of them to the full extent. The minimal set to create visual models is certainly the definition of a syntax and a visual notation together with at least a semantic description in the form of natural language explanations. This allows to create visual models that may even be processed by generic mechanisms and algorithms that do not require a further semantic specification. Many of the currently used standards for visual modeling languages, e.g. UML and BPMN, only contain such a minimal set and leave it to the modeler to determine the most suitable modeling procedure.

3.2 Conceptual Models and Ontologies

To describe our approach we also need to define the terms *conceptual model* and *ontology*. By a conceptual model we understand a visual representation of some aspects of the physical and social world for the purpose of human understanding and communication [4]. Based on the previous statements about the components of modeling languages, such a conceptual model is created based on a formal - in the sense of machine-processable - abstract and concrete syntax, which are specified by a schema or grammar, and a distinct graphical notation [4,3]. As it is not primarily directed towards machine processing, the definition of formal semantics is not compulsory but may be added if necessary, e.g. to conduct simulations. For defining the grammar of conceptual models it can be reverted to proprietary specifications such as the Eclipse modeling framework [12] or ALL [13] or standardized specifications such as the meta object facility (MOF) [14].

An ontology on the other hand can be characterized as "a shared and common understanding of some domain that can be communicated across people and computers" [15][p.184]. In contrast to conceptual models, ontologies are based on computer-usable definitions and are usually expressed in a logic-based language [16]. This makes them particularly useful for specifying and processing structured vocabularies that make the relationships between different terms explicit [17]. In addition, ontologies can today be easily interchanged using some of the widely used languages such as RDF, RDFS or the web ontology language (OWL) that come with a formal semantic specification that allow for automated reasoning mechanisms such as consistency checking and the classification of terms [18].

4 Conceptualization of a Semantic Annotation Modeling Language

Based on these foundations the process of developing a modeling language for semantically annotating arbitrary types of conceptual models can now be described. In particular we will investigate the theoretical foundations that were considered at the beginning, the formal considerations for realizing the modeling language in a way that can be processed by machines and the technical characteristics that needed to be taken into account.

4.1 Theoretical Foundations

As there are several approaches available that discuss the semantic annotation of conceptual models - in particular business process models - it was first investigated how semantic annotations have been conducted previously and which of the described techniques could be reused for our purposes. Thereby, two main directions could be identified - see also figure 2: The first direction concerns the *translation* of all model information into an ontology language that provides formal semantics, e.g. [19,8]. By enriching the resulting ontology skeleton with additional information about the semantic contents of the models, a machine processable representation can be established. To illustrate this with an example, consider the representation of a business process as an event driven process chain (EPC), c.f. [19]. To translate such a process into an ontology, at first the modeling language for EPCs is translated into ontology concepts, e.g. OWL classes. The resulting ontology can then be refined in OWL, for example by defining the "control flow" properties that connect "functions" and "events" of the EPC as a transitive property. Based on the formal semantics defined for OWL a reasoner can thus correctly interpret that instances of functions and events that are connected with "subsequent" properties are transitively connected to each other.

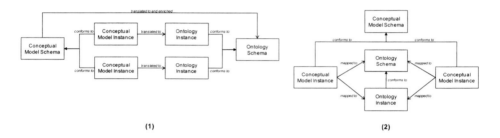

Fig. 2. Two Variants for Semantic Annotations of Conceptual Models

The second direction that can be found in the literature on semantic annotations for conceptual models is characterized by using mapping relations between the elements of a conceptual model and concepts in an ontology, e.g. [20,21,22]. This permits to process the elements in the ontology using formal semantics and thus detect for example ontology concepts that are similar to a concept that participates in such a mapping. Based on this information, the mappings from these similar ontology concepts to the same or other conceptual models can then be used to detect similar elements on the side of conceptual models, as e.g. described by [20].

Although these directions have been described primarily in the context of business process modeling so far, they seemed to be applicable also to other conceptual modeling languages. However, the literature on the application of these approaches to practical scenarios that would allow an evaluation of which of the approaches may be beneficial compared to the other is not yet available. At best, descriptions about the successful application to concrete use cases can be found, e.g. [23,21,22], thus illustrating potential advantages and shortcomings of the approaches. Therefore, it had to be decided which direction should be taken for our approach and we selected the second direction, i.e. the mapping between conceptual models and ontologies. The main reason for this choice was, that we envisaged that the approach would thus be more loosely coupled and could be more easily applied to arbitrary conceptual modeling languages. This loose coupling mainly stems from the fact that no semantic enrichment of the schema of the conceptual models is necessary but that only a mapping has to be defined.

The next theoretical consideration concerned the choice of the language for specifying ontologies. As Obrst has pointed out there is a spectrum of languages available that can be used for this purpose, each with its own advantages and pitfalls [16]. As we wanted to keep our approach as flexible as possible we chose the web ontology language (OWL) for representing ontologies. OWL is widely used in several domains, comes in the form of an official standard by the W3C and is well supported by a range of tools and APIs. In addition, it can serve various goals of using semantic annotations for conceptual models such as the building of formal thesauri, the representation of complex domain knowledge in a formal, machine processable way or as a starting point for executing queries on the formal specifications and the definition of rules, e.g. by using the semantic web rule language SWRL [24,25].

4.2 Formal Considerations

Based on the theoretical choices for using a mapping approach to the web ontology language, the next part was the actual translation of these choices into a concrete modeling language that would be able to use these concepts. Thus, it had to be decided how the mapping should be formally defined in terms of a modeling language and how an ontology in the OWL format should be represented. At the same time it should be ensured that the models that would result from using such a modeling language could be easily processed in a meaningful way. To represent OWL ontologies in the form of models several solutions have been described in the past. These include for example the ontology definition meta model by OMG [26] and a number of prototypes that originated from research projects, e.g. [27,21]. For the purposes of semantic annotations we chose to re-use a previously developed implementation that allows to represent OWL ontologies in the form of visual models but does not itself require the implementation of formal semantic restrictions [28]. In particular, this approach provides algorithms that allow to exchange representations of OWL ontologies with the Protégé ontology management platform. Thereby, the formal semantic restrictions are enforced on the Protégé platform and its attached reasoners and the ontologies are only represented in the modeling environment. To conduct reasoning tasks, requests can thus be sent to Protégé and the results then transferred back into the modeling environment. This not only permits to reuse already developed algorithmic solutions, e.g. for the similarity matching between concepts of an ontology, but also as a basis for advanced manipulations of the ontology concepts such as the execution of semantic queries or rules on the side of Protégé, e.g. by using the SPARQL or SWRL extensions [25].

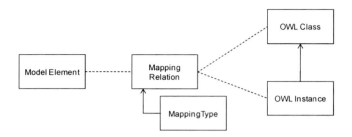

Fig. 3. Theoretical Conception of the Semantic Annotation Approach

To illustrate the path of developing the formal description of the semantic annotation approach, we will describe three evolution steps for realizing a modeling language for semantic annotations. Thereby we intend to show what considerations have to be made for creating the modeling language. In figure 3 the fundamental idea of the approach is shown: For any kind of model element a mapping relation is defined to either an OWL class or an instance of an OWL class. To keep the illustration simple we omitted the possibility of creating mappings to properties. Furthermore, the mapping relation can be detailed by a mapping type, which defines whether the mapped ontology entity *is equal*, *broader* or *narrower* to the meaning of the model element or *refers to* a particular meaning of an ontology entity.

Based on this idea, a first variant for translating these concepts into a modeling language is shown in figure 4. The left part in figure 4 shows the concrete syntax and according visual representation of a sample part of a business process model. It contains an *activity* element, a *decision* element and a *subsequent* relation between the two. In addition, *name* attributes with the values "Write letter"

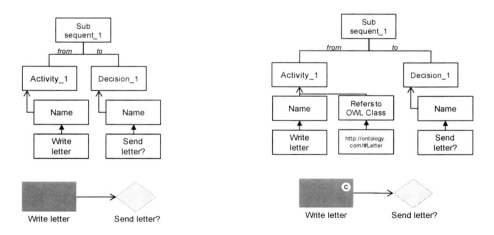

Fig. 4. Sample of an Excerpt of a Conceptual Business Process Model and a Variant for a Semantic Annotation

and "Send letter?" are linked to the model elements. As a first variant, the set of attributes for activities can be extended to give users of the modeling language the possibility to specify an OWL class that stands for the refers-to mapping type. If a value for such an attribute is present it can also be used to change the visual representation accordingly as shown on the right side of figure 4.

Although this first variant contains already all necessary information for the mapping between model elements and ontology concepts and could be directly processed by algorithms, it has several limitations. One limitation is that the original modeling language needs to be extended with an attribute to contain the mapping to the ontology concepts. This may not pose a serious limitation for many modeling languages, but it may lead to difficulties if certain algorithms depend on the original state of the modeling language and may need to be adapted in case of a modification. Another limitation is that for each annotation the exact reference to the ontology concepts needs to be known, i.e. the user of the modeling language has to know the URI of the ontology concept and insert it as an attribute value. Although this could be resolved on the user interface level, it seemed worthwhile to investigate further options for a better representation.

Based on these considerations a second variant was created as depicted in figure 5. It features a separate model type for representing the information contained in OWL ontologies. As mentioned above it does however not include any formal semantic restrictions but just presents the syntactic information

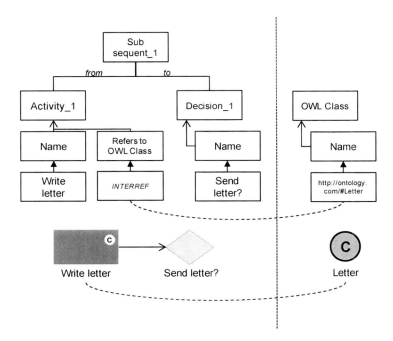

Fig. 5. Variant of a Semantic Annotations using a Model-based Ontology Representation

contained in an OWL ontology. For the example here, the OWL representation has been simplified to highlight the key aspects. In this way, only an *OWL Class* model element and a name attribute are shown. In a similar fashion also OWL properties and instances could be represented. However, the presented information is already sufficient to enable users to map the extended modeling language for a business process model to the OWL model representation. In contrast to the first variant, a user can easily select the ontology concepts that shall be used for the annotation without knowing about the exact reference of the ontology concepts. The ontology representation on the right side can thereby either created by hand - e.g. by an expert user - or imported from an ontology toolkit such as Protégé by using an import mechanism. Due to the lack of formal semantics in the model representation, any modifications of the ontology relationships must however be checked using an external source, e.g. through a reasoner attached to Protégé.

Despite the progress that could be made with the second iteration, the problem of modifying the original modeling language had not been solved. This led to a third iteration as described in figure 6. Here, the loose coupling between the original modeling language, the annotations, and the ontology representation is fully achieved. This is accomplished by introducing a third model type besides the business process model and the ontology model: This *annotation model type* contains references to both the elements of the modeling language that shall be annotated and the ontology model. It also permits to specify the annotation type - shown in figure 6 again by the example of the *Refers-to* annotation type. As the annotation model type provides all necessary information no modification of the original modeling language is necessary. This approach is similar to previously discussed approaches in the context of model weaving [29], however

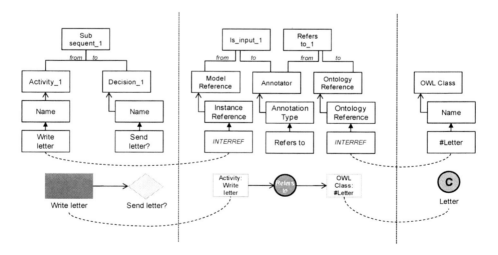

Fig. 6. Resulting Final Variant Using Two Additional Model Types for the Semantic Annotation

we use an explicit visual representation for the annotation model type. Thereby, a user can edit the annotations in a visual form without having to deal with a formal specification language.

4.3 Technical Characteristics

Besides the formal considerations for the conception of the modeling language also certain technical characteristics need to be taken into account. This stems from the fact that in case the modeling language shall be implemented in software, a translation from the abstract formal definitions into a concrete programming or machine processable description language needs to be accomplished. For this purpose it can be chosen from two directions: Either the modeling language is built from scratch using a standard programming language such as Java or C++ or some modeling tools such as specific programming APIs or a meta modeling platform are used. Although implementing the modeling language in a programming language from scratch may offer a maximum degree of freedom, it is certainly not an efficient way to do so when taking into account all the necessary details for the user interface, logic, and data storage level of such an application. And even if an existing platform or API is used, there are still several technical choices that need to be made.

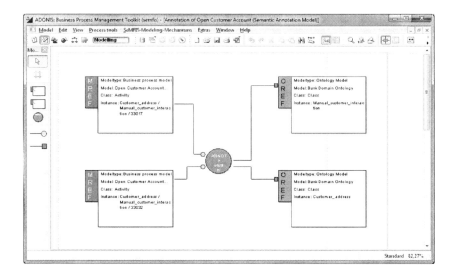

Fig. 7. Screenshot of the Implementation of the Semantic Annotation Model

For the technical realization of the described semantic annotation modeling language we used the ADOxx[1] meta modeling platform that is provided for free by the www.openmodels.at community. The choice for this platform was mainly

---
[1] ADOxx is a registered trademark of BOC AG.

based on its extensive funcationalities for implementing modeling languages, its industry ready scalability and robustness as well as existing skills on the side of the authors with its proprietary configuration languages ALL, ADL, and GRAPHREP [13]. The platform offers many options for implementing arbitrary types of visual modeling languages. To highlight some of the technical characteristics we will discuss two aspects: the user interface level and the aspects of data exchange and storage. For the user interface level it had to be taken into account that the semantic annotations can be easily created by hand and that the visual representation offers some guidance to the users. This concerned in particular the representation of the elements that reference the model elements and the ontology elements - see figure 7. It was therefore decided to integrate the details of the reference such as the model type, the model instance, the referenced class, and the referenced instance into the visual representation. Thus, the user can immediately see without further interaction what the reference stands for. The same considerations were applied for the references to ontology models. Another aspect of the user interface level that we would like to highlight is the choice of the colors: Here the decisive factor was that the user should be able to easily distinguish the elements from each other. Therefore different colors were chosen for the *model reference* and the *ontology reference* elements and for the two relations, the *is input* relation and the *refers to* relation. The choice for the shapes was not driven by any particular consideration but was targeted towards a neutral representation that would not evoke any references to existing symbols.

In regard to the data exchange and storage aspects the used meta modeling platform offered several functionalities that helped to focus on the conceptualization of the modeling language itself. Thus, it had not to be taken into account how the modeling language in the form of a meta model nor the actual model instances are stored in a database as the platform would handle that automatically and in an efficient way. The same applied to the use of import and export interfaces for exchanging ontology models with the Protégé platform. ADOxx provides a generic XML format for importing and exporting models that could be easily created by a specifically developed plugin for Protégé. If these functionalities had not been available particular effort would have been required to implement according database and XML schemata.

Also in terms of scalability and applicability to real scenarios, the choice for the ADOxx platform provides several advantages. These include the fact that ADOxx has been applied to many use cases in industry where several domain specific modeling languages (DSML) have been developed [30]. The proposed approach for using semantic annotations can be easily adapted to support a variety of existing other modeling languages and practical scenarios. In addition, also technical functionalities in regard to programmatic access to the models provide further opportunities. It is thus planned to use the WSDL interface for ADOxx to develop a web-based annotation tool. A first prototype for this approach that is based on the Google Web Toolkit and the SmartGWT[2] API is currently under development and will be shortly available [31,32]. Based on

---

[2] SmartGWT is a registered trademark of Isomorphic Software.

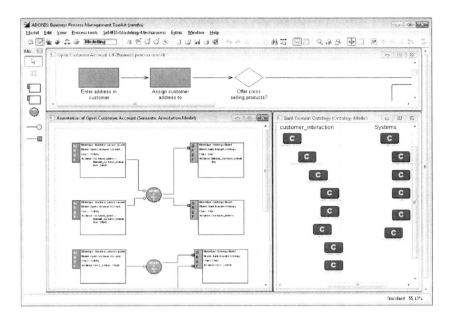

Fig. 8. Screenshot of the Implementation on the ADOxx Platform

these developments it is then envisaged to further investigate and advance the scalability of the approach by making it available for a wider audience on the web.

For the further evaluation of the implementation of the semantic annotation modeling language it will be made freely available in the course of the SeMFIS project on the www.openmodels.at platform[3]. Thereby, it is envisaged to receive further feedback from the community, especially in regard to the scalability and practical applicability of the approach.

5 Conclusion and Outlook

With the above description that highlighted some of the key choices during the development of the semantic annotation modeling language it can now be discussed which implications such a description may have. Clearly, the way how modeling languages are being realized today is not - or maybe not yet - a process that adheres to a well-defined reproducable process. Many of the choices that are made during the development are currently more based on intuition and previous experience than on a sound theoretical foundation. However, there are some parts in the development process where either existing theoretical approaches could be directly applied or where it seems worthwhile of developing them.

In particular we see three parts where this is the case: The first and probably most obvious concerns the choice of the graphical representation of the elements

---
[3] See http://openmodels.at/web/semfis/

and relations of a modeling language. For a long time several areas of science have studied the meaning of signs, the perception of color or the cultural implications that follow from this. It has already been described how systems could be realized that support the creators of modeling languages in choosing appropriate visual representations for this purpose [5]. This could be further developed and generate a direct benefit for the conceptualization of modeling languages in general.

Another part where the use of existing theories and their further adaptation to the conceptualization of modeling languages may be beneficial is the optimization of the syntax of the modeling language. The field of databases developed a large number of optimization techniques that may be able to serve as starting points for further developments. Similar to the principles of normalization and optimization of relational models [33], one could imagine also a theoretical approach for optimizing the syntactic representation of a visual modeling language. As described by the iterations that were presented in section 4 such an optimization needs to take into account several dimensions at the same time to be successful. It would not only have to focus on an efficient implementation in terms of a data structure, but the data efficiency may even be sacrificed to a certain extent to allow for a better user experience or a better application of algorithms.

The third aspect that is probably the most difficult to achieve and that has not been considered so far is the tighter collaboration with prospective real users of the modeling language. Although this is usually hard to achieve for scientists who are not tightly integrated with industry - e.g. based on common projects as it is done in consortium research [34] - this seems to be the only way to enhance the conceptualization process in terms of real usability. By receiving continuous feedback of the future users and the immediate, structured response to the needs expressed therein, is likely to be the sole option for arriving at a quasi-optimal solution that not only has an academic impact. For this purpose new developments in the fields of crowd-sourcing and social network approaches could bring about interesting options for realizing such tasks also on a low-budget basis and for integrating professionals in scientific development processes.

Acknowledgements

We would like to thank the three anonymous reviewers for their very constructive and valuable comments. The work on this paper has been funded by the Austrian Science Fund (FWF) in the course of an Erwin-Schrödinger-Fellowship grant number J3028-N23.

References

1. Object Management Group OMG: OMG Unified Modeling Language (OMG UML), Infrastructure, V2.1.2 (2007), http://www.omg.org/spec/UML/2.1.2/Infrastructure/PDF/ (accessed March 01, 2011)

2. Object Management Group (OMG): Business Process Model and Notation (BPMN) Version 2.0 (2011), http://www.omg.org/spec/BPMN/2.0/PDF/ (accessed March 01, 2011)
3. Wand, Y., Weber, R.: Research Commentary: Information Systems and Conceptual Modeling - A Research Agenda. Information Systems Research 13(4), 363–376 (2002)
4. Mylopoulos, J.: Conceptual Modeling and Telos. In: Loucopoulos, P., Zicari, R. (eds.) Conceptual Modelling, Databases and CASE: An Integrated View of Information Systems Development, pp. 49–68. Wiley, Chichester (1992)
5. Fill, H.G.: Visualisation for Semantic Information Systems. Gabler (2009)
6. Peleg, M., Tu, S.: Design Patterns for Clinical Guidelines. Artificial Intelligence in Medicine 47(1), 1–24 (2009)
7. Becker, J., Breuker, D., Pfeiffer, D., Raeckers, M.: Constructing Comparable Business Process Models with Domain Specific Languages - An Empirical Evaluation. In: 17th European Conference on Information Systems (ECIS), Verona, Italy (2009)
8. Ehrig, M., Koschmider, A., Oberweis, A.: Measuring Similarity between Semantic Business Process Models. In: Roddick, J., Hinze, A. (eds.) Proceedings of the Fourth Asia-Pacific Conference on Conceptual Modelling (APCCM 2007). Australian Computer Science Communications, vol. 67, pp. 71–80. ACM, New York (2007)
9. Hepp, M., Leymann, F., Domingue, J., Wahler, A., Fensel, D.: Semantic business process management: a vision towards using semantic web services for business process management. In: IEEE International Conference on e-Business Engineering, 2005, ICEBE 2005, pp. 535–540 (2005)
10. Governatori, G., Hoffmann, J., Sadiq, S., Weber, I.: Detecting Regulatory Compliance for Business Process Models through Semantic Annotations. In: 4th International Workshop on Business Process Design, Milan (2008)
11. Karagiannis, D., Kühn, H.: Metamodelling platforms. In: Bauknecht, K., Tjoa, A.M., Quirchmayr, G. (eds.) EC-Web 2002. LNCS, vol. 2455, p. 182. Springer, Heidelberg (2002)
12. McNeill, K.: Metamodeling with EMF: Generating concrete, reusable Java snippets (2008), http://www.ibm.com/developerworks/library/os-eclipse-emfmetamodel/index.html?S_TACT=105AGX44&S_CMP=EDU
13. Fill, H.G.: UML Statechart Diagrams on the ADONIS Metamodeling Platform. Electronic Notes in Theoretical Computer Science 127(1), 27–36 (2004)
14. OMG, O.M.G.: Meta Object Facility (MOF) Specification 2.0 (2006)
15. Studer, R., Benjamins, R., Fensel, D.: Knowledge Engineering: Principles and methods. Data & Knowledge Engineering 25, 161–197 (1998)
16. Obrst, L.: Ontologies for semantically interoperable systems. In: Proceedings of the 12th International Conference on Information and Knowledge Management. ACM Press, New Orleans (2003)
17. Horrocks, I., Patel-Schneider, P., Van Harmelen, F.: From SHIQ and RDF to OWL: The Making of a Web Ontology Language. Web Semantics: Science, Services and Agents on the World Wide Web 1(1), 7–26 (2003)
18. W3C: OWL Web Ontology Language - Overview W3C Recommendation 10 February 2004 (2004), http://www.w3.org/TR/owl-features/ (accessed September 16, 2005)
19. Thomas, O., Fellmann, M.: Semantic Business Process Management: Ontology-based Process Modeling Using Event-Driven Process Chains. IBIS 2(1), 29–44 (2007)

20. Hoefferer, P.: Achieving Business Process Model Interoperability Using Metamodels and Ontologies. In: Oesterle, H., Schelp, J., Winter, R. (eds.) 15th European Conference on Information Systems (ECIS 2007), University of St. Gallen, St. Gallen, pp. 1620–1631 (2007)
21. Fill, H.G.: Design of Semantic Information Systems using a Model-based Approach. In: AAAI Spring Symposium. Stanford University, CA (2009)
22. Fill, H.G., Reischl, I.: An Approach for Managing Clinical Trial Applications using Semantic Information Models. In: Rinderle-Ma, S., Sadiq, S., Leymann, F. (eds.) Business Process Management Workshops - BPM 2009. Lecture Notes in Business Information Processing. Springer, Ulm (2009)
23. De Francisco, D., Grenon, P.: Enhancing telecommunication business process representation and integration with ontologised industry standards. In: Hepp, M., Hinkelmann, K., Stojanovic, N. (eds.) Proceedings of the 4th International Workshop on Semantic Business Process Management (SBPM 2009). ACM, New York (2009)
24. Horrocks, I., Patel-Schneider, P., Boley, H., Tabet, S., Grosof, B., Dean, M.: SWRL: A Semantic Web Rule Language Combining OWL and RuleML (2004), http://www.w3.org/Submission/SWRL/ (accessed September 16, 2007)
25. O'Connor, M., Knublauch, H., Tu, S., Musen, M.A.: Writing Rules for the Semantic Web Using SWRL and Jess. In: Protégé with Rules Workshop, Held with 8th International Protégé Conference, Madrid, Spain (2005)
26. OMG, O.M.G.: Ontology Definition Metamodel, Third Revised Submission to OMG/ RFP ad/2003-03-40. Technical report (2005), http://www.omg.org/docs/ad/05-08-01.pdf (accessed September 16, 2005)
27. Leutgeb, A., Utz, W., Woitsch, R., Fill, H.G.: Adaptive Processes in E-Government - A Field Report about Semantic-based Approaches from the EU-Project FIT. In: Proceedings of the International Conference on Enterprise Information Systems (ICEIS 2007). INSTICC, Funchal, Madeira, Portugal, , pp. 264–269 (2007)
28. Fill, H.G., Burzynski, P.: Integrating Ontology Models and Conceptual Models using a Meta Modeling Approach. In: 11th International Protégé Conference, Amsterdam (2009)
29. Del Fabro, M.D., Valduriez, P.: Semi-automatic model integration using matching transformations and weaving models. In: SAC 2007 Proceedings of the 2007 ACM Symposium on Applied Computing. ACM, New York (2007)
30. BPTrends: The 2005 EA, Process Modeling and Simulation Tools Report - Adonis Version 3.81 (2005), http://www.boc-group.com/info-center/downloads/detail/resource/bptrends-review-of-adonis/ (accessed March 30, 2011)
31. Smeets, B., Boness, U., Bankras, R.: Beginning Google Web Toolkit - From Novice to Professional. Apress (2008)
32. Software, I.: Smart GWT(TM) Quick Start Guide - Smart GWT v2.4 November 2010 (2010), http://www.smartclient.com/releases/SmartGWT_Quick_Start_Guide.pdf (accessed March 30, 2011)
33. Codd, E.: A relational model of data for large shared data banks. Communications of the ACM 13(6), 377–387 (1970)
34. Oesterle, H., Otto, B.: Consortium Research - A Method for Researcher-Practitioner Collaboration in Design-Oriented IS Research. Business & Information Systems Engineering 5/2010 (2010)

Modeling and Analyzing Non-Functional Properties to Support Software Integration

Henning Agt[1], Gregor Bauhoff[2], Ralf-D. Kutsche[1], and Nikola Milanovic[2]

[1] Technische Universität Berlin
{henning.agt,ralf-detlef.kutsche}@tu-berlin.de
[2] Model Labs GmbH
{gregor.bauhoff,nikola.milanovic}@modellabs.de

Abstract. Software integration is one of the major needs as well as cost driving factors in the software industry today. Still, very few established methodologies exist, especially those addressing integration with respect to non-functional properties. Industry studies show that disregarded and hidden non-functional incompatibilities between systems and their interfaces are the constant source of errors and costly workarounds. We introduce a model-based process that allows dynamic definition of non-functional properties in the context of software integration, present a NFP taxonomy, and propose a method for formal analysis of interface incompatibilities with respect to these properties.

1 Introduction

Software and data integration practice is usually focused on structural and communication compatibility conflicts that require transformation of data types and structures and connection of communication channels. Integration frameworks and tools exist which address these issues to some extent (e. g., [1,2,3]). However, non-functional properties (NFP), such as reliability, availability, security, timeliness and cost play the crucial role in software integration when it comes to satisfying business process requirements. Their analysis is either neglected or informal, following best practices. Sometimes this is not enough as non-functional incompatibilities may compromise not only the quality of integration solution, but also limit its functionality.

For these reasons, as part of the research project BIZYCLE[1], we investigate in large-scale the potential of model-based software and data integration methodologies, tool support and practical applicability for different industrial domains (the consortium comprises of six system integrators from health, publishing and media, facility management, production and logistics sectors). We have developed an MDA-based methodology [4,5], we call it the BIZYCLE integration process, to systematically model integration projects at different levels of abstraction in order to achieve automatic analysis, code generation and integration. In this section we cover the basic aspects of the process and in the

---

[1] This work is partially supported by the Bundesministerium für Bildung und Forschung BMBF under grant number (Förderkennzeichen) 03WKBB1B.

remainder of the paper we concentrate on how to use models of non-functional properties to facilitate integration compatibility checks.

The essence of the BIZYCLE integration process is to provide multilevel integration abstractions and to make software integration partially automatic. The levels of abstraction are computational independent model (CIM), platform specific model (PSM) and platform independent model (PIM) level. The CIM level captures the integration business process. Existing systems to be integrated, interfaces and their properties realizing an integration scenario are described at the PSM level. In contrast to the usual MDA philosophy, all PSM models are transformed to the PIM level, which represents a common abstraction level. The PIM level is used to perform an integration conflict analysis to discover incompatible interfaces. Appropriate connector (mediator) model and code for required connector components are generated based on results of the conflict analysis. Our conflict analysis addresses structural, behavioral, communication, semantic and non-functional property mismatches. For example, the semantic conflict analysis [6] is carried out using ontology annotations and reasoning with Prolog.

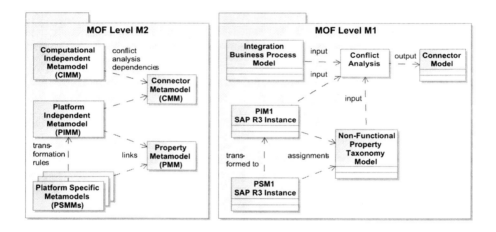

Fig. 1. BIZYCLE modeling methodology overview (excerpt)

Figure 1 presents part of our modeling methodology [7,5] and how NFP modeling is integrated. Dependencies between the framework's metamodels at the MOF M2 level are shown on the left side of the figure. Example models at the M1 level are given on the right (due to space reasons the figure includes only one PSM and PIM model, usually integration projects involve two or more systems). Our integration framework offers several metamodels and respective model editors on platform specific level to describe systems interfaces (PSMMs). We currently support SAP R/3 ERP systems, J2EE applications, SQL-based relational database systems, Web Services and XML Schema based files. A set of transformation rules for each platform is used to perform model transformations to common abstraction level with a single metamodel (PIMM). The PIMM and all PSMMs are linked to the Property Metamodel (PMM) presented in this paper to be able to associate NFPs to model elements at these abstraction levels. The Connector Metamodel (CMM) provides means to express conflict analysis' results in terms of Enterprise Application Integration (EAI) patterns [8].

In this paper we report our first practical experiences with model-based system integration with respect to NFPs. The rest of the paper is organized as follows: Section 2 presents a metamodel for expressing user-defined non-functional properties, their categories and measurement units. We focus on modeling of non-functional properties in a general way. Compared to the OMG QFTP specification [9] we are not limited to Quality of Service characteristics and UML based models. Additionally, we offer explicit modeling of measurement units to enable model-based comparison and calculation of NFPs. Section 3 describes a taxonomy with non-functional properties which we identified as relevant in the software integration context. It was implemented using our NFP metamodel. Section 4 proposes a method for formal analysis of interface incompatibilities with respect to these properties. Related work and conclusion are given in Section 5 and 6.

2 Non-Functional Property Metamodel

In order to model non-functional properties in our integration framework, we propose a property metamodel (PMM) for expressing NFPs, their categories and units of measurement and assigning them to other model elements. The metamodel is implemented in our integration framework using the Eclipse Modeling Framework. In the following we use `typewriter` font to refer to metamodel classes and attributes and describe examples on instance level with *italic* font.

Figure 2 gives abstract syntax of the property metamodel to create property categories (e.g., *performance*), non-functional properties (such as *throughput*) and units of measurement (such as *Mbit/s*).

Basic structural Features. Properties and measurement units are modeled separately and are grouped into categories. The categories and their elements together form the `PropertyModel`. A `NamedElement` metaclass (not shown in the Figure) passes attributes `+shortName:String[1]` (for abbreviations, e.g., *MTTF*) and `+longName:String[1]` (for full names, e.g., *Mean Time To Failure*) to most of the classes.

Properties. The `Property` metaclass owns the `scope`-attribute to define NFP validity. The `PropertyScope` can be one of the following values:

- `System`-wide (e.g., *mean time to repair* of a database system)
- `Interface`-wide (e.g., *availability* of a Web service)
- `Function`-related (e.g., *cost per invocation* of a Web service operation)
- `Parameter`-related (e.g., *accuracy* of a J2EE component method's return value)

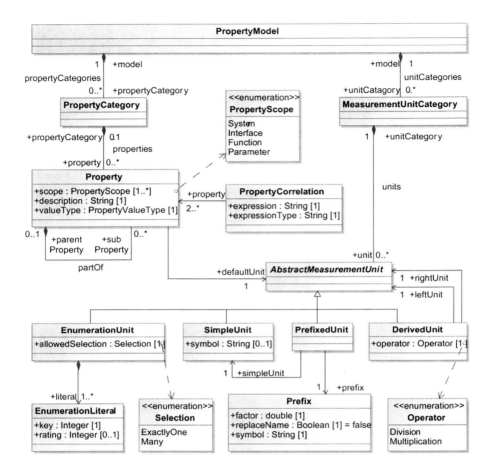

Fig. 2. Property Metamodel - Properties and units of measurement

The `description`-attribute includes additional explanatory text of the property. The attribute `valueType` constraints the value kind of a property to support comparison: character-based values (`String`), floating point numbers (`Double`), integer-based representations (`Long`) and `Boolean`-values. Properties can be nested with the `partOf`-relation. A property is associated with a default unit, which is the standard unit for property assignment.

Dependencies between properties can be declared with `PropertyCorrelation`. It is evaluated at runtime and can contain mathematical or boolean `expressions`. For instance, the calculation rule for availability ($A = \frac{MTTF}{MTTF+MTTR}$) can be expressed with MathML Content Markup [10] using property names as variables.

Measurement Units. The metamodel offers four units types to build units of measurement. The `SimpleUnit` is used to create basic SI-units [11] or ISO 80000

units such as *second* or *bit*. Additionally to shortName and longName attributes, a symbolic representation of a unit can be specified, if available.

PrefixedUnits are created from simple ones by combining them with Unit-Multiple. Usually a prefix is added in front of the unit name (e.g., metric prefix *kilo*, binary prefix *kibi*). A prefix of a unit is represented by a factor and a symbol. Contrary, there exist also non-SI measurement units that replace the whole unit name (e.g., *minute*). The change of the name can be controlled by the replaceName-attribute.

Composed units are modeled with the DerivedUnit[2] metaclass. It combines left- and right-handed units with an Operator. Reuse and nesting of simple units, prefixed units and derived units is allowed to build all kinds of measurement units (e.g., kg/m^3).

Finally, the EnumerationUnit describes possible values of a property as a set of EnumerationLiterals for non-numeric NFPs. The allowedSelection-attribute declares whether a property assignment must use exactly one literal or can use many literals. The key-attribute of the EnumerationLiteral is an additional unique numeric code. The rating attribute can assess a literal (e.g., to assess encryption algorithms). For example, we use enumerations to model ISO 4217 currency names.

Assigning Properties. On meta level, the PropertyAssignment (Figure 3) is the link between the actual non-functional property and elements of other metamodels that shall be annotated with NFPs. The type-attribute handles whether the property is offered/provided by the system or interface (e.g., *provided uptime*), or expected/required from other systems (e.g., *required network encryption*). Property values are either given as a single value (PropertyValue), as PropertyValueRange (e.g., minimum and maximum) or as a set of single values (PropertyValueSet). In case the default unit shall be overridden, the unitModifier is used (constrained to use different prefixes only). Enumeration unit literals are chosen with enumLiteralSelection (e.g., selecting *EUR* currency for a cost property from the currency code enumeration).

Example of a Property Assignment. In this paragraph, we demonstrate how the connection between different metamodels works. We have developed a platform specific metamodel [5] to describe interfaces of SAP R/3 enterprise resource planning systems (system access, communication channels, method signatures, parameter types, etc.). Upper part of Figure 4 presents the established link between the property metamodel and the SAP metamodel.

The SAP metamodel contains a metaclass SAP_R3 that represents a whole SAP R/3 system. SAP_R3_Interfaces are used to access certain parts of the system. We establish an association between PropertyAssignment and SAP_R3

---

[2] In the SI unit system and related ISO specifications the term *derived unit* usually refers to a fixed set of measurement units that have been derived from the SI base units. Here we use the term in a more general object-oriented way. Derived units are units that can be composed from other units using a formula.

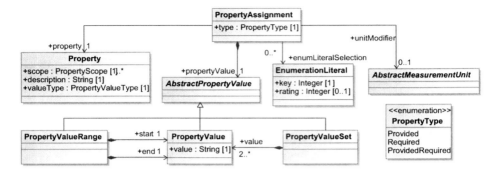

Fig. 3. PMM - Property assignment

metaclass to be able to assign any user-defined NFP to a concrete SAP installation. In our implementation based on the Eclipse Modeling Framework we use attributes that link between different Ecore files.

Lower part of Figure 4 shows an example of a property assignment on model level. We use object diagram notation to represent the instances. Instances *Server 1* and *purchase management* on the left side belong to a platform specific model of a concrete SAP R/3 system. Right part of the figure depicts excerpt of our property taxonomy for *Throughput* and the property assignment. The model contains two simple units *bit* and *second*. The prefixed unit is *Mbit*. Finally, the derived unit constitutes *Mbit/s*, the default unit for the *Throughput* property. The assignment links *Throughput* to *Server 1* and associates a value of *100*.

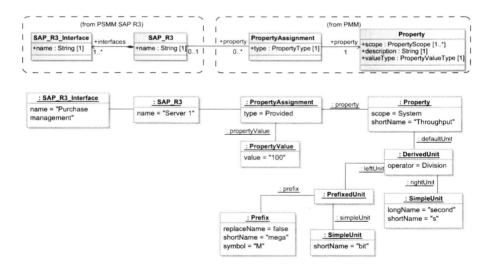

Fig. 4. Assignment example - SAP R/3 Server 1 provides 100 Mbit/s throughput

3 Non-Functional Properties in Software Integration

In this section we present a taxonomy of NFPs which we identified as relevant in the software integration context (excerpt is given in Figure 5). The taxonomy is modeled using the metamodel described in the previous section. It is not intended to be complete, but will be used here as a starting point to discuss modeling of non-functional aspects of software systems, interfaces, parameters and connectors, evaluate integration solutions, compute overall properties, detect non-functional mismatches and rank integration alternatives.

Entries of taxonomy's first level are property categories that thematically group NFPs defined at the second level. The third level (not shown in the picture) characterizes each property with description, type (e. g., float values), scope and the default unit (e. g., milliseconds for latency or currency codes for cost per invocation). Units are described according to standards such as ISO 80000-3:2006 (time), ISO 80000-13:2008 (IT units), ISO 8601 (date) or ISO 4217 (currency codes). In the following we provide more details on each property category.

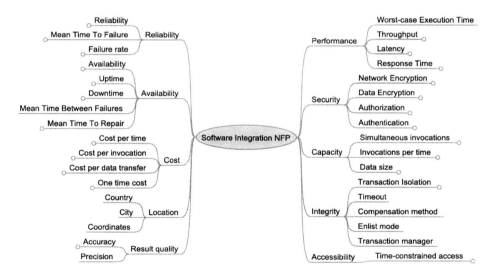

Fig. 5. Taxonomy of software integration non-functional properties (excerpt)

Reliability incorporates properties related to the ability of a system or component to perform its required functions under stated conditions for a specified period of time. Reliability is the probability that a system operates without failure for a given time t. Usually, steady-state reliability is used to characterize integrated systems, where observed interval is the system's lifetime. Reliability attributes such as *failure-rate* (λ) and *mean time to system failure (MTTF)* can also be specified.

Availability is similar to reliability, with one important exception: it allows for a system to fail and to be repaired. Thus, additional properties appear in this category: *mean time to repair (MTTR)*, *mean time between failures (MTBF)* as well as average *uptime/downtime* per year. Using this category, fault-tolerant lifecycle of integrated systems and their components can be analyzed.

Cost related NFP are used to compare different software integration alternatives. For example, the comparison of *cost per data transfer*-properties is achieved by specifying their unit in terms of a currency code in relation with the base unit byte with metric or binary prefix. Values with different currencies and different amounts of data volumes can be compared by determining the current exchange rate and by converting the units.

Performance category includes properties that are either bandwidth or timing related. They enable detection of possible integration bottlenecks and allow investigation of connector features such as caching as well as timing constraints.

Security category describes encryption and access control related properties. For example, *network encryption* property consists of three sub-properties *strength*, *protocol* and *technology*. Encryption strength can be directly compared, while protocols have to be evaluated based on sets of provided and required enumerations, correlations or rating (e. g., SHA vs. RIPEMD).

Capacity properties are considered to avoid system overloads during integration. For example, *data size* property specifies the maximum amount of data that can be passed to a system at once (value type: integer, default unit: megabyte). Together with *throughput*, duration of integration runs can be thus analyzed.

Integrity describes transactional behavior. *Isolation level* supports read uncommitted, read committed, repeatable read and serializable levels. *Timeout* defines system or interface timeout which can be used to discover timing mismatches, e. g., if a service with 1 hour timeout is waiting for a service with 1 day WCET, there is a timing conflict.

Location category describes geographical system/service location, as it may be necessary to determine validity of an integration scenario. For example, confidential data storage may be restricted to particular countries, because of legal considerations. To enable this, we include country name and its ISO code, as well as city and GPS coordinates of the system location.

Result quality describes attributes of the data/messages produced by a system. *Accuracy* represents calculation correctness (e. g., number of decimal places or maximal guaranteed computation error), while *precision* is the measure of the system output quality which may be gathered and evaluated statistically over a period of time, potentially also by users (in form of a reputation scale).

Accessibility is expressed by *time-constrained access*: it represents concrete time intervals or periodic time slots in which a system is accessible for integration tasks (e. g., Extract-Transform-Load tasks on Sundays 0:00-5:00 a.m.).

Figure 6 shows our NFP editor implementation using the plug-in and view architecture of Eclipse and EMF API to manipulate the models. Here we show the annotation of an SAP R/3 system interface with different availability and reliability NFPs and their values.

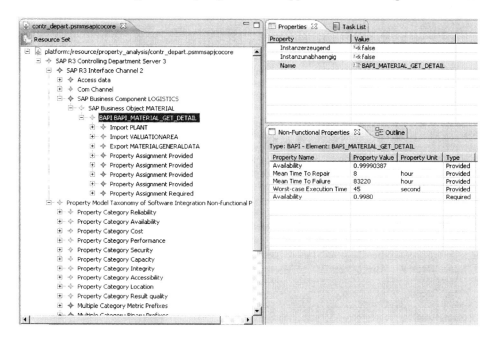

Fig. 6. Non-functional properties editor

4 Non-Functional Property Conflict Analysis

The task of NFP analysis is to determine if there are conflicts (i.e. incompatibilities or mismatches) between systems with respect to modeled non-functional properties. It is especially important in those integration cases where systems are functionally compatible, but hidden non-functional incompatibility compromises the integration solution. We provide the following case study: Figure 7 shows an instance of a so called connector model that describes message-based communication between the systems. The connector model is used in the last phase of the BIZYCLE integration process and is mostly generated from the models at the CIM level (integration business process) and the PIM level (systems and interfaces on a common abstraction level) and from the other conflict analysis phases (e.g., semantic or data type analysis [6,7]). In that last phase we treat all data exchanged between the systems as messages.

Figure 7 depicts different types of components: *Application Endpoints* representing the integrated systems and Message Processors, equivalent to EAI patterns [8] such as *Aggregators*, *Routers* or *Splitters* that mediate between application endpoints and route and transform messages. The components have *Ports* (P) and communicate via *Channels* (C). A complete language description can be found in [12]. The given connector model describes integration scenario with 4 systems: S_1, S_2, S_3 and S_4 which are annotated with (among others) non-functional descriptions, as explained in the previous sections. Based on the

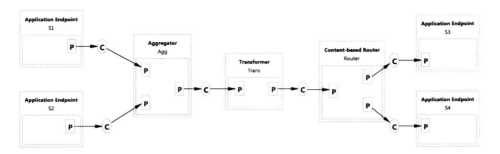

Fig. 7. Case study connector model

connector model, in the process of model transformation we generate an analysis model to investigate NFP mismatches.

The analysis model describes structural dependencies between connector components, with respect to NFP. The connector model is treated as a graph where application endpoints and message processors are vertices and channels are edges. Sets of source (S) and destination (D) vertices are identified first (in our example $\{S_1, S_2\} \in S$ and $\{S_3, S_4\} \in D$). Then all paths between S and D are discovered, using the standard algorithm for the detection of all paths between two vertices in a graph [13]. For each independent path that is discovered, a Boolean expression is derived: all vertices and edges on the path are connected with $\wedge$ if they belong to the same path. If more independent paths exist, they are connected with $\vee$. In our example, generated Boolean expression is:

$$S_1 \wedge S_2 \wedge Agg \wedge Trans \wedge Router \wedge (S_3 \vee S_4) \tag{1}$$

Note that we did not include channels in this analysis, assuming that they are ideal. After this step, Boolean expressions are minimized using the idempotence, associativity and distributivity rules of the Boolean algebra. Minimized equations may then be used for verification of several non-functional properties, such as cost, reliability and availability. We demonstrate how to analyse the latter.

For the purpose of availability analysis, Boolean expression is further transformed into reliability block diagram (RBD), which is the graph with following semantics: if elements are placed in series, they are statically dependent on each other. Otherwise, if they are placed in parallel, they are independent. The rules for this transformation are:

- The blocks of RBD model are all terms appearing in the minimized Boolean expression.
- If two terms are connected with the operator $\wedge$, RBD blocks are generated for both terms and placed into serial configuration.
- If two terms are connected with the operator $\vee$, RBD blocks are generated for both terms and places into parallel configuration.

After all block elements have been generated, each model element is parameterized with $MTTF$ and $MTTR$ parameters from the NFP annotation model.

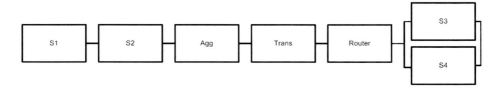

Fig. 8. Reliability block diagram model

This enables calculation of availability A of each model element (Table 1). The RBD equivalent of the connector model from Figure 7 is given in Figure 8.

Availability of each model element is calculated as:

$$A = \frac{MTTF}{MTTF + MTTR} \qquad (2)$$

Availability of series (A_S) and parallel (A_P) configuration of N elements (A_i) is calculated as (we do not address further issues regarding availability models as it is out of scope of this paper):

$$A_S = \prod_{i=1}^{N} A_i, A_P = 1 - \prod_{i=1}^{N}(1 - A_i) \qquad (3)$$

Exponential distribution is further assumed. Note once again that MTTR and MTTF parameters come from the non-functional annotation model, which has to be created manually as shown in Figure 6 or generated automatically based on historical and statistical data for systems/connector components. There are also numerous industrial studies listing these parameters for various system/software classes [14,15].

Instead of solving the model manually, for the purpose of availability analysis we generate RBD models for the external solver (Sharpe [16]), and obtain evaluation results for the connector availability shown in the row *Connector* of Table 1. This is the provided availability of the entire connector component which can now be compared with the required availability, if one was specified in the requirements specification phase.

Based on the analysis we can assert that the connector will run on the average for more than 2000 hours before it fails. Furthermore, connector repair will take more than 3 hours on the average. This also means that the connector based on the properties of its constituent parts and integrated systems will experience additional 12 hours of unplanned downtime per year. This is critical information for the integration scenario, because although the systems S_1, S_2, S_3 and S_4 may be functionally compatible, the requirement of the integration scenario may be that no more than 10 hours of unplanned downtime is allowed. In this case non-functional incompatibility would be detected.

Another possibility is to directly compare provided availability of source systems (S_1, S_2) and connector parts and determine if required availability of target systems (S_3, S_4) is satisfied. This is easy to do using the generated model

Table 1. Availability analysis results

	MTTF	MTTR	A
S_1	8760	0.6	0,99993151
S_2	8760	9	0,99897365
Agg	14400	2	0,99986113
$Trans$	18000	2	0,99988890
$Router$	9000	2	0,99977782
S_3	83220	8	0,99990387
S_4	83220	15	0,99981978
$Connector$	**2153.2**	**3.38**	**0.99854460**

by removing S_3 and S_4 from the model, reevaluating it and comparing the obtained value with required availability for S_3 and S_4. Steady-state availability of the system thus obtained is 0.99854462. Note that it does not differ greatly from the overall provided connector availability, because S_3 and S_4 are highly-available redundant data stores. Nevertheless, assume that required availability of S_3 and S_4 is 0.9980 and 0.9990 respectively. While availability requirements of S_3 are satisfied, it is obvious that S_4 will not guarantee correct operations as the rest of the system is not stable enough. This kind of incompatibility is very difficult, if not impossible, to determine using current system integration methods. As already noted, this approach may be used for equivalent calculation/matching of other non-functional properties, such as costs or accuracy. Properties, such as WCET or throughput, can be analyzed using a dynamic analysis model (i. e., Petri nets).

5 Related Work

Non-functional aspects in software integration relate to several research areas, i.e., requirements engineering, software engineering, service-oriented architecture, component-based development and model-driven development, in which non-functional properties/requirements (NFP/NFR), quality of service (QoS) attributes, and constraints are described, computed and analyzed. Glinz [17] surveys definitions of theses terms in relation to requirements engineering. We addressed non-functional properties with respect to software integration. Similar efforts in other contexts have been made: [18] discusses definitions and taxonomies of dependability and security in the context of faults, errors and failures. A Quality of Service catalog with regard to component-based software development is given in [19]. Several NFP ontologies exist, for example [20] compares existing solutions, such as OWL-QoS and QoSOnt.

Software integration research is today closely coupled with Web services. Several proposals have been made for NFP extensions of Web service descriptions, either XML-based [21,22] or as UML profiles to support graphical modeling of non-functional aspects in SOA [23]. Similar extensions are used for Web service discovery, matchmaking (e. g., DIANE framework [24]) and selection (a survey can be found in [25]). The tool Ark [23] also supports application code generation with respect to non-functional properties.

Description and analysis of non-functional properties plays an important role in software development based on MDA. [26] and [27] contribute frameworks that propose additional analysis models on CIM, PIM and PSM levels to validate non-functional properties on different levels of abstraction.

Apart from Web service extensions, metamodels for non-functional property specification exist. A survey of existing solutions for general non-functional property specification can be found in [28]. The OMG QFTP specification [9] provides an UML profile for QoS modeling that enables association of requirements and properties to UML model elements. Currently QFTP only offers abstract syntax for QoS models and is intended to be used in real-time domain (as well as the related specification MARTE). In the context of development of distributed components [29] defines the Component Quality Modelling Language (CQML), relates its usage to several different development scenarios and provides computational support for QoS managing and monitoring. Both CQML and QFTP have very limited support for modeling units of measurement (informative only and string-based respectively).

Similar to our approach, [30] provides a framework for NFP in component-based environment. It extends interface (IDL) and architecture (ADL) description languages to describe NFP at design time and then compare provided and required NFP at runtime. Only three properties are supported (performance, reliability, availability). [31] analyzes NFR of provided and required component interfaces. Additionally they provide tactics to resolve mismatches. The framework is process-oriented (manual steps done by a developer) in which capabilities of components are expressed and compared as goals.

Currently, we are not aware of an integrated solution that supports all the features we presented. Our solution is not restricted to Web service technology, UML profiles (assuming system models in UML) or textual IDLs and supports automatic analysis of non-functional mismatches as well as overall NFP computation. We provide ready-to-use property model for assignments based on the NFP metamodel that can be easily used and extended in model-based environments. It also overcomes weak unit modeling support of other solutions.

6 Conclusion

We presented part of the BIZYCLE integration framework which addresses system integration with respect to non-functional properties using model-driven methods and tools. The main advantage of the proposed solution is the ability to dynamically create new NFP and include them into analysis. Based on the NFP metamodel, it is possible to define relevant information necessary for further formal analysis – we presented an example of transforming integration models into reliability block diagrams to analyze availability. The project, in its present form, has been included into our Model-based Integration Framework (MBIF) tool and is undergoing industrial evaluation within our project consortium.

One challenge that remains however, is to perform analysis of multiple (possibly conflicting) NFP for a single scenario. The idea is to be able to derive optimal system configuration with respect to more than one NFP (e.g., cost, execution time and availability) for a given integration setup. Additional problems related to optimization with multiple criteria and goals arise that we plan to address using the proposed framework in the future work.

References

1. Rahm, E., Bernstein, P.: A survey of approaches to automatic schema matching. VLDB Journal 10(4), 334–350 (2001)
2. InterSystems: Ensemble data transformation language (2009), http://docs.intersystems.com/documentation/ensemble/20091/pdfs/EDTL.pdf
3. E2E Technologies Ltd: E2E Bridge, http://www.e2ebridge.com/en/e2e.asp
4. Kutsche, R., Milanovic, N.: (Meta-)Models, Tools and Infrastructures for Business Application Integration. In: UNISCON 2008. Springer, Heidelberg (2008)
5. Agt, H., Bauhoff, G., Cartsburg, M., Kumpe, D., Kutsche, R., Milanovic, N.: Metamodeling Foundation for Software and Data Integration. In: Proc. ISTA (2009)
6. Agt, H., Bauhoff, G., Kutsche, R.D., Milanovic, N., Widiker, J.: Semantic Annotation and Conflict Analysis for Information System Integration. In: Proceedings of the MDTPI at ECMFA 2010 (2010)
7. Kutsche, R., Milanovic, N., Bauhoff, G., Baum, T., Cartsburg, M., Kumpe, D., Widiker, J.: BIZYCLE: Model-based Interoperability Platform for Software and Data Integration. In: Proceedings of the MDTPI at ECMDA (2008)
8. Hohpe, G., Woolf, B.: Enterprise Integration Patterns. Addison-Wesley, Reading (2003)
9. OMG: Uml profile for modeling quality of service and fault tolerance characteristics and mechanisms (2008), http://www.omg.org/spec/QFTP/
10. W3C Recommendation: Mathematical Markup Language (MathML) Version 2.0, 2nd edn. (2003), http://www.w3.org/TR/MathML2
11. International Bureau of Weights and Measures: The International System of Units (SI), 8th edn. (2006)
12. Shtelma, M., Cartsburg, M., Milanovic, N.: Executable domain specific language for message-based system integration. In: Schürr, A., Selic, B. (eds.) MODELS 2009. LNCS, vol. 5795, pp. 622–626. Springer, Heidelberg (2009)
13. Thorelli, L.: An algorithm for computing all paths in a graph. Scientific Notes, BIT 6 (1966)
14. Yankee Group: Global Server Operating System Reliability Survey 2007-2008 (2008)
15. Scheer, G.W., Dolezilek, D.J.: Comparing the Reliability of Ethernet Network Topologies in Substation control and Monitoring Networks. Schweitzer Engineering Laboratories TR 6103 (2004)
16. Sahner, R., Trivedi, K., Puliafito, A.: Performance and Reliability Analysis of Computer Systems. Kluwer Academic Publishers, Dordrecht (2002)
17. Glinz, M.: On non-functional requirements. In: 15th IEEE International Requirements Engineering Conference, RE 2007 (2007)
18. Laprie, J.C., Randell, B.: Basic concepts and taxonomy of dependable and secure computing. IEEE Trans. Dependable Secur. Comput. 1(1), 11–33 (2004)

19. Brahnmath, G., Raje, R., Olson, A., Bryant, B., Auguston, M., Burt, C.: A quality of service catalog for software components. In: Proceedings of the Southeastern Software Engineering Conference, Alabama, pp. 513–520 (2002)
20. Dobson, G., Sanchez-Macian, A.: Towards unified qos/sla ontologies. In: SCW 2006: Proceedings of the IEEE Services Computing Workshops, pp. 169–174. IEEE Computer Society, Washington, DC, USA (2006)
21. Toma, I., Foxvog, D., Paoli, F.D., Comerio, M., Palmonari, M., Maurino, A.: WSMO Deliverable: Non-Functional Properties in Web Services. Technical report, STI International (2008)
22. Paoli, F.D., Palmonari, M., Comerio, M., Maurino, A.: A meta-model for non-functional property descriptions of web services. In: ICWS 2008: Proceedings of the 2008 IEEE International Conference on Web Services, pp. 393–400. IEEE Computer Society, Washington, DC, USA (2008)
23. Wada, H., Suzuki, J., Oba, K.: A model-driven development framework for non-functional aspects in service oriented architecture. Int. J. Web Service Res. 5(4), 1–31 (2008)
24. Hamdy, M., König-Ries, B., Küster, U.: Non-functional parameters as first class citizens in service description and matchmaking - an integrated approach. In: Di Nitto, E., Ripeanu, M. (eds.) ICSOC 2007. LNCS, vol. 4907, pp. 93–104. Springer, Heidelberg (2009)
25. Yu, H., Reiff-Marganiec, S.: Non-functional property based service selection: A survey and classification of approaches. In: NFPSLA-SOC 2008,CEUR-WS, Ireland, Dublin (2008)
26. Jonkers, H., Iacob, M.E., Lankhorst, M.M., Strating, P.: Integration and analysis of functional and non-functional aspects in model-driven e-service development. In: EDOC 2005. IEEE Computer Society, Washington, DC, USA (2005)
27. Cortellessa, V., Di Marco, A., Inverardi, P.: Integrating performance and reliability analysis in a non-functional MDA framework. In: Dwyer, M.B., Lopes, A. (eds.) FASE 2007. LNCS, vol. 4422, pp. 57–71. Springer, Heidelberg (2007)
28. Colin, S., Maskoor, A., Lanoix, A., Souquiéres, J.: A synthesis of existing approaches to specify non-functional properties. Technical report, Universit Nancy II (2008)
29. Aagedal, J.O.: Quality of Service Support in Development of Distributed Systems. PhD thesis, University of Oslo (2001)
30. Saleh, A., Justo, G.R.R., Winter, S.: Non-functional oriented dynamic integration of distributed components. Electr. Notes Theor. Comput. Sci. 68(3) (2003)
31. Supakkul, S., Oladimeji, E., Chung, L.: Toward component non-functional interoperability analysis: A uml-based and goal-oriented approach. In: IEEE International Conference on Information Reuse and Integration (2006)

Preface DsE@CAiSE 2011

Domain specific Engineering addresses the tools, methods and technologies that are used to tackle issues of complexity, scalability, quality and maintainability of modern software systems. Domain specific Engineering seeks to use techniques that raise abstraction levels away from general purpose software engineering technologies towards representations that are tailored to particular application domains. A domain in this context can be defined as an area of knowledge that uses common concepts for describing phenomena, requirements, problems, capabilities, and solutions.

Although being applicable to different engineering disciplines, domain specific engineering methods and domain specific languages (DSL) receive nowadays special attention from the information systems and software engineering communities who deal with artifact reuse, application validation, domain knowledge representation, ways to capture and manage variability, and guidelines for creating consistent and correct applications and systems in certain domains. The aim of all these up-and-coming methods and techniques is to help reduce time-to-market, product cost, and projects risks on one hand, and help improve product quality and performance on a consistent basis on the other hand.

As an interdisciplinary field, domain specific engineering deals with various topics such as semantic foundations, development and management of domain assets, technology support, language design, and theoretical and empirical evaluation of domain specific engineering techniques.

The purpose of this workshop is to bring together researchers and practitioners in the area of domain specific engineering in order to identify possible points of synergy, common problems and solutions, and visions for the future of the area. In particular, the workshop accepted 4 papers dealing with the development and usage of domain specific metamodels, ontologies, and languages:

1. Moharram Challenger, Sinem Getir, Sebla Demirkol and Geylani Kardas. A Domain Specific Metamodel for Semantic Web enabled Multi-agent Systems.
2. Thomas Janke. Ontology engineering based on Domain specific languages and the application of Ontology design patterns.
3. André Zwanziger. Reconstructing the Blade Technology Domain with Grounded Theory.
4. Raphael Romeikat and Bernhard Bauer. Specification and Refinement of Domain-Specific ECA Policies.

The workshop also had an invited talk given by Øystein Haugen from SINTEF and University of Oslo, Norway and entitled "Domain specific languages and standardization – friends or foes?".

Iris Reinhartz-Berger, Arnon Sturm, Yair Wand,
Jorn Bettin, Tony Clark, and Sholom Cohen
DsE@CAiSE'2011 Organizers

For more information on the workshop, see our website http://www.domainengineering.org/DsE@CAiSE11, or contact Iris Reinhartz-Berger (iris@is.haifa.ac.il) or Arnon Sturm (sturm@bgu.ac.il)

Organization

DsE@CAiSE'11 Organizers

Iris Reinhartz-Berger
University of Haifa,
Israel

Arnon Sturm
Ben Gurion University of
the Negev, Israel

Yair Wand,
University of British
Columbia, Canada

Jorn Bettin
Sofismo, Switzerland

Tony Clark
Thames Valley
University, UK

Sholom Cohen,
Software Engineering
Institute, Carnegie
Mellon University, USA

Program committee

Colin Atkinson	University of Mannheim, Germany
Kim Dae-Kyoo	Oakland University, USA
Joerg Evermann	Memorial University of Newfoundland, Canada
Jeff Gray	University of Alabama, USA
Jaejoon Lee	Lancaster University, UK
David Lorenz	Open University, Israel
Klaus Pohl	University of Duisburg-Essen, Germany
Julia Rubin	IBM Haifa Research Labs, Israel
Lior Schachter	Open University, Israel
Klaus Schmid	University of Hildesheim, Germany
Pnina Soffer	University of Haifa, Israel
Juha-Pekka Tolvanen	MetaCase, Finland
Gabi Zodik	IBM Haifa Research Labs, Israel

Additional reviewers

Oren Mishali	Open University, Israel
Andre Heuer	University of Duisburg-Essen, Germany

Domain Specific Languages and Standardization: Friends or Foes? – Invited Talk for DsE@CAiSE2011

Øystein Haugen

SINTEF and Department of Informatics, University of Oslo, Norway
oystein.haugen@sintef.no

Abstract. Domain specific languages capture the domain knowledge through the constructs of the language, but making a good language takes more than combining a set of domain concepts in some random fashion. Creating a good language – which does take time and maturing – requires knowledge also from the domain of language design.

It turns out that general abstraction concepts are useful for many different domains and most probably it will be beneficial to find ways to reuse such concepts in the domain specific languages. But there are challenges.

The general constructs should be recognizable as general even in a domain specific context. The general constructs may need adaptation to the domain specific ones. Still the reuse of general constructs should be such that implementing the domain specific language should not be made increasingly difficult. How many domain specific languages you have seen including well established concepts like inheritance and overriding?

The talk will show one way to compromise between the domain specific and the general standardizable through the example of a common variability language now under standardization in OMG. We will consider the advantages and challenges in greater detail and discuss alternative approaches. The talk will give a number of examples of domain specific as well as general languages, their creation and evolution as well as their implementation.

About the author. Dr. Øystein Haugen is Senior Researcher at SINTEF and part time Associate Professor at University of Oslo. He has earlier worked in industrial research in a small startup company with typographic systems, in large multinational companies ABB and Ericsson with methods and languages for system development and design.

He has worked with developing languages and with implementing language. He started working with making a computer microprogrammed to run the first object-oriented language Simula as efficiently as possible. He went on to taking part in the development of SDL (Specification and Description Language) in the ITU (International Telecom Union). Then he led the development of MSC (Message Sequence Charts) to the MSC-2000 version of the language and subsequently turned his attention to UML where he chaperoned the changes to the sequence diagrams in the UML 2.0 revision.

He is now leading the work on the Common Variability Language standardization within OMG.

Ontology Engineering Based on Domain Specific Languages and the Application of Ontology Design Patterns

Thomas Janke

SAP Research Dresden, Germany
thomas.janke@sap.com

Abstract. Knowledge management is a key success factor for companies. It can be facilitated by building information systems based on semantic technologies and herewith gain the profits of describing knowledge in a machine processable and exchangeable way. The problem companies are facing today is that ontology engineering still is a very complex and challenging task. Modeling high quality ontologies, in the sense of using the best suited language for the domain of interest with respect to available modeling constructs as well as applying established modeling best practices, is very difficult. This is especially true for domain experts who normally have no or just limited knowledge about the underlying logical formalisms. The model driven ontology engineering platform presented in this paper tackles those problem in two ways: 1) Domain specific languages (DSL) are provided which abstract from concrete ontology languages and hereby simplify ontology modeling for domain experts. 2) Ontology design patterns (ODP)[7], which describe best practices for ontology engineering, are applied automatically and transparently during ontology generation. In order to examine the feasibility of this approach, a prototype has been developed on top of the Eclipse Modeling Project (EMP).

Keywords: Domain Specific Languages, Ontology Engineering, Domain Specific Knowledge Engineering, Ontology Design Patterns.

1 Introduction

Ontology engineering is hard to master. The reasons for that are manifold and cover methodical as well as technological issues. The ontology engineering platform presented in this paper has been designed and implemented based on the assumption that the most severe problem comes with the fact that ontology engineers need to have a well-founded knowledge about the underlying logical formalisms (frames, first order logic, description logics, semantic networks, etc.) in order to model high-quality ontologies. Important aspects are the selection of the most appropriate language for a given scenario from the pool of available ontology languages (RDF(S), OWL, Topic Maps, F-Logic, etc.) as well as the knowledge about where to find and how to apply established modeling best practices. Typically, this cannot be assumed to be true or is at least difficult for people that do not have a grounded logical background. This fact stands in a vast contrast to the idea that domain experts should be capable of describing their field of expertise by using ontologies as their modeling language[7]. Today, this gap can only be filled by an intense collaboration of domain experts and ontology engineers, whereas the latter first need to understand the experts knowledge, to be able to then express this as formal descriptions. This approach leads to high costs in terms of both: development time and money to buy the expertise needed for ontology engineering.

To overcome or at least mitigate this situation, an ontology engineering platform, based on domain specific languages, the transparent application of ODPs and the concepts of model driven development (MDD), is proposed in this paper. It enables domain experts to model their domain of expertise using a domain specific language instead of general purpose ontology languages. The provided DSL abstracts from concrete ontology languages and incorporates terms and concepts the domain expert is familiar with. Based on this description, concrete ontologies in various languages can be generated. The transformations used to create those ontologies are provided by ontology experts. Therefore, they are designed in a way, that well known and documented modeling best practices, so called ontology design patterns, are reflected properly. The main benefits of such an approach are twofold. On the one hand it simplifies the modeling of ontologies for domain experts and on the other hand, by automatically and transparently applying best practices, it leads to higher modeling quality.

The paper is structured in the following way: Related research fields are introduced and preliminary contributions are refined from the envisioned platform. Thereafter, the architecture of the approach is described in more detail, the applied meta models are introduced, the developed domain specific language is discussed and a model editor is presented. Finally, the contributions are summarized, results are discussed and an outlook on future work is given.

2 Related Work

The combination of domain specific languages and ontologies has been discussed in various publications, for example [13] and [14]. The main focus of this research lies on how to improve the engineering of DSLs with the help of ontologies, facilitating their formal semantics. In contrast, the approach described in this paper uses domain specific languages to abstract from concrete ontology languages in order to simplify ontology engineering and improve ontology quality by transparently applying ontology design patterns.

ODPs are, in analogy to software design patterns, reusable, successful solutions to recurrent modeling problems[4]. The application of design patterns in the field of ontology engineering has been discussed in many publications[10,12,6,8,5] and attracts a growing community[2]. ODPs are also addressed by a dedicated W3C working group[3]. Following the classification of patterns given in [7], the platform introduced in this paper addresses so called *Transformational*

Ontology Patterns. They translate expressions from one language into another, trying to approximate the semantics of the source language. An example for such a pattern is the handling of n-ary relations, which are not supported as first level language primitives in OWL and RDF(S). Both of them only support binary relations. Nevertheless, there are published best practices how to model n-ary relations, for example by the W3C[1]. Another example of a design pattern is the description on how to model inverse relations. They are supported as default language constructs by OWL but not, for example, by F-Logic. However, there are best practices how to model inverse relations in F-Logic too. Whereas those patterns are a good starting point for optimizing ontology modeling by applying modeling best practices, they still put certain demands on domain experts. First of all, they need to be aware of ODPs, then they have to find the adequate pattern for a special task as well as understand its semantic and finally they have to apply the pattern manually. The platform presented in this paper offers authors of ODPs the possibility to provide their patterns not only in text form but also in an executable way.

3 Architecture of the Ontology Engineering Platform

This paper introduces an ontology engineering platform based on textual domain specific languages and ontology generation on top of ontology design patterns. The overall architecture of the platform is illustrated in Fig. 1. Ontologies are modeled with the help of domain specific languages. Those languages offer a textual syntax, containing keywords and concepts well understood in the particular domain they are designed for. The domain specific descriptions, in turn, are mapped to a common ontology model. Based on this model, concrete ontologies can be generated. Due to the fact that the platform is designed based on concepts and frameworks for model driven development, this is realized by means of model to model transformations. The latter are defined based on the common ontology meta model and the meta models of concrete ontology languages. In the architecture presented in Fig. 1, the OWL meta model is listed as an example. Each transformation is reflected by a collection of ontology design patterns. Those patterns are modular in the sense that each and every pattern describes a distinct and self-contained modeling best practice. Examples for patterns are n-ary relations, inverse relations, transitive relations, cardinality constraints for properties and transitive reduction. In order to apply a pattern to the transformation process and herewith execute it during ontology generation, the pattern has to be registered to the transformation runtime.

The architecture has been implemented based on components developed in the Eclipse Modeling Project (EMP) and its sub projects. Hence, Ecore has been used to define the common ontology meta model depicted in Fig. 1. Furthermore, EMF tooling has been used to develop a modular model transformation framework, which is the main component in the ontology generation module. In addition, the Xtext[1] framework has been used to develop a domain specific

---

[1] http://www.eclipse.org/Xtext/

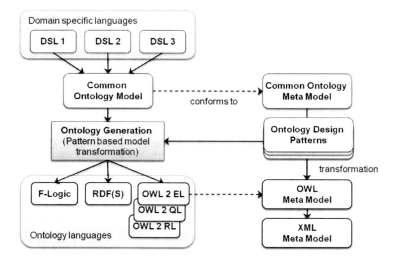

Fig. 1. A model driven ontology engineering platform based on ODPs

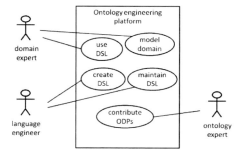

Fig. 2. Actors and use cases involved in the ontology engineering process

language for creating common ontology models and to generate an Eclipse editor to support domain modeling by offering syntax checking and code completion.

As depicted in Fig. 2, the platform allows for separating concerns along the competencies of all stakeholders involved in the modeling process. The domain expert is responsible for modeling his domain by using the provided domain specific language. The language engineer, in turn, concentrates on designing and maintaining the DSL with respect to the requirements of the given domain. In order to do that, he must not be an ontology engineer but only understand the common ontology model. Apart from that, he still needs to do a requirements analysis together with the domain expert in order to design a suitable language. Nevertheless, after this initial effort, domain experts can model and maintain their domain without further assistance. The third stakeholder involved are ontology experts which, using the interface given by the common ontology model, can contribute their knowledge by means of ODPs.

4 Applied Ontology Meta Models

The prototype is based on 4 meta models: meta models for RDF(S) and OWL as well as a XML meta model and the common ontology meta model developed as part of the prototype.

The XML meta model is provided by the AMMA[2] project as the standard meta model used to read and write XML models. The two ontology meta models are part of an Atlas Transformation Language (ATL) use case[3] published by the SIDo Group of the L3I[4] showing how to transform UML models into ontologies.

The common ontology meta model is used as a pivot language to describe the domain of interest and therefore is used as the starting point for model transformations to the concrete ontology meta models. As a result, all ontology design pattern implementations describe transformations from elements of this model to elements of the OWL and RDF(S) meta model, respectively. Therefore, every domain specific language developed in the context of this platform is free to reflect as many language features provided by the common meta model as needed. Whereas some domains may only require a small subset of language construct, others may need all of them to be provided.

The meta model developed in order to show the feasibility of the approach supports the following modeling primitives: *entities* and *entity hierarchies*, *attributes*, *relations* and *relation hierarchies*, *inverse relations*, *transitive relations*, *functional relations*, *n-ary relations* and *relation cardinalities*. Moreover, *namespaces* and *imports of other models* can be expressed. Although this collection of primitives reflects only a subset of features provided by common ontology languages, its expressivity is sufficient to model widely spread and used ontologies like Friend of a Friend (FOAF) or Dublin Core (DC). Moreover, it is adequate to apply a number of patterns for various languages as a proof of concept for the approach. In later iterations, it needs to be evaluated how to add more complex primitives like rules, annotations for instances and other axioms.

Apart from that, it is important to mention that this abstraction comes at a price: first, the common model will not be as expressive as concrete ontology languages, and second, the transformation from the common model to a concrete ontology model can only *approximate* the semantics of the applied primitive[7]. Nevertheless, the existence and the spread of such patterns[2,3,11,9] shows that this fact is acceptable in many real world scenarios and applications.

5 Design of Domain Specific Languages

In order to provide appropriate tool support for both - language engineering and domain modeling - Xtext has been used in the prototype to specify an easy to use ontology DSL. The Xtext framework supports the definition of languages and, beyond that, offers tooling to generate the whole language infrastructure,

---

[2] AtlanMod Model Management Architecture.
[3] http://www.eclipse.org/m2m/atl/usecases/ODMImplementation/#download
[4] http://l3i.univ-larochelle.fr/

including parser implementations as well as Eclipse-based editors with code completion and syntax checking. The concrete syntax for the developed language is specified using the Xtext grammar language. The abstract syntax is given by means of the meta models that are going to be populated by an automatically generated parser. Specifically, this means that ontology models, described in the developed language, are parsed and corresponding models, which conform to the common ontology meta model, introduced in Sect. 4, are instantiated. Using this approach, multiple DSLs can be specified, all based on one common ontology meta model. Due to the fact that Xtext is based on EMF, besides textual languages, also editors supporting graphical notations can easily be derived, for example by applying the Graphical Modeling Framework (GMF).

As outlined in Fig. 2, a domain specific language needs to be designed by a language engineer reflecting the requirements of the given domain. Therefore, an analysis must, among others, answer the following questions:

- What primitives, for example transitivity or constraints for relations, are needed in order to describe the domain?
- Are there any models that need to be reused or imported?
- What are common queries to be answered with the help of the ontology?

At the time of writing, we conduct a requirement analysis in the domain of software quality engineering for embedded devices. The results will be used to develop a methodology for building DSLs on top of the common ontology model for various domains. Additionally, the outlined approach can be further evaluated based on the experiences gained in this domain.

The language developed as part of the prototype, in its early state, is not yet bound to a specific domain but rather offers keywords still close to common ontology concepts. As a consequence, there are keywords like *ontology*, *concept* and *property*. Nevertheless, it illustrates already, how certain ontology primitives can be encapsulated and shielded from the domain expert by means of abstraction. Listing 1.1 contains a simplified example of the current modeling language.

```
ontology 'http://demo' {
   //import owl ontology
   import "../ontologies/foaf.owl"
   // import another domain model
   import "../ontologies/bookstore.oml"

   concept Customer {
      property name : string
      property account : "http://xmlns.com/foaf/0.1/#OnlineAccount"
      // n-ary relation
      property bought contained as 'Purchase' : Book as 'item', Store
         [1,1]
   }
}
```

Listing 1.1. Simplified ontology model

At first, an ontology is defined given a unique name. An obvious pattern implementation takes this name and uses it as the base URI of the ontology. Subsequently, two imports are defined: the first one is referencing an OWL ontology, namely FOAF, and the second one refers to another domain model described using the same domain specific language. Imports are used to enable and foster reuse of existing ontologies, which is a key concept of ontologies with respect to their goal to provide shared vocabularies. As shown here, imports across different ontology languages are possible. The current prototype supports imports by means of exposing all concepts defined in the referenced ontologies to the importing model. In the given example, this is illustrated by the *account* property, which is defined for the concept *Customer*. The property references the concept *OnlineAccount*, which is not part of the actual ontology but is imported from the FOAF ontology as its range. The same applies for the concepts *Book* and *Store* which both are defined in the cross referenced *bookstore* ontology. The developed editor supports those kind of imports by offering full auto completion for concept names. The patterns responsible for mapping the concept of imports to the corresponding RDF(S) and OWL models are very similar. Both of them generate a property range containing the fully qualified concept URI of the cross referenced concept. In addition, the OWL pattern generates an import statement making use of the `owl:import` property. The latter is not available in RDF(S) and is therefore omitted in those ontologies.

The last property defined in the ontology is an example of a n-ary relation which can be expressed in two different ways: Either a normal property definition is extended by the `contained` keyword or more than one concept and simple data type, respectively, are defined as the property range. Additionally, a cardinality constraint is posed on *Store* using the common min-max notation. Given that, the *bought* property is defined as an n:n:1 relation. Fig. 3 illustrates one of the patterns implemented to realize n-ary relations in the prototype. It is based on a best practice recommended by the W3C[1]. In order to model the n-ary relation *bought*, a new "link" concept named *Purchase* is introduced, which takes the role of the respective relation. The specific name has been specified with the help of the `as` keyword. If this would not have been the case, a name would have been automatically generated. The link concept is used as a domain for three newly introduced properties, namely *item*, *has_Store* and *has_Customer*. Whereas the last two have generated names, the *item* property has been labeled explicitly,

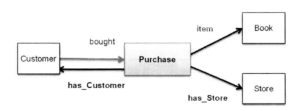

Fig. 3. Pattern for n-ary relations

again using the `as` keyword. For languages that support inverse relations, the *bought* and the *has_Customer* relations are additionally marked as inverse.

The cardinality constraint on *Store* can only be reflected in OWL ontologies, while RDF(S) does not support such restrictions. Therefore, two different patterns have to be applied. In OWL, a constraint on *has_Store* is generated, using `owl:cardinality`. For RDF(S), missing constraints are documented in the ontology by means of comments. Those annotations may later be used to implement the missing functionality on top of the ontology in the business logic layer of the targeted application. Cardinality constraints posed on non n-ary relations are handled in the same way. In OWL, `owl:minCardinality` and `owl:maxCardinality` are used to reflect those constraints in a concrete ontology.

6 A Domain Specific Ontology Editor

In addition to the model transformation framework and the common ontology meta model, an editor (see Fig. 4) is provided which supports the development of domain models using a textual domain specific language. The corresponding Eclipse plugin is based on an editor generated by the Xtext framework for the grammar of a given DSL. On top of that, the editor has been extended by various features, like code completion support for concepts imported from OWL and RDF(S) ontology files.

Fig. 4. A domain specific ontology editor

In order to seamlessly integrate the ontology generation process, project builders for OWL and RDF(S) ontologies are provided additionally. They are responsible for transforming the model described in the editor into its corresponding ontology models and are triggered by the model build process. As a result, corresponding OWL and RDF(S) ontologies are generated automatically and stored in XML format whenever the model has been modified, ensuring the liveness of the models during their maintenance. The modeling as well as the transformation process is assisted by markers for errors and warnings. Furthermore, wizards for creating new modeling projects as well as domain model files are provided. Based on this tool chain, domain experts are enabled to model their domain of interest in a domain specific language getting ontologies, modeled by applying well established best practices, in various languages as a result.

7 Summary and Future Work

Modeling high-quality ontologies is very challenging, especially for non-expert without a grounded knowledge about the underlying logical formalisms. This applies to both, selecting the most suitable ontology language and applying modeling best practices. In order to tackle those problems, an ontology engineering platform based on domain specific languages and ontology design patterns has been introduced. It aims at simplifying the ontology modeling process for domain experts by providing domain specific modeling languages which abstract from concrete ontology languages. Based on that abstraction, provided by means of a common ontology meta model, ontologies in various languages can be generated from the very same domain description. Moreover, ontology design patterns, which are published and widely accepted modeling best practices, are transparently and automatically applied during the ontology generation process, helping to increases the modeling quality of the emitted ontologies. In order to show the feasibility of the outlined approach, a prototype has been developed which covers the most important aspects and components required for a fully functional modeling platform. This also includes the design and implementation of a modular and extensible model to model transformation framework.

Whereas the experiences gained while designing and implementing the outlined prototype are promising, the suitability of the proposed platform can only be validated if the common ontology model and the DSLs provided have a appropriate expressivity. The ontology design patterns introduced in this paper and implemented as part of the prototype are a good starting point in order to show the benefits of the platform and to trigger further discussions and development. Further patterns and ontology model extension need to be developed on top of the provided platform. Suitable candidates for the ongoing development are annotations for triples (e.g., via reification), rules and the import of properties defined in external ontologies.

Furthermore, the modeling language introduced is this paper has to be extended to better reflect the specifics of a certain domain. In order to achieve that and to evaluate the platform in a real life use case, we started the development of such a language in the domain of ambient assisted living. The workbench will be used in order to model the interfaces as well as data quality aspects of embedded devices. The results of this work will help to compile additional requirements and to review the proposed approach.

Another aspect that needs to be investigated with regard to the real life applicability of the platform is how to sufficiently support editing of generated ontologies. This is a rather general problem of model driven approaches. In this particular domain it means that manual changes should not be overwritten during regeneration of the corresponding ontology. As a result, the ontology generation component has to be aware of manual changes. Proposals for potential solution can probably be derived from the implementation of the EMF code generation framework.

References

1. Defining N-ary Relations on the Semantic Web, http://www.w3.org/TR/swbp-n-aryRelations/
2. Ontology Design Patterns, http://ontologydesignpatterns.org
3. Semantic Web Best Practices and Deployment Working Group (2001), http://www.w3.org/2001/sw/BestPractices/
4. Blomqvist, E.: D2.5.2: Pattern based ontology design: methodology and software support, NeOn project (2010)
5. Blomqvist, E.: Ontology patterns: Typology and experiences from design pattern development. In: Linköping Electronic Conference Proceedings, pp. 55–64. Linköping University Electronic Press, Linköpings universitet (2010)
6. Blomqvist, E., Sandkuhl, K.: Patterns in ontology engineering: Classification of ontology patterns. In: ICEIS, vol. 3, pp. 413–416 (2005)
7. Gangemi, A., Presutti, V.: Ontology Design Patterns ODP. International Handbooks on Information Systems. In: Handbook on Ontologies, Springer, Heidelberg (2009)
8. Presutti, V., Gangemi, A.: Content ontology design patterns as practical building blocks for web ontologies. In: Li, Q., Spaccapietra, S., Yu, E., Olivé, A. (eds.) ER 2008. LNCS, vol. 5231, pp. 128–141. Springer, Heidelberg (2008)
9. Presutti, V., Gangemi, A., David, S., Aguado de Cea, G., Suarez Figueroa, M.-C., Montiel-Ponsoda, E., Poveda, M.: D2.5.1: Library of design patterns for collaborative development of networked ontologies, NeOn project (2008)
10. Staab, S., Erdmann, M., Maedche, A.: Engineering ontologies using semantic patterns. Ontologies and Information Sharing (2001)
11. Suarez Figueroa, M.-C., Brockmans, S., Gangemi, A., Gómez-Pérez, A., Lehmann, J., Lewen, H., Presutti, V., Sabou, M.: D5.1.1: NeOn Modelling Components, NeOn project (2007)
12. Svátek, V.: Design patterns for semantic web ontologies: Motivation and discussion. In: 7th Conference on Business Information Systems, Poznan (2004)
13. Tairas, R., Mernik, M., Gray, J.: Models in software engineering. In: Chaudron, M.R. (ed.) Using Ontology in the Domain Analysis of Domain-Specific Languages, pp. 332–342. Springer, Heidelberg (2009) ISBN: 978-3-642-01647-9
14. Walter, T., Silva Parreiras, F., Staab, S.: OntoDSL: An ontology-based framework for domain-specific languages. In: Schürr, A., Selic, B. (eds.) MODELS 2009. LNCS, vol. 5795, pp. 408–422. Springer, Heidelberg (2009)

A Domain Specific Metamodel for Semantic Web Enabled Multi-Agent Systems

Moharram Challenger, Sinem Getir, Sebla Demirkol, and Geylani Kardas

International Computer Institute, Ege University, 35100, Bornova, Izmir, Turkey
moharram.challenger@mail.ege.edu.tr,
{sinem.getir,sebla.demirkol,geylani.kardas}@ege.edu.tr

Abstract. Autonomous, responsive and proactive nature of agents makes development of agent-based software systems more complex than other software systems. A Domain Specific Modeling Language (DSML) may provide the required abstraction and hence support a more fruitful methodology for the development of MASs especially working on the new challenging environments such as the Semantic Web. In this paper, we introduce a domain specific metamodel for MASs working on the Semantic Web. This new metamodel paves the way for definition of an abstract syntax and a concrete syntax for a future DSML of agent systems. Achieved DSML syntax is supported with a graphical modeling toolkit.

Keywords: metamodel, domain specific modeling language, multi-agent system, semantic web.

1 Introduction

Development of intelligent software agents keeps its emphasis on both artificial intelligence and software engineering research areas. In its widely-accepted definition, an agent is an encapsulated computer system (mostly a software system) situated in some environment, and that is capable of flexible autonomous action in this environment in order to meet its design objectives [1]. These autonomous, reactive and proactive agents have also social ability and interact with other agents and humans in order to complete their own problem solving. They may also behave in a cooperative manner and collaborate with other agents to solve common problems. To perform their tasks and interact with each other, intelligent agents constitute systems called Multi-agent systems (MAS).

Considering abovementioned characteristics, the implementation of agent systems is naturally a complex task. In addition, internal agent behaviour model and interaction within the agent organizations become even more complex and hard to implement when new requirements and interactions for new agent environments such as the Semantic Web [2] are taken into account. Semantic Web brought a new vision into agent research. This new generation Web aims to improve World Wide Web (WWW) such that web page contents are interpreted with ontologies. It is apparent that the interpretation in question will be realized by autonomous computational entities –so agents- to handle the semantic content on behalf of their human users. Software agents are planned to collect Web content from diverse sources, process the information and exchange the results. Autonomous agents can also evaluate semantic data and collaborate with semantically defined entities of the Semantic Web such as semantic web services by using content languages [3].

In [4], we discuss how domain specific engineering can provide easy and rapid construction of Semantic Web enabled MASs and introduce a preliminary domain specific modeling language (DSML), called *Semantic web Enabled Agent Modeling Language (SEA_ML)*, for model driven development of such agent systems. As a domain specific language (DSL), SEA_ML should provide complete definitions for its abstract syntax, concrete syntax and formal semantics.

It is well-known that the abstract syntax of a language describes the vocabulary of concepts provided by the language and how they may be combined to form models or programs. It consists of a set of provided concepts and their relationships to other concepts [5]. On the other hand, a concrete syntax can be defined as a set of notations that facilitates the presentation and construction of the language. This set of notations can be given in a textual or visual manner. A metamodel that describes the meta-entities and their relationships for a domain can naturally provide a base for the definition of such an abstract syntax and also a concrete syntax. Therefore, in this paper, we introduce a domain specific metamodel for agent systems working on the Semantic Web and describe how it paves the way for the definition of both abstract and visual concrete syntax of SEA_ML. A graphical modeling toolkit for SEA_ML concrete syntax, which is based on Eclipse Graphical Modeling Framework (GMF)[1], is also discussed in this paper.

Rest of the paper is organized as follows: Section 2 discusses the metamodel and SEA_ML's abstract syntax. Section 3 covers the SEA_ML's concrete syntax. Section 4 includes the related work and Section 5 concludes the paper.

2 Metamodel for Semantic Web enabled MASs

The platform independent metamodel, which represents the abstract syntax of SEA_ML, focuses on both modeling the internal agent architecture and MAS organization. Revision of our previous metamodel given in [3] and enhancement of its modeling features have produced the brand new metamodel for SEA_ML abstract syntax within this study. Object Management Group's Ontology Definition Metamodel (ODM)[2] has been plugged into the new metamodel to help in the definition of ontological concepts. Besides, in addition to the reactive planning, the new metamodel supports modeling of Belief-Desire-Intention (BDI) Agents [6] with new meta-entities and their relations.

To provide clear understanding and efficient use, the new metamodel is divided into six viewpoints each describing different aspects of Semantic Web enabled MASs. These viewpoints are listed as follows:

---

[1] Eclipse Graphical Modeling Framework, http://www.eclipse.org/gmf (last access: Feb. 2011).
[2] Ontology Definition Metamodel, http://www.omg.org/spec/ODM/1.0/ (last access: Feb. 2011).

1. *Semantic Web Agent's Internal Viewpoint*: This viewpoint is related to the internal structures of semantic web agents and defines entities and their relations required for the construction of agents. It covers both reactive and BDI agent architectures.
2. *Protocol Viewpoint*: This aspect of the metamodel expresses the interactions and communications in a MAS by taking agent's roles and behaviours into account.
3. *MAS and Organizational Viewpoint*: This viewpoint solely deals with the construction of a MAS as a whole. It includes main blocks which compose the complex system as an organization.
4. *Role and Behaviour Viewpoint*: This perspective delves into the complex controlling structure of the agents. Agent plans and behaviours with all of their attributes are modeled.
5. *Environmental and Services Viewpoint*: Agents may need to access some resources (e.g. ontologies, knowledgebases, discovery and execution services) in their environment. Use of resources and interaction of agents with their surroundings are covered in this viewpoint.
6. *Agent - Semantic Web Service (SWS) Interaction Viewpoint*: It is probably the most important viewpoint of the metamodel. Interaction of semantic web agents with SWSs is described. Entities and relations for service discovery, agreement and execution are defined. Also internal structure of SWSs is modeled within this viewpoint.

We use Kernel MetaMetaModel (KM3) notation from ATL toolkit[3] to define our proposed metamodel (and hence SEA_ML abstract syntax) textually. A KM3 class is provided for each entity and associations between each entity of the metamodel are represented with "reference" labels. Role name of each model element and number of instances are also given for every association. In addition to the neat presentation of the abstract syntax, the utilization of the KM3 notation also enables us to employ our MAS metamodel as source or target models in various model-to-model transformations and provides automatic generation of the platform dependent counterparts of the MAS models for different agent deployment platforms (see [3] and [4] for further information). Each viewpoint of the metamodel is discussed in the following subsections. Due to space limitations only the first and the sixth viewpoints' visual representations are given.

2.1 Semantic Web Agent's Internal Viewpoint

This viewpoint focuses on the internal structure of every agent in a MAS organization. Partial metamodel, which represents this viewpoint, is given in Fig. 1. *Semantic Web Agent* in the SEA_ML abstract syntax stands for each agent in Semantic Web enabled MAS. A Semantic Web Agent is an autonomous entity which is capable of interaction with both other agents and semantic web services within the environment. They play roles and use ontologies to maintain their internal knowledge and infer about the environment based on the known facts. Semantic Web Agents can be

---

[3] Atlas Transformation Language Toolkit, http://www.eclipse.org/atl/ (last access: Feb. 2011).

associated with more than one *Role* at the same point at any time (multiple classification) and can change roles over time (dynamic classification). An agent can play role in various environments, have various states (*Agent State*) and owns a type (*Agent Type*) during his execution.

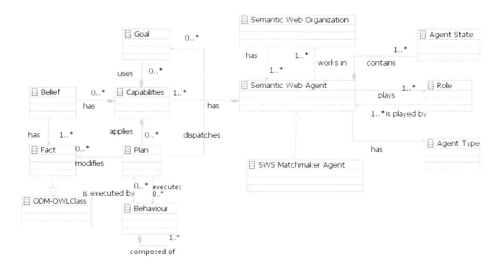

Fig. 1. Semantic Web Agent's Internal Viewpoint

Metamodel supports both reactive and BDI agents. BDI was first proposed by Bratman [6] and used in many agent systems. In a BDI architecture, an agent decides on which Goals to achieve and how to achieve them. Beliefs represent the information an agent has about its surroundings, while Desires correspond to the things that an agent would like to see achieved. Intentions, which are deliberative attitudes of agents, include the agent planning mechanism in order to achieve goals. Taking into consideration of concrete BDI agent frameworks (such as JADEX[4] and JACK[5]), we propose an entity called *Capabilities* which includes each agent's *Goals*, *Plans* and *Beliefs* about the surrounding. Each Belief is composed of one or more *Facts*. For the Semantic Web environment, each fact is an ontological entity and they are modeled as an extension of *OWLClass* from ODM in the metamodel. Semantic Web Agents apply *Plans* to perform their tasks. Each plan executes one or more agent *Behaviours* and goals are achieved during this execution.

On the other hand, agents need to communicate with a service registry in order to discover service capabilities. Hence, the model includes a specialized agent entity, called *SWS Matchmaker Agent*. This entity represents the matchmaker agents which store the capability advertisements of semantic web services within a MAS and match those capabilities with service requirements sent by the other platform agents.

---

[4] JADEX BDI Agent, http://jadex-agents.informatik.uni-hamburg.de/ (last access: Feb. 2011).
[5] JACK Autonomous Software, http://www.agent-software.com.au/ (last access: Feb. 2011).

2.2 Protocol Viewpoint

This viewpoint focuses on agent communications and interactions in a MAS and defines entities and relations such as *Protocol, Interaction, Message* and *Message Type*. Agents communicate with each other based on their social ability. A *Protocol* in a role uses several *Interaction*s to be realized. Each interaction, by itself, consists of some *Message* submissions which are triggered by agent behaviours. Each of the messages should have a Message Type such as inform, request, and acknowledgement. Within a behaviour definition an agent can send or receive a message from other agents.

Protocol viewpoint supports abstraction of commonly-used MAS interaction and messaging approaches. For instance, interactions of agents, which apply the well-known "Contract Net Protocol" (CNP) [7], can be modeled by using this metamodel. CNP as its own can be an instance of the *Interaction* entity. Each communication between initiator and participant agents can be a *Message* and has *Message Type*s such as call-for-proposal (cfp), refuse, propose, reject, and accept. Likewise, messages and message types, defined by IEEE Foundation for Intelligent Physical Agents (FIPA) Agent Communication Language (ACL) specification[6], can be described in meta-level by using the entities given in this metamodel.

2.3 MAS and Organizational Viewpoint

Structure and organization of a MAS are modeled within this viewpoint. *Semantic Web Organization* entity of SEA_ML metamodel is a composition of Semantic Web Agents which is constituted according to the organizational roles of those agents. An agent cooperates with one or more agents inside an organization and he may also reside in more than one organization. Moreover, a Semantic Web Organization can include several agents at any time and each organization can be composed of several sub-organizations. A Semantic Web Organization is inconceivable without ontologies. An ontology represents any information gathering and reasoning resource for MAS members. Collection of the ontologies creates knowledgebase of the MAS that provides domain context. These ontologies are represented in SEA_ML models as *Organization Ontology* instances.

2.4 Role and Behaviour Viewpoint

Semantic web agents can play roles and use ontologies to maintain their internal knowledge and infer about the environment based on the known facts. They can also use several roles at any time and can alter these roles over time. Task definitions and related task execution processes of Semantic Web agents are modeled with *Behaviour* concepts. *Role* is a general model entity and it should be specialized in the metamodel according to task definitions of architectural and domain based roles: An *Architectural Role* defines a mandatory Semantic Web enabled MAS role (e.g. registration or ontology mediator) that should be played at least one agent inside the platform regardless of the organization context whereas a *Domain Role* completely depends on the

---

[6] FIPA Agent Communication Language Message Structure Specification, http://www.fipa.org/specs/fipa00061/ (last access: Feb. 2011)

requirements and task definitions of a specific Semantic Web Organization created for a specific business domain. Inside a domain role, an agent uses a *Role Ontology* which is defined for the related domain concepts and their relations. An agent participates within a communication or task *Scenario* over the role(s) he plays. One role includes several agent Behaviours and each Behaviour is composed of many *Task*s. Each Task also covers one or more atomic *Action*s (such as sending a message to another agent or querying an ontology).

2.5 Environmental and Services Viewpoint

This viewpoint focuses on agents' use of resources and environmental interactions. SEA_ML's core concepts defined for this viewpoint can be listed as follows: *Environment, Resource, Permission Table, Service, Semantic Web Service* and *Service Ontology*. An agent can access many *Environment*s during his execution and an environment can include many *Resource*s, (e.g. database, network device) with their access permissions in *Permission Table*s.

An environment also includes *Semantic Web Service*s. A Semantic Web Service represents any service (except agent services) whose capabilities and interactions are semantically described within a Semantic Web enabled MAS. A Semantic Web Service composes one or more *Service* entities. Each service may be a web service or another service with predefined invocation protocol in real-life implementation. But they should have a semantic web interface to be used by autonomous agents of the platform. It should be noted that association between the semantic web agents and the services is provided over the agent *Role* entities in the metamodel. Because agents interact with semantic web services, depending on their roles defined inside the organization [3]. Semantic interfaces and capabilities of Semantic Web Services are described according to *Service Ontologies*.

2.6 Agent - Semantic Web Service Interaction Viewpoint

Perhaps the most important viewpoint of SEA_ML metamodel is the one which models the interaction between agents and SWSs. Concepts and their relations for appropriate service discovery, agreement with the selected service and execution of the service are all defined. Furthermore, internal structure of SWSs is modeled inside this viewpoint.

Fig. 2 portrays the agent – SWS interaction viewpoint of SEA_ML. Since, *Semantic Web Agent, Role, Registry Role, Plan, Behaviour* and *SWS Matchmaker Agent* concepts are imported from above discussed viewpoints, they will only be referenced when their relations between core concepts of this viewpoint are discussed.

Semantic web service modeling approaches (e.g. OWL-S[7]) mostly describe services by three semantic documents: Service Interface, Process Model and Physical Grounding. Service Interface is the capability representation of the service in which service inputs, outputs and any other necessary service descriptions are listed. Process Model describes internal composition and execution dynamics of the service. Finally, Physical Grounding defines invocation protocol of the web service. These Semantic

---

[7] OWL-S: Semantic Markup for Web Services, http://www.w3.org/Submission/OWL-S/ (last access: Feb. 2011).

Web Service components are given in our metamodel with *Interface, Process* and *Grounding* entities respectively. *Input, Output, Precondition* and *Effect* (a.k.a. IOPE) definitions used by these Semantic Web Service components are also defined. The metamodel imports *OWLClass* meta-entity from the OMG's ODM as the base class for the semantic properties (mainly IOPE) of the semantic web services. Since the operational part of today's semantic services is mostly a web service, *Web Service* concept is also included in the metamodel and associated with the grounding mechanism.

Semantic Web Agents apply *Plan*s to perform their tasks. In order to discover, negotiate and execute Semantic Web Services dynamically, three extensions of the Plan entity are defined in the metamodel. *Semantic Service (SS) Finder Plan* is a Plan in which discovery of candidate semantic web services takes place. *SS Agreement Plan* involves the negotiation on QoS metrics of the service (e.g. service execution cost, running time, location) and agreement settlement. After service discovery and negotiation, the agent applies the *SS Executor Plan* for executing appropriate semantic web services.

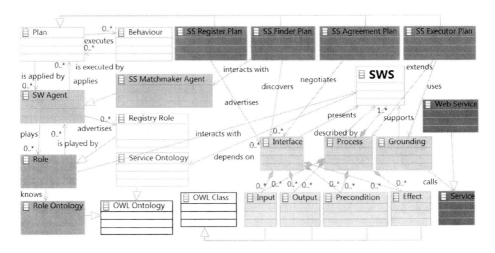

Fig. 2. Agent - Semantic Web Service Interaction Viewpoint

As discussed before, *Semantic Service Matchmaker Agent*s represent service registries for agents to discover service capabilities. During their executions, they apply *SS Register Plan*s.

3 SEA_ML's Concrete Syntax

While specification of abstract syntax includes the concepts that are represented in the language and the relationships between those concepts, concrete syntax definition provides a mapping between meta-elements and their textual or graphical representations. In this study, we propose a graphical concrete syntax for SEA_ML.

KM3 representation of SEA_ML metamodel has been converted to an Ecore representation and graphical notation for each language concept and relation has been chosen. Table 1 lists graphical notations for some SEA_ML concepts.

After choosing the graphical notation, we used Eclipse GMF to tie the domain concepts (supplied by the abstract syntax of SEA_ML) in Ecore format and their notations together. Achieved artifact is a graphical editor in which agent developers may design models for each viewpoint of required MAS conforming to the concrete syntax of SEA_ML. Screenshot in Fig. 3 illustrates use of the editor for modeling agent - semantic web service viewpoint of a multi-agent electronic barter (e-barter) system.

Table 1. Some of the concepts and their notations for the concrete syntax of SEA_ML

Concept	Notation	Concept	Notation
Semantic Web Agent		Semantic Web Organization	
Role		Belief	
Goal		Semantic Web Service	
Plan		Agent State	
Capabilities		Behaviour	

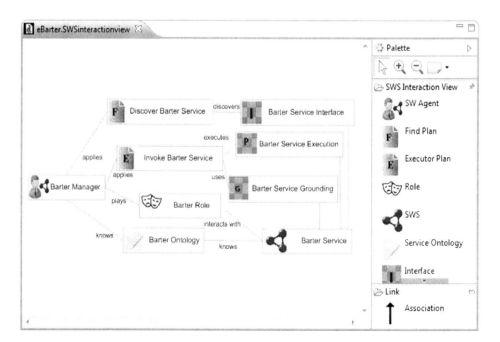

Fig. 3. Modeling agent-SWS viewpoint of a multi-agent e-barter system

An agent-based e-barter system consists of agents that exchange goods or services for their owners without using any currency. In our example, Barter Manager agent (shown in Fig. 3) manages all trades in the system. This agent is responsible for collecting barter proposals, matching proper barter proposals and tracking the bargaining process between customer agents. In order to infer about semantic closeness between offered and purchased items based on the defined ontologies, barter manager may use a SWS called Barter Service. Conforming to his Barter Role definition, Barter Manager needs to discover the proper SWS, interacts with the candidate service and realizes the exact execution of the SWS after an agreement. Fig. 3 shows how the related interaction can be modeled by using the concrete syntax constructs of SEA_ML. More information on this case study can be found in [4].

4 Related Work

Recent work on metamodeling of agent systems mostly considers definition of metamodels specific for some MAS development methodologies or generation of platform independent agent metamodels. For instance, Bernon et al. [8] give metamodels for MAS development methodologies called ADELFE, Gaia and PASSI. They introduce a unified metamodel composed by merging the most significant contributions of these methodologies. A similar study [9] introduces a metamodel for SODA agent development methodology. The study aims to model interaction and social aspects of the SODA and defines a metamodel considering these aspects. However, those metamodels are just formal representations for the concepts of the related methodologies and they are not suitable for the general MAS modeling.

FAML metamodel, introduced in [10], is in fact a synthesis of various existing metamodels for agent systems. Design time and runtime concepts for MASs are given and validation of these concepts is provided with their use in again various MAS development methodologies. Platform independent metamodel, proposed in [11] groups agent modeling concepts in various viewpoints in the same manner with our study. But neither [10] nor [11] consider a DSML specification for MAS development.

The syntax proposed in [5] is perhaps the most related work with our study. At first, the abstract syntax of a MAS DSML is represented by a platform independent metamodel and then a visual concrete syntax is defined based on the given concepts and their notations. However generated syntax does not support both agents on the Semantic Web and the interaction of Semantic Web enabled agents with their environment.

5 Conclusion

A metamodel for the domain of MASs working on the Semantic Web is discussed. Taking into consideration of internal agent architectures, metamodel supports both reactive and BDI agent structures. For MAS perspective, agent communication protocols can be modeled with the proposed metamodel. Also interactions of agents with each other and semantic entities such as SWS are supported. Proposed metamodel presents an abstract syntax and causes the derivation of a graphical concrete syntax for a DSML for Semantic Web enabled MASs, called SEA_ML. Achieved syntax is supported with an Eclipse GMF-based toolkit. Future work consists of the formal representation of the semantics for SEA_ML and development of an integrated tool to support all features of SEA_ML.

Acknowledgements

This study is funded by The Scientific and Technological Research Council of Turkey (TUBITAK) Electric, Electronic and Informatics Research Group (EEEAG) under grant 109E125.

References

1. Wooldrige, M., Jennings, N.R.: Intelligent agents: theory and practice. Knowl. Eng. Rev. 10(2), 115–152 (1995)
2. Berners-Lee, T., Hendler, J., Lassila, O.: The Semantic Web. Sci. Am. 284(5), 34–43 (2001)
3. Kardas, G., Goknil, A., Dikenelli, O., Topaloglu, N.Y.: Model Driven Development of Semantic Web Enabled Multi-agent Systems. Int. J. Coop. Inf. Syst. 18(2), 261–308 (2009)
4. Kardas, G., Demirezen, Z., Challenger, M.: Towards a DSML for Semantic Web enabled Multi-agent Systems. In: International Workshop on Formalization of Modeling Languages, Held in Conjunction with the 24th European Conference on Object-Oriented Programming (ECOOP 2010), pp. 1–5. ACM Press, New York (2010)
5. Warwas, S., Hahn, C.: The concrete syntax of the platform independent modeling language for multiagent systems. In: Agent-Based Technologies and Applications for Enterprise Interoperability, Held in Conjunction with the 7th Int. Conf. on Autonomous Agents and Multiagent Systems, AAMAS 2008 (2008)
6. Bratman, M.E.: Intention, Plans, and Practical Reason. Harvard University Press, Cambridge (1987)
7. Smith, R.G.: The Contract Net Protocol: High-level Communication and Control in a Distributed Problem Solver. IEEE T. Comput. 29(12), 1104–1113 (1980)
8. Bernon, C., Cossentino, M., Gleizes, M.-P., Turci, P., Zambonelli, F.: A Study of Some Multi-agent Meta-models. In: Odell, J.J., Giorgini, P., Müller, J.P. (eds.) AOSE 2004. LNCS, vol. 3382, pp. 62–77. Springer, Heidelberg (2005)
9. Molesini, A., Denti, E., Omicini, A.: MAS Meta-models on Test: UML vs. OPM in the SODA Case Study. In: Pěchouček, M., Petta, P., Varga, L.Z. (eds.) CEEMAS 2005. LNCS (LNAI), vol. 3690, pp. 163–172. Springer, Heidelberg (2005)
10. Beydoun, G., Low, G.C., Henderson-Sellers, B., Mouratidis, H., Gómez-Sanz, J.J., Pavon, J., Gonzalez-Perez, C.: FAML: A Generic Metamodel for MAS Development. IEEE T. Software Eng. 35(6), 841–863 (2009)
11. Hahn, C., Madrigal-Mora, C., Fischer, K.: A platform-independent metamodel for multi-agent systems. Auton. Agent. Multi-Ag. 18(2), 239–266 (2009)

Reconstructing the Blade Technology Domain with Grounded Theory

André Zwanziger

Institute for Technical and Business Information Systems,
Department of Computer Science,
Otto-von-Guericke Universität, Magdeburg, Germany
andre.zwanziger@ovgu.de
http://www.ovgu.de/

Abstract. Domain models are often reconstructed from different resources and contain domain elements, their properties and relationships. Ideally, the domain creation process is made transparent, so that each decision in the creation process can be traced back to the original source. One way to reach this goal is to use qualitative content analysis methods, e.g. the Grounded Theory. In this paper, the Grounded Theory is applied to the domain of IT infrastructures especially the blade technology and shows the necessary steps to extract a domain model from arbitrary documents.

Keywords: Grounded Theory, IT infrastructure, blade technology, domain engineering.

1 Introduction

One central question in domain engineering focusses on how a domain model can be extracted from a given field of application and/or its context. Starting from various definitions of the term "domain" e.g. [2,11,6,12] it can be stated that many authors assume that most domains already exist. The domains are often implicitly given or hidden in various documents (e.g. specifications, requirement documents, textbooks, source code, and/or standards) and very well known and understood by domain experts. The challenge for domain language creators therefore is to externalize this knowledge from given sources and to build a widely accepted model with an appropriate abstract and concrete syntax.

One way to externalize this knowledge for a domain model (or product family) are commonality and variability analysis [11]. Both methods require existing products and/or product families, which are compared and result in a list of domain elements as well as a list of variation points. In [11] three different kinds of commonality and variability analysis are proposed: (1) The application requirement matrix based analysis contrasts a list of requirements with different products and marks requirements as mandatory or optional for a given product. If all products have the same mandatory requirement, the requirement belongs to a domain. (2) The priority based analysis involves different stakeholders in the domain analysis process. The stakeholders are asked to prioritise predefined requirements for different products. Basic and high-rated requirements constitute the basis of the domain model. (3) The Check-list based analysis sets out from a given list of requirements that must be considered for the domain model. Another existing method is "abstracting away" characteristics from domain elements that potentially vary in the quality of the elements [5]. Finally, intuitive ways to elaborate a domain model, being made by one expert or agreed by a group of experts can be mentioned as possible method.

While intuitive methods are mainly the subject of implicit rules commonality and variability analysis and the abstraction mechanism follow more explicit rules. However, the basic question still remains, how the initial resources for the analysis are created. Commonality and variability analysis need a list of requirements or (in other analysis settings) features, use cases or components. The same issue occurs in the case of abstracting model elements, because a list of "to be abstracted" elements is required as a basis of the analysis.

Extracting those initial analysis items from arbitrary sources is usually examplary for social science methods, e.g. Grounded Theory [4] or qualitative content analysis [8]. Commencing with a predefined research question, different sources are selected, gradually analysed, interpreted, and result in a model that explains a social phenomenon. Applied to the field of domain analysis the research question is how a domain is structured (which elements exist, which properties do the elements consist of, which relationships exist between the elements). A possible result of the analysis can be a structural model, such as an UML class diagram, an Entity Relationship diagram, or a Feature diagram etc. that describes the domain.

In this paper, the Grounded Theory is applied to the field of IT infrastructures and is used to reconstruct a vendor neutral domain model for the blade technology. Section 2 introduces the overall application field of IT infrastructures and is narrowed to the blade technology. In section 3 the Grounded Theory is explained and applied to the domain of blade technology. Further, in section 4 the domain model is derived from the analysed data. Finally, the paper closes with a conclusion and outlook in section 5.

2   IT Infrastructures

In the context of this research, IT infrastructures are defined as all hardware and software entities, as well as facilities that are needed to run end user applications [10]. Hardware comprises computing and storage systems (e.g. blades, storage area networks), network technology (e.g. switches, cables), peripheral equipment (e.g. keyboards, printers), and additional equipment that is required to run the hardware (e.g. racks, uninterruptible power supplies). Software encompasses system software (e.g. operating systems) and basic software (e.g. databases, middleware systems). Additionally, IT infrastructures include rooms and buildings that are specially equipped to run hardware (e.g. data centers with heating, ventilation, and air conditioning (HVAC), redundant power supplies).

In most cases, IT infrastructures are operated in a managed system environment to ensure a demanded service level complying with a financial budget. Managed system environments comprise organisational aspects (product lifecycle phases, typical processes within the phases and responsible persons) as well as supporting technical applications (e.g. configuration management systems, monitoring tools). Changes in a managed system environment involve different stakeholders from different domains and needs to be coordinated in various directions. Here, models can help for the following purposes: (1) models enhance the *communication* between stakeholders through standardized language and graphical symbols. (2) Models *document* decisions made in the software introduction process and act as reference for future changes of the IT infrastructure. (3) Models can be *validated* to ensure the correctness of the required structure at an early stage of the deployment process. (4) Models can be used to *analyse* the behaviour in case of an incident or error, and (5) models can be used to *generate* artifacts that are used at runtime (e.g. configuration files) or to define a target state of the IT infrastructure in a managed system environment (e.g. configuration management system).

Even though these modeling purposes emerge, a gap between general purpose modeling languages (e.g. UML [9], Archimate [7]) and detailed class models for the management of IT infrastructures (e.g. Common Information Model [3]) can be identified. UML and Archimate define abstract modeling elements such as *node* and *device* on which *artifacts* can be deployed. Nodes and devices can be connected with a special dependency relationship called *Communication Path*. By default, these modeling elements do not include any additional, characterizing attributes. On the other hand, the Common Information Model (CIM) contains vendor independent, concrete type definitions for several (low-level) IT infrastructure elements with detailed attributes and operations (such as *CIM_Processor* or *CIM_PCIController*). Low-level refers to the fact, that most of these elements are configurable building blocks in a higher-level (fully-functional) computing system. Higher-level structures such as rack-mountable computing servers, switches or storage systems are not defined in CIM. In both cases, modelling IT infrastructures lacks concrete model elements, that are very well known by IT infrastructure domain experts (e.g. system administrators). A (set of) domain specific language(s) for IT infrastructures could help to close this gap.

Due to the vast amount of IT infrastructure components, the focus for a qualitative analysis in this paper is set on the blade technology. Blade technology is widely used in data centers as compact computing units. It consists of highly configurable elements and forms a well defined (sub-) domain of its own inside IT infrastructures. Moreover, there are many vendors for the blade technology, but each vendor has their own naming for similar products. Even though, blade products are incompatible between vendors in most cases, there are apparent similarities among products from different vendors and therefore a suitable field for domain engineering.

3 Qualitative Content Analysis with Grounded Theory

The goal of the Grounded theory is to develop a theory, that is based on systematically analysed data [4]. It has its origin in social science and is used to discover theories that explain social phenomena. Starting from a research question, different documents (e.g. transcribed interviews) are analyzed line by line and categories, their properties and relationships are elaborated [13]. During the analysis process, all documents are compared continuously and coded in three stages: (1) The goal of the *open coding* is to find categories and their properties in the documents. (2) The *axial coding* stage reveals relationships between categories and (3) the *selective coding* stage is to identify the core category and systematically relates it to other categories to find "hidden" relationships. During the coding stages, all documents are marked with text notes that refer to categories, properties, and/or relationships and thereby ensure a traceable decision making process.

Even though, the theoretic models in social science differ from the expected results of the domain engineering process, all coding stages can be applied with slight changes to the domain analysis process. Depending on the intended meta-model of the domain model, categories from the open coding can be seen as domain elements, such as classes, entities or features. Attributes and their types can be related to the intended domain elements and form the internal structure of a domain element. Relations between domain elements can be gained in the axial coding stage. Here, relations defined in the meta-model determine a starting point for the analysis. The third coding stage differs most from the original approach, due to the fact, that a domain model typically contains many elements on the same level of abstraction. Here, the relation of domain elements to other domains is the more interesting part for domain engineering, which leads to an integration of the new domain into existing domains.

In the context of this paper, the *research question* is how the blade technology can be structured in a vendor independent domain model. To further narrow the focus of the research question, the following analysis questions have been formulated in two categories: (1) *Structural Questions:* (a) What kind of single marketable/configurable components exist for the blade technology? (b) Which properties and their characteristics are named for each item/in relation to other items? (c) How are the components related to each other (dependency, aggregation, composition, specialization)? (d) Which cardinality (min/max) do the items have in relation to each other? (2) *Physical Characteristics:* (a) Which measures are used to describe the physical characteristics of each item? (b) Which measures are used to describe the environment of each item in operating and non-operating mode?

The next step is to obtain an appropriate *set of data* that forms the basis of the analysis. Here, Gartner's magic quadrant about blade server technology was the starting point for the document collection [1]. All listed vendors in the study have an international market presence and a sales volume of at least

$5 million in 2010. All vendors have been categorized into one sector of the quadrant, market leaders, niche players, visionary players. The fourth sector, challengers, remained empty in the study. To create a widely applicable domain model, the two market leaders HP and IBM, a visionary player (Cisco) and a niche player (Oracle) have been chosen for this analysis. In the next step, each vendor's product family for blade technology was investigated and specification documents have been retrieved from the public websites. Even though, most vendors offer more than one product relevant for this analysis, the vendor's product specification documents barely differ from each other. Therefore, it was sufficient to select one product and its specification from each vendor. In the following, the coding stages for two domain elements (BladeChassis and Blade) are described.

In the *open coding* stage of the analysis, all specification documents for BladeChassis and Blades have been compared and marked with categories, which can be aligned with the two parts of the analysis questions. Structural elements for BladeChassis contained information about (A) Blades, (B) Interconnects, (C) Fans, and (D) Power Supplies. Further information given in the specifications have been classified into the category (E) Other. Structural elements for Blades have been annotated with a lower case letter and comprise information about (a) Processors, (b) Memory, (c) Expansion Cards, (d) Storage Volumes, (e) Network Adapters, and (f) Other data. The physical characteristics for both domain elements comprise the following categories: (1) Dimension (height, depth, width), (2) Temperature, (3) Humidity, (4) Altitude, (5) Weight, and (6) Other. The category identifiers and the corresponding specification entries for each product are listed in Tables 1 and 2 for BladeChassis and Blades.

Parallel to the open coding stage, the *axial coding* has been performed to the specification documents and revealed the dependencies between domain elements. On the one hand, the structural information in the tables automatically relates different domain elements to each other. On the other hand, the relationship's cardinality has been coded in Table 1 in squared brackets to give a more precise understanding of the relationship. If no lower or upper cardinality could be determined from the specifications, a dash is printed as value.

During the axial coding phase two basic architectural differences have been discovered. HP, IBM and Cisco provide Blades, which contain slots for Expansion Cards. Expansion cards are mostly used to equip Blade servers with additional network adapters (such as Ethernet and Fibre Channel). In Oracle's blade technology, these expansion cards are not built into the Blades, but into the BladeChassis.

In the *selective coding* stage, all identified elements were compared with classes of the Common Information Model (CIM) to integrate the blade technology domain into an existing framework. The categories (C) Fan, (D) Power Supply, (a) Processor, (b) Memory, (d) Storage Volume, and (e) Network Adapter already exist in CIM and provide nearly all properties found in the specification documents. Therefore, these classes are subject to reuse in the domain model.

Table 1. Categories and assigned specification entries for the domain element Blade Chassis

Vendor / Product	Structural Information [min/max cardinality]	Physical Characteristics [Unit]
Cisco UCS 5100 Series Blade Server[1]	(A) Blade Server slots [-/8] (E) Fabric Extender slots [-/2] (B) Fabric Interconnects [-/4] (D) Four hot-swappable, redundant, power supplies, with IEC-320 C20 connections (C) hot-swappable fans [-/8] (E) Backplane with 1.2 Tb of aggregate throughput [1/1]	(1) Height / Width / Depth [in inch/cm; Height also in Rack Units] (2) Temperature (operating/non-operating) [in F/C] (3) Humidity (operating/non-operating) [in %] (4) Altitude (operating/non-operating) [in ft/m]

HP Blade System c3000 Enclosure[2]	(A) Device Bays
	  – full-height [-/4]
	  – half-height [-/8]
	  – mixed-configuration (true, false)
	(B) Interconnect Bays [-/4]
	(C) redundant fans
	(D) power connectors
	  – AC: c13/c14 [-/6]
	  – DC: D-SUB Power 3W3 [-/-]
		(6) rackable
		(1) Height / Width / Depth [in inch/mm]

IBM BladeCenter E[3]	(A) Blade bays [-/14] (B) Switch modules [-/4] (D) Power supply modules [-/4] hot-swap and redundant with load-balancing and failover capabilities (C) hot-swap and redundant blowers [2/-] (E) DVD multi-burner [0/1] (E) I/O-Ports: Keyboard, video, mouse, Ethernet, USB	(1) Height [in Rack Units] (6) Form factor (Rack-mount)
Oracle Sun Blade 6000 Series[4]	(A) server modules [-/10] (B) Network Express Modules [-/2] (D) AC power supply [-/4] – hot-swappable, load-sharing, load-balancing (C) fans: rear, front	(1) Height / Depth / Width [in mm/inch; Height also in U] (2) Temperature (operating / non-operating) [in C/F] (2) Optimum ambient [in C/F] (3) Relative Humidity (operating / non-operating) [in %] (4) Altitude (operating / non-operating) [in m/ft] (6) Sine-Vibration (operating / non-operating) [in G] (6) Shock [in G] (6) acoustic noise [in B] (5) Weight (fully loaded, empty) [in kg/lbs]

[1] http://www.cisco.com/en/US/prod/collateral/ps10265/ps10279/data_sheet_c78-526830.pdf
[2] http://h20195.www2.hp.com/v2/GetPDF.aspx/4AA0-5978ENW.pdf
[3] ftp://public.dhe.ibm.com/common/ssi/ecm/en/bld03018usen/BLD03018USEN.PDF
[4] http://www.oracle.com/us/products/servers-storage/servers/blades/033613.pdf
(Last access of websites on March, 7th 2011.)

Table 2. Categories and assigned specification entries for the domain element Blade

	Cisco UCS B250 M2[5]	HP ProLiant 620c G7[6]	IBM BladeCenter HX5[7]	Oracle Sun Blade X6275 M2[8]
Structural Information	(a) Processor: – Type – Amount (min/max) (b) Memory: – Amount of Memory Slots – Type of Memory Slots (c) Mezzanine – Amount (max) – Supported Cards (d) Hard disk drives (Storage) – Amount – Type – hot swappable – size of hdd (in inch)	(a) Processor: – Number of Processors – Maximum number of cores – Supported Processors – Cache / processor [in MB] – Processor speed [in GHz] (b) Memory – Memory Type – Standard Memory – Maximum Memory – Memory Slots (e) Network and I/O – Network Adapter (integrated) – Amount of I/O Expansion Slots – Standard/Maximum I/O bandwidth – Networking and I/O options (d) Storage – Storage type – Amount – Storage controller – Storage options	(a) Processor: – Amount (std/max) – Amount of Cores – Processor speed [in GHz] (a) Cache per processor [in MB] (b) Memory – Amount of DIMM slots – DIMM Type – DIMM speed [in MHz] (c) Expansion Slots – Amount of slots – Supported Types (d) Disk Bays (Storage) – Amount of devices – hot-swappable (true/false) – max storage (e) Type of network interface (f) Raid support	(a) Processor – Amount – Type (a) Cache per Processor / Core [in kB or MB] (b) Memory – DIMM Type – DIMM Speed – Amount of DIMM slots – Max Amount of RAM [in GB] (e) Network interfaces on board (d) Storage – Type – Connection Speed (f) Graphics controller (c) Midplane I/O – Extension I/O cards Type (f) Front Panel I/O (VGA, Serial Console, USB ports)
Physical Characteristics [Unit]	(2) Temperature (operating / non-operating) [in F/C] (3) Humidity (operating / non-operating) [in %] (4) Altitude (operating / non-operating) [in ft/m]	(1) Form factor (Full-height, single-wide)	(1) Form factor (single/double-wide)	(1) Height / Width / Depth [in mm/inch] (5) Max Weight [in kg/lbs]

[5] http://www.cisco.com/en/US/prod/collateral/ps10265/ps10280/ps10915/data_sheet_c78-588109.pdf
[6] http://h20341.www2.hp.com/enterprise/downloads/4AA3-0959ENW.PDF
[7] ftp://public.dhe.ibm.com/common/ssi/ecm/en/bld03032usen/BLD03032USEN.PDF
[8] http://www.oracle.com/us/products/servers-storage/servers/blades/sun-blade-x6275-m2-server-ds-182643.pdf
(Last access of websites on March, 7th 2011.)

4 Deriving a Domain Model

Generally, the determined categories of the analysis serve as a basis to directly derive domain model elements. In this paper, the domain model is represented as UML class diagram, even though other representations (such as Entity Relationship or Feature diagrams) are also applicable.

The internal structure of the blade technology domain is shown in Figure 1. The class BladeChassis contains zero to many Blades and Interconnects and holds two aggregation relationships to the classes CIM_PowerSupply and CIM_Fan. The classes PowerSupply and Fan are imported from the Common Information Model, which is indicated by the CIM_ prefix in the class name. The class CIM_Fan is specialized in an own class Fan, which holds the two additional attributes redundantConfiguration and hotSwappable, that could be identified during the open coding stage of the analysis.

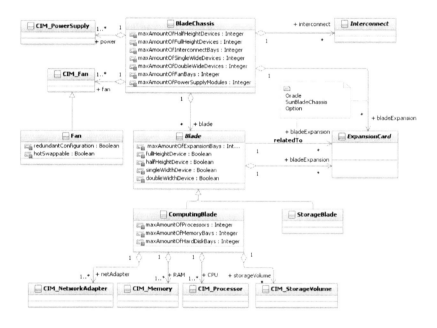

Fig. 1. Reconstructed Domain Model for the Blade Center Technology

During the product family investigation, the two blade types ComputingBlade and StorageBlade could be identified and are specialized in the domain model from the abstract class Blade. The class ComputingBlade is composed of the CIM classes CIM_NetworkAdapter, CIM_Memory, and CIM_Processor, whereby each relationship has a one to many cardinality. ComputingBlades can have storage volumes, but can also be operated in a disk-less mode with network boot option. Therefore, only a zero to many aggregation relationship is modeled to the class `CIM_StorageVolume`. Due to space limitations `StorageBlade`s can also be subject for future analysis and are not documented in detail here.

Both classes `BladeChassis` and `Blade` have an aggregation relationship to the abstract class `ExpansionCard`. During the axial coding stage, an architectural difference concerning the expansion cards has been elaborated, so that an expansion card can be modeled (a) as part of a blade and (b) as part of the blade chassis. In the latter case, an additional dependency relation between the classes `Blade` and `ExpansionCard` is used to assign an expansion card to a blade.

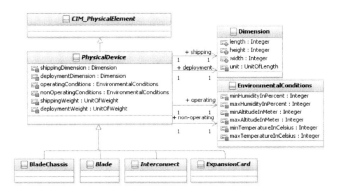

Fig. 2. Physical characteristics and type hierarchy of domain elements

In Figure 2 the domain elements `BladeChassis`, `Blade`, `Interconnect`, and `ExpansionCard` are shown in a second class diagram revealing the type hierarchy and the physical characteristics of the domain. All elements are derived from the abstract domain class `PhysicalDevice`, which itself is a specialization of `CIM_PhysicalElement` from the CIM framework. Even though all categories still can be seen as own classes, the model in Figure 2 comprises most physical characteristics into one class `EnvironmentalConditions`. The class `PhysicalDevice` holds two dependency relationships to the class `EnvironmentalConditions` that specify the conditions in operating and non-operating mode. The class `Dimension` is also referred with two dependencies from `PhysicalDevice` and is used to model the physical space of each object during shipping and deployment.

5 Conclusion and Outlook

The Grounded Theory approach enables domain engineers to extract domain models from arbitrary resources in a structured way. It extends the set of existing approaches for domain engineering and can be applied especially if handbooks, specifications or expert interviews are the main resources to create or reconstruct a domain model. Advanced concepts of the method (such as theoretic sampling or sensitivity analysis) have not been discussed in this article, but help to refine the domain model after a first version has been created.

For domain engineering, the content analysis methods (coding stages) of the Grounded Theory have been slightly adapted. The open coding stage, still remains to detect categories from arbitrary resources. All detected categories can be seen as structural elements such as UML classes. The axial coding stage was also left unchanged in its intention and aims on finding relationships between the structural elements. The selective coding was redefined to integrate existing domain models and is intended to find software reuse options in this case.

Finally, the approach is not limited to IT infrastructures and can be used for various domains. Nonetheless, the domain of IT infrastructure is a promising subject for future domain analysis. The blade technology domain is only a small piece of a bunch of IT infrastructure elements and further domain models can support many processes during deployment, operation and change.

References

1. Butler, A., Weiss, G.J.: Magic Quadrant for Blade Servers. Gartner RAS Core Research Note G00207244. Gartner (2011)
2. Clements, P., Northrop, L.: Software Product Lines: Practices and Patterns. Addison-Wesley, Pearson Education, Boston (2002)
3. Distributed Management Task Force: Common Information Model Specification. Version 2.28.0 (2010), http://dmtf.org/standards/cim/cim_schema_v2280 (March 7, 2011)
4. Glaser, B.G., Strauss, A.C.: Discovery of Grounded Theory. Strategies for Qualitative Research. Aldine Transaction (1967)
5. Kang, K.C., Cohen, S.G., Hess, J.A., Novak, W.E., Spencer Patterson, A.: Feature-Oriented Domain Analysis (FODA) Feasibility Study. Technical Report No. CMU/SEI-90-TR-21, Software Engineering Institute, Carnegie Mellon University, Pittsburgh, Pennsylvania, USA (1990)
6. Kelly, S., Tolvanen, J.-P.: Domain Specific Modeling. John Wiley & Sons, Inc., Hoboken (2008)
7. Lankhorst, M.: Enterprise Architecture at Work: Modelling, Communication, and Analysis. Springer, Heidelberg (2005)
8. Mayring, P.: Qualitative Inhaltsanalyse: Grundlagen und Techniken. 10., neu ausgestattete Auflage; Beltz Verlag (2008)
9. Object Management Group: Unified Modeling Language: Superstructure. Version 2.1.1 (non-change bar) (2007)
10. Patig, S.: IT-Infrastruktur. In: Kurbel, K., Becker, J., Gronau, N., Sinz, E., Suhl, L. (eds.) Lexikon der Wirtschaftsinformatik. Oldenbourg, München (2009)
11. Pohl, K., Böckle, G., van der Linden, F.: Software Product Line Engineering: Foundations, Principles, and Techniques. Springer, Heidelberg (2005)
12. Reinhartz-Berger, I., Sturm, A.: Utilizing domain models for application design and validation. In: Information and Software Technology, vol. 51, pp. 1275–1289. Elsevier B.V., Amsterdam (2009)
13. Strauss, A.C., Corbin, J.M.: Basics of Qualitative Research: Grounded Theory Procedures and Techniques, 2nd edn. Sage Publications, Inc., Thousand Oaks (1990)

Specification and Refinement of Domain-Specific ECA Policies

Raphael Romeikat and Bernhard Bauer

University of Augsburg, Institute of Computer Science, Augsburg, Germany
{romeikat,bauer}@ds-lab.org

Abstract. Policy-based management is a flexible approach for the management of complex systems as policies make context-sensitive and automated decisions. For the effective development of policies it is desired to specify policies at a high level of abstraction initially, and to refine them until they are represented in a machine-executable way. We present an approach for the specification and the automated refinement of domain-specific event-condition-action (ECA) policies. Domain-specific policies use domain-specific concepts within their event, condition, and action parts. The approach is generic as it can be applied to any domain and supports a flexible number of abstraction layers. It is applied to the network management domain and demonstrated with policies for signal quality management in a mobile network.

1 Introduction

Policies represent a promising technique for realizing autonomic capabilities within managed objects as they allow for a high level of automation and abstraction. Policy-based management has gained attention in research and industry as a management paradigm as it allows administrators to adapt the behavior of a system without changing source code or considering technical details. A system can continuously be adjusted to externally imposed constraints by changing the determining policies [1]. A well-known application area is network management, where policies are widely used for performing configuration processes. The usage of policy-based systems for the management of mobile networks was recently considered in [2–7].

The event-condition-action (ECA) model is a common way to specify policies. ECA policies represent reaction rules that specify the reactive behavior of a system. An ECA policy correlates a set of events, a set of conditions, and a set of actions to specify the reaction to a certain situation. The conditions are evaluated on the occurrence of an event and determine whether the policy is applicable or not in that particular situation. The actions are only executed if the conditions are met. Multiple policy frameworks share this model as for example Ponder2 [8].

Policy-based management is a layered approach where policies exist at different levels of abstraction. For simple systems it might be sufficient to have one or two abstraction levels only, one with a business view and another one with a technical view. For larger systems or systems in a complex domain it is reasonable to introduce additional levels between the business and the technical level in order to allow for domain and policy representation at intermediate abstraction levels. Strassner defines a flexible number of abstraction layers as the Policy Continuum [2]. The idea is to specify and manage policies at each level in a domain-specific terminology, and to refine them from a business level down to a technical level.

The process of providing a lower-level representation of a higher-level policy is called policy refinement. Policy refinement is a non-trivial task as different abstraction levels must be passed. Refinement is usually performed manually by passing policies from one level down to the next one and re-writing them with the means of the lower level. To address this we present a generic approach for the specification and automated refinement of domain-specific ECA policies. Automated refinement at runtime allows to control the actual system behavior by changing high-level models instead of their implementation.

This paper is structured as follows. Section 2 provides a scenario from the network management domain that is used as running example. Section 3 describes how domain-specific policies are modeled at a high level. The refinement of those policies is described in section 4. Related work is discussed in section 5. The paper concludes with a summary and future work in section 6.

2 Example Scenario

The signal quality of wireless connections in a communication system is subject to frequent fluctuations. There are various reasons for such fluctuations such as position changes of cell phones or changing weather conditions which impact the transmission. One possibility to react to fluctuating signal quality is adjusting transmission power (TXP) as power proportionally influences signal quality between an antenna and a cell phone.

The scenario now raises two objectives, amongst others. On the one hand, transmission power should be rather high in order to ensure good signal quality and to avoid connection losses. On the other hand, transmission power should be rather low in order to avoid unnecessary power consumption. As transmission power also influences the coverage area of the cells, a too high or too low setting can result in an undesired state of the network [7]. Therefore, a good tradeoff between transmission power and signal quality is desired.

In order to manage the behavior of the communication system we introduce a policy-based approach. Two ECA policies *lowQuality* and *highQuality* are responsible for adjusting the transmission power of the antenna. From a conceptual point of view the transmission power of an antenna can be increased and decreased. Changes in the signal quality are indicated by an event that contains the International Mobile Equipment Identity (IMEI) as unique identifier of the respective cell phone and the old and new value of the signal quality. The two policies are triggered whenever that event occurs and in their conditions they check the values of signal quality enclosed in the event. If the signal quality falls below a critical value, the *lowQuality* policy increases the transmission power of the antenna. The other way round, the *highQuality* policy decrease the transmission power if the signal quality goes beyond a critical value.

The behavior of the communication system can then be adjusted at runtime via the policies. The accepted range of signal quality between the two critical values is specified in the policies conditions. Changing those critical values is possible at any time and has an immediate effect on the transmission power and signal quality.

3 Policy Specification

Different models are used at different abstraction layers in order to specify domain-specific policies as illustrated in figure 1. The domain model allows domain experts to specify domain-specific concepts that are available in a system. The policy model allows policy experts to specify policies that are used to manage a system. The linking model allows policy and domain experts to link the policy model to the domain model in order to use the domain-specific concepts within the policies. Those models can also be regarded as parts of one large model. For each of them a metamodel exists that defines the structure of the model. Two layers i and j are shown exemplarily in figure 1 with layer i providing a higher level and layer j providing a lower level of abstraction.

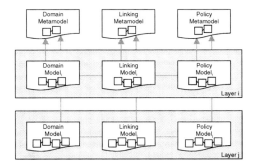

Fig. 1. Policy specification

3.1 Domain Modeling

Different expert groups are involved in the management of a system such as business managers or system administrators. Depending on their focus and their background, members of an expert group have a particular view on the system and they use special terminology to describe their knowledge. The *domain* represents a common understanding of those expert groups and covers the context of a system.

Any relevant information about the domain is covered by the *domain model*. The domain model covers the domain-specific concepts across all abstraction layers and specifies which domain-specific concepts are available. Its purpose is to specify domain knowledge independently from any policies, which will later control a system in that domain. Thus it represents the basis for building policies, which will then use domain concepts in their event, condition, and action parts. The domain model offers a particular view at any layer, which only contains the part of the domain model that is relevant at the respective layer. Figure 3 shows the domain model of the example scenario with two layers. The domain model is an instance of the *domain metamodel*, which allows to specify domain models in a way that is more expressive than just a domain-specific vocabulary and close to the structure of an ontology. For this purpose, the metamodel represents domain-specific knowledge as shown in figure 2. It represents the abstract syntax of the domain, i.e. it defines the structure of the domain model.

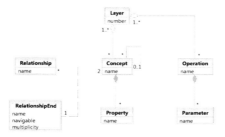

Fig. 2. Domain metamodel

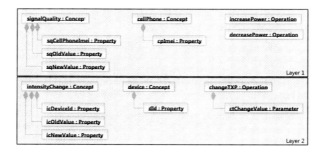

Fig. 3. Domain model

3.2 Policy Modeling

In the same way as expert groups have a particular view onto the domain, they also have a particular view onto the policies that control a system in that domain. A business expert e.g. uses a different terminology to express a policy than a system administrator does for the same policy. Also, a business policy might be represented by several technical policies at a lower abstraction layer.

Any information about the policies is covered by the *policy model*. The policy model offers a particular view at any layer, which only contains the part of the policy model that is relevant at the respective layer. Figure 5 shows an excerpt of the policy model at the first layer of the example scenario. The policy model is an instance of the *policy metamodel*, which contains the essential aspects required to specify basic ECA policies. It is shown in figure 4 and represents the abstract syntax of policies, i.e. it defines the structure of the policy model.

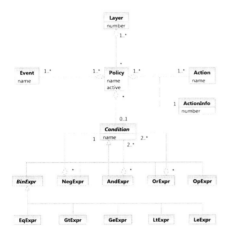
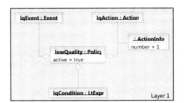

Fig. 4. Policy metamodel   **Fig. 5.** Policy model (excerpt)

3.3 Domain-Specific Policy Modeling

Domain and policies have been modeled independently from each other so far. The domain is specified as the domain model and policies are specified as the policy model. Now, both models must be combined in order to refer to the domain within the policies. For this purpose, a third model enables policies to refer to domain-specific information in their event, condition, and action part.

Any information about how domain-specific information is used within the policies is covered by the *linking model*. It specifies how the domain and the policy model are linked to each other. For this purpose, it allows to create links from the entities in the policy model to the entities in the domain model at the respective layers. The linking model offers a particular view at any layer, which only contains the links that are relevant at the respective layer. Figure 7 shows an excerpt of the linking model at the first layer of the example scenario. The linking model is an instance of the *linking metamodel*, which provides means to create links from the policy model to the domain model as shown in figure 6. It represents the abstract syntax of the links, i.e. it defines the structure of the linking model.

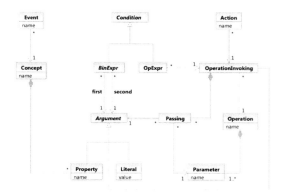 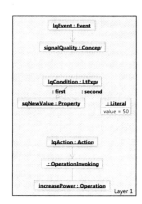

Fig. 6. Linking Metamodel   **Fig. 7.** Linking model (excerpt)

4 Policy Refinement

The formalization of domain-specific knowledge within the domain model allows to formalize the refinement of the domain from a higher to a lower layer as illustrated in figure 8. Refinement of the domain is the basis for the automated generation of refined policies in that domain.

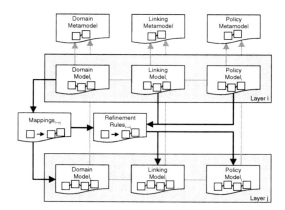

Fig. 8. Policy refinement

When going down the abstraction layers the representation of a higher-layer entity can remain the same at a lower layer or it can change completely. Refinement of the domain means mapping its representation from a higher layer to another representation at a lower layer. The possible structural changes through refinement are expressed by a set of mapping patterns. These patterns specify how the lower-layer representation of entities is derived from their higher-layer

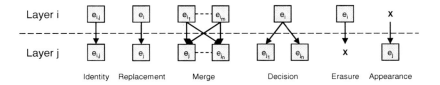

Fig. 9. Mapping patterns

representation. The available patterns are called *identity*, *replacement*, *merge*, *decision*, *erasure*, and *appearance* and are illustrated in figure 9.

A concrete mapping of one layer to another one is established by instantiation of the refinement patterns with the relevant entities at the respective layers. An instantiated pattern is simply called *mapping*. Figure 10 shows the mappings to refine the *lowQuality* policy of the example scenario in a textual syntax. The mappings once define refinement information within the domain and are then used for the automated refinement of policies in that domain.

$$signalQuality \mapsto intensityChange \text{ (replacement)}$$
$$sqNewValue \mapsto icNewValue \text{ (replacement)}$$
$$increasePower \mapsto changeTXP \text{ (replacement)}$$
$$undef \mapsto ctChangeValue \text{ (appearance)}$$
$$increasePower() \mapsto changeTXP(0.5) \text{ (merge)}$$

Fig. 10. Mappings (excerpt)

The generation of refined policies is divided into two parts as illustrated in figure 8. First, refinement rules are generated from the mappings. This part is only performed once after the set of mappings has been specified or modified. A refinement rule from layer i to layer j represents a model transformation that takes a policy and a linking model from layer i as input and produces a refined policy and a refined linking model at layer j as output. The left hand side (LHS) represents the input and the right hand side (RHS) represents the output of the transformation. Due to the different semantics of events, conditions, and actions, the impact of a mapping on a domain-specific policy depends from whether the entities of that mapping appear in the event, conditon, or action part of the policy. Therefore, one mapping results in three different refinement rules, one processing the event part, one the condition part, and one the action part.

Second, refined policies are generated by applying the refinement rules to the policy and the linking model. This part is be performed every time when a policy is added, modified, or deleted. In order to generate refined policies the refinement rules are applied to the policy and the linking model in a particular sequence. That sequence is determined by a pattern matching algorithm. The algorithm starts with the highest layer and generates the refined policies at one layer below. For any refinement rule that applies to those layers it matches the LHS to any combination of entities in the policy and linking model of the highest layer. Whenever a match is found, it invokes the matching refinement rule, which then generates the refined policy according to its RHS. This process is repeated until no more refinement rule can be applied to the highest layer. The intermediate result is a refined policy and linking model at one layer below. As the algorithm works on a copy of the policies, the policies of the highest layer remain and the refined policies are added to the models. The algorithm then processes the subsequent lower layers one after another in their ordering of abstraction and finally produces a refined policy and linking model at the lowest abstraction layer.

Figures 11 and 12 show an excerpt of the refined policy and linking models of the example scenario. During refinement the policy model remains the same as the structure of the policy is not affected by the mappings. However, the linking model is automatically changed and the policies are now linked to the domain entities of the lower layer. The event of the *lowQuality* policy is no more linked to the *signalQuality* concept, but to *intensityChange* one. The policy condition is no more linked to the *sqNewValue* property, but to the *icNewValue* one. These changes are caused by the respective replacement mappings. The policy action is no more linked to the *increasePower* operation, but to the *changeTXP* one and a literal value is passed to the *ctChangeValue* parameter of that operation. This change is caused by the respective appearance and merge mappings.

Fig. 11. Policy model (excerpt)

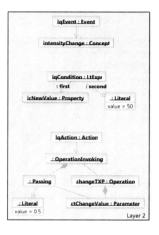

Fig. 12. Linking model (excerpt)

5 Related Work

The authors of [9] present a model-driven approach to design policies and integrate them into the software development process. The approach is based on MDE concepts and uses a UML profile for modeling policies. GPML supports different types of policy and ECA policies are represented by the obligation policy type. The ability to define a particular vocabulary allows to adapt policies to different domains. Policies are modeled at a low level of abstraction and cannot be refined.

The CIM Policy Model [10] by the Distributed Management Task Force (DMTF) addresses the management of complex multi-vendor environments with a huge number of heterogeneous devices. Policies are specified in a language-independent way and abstract from hardware characteristics. A UML profile is provided for the graphical representation of policies. The CIM Policy Model is a domain-specific model with a focus on network management. Different abstraction levels and policy refinement are not supported.

A refinement approach that focuses on policies in the autonomic networking domain is presented in [4]. Policies represent configuration settings and are used for automated network and resource configuration. A simple policy language offers a fixed terminology to specify domain-specific policies. Event-based policies are not supported. Policies are represented at five levels of a Policy Continuum and each layer offers a sub-set of that terminology. A wizard provides a graphical user interface to specify configuration policies on the highest level. Those policies are automatically refined into concrete configuration commands on a per-device basis. For this purpose, XSLT transformations replace higher-level objects with the respective objects at the lower levels.

6 Conclusion

A domain-specific approach for the specification and refinement of ECA policies was presented in this paper. The usage of models allows to specify policies at a high level of abstraction initially and avoids the direct implementation of policies at a technical level. High-level policies are made executable through refinement into a machine-executable representation. This allows to control the actual system behavior at runtime by changing the high-level models. The approach is novel as it is generic with respect to the domain, to the language, and to the number of abstraction levels and is nevertheless fully automated. No working solution has been known yet that realizes policy refinement in an automated way and that is not specifically tailored to a particular problem or domain.

Models in the approach do not only serve specification or documentation purposes, but are essential artifacts of the policy development process that initially starts with non-executable business policies and results in their technical and executable representation. The separation of knowledge into different models or model parts allows for an effective collaboration of domain and policy experts. The usage of different abstraction layers facilitates the collaboration of business and technical experts. Mapping patterns allow to generate refined ECA policies in an automated way and generation of refined policies helps to consolidate development effort. The approach is generic as it can be applied to any domain and any number of abstraction levels. It is also extensible and e.g. allows to integrate additional mapping patterns in order to cover dependencies that cannot be addressed with the provided patterns.

Tool support is subject to future work. A prototype of a graphical policy editor has already been developed [11, 12] and is to be developed further. This involves a modeling the domain, specifying the mappings, and modeling policies in that domain. The editor should trigger the policy refinement process after a policy was changed and generate code for existing policy languages.

References

1. Damianou, N., Dulay, N., Lupu, E.C., Sloman, M.: The Ponder Policy Specification Language. In: Sloman, M., Lobo, J., Lupu, E.C. (eds.) POLICY 2001. LNCS, vol. 1995, pp. 18–38. Springer, Heidelberg (2001)
2. Strassner, J.: Policy-Based Network Management: Solutions for the Next Generation. Morgan Kaufmann Publishers, San Francisco (2003)
3. Strassner, J.: DEN-ng: Achieving Business-Driven Network Management. In: 8th Network Operations and Management Symposium, pp. 753–766. IEEE CS, Los Alamitos (2002)
4. van der Meer, S., Davy, A., Davy, S., Carroll, R., Jennings, B., Strassner, J.: Autonomic Networking: Prototype Implementation of the Policy Continuum. In: 1st International Workshop on Broadband Convergence Networks, pp. 1–10 (April 2006)
5. Bandh, T., Sanneck, H., Schmelz, L.C., Carle, G.: Automated Real-time Performance Management in Mobile Networks. In: 1st WoWMoM Workshop on Autonomic Wireless Access, pp. 1–7. IEEE CS, Los Alamitos (2007)
6. Romeikat, R., Bauer, B., Bandh, T., Carle, G., Sanneck, H., Schmelz, L.-C.: Policy-driven Workflows for Mobile Network Management Automation. In: 6th International Wireless Communications and Mobile Computing Conference, pp. 1111–1115. ACM, New York (2010)
7. Bandh, T., Romeikat, R., Sanneck, H.: Policy-based Coordination and Management of SON Functions. In: 12th International Symposium on Integrated Network Management (May 2011) (to be published)
8. Twidle, K., Lupu, E., Dulay, N., Sloman, M.: Ponder2 - A Policy Environment for Autonomous Pervasive Systems. In: 9th Workshop on Policies for Distributed Systems and Networks, pp. 245–246. IEEE CS, Los Alamitos (2008)
9. Kaviani, N., Gasevic, D., Milanovic, M., Hatala, M., Mohabbati, B.: Model-Driven Engineering of a General Policy Modeling Language. In: 9th Workshop on Policies for Distributed Systems and Networks, pp. 101–104. IEEE CS, Los Alamitos (2008)
10. Distributed Management Task Force: CIM Policy Model White Paper. DSP0108 (June 2003)
11. University of Augsburg: PolicyModeler (August 2009), http://policymodeler.sf.net
12. Romeikat, R., Sinsel, M., Bauer, B.: Transformation of Graphical ECA Policies into Executable PonderTalk Code. In: Governatori, G., Hall, J., Paschke, A. (eds.) RuleML 2009. LNCS, vol. 5858, pp. 193–207. Springer, Heidelberg (2009)

Preface GRCIS 2011

Marta Indulska[1], Michael zur Muehlen[2], Shazia Sadiq[1], and Sietse Overbeek[3]

[1] The University of Queensland, Brisbane, Australia
[2] Stevens Institute of Technology, Hoboken, USA
[3] Delft University of Technology, Delft, The Netherlands
m.indulska@business.uq.edu.au,
Michael.zurMuehlen@stevens.edu,
shazia@itee.uq.edu.au,
S.J.Overbeek@tudelft.nl

The importance of governance and associated issues of compliance and risk management is well recognized in enterprise systems. This importance has dramatically increased over the last few years as a result of numerous events that led to some of the largest scandals in corporate history. The governance, risk and compliance market is estimated to be worth over $32 billion. Tool support for governance, risk and compliance related initiatives is provided by over 100 software vendors, however, while the tools have on average tripled in price since 2003, they are often insufficient to meet organizational needs. At the same time, there is an increasing complexity in the facilitation of compliant business processes, which stems from an increasing number of regulations, frequent and dynamic changes, as well as shared processes and services executing in highly decentralized environments.

In the age of outsourcing, dynamic business networks, and global commerce, it is inevitable that organizations will need to develop methods, tools and techniques to design, engineer, and assess processes and services that meet regulatory, standard and contractual obligations. Governance, Risk and Compliance (GRC) can be expected to play a significant part in several applications. This area is emerging as a critical and challenging area of research and innovation. It introduces, among others, the need for new or adapted modeling approaches for compliance requirements, extension of process and service modeling and execution frameworks for compliance and risk management, and detection of policy violations. In addition, it introduces questions relating specifically to the use of technology to support compliance management. For example, how auditors and regulators can put into use techniques like continuous monitoring and data analysis to assess whether an organization complies with relevant rules and regulations, or how technology can be used to support assessment of design and operational effectiveness of controls.

The GRCIS workshop series aims to make a consolidated contribution in the form of new and extended methods that address the challenges of governance, risk and compliance in information systems.

Patterns for Understanding Control Requirements for Information Systems for Governance, Risk Management, and Compliance (GRC IS)

Manuel Wiesche[1], Carolin Berwing[2], Michael Schermann[1], and Helmut Krcmar[1]

[1] Chair for Information Systems, Technische Universität München
Boltzmannstraße 3, 85748 Garching, Germany
{wiesche,michael.schermann,krcmar}@in.tum.de
[2] Daiichi Sankyo Europe GmbH
Zielstattstr. 48, 81379 München, Germany
caro_berwing@yahoo.de

Abstract. Companies face a plethora of regulations, standards, and best practice frameworks for governance, risk management and compliance. Information systems (IS) for planning, controlling, and reporting on the compliance with these requirements are known as governance, risk management, and compliance (GRC) IS. However, the challenge lies in mapping control requirements with functionality of GRC IS. In this paper, we review existing regulations and derive a framework for key control requirements. We develop a pattern-based approach that allows to systematically evaluate GRC IS based on the current regulatory situation. We evaluate the pattern catalogue by classifying an existing GRC portfolio. As implications for research, we associate existing control requirements and GRC information systems. As implications for practice, we provide decision support for the selection of GRC IS, depending on situational factors and the expected value proposition. In sum, our framework adds to the understanding of the effects of GRC IS.

Keywords: Governance, Risk Management, Compliance, GRC, patterns, software evaluation.

1 Introduction

Internationally acting companies face the challenge of meeting an overabundance of governance regulations and reporting on the compliance with these regulations [1-3]. Even nationwide, legislators require companies to account for compliance with multiple regulations. Assuring compliance has turned into one of the key objectives of any chief financial officer (CFO).

Information systems dedicated to plan, control, and report on the compliance with regulations create significant potentials for coping with regulations more effectively [3, 4]. Commonly, features of such information systems are discussed under the label of GRC (governance, risk management, and compliance). Driven by regulatory compliance, companies established such GRC IS to prevent fines and penalties imposed by regulatory agencies [1]. Today, companies focus on integrated solutions of GRC without a clear value proposition for their individual situation [5]. Still, market research predicts that US-based companies spend almost $30B on GRC related technology and solutions [6] and its importance continues to grow [7].

Organizations face both, a variety of requirements [3, 8] and a broad portfolio of GRC IS with different emphasis [5, 9, 10]. Executives have to rely on product presentations, progress reports from other users, and consulting services to determine an application's potential to meet control requirements. However, they often lack understanding of which application can fulfill a certain control regulation [5, 8, 9]. Hence, there are no methods, guidelines, or procedures for executives to evaluate the potential of compliance assurance through existing GRC IS. This article aims at answering the following research question: *How can control requirements be classified to evaluate existing information systems in the field of GRC?* Our research provides a pattern catalogue, which summarizes central aspects of control requirements. It serves for evaluating potentials and shortcomings of GRC IS with the help of the predefined patterns.

The remainder of this paper is structured as follows: in the first section we develop a conceptual framework of pertinent control requirements for GRC IS. Then we discuss a pattern catalogue for compliance assurance and present two control pattern candidates. We explore SAP GRC 10.0, a prominent GRC IS, using the patterns. We discuss the results and provide implications for practice and research. The paper finishes with a conclusion and an outlook on future research activities.

2 A Framework of Control Requirements for GRC IS

In this section, we introduce the terms governance and compliance. We develop a conceptualization of control requirements through constructing a control requirements framework. We review existing control regulations and classify them according to the proposed framework.

All efforts management takes in seeking to assure stakeholders that they get a return on their investments can be defined as corporate governance (CG) [11]. Due to regional and industry specific conditions, CG cannot be implemented based on an internationally and intersectorally valid system. It is rather a system of internationally recognized regulations and national requirements, which need to be integrated into an organizational framework. Implementing CG within an organization depends on various factors, which we suggest to structure in three dimensions: (1) the inner circumstances of a company, (2) the national environment including its habits, and (3) regulatory obligations, laws, and standards.

Although there is no formal or generally accepted definition, the understanding of compliance as duty of the board to ensure abidance of legal requirements and internal guidelines and assure appropriate behavior through the employees is out of question. Starting with financial constraints in the 1980s, today various GRC regulations, guidelines, standards, and frameworks have been developed, which organizations have to comply to.

These control requirements can be structured by the dimensions liability, area of responsibility and addressee. Regarding the dimension *liability*, requirements can be differentiated in either obligatory or recommended. *Area of responsibility* encompasses organizational setting, business processes and IT. Regarding *addressee*, GRC regulations can address internal and external dimensions.

The following examples shall demonstrate the broad scope and variety of GRC requirements: To be in compliance with e.g. the Sarbanes-Oxley Act (SOX), chief executives have to verify the accuracy and timely reporting of their financial results and establish procedures and controls which ensure the quality and integrity of their financial data [3]. On the other hand, privacy regulations require adequate data storage ensuring integrity and confidentiality. Furthermore, governance guidelines provide best practices for IS management and demand sound risk management.

We reviewed existing legal constraints, CG standards, corporate governance frameworks, IT-security and accounting standards, and selected pertinent industry-specific regulations from banking, insurance, medical, and chemical industry to provide an overview of this plethora of the diverse existing control requirements.[1] We classified them according to the dimensions introduced above.

In order to successfully comply with these regulations, various controls exist which cover the three management functions governance, risk management and reporting (Fig. 1). Governance controls include performance measurement, stakeholder integration, and audit. Risk management controls vary from implementing internal control systems, segregation of duties, and IT alignment. Reporting controls include proper book-keeping, internal audit, and archiving.

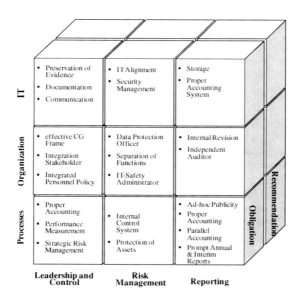

Fig. 1. Overview of categorized control activities

---

[1] In the field of laws, regulations, and standards for external addressees, we reviewed CobiT, COSO II, CGK, GxP, ISO 27000, IT-GSHB, ITIL, OECD principles, OCEG Redbook, EU guidelines 4,7 & 8, IFRS / IAS and US GAAP. Regarding internal addresses, we reviewed Basel III, DCGK, the German privacy regulations, KonTraG, MaRisk, BilReG, Solvency II, SOX, Liability, Market constraints, EU guidelines 4,7 & 8, FDA 21 CFR Teil 11, GDPdU, GoBS, and UMAG.

3 Establishing a Pattern Catalogue of Control Effectiveness

Since organizations face a vast amount of guidelines to comply with, we focus on a pattern repository that might serve as the distilled integration of control requirements. The patterns which will be introduced in the following, provide concrete requirements for IS functionality.

The term pattern was originally made up by Alexander [12] in the field of architecture and was formally defined as „IF: X THEN: Z / PROBLEM: Y". A pattern can be defined as the description of a reusable solution to a problem in a way that the solution can be used in similar situations. A pattern comprises the following elements [12]: the *context* comprises causes which lead to the problem described in a pattern and the conditions under which the problem occurs. The context should support acquiring the relevance of a pattern. The *problem* is described by explaining contradictions which cause the problem. The next section of a pattern explains the proposed *solution* by dissolving the elements described before. In order to make the patterns more actionable for software evaluation, we extended these dimensions by the elements *alias*, meaning alternative description, *aim* as key goal of the pattern, *regulation* as the names of the guidelines the pattern was derived from, *consequence* as positive and negative effects, and *related patterns* to describe how this pattern relates to others.

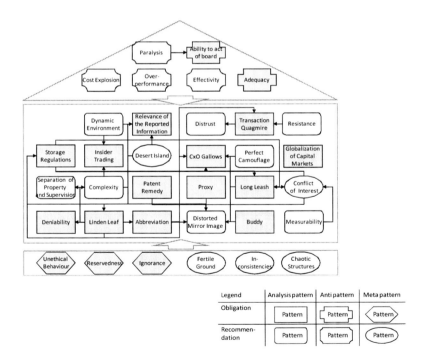

Fig. 2. A control pattern catalogue for structuring capabilities of GRC IS

To develop the patterns, we followed the suggestions of Buschmann et al. [13]: we reviewed existing guidelines, laws, best practices, and standards and classified them into the categories mentioned above. We reviewed what the guidelines, laws, best practices, and standards described as type of result and matched it to the identified control activities. We matched the requirements with the activities and used the description of the activities to define the supporting and enabling function of information systems. In general, GRC IS can provide real-time data processing, automation, and flexibility in the fields of reporting, logging, communication, simulation, central repository, role-based authorization systems, workflow, and archiving. Having the knowledge about the requirements, necessary activities and IS potentials, we developed a catalogue of 35 patterns to evaluate the potential of GRC IS (figure 2).

We identified four types of patterns as introduced in the literature: analysis patterns, anti patterns, Meta pattern, and modules. *Analysis patterns* support communicating and documenting domain knowledge. They ensure proper conceptualizing by helping understand the underlying business problem and define the requirements [14]. *Anti patterns* are negative examples of already implemented solutions, which include recommendations on how to fix it properly [15]. *Meta patterns* are general patterns which are universal and can therefore be used in various contexts [16]. *Modules* support in classifying existing patterns. Each module is a collection of single patterns, which can individually be seen as a pattern catalogue.

To evaluate existing software solutions for GRC, it is important to evaluate the overall potential from management perspective. Management must be able to understand the interplay between certain patterns to reveal the differing value propositions while evaluating GRC IS. Therefore, we propose the following eight categories to structure the control patterns: an effective corporate governance framework, preservation of evidence, segregation of duties, safety of assets, reporting, and corporate management under consideration of profitability and quality. By showing the various relationships between the different patterns the reader is offered a "navigator" for the complex area of corporate governance (figure 3).

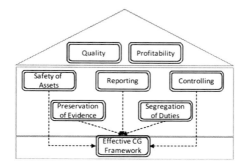

Fig. 3. Categories to structure control requirements

In the following, we will introduce two patterns to demonstrate the way the patterns are defined and structured. The patterns are structured according to the underlying modules (figure 2). The pattern *adequacy* is settled in the context of

Table 1. Patterns of Compliance Assurance

Name	adequacy	shortcut
Alias	underperformance	effectiveness
Aim	establish security	supervising employee's behavior with controls
Context	It is applied in the context of evaluating the effectiveness of the internal control systems. Since requirements are manifold and the organizational characteristics vary, annual audit also incorporates evaluating control effectiveness and adequacy of internal control system.	Employees conduct compliance work on top of their regular task, without a clear direct benefit. Caused by lack of time or disbelief, employees do not conduct compliance tasks properly or at all, which endangers successful audits.
Problem	The annual audit evaluates the existing internal control system ex-post. Found contradictions might require fundamental adoptions within CG which usually cannot be changed spontaneously and resulting in the auditors refuse the certificate. This situation of non-compliance affects stakeholder relationships and harms the external image.	In the annual financial statement a function check is conducted to reveal the effective match of control and associated risk. It refers to the fact that not only proper controls have to be proposed within the organization but also need to actually be implemented.
Solution	A solution for this issue would be continuous auditing. Internal resources including internal auditors can conduct a final rehearsal of the annual financial statement. Special focus should be laid on top management support to ensure cooperation with internal audit and communicate the importance of such topics.	The pattern provides a solution through workflow-based systems. Such systems services as reminder and provides guidance for employees to conduct compliance work properly. Such systems then document the accurate execution of the compliance task.
Consequence	+ continuous information on implementation of CG and audit acceptability - additional effort for testing and customizing	+ guarantee of the execution of compliance tasks within a reasonable period of time - requirement of initial effort for defining and implementing the system - reduced process performance
regulation	Basel III, IDW PS-330, MaRisk, SOX	MaRisk, SOX
related patterns	Distrust, Preservation of Evidence, Distorted Mirror Image, Ignorance, Adequacy, Long Leash, Buddy, Linden Leaf	Cost Explosion, Chaotic Structures, Abbreviation, Distorted Mirror Image, Linden Leaf, CxO-Gallow, Fertile Ground

quality-module and can also be described with the term underperformance (second column in table 2). The pattern *shortcut* can be classified in the prominent module segregation of duties with the aim of supervising employee's behavior with controls (third column in table 2).

Table 2. Evaluation of SAP GRC 10.0 with control patterns

Pattern		abbreviation	deniability	adequacy	storage obligations	buddy	CxO-gallows	relevance of the information given	Globalization of capital markets	ability to act of board	insider trading	conflict of interest	(long) leash	Linden leaf	easy solution	transaction quagmire	proxy	unethical behaviour	ignorance	reservedness	chaotic structures	dynamic environment	effectiveness	desert island	fertile ground	inconsistencies	complexity	sky-rocketing costs	paralysis	measurability	suspicion	overperformance	perfect camouflage	separation of property and control	Distorted mirror image	resistance
Access Control	RAR		◔		◑◔				◑							◑◑			●◑			◑◑				◑◑◔	◑		◑							◐
	ERM		◔	◑◔													◑◑			◑◑			◑◑				◑◔◔	◑		◐							○
	SUP	◔	◔◔◔					●								◑◑			●●			◑◑				○◑◑	◑		◑							○
	CUP		◔														◑◑			◑◑			◑◑				○◑◑	◑		◑							○
Process Control		●●◑◔◑●◔						◑		◑●◑●◔◑				○◑◑◑◑◑			◑◑●	◑						◑
GTS			○◑◔		◔		◑						◑			◑							◑			◑		◑ ○◑		○						
Environmental			○◑◔		◔		◑									◑										◑◑◑	◑									
Risk Management		◔		◑			◑						◑◑		◑				◑●◑◑			●◑◑			◑◐●			◐								

Legend: insufficient ○ to some extent ◔ partly ◑ adequately ◐ innovative ●

4 Exploring GRC Solutions with Control Patterns

In this section, we will use the derived pattern catalogue to evaluate a popular GRC IS. Therefore, we use the recently launched SAP BusinessObjects GRC 10.0 solution portfolio. The predecessor of this portfolio has been ranked as visionary within Gartner's most recent magic quadrant [9]. After giving a short summary of the functionality of the particular modules, we will use the SAP GRC portfolio to reflect the control patterns.

As leading supplier of enterprise software, SAP integrated existing compliance applications into the GRC portfolio in 2006. The GRC portfolio consists of five functional elements (rows in table 3). Access Control allows securing segregation of duties, compliant provisioning, and consists of the functional elements Risk Analysis and Remediation (RAR) for implementing and monitoring access guidelines, Enterprise Role Management (ERM) for defining and managing organizational roles, Compliant User Provisioning (CUP) for assigning these roles to users, and Superuser Privilege Management (SUP), allowing automated and fully documented fire fighter solutions for emergency access. Process Control allows managing the internal control systems and consists of control documentation, control analysis, certificates and reporting. Global Trade Services (GTS) allows securing cross border transactions. The module Environmental ensures environmental execution and legal compliance. Finally, the aggregating Risk Management allows the strategic detection of risks and control monitoring across the organization. In addition to using the aforementioned systems as data source, it provides a global risk management process as suggested by best practice frameworks, which complies with legal requirements.

We used test installations and existing documentation to understand the functionality of each module as a basis to evaluate the developed patterns. We assessed the potential of each module for each pattern by means of the following criteria: *insufficient* when the underlying problem is not addressed at all, *to some extent* when the problem is mentioned, but not solved, *partly*, when the problem is solved at least in parts, *adequately*, when the problem is solved with the help of the system, *innovative* when an existing solution is used for a new problem-context combination. The results are displayed in table 3.

The results in table 3 reveal that the SAP GRC portfolio has strengths and weaknesses in implementing certain patterns. Especially the patterns CxO-gallows, transaction quagmire, shortcut, chaotic structures, dynamic environment, and complexity are implemented with innovative ideas and solutions, which can provide competitive advantages. Then again, the SAP portfolio reveals gaps regarding the patterns unethical behavior, ignorance, reservedness, globalization of capital markets, and distorted mirror image which are addressed, but lack proper implementation. Further analyses of these patterns reveal that the potential of IS in the context of these patterns can only be established through proper governance and organizational structure. A satisfactory result could be obtained by e.g. combining further solutions of SAP like ERP Financials or ERP Human Capital Management and integration into organizational structures.

5 Discussion

In this section we will discuss the potentials of this pattern-based approach regarding the integrated perspective on compliance to balance and resolve conflicts and how this approach enables the determination of GRC effectiveness. We further discuss three implications of applying the pattern catalogue to an existing GRC portfolio.

The developed pattern catalogue provides an overview on control objectives, which GRC IS should address in order to meet control requirements. The pattern catalogue serves as a road map for executives to get an overall perspective over possible control activities. Especially the developed module structure allows navigating through solutions for specific control objectives. This allows the evaluation of potential initiatives depending on their degree of effectiveness within this specific situation and potential of integration with other initiatives. Inefficient applications can be identified easily and duplication of effort can be avoided.

The developed patterns are therefore not only useful to analyze GRC IS value propositions through elaborating actionable control requirements, but also show the need to balance and resolve conflicts. Management has to balance contradictory patterns, e.g. distrust and overperformance, ignorance and paralysis, or transaction quagmire and patent remedy. Using the developed pattern catalogue enables management to prioritize and decide in every situation without losing the integrated perspective.

The integrated perspective further helps reveal GRC IS effectiveness. For example the introduced adequacy pattern ensures an economic perspective on implementing GRC IS. Implementing too much functionality in terms of governance, risk management, and compliance will not only reduce an employee's performance, but also limits his or her motivation regarding the tasks they have to complete. Therefore, using the pattern catalogue allows executives to determine the optimal degree of governance, control, risk management, and reporting, necessary to both create transparency and to run a value adding company effectively.

Companies benefit in three ways from applying the patterns to an existing GRC IS. First, it shows that the developed patterns are useful and can be found within existing applications. It further reveals the patterns which are covered by the given application. In the case of SAP GRC 10.0, not all patterns are covered. Third, applying the patterns to an existing GRC IS and analyzing the underlying concepts reveals that some patterns are not suitable for the automatic approach of GRC IS. The pattern for ensuring the board's ability to act and the anti pattern paralysis require effective organizational structure and integration and cannot be implemented within GRC IS.

This research contributes to the body of knowledge by consolidating requirements for GRC IS through conducting a regulations-driven approach. We thoroughly connect existing requirements with information systems, which are designed to support meeting these requirements. Our research indicates that requirements can be synthesized into a defined set of capabilities, which are necessary to meet the considered regulations. We aid practitioners to soundly evaluate existing GRC IS depending on their individual requirements. The actionable patterns allow the implementation of an output-oriented evaluation of GRC tools. This research contributes to theory by bridging the gap between actual control regulations and GRC IS through developing requirements and integrating them into patterns. We further show that GRC IS are not suitable to solely fulfill each regulation without an adequate organizational integration.

Limitations of this research include the fact that laws, regulations, and standards were selected from German perspective. We further used an IS perspective on laws, guidelines, regulations, and standards. This could be enhanced with various other regulations from other fields, which might lead to new patterns which should also be taken into account. In order to reflect the patterns, we concentrated on evaluating one software portfolio. Evaluating more vendors might derive further interesting insights into the usability of the patterns. Nevertheless, the pure functionality of software modules does not guarantee proper compliance work within organizations. The patterns might be integrated with additional research on workarounds where employees bypass the established controls within the systems [17].

6 Conclusion

In this article, we reveal a solution to bridge the gap between complex control requirements and information systems, which support meeting these requirements. We showed the variety of differing requirements and the complex task of understanding how specific applications meet certain requirements. Hence, we developed a framework to classify control requirements and derived 35 control patterns. Here we introduced two control patterns and demonstrated the benefits of using such patterns in synthesizing the variety of regulations and determining the potentials of GRC IS. Although our research is still in progress, our pattern-based approach already supports evaluating GRC IS for their potential to fulfill specific control requirements.

Acknowledgments. We thank SAP AG for funding this project as part of the collaborative research centre 'CVLBA - Center for Very Large Business Applications'.

References

1. Parry, E.: SOX Wars: CIOs share ideas, fears on Sarbanes-Oxley compliance. SearchCIO.com (7) (2004)
2. Ashbaugh-Skaife, H., Collins, D., Kinney Jr., W., LaFond, R.: The effect of SOX internal control deficiencies and their remediation on accrual quality. The Accounting Review 83(1), 217–250 (2008)
3. Volonino, L., Gessner, G.H., Kermis, G.F.: Holistic Compliance with Sarbanes-Oxley. Communications of the Association for Information Systems 14 (2004)
4. Fisher, J.: Compliance in the Performance Management Context: What technologies could simplify compliance and automate information gathering? Bank, Accounting & Finance 20(4), 41–49 (2007)
5. Wiesche, M., Schermann, M., Krcmar, H.: Exploring the contribution of information technology to Governance, Risk, and Compliance (GRC) initiatives. Paper to be presented at the 19th European Conference on Information Systems (ECIS), Helsinki, Finland (2011)
6. Hagerty, J., Kraus, B.: GRC in 2010: $29.8B. In: Spending Sparked by Risk, Visibility, and Efficiency, Boston, MA, p. 12 (2009)
7. OpenPages, Risk Management Investments to Rise in 2010 (2009)
8. Syed Abdullah, S.N.H., Induslka, M., Shazia, S.: A study of compliance management in information systems research. In: ECIS 2009 Proceedings (2009)
9. Heiser, J.: Hype Cycle for Governance, Risk and Compliance Technologies. In: Gartner Hype Cycles (2010), Gartner Research Report G00205229
10. Teubner, R.A., Feller, T.: Informationstechnologie, Governance und Compliance. Wirtschaftsinformatik 50(5), 400–407 (2008)
11. Shleifer, A., Vishny, R.W.: A survey of corporate governance. Journal of Finance 52(2), 737–783 (1997)
12. Alexander, C.: The timeless way of building. Oxford University Press, New York (1979)
13. Buschmann, F., et al.: A System of Patterns: Pattern-Oriented Software Architecture: A System of Patterns. John Wiley & Sons Inc., Chichester (1996)
14. Fowler, M.: Analysis Patterns: reusable object models. Addison-Wesley, Reading (1997)
15. Brown, W.J. (ed.): AntiPatterns: refactoring software, architectures, and projects in crisis, vol. 20. Wiley, Chichester (1998)
16. Pree, W., Sikora, H.: Design patterns for object-oriented software development. In: ICSE 1997 Proceedings of the 19th International Conference on Software Engineering. ACM, New York (1997)
17. Ignatiadis, I., Nandhakumar, J.: The Effect of ERP System Workarounds on Organizational Control: An interpretivist case study. Scandinavian Journal of Information Systems 21(2), 3 (2009)

Exploring Features of a Full-Coverage Integrated Solution for Business Process Compliance*

Cristina Cabanillas, Manuel Resinas, and Antonio Ruiz-Cortés

Universidad de Sevilla, Spain
{cristinacabanillas,resinas,aruiz}@us.es

Abstract. The last few years have seen the introduction of several techniques for automatically tackling some aspects of compliance checking between business processes and business rules. Some of them are quite robust and mature and are provided with software support that partially or fully implement them. However, as far as we know there is not yet a tool that provides for the complete management of business process compliance in the whole lifecycle of business processes. The goal of this paper is to move towards an integrated *business process compliance management system (BPCMS)* on the basis of current literature and existing support. For this purpose, we present a description of some compliance-related features such a system should have in order to provide full coverage of the business process lifecycle, from compliance aware business process design to the audit process. Hints about what existing approaches can fit in each feature and challenges for future work are also provided.

Keywords: business process compliance, feature analysis, compliance management system, integration framework, business process lifecycle.

1 Introduction

Much work has been published on business process compliance in the last decade. Many organizations are concerned with ensuring compliance between business processes and regulations, and this has awoken the interest of many researchers. There are some well-defined and automatically supported approaches for Post-Design Time Compliance Checking (PDTCC) [1,2], for Run-Time Compliance Checking (RTCC) [3], and for Backward Compliance Checking (BCC) [4,5]. However, most of these approaches focus both on a specific kind of compliance rules (e.g. those concerning only control flow) and on a concrete checking moment (being it before, during or after the execution of a business process).

So, compliance checking techniques have been developed but, to the best of our knowledge, a compliance management system that gives support to the

---

* This work has been partially supported by the European Commission (FEDER), Spanish Government under the CICYT project SETI (TIN2009-07366); and projects THEOS (TIC-5906) and ISABEL (P07-TIC-2533) funded by the Andalusian Local Government.

whole lifecycle of business processes is still missing. Coming up with a system that puts them all together would be very useful for several reasons: (i) some of the developed techniques for compliance checking are complementary, i.e. some approaches complement the results of other approaches; (ii) applying compliance mechanisms addressing only a part of the aspects of a business process and/or in a single period of time (i.e. design time or run time) does not guarantee that the business processes of an organization are compliant with all the rules they have to fulfill; and (iii) a system that controls all kinds of business process compliance would help organizations to be prepared for audits, and would make auditors' work easier.

With this paper we pretend to walk a step forward in this direction by presenting a description of some compliance-related features a *business process compliance management system (BPCMS)* should have in order to provide full coverage of the business process lifecycle, from compliance aware business process design to post-execution evaluation, including audit process as well. Besides specifying the desired features of a BPCMS, hints about what existing approaches for business process compliance checking can fit in each feature and challenges for future work are also provided. We build on the existing literature about business process compliance to carry out this work.

The paper is structured as follows: Section 2 presents a view of a compliance-aware business process lifecycle; in Section 3 we explain some features required to provide full-coverage of the lifecycle, jointly with an outline of the main literature analysed to perform this work; Section 4 contains some conclusions and several challenges that must be faced to develop a full-coverage integrated BPCMS.

2   Compliance-Aware Business Process Lifecycle

We have extended the business process lifecycle described by Weske [6] to make it compliance-aware, i.e., to include aspects related to business process compliance. We rely on the descriptions provided by Weske to briefly define each phase of the business process lifecyle and foresee the aspects it would require to be compliance-aware. There are so-called compliance lifecycles in literature, such as the one in [3,7]. This lifecycle differs from our proposal in that it is directly focused on compliance, while we focus on business process management.

In the *design phase* business processes are identified, reviewed, validated, and represented by business process models using a particular notation. Collaborative capabilities for the jointly modelling of the processes and design assistance would be helpful to design compliant business processes.

In the *analysis phase* business process models are analysed by means of validation, simulation and/or verification techniques, and improved so that they actually represent the desired business processes and that they do not contain any undesired properties. Regarding compliance, capabilities to carry out compliance checkings, to have corrective advising and to perform simulation of compliance issues are required.

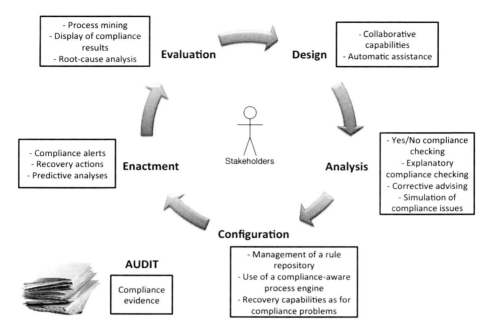

Fig. 1. Compliance-aware business process lifecycle

Once the business process models are designed and verified, the business processes need to be implemented. An implementation platform is chosen during the *configuration phase*, and it is configured together with the employees system interactions and the integration of software systems existing in the organization and the business process management system. Mechanisms to manage rule repositories and a compliance-aware process engine have to be considered during the configuration phase. Then, the implementation of the business processes needs to be tested, so integration and performance tests are carried out.

The process *enactment phase* encompasses the actual run time of the business process, in which process monitoring plays an important role for providing accurate information on the status of business process instances. Once again, mechanisms to check business process compliance at run time, to alert about found problems, to recover from violations and to predict possible future proplems are required.

Finally, the *evaluation phase* uses information available to evaluate and improve business process models and their implementations. Execution logs are evaluated using business activity monitoring (BAM) and process mining techniques. These techniques have to be extended to include compliance aspects, root-cause analyses should be carried out, and the ability of displaying the results of compliance analyses should be considered.

Figure 1 shows what we are calling *compliance-aware business process lifecycle*. As depicted, the five phases of the business process lifecycle described in [6] are surrounded by compliance-related features. These are some *specific* features a BPCMS should provide in each phase to include compliance issues in business process management. They will be explained in detail in Section 3. We have included *audit* as an element external to the lifecycle because it makes sense in compliance domain but it does not in generic business process management. Proofs that provide compliance evidence are necessary to perform audits.

3 Features for Compliance Support

This section contains a description of the features required in every phase of the compliance-aware business process lifecycle introduced above. These are the desired features of a full-coverage BPCMS.

3.1 Design

Creating business processes aware of compliance is the first step towards ensuring that processes fulfill the business rules imposed to an organization by regulations and legislations, by normative rules that help guarantee business quality such as ISO/IEC 20000, and by the organization itself. Two groups of features have been identified:

- **Collaborative capabilities.** Joining processes and rules is a complex task, which demands great expertise about the specific business processes carried out in an organization, the rules that must be fulfilled and their application to these business processes. Not making a clear separation between *what business processes must do* and *the features introduced because of the inclusion of rules* may affect the resulting business process models negatively. It means that when modelling business processes aware of compliance issues, the modeller must not disregard the final goal of the process and the services it has to provide to the organization in order to avoid changing its behaviour because of the rules. To prevent this problem, a *business expert* and a *compliance expert* should put their effort on respectively identifying and modelling business processes, and interpreting and modelling business rules, and then put together the individual work with the aim of providing a single *compliance-aware business process model*. Specific definitions for these two roles can be found in [8]. Offering collaborative design support (i.e. collaborative business process modelling) and social capabilities such as those characteristic of wikis and social networks (e.g. addition of comments and forums) would be desirable.
- **Automatic assistance.** An alternative that does not require the existence of separate roles consists of providing the tool with a suggestion mechanism that automatically assists the modeller during the design of the process to make it comply with the business rules. For this to be possible the rules must have been previously defined, which in turn requires minimally knowing the activities the business process is made up of beforehand. To the best of our knowledge, there is not yet a tool that provides this design assistance to the user with the aim of modelling compliant business processes.

3.2 Analysis

Performing compliance checking after the design of a business process is necessary to avoid behavioural problems at run time, as well as to ensure that all the proofs necessary to successfully pass subsequent compliance audits will be created during execution. Seeking compliance problems requires examining the behaviour of the process regarding semantics, that is, analysing the process from execution perspective to find out unexpected behaviours, e.g. mandatory activities that may not be executed due to XOR splits. This matter, together with the fact that full compliance checking must consider rules involving the four following aspects of business process: control flow, data, time and resources, makes the full analysis of compliance-aware business process models quite difficult. This is the main reason why most of the existing approaches for compliance checking deal only with control flow issues [1, 2, 4, 9, 10, 11, 12]. However, addressing data aspects is increasingly awaking the interest of researchers [13]. For instance, Cabanillas et al. have developed a procedure aimed at making data-related compliance checking easier by automatically generating a data-centered view of business processes [14]. This view can be used as input of algorithms to check for data-related compliance problems such as those described in [15]. Taking all this into account, a full-coverage BPCMS should contain the next features:

- **Yes/No compliance checking.** Sometimes the analyst requires quickly finding out whether a business process model is compliant with rules without going into detail. Therefore, this requirement should be available both to check for a single rule and to check for the whole set of rules that have to be applied to the business process. Some approaches supporting Yes/No response are described in [1, 9, 10].
- **Explanatory compliance checking.** Giving an explanation of an identified problem is very useful to the analyst and/or modeller of the business process. Most of the existing approaches, out of those that include this feature, expose the explanations in the form of *counterexamples*, i.e., a demonstration or example of how a rule can be violated. This output must be as real as possible, meaning that the counterexample must be traced back to the business process model in order to comprehend what it actually means, no matters what the formalism to detect the compliance problem was. For example, OPAL [2] applies model-checking algorithms to check business process compliance and, in case of violations, it returns counterexamples to demonstrate the existence of such problems. Root-cause analyses can be used to explain compliance violations as well [16].
- **Corrective advising.** Having at disposal an assistant that guides the user towards solving the compliance problems detected would be useful (and helpful) to complement the two previous features. Ideally, more than one corrective action may be suggested to the user, who can choose how to repair violations. In [17], Ghose et al. present an approach to detect and repair non-compliant business processes.

- **Simulation of compliance issues.** Including a simulator of business process execution that takes compliance issues into account can help detect unexpected behaviour by simulating the execution of the business processes (step by step) with value configurations obtained from the analysis of previous executions or from the specific domain knowledge of the analyst.

3.3 Configuration

Before executing a business process its instrumentation is required, i.e., it is important to configure the BPCMS as for the following features:

- **Management of a rule repository.** Although it has already been glimpsed in the features of the previous two phases, having a repository of rules and enabling the system to access it is of utmost importance. In this phase, mechanisms to select the business rules that have to be checked at run time and to configure other parameters referring to the compliance rules that have to applied are required.
- **Use of a compliance-aware process engine.** As we need to keep a trace of business process execution for post-execution checks, it is necessary to set at which moments of a business process execution the events to be stored will be triggered (compliance evidence included), how they will be captured and processed by the process engine, and the way they will be stored.
- **Recovery capabilities as for compliance problems.** The BPCMS must allow selecting the recovery actions that can be applied at run time for a specific business process in case of compliance violation, from all the possible recovery actions.

3.4 Enactment

RTCC has barely been addressed in compliance-related work. The work in [3] and [18] are two of the few approaches we have found regarding compliance checking at run time. However, no mention to the features desired for this phase of business process lifecycle is included in them. During the execution of a business process the BPCMS must ensure the appropriate rules are being fulfilled and the compliance evidence necessary for subsequent audits is being created. Furthermore, the next features must be part of the BPCMS:

- **Compliance alerts.** The tool must be enabled to show alerts about compliance problems arised at run time, as well as to automatically send notifications about them to the person in charge.
- **Recovery actions.** Besides the appropriate alerts, the execution of a business process can either continue after a compliance violation, either ignoring the problem or after the necessary recovery action(s), or get blocked until being manually revised and/or repaired. Namiri et al. present some recovery actions to be considered (including some of the aforementioned) [8].

– **Predictive analyses.** The system must be able to be ahead of future problems that may occur during the execution of a process instance, thus preventing their appearance by means of proper alerts that cause human reactions or by automatically performing recovery actions. This predictive analyses can be carried out from history logs containing previous instance executions.

3.5 Evaluation

Several techniques can be carried out to assess the degree of compliance of a business process execution:

– **Process mining.** After the execution of a process instance all the information generated must be in an event log. Logs will contain all the information necessary to cover the four aspects of the business processes mentioned before in this paper. Van der Aalst et al. have defined a business process compliance checker that performs BCC from logs by means of process mining [5]. It is implemented in tool LTL Checker, a plugin of ProM[1]. However, temporal constraints seem to be unconsidered in this approach. Another BCC approach is explained in [4], where Rozinat et al. introduce tool Conformance Checker (also included in ProM), which compares an a-priori business process model with the observed reality stored in some MXML log. This technique addresses only control flow.
– **Display of compliance results.** Once compliance has been checked, a mechanism to show the results is necessary. The use of a *Compliance Governance Dashboard (CGD)* that lets the user choose among several levels of abstraction, so all the information required to perform both internal and external audits can be drilled down, would be very useful [7].
– **Root-cause analysis.** From event logs and CGDs, root-cause analyses can be performed. These analyses study the behaviour of instances of a business process to find out the cause of compliance violations, i.e., give explanations. Rodriguez et al. carry out root-cause analyses based on decision trees from CGDs in [20], with the support of the EU research projects COMPAS and MASTER. From the analysis results, the system should also offer suggestions about corrective actions that help avoid compliance problems in future executions of a business process.

3.6 Audit

The system must be prepared to allow the execution of internal audits aimed at performing routine controls by the organization, and external audits carried out by compliance experts unconnected with the organization and responsible for checking whether this complies with the rules. Proofs for compliance can be given in the form of documents that corroborate the business process is being executed in accordance with the corresponding compliance rules. As stated in [21], "documentation is a key element of each audit. Important objectives of documentation include providing evidence [...] This results in a number of different tasks, including

---

[1] ProM is an extensible framework for process mining [19].

Table 1. Existing feature coverage of the desirable features of a full-coverage BPCMS

Compliance-aware BP lifecycle phase	Feature	Coverage	Implementation
Design	Collaborative capabilities		
	Automatic assistance		
Analysis	Yes/No compliance checking	[1] [9] [10] [11] [12] [15]	[1] [9] [10] [11] [12] [15]
	Explanatory compliance checking	[2] [16]	[2] [16]
	Corrective advising	[16] [17]	[16] [17]
	Simulation of compliance issues		
Configuration	Management of a rule repository		
	Use of a compliance-aware process engine	[3]	[3]
	Recovery capabilities as for compliance problems		
Enactment	Compliance alerts	[8]	
	Recovery actions	[8]	
	Predictive analyses		
Evaluation	Process mining	[4] [5]	[4] [5]
	Display of compliance results	[7]	[7]
	Root-cause analysis	[20]	[20]
Audit	Compliance evidence		

ensuring the completeness of the information, the traceability of the findings and recommendations, and providing a safeguard function. [...] The concept of audit is inseparable from documentation". This need of evidence is also remarked in normative rules such as ISO/IEC 20000, which calls for the storage of reports to prove compliance. The structure and storage of proofs must be perfectly defined.

4 Conclusions and Open Challenges

Although guaranteeing business process compliance may be impossible, if an organization limits the scope of compliance checking to one of the phases of business process lifecycle, ensuring that their business processes comply with all the rules the organization is subjected to becomes even harder. In this paper we have walked a step towards the definition of a BPCMS that covers the whole business process lifecycle by defining some compliance-related features the system should contain in every phase to ease the fulfillment of rules. The features have been gathered from existing literature.

Table 1 collects the aforementioned features, together with existing approaches that could be used to cover them. Blank cells represent features never addressed before. As shown in the table, there are not yet approaches to deal with compliance-aware business process design as understood in this paper. Approaches facing analysis phase focus on compliance checking and do not consider simulation functionalities. Specific work on configuration of a BPCMS should be done. As far as enactment phase is concerned, some approaches mention the use of alerts and recovery actions, but there is not yet a full implementation of these features. Predictive analysis is still to be done. However, features mentioned for evaluation are widely covered by current approaches. The collection of compliance evidence during business process execution is also disregarded in existing business process compliance related literature.

It is important to notice that in this paper we refer only to compliance-related features. Tool-related features such as scalability, efficiency and performance are out of its scope. Also the identification of candidate languages for modelling and executing processes, and the description of specific methods for compliance checking are beyond.

From this study we can conclude that many features are required for a BPCMS to cover the whole business process lifecycle, and only some of them have been partially described and/or implemented so far in literature. This reiterates the need of an integration framework that provides a full view of business process compliance management, both covering all the lifecycle phases and taking into account all the elements involved in business processes. Great efforts should be done to integrate all the existing solutions in such a framework.

In our opinion, the main challenges towards the design and development of a full-coverage integrated BPCMS are the following:

- We believe it would be interesting to provide solutions for all the blank cells present in Table 1, since having all the features described in Section 3 would be helpful to manage business process compliance. The empirical study carried out in [22] can complement the study we have performed giving an organization-centered perspective, thus showing the most critical features.
- Design an integration framework prepared to provide for compliance management in the whole business process lifecycle. For this purpose, assessing whether existing support tools can be integrated is necessary.
- Define a minimum catalogue of compliance rules the initial version of the system must cover and a language expressive enough to allow specifying the set of rules contained if the catalogue.
- Design an accessible, usable and friendly user interface (UI) for the system.
- Integrate the system with existing systems. In real scenarios instrumenting the process engine is not enough. Besides, events and proofs are spread over the different applications of the organization, so their integration with the BPCMS is required.

References

1. Awad, A., Decker, G., Weske, M.: Efficient compliance checking using bpmn-q and temporal logic. In: Dumas, M., Reichert, M., Shan, M.-C. (eds.) BPM 2008. LNCS, vol. 5240, pp. 326–341. Springer, Heidelberg (2008)
2. Liu, Y., Müller, S., Xu, K.: A static compliance-checking framework for business process models. IBM Systems Journal 46(2), 335–362 (2007)
3. Birukou, A., D'Andrea, V., Leymann, F., Serafinski, J., Silveira, P., Strauch, S., Tluczek, M.: An integrated solution for runtime compliance governance in SOA. In: Maglio, P.P., Weske, M., Yang, J., Fantinato, M. (eds.) ICSOC 2010. LNCS, vol. 6470, pp. 122–136. Springer, Heidelberg (2010)
4. Rozinat, A., van der Aalst, W.M.P.: Conformance checking of processes based on monitoring real behavior. Information Systems 33(1), 64–95 (2008)

5. van der Aalst, W.M.P., de Beer, H.T., van Dongen, B.F.: Process mining and verification of properties: An approach based on temporal logic. In: Chung, S. (ed.) OTM 2005. LNCS, vol. 3760, pp. 130–147. Springer, Heidelberg (2005)
6. Weske, M.: Business Process Management: Concepts, Languages, Architectures. Springer, Heidelberg (2007)
7. Silveira, P., Rodriguez, C., Casati, F., Daniel, F., D'Andrea, V., Worledge, C., Taheri, Z.: On the design of compliance governance dashboards for effective compliance and audit management. In: Workshop on Non-Functional Properties and SLA Management in Service-Oriented Computing (NFPSLAM-SOC) (2009)
8. Namiri, K., Stojanovic, N.: Using control patterns in business processes compliance. In: Weske, M., Hacid, M.-S., Godart, C. (eds.) WISE Workshops 2007. LNCS, vol. 4832, pp. 178–190. Springer, Heidelberg (2007)
9. Förster, A., Engels, G., Schattkowsky, T., Straeten, R.V.D.: Verification of business process quality constraints based on visual process patterns. In: TASE, pp. 197–208 (2007)
10. Governatori, G., Milosevic, Z., Sadiq, S.W.: Compliance checking between business processes and business contracts. In: EDOC, pp. 221–232 (2006)
11. Lu, R., Sadiq, S., Governatori, G.: Compliance aware business process design. In: Workshop on Business Process Design, BPD (2007)
12. Weber, I., Governatori, G., Hoffmann, J.: Approximate compliance checking for annotated process models. In: Workshop on Governance, Risk and Compliance, GRCIS (2008)
13. Sadiq, S., Orlowska, M.E., Sadiq, W., Foulger, C.: Data flow and validation in workflow modelling. In: ADC. CRPIT, vol. 27, pp. 207–214 (2004)
14. Cabanillas, C., Resinas, M., Ruiz-Cortés, A., Awad, A.: Automatic generation of a data-centered view of business processes. In: Mouratidis, H., Rolland, C. (eds.) CAiSE 2011. LNCS, vol. 6741, pp. 352–366. Springer, Heidelberg (2011)
15. Ryndina, K., Kuster, J., Gall, H.: Consistency of business process models and object life cycles. In: Models in Software Engineering, pp. 80–90 (2007)
16. Elgammal, A., Turetken, O., van den Heuvel, W.-J., Papazoglou, M.: Root-cause analysis of design-time compliance violations on the basis of property patterns. In: Maglio, P.P., Weske, M., Yang, J., Fantinato, M. (eds.) ICSOC 2010. LNCS, vol. 6470, pp. 17–31. Springer, Heidelberg (2010)
17. Ghose, A.K., Koliadis, G.: Auditing business process compliance. In: Krämer, B.J., Lin, K.-J., Narasimhan, P. (eds.) ICSOC 2007. LNCS, vol. 4749, pp. 169–180. Springer, Heidelberg (2007)
18. Kharbili, M.E., Stein, S.: Policy-based semantic compliance checking for business process management. In: MobIS Workshops. CEUR Workshop Proceedings, vol. 420, pp. 178–192 (2008)
19. Medeiros, A., Weijters, T.: Prom framework tutorial (2009), http://prom.win.tue.nl/research/wiki/prom/tutorials
20. Rodríguez, C., Silveira, P., Daniel, F., Casati, F.: Analyzing compliance of service-based business processes for root-cause analysis and prediction. In: ICWE Workshops, pp. 277–288 (2010)
21. Kagermann, H., Kinney, W., Küting, K., Weber, C.-P.: Documentation in internal audit. In: Internal Audit Handbook, pp. 432–440. Springer, Heidelberg (2008)
22. Syed Abdullah, N., Sadiq, S., Indulska, M.: Emerging challenges in information systems research for regulatory compliance management. In: Pernici, B. (ed.) CAiSE 2010. LNCS, vol. 6051, pp. 251–265. Springer, Heidelberg (2010)

A Systematic Review of Compliance Measurement Based on Goals and Indicators

Azalia Shamsaei, Daniel Amyot, and Alireza Pourshahid

SITE, University of Ottawa, 800 King Edward, Ottawa, ON, K1N 6N5, Canada
{asham092,damyot,apour024}@uottawa.ca

Abstract. Business process compliance management is an important part of corporate governance as it helps meet objectives while avoiding consequences and penalties. Although there is much research in this area, we believe goal-oriented compliance management using Key Performance Indicators (KPIs) to measure the compliance level of organizations is an area that can be further developed. To investigate this hypothesis, we undertook a systematic literature review, querying four major search engines and performing manual searches in related workshops and citations. From a research body consisting of 198 articles and their references, we have systematically selected 32 papers. We grouped these papers into five categories and highlighted their main contributions. The results show that all selected papers were written in the last five years, and that few effectively represent compliance results using dashboards or similar tools. Although all individual pieces are available, no existing solution yet combines goals with KPIs for measuring the overall compliance level of an organization.

Keywords: Systematic Review, Business Process, Goal Modeling, Legal Compliance, Key Performance Indicator.

1 Introduction

Ensuring that business processes comply with legislation, regulations, and policies is a very important activity. Every year, organizations invest time and money to ensure business process compliance (BPC). According to a survey by the Illinois Banker Association [9] in 2010, among the 128 banks who responded, over 54% spend 5% of their annual operating expenses on compliance and internal audits, 40% spend between 5% and 20% on compliance, while 4% spend more than 20% on compliance.

Compliance management becomes complex due to an overwhelming number of regulations introduced each year. With so many rules to follow, large organizations face difficult challenges when measuring business process compliance levels in a quantitative way. They also have a hard time assessing the impact of making their business processes compliant to organization goals and finding suitable tradeoffs.

While there is ongoing research on BPC, the lack of comprehensive techniques for *measuring* the level of business process compliance against regulations while considering *processes* and *goals* motivates us to conduct a systematic literature review in this area. The objective of our review is the systematic selection and characterization of literature that focuses on BPC. The research questions we address in this paper are:

- What are the methods based on Key Performance Indicators (KPIs) used for measuring the compliance of business processes against policies and laws?
- What goal-oriented modeling methods are used for compliance measurement?

Although some systematic literature reviews have been done in the field of compliance management [1, 5], these reviews are limited to the information systems domain or focus on the compliance assessment of business process instances to process definitions (without consideration for legal aspects or means to reason about tradeoffs with other organization goals). Hence, they do not answer our research questions.

In our research, we followed the approach proposed by Kitchenham [15] for systematic literature reviews. We divided our method into three main phases, shown in Fig. 1. The first phase is the selection of the related work, the second is the analysis of the selected material, and the third is the detailed review of relevant papers.

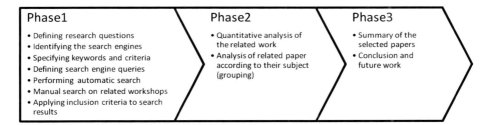

Fig. 1. Research Method

This paper is organized as follows. Section 2 details the first phase on paper selection. Section 3 categorizes and analyzes the selected papers. A summary of the most important papers is presented in section 4, followed by our conclusions in section 5.

2 Phase 1: Selection of Related Work

This phase identifies the search engines, selection criteria, and inclusion criteria.

2.1 Identification of Search Engines and Other Sources

We considered four popular IT search engines for this research, including SpringerLink, IEEE Xplorer, and the ACM Digital Library. Google Scholar was also included in order to cover a broader range of domains (e.g., management and auditing) and venues. In addition, a manual search was done for the following workshops: i* Workshop (for goal modeling) and GRCIS (for regulatory compliance). We also extended the initial selection with relevant articles that have been cited in the papers found. We did not scope the review to a particular time period. The data set consisted of 142 papers from the search results and 56 papers from the manual inspection. Since not all papers found by the search engines were related to our research questions, we defined selection criteria, discussed in the next section, to filter out the first set of results.

2.2 Selection Criteria

We were looking for papers focusing on goal modeling approaches and/or KPIs for measuring compliance of processes with regards to regulations or policies. We chose five main sets of keywords for defining the search engine queries as well as the final filtering of the search results. The reviewed articles should at least focus on *Compliance*, *Business Process*, *Legal/Law/Policy*, *KPI*, and *Goal Modeling*.

Using these five selection criteria, we formally defined keywords and queries for the search engines. The main abstract query is (goal AND compliance AND (law OR legal OR policy) AND ("performance indicator" OR KPI OR "compliance indicator") AND "business process" AND model), used for all search engines except for Google Scholar. The latter returned thousands of unrelated papers with the aforementioned keywords; therefore we decided to narrow down the results by replacing "business process" keyword with "business process compliance". In addition we tried a simpler query ("Business process compliance" AND "Goal" AND ("KPI" OR "Indicator")) on all four search engines, but most articles found were the same as in the first set of queries, and only 8 new articles were found. A manual search of the two related workshops led to an additional 56 papers. The search results are illustrated in Table 1.

Table 1. Automatic and Manual Search Results

	Springer	IEEE	ACM	Google Scholar	GRCIS	iSTAR	Simpler Query	Cited	Total
Search Result	44	45	20	25	13	43	8	0	198
Finally Selected	2	7	4	8	4	2	0	5	32

2.3 Inclusion/Exclusion Criteria and Procedures

In this step, we reviewed each of the 198 papers by reading the abstracts and conclusions. A paper was included if any of the following were true:

- It was related to compliance of processes or legal/policy compliance.
- It used KPI for any kind of measurement not just BPC (e.g., for process performance or for assessing the security of a complex process).
- It was related to stakeholder or organization goals (goal-oriented).

The last two aforementioned criteria were defined to improve our understanding of the other applications of goal-oriented and KPI-based approaches. Furthermore, a paper was excluded if any of the following were true:

- It discussed compliance but not in relation to business processes or to the legal/policy domain (e.g., network compliance).
- The paper was not written in English.

Finally, after considering all the papers against the above criteria, we selected 32 papers for the next phase for further analysis and detailed review. Table 2 lists all 32 papers, the criteria (keywords) they satisfy, and the five categories introduced in section 3.

Table 2. Selected Papers and Criteria

Category	Paper	Goal	Business Process	Compliance Modeling	Process Modeling	Law/Legal /Policy/Rule	Compliance	Indicator /KPI
Compliance framework and standards	[33]	No	No	No	No	Yes	Yes	No
	[11]	No	Yes	No	Yes	Yes	Yes	No
	[12]	No	Yes	No	Yes	Yes	Yes	No
	[14]	No	Yes	No	Yes	Yes	Yes	No
	[13]	No	Yes	No	Yes	Yes	Yes	No
	[17]	No	Yes	No	Yes	Yes	Yes	No
	[16]	No	No	No	No	No	Yes	No
Measure of compliance levels	[26]	No	Yes	No	Yes	Yes	Yes	No
	[18]	No	Yes	No	Yes	Yes	Yes	No
	[37]	No	Yes	No	No	Yes	Yes	Yes
	[34]	Yes	Yes	Yes	Yes	Yes	Yes	Yes
Discovery and controls of non-compliant business processes	[27]	No	Yes	No	No	Yes	Yes	No
	[36]	No	Yes	Yes	Yes	Yes	Yes	No
	[21]	Yes	Yes	Yes	Yes	Yes	Yes	No
	[7]	Yes	Yes	Yes	Yes	Yes	Yes	No
	[8]	Yes	Yes	Yes	Yes	Yes	Yes	No
	[35]	No	Yes	No	No	Yes	Yes	Yes
	[2]	No	Yes	No	Yes	Yes	Yes	No
	[38]	No	Yes	No	Yes	Yes	Yes	No
Goal-oriented techniques and KPI	[32]	Yes	Yes	Yes	Yes	Yes	Yes	Yes
	[31]	Yes	Yes	No	Yes	No	No	Yes
	[28]	Yes	Yes	No	Yes	Yes	No	Yes
	[4]	No	No	No	No	No	No	Yes
	[23]	No	No	No	No	Yes	No	Yes
	[6]	No	Yes	No	No	Yes	No	Yes
	[25]	Yes	No	No	No	No	Yes	No
	[24]	Yes	Yes	No	Yes	No	No	No
	[3]	Yes	Yes	No	Yes	No	No	No
Others	[22]	No	Yes	No	Yes	No	No	Yes
	[29]	No	Yes	No	No	Yes	Yes	Yes
	[19]	No	No	No	No	No	Yes	Yes
	[20]	No	No	No	No	No	Yes	Yes

3 Phase 2: Analysis of Related Work

In this phase, we analyzed the selected papers in two ways. First, we performed a quantitative analysis to show the distribution of the articles over the years. We observed that the selected papers were all published after 2006. The second analysis is the main contribution of this literature review. After careful analysis of the papers' contents, we grouped the papers into five categories considering their subject and our research questions.

- *Compliance frameworks and standards*: This category includes papers that suggest a framework for regulatory compliance or compare standards (see 4.1).
- *Measurement of compliance levels*: Approaches that not only discover non-compliant business processes but also measure their compliance level qualitatively and/or quantitatively (see 4.2).
- *Discovery and control of non-compliant business processes*: Approaches for discovering and controlling non-compliant business processes that however do not suggest solutions for measuring compliance levels (see 4.3).
- *Goal-oriented techniques and KPI*: Papers using goal-oriented techniques and KPI measurements for applications not related to compliance (see 4.4).
- *Others*: Papers related to compliance not appropriate for any of the previous compliance related categories (see 4.5).

4 Phase 3: Summary of Selected Papers

4.3 Compliance Frameworks and Standards

There are a number of methodologies and standards for IT security and governance helping companies increase IT efficiency and meet regulatory requirements. Radovanovic et al. [33] compare several. According to a survey referred in their work, out of 1865 companies, 69% use COBIT for IT governance, 11% use ITIL for its best practices in IT services management, and 12% use ISO 27002 for IT security. These standards are used for internal audits and IT process improvement, as well as addressing legal requirements such as protection and non-disclosure of personal data and the Sarbanes-Oxley Act (SOX).

Karagiannis et al. [11] propose a six-step business process modelling approach for SOX regulatory compliance. This approach relies on detecting risks in processes (related to a particular section of the SOX regulations) and addressing them by defining controls. In addition, they design extensive test cycles to verify compliance. If the test results show a gap, then a redesign step is considered to address the detected issues. They also propose the use of a business process management (BPM) platform called ADONIS as the supporting tool for the methodology [12].

Kharbili and Stein [13, 14] define high-level requirements and an architecture for compliance management. They introduce a three-layer-architecture: 1) one to document and model policies, 2) one for design-time artifacts such as process models and business rules, and 3) one for the execution of both processes and rules. Furthermore, they propose transforming regulations into semantic policies, and then transforming semantic policies into semantic business rules, and then a final transformation into operational rules which can be used to automate processes. They also discuss eight dimensions used to assess a compliance management system.

Ly et al. [17] propose the fundamental requirements for process management systems' compliance with rules/policies. In addition, they assess the existing frameworks with respect to the proposed requirements.

Finally, Koliads and Ghose [16] describe a compliance program, a set of management processes, helping organizations with regulation compliance. In their context, a compliance program should be able to discover compliance obligations and to report on the overall compliance of the organization. In addition, it should have a mechanism for improving non-compliant processes and be able to identify, measure, and mitigate risks.

4.2 Measurement of Compliance Levels

Morrison et al. [26] define a method for measuring the degree of compliance of processes with respect to both crisp and imprecise compliance requirements. Their method relies on creating a compliance scale model that allows measurement of both qualitative and quantitative values for a particular process instance. Although this method can assess the level of compliance of a process, it requires a lot of preparatory work to determine the compliance scales.

Lu et al. [18] propose a method for measuring BPC against control rules defined using control objectives from different sources (e.g., regulations or partner contracts) and are modeled using FCL (Formal Contract Language). They define concepts of ideal semantics for control rules in order to categorize various degrees of compliance between processes and rules. They categorize them into four groups including ideal, sub-ideal, irrelevant, and non-compliant situations. They calculate both ideal and sub-ideal compliance degrees of businesses processes against control rules to evaluate how well the process model supports control rules.

Silveira et al. [37] suggest a compliance governance dashboard (CGD), with *key compliance indicators (KCI) used to measure the compliance level of processes*. Their CGD consists of different levels of abstraction. The top-level page shows the most critical regulatory and policy indicators, the compliance level of the main processes, as well as an overall compliance level for the organization. One can drill down to see more details and analyze the compliance of individual process atomic units in various business units. Furthermore, one can view compliance violation reports consisting of all the information reported to internal and external auditors.

Rifaut and Dubois [34] propose a method to combine and model the regulations and business requirements for processes. They combine tabular requirements with i^* goal models, where they model *purposes*, and decompose them all the way down to indicators used to assess and measure the success of processes. This framework can be used prior to the design and implementation of a process, as well as later on for monitoring and controlling the compliance of processes.

4.3 Discovery and Control of Non-compliant Business Processes

Namiri and Stojanovic [27] propose a formal logic-based framework for managing BPC. They identify significant accounts (e.g., Inventory) with major impact on financial reporting. Afterwards, they identify all relevant risks (e.g., customer order rejection) and processes (e.g., warehousing and purchasing process). Finally, they define a set of controls for these risks, and suggest properties focusing on relationships between the accounts, controls, processes, and risks.

Sadiq et al. [36] propose a structured approach bringing together compliance control objectives and process models. Control objectives are modeled through a modal logic based on FCL. They also propose four types of control tags (i.e., flow, data, resource, and time) used to visually annotate process models and illustrate the aspects of a process controlled by control objectives.

Marino et al. [21] check BPC at design time to detect sources of non-compliant. They define control objectives, derived from both regulations and business objectives/goals, at a high level and refine them into lower-level functions and procedures (activity controls) implemented in the form of control processes. In addition, they propose an algorithm used to perform bottom-up satisfaction analysis of control objectives. A second algorithm is suggested to detect the impact of process activities on the control objects in terms of satisfaction and compliance.

Ghanavati et al. [7, 8] propose a requirements management framework for BPC based on the User Requirements Notation (URN) [10]. In this framework, the legal requirements and organization goals are modeled using URN's Goal-oriented Requirement Language and business processes with URN's Use Case Maps. In addition, the models are linked to policies and legal documents using a commercial requirement management system. Several types of links between organizational and legal models are defined to detect non-compliant and react to changes in the law.

Rodriguez et al. [35] build on the results obtained from CGD [37] using a decision tree algorithm and data mining to analyze, predict, and explain non-compliant process instances. They successfully apply their method to a drug dispensation process.

Awad et al. [2] propose a method for automatic detection and resolution of compliance violation in process models using patterns. This is a great step toward addressing maintenance issues in process compliance space. Weber et al. [38] propose an approach for validating a process against a set of predefined constraints. The objective of this work is to detect states of the process execution violating the defined rules.

4.4 Goal-Oriented Techniques and KPI

Pourshahid et al. [32] extend URN to validate processes from both performance and compliance points of view. In addition, [31] use the aspect-oriented extensions to URN to improve processes dynamically using KPIs and redesign patterns.

Nigam et al. [28] suggest an artifact-centric approach for BPM. They model the high-level business goals that drive operational goals as well as the KPIs used to manage and monitor operational artifacts. In addition, they formally introduce the concept of a management rule, defined to react to events occurring in the organizations. Boehmer [4] also uses efficiency and effectiveness KPIs to evaluate and measure the value of an investment to prevent risk in the implementation of an Information Security Management System based on ISO 27001. Martin and Refai [23] propose a framework for measuring and monitoring IT security performance using metrics.

Dang et al. [6] describe an ontological framework for designing healthcare processes, resources, and rules. Their framework contains five different views of a hospital as well as the relations between components of these views. KPIs' view is used to monitor and evaluate performance from different perspectives.

Morandini et al. [25] summarize three goal-oriented research areas ongoing at the University of Trento, i.e., system requirements for compliance with laws, the selection of the best design patterns during system design, and self-adaptive systems using software agents that select alternative paths at run-time to achieve system goals.

Martinez et al. [24] propose a goal-based approach (using TROPOS) to monitor and assess the impact of processes on enterprise and actor goals. Furthermore, Popova and Sharpanskykh [30] very recently proposed a framework for modeling organization goals based on KPIs. Behnam et al. [3] use a goal-driven development method, considering both organization and system goals, to design and develop patient surveillance software for monitoring adverse events.

4.5 Others

Compliance has a critical role in outsourcing environments where trust between clients and contractors can be an issue. Massacci and Yautsiukhin [22] use indicators to assess the security of a complex process in such situations. They use Key Assurance Indicators (KAI) to show how client goals are met, and Key Security Indicators (KSI) to measure the security techniques utilized by contractors. According to Pasic et al. [29], KAI can be used to evaluate process compliance and KSI can illustrate the quality of the control processes used to achieve compliance.

Mahnic *et al.* [19, 20] discuss the compliance of AGIT (AGIle software developmenT) against COBIT with regards to indicators. AGIT models consist of indicators for the performance of a Scrum development process. The authors compare AGIT indicators with COBIT indicators to check whether the latter are measurable using AGIT. Finally, they propose adding new indicators to AGIT to cover the gaps.

5 Conclusions and Opportunities

This paper reports on a systematic literature review that addresses two questions: *Have KPIs been used for compliance measurement?* and *Are there any goal-oriented methods for compliance measurement?* Although the answer is yes to both questions, no available solution yet combines goals with KPIs for measuring the overall compliance of organizations.

We have grouped the 32 selected papers into five categories. The first one focuses on compliance frameworks, reference models, and standards, and it can be used as general guidelines for assessing compliance management frameworks. The next category targets the measurement of compliance levels of processes. The two papers most related to our research topic here are [37], which suggests a dashboard/KPI approach to measure the overall compliance of an organization, and [34], which proposes a goal-oriented process assessment model capturing and measuring process requirements. Although the approach in [34] addresses both of our research questions, the paper does not identify how KPI values are measured and does not suggest a method for measuring the overall compliance level of the organization. In the category related to non-compliant business processes, some papers propose logic-based frameworks for modeling controls and rules whereas others use goal-oriented languages such as URN or *i**. The goal-oriented and KPI category cover papers with approaches in research areas not related to compliance. Finally, the last category discusses papers related to compliance that are not appropriate for any other category.

Research on BPC has increased significantly in the past 5 years. Much of the research uses control objectives as a means of expressing compliance goals for business processes, while internal controls are used as means to make processes compliant. Also, several goal-oriented and measurement (KPI)-based approaches to manage and control compliance in organizations have been proposed. These two types of approaches are similar in the sense that in both cases, regulation requirements are imposed on processes as process objectives. None of these approaches, however, provides a final qualitative indicator on the compliance level of organizations. This would be a key enabler for upper management to analyze the current state of the organization and plan for the future. As a result, an important item for the research agenda in this area is the qualitative measurement of the level of compliance in organizations. Future work should tackle the combination of KPIs with goal-oriented approaches, possibly using business intelligence applications for visualization and reporting to provide the infrastructure for measuring and monitoring the compliance level of organizations.

Acknowledgments. This research was supported by the Business Intelligence Network, a strategic network funded by NSERC (Canada). We also thank Gunter Mussbacher, Liam Peyton, and Michael Weiss for reviewing and commenting this paper.

References

1. Abdullah, S., Hikmi, S., Indulska, M., Sadiq, S.: A study of compliance management in information systems research. In: 17th ECIS, Verona, Italy, pp. 1–10 (2009)
2. Awad, A., Smirnov, S., Weske, M.: Towards Resolving Compliance Violations in Business Process Models. In: GRCIS 2009, Netherlands. CEUR-WS.org, vol. 459 (2009)
3. Behnam, S.A., Amyot, D., Forster, A.J., Peyton, L., Shamsaei, A.: Goal-driven development of a patient surveillance application for improving patient safety. In: Babin, G., Kropf, P., Weiss, M. (eds.) E-Technologies: Innovation in an Open World. LNCS, vol. 26, pp. 65–76. Springer, Heidelberg (2009)
4. Boehmer, W.: Cost-Benefits Trade-Off Analysis of an ISM Based on ISO 27001. In: ARES 2009, Fukuoka, Japan, pp. 392–399 (2009)
5. Cleven, A., Winter, R.: Regulatory compliance in information systems research – literature analysis and research agenda. In: Halpin, T., Krogstie, J., Nurcan, S., Proper, E., Schmidt, R., Soffer, P., Ukor, R. (eds.) Enterprise, Business-Process and Information Systems Modeling. LNBIP, vol. 29, pp. 174–186. Springer, Heidelberg (2009)
6. Dang, J., Hedayati, A., Hampel, K., Toklu, C.: An ontological knowledge framework for adaptive medical workflow. In: JBI, vol. 41, pp. 829–836. Elsevier Science, Amsterdam (2008)
7. Ghanavati, S., Amyot, D., Peyton, L.: Towards a framework for tracking legal compliance in healthcare. In: Krogstie, J., Opdahl, A.L., Sindre, G. (eds.) CAiSE 2007 and WES 2007. LNCS, vol. 4495, pp. 218–232. Springer, Heidelberg (2007)
8. Ghanavati, S.: A Compliance Framework for Business Processes Based on URN, M.Sc. thesis, University of Ottawa, Canada (2007)
9. Illinois Banker Association, IBA Survey on Impact of Dodd-Frank Act (2010), http://www.ilbanker.com/Adobe/GR/Washington_Visit_ExecSummary_2010.pdf
10. ITU-T: Recommendation Z.151 (11/08), User Requirements Notation (URN) – Language definition (2008), http://www.itu.int/rec/T-REC-Z.151/en
11. Karagiannis, D., Mylopoulos, J., Schwab, M.: Business Process-Based Regulation Compliance: The Case of the Sarbanes-Oxley Act. In: RE 2007, pp. 315–321. IEEE, India (2007)
12. Karagiannis, D.: A Business Process-Based Modelling Extension for Regulatory Compliance. In: MKWI 2008, pp. 1159–1173. GITO-Verlag, Berlin (2008)
13. Kharbili, M.E., Stein, S.: Policy-Based Semantic Compliance Checking for Business Process Management. In: MobIS 2008, Germany. CEUR-WS.org, pp. 178–192 (2008)
14. Kharbili, M.E., Stein, S., Markovic, I., Pulvermuller, E.: Towards a Framework for Semantic Business Process Compliance Management. In: GRCIS 2008, France, pp. 1–15 (2008)
15. Kitchenham, B.: Procedures for performing systematic reviews. Technical Report, Keele University and NICTA, Staffordshire, UK (2004)
16. Koliads, G., Ghose, A.: Service Compliance: Towards Electronic Compliance Programs. Technical Report, Decision Systems Lab, University of Wollongong, Australia (2008)
17. Ly, L.T., Göser, K., Rinderle-Ma, S., Dadam, P.: Compliance of Semantic Constraints A Requirements Analysis for Process Management Systems. In: GRCIS 2008, Montpellier, France. CEUR-WS.org, pp. 31–45 (2008)
18. Lu, R., Sadiq, S., Governatori, G.: Measurement of Compliance Distance in Business Processes. Info. Sys. Management 25, 344–355 (2008)
19. Mahnic, V., Zabkar, N.: Using cobit indicators for measuring scrum-based software development. WSEAS Trans. on Computers 7(10), 1605–1617 (2008)

20. Mahnic, V., Zabkar, N.: Assessing Scrum-based software development process measurement from COBIT perspective. In: ICCOMP 2008, 12th WSEAS International Conference on Computers, pp. 589–594. WSEAS, Stevens Point (2008)
21. Marino, D., Massacci, F., Micheletti, A., Rassadko, N., Neuhaus, S.: Satisfaction of control objectives by control processes. In: Baresi, L., Chi, C.-H., Suzuki, J. (eds.) ICSOC-ServiceWave 2009. LNCS, vol. 5900, pp. 531–545. Springer, Heidelberg (2009)
22. Massacci, F., Yautsiukhin, A.: An algorithm for the appraisal of assurance indicators for complex business processes. In: QoP 2007, pp. 22–27. ACM, Chicago (2010)
23. Martin, C., Refai, M.: A Policy-Based Metrics Framework for Information Security Performance Measurement. In: 2nd IEEE/IFIP BDIM 2007, Munich, pp. 94–101 (2007)
24. Martinez, A., Gonzalez, N., Estrada, H.: A Goal-Oriented Approach for Workflow Monitoring. In: Fourth Int. i* Workshop, Tunisia. CEUR-WS.org, pp. 118–122 (2010)
25. Morandini, M., Sabatucci, L., Siena, A., Mylopouslos, S., Penserini, L., Perini, A., Susi, A.: On the use of the Goal-Oriented Paradigm for System Design and Law Compliance Reasoning. In: Fourth Int. i* Workshop, Tunisia. CEUR-WS.org, pp. 71–75 (2010)
26. Morrison, E., Ghose, A., Koliadis, G.: Dealing With Imprecise Compliance Requirements. In: EDOCW, pp. 6–14. IEEE CS, New Zealand (2009)
27. Namiri, K., Stojanovic, N.: Towards A Formal Framework for Business Process Compliance. In: MKWI 2008, pp. 1185–1196. GITO-Verlag, Berlin (2008)
28. Nigam, A., Jeng, J., Chao, T., Chang, H.: Managed Business Artifacts. In: 2008 IEEE International Conference on e-Business Engineering, China, pp. 390–395 (2008)
29. Pasic, A., Bareno, J., Gallego-Nicasio, B., Torres, R., Fernandez, D.: Trust and Compliance Management Models in Emerging Outsourcing Environments. In: SSeW. IFIP AICT, vol. 341, pp. 237–248. Springer, Boston (2010)
30. Popova, V., Sharpanskykh, A.: Formal modelling of organisational goals based on performance indicators. Data & Knowledge Engineering 70, 335–364 (2011)
31. Pourshahid, A., Mussbacher, G., Amyot, D., Weiss, M.: An aspect-oriented framework for business process improvement. In: Babin, G., Kropf, P., Weiss, M. (eds.) E-Technologies: Innovation in an Open World. LNBIP, vol. 26, pp. 290–305. Springer, Heidelberg (2009)
32. Pourshahid, A., Amyot, D., Peyton, L., Ghanavati, S., Chen, P., Weiss, M., Foster, A.: Business process management with the User Requirements Notation. In: ECR, vol. 9(4), pp. 269–316. Kluwer Academic Publishers, Norwell (2009)
33. Radovanovic, D., Radojevic, T., Lucic, D., Sarac, M.: IT audit in accordance with COBIT standard. In: Proceedings of the 33rd Convention, MIPRO 2010, Croatia, pp. 1137–1141 (2010)
34. Rifaut, A., Dubois, E.: Using Goal-Oriented Requirements Engineering for Improving the Quality of ISO/IEC 15504 based Compliance Assessment Frameworks. In: 16th IEEE RE 2008, Barcelona, Catalunya, Spain, pp. 33–42 (2008)
35. Rodríguez, C., Silveira, P., Daniel, F., Casati, F.: Analyzing compliance of service-based business processes for root-cause analysis and prediction. In: Daniel, F., Facca, F.M. (eds.) ICWE 2010. LNCS, vol. 6385, pp. 277–288. Springer, Heidelberg (2010)
36. Sadiq, S.W., Governatori, G., Namiri, K.: Modeling control objectives for business process compliance. In: Alonso, G., Dadam, P., Rosemann, M. (eds.) BPM 2007. LNCS, vol. 4714, pp. 149–164. Springer, Heidelberg (2007)
37. Silveira, P., Rodriguez, C., Casati, F., Daniel, F., D'Andrea, V., Worledge, C., Taheri, Z.: On the design of Compliance Governance Dashboards for Effective Compliance and Audit Management. In: ICSOC-ServiceWave 2009. LNCS, vol. 5900, pp. 208–217. Springer, Stockholm (2009)
38. Weber, I., Governatori, G., Hoffmann, J.: Approximate compliance checking for annotated process models. In: GRCIS 2008, France. CEUR-WS.org, pp. 46–60 (2008)

Continuous Control Monitoring-Based Regulation: A Case in the Meat Processing Industry

Joris Hulstijn[1,3], Rob Christiaanse[2], Nitesh Bharosa[1], Friso Schmid[3], Remco van Wijk[1,3], Marijn Janssen[1], and Yao-Hua Tan[1]

[1] Delft University of Technology
[2] VU University
[3] Thauris B.V., The Hague
j.hulstijn@tudelft.nl

Abstract. Regulation based on Continuous Control Monitoring could reduce the administrative burden for companies. Often, companies already have elaborate internal control and quality management systems. Instead of periodic physical inspections, regulatory supervision can partly be automated and performed on a continuous basis. The regulator gets access to a validated copy of key data elements from the company's internal information systems, which serve as indicator of compliance to specific control objectives. In this paper we describe an information architecture for continuous control monitoring, and show how it can be applied to supervision of regulatory compliance. The approach is illustrated by a pilot project in the Netherlands of applying continuous control monitoring to food safety regulations in the meat processing industry. Participants concluded that the approach is technically feasible but requires a different mindset towards regulation, and a clear business case.

Keywords: Regulatory Compliance, Continuous Control Monitoring.

1 Introduction

In the wake of the financial crisis there is a call for more and more stringent regulation on financial institutions. Also in other sectors such as health care or food processing, there is an increase of governance guidelines and regulations. In particular after incidents, new regulation is introduced. Power [1] calls this the audit society. As a result, companies must keep an increasing amount of records to demonstrate compliance with laws and regulations, as well as corporate standards and guidelines. Regulators, on the other hand, are under political pressure to provide more security, i.e. reduce risks for society [2], while reducing costs and administrative burden for businesses. One way to deal with these contradictory regulatory demands is by information systems. In particular, information systems may help with evidence collection and analysis. Key data elements which are indicators of compliance to specific control objectives are monitored automatically, on a continuous basis. This approach is called *continuous assurance* or *continuous control monitoring* (CCM) [3-5]. CCM can be applied to any kind of control system, be it financial, quality or safety related. We are especially interested in the following research question:

How can we apply continuous control monitoring to improve regulatory compliance?

In this paper we discuss five design principles (pillars) for continuous control monitoring, and show how they can be applied to improve regulatory compliance. When CCM is specifically applied to control objectives derived from laws and regulations, we call it Continuous Control Monitoring-based Regulation (CCM-R).

Consider the norm in the meat processing industry that, in order to prevent diseases like BSE, animal waste may not re-enter the food chain. To demonstrate adherence to this norm we need to oversee the whole supply chain. By using a standard data representation format like XBRL with a shared semantics, we can compare data from different parties, even when underlying commercial data is stored in different formats. This allows reconciliation over the supply chain and makes it possible to verify completeness as well as accuracy. To model the flow of goods we use Starreveld's [6] value cycle. For example, the sum total of waste from slaughterhouses in a region, should equal the sum total of waste entering the certified destruction company for that region. If not, some waste is not accounted for. To detect unreported waste for a slaughterhouse requires spanning reconciliation: comparing the ingoing (animals) and the outgoing flow of goods (meat products and waste), according to normative ratios.

The design principles are illustrated by a pilot project of applying CCM-R in the meat processing industry in the Netherlands. The pilot shows that developing a system for CCM-R is a complex social process. We discuss technical design issues as well as challenges concerning legal and social aspects.

The remainder of the paper is structured as follows. In Section 2 we discuss our vision of continuous control monitoring, and show how it can be applied to regulatory compliance. In Section 3 we discuss the pilot project in the meat processing industry. The paper concludes with lessons learned.

2 Continuous Control Monitoring-Based Regulation

In brief, our vision on CMM-R is as follows. On the basis of key performance indicators (KPI) the continuous control monitoring system verifies on behalf of the regulator whether production proceeds in a controlled manner and whether regulations are being followed. The monitoring system will signal exceptions and report them to the regulator. Irregularities must be explained – proactively or on the basis of additional queries by the regulator. In case of incidents, the system shows whether countermeasures were implemented successfully and production resumes its regular pattern. Companies which sign on to such a 'heartbeat monitor' signal that they are able to control the process and are willing to be transparent.

The CCM-R vision rests on five principles, or pillars: (1) automated verification, (2) continuous monitoring, (3) verification over the supply chain, (4) internal control and (5) regulatory policy. Although we believe all pillars are necessary to realize the full potential of CMM-R, the pillars can also be seen as dimensions which describe specific regulatory settings. For instance, without (5) we get commercial mechanisms for controlling quality in a supply chain. Without (3) we get regulation focused on individual companies. Without (1) and (2) we get old fashioned manual auditing.

2.1 Automated Verification

To verify controls build into computer systems, an auditor generally takes original data from the system and puts it into a simulation tool, which runs a set of test transactions. The simulation represents behaviour expected on the basis of standards and guidelines ('soll'). The results are compared to the results of actual behaviour ('ist'), taken from the computer system. Outcomes which do not align are called exceptions, which either need to be explained or dealt with. An exception may not necessarily amount to a violation. Guidelines could be incomplete or underspecified. For example, in supply chain management, the return flow of goods often raises exceptions. Guidelines do not specify under what account returns should be booked.

Parties need agreement about the key performance indicators to be verified, and about the specific norms or standards to verify them against. The indicators should be selected to provide evidence of the main control objectives, which are again derived from the original rules and regulations, as well as from requirements suggested by experts and other stakeholders. Note that not all data needs to be reported. For example, to measure hygiene, a general requirement for meat processing plants, only a few indicative microorganisms need to be measured and reported[1] [7].

We consider three ways in which compliance can be demonstrated, compare [8]. First, evidence of performance itself. For instance, low microorganism levels indicate that hygiene is being observed. Second, evidence of actions or control measures being in place, which should normally result in the stated objective. For instance, records that the floor is being cleaned regularly twice every day. Third, evidence of competence of staff, which should result in the objectives being actively observed. For instance, evidence that all staff have followed the hygiene-at-work course.

2.2 Continuous Monitoring

Vasarhelyi and colleagues [3-5, 9-11] have been an ardent proponent of what was initially called continuous auditing. Continuous auditing is defined as "a methodology for issuing audit reports simultaneously with, or a short period of time after, the occurrence of the relevant events" [12]. Crucial is the frequency of reports, and the fact that the flow of events may still be adjusted. The term continuous auditing may seem odd, suggesting a human auditor being present, but in fact it refers to continuous confrontation of data to a norm. The approach is also called continuous assurance [10], as the objective is to provide assurance that objectives are met, on the basis of a system of control measures and continuously monitoring their effectiveness.

In Figure 1 we show an architecture for continuous assurance adapted from [3]. Although very general, this overview already highlights some design choices. First, data is drawn from the company's enterprise information system at the application layer; not from the database. This would be impossible both for legal reasons (auditors may only access company data with approval) and security reasons (no one may access data directly, only through the application layer). Second, performance data is stored in a separate database, under control of the auditor. This database also contains the audit trail (way it was obtained). In this way the auditor can perform his

---

[1] For example E. Coli shows whether water is polluted with faecal material, and the presence in food of Staphylococcus Aureus generally indicates contamination from human handling.

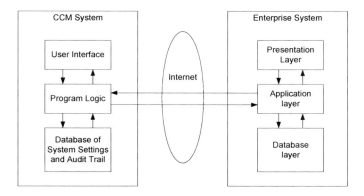

Fig. 1. Generic architecture for continuous assurance, based on Alles et al [3]

or her analysis independently of the host. Data can be queried, stored and retrieved using analytic tools built on top of a usual DBMS. Third, the CMM system is controlled by a module containing the 'Program Logic' specifying auditing behaviour: which data to take from the system, how to store and how to manipulate it. The complete CCM system is controlled by a user interface. More elaborate compliance architectures are provided by Lotz et al [13] and Accorsi et al [14].

Kogan et al. [5] discuss the trade-off between *control-oriented* and *data-oriented* procedures for continuous auditing. The first approach is also known as system-based auditing; it relies on a coherent system of internal control measures. Provided that such measures are in place, the idea is that less effort can be spent on substantive testing. Consider the audit risk model [15], but see [17] for a critical discussion.

audit risk = inherent risk × control risk × detection risk.

Inherent risk is the risk that misstatements or violations occur in the first place. This is beyond the control of the auditor. Control risk is the risk that control measures do not prevent, or detect and correct a misstatement or violation. Detection risk is the risk that remaining misstatements or violations are not detected by the auditor. In case of strong preventative internal controls, the auditor can perform less inspections or substantive tests, while keeping the net audit risk within acceptable boundaries. This suggests adopting application controls in information systems which leave little room for error or manipulation: *compliance by design* [16]. However, especially with modern business intelligence tools, focused data analysis can also be very powerful. Given basic data reliability guaranteed by information technology and the presence of irreplaceable preventative controls (i.e. segregation of duties, identification and authentication, audit trail), data analysis can establish misstatements efficiently.

2.3 Reasoning and Reconciliation over the Supply Chain

Once we have a continuous stream of performance data being monitored, there are several kinds of reasoning which can be used to establish compliance. Here is a brief overview of what can be done, for individual companies:

- **Time series and trends**: is performance improving? Is performance developing in a natural way, or are there abrupt changes, indicating bold interventions?
- **Alerts and red flagging**: when performance reaches some critical level, an automated signal can be generated. Sometimes, a combination of critical factors taken together may be evidence of an increased risk of a disruption.
- **Reconciliation:** different variables can be reconciled, based on the underlying causal, fiscal, or trading relationships [6, 17]. For example, the number of test samples in the laboratory for a given day, should equal the number of animals being slaughtered, as counted by independent sources.

Once we have data assembled from several different companies, spanning part of the supply chain, we can also perform the following kinds of reasoning.

- **Benchmarking**: comparing performance to peers in the same sector, or to previous performance of the same plant. For example, it could be determined that on average, for each animal, 4 kilograms is left over as Category 1 waste. This produces a normative ratio that can be used in reconciliation.
- **Reconciliation over the supply chain:** variables from different trading partners can be compared. Output from one party should equal the input for subsequent parties in the chain. In particular when some parts of the chain are controlled, this can be used to establish completeness, as well as accuracy of the reported data.

The underlying theory of reconciliation is based on Starreveld [6], commonly taught in Dutch accounting courses. See Blokdijk et al [18] for an English introduction. Our exposition here is based on Christiaanse and Hulstijn [19].

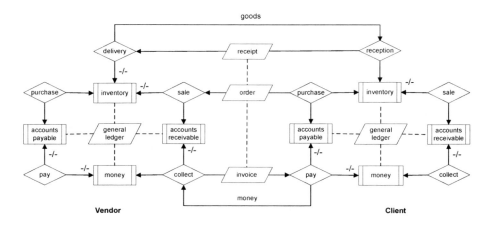

Fig. 2. Interconnected value cycles of vendor and client with communication

Essentially, each business can be modelled as a value cycle: interconnected flows of money and goods. Figure 2 shows two interconnected value-cycles of a vendor and a client, both trading companies. For other sectors (production, service industry), other typologies are known. We use the following notation. Decisions (authorizations) are indicated by a diamond. An actual decision is an event or change of state. Double rectangles are states of a certain value to the company, such as inventory or accounts payable. Records of states, i.e. accounts, are related through reconciliation relationships, indicated by dashed lines, which come together in the general ledger. Influence is indicated by arrows. The sign, '+' or '–/–', indicates an increment or decrement of the corresponding account, where '+' is often left out. Thus, a purchase leads to an increment of the accounts payable, while the purchased goods are added to the inventory. A sale leads to an increment of the accounts receivable and a decrement of the inventory, etc. Messages representing economic transactions are also shown. A typical reconciliation relationship (3-way match) holds between invoice, purchase order and receipt, i.e. evidence of the arrival of the goods.

In Starreveld's work [6] there are two general 'laws'. First, the *rational relationship between sacrificed and acquired goods* states that, for all events e such that $s <e> t$ in Fig 2, the values of s and t before and after an event are related in a rational way.

(1) $incr(e,t) = f \cdot decr(e,s)$, for some normative ratio f.

For example, if we look at a sales event, we have: *increase in accounts receivable = sales price • decrease in inventory*. Second, the *relationship between state and events* holds that, for all states s, the value at the end of a period should equal the value at the beginning, with all increments added, and decrements subtracted.

(2) $s_{begin} - s_{end} + \Sigma_e\ incr(e,s) - decr(e,s) = 0$

For example, inventory at the end of the day should equal inventory in the morning, with all goods received during the day added and all cleared goods subtracted.

A similar role to these laws is played by what Vasarhelyi et al [10] call continuity equations. Griffoen et al [17] use Petri nets and equation modeling to capture these constraints. Crucial is that these reconciliation equations can be used to verify compliance, also in non-financial domains. In commercial traffic, trading partners usually have *opposed interests*: a buyer prefers a low price and a high quality, a seller prefers the opposite. Therefore each party will carefully verify data. Original data from commercial traffic are therefore relatively trustworthy, at least more than reports filed with the only purpose of being compliant. This may be called the piggy-backing principle: compliance rides along on the back of commercial traffic [20].

2.4 Trust and Internal Control

Like in various other forms of self-regulation, e.g.[21, 22], in CCM-R the regulator must rely on evidence provided by the company being controlled. That means that the regulator should be able to distinguish those companies which are 'in control' and can be trusted to provide reliable information, from those which are not. Often this is achieved through some form of certification based on an elaborate audit. Compare AEO certification for trusted companies in European customs legislation [22].

When do we say that a company is 'in control'? One can take the feedback-control loop from engineering, and apply it to management. An influential exponent is Deming's plan-do-check-act cycle [23]. Similar ideas can be found in total quality management (TQM) [24]. The ability to learn and improve is a property of the organization as a whole. Capability maturity models (CMM) can be used to assess the maturity level of an organization in a specific domain, for instance software development [25]. CMM distinguishes the following levels: 1. Initial (ad hoc), 2. Repeatable, 3. Defined, 4. Managed, and 5. Optimizing. At level 3 and higher the organization is 'in control': they can make sure that business objectives are being met.

2.5 Regulatory Policy

Regulatory agencies are under pressure to cut costs, but on the other hand to protect the interests of society, such as safety, security and financial stability. In many cases, regulatory policies have developed historically and need not be optimal.

The regulator should try and spend most inspection and enforcing effort on those companies, which generate risks for society. The underlying decision to inspect, or after incidents, to enforce is *risk-based*. Based on evidence of company behaviour, location and kind of business, the likelihood and impact of violations are estimated.

Similar to responsive regulation [21], the regulatory policy is adjusted to the behaviour of the company being regulated (Table 1). A company should be both willing and able to comply. Being in control is an indicator of being able to be compliant. Companies which are not in control and not compliant are a risk to society, and should be guided towards the left, or else the license withdrawn. Companies which are in control, but not compliant, are apparently able, but not willing to comply. Here enforcement (sanctions) might work. Companies which are not in control, but (trying to be) compliant, should be assisted in improving their internal controls. The regulator could refer to best practices from branch organizations. Strict enforcement would be counter-productive. Finally, companies which are in control and compliant, need less regulatory intervention. Here the number of inspections can be reduced without fear for public safety.

Table 1. Regulatory approach towards companies based on being in control and compliant

	Compliant	Non Compliant
In Control	Advance Guard, => reduce inspection effort (e.g. less physical inspection)	Opportunistic, => enforce compliance (e.g. apply sanctions)
Not in Control	Struggling, either compliant by accident, or only with additional effort => assist in improving controls	Rough trade => put out of business (e.g. withdraw certificate)

In addition, in all cases the regulator must regularly audit the implementation of the CMM-R system and underlying internal controls, in order to make sure the system is not only internally consistent -- all transaction performed according to specification-- but also externally consistent: reported data actually connect to the real world.

3 Pilot Study: CCM-R in the Meat Processing Industry

We report on a recent proof of concept of CCM-R. Figure 3 gives a general overview of the parties involved in the meat processing industry in the Netherlands. On the left, the food chain starts with agriculture producing crops which are converted and sold as foodstuffs. Farms raise cattle or pork, which are slaughtered at the slaughterhouse and sliced into cuts by meat packing firms, according to demand from retail. Those pieces which are left over (by-products), as well as dead animals which are unfit for consumption (ill, contaminated by manure), are taken to a certified destruction company. Generally by-products are re-used industrially; for example gelatine is an important rest product. All parties keep computerized registrations of transport of goods, much of which is regulated. On the right we see the various regulators in the meat processing industry, among which the Food and Consumer Product Safety Authority (VWA) which oversees animal welfare and food safety.

The main safety concern in the meat processing industry is that animal waste and by-products not fit for human consumption, will not re-enter and contaminate the food chain. Among other reasons, this is to prevent illnesses like BSE (mad-cow disease). A strict separation is maintained between meat and by-products (red and blue factory lines). So called Category 1 and 2 by-products (for example some organ tissue like brains, bone marrow, unwashed intestines, semen, milk, contaminated meat) must be kept separate. This material may only be transported and be disposed of through the services of a certified destructor firm, see EC 1774/2002 [26]. Category 3 by-products (like left-over meat, blood, hide, hoofs, etc. of healthy animals) may be transported and processed by category 3 destructors, of which there are several.

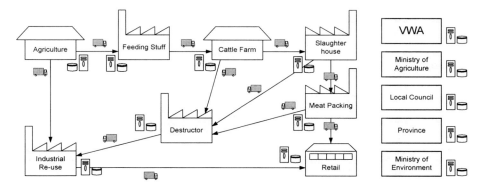

Fig. 4. Simplified overview of the flow of goods in the meat processing industry

3.2 Pilot Project

To test the viability of CMM-R in the meat processing industry a number of parties collaborated to develop a proof of concept[2]. Participants were two slaughterhouses, one for pork and one for beef, a Category 1 and 2 destruction plant, a Category 3 destruction plant, the Food and Consumer Product Safety Authority (VWA). The pilot focuses on information being exchanged concerning regulations EC 1774/2002 [26] explained above, and EC 2073/2005 [27], which is about microbiological criteria for food, in order to promote hygiene and protect public health. A project organization

---

[2] See: http://sggv.nl/casussen/sggv-in-de-vleesindustrie/omschrijving, accessed 02/Feb/2011.

was set-up, with experts on the regulatory domain (by-products, microbiological criteria), and experts of process optimization and technical support. The project took seven months, during which requirements were drawn, prototypes build and tested, and a practice test was performed to the satisfaction of two auditors of VWA.

The pilot feasibility test used XBRL as standard data representation format, and the Netherlands Taxonomy (NT) as definitions for the semantics of reports. A specific extension of the taxonomy was developed for microorganism samples (EC 2073/2005) and by-products bookkeeping (EC 1774/2002). Although it may seem a long detour to use a data standard intended for financial reporting in the meat processing industry, it turned out to be a good choice. Required knowledge about meat processing was limited to knowledge of the way a piece of meat is classified as category 1 or 2 (must be destroyed) or category 3 (may be re-used), and to how microorganism samples are being taken. Required expertise relates to the practices used to make sure records are also externally consistent, i.e. connect to reality.

The pilot used a gateway for secure exchange of compliance reports, built according to the GEIN reference architecture (GEneric INfrastructure) used in Dutch Government. The same architecture is used in the gateway for uploading XBRL reports to Dutch government agencies, like tax office, bureau of statistics and filing the annual financial statements. The gateway is built using open standards, in particular services for SOAP and web interface definitions, and BPMN for process definitions (both manual and technical). The gateway also provides database functionality for storing, querying and retrieving messages, and for archiving.

3.3 Results

Participants in the pilot feasibility test concluded that the CCM-R concept is indeed viable, in the sense that the XBRL data definitions, message reports, interface connections and auditing procedures performed as intended.

However, participants also agreed that to make this into a success, a mind-shift is needed. Many auditors in VWA are trained as veterinary surgeons. They have always been checking meat processing from within the slaughterhouse. From numerous incidents, they have learned to mistrust meat processing firms. As all good auditors, they are sceptical by nature, whereas CCM-R requires a certain level of trust in the professional conduct of meat processing firms. A particular example concerned the audit of the practice test. How do you audit something new? The auditors who had to assess the proof of concept found it hard to come up with suitable assessment criteria. This underlines the need for a general audit model suitable for CCM solutions.

Another outcome concerns the business case. The pilot project was funded by the Ministry of Economic Affairs. In a real situation, meat processing firms would need a clear incentive – reduced inspections – in order to join. One participant in the project already has a very elaborate quality management system. They would like CCM-R to force less advanced and cheaper competitors out. Another participant entered the project much more opportunistically: they can see the economic benefit of less physical inspections. Currently, inspections are compulsory and performed by VWA, but paid by the meat processing firms themselves.

4 Conclusions

Continuous control monitoring can be applied to regulatory compliance, to make it more efficient and possibly more effective. In this paper we presented five 'pillars' of applying CMM to business regulation: (1) automated verification, (2) continuous monitoring, (3) verification over the supply chain, (4) internal control and (5) regulatory policy. These pillars can also be seen as independent dimensions characterizing specific regulatory situations. For instance, without (4) we get direct supervision of performance by the regulator, as for instance in monitoring pollution.

A pilot study in the Netherlands shows that CCM is technically feasible. In particular, existing data representation formats and message infrastructure protocols can be either reused or can be relatively easily adapted where needed (XBRL). Legal barriers can be overcome, by having the company voluntarily supply data, instead of the regulator pulling data out of commercial systems directly. Furthermore the pilot project illustrates the general idea: that CMM allows for more effective audits, with less physical inspections and therefore in the long run potentially less costs.

On the other hand, the pilot has revealed some non-technical challenges in the realization of CCM-R. A significant challenge is that of trust. Like other forms of self-regulation, CCM requires trust in the reliability of the data supplied by the company. Auditors are sceptical about reliability of automated controls. In addition, there is a need for a general audit model which fits system-based auditing approaches and CCM solutions. Another potential barrier is uncertainty about investments and the business case for joining a scheme like CCM-R.

Acknowledgments. We would like to thank the Food and Consumer Product Safety Authority (VWA) for their cooperation in this project.

References

1. Power, M.: The Audit Society: Rituals of Verification. Oxford University Press, Oxford (1997)
2. Beck, U.: Risk society – Towards a new modernity. Sage, London (1992)
3. Alles, M., et al.: Continuous monitoring of business process controls: A pilot implementation at Siemens. Accounting Information Systems 7, 137–161 (2006)
4. Alles, M., Kogan, A., Vasarhelyi, M.: Putting Continuous Auditing Theory Into Practice. Journal of Information Systems 22(2), 195–214 (2008)
5. Kogan, A., Sudit, E.F., Vasarhelyi, M.: Continuous online auditing: a program of research. Journal of Information Systems 13(2), 87–103 (1999)
6. Starreveld, R.W., de Mare, B., Joels, E.: Bestuurlijke Informatieverzorging (in Dutch), Samsom, Alphen aan den Rijn, vol. 1 (1994)
7. Notermans, S.H.W., Mead, G.C.: Microbiological Contamination of Food: Analytical Aspects. In: International Food Safety Handbook, pp. 549–566 (1999)
8. Eisenhardt, K.M.: Control: Organizational and Economic Approaches. Management Science 31(2), 134–149 (1985)
9. Vasarhelyi, M.A., Halper, F.B.: The Continuous Audit of Online Systems. Auditing: A Journal of Practice and Theory 10(1), 110–125 (1991)

10. Vasarhelyi, M.A., Alles, M., Kogan, A.: Principles of analytic monitoring for continuous assurance. J. of Emerging Technologies in Accounting 1(1), 1–21 (2004)
11. Alles, M.A., Kogan, A., Vasarhelyi, M.A.: Feasibility and economics of continuous assurance. Auditing: A Journal of Practice and Theory 21(1), 125–138 (2002)
12. CICA/AICPA, Continuous auditing, Research report, The Canadian Institute of Chartered Accountants (CICA), Toronto, Canada (1999)
13. Lotz, V., et al.: Towards Systematic Achievement of Compliance in Service-Orientied Architectures: The MASTER Approach. Wirtschaftsinformatik 50(5), 383–391 (2008)
14. Accorsi, R., Sato, Y., Kai, S.: Compliance monitor for early warning risk determination. Wirtschaftsinformatik 50(5), 375–382 (2008)
15. Knechel, W., salterio, S., Ballou, B.: Auditing: Assurance and Risk, 3rd edn. Thomson Learning, Cincinatti (2007)
16. Governatori, G., Sadiq, S.: The journey to business process compliance. In: Handbook of Research on Business Process Management, pp. 426–445. IGI Global (2009)
17. Griffioen, P.R., Elsas, P.I., van de Riet, R.P.: Analyzing Enterprises: the value-cycle approach. In: Database and Expert Systems Applications, pp. 685–697. Springer, Heidelberg (2000)
18. Blokdijk, J.H., Drieënhuizen, F., Wallage, P.H.: Reflections on auditing theory, a contribution from the Netherlands. Limperg Instituut, Amsterdam (1995)
19. Christiaanse, R., Hulstijn, J.: Neo-Classical Principles for Information Integrity. Faculty of Technology, Policy and Management, Delft University of Technology (2011)
20. Tan, Y.H., et al. (eds.): Accelerating Global Supply Chains with IT-Innovation. Springer, Berlin (2011)
21. Ayres, I., Braithwaite, J.: Responsive Regulation: Transcending the Deregulation Debate. Oxford University Press, Oxford (1992)
22. Burgemeestre, B., Hulstijn, J., Tan, Y.-H.: Rule-based versus Principle-based Regulatory Compliance. In: Governatori (ed.) JURIX 2009, pp. 37–46. IOS Press, Amsterdam (2009)
23. Deming, W.E.: Out of the Crisis. MIT Center for Advanced Engineering Study (1986)
24. Hackman, J.R., Wageman, R.: Total quality management: empirical, conceptual, and practical issues. Administrative Science Quarterly 40, 309–342 (1995)
25. Paulk, M.C., et al.: The Capability Maturity Model: Guidelines for Improving the Software Process. Addison-Wesley, Reading (1995)
26. EC, Regulation No 1774/2002 laying down health rules concerning animal by-products not intended for human consumption, European Parliament and the Council (2002)
27. EC, Regulation No 2073/2005 on Microbiological criteria for foodstuffs, The Commission of the European Communities (2005)

Semantic Representation of Process and Service Compliance – A Case Study in Emergency Planning

Aygul Gabdulkhakova[1], Birgitta König-Ries[1], and Norris Syed Abdullah[2]

[1] Friedrich-Schiller-University Jena, Germany
{aygul.gabdulkhakova,birgitta.koenig-ries}@uni-jena.de
[2] The University of Queensland, Brisbane, Australia
norris@itee.uq.edu.au

Abstract. Emergency events like natural disasters and large scale accidents pose a number of challenges to handle. The requirement to coordinate a wide range of organizations and activities, public and private, to provide efficient help for the victims can often be complicated by the need to comply with requisite policies and procedures. Current process and service models that represent domains such as emergency planning do not provide sufficient artefacts with respect to compliance requirements. In this paper, we argue that techniques for compliance management in business processes can be applied to the emergency domain. We provide a high level model for the representation of compliance requirements within business processes and services. Hence, we demonstrate the application of the model in the emergency planning domain. Finally, we present an analysis derived from the case study that identifies the current limitations and requirements for semantic extensions of process and service models in order to cater for compliance.

Keywords: emergency management, SOA, semantic web services, and compliance management.

1 Introduction

The organizations involved in mass casualty incidents (MCI), i.e., police, medical services, and fire and rescue forces, are faced with manifold challenges. A mass casualty incident (MCI) is a special incident in which the personnel and equipment of the rescue forces at the scene are overwhelmed by the number and severity of casualties at that incident. The main problem for the operations manager in such situations is to manage the gap between actually available resources and necessary resources [1]. Typically, this assignment needs to be done on-the-fly once the disaster has occurred: While for some disasters (e.g., a fire in a football stadium), rather detailed emergency plans can be developed beforehand, there are also numerous disasters where this is not the case. Consider, e.g., hurricanes or traffic accidents. These disasters can occur anywhere and can vary widely in severity. Depending on the exact location, access to the accident site will differ, the number, experience, and equipment of available emergency personnel and volunteers will also depend on the location. Often, only limited information about the incident will be available in the beginning. More information about the situation will become known over time, only.

Thus, a system is needed that can efficiently assign emergency personnel and equipment to the necessary tasks according to their abilities and organizational structures (police, medical services, fire and rescue services). The SpeedUp project [www.speedup.uni-jena.de] aims to develop a framework that provides IT-support for the cooperation and communication of emergency management organizations. Up to now, such cooperation is achieved more or less manually by orally exchanging information or exchanging print outs. In the case of scenarios such as mass casualty incidents, however, personal consultations or the procurement and dispatch of documents are virtually impossible to manage. Processes are inefficient and precious time is lost as a result: factors that, in the worst case, raise the number of victims. In our ongoing work, we are investigating the possibility to dynamically map emergency management processes to varying underlying resources using semantic web service technology. The aim is to (semi-)automatically compose processes using the available resources.

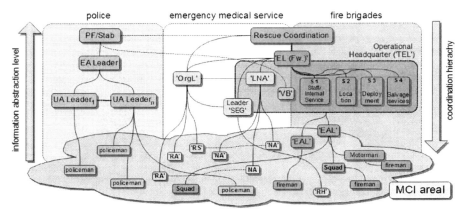

EA Leader – leader of an operational area; *UA Leader* – subsection leader; *EL* – local operation manager; *S 1- S4* – functional areas; *OrgL* - Organizational Medical Leader; *LNA* - Leading Emergency Doctor; *RH* – Emergency Medical Technician; *RA* – Paramedic; *RS* - Emergency Medical Technician; *NA* – Emergency Doctor; *EAL* – leader of an operational area; *VB* – liaison officer; *PF (Polizeifuehrer)/Stab* – commander of police/ Crisis Management Group (CMG).

Fig. 1. Core roles within organizations in the MCI scenario

It is important, however, that these processes and the assigned resources do not only meet functional requirements, but also obey the rules and standards governing emergency organizations. Consider an accident on a motorway with a number of injured people. In handling this situation, at least fire fighters, first aid personnel, and police will be involved and special management structures will be established between them. For example, the police use a Special Organisational Structure, while the fire and emergency medical services establish a Technical Operation Management respectively OrgL (organisational medical leader) and LNA (leading emergency doctor) (see Figure 1). Different roles in this structure are assigned with different rights based on legal requirements or organizational rules. A special characteristic in such a scenario is that the operation managers should handle tasks whose goals arise and can quickly change during the mission itself [2]. So, the basic idea is to develop a mechanism that supports operation managers in achieving those goals by (semi-)automatically assigning or suggesting appropriate resources and at the same time ensures that existing rules, such as access restrictions on a particular personal data, commands are given by authorized personnel etc., are obeyed by the dynamically created processes. In this paper, we propose such a system based on semantic web service technology. Resources are modeled as services and will be discovered and bound at run time. To achieve this, services need to be described in a machine-processable manner. In addition, we need to make sure that only services that meet rules and regulations are used within a process. Here, we argue that techniques for compliance management known from BPM can be adapted to our domain. In the remainder of the paper, we discuss how this can be achieved. First, we introduce the semantic service descriptions we use. Second, we look at compliance requirements in our domain and discuss how they could be formalized. Finally, we present our architecture that brings together the different building blocks. Thereafter, we will give an overview of the related work and conclude.

2 Semantic Service Descriptions

We have decided to base our system on a service oriented architecture with semantic, i.e., machine-processable service descriptions, as this is an ideal architecture to support flexibility and robustness in dynamic situations. These descriptions enable an automatic assignment of suitable service offers to service requests. In case a service is no longer available, performs badly or inadequate in a certain situation, another service offer can be chosen without affecting the overall behavior.

To describe services semantically, we use the DIANE Service Description language (DSD) and its matchmaker [3] to provide such descriptions and to automatically match service requests and offers in order to find the most appropriate pairing for both. The language is not based on one of the existing ontology or logic languages such as the often used description logic or f-logic, but uses an ontology language and a reasoning mechanism that is specialized for service discovery: the DIANE Elements (DE). Service offers are described as sets of required preconditions and achieved effects. By the introduction of variables, DSD allows to seamlessly integrate the descriptions of which functionality is provided and the form of message flow, *viz.*, which inputs a service expects and which outputs it is able to produce. DSD descriptions of both offers and requests are basically directed graphs. The matchmaker traverses the request graph and tries to find and configure matching offers by implementing a subset test. This powerful and efficient matchmaker is at the heart of the accompanying semantic service middleware that supports the whole process of service matching, selection, and automatic invocation [3].

Figure 2 illustrates an example of a service offer that allows transmitting a text message (e.g., information about number of affected persons) from the leading emergency doctor to the organizational medical leader. The description tells that the effect of the service execution will be that a text message (*TextMessage* is an input

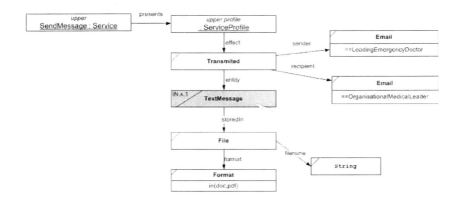

Fig. 2. Service Offer *"SendMessage"*

parameter of the service) will be sent from the leading emergency doctor to the organizational medical leader. This message needs to be in *.doc* or *.pdf* format and the filename needs to be provided as an input. Service requests are formulated similarly and are then automatically matched with all available service offers to find the best matching currently available service.

We envision emergency personnel to have access to a tool that will trigger service requests at certain steps in emergency management process. For instance, in the event that leading emergency doctor may want to inform the organizational medical leader about the number of victims. The tool will automatically create an appropriate service request from this. This request will then be matched with the available service offers. Such offers might include services totally unrelated to the task at hand, e.g. a service scheduling an ambulance, but also a number of services more or less suitable to achieve the given goal, e.g. the service offer above, but also a service that creates a wireless link, a service that ensures that the information is transmitted by a messenger etc. Unfortunately, requests that look very similar from the semantic service description and matchmaking point of view, may require the usage of very different services in order to meet compliance requirements. For instance, if the leading emergency doctor wants to communicate just the number of victims, she may be able to use a different service (e.g., a volunteer messenger or a wireless transmission) than when she also wants to communicate personal information about those victims.

In the next section we will describe in more detail how the association between internal controls and process tasks or services can be done.

3 Compliance in Emergency Management

As described above, our current matchmaker is able to take functional and non-functional aspects reflected in the service offer and request descriptions into account to find the best matching services. The matchmaker, however, is not able to take into account rules and regulations that are defined elsewhere. Here, we propose to integrate tools developed in the context of compliance management in BPM. In this section, we describe how concepts known there can be applied to our domain.

Let us consider the following example: Article §10 of the Medical Association's professional code of conduct in Germany states that the leading medical doctor evaluates the operational picture: progress of the care of the patients on-site, the condition of the patients and the evacuation of the patients on-site. According to §163 StPO (*German Code on Criminal Procedure*), he is prohibited from spreading this information to other organisations (e.g., police). Unfortunately, not all emergency staff manages those requirements carefully or is even fully aware of them. Therefore, we suggest to start with formalizing the compliance requirements. We propose the use of formalisation as in [4] to facilitate the extension of service descriptions. In [4], the work examined the semantics of the contract conditions with reference to behavioural expressions which then they referred to as deontic constraints. Deontic constraints express what parties to the contact are required to perform (obligations), what they are allowed to do (permissions), or what they are not allowed to do (prohibitions). As a result, we derive compliance rules in form of machine readable statements/rules as follows: *(1) Service Obligation* - what must the services be able to deliver or produce? *(2) Service Prohibition* - what must the service not deliver or produce? *(3) Service Delegation* - what is permissible for the service to deliver or produce or substitute in terms of its output?

Consider our example about transmitting a message about affected persons from the leading emergency doctor to the organizational medical leader. An organizational medical leader leads the subordinate forces and is responsible for the best possible care of the patients. The subordinate forces forward information to the organizational medical leader. Thus, transmitting information about affected persons to the organizational medical leader from the leading emergency doctor is allowed and in this case the warranted connection is via an e-mail service (§ 203 StGB (*The German Criminal Code*) "...Transmitting patient's data ... via telephone or radio connection is basically forbidden"). These rules can be regarded as compliance rules. For instance, the Service Obligation part could capture the following requirements:

- Triage documentation, i.e., the estimation of victims injury in order to determine the priority of patients treatments based on the severity of their condition;
- Medical documentation of patients;
- Organization of ambulance movement according to the destination of patients.

In the Service Prohibition part will be a statement on what the service must not produce; regarding our example:

- Transmitting patient's data to other organizations (e.g., police, fire brigades) and
- Transmitting patient's data via telephone or radio connection.

The Service Delegation part will contain statements on what is acceptable to be substituted and describes the tasks to be executed in Compliance Management component. In our case these substitutes can be:

- Assignment of an identification number of patient (without supporting any medical documentation e.g. patient diagnose) to police in accordance with official call;
- Providing e-mail services as option for transmitting patient's data between leading emergency doctor and organizational medical leader.

In the following, we show the examples of formalization for part of emergency services rules involving patient's data protection namely R1, R2, and R3. R1 represents compliance rule formalization specifying leading emergency doctor (LNA) has the obligation (O) to safe keep patient's data. In the event of violation ($\otimes$), LNA is obligated (O) to pay fine. Another formalization, R2 shows that LNA is prohibited ($O\neg$) to send patient's data to Non-Medical Agencies (NMA). We complete this with service delegation in R3 where LNA is permitted (P) to send patient data through e-mail to Organizational Medical Leader (OrgL).

- R1 (Service Obligation): PatientData, O_{LNA} Safekeep $\otimes$ O_{LNA} PayFine.
- R2 (Service Prohibition): PatientData, $O\neg_{LNA}$ SendtoNonMedicalAgencies.
- R3 (Service Delegation): PatientData, P_{LNA} SendEmailtoOrgL.

The examples have demonstrated how we use compliance rules to capture requirements in the emergency management domain. While semantic services provide the basis for dynamic process composition, in many settings, it is inadequate to find a functionally correct process and at the same time adhere to surroundings constraints (legal, etc.). Using compliance rules (in addition to the service descriptions) can provide us with the ability to dynamically allocate resources, execute services/substitutes, etc. in critical situation without violating required policies and guidelines.

4 Solution Architecture

In this section we present the overall architecture for representation of compliance requirements for emergency management.

In order to assist such dynamic environments, a system has to combine expertise about dynamically creating processes and expertise to generically describe and enforce compliance to reach the next level towards automatic process management. Figure 3 shows the interplay between the AI planner, the service component and the compliance management component: While the planning component will create processes that will solve given tasks, the service component will find concrete resources that are needed to execute these services. Service offers and service requests are not initially designed to fit together but are matched at run time by the service oriented software. In order to match a service request with a service offer, we have a service repository. It manages a list of all currently available services. To keep the repository up to date, service providers have the task to announce just offered services as well as services that are not available anymore. Service requests have the possibility to search in the repository for services providing certain functionality. In order to ensure that only service that match functionally and do not violate any rules and regulations, a compliance management component is needed. This component allows an on-the-fly compliance check and ensures that existing rules are fulfilled.

Emergency organizations typically involve a collection of business process tasks performed to accomplish the offered service. Considering that, we employ the use of ontological alignment and process model enrichment proposed by [5] in our solution. According to [5], process model enrichment will provide a better understanding of the interaction between process model and compliance rules (through improved visualisation of controls on the process model). Therefore, we start our compliance

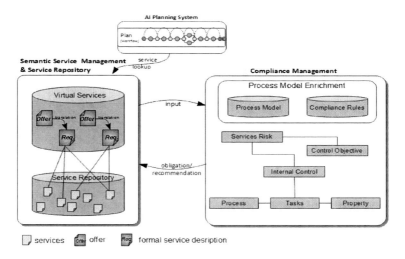

Fig. 3. System Architecture

management by identifying the associated compliance rules (regulation/standard) for a particular business process. Then, we proceed with the identification of risks for a particular service with regard to (violation of) compliance rules for the offered services. This will facilitate the identification of compliance obligation associated with a particular service or so called control objectives.

Following this, specific internal controls (specific activities/checks etc. that will be undertaken to fulfill a control objective) are designed and associated with the requisite control objectives and identified services risk. The fulfillment of control objectives will ensure the service process is free from the determined risks, or at least operates at a mitigated level of risk. To describe the relationship between internal controls and tasks, we observe that there are several controls that are applicable to a particular task. For each task there are a number of properties which represent the instance of a particular task. For instance, in emergency services the property may represent particular emergency staff roles or particular condition and/or time when a particular service is performed. By completing the ontological alignment and the process model enrichment, the emergency services and processes are explicitly associated with internal controls and hence with compliance obligations (or control objectives). This will facilitate the creation of low risk or risk free processes for a particular service adhering to compliance rules.

5 Related Work

In the last twenty years, many projects dealt with support in MCI and other emergency scenarios and many used a similar combination of technologies as SpeedUp does. Examples include SHARE [6], CoSAR-TS [7], MobiKat [8] and the Emergency Management System [9]. However, despite clear indications for the need [10, 11], to the best of our knowledge, none of these projects aims to provide sufficient artefacts with respect to compliance management for different types of rescue forces for managing MCI scenarios.

Efforts towards supporting the modeling of business process to meet compliance requirements have been established by a number of prior research works. In particular, [5] introduces an approach that provides the capability to capture compliance requirements through a generic requirements modeling framework. In their approach [5] also introduce the use of Formal Contract Language (FCL) as formalism to represent the declarative nature of compliance requirements. The formalization of process models is also supported by [12] that present formalism for annotated process models for the purpose of compliance checking. Another work by [13] provides an interesting method for integrating risks in business processes. The proposed technique for "risk-aware" business process models is developed for EPCs (Event Process Chains) using an extended notation. Similarly [14] present a logical language PENELOPE, that provides the ability to verify temporal constraints arising from compliance requirements on affected business processes. Distinct from the above works, the contribution of this paper has been on firstly providing an overall methodology for a model driven approach to business process compliance, and secondly on a structured technique for process model enrichment based on formal modeling of control objectives. Another significant research also exists on the modeling of control flow in business processes, particularly in the use of patterns to identify commonly used constructs [www.workflowpatterns.com]. On a similar note, [15] provide temporal rule patterns for regulatory policies, although the objective of this work is to facilitate event monitoring rather than the usage of the patterns for support of design time activities.

The most closely related work with regard to discovery is the WSMO-MX Matchmaker [16]. WSMO-MX is a hybrid matchmaker for WSML services that borrows the graph-matching approach from the DSD Matchmaker, but combines it with other concepts developed within other matchmakers which the DSD Matchmaker is lacking. What distinguishes the DSD Matchmaker most from WSMO-MX, as from most other discovery approaches is DSD's concept of precise fine-grained preferences and ranking. Most matchers proposed for OWL-S (see e.g. [17] for a typical example) rely on the subsumption matching of inputs and outputs described above and do not take the effects of the service into account. The recent matcher proposed in [18] additionally matches service product and classification. In contrast, DSD's matching is purely state-based. This has two advantages: (1) compares whether a service provides the desired effect or not and (2) DSD can abstract from differing interface and find functionally matching services even if their interface differ.

For WSMO, a discovery mechanism that abstracts from the individual effect to a desired, more generic goal is proposed. In [19] the developers argue that this abstraction is necessary due to performance considerations. Likewise, OWL-S [20], e.g., inherits difficulties with reasoning on the instance level from the description logics it is based on. Tools for OWL-S thus tend to not use instance information. However, contrary to DSD both approaches do not differentiate between a description of an offered and a requested service and rely on ontologies and heavy-weight logics (like description logics or frame logics). Thus, when searching for a service in dynamic and unreliable environments, it would be difficult to describe what should happen in cases where, e. g., information is missing or not fully matching.

6 Conclusion

In this paper we have presented a high level model for the representation of compliance requirements technologies which are essential for building up IT-support for operation managers in large-scale MCI scenarios. We described the components, their functionalities in the modeling and execution phases. In our current approach, a model for representing compliance requirements is build through the extension of service descriptions in form of machine readable statement/rule. Most parts of the architecture are still in development and need additional scientific investigations such as the usage of these extensions in the matching process and the role of these extensions at service execution time. Currently, we are integrating the building blocks of our solution into a common prototype which will then be tested in a real-life setting.

Acknowledgements. The work described here has been partially funded by the Federal Government's program Research for Civil Security (call "rescue and protection of people") by the German Federal Ministry of Education and Research (http://www.speedup.uni-jena.de) and German Academic Research Service (DAAD).

We would like to thank our SpeedUp project partners from the Intercultural Business Communication (IWK) department, University of Jena (Germany) especially Yeliz Yildirim-Krannig, Mareike Mähler, and Fabian Wucholt who have provided us with important insights into intra- and inter-organizational interaction and contents of communication in MCIs. We also would like to acknowledge Shazia Sadiq from School of Information Technology and Electrical Engineering, The University of Queensland for her invaluable input in this research.

References

1. Peter, H.: Die Leitstelle beim MANV. Stumpf + Kossendey Verlagsgesellschaft mbH (2001)
2. Kemper, H.: Führen und Leiten im Einsatz. Ecomed, 3. Auflage 2008 (2008)
3. Kuester, U., Koenig-Ries, B., Klein, M., Stern, M.: DIANE - A Matchmaking-Centered Framework for Automated Service Discovery, Composition, Binding and Invocation on the Web. Special Issue of IJEC (International Journal of Electronic Commerce) on Semantic Matchmaking and Retrieval (2007)
4. Governatori, G., Milosevic, Z., Sadiq, S., Orlowska, M.: On Compliance of Business Processes with Business Contracts Technical Report, School of Information Technology and Electrical Engineering, The University of Queensland (2006)
5. Sadiq, S., Governatori, G., Namiri, K.: Modeling Control Objectives for Business Process Compliance. In: Alonso, G., Dadam, P., Rosemann, M. (eds.) BPM 2007. LNCS, vol. 4714, Springer, Heidelberg (2007)
6. Konstantopoulos, S., Pottebaum, J., Schon, J., Schneider, D., Winkler, T., Paliouras, G., Koch, R.: Ontology-Based Rescue Operation Management, pp. 112–121 (2009)
7. Tate, A., Dalton, J., Bradshaw, J.M., Uszok, A.: Coalition Search and Rescue - Task Support: Intelligent Task Achieving Agents on the Semantic Web. Technical report, Artificial Intelligence Applications Institute The University of Edinburgh and Florida Institute for Human & Machine Cognition, IHMC (2004)

8. Danowski, K.: MobiKat - Integriertes System zur Untersttzung der Katastrophenbewältigung und der alltäglichen Gefahrenabwehr. Fraunhofer-Institut für Verkehrs- und Infrastruktursysteme IVI Infoblatt (2007)
9. Rausch, A., Niebuhr, D., Schindler, M., Herrling, D.: Emergency Management System. In: Proceedings of the International Conference on Pervasive Services 2009 (ICSP 2009), Clausthal University of Technology, Department of Informatics - Software Systems Engineering Research Group (2009)
10. Robillard, J., Sambrook, R.: USAF Emergency and Incident Management Systems: A Systematic Analysis of Functional Requirements (2008),
    http://www.uccs.edu/~rsambroo//Research/EIM_REQS.pdf
11. Lanfranchi, V., Ireson, N.: User requirements for a collective intelligence emergency response system. In: BCS-HCI 2009: Proceedings of the 23rd British HCI Group Annual Conference on People and Computers, pp. 198–203. British Computer Society, Swinton (2009)
12. Weber, I., Governatori, G., Hoffmann, J.: Approximate Compliance Checking for Annotated Process Models. In: 1st International Workshop on Governance, Risk and Compliance - Applications in Information Systems (GRCIS 2008) Held in Conjunction with the CAiSE 2008 Conference, Montpellier, France (2008)
13. Padmanabhan, V., Governatori, G., Sadiq, S., Colomb, R., Rotolo, A.: Process Modeling: The Deontic Way. In: Stumptner, M., Hartmann, S., Kiyoki, Y. (eds.) Australia-Pacific Conference on Conceptual Modeling, CRPIT, vol. 53, pp. 75–84 (2006)
14. Goedertier, S., Vanthienen, S.: Designing Compliant Business Processes with Obligations and Permissions. In: Eder, J., Dustdar, S., et al. (eds.) BPM Workshops 2006. LNCS, vol. 4103, pp. 5–14. Springer, Heidelberg (2006)
15. Giblin, C., Muller, S., Pfitzmann, B.: From Regulatory Policies to Event Monitoring Rules: Towards Model Driven Compliance Automation. IBM Research Report. Zurich Research Laboratory (October 2006)
16. Kaufer, F., Klusch, M.: WSMO-MX: A Logic Programming Based Hybrid Service Matchmaker. In: Proceedings of the 4th IEEE European Conference on Web Services (ECOWS 2006), Zürich, Switzerland (December 2006)
17. Paolucci, M., Kawamura, T., Payne, T.R., Sycara, K.P.: Semantic Matching of Web Services Capabilities. In: Horrocks, I., Hendler, J.A. (eds.) ISWC 2002. LNCS, vol. 2342, pp. 333–347. Springer, Heidelberg (2002)
18. Srinivasan, N., Paolucci, M., Sycara, K.: Semantic Web Service Discovery in the OWL-S IDE. In: Proceedings of the 39th Annual Hawaii International Conference on System Sciences, vol. 06. IEEE Computer Society, Los Alamitos (2006)
19. Keller, U., Lara, R., Polleres, A., Toma, I., Kifer, M., Fensel, M.: WSMO Web Service Discovery - WSML Working Draft 12 11 2004. Technical Report, DERI (2004)
20. Burstein, M.H., Hobbs, J.R., Lassila, O., Martin, D.L., McDermott, D.V., McIlraith, S.A., Narayanan, S., Paolucci, M., Payne, T.R., Sycara, K.P.: DAML-S: Web Service Description for the Semantic Web. In: Horrocks, I., Hendler, J. (eds.) ISWC 2002. LNCS, vol. 2342, p. 348. Springer, Heidelberg (2002)

A Framework for Organizational Compliance Management Tactics

Ralph Foorthuis[1] and Rik Bos[2]

[1] UWV, Business Services, La Guardiaweg 116, 1040 HG Amsterdam, The Netherlands
Ralph.Foorthuis@uwv.nl
[2] Utrecht University, Information and Computing Sciences, Princetonplein 5, 3584 CC Utrecht, The Netherlands
R.Bos@cs.uu.nl

Abstract. Organizational compliance with laws, industrial standards, procedures and enterprise architectures has become a highly relevant topic for both practitioners and academics. However, both the fundamental insights into compliance as a concept and the tactics for bringing an organization into a compliant state have been described in a fragmented manner. Using literature from various disciplines, this paper presents two contributions. First, it describes the fundamental concepts regarding compliance. Second, it presents a framework in which the various tactics for achieving organizational compliance can be positioned.

Keywords. Compliance management, governance, tactics, literature overview.

1 Introduction

With the advent of stricter legal demands, industrial best practices and prescriptive enterprise architectures, the topic of organizational compliance has become highly relevant for both practitioners and academics [1,2,3,4]. Organizational compliance can relate to various types and levels of prescriptive systems. International and domestic laws and regulations, industry-wide standards and best practices, organizational rules and procedures, and enterprise architecture principles and models can all require organizational units, projects and employees to conform to norms.

The topic of compliance has fascinated scholars for centuries. As early as the 1600s, Thomas Hobbes touched on the delicate issue of the *compliance problem* [5,6,7]. He stated that, although compliance with contracts may be better for the group as a whole and it may be in an individual actor's best interest to agree to contracts, it may very well not be in his interest to actually comply with them. Following this logic, it is necessary for policy makers to actively pursue and monitor compliance. This is also true in an organizational context, as compliance with norms may be in the best interest of the organization as a whole, but may not lead to optimal results from the perspective of the complying individuals, projects and departments. This is not merely a philosophical stance, as several studies demonstrate that non-compliance in organizations is widespread [3,8,9]. This makes compliance a strategic issue in the current era, especially considering the high costs organizations have to pay for their non-conformance. With regulations such as the Sarbanes-Oxley Act, organizations and individual CEOs and CIOs face severe penalties for non-compliance [10,11]. In addition, scandals and unethical firm behavior can severely damage an organization due to unsatisfied customers, shareholders, employees and other stakeholders [1,12]. On the other hand, demonstrating compliance with regulations, industrial best practices and ethical norms can yield a good reputation and the benefits that come with it, such as attracting large institutional investors and customers [2,9,12].

However, organizations have difficulties implementing their compliance management approaches [13,14]. At the same time, both the compliance stimulating tactics that comprise these approaches and the fundamental concepts regarding compliance have been described in the literature in a fragmented manner, from different perspectives and in distinct academic disciplines. Consequently, there is a need for a structured overview of generic ways in which compliance can be achieved and maintained.

The preliminary results presented in this paper are part of a larger research project, set out to identify compliance tactics acknowledged in literature from various disciplines and to offer an approach for developing an organizational compliance management strategy. This paper lays the foundations for such a research project by answering two research questions: *What are the fundamental concepts in compliance?* and *How can compliance tactics be categorized?* Our goal in presenting the preliminary results, besides the aforementioned relevance to academia and practice, is to obtain feedback that may be used in the ongoing research.

This article proceeds as follows. In section 2, our research approach is described. Section 3 defines and discusses fundamental compliance concepts. Section 4 introduces the Compliance Tactics Framework with the example tactics positioned within it to demonstrate the framework. Section 5 is for discussion and conclusions.

2 Research Approach

We employed a literature study for our research, as this provides an appropriate method to investigate the fundamentals of compliance and consequently develop the framework in which to position the identified tactics for achieving compliance. A literature study is also well-suited to identify the wide array of techniques devised in distinct disciplines. Science can benefit from drawing from different fields, as a topic can be enriched by the exposure to distinct and potentially relevant theoretical backgrounds [cf. 15,16]. The main disciplines we have drawn upon are law, philosophy, business studies, information systems and social psychology.

Due to space restrictions, we can only briefly describe our approach, but we have incorporated the following elements [cf. 16,17,18,19]. The most important search terms were "compliance", "conformance", "conformity", and combinations such as "compliance management" and "organi[z|s]ational compliance". The search was conducted in academic indexing services, such as JSTOR and PiCarta, but also in broader listings such as GoogleScholar. The literature was collected by the principal researcher and an information specialist of Statistics Netherlands. As the nature of the study was less a 'truth finding' mission than a broad and open-minded identification effort, quality criteria for journals and conferences could not be too strict. Nonetheless, the norm was that a publication be academically peer reviewed, unless a technical report or practitioner publication yielded a unique insight. A literature database was created, allowing systematic storage of information on the collected publications during the actual review process undertaken. The database was based on the concept matrix of [16] and the data extraction guidelines of [18,19]. It contained information such as the titles, authors, unit of analysis and substantive conceptual contribution. In addition, a review protocol was established to ensure that the review process was carried out in a systematic fashion. As publications were reviewed, relevant texts were added to the preliminary tactics overview, which was coded by using the method of [17]. In our study, a code represented a (candidate) tactic. Using *first-level coding*, a preliminary categorization was conducted, resulting in summarized pieces of data and their respective codes. After 35 publications had been reviewed an iterative and creative process of *pattern coding* was initialized to run parallel with the continuing review and first-level coding activities, resulting in a more mature categorization of tactics. At the time of writing, we had reviewed 54 publications. This resulted in the framework and the set of example tactics as presented in section 4 of this paper.

3 Fundamentals of Compliance

This section defines and discusses key concepts, such as compliance, actors, norms and policies. In addition, the nature of compliance is explored in more detail, showing the insights used to structure the framework.

3.1 Compliance: Key Concepts and Definitions

We define *compliance* as a state of accordance between an actor's behavior or products on the one side, and predefined explicit rules, procedures, conventions, standards, guidelines, principles, legislation or other norms on the other [cf. 4,20,21,22]. Although we do not focus on compliance with the implicit, broader spirit of the norms, we do acknowledge relatively (high-level) principles as norms – on the condition that they be made explicit. A compliant state can be achieved regardless of the motivations, causes or circumstances that have lead to it [20,21]. In our view, therefore, an actor can be compliant without internalizing the norms and without necessarily changing his beliefs or behavior. Furthermore, unintentional compliance is also compliance. Finally, compliance should be distinguished from effectiveness, as a compliant state need not necessarily result in achieving the desired end goals [20,21].

We will use the term *conformity* here as equivalent to compliance, as it has been used inconsistently in the literature. We will elaborate on this below. Similar to compliance, conformity is regularly used as adherence to prescribed rules [3,21,23, 24,25,26]. Compliance has also been contrasted with conformity, with the former following an explicit or implicit request, and the latter referring to a state of accordance in the absence of a request [27]. In this context, conformity is sometimes said to necessarily involve a change in belief or behavior [28,29], whereas an actor can be compliant without a position change (see above). Finally, according to [30] compliance is a form of conformity, representing public instead of private agreement. The term *conformance*, likewise, is not used in a single, specific manner [cf. 23,31,32]. Therefore, unless specified otherwise, we will use the terms compliance, conformity and conformance interchangeably (using the definition presented at the beginning of section 3.1).

We define an *actor* as a person or organizational entity who acts within an organization, is equipped with cognitive capabilities, preferences, beliefs, values and at least some degree of autonomy [6,35,36]. As such, an actor can be e.g. an organizational unit, a project or an individual employee. In the context of this paper, an actor is expected to comply with the norms. See section 3.2 for more on actors.

The terms *norms* and *prescriptions* are used interchangeably here, serving as general denotations that encompass more specific forms such as laws, standards, rules, principles and guidelines. Therefore, norms or prescriptions can refer to general, abstract (but explicit) principles or to detailed rules – or anything in between. They can also refer to prohibitive norms (so-called proscriptions). Furthermore, they can be legally required or voluntary by nature. Norms can relate to both behavior and products. Requiring a project to use the organization's standard system development method is an example of rules relating to behavior. Requiring the IT-systems delivered by the project to comply with enterprise-wide quality standards is an example of rules relating to products. Finally, norms can (and probably will) change as time progresses. A set of norms is referred to here as a *policy*.

When applying norms or assessing them on conformance, several aspects should be taken into account [4]. A prescription should be applied *correctly*. Its use, or lack of it, should also be *justified* (relevant) in the respective situation. Another issue is whether related prescriptions are applied *consistently*. A final concern is whether the *complete* set of (mandatory) norms is applied, as opposed to merely a convenient subset.

Another interesting aspect concerns whether norms are *mandatory* or not. In practice, not all norms are (e.g. industrial best practices or some enterprise architecture principles). Adherence to the norms then is more akin to the narrow sense of conformity as defined by [27], i.e. adherence without a request. Even when norms are mandatory, they are not always perceived as such in practice [33].

A distinction can be made between two types of non-compliance [cf. 24,34]. First, a *transgression* refers to a situation in which a norm is not complied with, e.g. by breaking a law or rule. A reason for this might be that the actor in question had no interest in conforming to this specific norm or simply did not know how to comply. Secondly, *subversion* refers to a situation in which an actor, for his own individual interest, attempts to undermine the entire compliance system itself, or at least an essential part of its norms. For example, when the implementation of standards is carried out in such a fashion as to demonstrate their inferiority and the need to abandon them altogether. In an organizational context, subversion might point to fundamental political problems, structural conflicts of interest or competing norm systems. An organization that is the result of a merger, for example, may have competing sets of architectural standards.

A *compliance tactic* is a measure that can be taken, or a technique or mechanism that can be used, to encourage compliance of relevant actors [cf. 37]. Tactics can be preventative, detective and corrective in nature [13]. As one tactic is typically not sufficient to obtain compliance, multiple tactics need to be combined into a coherent strategy. A *compliance management strategy*, therefore, is a general plan featuring a consistent set of compliance tactics that aims to bring the organization to a state that is compliant with relevant norms, at least to a sufficient level. Such a strategy can aim to achieve *holistic compliance*, addressing three concerns: coherent instead of fragmented compliance efforts [10,38], a long-term scope [13], and the ability to cover multiple laws, standards frameworks or internal procedures at the same time.

3.2 The Nature of Compliance

In this section we will discuss some fundamental insights into compliance that will form the basis for our framework. The literature on compliance distinguishes between two broad types of theory, namely rationalist and normative approaches [3,6,9,20,21, 39,40,41]. These theories provide distinct insights into compliance-related behavior and underlying motivations of states, firms and individuals. *Rationalist models* focus on the actor's calculation of benefits and costs in his decision on whether or not to comply. This approach sees actors as choosing rationally among alternatives. Game theory is a regularly used lens here to analyze behavioral motivations, using the prisoner's dilemma to model the Hobbesian compliance problem [6,42]. In this light, incentives and disincentives will alter the outcome of the actor's calculation. Therefore, one major approach used here is enforcement (or command-and-control), in which unwanted behavior is deterred by means of punishment. Rewards are an additional means in the rationalistic perspective, stimulating compliance by changing the cost-benefit calculation to the actor's advantage.

As a second perspective, *normative models* focus on cooperation and assistance as a way of stimulating compliance [9,20,21,39]. This approach views actions as based on identities, roles, obligations, and considerations of appropriate, fair and legitimate action. Normative theories do not take the stance that an actor's behavior is irrational, but tend to broaden the scope to prevent reducing the discussion to costs and benefits. Actors are imagined to follow the institutionalized rules and practices that link particular identities to particular situations. These rules need to be internalized and viewed as legitimate by those subject to them. It is acknowledged that compliance may be hindered if rules are ambiguous, complex or continuously changing, or if they are too numerous or not easily available. Non-compliance may also be the inadvertent result of deficient routines or a lack of capacity, knowledge or commitment. For all these reasons, non-compliance should be 'managed' instead of being sanctioned. Methods to increase compliance therefore often focus on increasing the actor's capacity to comply. This is effectuated by cooperating, providing support and encouraging shared discourse in order to render rules clearer, more persuasive and easier to commit to.

Rational and normative models are not mutually exclusive, but rather complement each other and provide different lenses for analyzing influences on compliance behavior [3,9,20]. Both perspectives are relevant to our research. For example, organization-wide standards may be dismissed for rational reasons, as conforming to them may take additional time and effort. Or it may be that the organizational units and employees value their identity as "professionals" or their role as "managers". Also, public organizations may feel "obliged", or consider it "appropriate" not to spend tax payers' money unnecessarily.

Although theories from both the rational and normative perspective often regard actors that need to comply as unitary agents, a comprehensive perspective on compliance also needs to be able to disaggregate an actor into multiple sub-actors [9,20,39]. An organization is comprised of structural units, such as departments and their sub-units, and temporary initiatives, such as programs and their projects and teams. Furthermore, all of these entities will have individual members. Motivations for compliance-related behavior may differ between these different (sub-)actors [9]. We deal with this issue in our study by acknowledging three conceptual levels. First, the level of the enterprise as a whole, in which "enterprise" can be taken to mean the entire organization, a division or even a network of organizations [cf. 31]. This is the level at which the internal policy makers are located and at which the policies are determined – although there may obviously be pressure from higher (external) levels, in the form of laws and industrial best practices. The second level accommodates various types of collectives that are expected to comply. They exist within the enterprise, such as departments and their sub-units and programs and their projects and teams. These collectives typically have a more local scope and may have a political agenda that can, at least in part, be inconsistent with the wider enterprise and its policies. The third level is that of individuals, who may themselves be expected to comply (e.g. in the case of information security procedures) or who may be part of a collective that is requested to comply (e.g. in the case of a project implementing a system that records privacy-sensitive information). In both cases, the decisions and behavior of individuals are determinants of actual compliance.

4 The Compliance Tactics Framework

Based on the fundamental insights discussed above, this section presents the framework within which the tactics used to stimulate compliance can be positioned. On the horizontal dimension, the characteristics of both the rationalist and the normative compliance approaches are used as defining elements. As these types of theory provide different perspectives on behavioral motivations for compliance, they can accommodate tactics of a different nature. The rationalist perspective puts forward *inducements* (incentives or rewards) and *enforcement* (disincentives or penalties), whereas the normative perspective offers *management* of compliance (cooperation and assistance). The vertical dimension represents the organizational level at which

		Compliance Management Approach		
		Inducements	Enforcement	Management
Organizational Level	Enterprise	Mandating compliance officers to give incentives	Developing guidelines for punishment	Reflecting on culture in terms of compliance
	Collective	Paying for expenses	Rejecting the project deliverable	Conducting compliance assessments
	Individual	Offering financial rewards	Creating social disincentives	Providing performance feedback

Fig. 1. The Compliance Tactics Framework

the tactics are applied, i.e. the level at which the effort is made (note that it does not necessarily denote the actor at which the tactic is directed). The *enterprise* level is the level at which the internal policy and its norms are formulated. This is also the level at which the compliance management strategy is developed and at which top management, compliance officers and organization-wide auditors operate. The *collective* level represents organizational units and temporary initiatives, such as projects, that need to conform. The *individual* level accommodates individual employees that are expected to comply. Figure 1 gives a visual representation of the framework. The examples positioned within it are discussed in detail below.

The framework can be used to position and characterize *individual tactics*. However, the framework can also be used to analyze or develop an organization's *compliance management strategy*, which is a general, integrated plan consisting of multiple tactics with the intention of achieving a satisfactory level of organizational compliance. As a strategy utilizes multiple tactics, it typically covers multiple cells of the framework.

Examples of Tactics Used in Compliance Management

This section will present examples of compliance tactics for each cell. Tactics are represented by italic text and can be found in the visualized framework. A first tactic at the enterprise level is *mandating compliance officers to give incentives*. A problem for those directly responsible for achieving compliance, e.g. security officers, is that they often have no line authority over relevant employees, including transgressors [9,33]. This will mean specifically that it will be very difficult for them to punish non-complying employees themselves. Rewarding complying employees, however, can be expected to be a less sensitive issue due to its positive character. Related to enforcement, *developing guidelines for punishment* results in enterprise-level standards, which should prevent penalties being given arbitrarily and inconsistently throughout the organization. This will increase the level of perceived fairness and consistency of the procedures (i.e. procedural justice), which is a significant determinant of compliance [9,3,40]. Making norms and conditions explicit may also increase their perceived 'mandatoriness', which can further increase compliance levels [33]. As a management tactic at the enterprise level, the organization can *reflect on its culture in terms of compliance*. This can be seen as a comprehensive and deep diagnosis of the corporate culture and its behavior in terms of compliance and ethics [12]. This need not be an incidental affair, but can be part of an ongoing process. As part of this, one goal would be to gain insight into the degree of policy-induced compliance (i.e. compliance *because* of the compliance system) versus externally determined compliance (e.g. a shift in values at the societal level) [21]. Reflecting also entails understanding non-compliance, which might be the result of high compliance costs, lack of technical knowledge or complex, ambiguous or difficult-to-find rules [20,21,39]. All these insights should inform the development of a new compliance management strategy.

As an incentive on the collective level, certain *expenses might be paid for*, as a reward for compliance. The IT costs of a project, for example, are sometimes paid for out of an enterprise-level budget on the condition that it conforms to the enterprise architecture prescriptions [4,37]. Alternatively, a project or department could be punished for non-compliance by *rejecting the project deliverable* [43]. This can occur, for example, if a software solution that is developed is not described in sufficient detail to meet the standards set by the party responsible for maintaining it in production (especially if this is an external party). Rejection need not be final, since the deliverable may be accepted after reworking it in accordance with the norms. In addition, *compliance assessments* of processes, systems and projects are conducted to verify whether the norms are actually complied with in practice [4,26,44]. The results of such an assessment or audit can be reason to take corrective action. The object of scrutiny here can be behavior, such as when it is verified whether a project conforms to the rules of the relevant project management or systems development methodology. In addition, an assessment can verify product quality by reviewing the project's design documents or by checking the delivered output of a production process against the quality standards. Because of our definition of compliance, what is central in an assessment is whether the behavior and products are consistent with the norms, not if they are consistent as a result of the norms (this latter issue can be explored in the reflecting tactic). A recent survey ($n=293$) found the use of compliance assessments to be the most important determinant of conformance of projects to enterprise architecture prescriptions, probably due to a desire to avoid confrontation [37].

Offering financial rewards is an example of a rewarding tactic at the individual level. This can take a variety of forms, such as pay raises, promotions, awards, bonuses, days off and paid vacations [41,45]. An example of penalties for individuals is *creating social disincentives*. As these tend to be intangible, they might take the form of reprimands, 'naming and shaming', suspension, unfavorable mention in oral or written assessments and the consequent loss of reputation and status [9,11,41]. *Providing performance feedback* is a proven and inexpensive management tactic for improving employee behavior [45,46]. This tactic derives its power from providing the employee with objective information on his performance, preferably presented in an immediate, positive and specific fashion, with a focus on the task rather than the person. The information can trigger a performance-improving reaction within the employee, for example because he is encouraged to reduce the discrepancy between his performance and the standard or because of an inner motivation to raise the bar.

5 Conclusions and Outlook

This paper offers two contributions. First, we presented fundamental definitions and concepts in compliance management, based on insights from distinct academic fields. Second, we developed a framework for characterizing and categorizing compliance tactics, including an example of each category. This research is continuing, as we are currently in the process of identifying more tactics and positioning them within the framework, and studying how the framework can inform a compliance strategy.

Acknowledgements. The authors thank Annemarie Koomen, Erika Streefland, Sjaak Brinkkemper, Wiel Bruls, Nico Brand, Marlies van Steenbergen and Remko Helms.

References

1. Harris, J., Cummings, M.: Compliance issues and IS degree programs. Journal of Computing Sciences in Colleges 23(1) (2007)
2. Emmerich, W., Finkelstein, A., Montangero, C., Antonelli, S., Armitage, S., Stevens, R.: Managing Standards Compliance. IEEE Transactions on Software Engineering 25(6), 836–851 (1999)

3. Tyler, T.R., Blader, S.L.: Can Businesses Effectively Regulate Employee Conduct? The Antecents of Rule Following in Work Settings. The Academy of Management Journal 48(6), 1143–1158 (2005)
4. Foorthuis, R.M., Hofman, F., Brinkkemper, S., Bos, R.: Assessing Business and IT Projects on Compliance with Enterprise Architecture. In: Proceedings of GRCIS 2009, CAISE Workshop on Governance, Risk and Compliance of Information Systems (2009)
5. Gauthier, D.: Why Contractarianism? In: Vallentyne, P. (ed.) Contractarianism and Rational Choice: Essays on David Gauthier's Morals by Agreement, pp. 15–30. Cambridge University Press, Cambridge (1991)
6. Hollis, M.: The Philosophy of Social Science: An Introduction. Cambridge University Press, Cambridge (1994)
7. Hartman, E.M.: Organizational Ethics and the Good Life. Oxford University Press, New York (1996)
8. Healy, M., Iles, J.: The Establishment and Enforcement of Codes. Journal of Business Ethics 39, 117–124 (2002)
9. Malloy, T.F.: Regulation, Compliance and the Firm. Temple Law Review 76 (2003)
10. Volonino, L., Gessner, G.H., Kermis, G.F.: Holistic Compliance with Sarbanes-Oxley. Communications of the AIS 14(1), 219–233 (2004)
11. Braganza, A., Franken, A.: SOX, Compliance, and Power Relationships. Communications of the ACM 50(9), 97–102 (2007)
12. Rossouw, G.J., Van Vuuren, L.J.: Modes of Managing Morality: A Descriptive Model of Strategies for Managing Ethics. Journal of Business Ethics 46, 389–402 (2003)
13. Sadiq, S., Indulska, M.: The Compliance Enabled Enterprise: Process is the Product. Compliance and Regulatory Journal 5, 27–31 (2008)
14. Hurley, J.: The Struggle to Manage Security Compliance for Multiple Regulations. White Paper, Symantec (2004)
15. Malone, T.W., Crowston, K.: The Interdisciplinary Study of Coordination. ACM Computing Surveys 26(1) (1994)
16. Webster, J., Watson, R.T.: Analyzing the Past to Prepare for the Future: Writing a Literature Review. MIS Quarterly 26(2) (2002)
17. Miles, M.B., Huberman, A.M.: Qualitative Data Analysis, 2nd edn. Sage Publications, Thousand Oaks (1994)
18. Tranfield, D., Denyer, D., Smart, P.: Towards a Methodology for Developing Evidence-Informed Management Knowledge by Means of Systematic Review. British Journal of Management 14, 207–222 (2003)
19. Kitchenham, B., Brereton, O.P., Budgen, D., Turner, M., Bailey, J., Linkman, S.: Systematic literature reviews in software engineering – A systematic literature review. Information and Software Technology 51, 7–15 (2009)
20. Zaelke, D., Kaniaru, D., Kružíková, E.: Making Law Work: Environmental Compliance & Sustainable Development, vol. I & II. Cameron May Ltd., London (2005)
21. Mitchell, R.B.: Compliance Theory: An Overview. In: Cameron, J., Werksman, J., Roderick, P. (eds.) Improving Compliance with International Environmental Law. Earthscan, London (1996)
22. Kim, S.: IT compliance of industrial information systems: Technology management and industrial engineering perspective. Journal of Systems and Software 80(10) (2007)
23. Merton, R.K.: Social Theory and Social Structure. Free Press, New York (1957)
24. Schapiro, T.: Compliance, Complicity, and the Nature of Nonideal Conditions. The Journal of Philosophy C(7), 329–355 (2003)

25. Currie, W.: Institutionalization of IT Compliance: A Longitudinal Study. In: Proceedings of the 29th International Conference on Information Systems (ICIS 2008), Paris, France (2008)
26. Ellis, D., Barker, R., Potter, S., Pridgeon, C.: Information Audits, Communication Audits and Information Mapping: A Review and Survey. International Journal of Information Management 13(2), 134–151 (1993)
27. Cialdini, R.B., Goldstein, N.J.: Social Influence: Compliance and Conformity. Annual Review of Psychology 55, 591–621 (2004)
28. Zimbardo, P.G., Leippe, M.R.: The Psychology of Attitude Change and Social Influence. McGraw-Hill, New York (1991)
29. Rowe, F.: Are Decision Support Systems Getting People to Conform? The Impact of Work Organization and Segmentation on User Behaviour in a French Bank. Journal of Information Technology 20, 103–116 (2005)
30. Levine, J.M., Resnick, L.B.: Social Foundations of Cognition. Annual Review of Psychology 44, 585–612 (1993)
31. The Open Group: TOGAF Version 9: The Open Group Architecture Framework (2009)
32. Alter, S., Wright, R.: Validating Work System Principles for Use in Systems Analysis and Design. In: Proceedings of ICIS 2010, St. Louis, USA (2010)
33. Boss, S.R., Kirsch, L.J., Angermeier, I., Shingler, R.A., Wayne Boss, R.: If Someone is Watching, I'll Do What I'm Asked: Mandatoriness, Control, and Information Security. European Journal of Information Systems 18, 151–164 (2009)
34. Merriam-Webster: Merriam-Webster Online Dictionary, http://www.merriam-webster.com/dictionary/ (Date of access: January 22, 2011)
35. Jones, T.M.: Ethical Decision Making by Individuals in Organizations: An Issue-Contingent Model. The Academy of Management Review 16(2) (1991)
36. Thiroux, J.P.: Ethics: Theory and Practice. Glencoe Publishing Co., Inc., Encino (1977)
37. Foorthuis, R.M., Steenbergen, M., van Mushkudiani, N., Bruls, W., Brinkkemper, S., Bos, R.: On Course, But Not There Yet: Enterprise Architecture Conformance and Benefits in Systems Development. In: Proceedings of ICIS 2010, St. Louis, Missouri, USA (2010)
38. Cleven, A., Winter, R.: Regulatory Compliance in Information Systems Research: Literature Analysis and Research Agenda. In: Enterprise, Business-Process and Information Systems Modeling. LNBIP, vol. 29, pp. 174–186 (2009)
39. Chayes, A., Chayes, A.H.: On Compliance. International Organization 47(2), 175–205 (1993)
40. Li, H., Sarathy, R., Zhang, J.: Understanding Compliance with Use Policy: An Integrative Model Based on Command-and-Control and Self-Regulatory Approaches. In: Proceedings of ICIS 2010, St. Louis, USA (2010)
41. Bulgurcu, B., Cavusoglu, H., Benbasat, I.: Information Security Policy Compliance: An Empirical Study of Rationality-Based Beliefs and Information Security Awareness. MIS Quarterly 34(3), 523–548 (2010)
42. Kraus, J.S., Coleman, J.L.: Morality and the Theory of Rational Choice. Ethics 97(4), 715–749 (1987)
43. Project Management Institute: A Guide to the Project Management Body of Knowledge: PMBOK Guide, 3rd edn. Project Management Institute, Inc., Pennsylvania (2004)
44. Botha, H., Boon, J.A.: The Information Audit: Principles and Guidelines. Libri 53, 23–38 (2003)
45. Stajkovic, A.D., Luthans, F.: A Meta-Analysis of the Effects of Organizational Behavior Modification on Task Performance. The Academy of Management Journal 40 (1997)
46. Kluger, A.N., DeNisi, A.: The Effect of Feedback Interventions on Performance. Psychological Bulletin 119(2), 254–284 (1996)

Preface INISET 2011

In conjunction with the
23rd International Conference on Advanced Information System Engineering (CAISE 2011)
21.6.2011, London, UK
http://cdl.ifs.tuwien.ac.at/iniset2011

Modern large-scale IS engineering projects typically involve the cooperation of a wide range of systems and tools that use different technical platforms and heterogeneous data models. Today's system integration technologies are suitable to bridge most of the technical and semantic gaps between these systems and tools. However, error-prone and time-consuming human work (e.g., manually copying information from one tool to another) is often needed to handle integration concerns at the interfaces of the different tools.

Typically each engineering role (e.g., electrical engineer or software engineer) has a tailored tool set that works on data relevant to the engineer's tasks. In order to support the data exchange between these engineering tools, an additional component is needed. In a typical process step in the engineering process an engineer exports data from his tool to a transfer document (e.g., PDF of data table) and integrates this document in a common repository accessible by a set of partner engineering tools. The major challenges here are on the one hand side in the identification and description of tool data that should be extracted from tools and made available to other tools. On the other hand side, the data integration itself poses another huge challenge, since it is often not possible to agree on a common data schema agreed on by all tools, and additionally all engineers working with the tools want to stick with their well-known terms and notations.

The goal of the workshop was the investigation of methods and techniques for the technical and semantic integration of multi-vendor (heterogeneous) engineering tools to improve effectiveness and efficiency of engineering projects. The workshop received submissions related to a reference model for the integration of complex tool landscapes, which can be used for reasoning, and about the integration of log file information for process mining using a genetic algorithm inspired technique.

Tool Integration beyond Wasserman

Fredrik Asplund, Matthias Biehl, Jad El-Khoury, and Martin Törngren

KTH, Brinellvägen 83, 10044 Stockholm, Sweden
{fasplund,biehl,jad,martint}@kth.se

Abstract. The typical development environment today consists of many specialized development tools, which are partially integrated, forming a complex tool landscape with partial integration. Traditional approaches for reasoning about tool integration are insufficient to measure the degree of integration and integration optimality in today's complex tool landscape. This paper presents a reference model that introduces dependencies between, and metrics for, integration aspects to overcome this problem. This model is used to conceive a method for reasoning about tool integration and identify improvements in an industrial case study. Based on this we are able to conclude that our reference model does not detract value from the principles that it is based on, instead it highlights improvements that were not well visible earlier. We conclude the paper by discussing open issues for our reference model, namely if it is suitable to use during the creation of new systems, if the used integration aspects can be subdivided further to support the analysis of secondary issues related to integration, difficulties related to the state dependency between the data and process aspects within the context of developing embedded systems and the analysis of non-functional requirements to support tool integration.

Keywords: Tool Integration, Model-based Tool Integration, Model-based Development, Integrated Development Environments.

1 Introduction

We work within the domain of embedded systems. In this domain there is traditionally a strong emphasis on ensuring system quality throughout the development process. This is due to embedded systems, through their close interaction with the environment in domains such as transportation and automation, have a strong presence of requirements on safety, availability, performance, etc. To ensure relevant expert knowledge development efforts are therefore often very much multidisciplinary, which leads to many stakeholders and a large diversity of tools. In development environments for embedded systems well functioning tool integration is needed to achieve seamless cooperation between tools to support the goals of the tool users. Due to it being unlikely that the whole system will be taken into account during every change done to improve tool integration this strive towards seamless cooperation typically leads to *islands of automation* (i.e. integrated groupings of tools). These islands support only specific parts of the *product life-cycle* and are heterogeneous environments that can vary drastically in the way they carry out tool integration.

We have used the principles that originated in [1] to build a reference model for reasoning about tool integration in these heterogeneous development environments (hereon after this is the *context* of which we speak), since we found the original principles insufficient for our work. The second section in this paper describes the reasons behind diverging from the original principles and how we do this by adding metrics and dependencies to the categories defined in [1].

The third section describes a method on approaching tool integration in our context. This is done both to exemplify our reference model and to allow for it being used in case studies.

In the fourth section we describe a case study.

In the fifth, and final, section we sum up our findings and point out the research directions in the greatest need of further effort.

2 Diverging from Wasserman

To facilitate the reasoning about tool integration in an existing system we need:

- A set of *categories* that divide an integration effort into parts that can be discussed in isolation. This is needed to structure the reasoning into manageable parts.
- A way to *measure* the degree of integration. This to needed to understand the state of the integration of a system.

- A notion of what *optimal* integration is. This is needed to know in which direction to move when improving a system.

[1] provides all of these, but before we settled on this set of principles we performed an extensive literature review to judge its current value. As will be apparent later in this section these principles figure prominently in literature throughout the last two decades, which is, in itself, promising. What made us finally decide was that [1] is being mentioned in literature reviews summarizing the most salient papers [2] and used as a reference to compare with when trying to build new research agendas for tool integration [3].

These principles are, however, not fully applicable in our context. In the following subsections we will discuss each of the requirements above as put forward in [1] and how we diverged from them when building our own reference model.

2.1 A Set of Categories

First, there are five widely accepted categories found in [1], namely the *control, data, platform, presentation* and *process integration* aspects (hereon after *aspects* is used to specifically indicate these five categories). For clarity we have listed the definitions of these aspects below. These definitions are in essence the same as the ones found in [1], with only minor updates to reflect our view of the discussion since the paper was published.

- Control integration is the degree to which tools can issue commands and notifications correctly to one another.

- Data integration is the degree to which tools can, in a meaningful way, access the complete data set available within the system of interest.
- Platform integration is the degree to which tools share a common environment.
- Presentation integration is the degree to which tools, in different contexts, can set up user interaction so that the tool input/and output is perceived correctly.
- Process integration is the degree to which interaction with tools can be supervised.

This decomposition is often used when structuring development efforts or case studies. Discussions often lead to which *technical mechanisms* (such as explicit message passing vs. message servers, etc., hereon after mentioned only as *mechanisms*) should be covered ([4]) or were used to address which integration aspect ([5], [6], [7], [8], [9], [10], [11]). These discussions often take a "broad" view of what the different aspects entail and discuss only the mechanisms actually used.

The aspects are used also in evaluative approaches. In [12] the aspects are used for categorizing, but combined with the notion of integration levels [13] to define the extent of the integration. An attempt is made to relate the different levels to several of the aspects. In the end this is again done by directly mapping different mechanisms to the different levels. In [14] all the aspects are pulled into one category where different groupings of mechanisms determine the level of integration.

So, while the aspects are widely used, they are used as vague categories. When exactness is needed the mechanisms are the preferred fallback. This is natural, since in [1] mechanisms are used as the measure of integration. Assigning different mechanisms to different aspects has with time also become the way of isolating the aspects from each other when exactness is needed.

2.2 A Way to Measure

There are two reasons why using mechanisms as the measure of integration is problematic for us. First, it does not allow discussing complex mechanisms that cover several aspects without the terminology becoming vague [15]. Secondly, this approach does not scale as the amount of mechanisms grows. Both of these problems are especially difficult in our context, since we deal with such heterogeneous environments. Therefore, to facilitate the reasoning about integration in our context, we have come up with a new *metric* for each of the aspects. These are described in the paragraphs below.

We define our metric of control integration as the number of unique services in a system. This we have picked up from the notation in [16] that the provision and use of services is the essence of this aspect. The possibility to achieve a high level of integration increases the finer the granularity of a systems services is.

We define our metric of data integration as the number of data interoperability sets in a system (a data interoperability set is a collection of syntax and semantic pairs that are related by links or transformations). This we have deduced from the discussions on data integration ([16], [17]) where data interoperability figures prominently. The possibility to achieve a high level of integration decrease when the number of data interoperability sets increase.

We define our metric of platform integration as the distinct platforms used in the system. The more platforms that have to be considered when analyzing the other aspects, the less possible it is to achieve a high level of integration.

We define our metric of presentation integration as the level to which users are forced to view or manipulate data in views they are not used to interact with. Most of the discussions about presentation integration are centered on the need for a common "look and feel" ([16], [18], [19]). However, in our context a specific user is usually not expected to use all of the tools present and thus a lot of different "look and feels" can exist without a major impact. The more data entities that are accessed in different views, pertaining to different development activities, the less possible it is to achieve a high level of integration.

We define our metric of process integration as the number of services that allow the end-user to know the state of the system when they signal completion (implicitly or explicitly). Process integration is mostly discussed in relation to frameworks put forward to facilitate the application of a process ([15], [20], [21], [22]), but we focus on process in its most simple form. The closer this metric comes to the total number of services, the better the possibility to achieve a high level of integration.

Our metrics, however, do not help us to isolate the aspects from each other. To be able to use them we also explicitly list the dependencies between the aspects.

The different services of control integration need to be reachable, which is a feature of platform integration. Data also needs to be reachable, which is a combined feature of control and platform integration. Control, data and platform integration limit the choices available for presentation integration. The logic of process integration will depend on control (process awareness) and data integration (state). These dependencies are visualized in *Figure 1*.

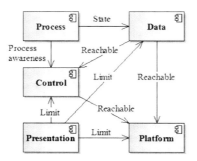

Fig. 1. Dependencies between aspects

We should treat the dependencies as entities in their own right and understand how they are handled. Then the aspects can be discussed and measured in isolation.

2.3 A Notion of Optimality

This leads us to the last issue, the notion of optimality. In [1] optimal tool integration is defined as when all tools agree on the mechanisms in regard to all aspects. This is of course true, but the price for and time to achieve such a homogeneous environment is likely to be large. We need a reference model which is able to point out what to focus on and in what order. The dependencies and our metrics work together to give our reference model this property.

The first indicator of optimality is the existence of as few dependencies *as possible* (process steps may for instance dictate a certain number of required dependencies). Fewer dependencies indicate both less need for and a greater possibility for integration between aspects. The structure of dependencies provides the order in which to deal with the aspects, from the aspect with no dependencies (platform) to the ones at the end of the dependency chains (presentation and process). A change at the beginning of a dependency chain will affect more entities than a change at the end of a chain. Our metrics are the secondary indicator of optimality.

3 A Method to Analyze Development Environments

To exemplify the reference model described in the previous section and to prepare the way for an upcoming case study we here describe a method for analyzing development environments. The description will make use of a fictional example of three islands of automation, shown in *Figure 2*.

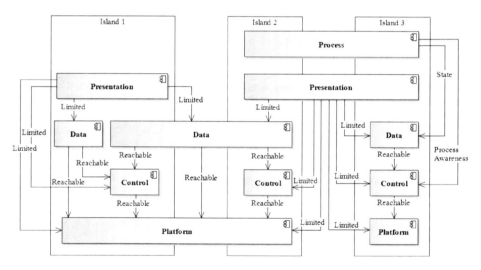

Fig. 2. A fictional example of three groupings of integrated tools illustrated through their integration aspects and dependencies

3.1 Identify the Member Sets and Their Dependencies

The first step is to identify all the sets of members of our metric sets (i.e. the sets of related data interoperability sets, the platforms used together, etc.) and their dependencies. *Figure 2* illustrates this.

The implications of the first three aspects (platform, control and data) in the dependency chain are obvious, but we note that they can be shared between islands. When none of these member sets are shared this implies a data artifact which is manually transferred between development steps (using a word processor or such). Less obvious is perhaps the sharing of a presentation and process member set. For a presentation member set this simply implies that the same abstractions are supported on both islands, perhaps by adhering to a standard (UML, etc.). For a process member set this implies that there is no possibility to identify distinct process states on the different islands, perhaps because the process is one of gradual refinement. The later could be equally well signaled by not listing a process member set (note the dependencies between control, data and process however, where there is none it implies that the completion of a process step cannot be known by the tools). We also note that data member sets can be shared even though control member sets are not; this simply implies the use of different data bases or such.

3.2 Reason about Aspects

The second step is to reason about the aspects on a more general level. This step is also undertaken to identify and investigate the non-functional requirements (available expertise, cost-effectiveness, etc.) that block the strive towards a homogeneous, non-fractured environment. If it is obvious that a large part of the non-functional requirements can be changed, then we can jump directly to reasoning about them and then start over afterwards (to avoid sub-optimization). Important issues not strictly dependent on the optimality of integration, such as data synchronization, interaction paradigms in use, etc, should also be discussed during this step.

3.3 Add Member Sets and Dependencies

The third step is to review missing member sets and dependencies, to see if something can be gained by introducing extra complexity. In our example this could consist of introducing separate, identifiable process steps on island 1 and 2.

3.4 Minimize the Number of Member Sets

The fourth step is to minimize the number of member sets, which entails both reducing the amount of dependencies and maximizing our metrics. In our example the former could consist of using the same database for all data on island 1 and 2, using the same platform set for all islands, etc. The later could consist of using fewer platforms on a particular island, increasing services that signal completion, etc.

3.5 Reason about Non-functional Requirements

The last step would be to reason about which of the existing non-functional requirements can be changed. A change in these opens up the possibility to reiterate the earlier steps to identify new opportunities for better tool integration. We have not found any suggestion on a structured approach to this, which is not surprising as for instance the lack of research into economical implications of tool integration have been noted in [3].

4 A Case Study

In this section we take a look at an industrial case study put forward by an industrial partner. The case aims to assess the impact of tool integration in a development environment aimed at multicore products and featuring HW/SW co-design. The product used to evaluate the development environment is a prototypical control system for an elevator. This control system is developed to be suitable for closed loop control where a number of sensor elements and actuators are connected by various interfaces. The system performs relevant actions depending on the input signals, the internal system state, the configurable logic, and operator commands. The development is to a large degree done according to the principles of *Model-based Development* (MBD).

Table 1. Original set of tools analyzed in the case study

Req. Engineering & Analysis	Design	Implementation	V&V
MS Word	Matlab/Simulink with RTW	Windriver Workbench	Matlab/ Simulink
Excel	Control Builder (1131)	Xlinx ISE	ModelSIM
MS Sourcesafe	MS Sourcesafe	MS Sourcesafe	MS Sourcesafe
PCVS	PCVS	PCVS	PCVS
	MS Word	GNU	
	Excel		

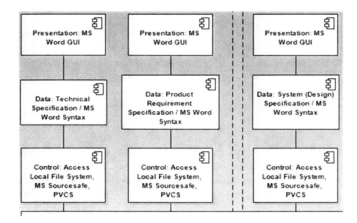

Fig. 3. Part of the visualization highlighting the data fragmentation

The total number of tools that figured in the original setup was 15. Out of these we limited ourselves to 11 (see *Table 1*), disregarding tools whose use was not clearly defined. The most obvious problem was the fragmented handling of data, both in regard to the data and control aspects (see *Figure 3*). In total we identified 12 separate data interoperability sets, all potentially handled separately from each other in 17 different development steps. The lack of process support was also obvious, since no process tool or integrated process support in the tools involved were used.

After identifying the original state of the development environment we analyzed it according to our method introduced in section 3 and came up with suggested improvements. However, there were few non-functional requirements defined for the case study. Therefore we had to evaluate our solution by contrasting it against suggested improvements by system engineers working at our industrial partner. The commonly identified improvements we analyzed in a first iteration consisting of relatively easily achieved integration improvements. Among the additional improvements we had identified we chose two (discussed further below) which will be the focus of further research and included them in a second iteration. Due to the lack of non-functional requirements we could not evaluate the worth of the remaining improvements highlighted by our reference model and removed them from the case study.

Due to the existence of a defined product life-cycle we could exchange the use of MS Word and Excel early in the development process with the use of Enterprise Architect. This allowed the start of MBD practices earlier than before. The use of EDA Simulator Link allowed us to link Hardware and Software Development. Together this shrank the total number of data interoperability sets to 4. The introduction of SVN and a MS Windows network similarly simplified the reachability of the data.

The first of the two improvements in the second iteration was to introduce traceability between requirements and design. This would shrink the total number of data interoperability sets even more, reducing error sources and increasing the possibility of verification and validation. The second improvement related to the lack of process support. This would entail introducing support for the process awareness dependency and moving the knowledge of the state of the process from inside the heads of the designers to the data.

4.1 Evaluating Our Reference Model

The critical issue is not the improvements of the development environment in the case study; it is how the use of our reference model compares to the use of [1] when searching for these improvements. To evaluate this we made use of integration weaknesses identified in the case study.

There were a total of 25 integration weaknesses identified by domain experts and developers using this tool chain on a daily basis. Note that 14 out of these 25 were not relevant for this comparison:

- 4 were domain issues such as the lack of a complete list of requirements. These were contained within the aspects in both reference models.
- 4 detailed secondary issues, i.e. workflow optimization, version control, etc.
- 1 was in direct conflict with a non-functional requirement we had identified.
- 5 were related to tools we had excluded from our analysis or were too vague to be analyzed.

7 of the remaining 11 integration weaknesses were equally visible in both reference models. Interestingly enough almost all of them related to data being handled inefficiently and in a segmented way. The remaining 4 were obvious in our reference model, but not when using the principles detailed in [1].

- While there was a development process, it was not rigorously defined. This relates to the lack of process state defined for the data, which we could identify since there was no state dependency for several of the process steps (see *Figure 4*).
- The process was customized by the different designers. This was identified like in the issue above, but due to missing process awareness dependencies.
- There was an unnecessary diversity in the tool solutions. The limitation dependency between presentation and data clearly identified the difference in tool boxes being used in the same development phase, but on different system parts (see *Figure 5*).
- Some data was not possible to access from relevant development steps, once again identified by the dependencies between presentation and data.

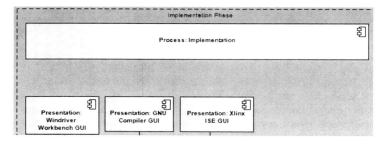

Fig. 4. Process step without dependencies to control or data

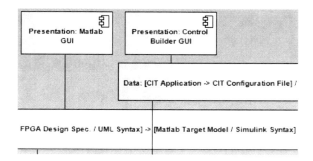

Fig. 5. Tool access related to relevant data

The completeness of our classification framework can be shown for this case study, as all 20 integration weaknesses could be identified and isolated to an aspect or dependency.

5 Discussion and Conclusion

We have found that we cannot apply the decomposition defined by Wasserman in [1] when reasoning about integration issues in the heterogeneous environments we work with. To solve this we have extended the set of principles in [1] into a new reference model. This model moves away from technical mechanisms as the measurement of integration. At a higher level of abstraction it instead focuses on reasoning around the dependencies between and metrics for integration aspects.

We have analyzed a limited case study to evaluate our reference model. For that case we found no sign of deterioration of the usefulness of the principles found in [1]. On the contrary, a number of integration weaknesses that would not have been obvious earlier were now highlighted. We were also able to break down and isolate all integration issues in the case study to individual aspects or dependencies.

Our ideas show promise, but there are a number of open questions. We think the most important of these are:

- Is our reference model suitable for decision support when building a new development environment? While the principles in [1] compare different mechanisms in an absolute way our reference model focuses on giving guidance on how to improve a system. To ensure the usefulness in this scenario our reference model should be applied to different architectures and platforms to identify how our metrics relate to them.
- The current metrics are very generic, while there are a number of secondary issues related to integration (data synchronization, data consistency, etc.). The later can be handled by checklists or multi-dimensional reference models, but these may limit users by only highlighting a subset of the relevant issues. Instead, some of the aspects could potentially be divided into parts if dependencies between these parts were identified. This could give guidance without limiting reasoning.
- In our experience, the identification of mechanisms to support the different aspects and dependencies is usually easy. It is however difficult for the state dependency between the data and process aspects, at least within the context of the development of embedded systems. This is due to difficulties in ascertaining the state of the data artifacts in relation to the development process. These difficulties are related to a diversity of issues, such as rules for artifact refinement, development metrics, requirements traceability, optimizing of different system aspects, etc. ForSyDe [23] is an example of a design methodology that takes this into account, but actual tool support is not easy to come by.

In addition there is one broader question that is not peculiar to our reference model, but which is critical to its use (as discussed in section 3):

- How non-functional requirements relate to tool integration is another very relevant topic which requires additional research. Are there separate aspects yet to be defined to support reasoning about these, and what are the involved dependencies in that case?

Acknowledgments

We thank all participants of the ARTEMIS iFEST project, who have given us continuous access to an additional breadth of expertise on and experience of software engineering in relation to the life-cycle of embedded systems.

Reference

1. Wasserman, A.L.: Tool Integration in Software Engineering Environments. In: Long, F. (ed.) Proceedings of the Software Engineering Environments: International Workshop on Environments, pp. 137–149. Springer, Chinon (September 1989)
2. Wicks, M.N.: Tool Integration within Software Engineering Environments: An Annotated Bibliography. HW-MACS-TR-0041. Heriot-Watt University, Edinburgh (2006)
3. Wicks, M.N., Dewar, R.G.: Controversy Corner: A new research agenda for tool integration. J. Syst. Software 80(9) (2007) ISSN: 0164-1212
4. Chen, M., Norman, R.J.: A Framework for Integrated CASE. IEEE Software 9(2) (1992) ISSN: 0740-7459
5. Gautier, B., et al.: Tool integration: experiences and directions. In: Proceedings of ICSE 1995. ACM, New York (1995) ISBN: 0-89791-708-1
6. Bao, Y., Horowitz, E.: A new approach to software tool interoperability. In: Proceedings of SAC 1996. ACM, New York (1996) ISBN: 0-89791-820-7
7. Best, C., Storey, M.-A., Michaud, J.: Designing a component-based framework for visualization in software engineering and knowledge engineering. In: Proceedings of SEKE 2002. ACM, New York (2001) ISBN: 1-58113-556-4
8. Wallace, E., Wallnau, K.C.: A situated evaluation of the Object Management Group's (OMG) Object Management Architecture (OMA). In: SIGPLAN Not., vol. 31(10). ACM, New York (1996) ISSN: 0362-1340
9. Reiss, S.P.: The Desert environment. ACM Trans. Softw. Eng. Methodol. 8(4) (1999) ISSN: 1049-331X
10. Mampilly, T., Ramnath, R., Irani, S.: PFAST: an eclipse-based integrated tool workbench for facilities design. In: Eclipse 2005: Proceedings of the 2005 OOPSLA Workshop on Eclipse Technology Exchange. ACM, New York (2005) ISBN: 1-59593-342-5
11. Biehl, M., DeJiu, C., Törngren, M.: Integrating safety analysis into the model-based development toolchain of automotive embedded systems. In: SIGPLAN Not., vol. 45(10). ACM, New York (2010) ISSN: 0362-1340
12. Cuthill, B.: Making sense of software engineering environment framework standards. In: StandardView. ACM, New York (1994) ISSN: 1067-9936
13. Brown, A.W., McDermid, J.A.: Learning from IPSE's mistakes. In: IEEE Software, vol. 9(2). IEEE Computer Society, Pittsburgh (1992) ISSN: 0740-7459
14. Baik, J., Boehm, B., Steece, B.M.: Disaggregating and Calibrating the CASE Tool Variable in COCOMO II. IEEE Trans. Softw. Eng. 28(11) (2002) ISSN: 0098-5589
15. Pohl, K., Weidenhaupt, K.: A contextual approach for process-integrated tools. SIGSOFT Softw. Eng. Notes 22(6) (1997) ISSN: 0163-5948
16. Thomas, I., Nejmeh, B.A.: Definitions of Tool Integration for Environments. IEEE Software 9(2), 29–35 (1992)
17. Holt, R.C., et al.: GXL: a graph-based standard exchange format for reengineering. Sci. Comput. Program. 60(2) (2006) ISSN: 0167-6423
18. Tilley, S.R.: The canonical activities of reverse engineering. Ann. Softw. Eng. 9(1-4) (2000) ISSN: 1022-7091
19. Stoeckle, H., Grundy, J., Hosking, J.: A framework for visual notation exchange. J. Vis. Lang. Comput. 16(3) (2005) ISSN: 1045-926X

20. Pohl, K., et al.: PRIME—toward process-integrated modeling environments. ACM Trans. Softw. Eng. Meth. 8(4) (1999) ISSN: 1049-331X
21. Endig, M., Jesko, D.: Engineering Processes - On An Approach To Realize A Dynamic Process Control. J. Integr. Des. Process Sci. 5(2) (2001) ISSN: 1092-0617
22. Sharon, D., Bell, R.: Tools that bind: creating integrated environments. IEEE Software 12(2) (March 1995)
23. Sander, I., Jantsch, A.: System modeling and transformational design refinement in ForSyDe. IEEE Transactions on Computer-Aided Design of Integrated Circuits and Systems 23(1) (2004)

Integrating Computer Log Files for Process Mining: A Genetic Algorithm Inspired Technique

Jan Claes and Geert Poels

Department of Management Information Systems and Operations Management
Faculty of Economics and Business Administration
Ghent University, Tweekerkenstraat 2, 9000 Ghent, Belgium
{jan.claes,geert.poels}@ugent.be

Abstract. Process mining techniques are applied to single computer log files. But many processes are supported by different software tools and are by consequence recorded into multiple log files. Therefore it would be interesting to find a way to automatically combine such a set of log files for one process. In this paper we describe a technique for merging log files based on a genetic algorithm. We show with a generated test case that this technique works and we give an extended overview of which research is needed to optimise and validate this technique.

Keywords: Tool-Support for Modeling, Business Process Modeling, Process Mining, Process Discovery, Log File Merging.

1 Introduction

When people are discussing organisational processes in a certain context they mostly want to find out how processes *should be*. A good starting point for such discussions is to discover processes as they *currently are*. This can be done by asking domain experts to model the organisation's current processes as they know or perceive them. This manual activity is, however, time-consuming [1] and subjective [1, 2].

Process discovery[1] techniques analyse actual process data, which can be found in computer log files, to automatically discover the underlying process. The main idea in process discovery techniques is that business processes are executed many times and thus log files contain many traces of the same process [2]. It is assumed that each trace contains the different events registered for one process execution in the correct order [3]. By searching for repeating patterns in these traces a general process flow can be discovered. An overview of process discovery and other process mining techniques can be found in [1-5].

Process mining techniques are developed to be applied to single computer log files. But many business processes are supported by different software tools and their

---

[1] The IEEE Task Force on Process Mining, consisting of major researchers and practitioners in the Process Mining field, decided to reserve the term *process mining* as an umbrella term for all techniques on process data and to use the term *process discovery* for techniques to reveal processes out of process data. (http://www.win.tue.nl/ieeetfpm/).

executions are by consequence recorded into multiple log files. Consider for example a back-end IT support process where support actions are logged through a ticketing system and changes to program code and documentation are logged using a version control system. Part of the process is registered in a first log file and the other part is registered in a second log file. We are not aware of any *automated* way to use both files at once for process mining in general and process discovery in particular.

Therefore, it would be interesting to find a way to automatically combine such a set of log files before process discovery techniques are applied. In this paper we describe a technique for merging log files containing different traces of the same process executions based on a genetic algorithm. Genetic algorithms are search heuristics inspired by natural selection and the principle of survival of the fittest [6]. We implemented our log file merging algorithm in the latest version of ProM [3], a well-known academic process mining tool, and used simulated test data to demonstrate its effectiveness for process discovery.

We start with a description of process discovery and its assumptions in Section 2, followed by a description of the research problem and the assumptions we make for its solution. Our genetic algorithm inspired technique for merging log files is presented in Section 3. The proof of concept application using a generated test case is presented in Section 4. To end the paper, an extended overview is given of which further research is needed to optimise and validate our solution in Section 5 and a conclusion is provided in Section 6.

2 Problem Description

2.1 Process Discovery

Process discovery is based on a number of assumptions [2]. First, process data needs to be available somehow, somewhere. Second, it should be possible to distinguish data from different executions and group the logged event data in traces (one trace per execution). Similarly, it has to be possible to distinguish events and therefore it is assumed that different events have different names [2]. However, an approach to discover processes with duplicate tasks, where different logged events have the same name, can be found in [7]. Third, the order of logged events should be clear [3], but it is not always strictly necessary to have exact timestamps (e.g. the Little Thumb technique does not use timestamps [8]). Of course, some process discovery techniques make more assumptions like *all data should be logged (completeness)* or *there should be no errors or noise in the logged data (correctness)* [5].

Given these assumptions it is possible to compose log files consisting of a group of traces which themselves consist of groups of ordered events. This is the starting point for process mining techniques [2]. In this paper, we focus mainly on process discovery techniques. These techniques look for repeating patterns in the traces of the log file. If an event A is immediately followed by an event B in every trace of the log, it can be assumed that in the underlying process task B always has to follow task A. This results in drawing an edge between A and B in the model of the discovered process. If A is in a number of traces immediately followed by B but in all other traces immediately preceded by B, it can be assumed that A and B are in parallel (i.e. and-split). If A is in a number of traces immediately followed by B (but not by C) and in all other traces immediately followed by C (but not by B), it can be assumed that after A comes B or C (i.e. or-split). This simplified example describes the basics of the α-algorithm [9], which is the basic theoretical algorithm for process discovery.

2.2 Merging Log Files

The availability of data on process executions is a logical assumption for automatic process discovery. Furthermore, it is also clear that if parts of the process are handled manually and these manual activities are not registered, it is almost impossible to recover these steps in the process with process discovery techniques. In some cases one could guess a hidden task in the discovered process [5]. But what if the process to be discovered is supported by multiple computer-based tools or systems and therefore parts of the process are recorded in another log file?

Consider for example the back-end IT support process in Fig. 1. Two types of support requests could reach the back-end unit: requests for change (RFC) and requests for information (RFI). All white tasks are supported by a ticketing system (e.g. Omnitracker) and all gray tasks can be discovered in the logging of a version control system (e.g. Subversion).

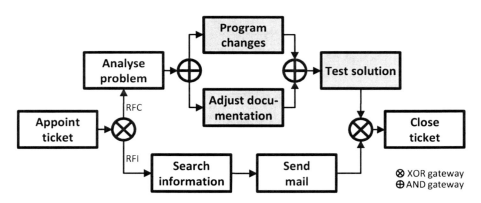

Fig. 1. Example process model for a back-end IT support process

All current process discovery (or even process mining) techniques start from a single event log file containing traces of ordered events that register the process executions. If execution traces are split up in different log files, then existing process discovery techniques can still be used provided that the different log files containing partial evidence of the process executions are first merged into one more complete log file.

We focus our solution on tackling the problem of one process whose executions are being logged in two log files, abstracting from more complex problems that are variations to this basic problem (e.g. more than two log files, more than one process). In other words, both log files contain partial data about executions of the same process. For the example process of Fig. 1, the execution of the white tasks is registered in one log and the execution of the gray tasks is registered in the other log. Our solution firstly links together the traces of both logs that belong to the same process execution and secondly merges the events of linked traces from both log files into one trace in the merged log.

In the solution proposed in this paper we make two additional assumptions. First, for the linking of traces in both logs we assume that the second log contains no process start events. This means that all traces from the second log are initiated in the first log. In our opinion, this assumption makes sense if processes have only one starting point (that is always supported by the same software and is thus logged in the same file). The linking problem is then reduced to linking each trace from the second log to only one trace from the first log containing the start event of the same process execution. This assumption includes that we know which of both logs is the first (containing all process start events). In the example shown in Fig. 1, the log maintained by the ticketing system contains the registered start events of the back-end IT support process executions. Hence, the problem reduces to linking each trace in the log of the version control system to one trace in the log of the ticketing system.

Second, for the merging of the events from the linked traces we assume that reliable and comparable timestamps for all events are available (we consider missing or incorrect time information to be noise).

- Timestamps are *reliable* if the events are logged when they occur (e.g. if a worker registers a phone call two hours late, the timestamp will probably not be reliable) and if they are logged correctly (e.g. not the case if the software itself has errors or if the operating system provides inaccurate time information to the software).
- Timestamps are *comparable* if their precision is (almost) equal (this is not the case if in one log file only dates were recorded and the other has millisecond precise time information) and if they are in the same time zone (or can be converted to the same time zone).

If these two conditions are met, we can simply order events from linked traces in chronological order. This makes sense because, given our assumptions, this is the order in which the events actually occurred. Hence, in our solution description we focus on the linking problem to find out which traces in both logs belong together.

3 Solution Design

Many factors can indicate whether traces from two logs relate to the same process execution (see 3.2.2). Instead of focussing on one such factor we incorporated multiple factors in our solution. The more elements indicate that two traces should be linked, the more certain we are that they in fact relate to the same process execution. To design our solution we looked for similar problems in other domains and found our inspiration in the principles of genetic algorithms.

3.1 Genetic Algorithms

Genetic algorithms are inspired by nature and rely on Darwin's principle of "survival of the fittest" [10]. A population of multiple solutions to a certain problem evolves from generation to generation with the goal to be optimised through generations.

A genetic algorithm starts with a totally random initial population. Each next generation is constructed with bits and pieces of the previous generation using crossover and mutation operators. Crossover means that random parts of two solutions are swapped and mutations are random changes in a solution. Mutation is needed to assure that lost parts can be recovered. To quantify the quality of solutions in a generation, a fitness function is used. Because the fitness score determines the chance to be selected as input for a next generation of solutions, consecutive generations tend to get better in every step (i.e. survival of the fittest). The algorithm ends when a termination condition is met. This is mostly when a certain measurable degree of correctness is achieved or when no more optimisation is established. The steps of a genetic algorithm can be summarised as: (i) initialisation, followed by a repeating sequence of (ii) selection based on the fitness function, (iii) reproduction using crossover and mutation, and ended by (iv) a termination condition.

For more information about genetic algorithms we refer to [6].

3.2 Genetic Algorithm Inspired Technique for Merging Computer Log Files

We start with a random combination of links between the traces contained in both logs. Then in each step we make random mutations by changing the links. We calculate the fitness score before and after all mutations of each step. We continue with the original version if the fitness diminished, otherwise we continue with the new version.

To compare with genetic algorithms, our solution can be regarded as a genetic algorithm with a solution population of size one. Only one combination of links (i.e. one solution) is used as a base for finding an optimal solution. Selection for reproduction and crossover are useless if there is only one element in the population. We end up with only initialisation, mutations evaluated by a fitness function and termination. The same simplified version of genetic algorithms is used for timetabling in Genetic Algorithm for Time Tabling (GATT) [11]. The expert reader will notice that because of the simplifications this technique is no real genetic algorithm anymore and for that reason we call it a *genetic algorithm inspired technique*.

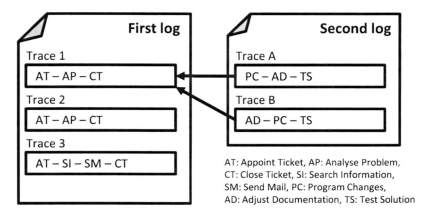

Fig. 2. Linking second traces (traces from the second log) to first traces (from the first log)

3.2.1 Initialisation

Because we assume each second trace (each trace in the second log) was initiated in the first log, we have to link each second trace to only one first trace (trace in the first log). We have to loop over all second traces and assign each of them to a random first trace. We do not assume that each first trace can initiate only one second trace which means that multiple second traces can be linked to the same first trace (see Fig. 2).

3.2.2 The Fitness Function

In each step we compare the fitness score before and after mutations to decide which version to continue with. As a result of not knowing the actual relation between the two log files we start from working hypotheses describing specific conditions that could indicate that two traces should be connected. We treat these different factors indicating traces from the two logs should be linked as rules of thumb, assuming that the combination of links between the traces of two logs with the highest combined score for all these factors is probably better than other combinations. Therefore we defined the fitness function such that the fitness score is the sum of the individual scores for each factor we identified (see Formula 1):

$$f = w_1 \sum STI_i + w_2 \sum TO_i + w_3 \sum EAV_i + w_4 \sum NLT_i + w_5 \sum TD_i . \quad (1)$$

If more information about the relation between the two logs is known, weights could be configured by the user to reflect the relative importance of each factor (w_1-w_5). The following factors were taken into account when defining our fitness function:

Same trace id (STI_i)

A first factor to indicate that two traces belong together is if they have the same trace id (i.e. the process execution is consistently identified in both logs). In this case the problem is rather trivial, because it's almost certain how to merge the two log files. But this is no reason to exclude the factor from our fitness function. If, exceptionally, two traces with the same trace id do not belong together (e.g. a customer number that matches with an invoice number), then another solution should score higher due to the other factors of the fitness function.

Trace order (TO_i)

Because we assume all second traces are originated in the first log, the first event of the second trace should occur after the first event of the first trace (given our assumption regarding the reliability and comparability of event timestamps). All trace links that violate this rule make the fitness score decrease. We call this a punishment score and implement this simply by adding a negative score to the overall fitness score (i.e. $TO_i \leq 0$).

Equal attribute values (EAV_i)

In many processes a reference number or code is used throughout the entire process. This is most probably the trace id. But maybe other numbers are passed from event to event. If this number is logged, we should search for matching values of event attributes. Note that attribute names do not need to correspond. The name for this number can be different in both logs (e.g. "invoice number" and "reference number") and matching attribute names is more challenging [12]. Also note that some attribute values may have equivalents in lots of traces (for example status *completed*). This would make barely any difference between different solutions, because almost all possible solutions would score higher.

Number of linked traces (NLT_i)

Although multiple second traces can be linked to the same first trace, we consider this to be reasonably exceptional and therefore give a punishment score (i.e. $NLT_i \leq 0$) for each additional second trace linked to the same first trace. As with almost all other factors this is only an indication. If a lot of other factors indicate that multiple second traces belong to the same first trace, the fitness function must be defined such (e.g. by adapting the weights of the different factors) that their combined score is more positive than the (negative) punishment score for this factor. In this way it is still possible, but less probable, to end up with different second traces for the same first trace.

Time distance (TD_i)

This factor focuses on the actual distance in time between two traces (i.e. the difference between the time stamps of the first events of both traces). If two second traces are candidates to be linked to a same first trace and the fitness score for all other factors is equal for both solutions, we think the one with the least time distance to the first trace is more likely to be the correct matching partner. Because we have no idea about the correct time distance we did not score the actual distance, but we simply add to the score if time distance decreased (i.e. $TD_i > 0$) and subtract to the score if time distance increased (i.e. $TD_i < 0$).

3.2.3 Mutation and Termination

We can be short about the remaining properties of our implementation of the genetic inspired algorithm. In each step we select a certain fixed amount of second traces and link them with another random first trace (this is a mutation). If the fitness function score at the end of this step is higher than before, we continue with this new link combination, otherwise we revert to the previous combination. As we are not (yet) searching for the fastest implementation of this algorithm we also use a fixed number of steps. There is no real termination condition. This can of course be changed later. When at a given point no progress is made in the last steps, it is perhaps better to stop the algorithm earlier.

4 Proof of Concept

We have tested our technique with a simulated example. The benefit of using simulation is that the correct solution (i.e. the process to be discovered) is known. Another advantage is that properties like time difference or noise can be controlled.

4.1 Example Model

Our example of a back-end IT support process (Fig. 3) is based on the same example model as in [5]. We generated two log files with 100 random executions of the process where the executions of tasks AT, AP, SI, SM and CT were logged in a first log file and the executions of tasks PC, AD and TS in the second file. We initially did not include noise, the executions did not overlap in time, and there was no structural unbalance in choosing one or the other path first for AND-split or selecting the path to be followed for an OR-split. Time differences between consecutive events were also random.

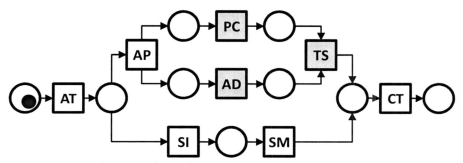

AT: Appoint Ticket, AP: Analyse Problem, PC: Program Changes, AD: Adjust Documentation
TS: Test Solution, SI: Search Information, SM: Send Mail, CT: Close Ticket

Fig. 3. Process model for our back-end IT support process example

4.2 Technical Implementation

We implemented our algorithm in the latest version of ProM [3] (ProM 6), a well-known academic process mining tool developed by the Process Mining Group at Eindhoven University of Technology. This tool can be downloaded from http://prom.sf.net.

Genetic algorithms can be optimised by narrowing down the candidates in each random choice [6]. Instead of starting with a totally random initial linking combination, we start with a combination where each second trace is linked to a first trace with which it has the highest individual fitness score (i.e. fitness score for this particular link rather than for the entire solution of links between the traces of both logs). We also think some factors of the fitness function (like same trace id and trace order) are stronger than others. Therefore we used different weights for individual factors. Finally, because we want to improve our solution in every step, we do not select random traces for change in the mutation step. Instead we randomly select a factor and then select a random trace for which we can improve this factor.

4.3 Tests and Results

We tested log files for 100 sample model executions with our implemented log file merging algorithm using 100,000 steps. We included the following attributes in our test logs: name, originator, status, and time[2]. Because there is no unbalance in choosing paths in the OR-split, the second log ends up with about 50 traces. For a simple example of 100 generated traces with no noise, no overlapping traces, and matching trace ids the result is shown in Fig. 4 (after mining with Heuristic Miner [8]). A log-to-log comparison shows that all traces were correctly linked and merged between both files.

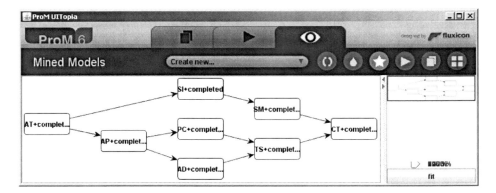

Fig. 4. Resulting model after merging and process discovery with Heuristic Miner [8]

In a second test run, we generated files for the same model with different properties:

- We added noise in the same way as described in [8]. One of four options is randomly selected: (i) delete minimum one and up to one third of events from the beginning of a trace, (ii) from the middle of a trace, (iii) from the end of a trace, or (iv) switch places of two random events in a trace. The noise percentage determines the chance a trace is influenced by noise in one of the four ways. We tested with 0, 10, 20 and 50% noise.
- Another property we varied is overlap. The overlap percentage determines the chance of each execution to start during the previous execution. With 10% overlap 10% of traces started before the previous one ended. We did tests with 0, 10, 20, 50, 75 and 100% overlap.
- Finally, we repeated each test with a set of log files where trace numbers did never match.

The results of our tests can be derived from Table 1 (for matching id numbers) and Table 2 (for non-matching id numbers). When traces run partly in parallel (overlap > 0%) and no matching trace numbers exist, there seems to be too little information left to find a proper solution.

We also performed tests with other amounts of process executions and with other simple models. Due to a page restriction we do not describe any of these other tests in this paper, but the test outcomes were similar to the results in Table 1 and Table 2.

---

[2] This corresponds to these extensions of XES ("an XML-based standard for event logs") used in ProM: concept:name (name), org:resource (originator), lifecycle:transition (status), and time:timestamp (time). (http://www.xes-standard.org/)

Table 1. Test results for matching ids with varying noise and overlap percentage (incorrect links in relation to total links identified)

Matching id	Overlap						
Noise	0	10	20	50	75	100	Mean
0	1/59	1/55	0/50	0/54	0/50	3/45	2%
10	0/49	0/43	0/62	0/50	0/46	0/54	0%
20	0/48	0/48	0/49	0/53	0/45	0/38	0%
50	0/46	0/54	0/64	0/56	0/41	0/49	0%
Mean	0%	0%	0%	0%	0%	2%	0%

Table 2. Test results for non-matching ids with varying noise percentage, overlap percentage (incorrect links in relation to total links identified)

No matching id	Overlap						
Noise	0	10	20	50	75	100	Mean
0	0/51	7/50	4/42	12/48	19/56	36/46	27%
10	0/57	1/44	0/49	10/57	14/46	27/50	17%
20	0/59	2/51	8/50	7/46	13/53	23/50	18%
50	1/47	6/53	1/47	13/56	16/46	27/50	21%
Mean	1%	8%	7%	20%	31%	58%	21%

5 Discussion

In the previous sections we presented our technique. In this section we discuss (i) performance of our solution, (ii) the assumptions we made, and (iii) the factors we used in the fitness function.

Performance of our implementation depends on m x $(2n_1 + 2n_2)$ = 100,000 x (100+100+50+50) = 3×10^7 sets of instructions to be executed (where m is the number of steps and n_1 and n_2 are the number of traces in the log files). If we would use a technique that looks for all possible solutions for merging each second trace to a first trace, $n_1^{n2} = 100^{50} = 10^{100}$ options should be checked (permutation with repetition of 50 elements out of a set of 100). This relates to the number of options in our solution as 3×10^{87} years to 4 minutes (about the mean time our algorithm ran in our tests). Off course, there may still be better solutions, we only claim to have found an optimal solution with an *acceptable* performance (for our example case).

Process mining is based on a number of assumptions (see 2.1). We made two additional assumptions (see 2.2). First, we assume the first log contains all process start events and we know which log is first. We expect to be able to drop this assumption later on.

The second assumption we made is the presence (and reliability and comparability) of event timestamps. We use this for matching traces and we really need this for merging traces. The only way to find out in which order events happened is to look at some time information. We think data is logged for different reasons, but is mostly concerned about what, who and when. Therefore in our opinion in most cases time information is logged, so the assumption focuses on reliability and comparability.

Whereas our assumption may seem narrower than the assumption of correct order in process discovery, we think to have widened the possibilities of process discovery because in our opinion time information is mostly available but getting all process data in one log file is more challenging.

We still need to complete research on which factors and weights to use. Maybe some factors should be omitted, maybe others should be added. For example one factor we are experimenting with is time difference. We now assume the difference between first events in first and second traces should be minimal, but we are not sure this assumption is totally correct. A better assumption could be that time difference between all first and second traces should be alike, whether it is a large difference or a small one. Mathematically this is translated into a minimisation of the standard deviation of all time differences of a combination.

We also relied on assumptions made in other process mining research like for instance the perspective on noise. In [8], for example, noise was incorporated as one of four options. One of these options is to "interchange two random chosen events" ([8], p13), but we are not convinced that this type of noise is common. We think an event could be logged too late, but it does not seem logical that another event would be logged earlier instead. We plan on looking into this kind of assumptions to verify applicability.

6 Conclusion

In this paper we presented a possible solution to still be able to use process mining techniques if process data is recorded in multiple log files. By merging the log files into a new log file all existing process mining techniques could still be used. Our technique is inspired by genetic algorithms and uses random operations which are evaluated by a combined score (see 3.1). We presented a possible set of factors to build up this score (see 3.2.2) and implemented the technique in the ProM tool (see 4.2). As a minimal form of evaluation we tested the implementation with generated files for a given model. We claim to have shown for at least one example case that this technique works and the test results are quite good (see 4.3). Lots of research has to be done to properly validate the technique and its implementation. We tried to give an overview and extended discussion of which elements need further research (see Section 5).

References

1. Rozinat, A., Mans, R.S., Song, M., Van Der Aalst, W.M.P.: Discovering Simulation Models. Information Systems 34, 305–327 (2009)
2. Van Der Aalst, W.M.P., Van Dongen, B.F., Herbst, J., Maruster, L., Schimm, G., Weijters, A.J.M.M.: A Survey of Issues and Approaches. Data & Knowledge Engineering 47, 237–267 (2003)
3. Van Dongen, B.F., De Medeiros, A.K.A., Verbeek, H.M.W., Weijters, A.J.M.M., Van Der Aalst, W.M.P.: The ProM Framework: A New Era in Process Mining Tool Support. In: Ciardo, G., Darondeau, P. (eds.) ICATPN 2005. LNCS, vol. 3536, pp. 444–454. Springer, Heidelberg (2005)

4. Van Der Aalst, W.M.P.: Challenges in Business Process Analysis, p. 27. Springer, Heidelberg (2008)
5. Van Der Aalst, W.M.P., Weijters, A.J.M.M.: Process Mining: A Research Agenda. Computers in Industry 53, 231–244 (2004)
6. Goldberg, D.E.: Genetic Algorithms in Search, Optimization, and Machine Learning. Addison-Wesley, Reading (1989)
7. Li, J., Liu, D., Yang, B.: Process Mining: Extending α-Algorithm to Mine Duplicate Tasks in Process Logs. In: Chang, K.C.-C., Wang, W., Chen, L., Ellis, C.A., Hsu, C.-H., Tsoi, A.C., Wang, H. (eds.) APWeb/WAIM 2007. LNCS, vol. 4537, pp. 396–407. Springer, Heidelberg (2007)
8. Weijters, A.J.M.M., Van Der Aalst, W.M.P.: Rediscovering Workflow Models from Event-based Data Using Little Thumb. Integrated Computer-Aided Engineering 10, 151–162 (2003)
9. Weijters, A.J.M.M., Van Der Aalst, W.M.P.: Process Mining: Discovering Workflow Models from Event-based Data. In: Belgium-Netherlands Conference on Artificial Intelligence, pp. 283–290. Citeseer (2001)
10. Darwin, C.: On the Origin of Species by Means of Natural Selection, or the Preservation of Favoured Races in the Struggle for Life. Murray, John, London (1869)
11. Ross, P., Hart, E., Corne, D.: Genetic algorithms and timetabling, pp. 755–771. Springer-Verlag New York, Inc., New York (2003)
12. Wang, J.R., Madnick, S.E.: The inter-database instance identification problem in integrating autonomous systems. Data Engineering, 46–55 (2002)

Preface IWSSA 2011

Diverse interacting information and software systems are needed by cities conducting large-scale events such as the Olympics, Worldcup Football, and the like. Some of these systems monitor and control utilities required for hosting the events including electricity, water supply, gas supply, etc., while others are used to monitor and control systems with wider geographic spread such as air traffic, sea and river traffic, and highway transportation systems. However, all these systems must be designed to operate in a coordinated and collaborative manner so that event organizers receive latest scenarios of the environment of the games and take appropriate actions which may include change of venue, postponement, or even cancellation of events. This is particularly relevant in view of threats to life and society in modern times. However, diverse information systems that monitor and control critical infrastructures do not collaborate by accident: collaboration, interoperability, reliability, and security need to be designed into such systems. Since architecture development is usually the first step in system or software design, designers need to address these non-functional requirements, which are sometimes conflicting or synergistic, in the architectures themselves. In particular, non-functional requirements and constraints take special relevance due to the new environments in which the systems themselves have to operate, i.e., some kind of combination of internet and pervasive systems.

The papers included in the proceedings address the explicit connection between requirements and architecture models through innovative techniques, methodologies, frameworks and processes. In particular, the selected papers cover important quality attributes of software systems ranging from users' requirements (security, reliability, usability, collaboration, etc.) to developers' requirements (reusability, change management and evolution, maintainability, scalability, etc.). These papers highlight what appears to be a clear trend in recent technologies (model-driven approaches, aspects, services, and business process modeling) towards developing quality architectures along different phases in the software lifecycle, namely: requirements modeling, design, implementation, validation, assessment, and maintenance.

Most papers include both theoretical content and real case studies for systems with varying scopes and applications, including enterprise systems, collaborative systems, mobile systems, and ubiquitous systems. We hope they will contribute to a successful workshop with the audience, presenters, and researchers participating in mutually beneficial discussion. We sincerely hope that the workshop will be an appropriate forum where the sharing of knowledge and experiences about system/software architectures promotes new advances in both research and development. We also hope that readers enjoy the papers selected for the proceedings.

This will be the 9th in the series of International Workshop on System/Software Architectures (IWSSA'11), and for the first time it is being held in association with the International Conference on Advanced Information Systems Engineering (CAiSE'11). As in the previous versions of this workshop, the present edition also received an excellent response with a total of twenty three abstract and paper submissions out of which, on the basis of reviews, seven papers were finally selected as full papers and three as short papers. This fact does not belittle the quality of the rest of the papers as the selection process was extremely competitive because of required acceptance rate. Actually, rejected papers were also well rated. We regret that we could not accommodate more papers, but we hope to be able to receive submissions of improved versions to subsequent editions of IWSSA.

We would like to sincerely thank CAiSE workshops chairs, Óscar Pastor and Camille Salinesi, for their constant help and support, IWSSA'11 Program Committee members for their excellent work and invaluable support during the review process, and most importantly authors of the papers for their very interesting and high quality contributions, which makes possible to organize successfully this workshop series every year.

April 2011

Lawrence Chung, University of Texas at Dallas (USA)
Kawtar Benghazi, University of Granada (Spain)
Nary Subramanian, University of Texas at Tyler (USA)
Manuel Noguera, University of Granada (Spain)

Ontology-Based Architectural Knowledge Representation: Structural Elements Module

David Ameller and Xavier Franch

Universitat Politècnica de Catalunya, Barcelona, Spain
{dameller,franch}@essi.upc.edu

Abstract. In the last years, Architectural Knowledge (AK) has emerged as a discipline for making explicit architects' knowledge and architectural decision-making processes. As a consolidated formalism for the representation of conceptual knowledge, ontologies have already been proposed for AK representation. Aligning with this trend, we are currently developing an ontology for AK representation named Arteon. The ontology is articulated in four modules and in this paper we focus on one of them, the structural module, that defines the elements necessary to build a software architecture. Therefore, we clarify the concepts of architectural view, framework and element, show their relationships, its accurate definition is required to drive architectural design in a prescribed way.

Keywords: Architectural Knowledge, Software Architecture, Architectural view, Ontology.

1 Introduction

The most important task of an architect is making Architectural Design Decisions (ADDs) [1]. In the current practice, architects made ADDs based on their experience and intuition which may hamper understandability, traceability, and reuse of ADDs. Even, this practice could be an important source of design errors. These errors at the preliminary stages of the software development, as many times has been said, are translated into high development costs, or they may simply imply the worst scenario, a project failure. One of the major reasons that bring us this situation is that Architectural Knowledge (AK) only resides in architects' minds, they do not normally document their decisions, nor the reasoning and alternatives considered either. On the research community side, during the last two decades, software architecture has evolved from just a structural representation in the 90s', to a huge methodological approach, and currently to a decisional centric approach [2].

All these approaches had in common one thing, the necessity to materialize AK. One benefit is that we could share and reuse this knowledge in different software projects or in a community of architects. In our case, we are going one step forward, we want to use this knowledge to guide and facilitate architects' the decision making processes. Eventually, it could bring more reliability to the process by surfacing new alternatives that were not initially considered by the

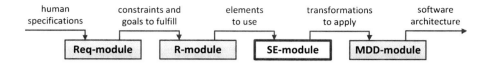

Fig. 1. Relationships between the four Arteon modules

architect. The natural evolution would be the integration of this functionality inside a Model-Driven Development (MDD) [3] process.

Among other alternatives we have chosen to use an ontology to represent AK. Ontologies have been successfully used in other domains where there was a necessity of knowledge representation (e.g., software engineering, artificial intelligence, semantic web, biomedicine, etc.). Our ontology, Arteon, is composed of four modules: Req-module, representing software requirements knowledge; R-module, reasoning and decision-making knowledge; SE-module, structural elements, views and frameworks knowledge; and MDD-module, MDD related knowledge. Although interconnected (see Fig. 1), the four modules are loosely coupled and highly cohesive enough to be used or reused separately.

The rest of this paper is divided in: related work in section 2, an overview of the SE-module in section 3, and the conclusions and future work in section 4.

2 Related Work

The essential role of ADDs in the architecture design process has been widely recognized [1,2,4]. Arteon may be considered a step towards this consolidation, but our position is that the decisional concepts should be isolated from the architectural elements, and in this way we can improve two kinds of knowledge independently. ADDs ontologies are more likely to be compared with the R-module instead of the SE-module that is the focus of this paper.

Few works use ontologies as the mechanism to represent the architectural knowledge focusing on the structural elements of the architecture:

- Akerman and Tyree [5] presented an ontology-based approach focused on ADDs but also includes part of the ontology, called "archirecture assets" which is simillar to the structural elements presented in this work, but their ontology lacks of key concepts such as view and style.
- ArchVoc [6] is an ontology for representing the architectural vocabulary. The terminology is classified in three main categories: architectural description (e.g., frameworks, views, and viewpoints), architectural design (patterns, styles, methodologies, etc.), and architectural requirements (non-functional requirements, and scenarios). Most of these concepts are present in Arteon, the non-appearing concepts such as anti-pattern do not have a direct use in the architectural design which is the final objective of Arteon.
- Pahl et al. [7] presented an ontology that focused on components and connectors as a general way to describe architectural styles. This ontology uses

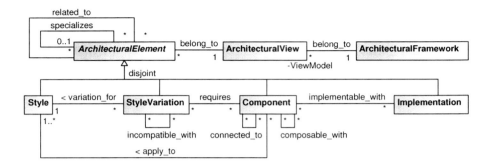

Fig. 2. SE-module conceptual model

a precise notation because the final objective is to provide a modeling language for architectural styles. The knowledge represented in Arteon could be used to produce models, but it is not intended to be used as a modeling language.

3 Arteon: SE-Module

In this section we focus on the SE-module of Arteon. In Fig. 2 we present the concepts of this module and the relationships among them, whilst in Fig. 3 we show an example of these concepts in a typical web-based application scenario. Most of these concepts are already known concepts in this community. But in fact we may find both minor discrepancies and major misconceptions in their use, therefore we should define them carefully (whenever possible, we simply adhere to some existent and widely-accepted definition). These are the most important concepts in the SE-module:

Architectural view. Representation of the whole system from the perspective of a related set of concerns [8]. Views are useful in large and complex architectures where trying to understand the whole architecture in a single representation could be, at least, a difficult task. In the example (Fig. 3) there are 4 views: logical, development, deployment, and platform. Views can be used to show the static parts of the system, such as the ones in the example, or behavioral aspects, such as the process view defined in [9]. Our ontology can be used for both static and behavioral views, but our current work is more oriented to the static views.

Architectural framework. Defines a set of views to represent the architecture, this set of views is also called *view model*. Examples of architectural frameworks are: RM-ODP [10] and "4+1" view model [9]. In the example (Fig. 3) we use a variation of the "4+1" view model that takes into account the platform view. Other frameworks such as TOGAF [11] and Zachman [12] are partially supported because they define the full structure of an enterprise and we are only interested in the software part.

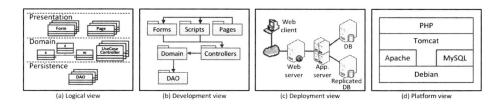

Fig. 3. Example of the representable knowledge in SE-module

Architectural element. Abstract concept that denotes the kinds of elements that architects may decide to use in their architectural solutions. We consider four kinds of elements: styles, style variations, components, and implementations (see next definitions for particularities). All kinds of elements share some characteristics: they can be specialized (e.g., 3-layer style is a specialization of layered style). They can establish relationships or dependencies with other elements from other views. Looking at Fig. 3 we can see some examples: Tomcat from the platform view is related to the application server, DAO classes are related to the DAO package, the scripts package is related to PHP, etc. Dependencies are especially useful to ensure the consistency of the architecture when a change is made.

Style. Architectural styles (also known as architectural patterns) were widely defined by [13] and [14]: "An architectural pattern is determined by a set of element types, a topological layout of the elements indicating their interrelation-ships, a set of semantic constraints and a set of interaction mechanisms". Styles should not be confused with design patterns, styles define the whole structure of an architecture for a concrete architectural view, while a design pattern could be applied to one or more parts of the architecture (normally in the same architectural view). In the example: in the logical view we use a 3-layer style; in the development view we use a web application style; in the deployment view we use a specialized client-server style, database and application server separated [15]; and in the platform view we use a stack solution style.

Style variation. In practice, it is common that architectures that do not follow a "pure" architectural style. Instead, they follow a main style accompanied with some variations (examples of these variations for the layered style can be seen in [16], p. 8). Normally, the architect applies several variations (some of them are alternatives, see the incompatible relationship in Fig. 2) to increase the satisfaction of the requirements. We can define a style variation as a minor style modification, e.g., a typical style variation is to apply a pattern in a concrete part of the architecture. In the example: the 3-layer style is modified with DAO and controllers patterns; the web deployment style is modified with a database replication; and the web platform style is modified with a FOSS variation. Currently we are not trying to deal with the complexity of using more than one style in one view, but in most cases one style accompanied with variations would suit.

Component. A component is a building block of an architectural view, examples could be: web server for the deployment view, layer for the logic view, or package for the development view. For each view, the style and the used variations will describe which components could be used and how the architecture is built. Components share two extra characteristics apart from the ones inherited from being architectural elements: first, components are connected to other components (e.g., presentation layer, that is a specialization of layer, is connected to the domain layer) and second, components can be composed by other components (e.g., layers in the logical view are composed by classes).

Implementation. Implementations are the real pieces that will make up the software architecture when it is implemented. This part of the knowledge is becoming important as nowadays most of the software is built using existing pieces of software (or hardware in some cases). In the example, the implementations would be: the classes implemented in some programming language, the package distribution provided by the programming language, the physical pieces of hardware where the system is deployed (e.g., a load balancer that is actually implemented by a device from Cisco Systems) and the concrete versions of the platform components. In the last two cases this knowledge could be reused in different architectures, and could be used to ensure the satisfaction of requirements or to detect incompatibilities. The non-reusable knowledge (e.g., implemented classes) would not be part of knowledge of this ontology.

To better understand the importance of this concept, we could think in Service Oriented Architectures (SOA). These architectures are composed of services that sometimes are already implemented by third-party companies. We can use the knowledge of the implemented services to design a SOA with more detail.

We think that using these concepts is enough to represent the AK needed in the decision-making process carried by the architects. This knowledge is also complemented by the rest of modules that compose Arteon, from the R-Module side we can specify properties for each element and establish relationships between elements and quality aspects and from the MDD-module side we can establish the relationships between the elements and the needed transformations (e.g., the transformation to support a technology or to implement some pattern).

4 Conclusions and Future Work

In this paper we have presented an ontology to represent AK, in particular the module that focus on the structural elements that compose an architecture. We have defined the concepts of this module, and used the typical web architecture as a driving example.

We will make improvements in Arteon, including the SE-module. For instance, we want to populate the ontology with SOA related AK, during this knowledge acquisition we may detect some domain specific details that are important in the decision-making process but not representable in the current state of the ontology.

Another branch of this work, already in progress, is to provide a tool support to manage AK and to guide the decision-making process. The current state of this tool can be consulted in: http://www.essi.upc.edu/~ocollell/architech

References

1. Jansen, A., Bosch, J.: Software architecture as a set of architectural design decisions. In: Proceedings of the 5th Working IEEE/IFIP Conference on Software Architecture, pp. 109–120. IEEE Computer Society Press, Washington, DC, USA (2005)
2. Kruchten, P., Capilla, R., Dueas, J.: The decision view's role in software architecture practice. IEEE Software 26(2), 36 (2009)
3. Atkinson, C., Kuhne, T.: Model-driven development: a metamodeling foundation. IEEE Software 20(5), 36–41 (2003)
4. Tyree, J., Akerman, A.: Architecture decisions: Demystifying architecture. IEEE Softw. 22, 19–27 (2005)
5. Akerman, A., Tyree, J.: Using ontology to support development of software architectures. IBM Syst. J. 45, 813–825 (2006)
6. Babu, T.L., Seetha Ramaiah, M., Prabhakar, T.V., Rambabu, D.: Archvoc–towards an ontology for software architecture. In: Workshop on SHAring and Reusing architectural Knowledge. SHARK-ADI. IEEE Computer Society Press, Los Alamitos (2007)
7. Pahl, C., Giesecke, S., Hasselbring, W.: Ontology-based modelling of architectural styles. Information and Software Technology 51(12), 1739-1749 (2009)
8. ISO/IEC 42010 (IEEE std.): Systems and Software engineering - Recomended practice for architectural description of software-intensive systems (2007)
9. Kruchten, P.: The 4+1 view model of architecture. IEEE Software 12, 42–50 (1995)
10. Farooqui, K., Logrippo, L., de Meer, J.: The iso reference model for open distributed processing: An introduction. Computer Networks and ISDN Systems 27(8), 1215–1229 (1995)
11. TOGAF. The Open Group Architecture Framework Version 9 (2009)
12. Zachman, J.A.: A framework for information systems architecture. IBM Syst. J. 26(3), 276–292 (1987)
13. Shaw, M., Garlan, D.: Software Architecture: Perspectives on an Emerging Discipline. Prentice-Hall, Englewood Cliffs (1996)
14. Bass, L., Clements, P., Kazman, R.: Software Architecture in Practice, 2nd edn. Addison-Wesley Professional, Reading (2003)
15. Ceri, S., Fraternali, P., Bongio, A., Brambilla, M., Comai, S., Matera, M.: Designing Data-Intensive Web Applications. Morgan Kaufmann Publishers Inc., San Francisco (2002)
16. Avgeriou, P., Zdun, U.: Architectural Patterns Revisited - a Pattern Language. In: Proceedings of the 10th European Conference on Pattern Languages of Programs (EuroPLoP 2005), Irsee, Germany (July 2005)

The Overall Value of Architecture Review in a Large Scale Software Organization

Sofia Sherman[1], Irit Hadar[1], Ethan Hadar[2], and John J. Harrison Jr.[2]

[1] Information Systems Department, University of Haifa,
Carmel Mountain 31905, Haifa, Israel
{shermans,hadari}@is.haifa.ac.il
[2] CTO Office, CA Technologies
{ethan.hadar,jay.harrison}@ca.com

Abstract. Software architecture review is an important part of architecture construction and evaluation, aimed at ensuring high-quality architecture thus leading to high-quality product. The literature recognizes the different benefits gained by architecture review. Yet, our empirical findings obtained in a large scale software organization show that (1) not all architects are fully aware of the review contribution, and (2) in addition to improving the quality of the architecture, the review encompasses other value propositions, such as promoting collaboration, knowledge sharing, and verifying alignment with the organization's strategy. The study presented in this paper is a first step in an ongoing research aimed at improving existing architecture review processes, methods and tools for enhancing the review's various contributions.

Keywords: Architecture review, architecture quality, architecture process, qualitative research.

1 Introduction

Software architecture establishes major design decisions which determine the system's development, deployment and evolution [1]. Architecture review is a critical phase in software architecture, aimed at ensuring the quality of a suggested architecture [2] and validating it meets the quality requirements [1]. While these are usually the defined objectives of the review, several researchers note that the review results in additional benefits. For example, Kazman and Bass state that the architecture review also has implications on social, organizational, managerial, and business aspects of the corporation [3]. Babar and Gorton determine that in addition to the benefits related to architecture quality, risks and requirements met, there are other benefits related to architecture documentation, project management, communication with stakeholder, and reuse [4].

The objective of the research presented in this paper is to identify software architects' perceptions regarding the value of architecture review. This objective is part of a larger research plan to enhance the architecture review process, methods and tools.

Understanding the desired outcomes of the review will guide us in identifying the different objectives of architecture review and deciding what elements of the review to focus on and enhance in order to increase its value.

The paper is organized as follows: the next section presents the empirical study we conducted and its findings. Next we describe the relevant existing literature and its alignment with our findings, and finally we discuss and conclude.

2 Empirical Study

2.1 Methodology and Settings

This exploratory study was conducted in a large scale, internationally distributed software firm. The main objective of this study was to identify software architects' perceptions with regard to the software architecture review value. When trying to learn a phenomenon and identify its characteristics, rather than corroborating predetermined hypothesis, it is appropriate to use qualitative research methods and tools [5]. In light of the research objective, the research tools and methods used in this study are based on the qualitative grounded theory approach [6].

The study was conducted using an online survey sent to architects within the firm. Prior to its distribution, the survey was validated by 3 experts from the firm whose field of expertise is relevant to the research topic [7]. We received back 70 appropriately completed responses from architects with an average of 7.5 years of experience in architecture practice.

The survey included different questions regarding the existing architecture process, and two questions related to architecture review[1]. The participants were first asked if they found that architecture reviews contribute to the overall quality of their project. The next question was only addressed to those who answered positively to the previous one, and requested the participants to describe the main contributions of the review. In order to identify the architects' unbiased perceptions, and consistently with the grounded theory approach, no predefined contributions were presented to the participants but rather they were asked to provide them themselves; the data collected underwent a qualitative analysis in which categories gradually emerged [6].

2.2 Findings

In the first question, roughly 75% (52 out of 70) of the participants indicated they found architecture reviews to contribute to the overall quality of their project. Each of these participants was requested to describe the main contributions of the review. Out of this group of 52 architects only 36 participants listed contributions, and most of them only indicated one or two such contributions. Using a qualitative data analysis method [6], we divided the written text to statements, each describing a single contribution. Table 1 presents the categories that emerged from our data analysis of the total of 55 relevant statements regarding the contributions of architecture review. Each category is briefly explained, an example or two are presented to illustrate it, and the number of statements that relate to the category is noted.

---

[1] A detailed description of the current architecture review process can be found in [9].

Table 1. The contributions of architecture review

Category	Explanation	Example	No. of statements
Architecture quality	The review improves the quality of the architecture.	"Covers potential customer and use cases to be supported in the products."	18
Knowledge sharing and reuse	Knowledge sharing between experts to be reused in different products.	"Reusability of design patterns or technology." "Share knowledge and best practices across products."	8
Diverse opinions	Getting "second opinion" on the suggested architecture.	"Allows having a second pair of eyes to look at the project." "Providing more directions of thought that are sometimes missed in a one person effort."	8
Organization strategy	Examining the architecture in the context of the bigger picture – the overall organization's strategy.	"Alignment with corporate strategy." "Ensures alignment of the product architecture with the future roadmap."	6
Early problem detection	The early timing of the review within the development process for identifying problems early on.	"Identify gaps or problem areas early in the game " "Ensures designs are vetted out before we get to the next phases"	4
Collaboration	Collaboration with other teams in the firm	"Identifying overlap, expertise in other teams and opportunities for synergy with other teams."	4
Reflection	Reflection on the architecture and its documentation as a part of preparation for the review.	"I think the review process reminds us to continually think about big picture items critical for enterprise software such as performance, scalability, component integration."	4
Architecture documentation	Documentation preparation as a part of preparation to the review process	"Questions asked will be asked by others and if documented, will offer a way to help the future support/developers."	3

3 Related Work

The architects who answered our questionnaire referred to contributions related to architecture quality as well as to other aspects, as shown in Table 1. The literature also refers to beneficial outcomes from architecture reviews which go beyond the architecture quality per se. In order to better understand the contributions stated by our subjects as well as provide additional validation to the identified categories above, we summarize below previous documented contributions of architecture review.

Architecture Quality: Architecture review significantly improves architecture, leading to delivering higher quality systems to customers at lower costs [1][4][8]. Specific benefits of architecture review to architecture quality include uncovering problems and conflicts in requirements and facilitating clear articulation of nonfunctional requirements [4], as well as providing critique for consistency and completeness [2].

Architecture Knowledge Sharing and Reuse: During architecture review, the architects have an opportunity to gain knowledge and identify knowledge gaps based on the feedback they receive. Identified knowledge gaps can be used for establishing training in relevant areas for architects, to promote cross-product knowledge and learning, and to "spread knowledge of proven practices in the company by using the review teams to capture these practices across projects" [2, p. 35]. Identifying opportunities for reuse of architectural artifacts and components was validated as one of the benefits of the review [4]. Sherman et al. propose a mechanism for knowledge reuse for architects and reviewers, capturing knowledge in form of review results, discussions and decisions [9].

Diverse Opinions: Architecture review usually involves different architecture experts from within and outside the team. The review enables leveraging of experienced people by using their expertise and experience to help other projects in the company [2]. Kazman and Bass describe the review as going beyond "just the reviewers reviewing the architecture – it's the entire group discovering aspects of the architecture" [3, p. 71]. Review teams usually include as reviewers people with the right skills and relevance to the project, but with different perspectives [8]. In certain review methods, the different stakeholders are required to collaborate as they each contribute their own perspective [1].

Organization Strategy: Architecture review is one of the management tools that align the architecture and related artifacts and processes with different aspects of the organization strategy. Architecture reviews help identify best practices across the organization, thereby improving the organization's quality and operation, let the company better manage software company suppliers, and provide management with better visibility into technical and project management issues [2].

Early Problem Detection: Most papers discussing architecture review mention the importance of early problem detection. Architecture review helps in identifying gaps and problems in an early stage of the development, which helps reducing the costs of development [1][2]. Early detection of problems that are provided in time to project management help them take more informed decisions [2][8][10].

Collaboration: Collaboration is hardly discussed in the literature as a value from the architecture review with few exceptions; Babar and Gorton list *Opening new communication channels among stakeholders* as one of the benefits of the review [4] and Sherman et al. discuss the importance of collaboration during the review process and propose a mechanism for collaboration between architects, reviewers and among them [9].

Architecture Documentation: As part of preparation for the architecture review, the architects prepare documentation describing the architecture, and based on previous experience try to be prepared for questions that will be asked and the typical criteria against which their work will be evaluated [8]. Improving architecture documentation quality and capturing the rationale for important design decisions was found to be one of the benefits of the review [4].

Reflection: Architects should treat architecture review as a learning opportunity which, along with its contribution to the project, fosters the organizational architects' professional development [8]. Reflection is one of the core contributions to the learning process and guides professionals to rethink their creations during and after the accomplishment of the creation process [11]. Hazzan refers to reflection in the context of software engineering and concludes that "as much as one improves one's reflective proficiency, one increases one's personal skills whether they are methodological, cognitive or social" [12]. Indeed, over time, preparation for review promotes stronger architectural skills [8].

4 Discussion

Seventy five percent of the architects we questioned believe the architecture review contributes to the overall quality of their project. Those who answered in the affirmative usually listed only one or two contributions, if any. This may indicate that while there is a partial consensus about the benefits in conducting architecture reviews, these benefits are not always obvious to the architects. This in turn may imply that the architecture review can be enhanced to better provide the expected contributions discussed in the literature.

Our findings of the perceived contributions are mostly consistent with those discussed in the literature. Some deviations, however, were found as follows. We identified a new category, reflection, which is not mentioned in the literature directly as a possible benefit from architecture review. The reflection guides architects to improve the architecture as a preparation for the review, leading them to scrutinize their architecture document and thinking about things they may neglect otherwise. Another contribution, more heavily emphasized in our findings than in the literature, is the collaboration among different development teams, including communication and knowledge sharing between teams. Our survey also shows architects referred to the importance of aligning the reviewed architecture with the business strategy and product-line roadmap, in addition to other organizational strategy related topics discussed in the literature. The emphasis on collaboration among teams, as well as on the specific aspect of product-line development strategy may stem from the fact that the survey was conducted in a large scale software organization.

Strengths and weaknesses: In this research we directly identified the architects' perceptions regarding architecture review contributions, without constraining them to predefined options. The main threat to validity stems from the fact that the study was conducted in a single, although large and globally distributed, company. For further generalization of these findings, surveys may be conducted in additional companies.

5 Conclusion

The study reported in this paper is part of an ongoing research aimed at enhancing the architecture review process, its methods and tools, in order to increase their value. The main goal of architecture review, as evident from literature as well as from our findings, is improving the quality of the architecture and the resulting product. However, many additional contributions are also indicated, such as promoting collaboration and knowledge sharing, and verifying alignment with the organization's strategy. Our next research step is to analyze existing review processes and supporting methods and tools, and identifying the contributions of each element of the review. Following that, we aim to enhance the review process to ensure the desired contributions are more easily obtained, while studying corresponding metrics to quantify these contributions.

Acknowledgement. We would like to acknowledge CA Labs, the research arm of CA Technologies, for their support.

References

1. Babar, M.A., Zhu, L., Jeffery, R.: A framework for classifying and comparing software architecture evaluation methods. In: Australian Software Engineering Conference, pp. 309–318 (2004)
2. Maranzano, J.F., Sandra, A., Rozsypal, S.A., Zimmerman, G.H., Warnken, G.W., Wirth, P.E., Weiss, D.M.: Architecture Reviews: Practice and Experience. IEEE Software 22(2), 34–43 (2005)
3. Kazman, R., Bass, L.: Making Architecture Reviews Work in the Real World. IEEE Software 19(1), 67–73 (2002)
4. Babar, M.A., Gorton, I.: Software Architecture Review: The State of Practice. IEEE Computer Society 42(7), 26–31 (2009)
5. Bassey, M.: Methods of Enquiry and the Conduct of Case Study Research. In: Case Study Research in Educational Settings, ch. 7, pp. 65–91. Open University Press, UK (1999)
6. Strauss, A., Corbin, J.: Grounded Theory Methodology: An Overview. In: Denzin, N.K., Lincoln, Y.S. (eds.) Handbook of Qualitative Research, ch. 1. Sage, Thousand Oaks (1994)
7. Sushil, S., Verma, N.: Questionnaire Validation Made Easy. European Journal of Scientific Research 46(2), 172–178 (2010)
8. Cook, D.: Architecture evaluation and review practices (2007), http://msdn.microsoft.com/en-us/library/bb896741.aspx (accessed, February 2010)
9. Sherman, S., Hadar, I., Levy, M.: Enhancing Software Architecture Review Process via Knowledge Management. In: Proceedings of the Sixteenth Americas Conference on Information Systems, Lima, Peru (2010)
10. Clements, P., Kazman, R., Klein, M.: Evaluating Software Architectures: Methods and Case Studies. Addison-Wesley, Reading (2001)
11. Schon, D.A.: Educating the Reflective Practitioner: Towards a New Design for Teaching and Learning in The Profession. Jossey-Bass, San Francisco (1987)
12. Hazzan, O.: The Reflective Practitioner Perspective in Software Engineering Education. The Journal of Systems and Software 63(3), 161–171 (2002)

Evaluating Complexity of Information System Architecture Using Fractals

Nary Subramanian

Department of Computer Science, The University of Texas at Tyler,
3900 University Blvd., Tyler, TX 75799, USA
nsubramanian@uttyler.edu

Abstract. Information systems collect, process, store, and output information for the benefit of their stakeholders. They range in scale from a simple smart phone to the world wide web. An architecture of an information system represents a high-level view of a specific facet of the system. An important view of the information system is provided by its information architecture that allows stakeholders visualize transfer of information among system components. Evaluation of complexity of this information architecture gives stakeholders a means of selecting the best architecture from an information standpoint. In this paper we propose to use fractal dimension as a means of evaluating complexity of information architecture of systems. Fractals are recurring patterns at multiple scales and fractals can be evaluated by means of their dimensions. In this paper, we model the information architecture as a fractal, compute its dimension, and determine its complexity. We develop the theory for fractal complexity evaluation, propose algorithms for practical application, and apply them to evaluate complexity of architectures.

Keywords: Information, Architecture, Evaluation, Complexity, Fractal.

1 Introduction

An information system is an arrangement of people, data, processes, and information technology that interact to collect, process, store, and provide as output the information needed to support an organization [1]. There are several different types of information systems such as transaction processing system or management information system, and they range in application scale from a simple app on a smart phone, through desktop applications and enterprise applications, to the world wide web itself. An important aspect of an information system is that each of them possesses an architecture that defines the high level view of an aspect of the system [2]. Therefore, there exists a system architecture, information architecture, hardware architecture, and infrastructure architecture for an information system. System architecture defines the high-level interactions between hardware, software, people, and data within an information system; information architecture defines the high-level view of information sources and sinks within a system – information includes both data and control flows in the system; hardware architecture defines the interactions between hardware components in the system; while infrastructure architecture defines the interaction between software and the hardware components on which software execute. In this paper we investigate complexity analysis of information architecture for information systems.

The information architecture of an information system consists of components, connections, patterns, and styles [3]. Components are the sources and sinks of information including elements such as data readers, cameras, human data entry sources, and displays; connections are data and control flows; styles are the layout of components and connections such as layered, object-oriented, or pipe-and-filter; while patterns are the repeating motif in the architecture such as IPO (input-process-output) or MVC (model-view-control) pattern. There is a class of patterns for information architectures that make those architectures distinct from others – we call this the fractal pattern. Fractals are mathematical objects that have a very specific property of hierarchy wherein higher elements in the hierarchy subsume the pattern of the lower ones. For example, in Fig. 1a, one can see several levels of hub-and-spoke pattern for a games information system used when conducting modern large-scale sports events such as Olympics [4, 5]. In this figure we can see several basic systems used for gathering athlete information in the field, including the False Start Control System, Automatic Photo Finish System, Transponder Control System, and Display Control System. These systems are connected to the respective physical devices such as the starter's gun, timers, video recording equipments, and display boards. These systems are each at level 1 in the hierarchy (indicated by $n = 1$ in the figure) and they are connected to Competition Result System- which will be at level 2 in the hierarchy (indicated by $n = 2$ in the figure). Similarly, at level 3, Competition Result System, Commentator Information System, Security System will all be connected to the Games Information System. In Fig. 1b, we see the repeater pattern (or transporter pattern) at several hierarchies for the human nervous system [6]: at level 1 we have axons carrying information between neurons, at level 2 we have nerves carrying information between sets of neurons and the spinal column, and at level 3 we have spinal column carrying information to the brain. It will be interesting to characterize the complexity of such information architectures using fractal complexity metrics.

Complexity is an important non-functional requirement for software architectures since the measure of complexity gives a good indication of the difficulty of maintaining the software system. Typically the more complex the software architecture the more difficult it is to maintain the software and since maintenance is the most expensive part of software operation, it will be of interest to software practitioners to have a measure of the complexity at the architecture level itself. Very few methods exist in literature for evaluating software architecture complexity. McCabe's cyclomatic complexity [7] is one of the oldest known methods for evaluating complexity when the detailed structure of software is known – however, since structure is typically not clear until detailed design, this method is not easily applied at the software architectural level. Extent of design pattern coverage in an architecture has been used to specify the complexity of architecture [8] using an Interactive Architecture Pattern Recognition System – however, patterns considered do not include the fractal types that is the subject of this paper. It has been proposed that architecture dependency graphs may be used for evaluating complexity [9] – however, it is not always apparent whether all dependencies have been covered in this method. Likewise a function point method has been specified in [10] – but relationship between function points and software architectures is not always straightforward. In this paper we use the fractal dimension as a measure of complexity of self-similar information architectures.

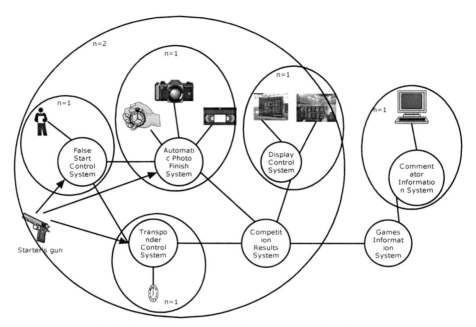

a. Two Fractal levels of Games Information System using Hub-and-Spoke Pattern

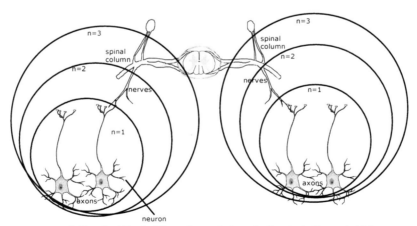

b. Three Fractal levels of Human Nervous System using Repeater (or Transporter) Pattern

Fig. 1. Fractal Nature of Certain Information Architectures

This paper is organized as follows: Section 2 discusses evaluation of information architecture complexity with fractals, Section 3 presents algorithms for complexity evaluation and computes the complexity of two practical systems, Section 4 discusses issues with complexity evaluation using fractals, and Section 5 summarizes the approach and provides directions for future research.

2 Fractal Math for Complexity Evaluation

Fractals seem to follow an emergent nature. As investigated by Mandelbrot [11, 12], halving the unit of measurement for length does not double the size of the item measured, in fact it increases more than double the original measurement. This property of fractal fits in well with the measurement of complexity since being a non-functional requirement makes complexity an emergent property as well [16]. The equation for measuring length of a coastline [13] using fractals is given in eq. 0,

$$P = kA^{D/2} .\qquad(0)$$

where P is the perimeter, A is the area, k is the constant of proportionality, and D is the fractal dimension. As discussed in [14], D is a good indicator of how complex the fractal is. For the purpose of evaluating complexity of information architectures we modify eq. 0 to the one in eq.1,

$$I = kN^{C/2} .\qquad(1)$$

where I is information, N is the number of components in the architecture, k is the constant of proportionality, and C is the complexity of the architecture.

Taking, natural logarithm on both sides, the above equation may be rewritten as

$$\ln I = \ln k + \frac{C}{2}\ln N \cdot \qquad(2)$$

In eq. 2, the complexity C is twice the slope of the line in the $\ln I$ and $\ln N$ plane. Therefore, if we plot a linear regression line in a plot on this plane, the slope of this line gives half the value of the complexity. Thus, we can define complexity of information architectures C as

$$C = 2 \times slope\ of\ regression\ line\ in\ logarithmic\ I\ and\ N\ plane \cdot \qquad(3)$$

Based on above definitions, we develop the following theorems.

Theorem 1. Complexity of Information Architectures (C) will satisfy the relation $0 \leq C \leq \infty$.

Discussion: By eq. 3, C is twice the slope of a regression line. Slope of a line follows the relation $0 \leq slope \leq \infty$ and, therefore, $0 \leq C \leq \infty$. This is different from the case in [15] wherein fractal dimension is constrained between 1 and 2 for the topological domain.

Theorem 2. Complexity of Information Architectures (C) with low throughput components will be closer to 0. Complexity of Information Architectures (C) with high throughput components will be closer to ∞.

Discussion: In eq. 2, when I is small for large values of N, the slope of the line will be low making C closer to 0. Likewise, in eq. 2, when I is large for small values of N, the slope of line will be high making C closer to ∞. This can be visualized better in Fig. 2 where the linear regression lines for both low throughput and high throughput environments are given.

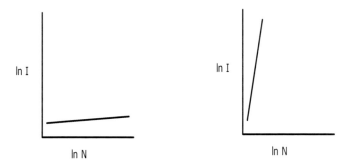

A. Linear Regression in Low Throughput Environment

B. Linear Regression in High Throughput Environment

Fig. 2. Figures for Visualizing Theorem 2

Theorem 3. The constant of proportionality k in eq. 2 equals the throughput in the trivial case, namely, when the architecture has only one component.

Discussion: In eq. 2, when $N = 1$, the resulting equation is

$$\ln I = \ln k \Rightarrow k = I . \tag{4}$$

Therefore, k defines the initial condition of the system when only one component has been included in the system.

Theorem 4. Complexity of Information Architectures (C) may be computed also by the following equation:

$$C = 2 \times \frac{\ln I'}{\ln N'} . \tag{5}$$

where I' is the maximum expected information throughput of the architecture corresponding to N', the maximum expected number of components in the architecture.

Discussion: Let's assume that components are added to the information architecture in the ascending order of their information throughput, where I is the information throughput of the first component, and I' the information throughput when N' components have been added. Then, by eq. 2 and Theorem 3, we have

$$\ln I' = \ln I + \frac{C}{2} \times \ln N' . \tag{6}$$

This is same as,

$$\ln \frac{I'}{I} = \frac{C}{2} \times \ln N'. \quad (7)$$

When $I' \gg I$, since items have been added in ascending order, eq. 7 can be written as,

$$C = 2 \times \frac{\ln I'}{\ln N'}. \quad (8)$$

Theorem 4 will allow us to develop the algorithm for evaluating complexity given in the next section.

3 Evaluating Information Architecture Complexity Using Fractals

There are two possible ways to evaluate complexity – where the information distribution patterns are known we can use eq. 3 to compute complexity and where the architectural elements' throughput are known we can use eq. 8 to compute complexity.

Algorithm 1: complexity evaluation when information distribution pattern is known:

1. Plot the data rates for the different devices on the logarithmic I vs. logarithmic N scale
2. Compute the linear regression that best fits the points plotted.
3. Complexity is, by eq. 3, twice the slope of this regression line.

Algorithm 2: complexity evaluation when throughput of individual elements of the architecture are known:

1. Include all data sources and sinks in the information architecture.
2. Include all control actuators in the information architecture.
3. For each data source, data sink, and control actuator estimate the approximate data rates.
4. Compute the total number of data sources, data sinks, and control actuators as N'.
5. Compute the total data rate as I'.
6. Calculate the complexity of information architecture by eq. 8.

3.1 Evaluation of Complexity of Computer Lab Network

The fractal pattern is also found in the computer network in a University. The data collected in the research lab at the Department of Computer Science at the University of Texas at Tyler at about 10 am on a weekday morning is shown in Table 1.

We apply Algorithm 1 above and obtain the graph of Fig. 3. The slope of the linear regression ($\ln I = 3.4379 + 0.2882 \ln N$) is 0.2882, which gives the complexity of the information architecture to be 0.5764 (since, by eq. 3, complexity is twice the slope).

Table 1. Information Throughput in a Computer Lab Network

No. of Nodes	Data in Kbps
1	50
3	50
4	120
5	50
6	75
6	225
8	200
10	1000
11	225
14	850
15	500

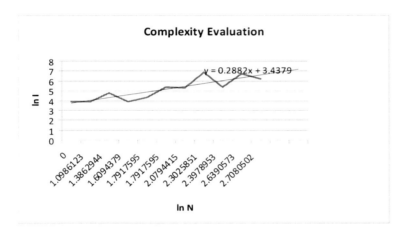

Fig. 3. Evaluation of Complexity by Linear Regression for Data in Table 1

3.2 Evaluation of Complexity of Games Information System

For the architecture given in Fig. 1a, for $n = 2$, data throughput for a few of practical subsystems are given in Table 2 (data obtained from [17, 18, 19, 20]).

Table 2. Components for Competition Results System in Fig. 1a

Item (Data/Control Source/Sink)	Data rate
Photo Finish System (MacFinish III Ethernet)	100Mb/s
False Start Control System (ASC2)	115kb/s
Display Control System (Nova Modular Color Display)	110kb/s
Transponder Control System (Swiss Timing using GPRS technology)	48kb/s
Total: 4	Total: 100.3Mb/s

Here we apply Algorithm 2 above and obtain, by eq. 8,

$$C = 2 \times \frac{\ln(100,300,000)}{\ln 4} = 26.58 \cdot \qquad (9)$$

In eq. 9, 100.3M has been expanded. This means that complexity is affected mostly by the high throughput subsystem and therefore special focus is needed for designing infrastructure and hardware architectures for high throughput subsystems.

4 Observations

Evaluation of complexity of information architectures by means of fractals gives us an approach to compare and classify software architectures. In our example evaluations, we evaluated complexity for information architectures without considering the level of the architecture in the hierarchy. Thus for the university research lab we evaluated complexity at level 1, while for the competition result system we evaluated the complexity at level 2. We assumed that algorithms for calculating complexity are independent of the hierarchical level though this will require further study.

In our discussion we have assumed information content (I) in information architectures to represent the rate of flow of data from data sources and data sinks, as well as flow of control from control sources and sinks (therefore, high data rate systems may influence computation as seen in the example in Section 3.2). However, if information is perceived as representing total data transferred or bandwidth used, then we may need to revisit equations in Section 2.

Theorem 3 equates the constant of proportionality with the initial state of architecture development. We need to investigate this further to ensure that the order in which the components are added to an architecture does not become a major factor in complexity evaluation. This is related to an assumption made in Theorem 4 where we assume the final information flow is much greater than the initial one - when this assumption fails the algorithms in Section 3 may need to be modified.

We have used one of the equations (eq. 0) possible for evaluating fractal complexity. There are other methods [11] to evaluate fractal complexity as well such as the rule complexity for generating fractals or the number of iterations needed to generate a fractal shape (indicated, to some extent, by the number n in Fig. 1); we need to explore the differences in complexity evaluation for information architectures using these methods as well.

Our algorithms for assessing fractal complexity of software architectures are relatively straightforward – as new components of software architecture become known, the changes to complexity may be dynamically evaluated. This permits the software architect develop a real-time complexity view of the system being developed.

5 Conclusion

Complexity of software architectures is an important non-functional requirement whose quantitative values will permit system architects to better estimate maintenance effort for the final system - the more complex the architecture is, the more it typically costs to maintain. Information architectures for information systems capture the interconnection of components that serve as control and data sources and sinks. There is a class of information systems whose information architectures display a self-similar pattern such as, for example, campus network systems, games information systems, and the human central nervous system. These self-similar architectures are similar to fractals and in this paper we employed fractal dimension to evaluate complexity of information architecture for such systems. We developed algorithms to evaluate complexity and applied it to practical systems. In this process we found that fractal-based evaluation provides a quantitative method for dynamically (re-)computing complexity for system under development. The complexity is evaluated as numbers in this process that allows for easy comparison between software architectures. Software architects can benefit from this method by being able to compare architectures and choosing the best option for the system being developed. Also, this evaluation will help architects determine those subsystems that need special focus during infrastructure and hardware architecture designs.

There are several lines of further research in this area. It will be interesting to observe if there are differences in the complexity evaluation when applied at different hierarchical levels in a fractal information architecture. Theorem 1 gives an open upper bound for complexity- it will be useful to practitioners if complexity bands may be identified for different classes of systems. Also it will be of interest to practitioners if fractal approach could be applied to other types of software architecture such as system architecture, infrastructure architecture, or hardware architecture. However, we believe that fractal approach to complexity evaluation helps practitioners in industry and academia to quickly compute complexity for information architectures.

Acknowledgement

We thank reviewers of the earlier version of this paper for their valuable suggestions and comments. The paper has been revised to more clearly present the results of complexity analysis employing fractals.

References

1. Whitten, J.L., Bentley, L.D.: Systems Analysis and Design Methods. McGraw Hill Irwin, New York (2007)
2. Eeles, P., Cripps, P.: The Process of Software Architecting. Addison Wesley, New Jersey (2010)
3. Shaw, M., Garlan, D.: Software Architecture: Perspectives on an Emerging Discipline. Prentice Hall, New Jersey (1996)
4. International Association of Athletic Federation, Competition Rules 2010-2011, http://www.iaaf.org/mm/Document/Competitions/TechnicalArea/05/47/81/20091027115916_httppostedfile_CompRules2010_web_26Oct09_17166.pdf
5. ATOS Origin, http://www.atosorigin.com/en-us/olympic-games/london_2012/default.htm

6. Martini, F.H., et al.: Fundamentals of Anatomy and Physiology. Prentice Hall, New Jersey (2001)
7. McCabe, T.J.: A Complexity Measure. IEEE Transactions on Software Engineering, SE-2(4), 308–320 (1976)
8. Kazman, R., Burth, M.: Assessing Architectural Complexity. In: 2nd Euromicro Conference on Software Maintenance and Reengineering, pp. 104–112. IEEE Press, Florence (1998)
9. Zhao, J.: On Assessing the Complexity of Software Architectures. In: 3rd International Workshop on Software Architecture, pp. 163–166. ACM, Orlando (1998)
10. AlSharif, M., Bond, W.P., Al-Otaiby, T.: Assessing the Complexity of Software Architecture. In: 42nd Annual Southeast Regional Conference, pp. 98–103. ACM, Huntsville (2004)
11. Mandelbrot, B.B.: The Fractal Geometry of Nature. W. H. Freeman & Company, New York (1977)
12. Fractals and the Fractal Dimension, http://www.vanderbilt.edu/AnS/psychology/cogsci/chaos/workshop/Fractals.html
13. Frohn, R.C.: Remote Sensing for Landscape Ecology: new metric indicators for monitoring, modeling, and Assessment of Ecosystems. CRC Press, Boca Raton (1998)
14. Fractal Dimension Index, http://www.trivisonno.com/fractal-dimension-index
15. O'Neill, R.V., et al.: Indices of landscape pattern. Landscape Ecology 1(3), 153–162 (1988)
16. Chung, L., Nixon, B.A., Yu, E., Mylopoulos, J.: Non-Functional Requirements in Software Engineering. Kluwer Academic Publishers, Boston (2000)
17. TimeTronics, http://www.timetronics.be/products/macfinish.php#MF3ETHERNET
18. Swiss Timing, http://www.swisstiming.com/Detail.559.0.html?&tx_stproducts_pi1[uid]=35&tx_stproducts_pi1[currentSport]=73&tx_stproducts_pi1[currentType]=69&cHash=38a140d0e844d9c7eafec8cc3c5fadb9
19. Swiss Timing, http://www.swisstiming.com/uploads/tx_stproducts/NOVA_MODULAR_COLOUR_DISPLAYS_3437.525.02-S9.pdf
20. Swiss Timing, http://www.swisstiming.com/Athletics.495.0.html

Towards a Reconfigurable Middleware Architecture for Pervasive Computing Systems

Gustavo G. Pascual, Lidia Fuentes, and Mónica Pinto

E.T.S.I. Informática, Universidad de Málaga
{gustavo,lff,pinto}@lcc.uma.es

Abstract. One of the main features of pervasive computing systems is that environment conditions are continuously changing. Therefore, these systems need to be dynamically reconfigured in order to properly adapt to their environment (context). An appropriate solution to provide reconfigurability is Aspect-Oriented Software Development. In this paper, we present an aspect-oriented middleware architecture for pervasive computing systems reconfiguration. Using our architecture, middleware services can be reconfigured by enabling/disabling optional functionalities or replacing the entire service with lighter implementations which are less resource consuming. In order to achieve dynamic reconfiguration, the most relevant middleware service is the context-monitoring service, which is needed to provide the middleware with information about the state of the environment. Thus, in this paper, we focus on the context-monitoring service, although the rest of the services are defined and reconfigured in a similar way and will be addressed in the future.

Keywords: Middleware, AOSD, Dynamic Reconfiguration, Monitoring.

1 Introduction

Pervasive computing systems have experienced an increased demand due to the evolution and popularity of mobile devices and embedded systems. Computing has moved then from desktops to highly dynamic environments. When the environment (context) of a system changes, the requirements that services need to satisfy can also change, so an adaptation is needed in order to fulfill these new requirements. Adaptation can involve enabling, disabling or modifying existing services. Furthermore, this process should be as transparent as possible to the services and applications. Therefore, this is a complex task and should be addressed by a middleware architecture that provides the monitorisation and dynamic reconfiguration services needed to achieve context-aware adaptation.

There are nowadays several middleware solutions that try to achieve dynamic adaptation. Some of them focus only on adapting the application level [1,2,3,4], while others also reconfigure the services of the middleware infrastructure [5,6,7,8]. However, a shortcoming of most of them is their lack of support to satisfactorily achieve highly relevant non-functional requirements in the development of pervasive computing systems, such as *flexibility* and *consistency* of the reconfigurations, *homogeneous reconfiguration* at both the middleware infrastructure and the application level, and contention of the *performance overhead* introduced by dynamic adaptation. Other requirements such as service distribution, mobility or fault tolerance are equally important and will be considered in future works.

In our approach, *flexibility* is achieved by using Aspect-Oriented Software Development (AOSD). AOSD is an appropriate technology for this purpose. Firstly, optional functionalities can be modelled as aspects, which are dynamically enabled/disabled or even woven/unwoven if the underlying AO platform supports it [9]. For example, if sensors were implemented as aspects, they could be disableds when they are no longer needed, releasing the resources used by those sensors. On the other hand, if new sensors are needed, they can be woven at runtime. Secondly, entire services can also be replaced by alternative implementations that better suit the current context conditions. However, in dynamic AO middlewares flexibility is usually achieved at the cost of *consistency*. This occurs, basically, because the possibility of incorporating any aspect at any place and at any moment of the execution of the system may seriously affect the system consistency (e.g. a configuration in which the communication between two components is encrypted but, although the Encryption aspect has been woven in the source component, the Decryption aspect has not been woven in the target). In these cases a consistency service [10] needs to be added to the middleware infrastructure in order to check that the incorporation/deletion of an aspect maintains the system in a consistent state. However, this supposes a runtime performance overload, especially relevant in the case of resource-constrained devices. In our approach, we try to find a compromise between flexibility and consistency by limiting the adaptations that can be performed in a particular service to the addition/deletion of aspects that have been previously identified, modelled and implemented for each middleware service.

Another shortcoming of AOSD is the *performance overhead* introduced by the dynamic weaving of aspects. Thus, the decision about the AO approach to be used in a middleware for pervasive computing systems is a key issue. In this paper we show an initial performance evaluation that will be completed with a more exhaustive study before deciding the particular mechanism to be used.

Summarising, this paper proposes an AO reconfigurable middleware architecture that perform context monitoring and reconfigure itself in order to adapt to the changes in the environment. Our architecture provides support for an homogeneous reconfiguration of all services, both the middleware infrastructure services and the applications running on top of the middleware infrastructure. Moreover, we use AOSD to provide more flexible and reconfigurable services, but still controlling the consistency and performance overload limitations usually introduced by AOSD. After this introduction, in Section 2 we present some related work and the requirements that our middleware architecture should address. Section 3 outlines our middleware architecture and service model, focusing on the context-monitoring service. An initial performance evaluation is done in Section 4. Conclusions and future work are presented in Section 5.

2 Motivation and Related Work

In this section we focus on those proposals of the state of the art that cover context management and reconfigurability. We also take into account whether these proposals provide consistency of the reconfigurations.

Regarding reconfiguration, most of the existing work [1,2,3,4] provide support for reconfiguration only of the application layer. The objective of these middlewares is to enable constrained devices to run complex tasks by offloading part of their execution on a resource-rich node connected through a wireless network. However, in these platforms, the middleware always takes the same amount of resources. Since our work focuses on reconfiguration at the middleware layer, our objective is clearly different. Some reconfigurable middlewares are RCSM [5], SOCAM [6], the work by Janik and Zielinski [7] and the architecture in the PhD thesis of Paspallis [8]. Throughout this section we focus on answering three questions: how do these works provide context gathering and management?; how flexible the reconfiguration is?, and how consistency is provided?

2.1 Context Gathering and Management

Middleware architectures should provide an efficient mechanism for gathering context from different kinds of sources (*context acquisition*). Usually, information will come from sensors (temperature, light, accelerometers, etc.), but it can also come from measuring of available resources of the device (CPU, memory, storage, network bandwidth, etc.). Context management should also provide some kind of context abstraction, like data aggregation or filtering (*context processing*). Sometimes a service needs context information that is produced in remote devices, orr due to the device constraints a context provider would be better instantiated in a remote node with more resources. The middleware architecture should provide support for deploying remote providers and for gathering remote context data transparently to the service or the application. Furthermore, when context is distributed, requirements like privacy and security arise.

Context acquisition is similar in most approaches, although using different terminology. For instance, RCSM has a lookup service to localise available sensors and context information is gathered from both sensors and the underlying operating system. SOCAM defines the concept of context providers, which can be internal – i.e. that are connected to physical sensors, or external – i.e. that get information from web servers and other information services. Similarly, in the work by Paspallis context is provided by pluggable components that are called *context plug-ins*. An important difference is introduced by those approaches using aspect-orientation. Concretely, in Janik and Zielinski context data is provided by sampling devices that are implemented as aspects and that can be woven/unwoven from the service as needed. The use of aspects allows an easier adaptation of the number and type of sampling devices. Another advantage of using aspects is that the source of context information can be any point of your system that needs to be monitored, even if the service was not initially designed as a context provider. An example would be the necessity of monitoring the number of threads created in a particular service. Using AOP to implement the sampling device, the only requirement would be to intercept those points in the service code that create a new thread. AOP allows doing that in a non-invasive way. Our approach is similar to this with the following differences: (1) our goal is to use AOP to separate as aspects not only the context providers but also any other crosscutting concern; (2) we provide an homogeneous model and thus the rest of middleware services (communication, mobility, etc.) will also be modelled following an AO approach, and (3) we will explicitly cope with the consistency and performance overhead issues of AOP.

Once the context is gathered, the main differences between the existing proposals is in the way in which the context processing is done. RCSM, for instance, introduces the concept of *situation* as a context abstraction, which consists of an aggregation of past context data. For example, presentation slides can be downloaded to the mobile phone "if the user is in the office", "his desktop computer is near" and the "class time is approaching", being each of these conditions a single situation. A similar approach is followed in the work of Janik and Zielinski, where monitoring agents collects the context information and forward it to a centralised observer. The information can then be stored, aggregated and filtered by some entities called *appenders*. A different approach is followed by both SOCAM and the work by Paspallis that defines a query language to consult the contextual information previously gathered. In SOCAM an Ontology Web Language (OWL) is used to discover and interpret the context. In the work by Paspallis they define an XML-based language called CQL that provides support for immediate and subscription-based access to context data. Each approach has its benefits and limitations, although none of them is adaptable enough in order to satisfy the necessities of all context-aware applications. In our approach, our intention is to take advantage of the flexibility offered by AOP in order to be able to support both approaches, adapting the context-aware service to the particular necessities of each application. This is however part of our ongoing work and thus it is out of the scope of this paper.

Finally, all the studied proposals provide some kind of support to access remote context. For instance, RCSM support the access of remote sensors using a context discovery protocol (R-CDP) and SOCAM includes a service location service that provides support for using external context providers. Additionally, in the work by Janik and Zielinksi and in the work by Paspallis, in addition to access to remote context, context providers can also be remotely instantiated. However, although privacy and security are two requirements identified as needed when context distribution is available, security is not provided in any of the proposals described here. Moreover, none of them support privacy, with the exception of the work by Paspallis that includes a privacy component in the architecture of its monitoring service. In our middleware, all services may be distributed according to the constraints introduced by the environment conditions, including the monitoring service. Privacy and security will be added to the service as aspects only when needed.

2.2 Middleware Reconfiguration

There are mainly two different levels of reconfiguration. The first one assumes that the components/services of the middleware infrastructure and application define a set of *configuration parameters* that can be modified at runtime in order to adapt their behaviour to the environment changes. In the second level, components/services can be enabled and disabled at runtime. This second approach is more complex, although it is also more powerful because resource consumption can be reduced when a service is no longer needed, and new functionalities can be enabled even when they were not initially expected to be needed.

In RCSM, reconfiguration is supported in context acquisition by modifying rules and situations. When a rule or a situation is changed, sensing units that are no longer needed can be disabled and new required sensing units be enabled. SOCAM provides reconfiguration in context providers, adding or removing sensors and modifying the information provided. The work of Janik and Zielinski integrates with AAOP, an AO model which provides support for specifying adaptability strategies. Strategies are modeled as a graph of states where each state defines an adaptation policy, which consists of a set of constraints (for example, maximum CPU time or maximum memory usage) and a set of conditions to change from active state to another one. Everytime that state is changed some actions can be executed (usually, sampling devices or application aspects are enabled or disabled). The monitoring system presented in this paper addresses reconfiguration in monitoring service by enabling/disabling sampling devices or modifying configuration parameters. This monitoring service, used together with AAOP, enables application reconfiguration (e.g. for satisfying non-functional goals). However, this approach lacks scalability because with each non-functional goal taken into account, the number of graph states is multiplied and it is very difficult to maintain. Finally, the architecture presented in the thesis of Paspallis is composed of loosely coupled components. A centralized component, called Context Manager, provides support for dynamically deploying or removing context plug-ins (i.e. context data providers). The Context Manager will analyze the received context data queries in order to decide which context plug-ins should be enabled or disabled.

In our approach our goal is to support both levels of reconfiguration. The first level will be achieved in a similar way to existing proposals. Regarding the second level, our approach will be similar to the work by Janik and Zielinski, in the sense that we also use AOP to implement the middleware service variabilities. The main difference is that our goal is to use aspects to model not only the addition/removal of sampling devices, but of any service behaviour susceptible to adaptation at runtime. We will provide more details further on the paper.

2.3 Consistency

In the related work presented in this section, only small changes are performed with reconfiguration operations, so there is no need to introduce mechanisms to ensure consistency. Some proposals (e.g. [11,12,13,14]) provide support for dynamic reconfiguration, but they don't ensure consistency, or it is only partially addressed. This lack of consistency support is the main motivation of the work by Surajbali [10], which proposes an AO middleware architecture that provides consistent dynamic reconfiguration. However, this architecture doesn't support context-awareness and it was not specifically designed to run on resource-constraints devices. The architecture proposed by Janik and Zielinski is focused on monitoring service. Since reconfiguration is limited to sampling devices and context data transformation, it is not necessary to provide mechanisms to ensure consistency. However, when the monitoring service is used together with the AAOP model, it provides support for reconfiguration of the application level too. In that case, the responsability of defining a graph of consistent states is delegated to the application developers. Finally, in the architecture presented by Paspallis, context plug-ins can be installed and uninstalled at runtime. Context plug-ins specify their provided and required context types. The only consistence mechanism provided is dependences checking between context plug-ins.

3 Middleware Architecture and Service Model

3.1 High-Level Middleware Architecture

Figure 1 shows our high level middleware architecture. We explicitly show the *Dynamic Reconfiguration Service* (DRS), the *Context-Monitoring Service* (CMS) and the *Aspect Management Service* (AMS). The rest of the services (e.g. distribution, communication, localisation, etc.) are all represented by the *Middleware Service* (MS). In our approach, the DRS provides support for services reconfiguration. Reconfigurations will be performed taking into account context information, which is provided by the CMS. Since DRS and CMS communicate through well known interfaces, and they don't depend on the internal services design, many services (both middleware and application services) can be built around this architecture, taking advantage of the dynamic reconfiguration and context-monitoring abilities in a homogeneous way. The AMS is the responsible for adding and removing aspects according to the contextual information gathered and processed by the CMS.

As shown in Figure 1, the high level architecture of the *Context-Monitoring Service* can be organised into two main components, according to the main tasks offered by this service: *Context Acquisition* and *Context Processing*. Context acquisition involves several tasks such as: (1) enabling and disabling context providers; (2) tracking available context providers; (3) registering new context providers and (4) context data gathering from context providers. Context processing consists of tasks such as: (1) maintaining context history; (2) providing context abstraction; (3) context information modelling and context query support; (4) sending contextual event notifications to subscribed services, and (5) tracking needed context information in order to request *Context Acquisition* to disable context providers that are no longer needed or to enable new ones.

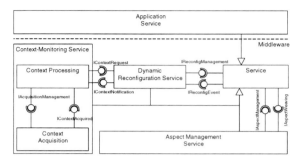

Fig. 1. Middleware Architecture

3.2 Service Model

One of the main contributions of this paper is our service model. In order to develop services that can be dynamically reconfigured in a homogeneous, flexible, consistent and efficient way, our approach proposes the use of a service development methodology based on the same principles of *Software Product Lines* (SPL) [15]. The main goal of a SPL is the definition of a family of products through the distinction between the functionalities that are common to all the products, and the variabilities introduced by each product in the family. The main difference with our approach is that our objective is not the definition of a family of products, but the definition of a family of consistent service configurations. We illustrate our proposal using the Context-Monitoring service as an example.

Our service development methodology begins with the identification of the service's functional and non-functional requirements and the definition of a feature model [16] representing all the functionalities of the service, including information about their dependencies and which ones are optional and which are mandatory. On an example, Figure 2 shows part of the feature model of the Context-Monitoring service. This service consists of two main features: *Context acquisition* and *Context processing*. Each of them can also be split to different sets of features. Context acquisition will be responsible for tracking all available context providers, so it should provide support for registering new context providers, enabling and disabling context providers and gathering all the data generated by the enabled context providers. Context providers are part of context acquisition, and they can be locally or remotely deployed. When context distribution is enabled using remote context providers, concerns like privacy and encryption should be taken into account. As can be seen in the figure, support for remote context providers is optional, because it is a feature that may introduce an overload and a consumption of networking and power resources. Another optional feature for context providers is the use of a *cache*. When obtaining of a sample of context information is expensive, performing probing every time that a value is asked for is not efficient and, depending on the requirements, returning a cached value could be more appropriate. On the other hand, context processing consists of some different features too. Context information requests should be analysed in order to enable the needed context providers and disable those that are no longer needed. This feature is called *required providers tracking*. The context information can be provided at low level (asking for a specific value of a provider measurement) or by using a context abstraction. Context abstraction provides support for high-level context, and we can distinguish two different approaches: simple combinations of low-level context information (defined as *situation* by some authors [5]) or more complex reasoning mechanisms like ontologies or context query languages [6,8]. Both approaches provide support for storing and accessing past context information (context history).

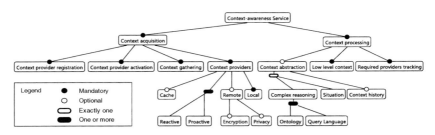

Fig. 2. Example of Context-Monitoring Service Model

Once the feature model has been specified, in the next step of our methodology an architecture of the service will be modelled according to that feature model. The architecture will consist of some mandatory components (the core architecture) and some optional ones that will be connected or not to the core architecture depending on the variabilities being included for each particular configuration. In our approach, we use AOSD to specify how the variable architecture is connected to the core architecture. Moreover, using AOSD the optional components are dynamically enabled and disabled depending on the features selected from the model. There are mainly two alternatives to model aspects at the architectural level. One of them is the use of an AO UML profile and the other one is the use of an AO ADL. In order to illustrate our approach, in this paper we use our Aspect-Oriented Architecture Description Language (AO-ADL) [17]. Note that other approaches may have also been used. Continuing with our example, Figure 3 shows part of the AO-ADL architecture of Context-Monitoring.

In this scenario, the *Context Gathering* component is responsible for collecting all the information generated by context providers. This example shows how this component communicates with a remote *Context Provider* using the *Distribution Service*. Context Providers are *aspects* that generate contextual information. This information can be measurements from physical sensors or from resources usage (CPU, memory, network, storage, battery, etc.) but, since context providers are aspects, they can also get information about applications or services (number of running threads, interaction between components, execution time, etc.), providing great versatility to the Context-Monitoring service.

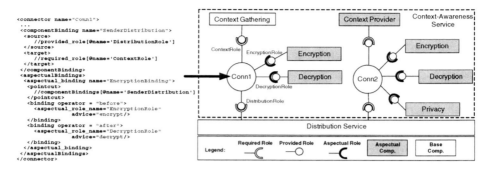

Fig. 3. Partial architecture of the context-monitoring service

The *Distribution Service* provides support to communicate with remote componentes/aspects. In order to establish a secure interaction with remote providers, the *Encryption*, *Decryption* and *Privacy* aspects have been woven. In this way, only authorised devices will gain access to the contextual information provided by that context provider. Furthermore, information will be encrypted/decrypted to secure data transmission over the network. There are two main benefits derived from the use of AOSD: (1) The *Context Gathering*, *Context Provider* and *Distribution Service* components are completely unaware of the *Encryption*, *Decryption* and *Privacy* aspects, being able to reuse them in different configurations of the service without any modification in their design/implementation. For instance, the same implementations of these components will be reused in both local and remote interactions. In the XML code on the left handside of Figure 3 you can see that the pointcuts (i.e. the place where aspects are injected) and the advice (i.e. the aspect behaviour being injected) are specified outside the components, as part of the connector; (2) *Encryption*, *Decryption* and *Privacy* can be easily added or removed from the service at runtime using the AO mechanisms offered by the middleware architecture.

3.3 Service Reconfiguration

Finally, DRS provides the interface *IReconfigManagement*, which can be used by services to manage their own reconfiguration. Services will provide DRS with (1) their service model; (2) a set of rules that define how and when they should be reconfigured and (3) the features initially selected from the service model.

Every service will define its own set of *reconfiguration rules*. These rules consist of a set of actions that will be performed if some *activation conditions* of context and service features are true. The actions can be enabling or disabling features of the service model. DRS will track the enabled features of each service and, when the conditions of a rule are met, it will process the actions defined for that rule taking into account the stored feature model of the service. After executing the actions of the rule, it may be that: (1) A new valid choice is generated. In that case, DRS will send a notification to the service through the interface *IReconfigEvent* indicating the new set of enabled features, and the service will map it as a new configuration of its components, and (2) An invalid choice is generated. Then, DRS will send a notification to the service indicating that it is not possible to find a proper configuration for the current context situation, and service will decide if it continues to use the same configuration, stops its execution or throws up an error.

For instance, continuing with our example in Figure 2, the feature model determines that only the *Encryption* and *Privacy* features can be dynamically added/removed from the interaction between the *Context Gathering* component and the *Context Provider* remote aspects. This means that the reconfiguration service will prevent any adaptation that was not previously contemplated during the service design. As another example, the feature model in Figure 2 does not contemplate the use of encryption and privacy when interaction with context providers is local. In our approach, this means that the adaptation of the service to incorporate those aspects in local interactions will be detected as a non-valid reconfiguration. Thus, using our service model we are able to provide more flexibility than those approaches where adaptation is based on predefined plans, while avoiding the consistency problems introduced by AO approaches, which allows the addition/removal of any aspect, even if the aspect's behaviour was not previously identified as part of the service during its design.

4 Performance Evaluation

As mentioned in Section 3, we use AOSD to manage the architecture's variability. There are some different mechanisms (JBoss AOP, Spring, etc...) that provide support for developing AO systems, although it is possible to design our own weaving mechanism. Since we focus on pervasive computing systems, it is critical to choose an efficient and scalable mechanism. To this end we have implemented a prototype of a weaving mechanism based on the AO-ADL connector, which is a first-class entity that contains the references of the aspects being injected in a particular component composition, and we have designed an evaluation scenario in order to evaluate the overhead introduced by our connector related to JBoss AOP and a direct communication between components. In our evaluation scenario there are two locally instantiated components *c1* and *c2*, where *c1* calls the operation *m1* provided by *c2*. This communication is instrumented by the weaving mechanism in order to apply a set of aspects before the operation *m1* is executed. Neither *m1* or the aspects perform any action, because we want to evaluate the overhead introduced by the weaving mechanism when it gets the aspects references and starts advices execution. In the case of direct communication, the operations defined in the aspects are executed by the component *c2*. We have measured the elapsed time when *m1* operation is called and this operation has finished. We have measured this for different number of aspects in order to know if these mechanisms are scalable. We have used an ASUS UL50AG laptop with an Intel ULV SU7300 CPU and 4 GB of RAM memory running 64-bit Windows 7 Home Premium. The results of the performance evaluation can be seen in Figure 4. Note that in Figure 4a the results are shown in microseconds and in

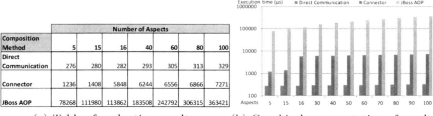

(a) Table of evaluation results   (b) Graphical representation of results

Fig. 4. Performance Evaluation Results

Figure 4b, the execution time is shown in a logarithmic scale. As was expected, direct communication introduces the least overhead, and it is nearly constant with respect to the increased number of aspects. However, in the direct communication approach, coordination mechanisms such as event notification would be necessary to provide reconfiguration support. As can be seen in Figure 4b, our implementation is scalable because, as it occurs in direct communication, if we increase the number of aspects, the overhead does not increase greatly. It's worth noting that, in our implementation, overhead increases significantly when the number of aspects reaches 16, although after that the overhead remains almost constant. This behaviour is related to the internal implementation of Java Reflection API and will be addressed in future work. Finally, it can be seen that the execution times measured when using JBoss AOP are much higher than the ones measured with the two previous approaches and, although it is also scalable, the overhead increase related to the number of aspects is higher than the measured in the previous approaches.

5   Conclusions and Future Work

We have presented an initial approach towards the definition of an AO context-aware middleware platform to reconfigure both middleware and application services at runtime. We focus particularly on pervasive applications running on resource-constrained devices. In order to do that, in this paper we focus on how to achieve a flexible, consistent and efficient approach. Our main contributions are the use of AOSD and the definition of a service model inspired in the principles of SPLs. There are still many open questions that we plan to answer as part of our future work. Firstly, we need to choose the AO mechanism. For that, we need to complete the evaluation presented in this paper addressing concerns such as consistency and reconfiguration performance before deciding the most efficient mechanism to be used in resource-constrained environments. Another relevant issue is the design of the reconfiguration service. There are many approaches managing the valid configurations in different ways (graphs, set of plans, etc). Some of them are not scalable and may negatively affect the reconfiguration service when simultaneously managing reconfigurations from multiple middleware services and applications. Thus, this is a very relevant decision and we need to analyse the different existing approaches by measuring its flexibility, scalability and performance overhead. Also, our service model needs to be refined and automated (for instance, using Model-Driven technologies), and different application scenarios need to be defined and implemented.

References

1. Chan, A., Chuang, S.: MobiPADS: a reflective middleware for context-aware mobile computing. IEEE Transactions on Software Engineering, 1072–1085 (2003)
2. Cuervo, E., et al.: Maui: Making smartphones last longer with code offload. In: Proceedings of the 8th International Conference on Mobile systems, Applications, and Services, pp. 49–62. ACM, New York (2010)
3. Giurgiu, I., et al.: Calling the cloud: enabling mobile phones as interfaces to cloud applications. In: Proceedings of the 10th International Conference on Middleware, pp. 1–20. Springer, Heidelberg (2009)
4. Team, C.D.: Codamos: Context-driven adaptation of mobile services, http://distrinet.cs.kuleuven.be/projects/CoDAMoS/
5. Yau, S.S., Huang, D., Gong, H., Seth, S.: Development and runtime support for situation-aware application software in ubiquitous computing environments. In: COMPSAC, pp. 452–457. IEEE, Los Alamitos (2004)
6. Gu, T., Pung, H., Zhang, D.: A service-oriented middleware for building context-aware services. Journal of Network and Computer Applications 28(1), 1–18 (2005)
7. Janik, A., Zielinski, K.: AAOP-based dynamically reconfigurable monitoring system. Information and Software Technology 52(4), 380–396 (2010)
8. Paspallis, N.: Middleware-based development of context-aware applications with reusable components. University of Cyprus (2009)
9. JBoss-AOP, http://www.jboss.org/jbossaop (last visited: February 2011)
10. Surajbali, B.: An aspect-oriented middleware architecture supporting consistent dynamic reconfiguration (2010) (status: published)
11. Grace, P., et al.: Deep middleware for the divergent grid. In: Proceedings of the International Conference on Middleware, pp. 334–353. Springer, Heidelberg (2005)
12. Hillman, J., Warren, I.: An open framework for dynamic reconfiguration. In: Proceedings of the 26th ICSE, pp. 594–603. IEEE Computer Society, Los Alamitos (2004)
13. Rasche, A., Polze, A.: Configuration and dynamic reconfiguration of component-based applications with microsoft. net (2003)
14. Vandewoude, Y.: Dynamically updating component-oriented systems (2007) (status: published)
15. Pohl, K., Böckle, G., der Linden, F.J.V.: Software Product Line Engineering: Foundations, Principles and Techniques. Springer, Heidelberg (September 2005)
16. Czarnecki, K., et al.: Formalizing cardinality-based feature models and their specialization. Software Process: Improvement and Practice (1), 7–29 (2005)
17. Pinto, M., Fuentes, L.: AO-ADL: An ADL for describing aspect-oriented architectures. Early Aspects: Current Challenges and Future Directions, 94–114 (2007)

A Reference Architecture for Building Semantic-Web Mediators*

Carlos R. Rivero, Inma Hernández, David Ruiz, and Rafael Corchuelo

University of Sevilla, Spain
{carlosrivero,inmahernandez,druiz,corchu}@us.es

Abstract. The Semantic Web comprises a large amount of distributed and heterogeneous ontologies, which have been developed by different communities, and there exists a need to integrate them. Mediators are pieces of software that help to perform this integration, which have been widely studied in the context of nested relational models. Unfortunately, mediators for databases that are modelled using ontologies have not been so widely studied. In this paper, we present a reference architecture for building semantic-web mediators. To the best of our knowledge, this is the first reference architecture in the bibliography that solves the integration problem as a whole, contrarily to existing approaches that focus on specific problems. Furthermore, we describe a case study that is contextualised in the digital libraries domain in which we realise the benefits of our reference architecture. Finally, we identify a number of best practices to build semantic-web mediators.

Keywords: Information Integration, Mediator, Semantic-web Technologies.

1 Introduction

The Semantic Web is gaining popularity day by day [48]. The best proof of this popularity is that there are a number of domains in which semantic-web technologies are becoming a de facto standard for representing and exchanging data, e.g., the Gene Ontology in the life sciences domain [4], SwetoDBLP in the digital libraries domain [1], FOAF in the people description domain [12], or DBPedia in multiple domains [6].

Semantic-web technologies comprise RDF, RDFS and OWL ontology languages to represent models and the data that populates them, and the SPARQL query language to query these data [3]. Ontologies are shared models by a number of communities that have been developed by consensus [8]. The development of an ontology is not a trivial task: to reach an agreement amongst one or more communities can be an unaffordable problem [22]. Due to this fact, there are a

---

* Supported by the European Commission (FEDER), the Spanish and the Andalusian R&D&I programmes (grants TIN2007-64119, P07-TIC-2602, P08-TIC-4100, TIN2008-04718-E, TIN2010-21744, TIN2010-09809-E, TIN2010-10811-E, and TIN2010-09988-E).

large variety of heterogeneous and distributed ontologies in the Semantic Web, and there is a need to integrate them [20,34].

Mediators are pieces of software that help to integrate data models [27]. This integration comprises two tasks: data integration and data translation. The former deals with answering queries posed over a target model using a set of source models only [13,21,27,52]. In this task, the target model is virtual and contains no data. The latter, also known as data exchange, consists of, based on user preferences, populating a target model with data that comes from a set of source models [15,18,36,47]. Therefore, the aim of this task is the materialisation of the target model. To perform these tasks, mediators rely on the use of mappings, which are relationships between source and target models [18,27,39].

Building and maintaining mappings is costly since users must write them, check whether they work as expected or not, making changes if necessary, and restart the loop [5,37]. Therefore, it is appealing to provide techniques for building and maintaining mappings automatically. To solve this problem, there are a number of approaches in the bibliography to automatically generate correspondences, i.e., uninterpreted mappings that have to be interpreted to perform the integration between source and target models [17,43].

Furthermore, other approaches are based on automatically-generated executable mappings, which encode the interpretation of correspondences into a query in a given query language, such as SQL, XSLT, XQuery or SPARQL [31,38,39,40]. Therefore, the data integration task is performed by rewriting queries over these executable mappings, and the data translation task is performed by executing them by means of a query engine.

Mediators have been widely studied in the context of (nested) relational models which represent trees [18,21,27,39,52]. Unfortunately, these mediators are not applicable to the semantic-web context due to a number of inherent differences between databases and ontologies [25,32,33,51]. Some examples of these inherent differences are the following:

- Structure: a nested relational model represents a tree in which there is a unique path from the root to every node. Contrarily, an ontology forms a graph in which may be zero, one or more paths connecting every two nodes.
- Optionality: in a nested relational model, an instance of a nested node exists if and only if the entire path from this node to the root exists. Contrarily, in an ontology, elements are optional by default, so it is not possible to assume that there exists a path that connects every two nodes.

In this paper, we present a reference architecture for building semantic-web mediators to solve these inherent differences. To the best of our knowledge, this is the first reference architecture in the bibliography that solves the integration problem as a whole, contrarily to existing approaches that focus on specific problems [15,20,28,29,30,47]. Furthermore, we survey a number of approaches in the bibliography that can be used to build various modules within our architecture. We also present a case study that is contextualised in the domain of digital libraries. Finally, after analysing existing approaches in the bibliography and devising our reference architecture, we identify a number of best practices to build semantic-web mediators.

This paper is organised as follows: Section 2 describes the related work. Section 3 presents our reference architecture for building semantic-web mediators. In Section 4, we describe a case study that is contextualised in the digital libraries domain. Finally, Section 5 recaps our main conclusions and present a number of best practices to build semantic-web mediators.

2 Related Work

In this section, we survey a number of approaches in the bibliography for building semantic-web mediators.

Maedche et al. [28,29] proposed a mediator that is based on the Semantic Bridge Ontology, i.e., an ontology that bridges the gap between source and target ontologies. This ontology allows to relate classes, properties, and instances by means of semantic bridges. Furthermore, they allow to combine these semantic bridges by means of specialisation, abstraction, composition or alternative. This mediator performs the data translation task using an ad-hoc technique, which consists of evaluating the instances of the Semantic Bridge Ontology to translate the data of the source ontologies into the target.

The mediator proposed by Dou et al. [15] is based on executable mappings, which are specified by hand and represented with the Web-PDDL language (that is a subset of first-order logic) devised by the authors. The mediator performs the data translation task by merging source and target ontologies into a single global ontology. Then, a reasoner devised by the authors is used over this global ontology, and it retains conclusions that are only expressed in the vocabulary of the target ontology. These conclusions compound the resulting target data.

Haase and Wang [20] proposed a mediator that is based on a reasoner devised by the authors, which is able to deal with distributed ontologies. Their approach builds on executable mappings that are expressed in OWL-DL, and it is assumed that they are known beforehand. A virtual ontology is created that merges source and target ontologies and the executable mappings. Finally, the data integration task is performed by reasoning over this virtual ontology with the user query, retrieving the target query results.

The mediator proposed by Serafini and Tamilin [47] focuses on the translation of class instances. Therefore, they use two types of correspondences, between classes and between individuals, and both are expressed using OWL-DL. In this approach, the data translation task is performed by using a reasoner to reclassify classes or individuals from the source ontology into the target.

Makris et al. [30] devised a mediator based on OWL that performs the data integration task by means of handcrafted executable mappings. These mappings are expressed using the alignment API proposed by Euzenat [16]. Then, a SPARQL query over the target ontology is rewritten using an ad-hoc query rewriting technique, which deals with graph pattern operators such as AND, UNION or OPTIONAL, and even with FILTER expressions.

To conclude, none of the existing approaches, as far as we know, solve the integration problem as a whole. They focus on algorithms to solve the data integration and/or data translation tasks, but none of them presents an architecture that includes all the problems that must be solved when building a mediator: the generation of mappings, the data integration task, the data translation task, and the technology to support it.

3 Reference Architecture

In this section, we describe our reference architecture to build semantic-web mediators. Furthermore, we identify a number of approaches in the bibliography that can be used to build various modules of this architecture.

Figure 1 shows our reference architecture that is divided in four main modules: Setup, Data Integration, Data Translation and Support. The Setup module deals with the automatic generation of mappings that relate source and target ontologies. Data Integration is responsible for retrieving data from the source ontologies by means of a query over the target ontology. The Data Translation module takes the data from the source ontologies and compounds it to generate target data. Finally, the Support module comprises a number of auxiliary components that are needed in the integration process. In the following subsections we describe these modules.

3.1 Setup

This module takes the source and target ontologies as input, and produces a set of mappings based on these ontologies.

Correspondence Generation deals with the process of specifying correspondences that may be defined in different ways, namely: handcrafted [15,30], handcrafted with the help of a graphical tool [2,42], automatically-generated [17,43], or automatically-generated by means of patterns [44].

Mapping Generation takes the source and target ontologies and a set of correspondences as input, and generate a number of mappings as output. Some approaches use correspondences as mappings, which must be interpreted to perform the data integration and data translation tasks. Existing semantic-web mediators interpret correspondences by means of ad-hoc techniques or reasoners, which hinder their applicability to real-world scenarios due to the low performance with medium or large amount of data of ad-hoc techniques and reasoners [15,20].

Other approaches use executable mappings that encode the interpretation of correspondences. The semantic-web mediator devised by Dou et al. [15] is based on handcrafted executable mappings. Popa et al. [39] devised a technique to generate executable mappings for nested relational models. In this technique, correspondences that are related by source and/or target restrictions are grouped to form executable mappings. Unfortunately, it is not applicable to the semantic-web context due to the inherent differences previously described. Qin et al. [40] devised a technique to generate executable mappings between OWL ontologies,

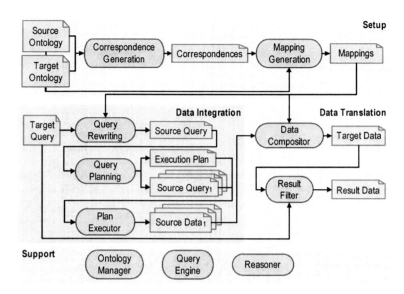

Fig. 1. Reference architecture of a semantic-web mediator based on executable mappings

which are represented in Datalog or SWRL. This technique takes a set of correspondences and a set of instance examples of the target ontology as input.

Polleres et al. [38] proposed the use of the SPARQL query language to represent executable mappings, but it has a number of issues, such as the optionality of properties, or the multi-typed instances. However, note that current semantic-web technologies have proved to be efficient in the management of large data volumes using SPARQL queries [7,46]. Consequently, technology is not an obstacle to the development of SPARQL executable mappings.

3.2 Data Integration

This module takes the mappings and a query over the target ontology as input, and it is responsible for rewriting and planning this query to retrieve source data. This process is divided into three tasks: Query Rewriting, Query Planning and Plan Executor.

Query Rewriting deals with the reformulation of the target query into a single query over source ontologies. This reformulation varies depending on the type of mappings. GAV mappings comprise one single clause of the target ontology and a number of clauses of the source ontologies [27]. In this case, the reformulation is performed by unfolding these mappings into the user query [35]. LAV mappings comprise a number of clauses of the target ontology and one single clause of one source ontology [27]. In this case, the reformulation is performed by applying the techniques of answering queries using views [21]. Finally, GLAV mappings comprise a number of clauses of both source and target ontologies [19]. In this case, the reformulation is performed using hybrid techniques from GAV and LAV [52]. Note that these techniques focus on nested relational models (specifically, Datalog and XML [21,52]); however, there is an increasing interest on SPARQL query rewriting in the semantic-web community [13,24].

Query Planning divides the source query into a number of queries, each of which affects only one source ontology. Furthermore, it generates a plan that specifies how these queries must be executed. In this context, Ives et al. [23] proposed a query planner that exploits the features of the source data for XML models. Thakkar et al. [50] focused on the automatic generation of parameterised executions plans that are exported as web services. Furthermore, they devised techniques that improve the efficiency of these plans by reducing the number of requests to data sources. Braga et al. [9] presented a framework to answer multi-domain queries, which can be answered by combining the data of one or more sources. Finally, Langegger et al. [26] and Quilitz and Leser [41] proposed techniques to answer SPARQL queries over distributed RDF sources.

Plan Executor is responsible for executing the previous plans by posing queries over source ontologies and retrieving their data. In this case, if the sources are web-based, it is mandatory to use wrappers to access to them [14]. These wrappers deal with one or more of the following problems: 1) form filling, in which the query over the source is used to fill in the search forms of the web application appropriately; 2) navigation, in which the resulting page after submitting a search form is navigated until pages that contain the information of interest are found; 3) information extraction, in which the information of interest is extracted and structured according to a given ontology; 4) verification, in which the retrieved information is checked for errors.

3.3 Data Translation

This module takes the mappings, the retrieved source data and the target query as input, and it is responsible for composing the result data of the target query.

Data Compositor takes the mappings and the source data as input, and generates target data as output. When using executable mappings, this task consists of executing these mappings by means of a query engine over source data to produce target data [39]. When using correspondences, this task is performed by interpreting correspondences using ad-hoc techniques or reasoners [15,28]. Note also that executable mappings can be automatically optimised by the query engine to achieve a better performance [31]. Furthermore, executable mappings and the query engine are independent, so we may choose any query engine to perform this task without changing the mappings [31].

Result Filter is needed in some cases since the source data retrieved by Data Integration module may comprise more information than the requested by the user query. Therefore, this task consists of executing the target query over the composed target data and applying other optimisations to this data to produce the final result of the target query.

3.4 Support

This module is orthogonal to the architecture and it provides a number of semantic-web technologies to support the development of semantic-web mediators.

Ontology Manager is responsible for the management of ontologies, which comprises an internal model to represent ontologies, a storage mechanism for ontologies, and operations to load from the file system to this internal model and conversely. Currently, there are a number of frameworks that manage ontologies such as Jena or Sesame [10,11]. Furthermore, it is important to notice that these frameworks have proved to be mature enough to cope with large volumes of data [7,46].

Query Engine deals with the management and execution of queries. Jena and Sesame frameworks incorporate modules to work with SPARQL queries and, consequently, Ontology Manager and Query Engine are implemented using the same semantic-web technologies. In this context, Schmidt et al. [45] studied the theoretical foundations of optimising SPARQL queries, which are the base of these engines.

Finally, Reasoner is able to make the knowledge explicit over a specific ontology, i.e., to infer new triples according to a set of rules. This is mandatory when working with the SPARQL query language since it only deals with plain RDF and does not implement RDFS/OWL semantics [3]. Pellet is an OWL-DL reasoner that is distributed alone [49], but there are other platforms that incorporate reasoners such as Jena or Oracle amongst others.

4 Case Study

In this section, we present a case study that uses a semantic-web mediator for integrating ontologies, which is contextualised in the digital libraries domain.

Figure 2 shows a scenario in which we integrate two source and target ontologies. On the one hand, the source ontology comprises two classes with no relation between them, which are *src:Article* and *src:Paper*. These classes model published articles and papers, respectively. Furthermore, these classes are related to three data properties, namely: *src:title*, which models the title of the article or paper; *src:journal*, which represents the title of the journal in which the article has been published; and *src:conference*, which stands for the conference in which the paper has been published.

On the other hand, the target ontology comprises three classes, which are the following: *tgt:Publication*, *tgt:Article*, which specialises *tgt:Publication*; and *tgt:Paper*, which also specialises *tgt:Publication*. These classes are related to two data properties: *tgt:title* and *tgt:host*. Behind each information integration scenario, there is an intention of change that reflects new user needs, i.e., the source model is the ontology before changes are applied, and the target ontology is the ontology after changes are applied. Behind this case study, there is an intention of change that consists of incorporating the source classes into the hierarchy of the target ontology: the classes in the source ontology are not related and, in the target ontology, these classes are part of a hierarchy.

A Reference Architecture for Building Semantic-Web Mediators 337

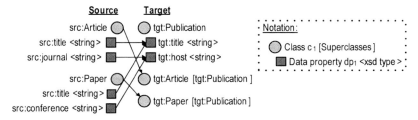

Fig. 2. Example of integration in the digital libraries domain

```
/* Translates Articles and          /* Translates Papers and
   titles */                           conferences */
M₁:                                 M₂:
CONSTRUCT{                          CONSTRUCT{
    ?tArticle  rdf:type  tgt:Article.   ?tPaper  rdf:type     tgt:Paper.
    ?tArticle  tgt:title  ?tTitle.      ?tPaper  tgt:conference  ?tConf.
} WHERE {                           } WHERE {
    ?sArticle  rdf:type  src:Article.   ?sPaper  rdf:type     src:Paper.
    ?sArticle  src:title  ?sTitle.      ?sPaper  src:conference  ?sConf.
} LET{                              } LET{
    ?tArticle := ?sArticle.             ?tPaper := ?sPaper.
    ?tTitle := ?sTitle.                 ?tConf := ?sConf.
}                                   }
```

Fig. 3. SPARQL mappings to integrate the ontologies of the case study

To build a mediator for this case study, the first step consists of building a set of correspondences amongst the elements of source and target ontologies. These correspondences are represented as arrows in Figure 2. Note that these correspondences are only visual aids to help reader to understand the case study. Correspondences are interpreted to get a number of mappings to perform the data integration or data translation tasks. However, the interpretation of these

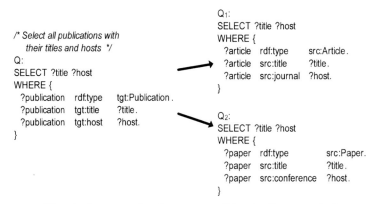

Fig. 4. An example of query rewriting in the case study

correspondences is not standardised: "correspondences are interpreted in distinct ways by different [mapping] systems" [39].

Then, the next step consists of automatically generating SPARQL executable mappings based on these correspondences. Figure 3 presents two examples of SPARQL executable mappings. It is important to notice that these mappings are CONSTRUCT queries [3], which comprise three parts: the WHERE, CONSTRUCT and LET clauses. The WHERE clause is used to retrieve data, the CONSTRUCT clause is used to compose data into the form of a RDF graph, and the LET clause contains a number of assignments. Note that these assignments are not allowed in standard SPARQL, but there are some implementations that support them such as the Jena framework.

In this phase, we are able to translate data from the source into the target ontology by executing the SPARQL executable mappings over the source ontologies by means of a query engine. The main benefit of using executable mappings is that the result is the same regardless the order of execution. Therefore, we have to consider no process or workflow to perform this translation: by executing these mappings in any order, we obtain the final target data.

Finally, assume that a user poses a query over the target ontology to retrieve publications with their titles and hosts, as shown in query Q of Figure 4. This query is rewritten and we obtain two queries Q_1 and Q_2, each of which affects one source class only. The rewriting of this query is based on the SPARQL executable mappings previously generated. Note that, in this case, the queries are of the SELECT type, each of which comprises a unique WHERE clause and a set of variables to be returned. This type of query retrieves a plain table of values for a set of triple patterns [3]. In this case, the execution plan is trivial since we pose Q_1 and Q_2, or conversely, to obtain the same result.

5 Conclusions

In this paper, we present a reference architecture to build semantic-web mediators that is, to the best of our knowledge, the first reference architecture in the bibliography that solves the integration problem as a whole, contrarily to existing approaches that focus on specific problems. Our architecture comprises four modules: Setup, Data Integration, Data Translation and Support. Setup module is responsible for generating uninterpreted mappings (also known as correspondences) or executable mappings. Data Integration takes a target query as input, and it deals with dividing the query into a number of queries, which are posed over the sources, and retrieving source data. Data Translation module takes this source data as input, and it interprets correspondences or executes executable mappings over it to produce target data. Finally, Support module deals with orthogonal semantic-web technologies for supporting semantic-web mediators.

After analysing existing approaches in the bibliography and devising our reference architecture, we identify a number of best practices to build semantic-web mediators, which are the following:

Building and maintaining mappings is costly since users must write them, check whether they work as expected or not, making changes if necessary, and restart the loop [5,37]. Therefore, it is appealing to provide techniques for building and maintaining mappings automatically. To solve this problem, there are a number of approaches in the bibliography to automatically generate correspondences, i.e., uninterpreted mappings that have to be interpreted to perform the integration between source and target models [17,43].

1. Automatic generation of mappings: handcrafted mappings are difficult to build and maintain, since they require the intervention from users. Consequently, semantic-web mediators should use techniques to automatically generate mappings.
2. Exploiting source capabilities in data integration: when rewriting and planning a target query into a number of source queries, semantic-web mediators should restrict as much as possible these source queries to extract as less irrelevant data as possible. Thanks to this, the data translation task is alleviated significantly.
3. Data translation by means of executable mappings: when using executable mappings, the data translation task consists of executing them by means of a query engine over the source data to produce target data. Semantic-web mediators should build on executable mappings since they encode the interpretation of correspondences, and we do not have to rely on ad-hoc and complex techniques to interpret them, i.e., to perform the data integration or data translation tasks.
4. Support for large data volumes: semantic-web data is growing day by day, and to solve real-world integration problems, semantic-web mediators should work with semantic-web technologies that support large data volumes. As we have seen (cf. Section 3), current semantic-web technologies are mature enough to cope with large data volumes.

References

1. Aleman-Meza, B., et al.: SwetoDblp ontology of computer science publications. J. Web Sem. 5(3) (2007)
2. Alexe, B., et al.: Muse: a system for understanding and designing mappings. In: SIGMOD Conference (2008)
3. Antoniou, G., van Harmelen, F.: A Semantic Web Primer, 2nd edn. (2008)
4. Ashburner, M., et al.: Gene Ontology: tool for the unification of biology. Nature genetics 25 (2000)
5. Bernstein, P.A., Haas, L.M.: Information integration in the enterprise. Commun. ACM 51(9) (2008)
6. Bizer, C., et al.: DBpedia - a crystallization point for the web of data. J. Web Sem. (2009)
7. Bizer, C., Schultz, A.: The berlin SPARQL benchmark. In: Int. J. Semantic Web Inf. Syst. (2009)
8. Bouquet, P., et al.: Contextualizing ontologies. J. Web Sem. 1(4) (2004)
9. Braga, D., et al.: Optimization of multi-domain queries on the web. PVLDB 1(1) (2008)

10. Broekstra, J., et al.: Sesame: A generic architecture for storing and querying RDF and RDF schema. In: International Semantic Web Conference (2002)
11. Carroll, J.J., et al.: Jena: implementing the semantic web recommendations. In: WWW (2004)
12. Celma, Ò., Serra, X.: FOAFing the music: Bridging the semantic gap in music recommendation. J. Web Sem. 6(4) (2008)
13. Correndo, G., et al.: SPARQL query rewriting for implementing data integration over linked data. In: EDBT/ICDT Workshops (2010)
14. de Viana, I.F., Hernandez, I., Jiménez, P., Rivero, C.R., Sleiman, H.A.: Integrating deep-web information sources. In: Demazeau, Y., Dignum, F., Corchado, J.M., Bajo, J., Corchuelo, R., Corchado, E., Fernández-Riverola, F., Julián, V.J., Pawlewski, P., Campbell, A. (eds.) Trends in PAAMS. Advances in Intelligent and Soft Computing, vol. 71, pp. 311–320. Springer, Heidelberg (2010)
15. Dou, D., et al.: Ontology translation on the semantic web. J. Data Semantics 2 (2005)
16. Euzenat, J.: An API for ontology alignment. In: International Semantic Web Conference (2004)
17. Euzenat, J., Shvaiko, P.: Ontology matching (2007)
18. Fagin, R., et al.: Data exchange: semantics and query answering. Theor. Comput. Sci. 336(1) (2005)
19. Friedman, M., et al.: Navigational plans for data integration. In: AAAI (1999)
20. Haase, P., Wang, Y.: A decentralized infrastructure for query answering over distributed ontologies. In: ACM Symposium on Applied Computing (2007)
21. Halevy, A.Y.: Answering queries using views: A survey. VLDB J. 10(4) (2001)
22. Halevy, A.Y., et al.: Piazza: data management infrastructure for semantic web applications. In: WWW (2003)
23. Ives, Z.G., et al.: Adapting to source properties in processing data integration queries. In: SIGMOD Conference (2004)
24. Jing, Y., et al.: SPARQL graph pattern rewriting for OWL-DL inference queries. Knowl. Inf. Syst. (2009)
25. Karvounarakis, G., et al.: Querying the semantic web with RQL. Computer Networks 42(5) (2003)
26. Langegger, A., Wöß, W., Blöchl, M.: A semantic web middleware for virtual data integration on the web. In: Bechhofer, S., Hauswirth, M., Hoffmann, J., Koubarakis, M. (eds.) ESWC 2008. LNCS, vol. 5021, pp. 493–507. Springer, Heidelberg (2008)
27. Lenzerini, M.: Data integration: A theoretical perspective. In: Symposium on Principles of Database Systems (2002)
28. Maedche, A., et al.: MAFRA - a MApping FRAmework for distributed ontologies. In: Knowledge Acquisition, Modeling and Management (2002)
29. Maedche, A., et al.: Managing multiple and distributed ontologies on the semantic web. VLDB J. 12(4) (2003)
30. Makris, K., Bikakis, N., Gioldasis, N., Tsinaraki, C., Christodoulakis, S.: Towards a mediator based on OWL and SPARQL. In: Lytras, M.D., Damiani, E., Carroll, J.M., Tennyson, R.D., Avison, D., Naeve, A., Dale, A., Lefrere, P., Tan, F., Sipior, J., Vossen, G. (eds.) WSKS 2009. LNCS, vol. 5736, pp. 326–335. Springer, Heidelberg (2009)
31. Miller, R.J., et al.: Schema mapping as query discovery. In: Very Large Data Bases (2000)
32. Motik, B., et al.: Bridging the gap between OWL and relational databases. J. Web Sem. 7(2) (2009)

33. Noy, N.F., Klein, M.C.A.: Ontology evolution: Not the same as schema evolution. Knowl. Inf. Syst. 6(4) (2004)
34. Noy, N.F., et al.: Making biomedical ontologies and ontology repositories work. IEEE Intelligent Systems 19(6) (2004)
35. Pan, A., et al.: The denodo data integration platform. In: Very Large Data Bases (2002)
36. Parreiras, F.S., et al.: Model driven specification of ontology translations. In: International Conference on Conceptual Modeling / the Entity Relationship Approach (2008)
37. Petropoulos, M., et al.: Exporting and interactively querying web service-accessed sources: The CLIDE system. ACM Trans. Database Syst. 32(4) (2007)
38. Polleres, A., Scharffe, F., Schindlauer, R.: SPARQL++ for mapping between RDF vocabularies. In: Chung, S. (ed.) OTM 2007, Part I. LNCS, vol. 4803, pp. 878–896. Springer, Heidelberg (2007)
39. Popa, L., et al.: Translating web data. In: Very Large Data Bases (2002)
40. Qin, H., Dou, D., LePendu, P.: Discovering executable semantic mappings between ontologies. In: Chung, S. (ed.) OTM 2007, Part I. LNCS, vol. 4803, pp. 832–849. Springer, Heidelberg (2007)
41. Quilitz, B., Leser, U.: Querying distributed RDF data sources with SPARQL. In: Bechhofer, S., Hauswirth, M., Hoffmann, J., Koubarakis, M. (eds.) ESWC 2008. LNCS, vol. 5021, pp. 524–538. Springer, Heidelberg (2008)
42. Raffio, A., et al.: Clip: a tool for mapping hierarchical schemas. In: SIGMOD Conference (2008)
43. Rahm, E., Bernstein, P.A.: A survey of approaches to automatic schema matching. VLDB J. 10(4) (2001)
44. Scharffe, F., et al.: Towards design patterns for ontology alignment. In: ACM Symposium on Applied Computing (2008)
45. Schmidt, M., et al.: Foundations of SPARQL query optimization. In: ICDT (2010)
46. Schmidt, M., et al.: SP^{2}Bench: A SPARQL performance benchmark. In: International Conference on Data Engineering (2009)
47. Serafini, L., Tamilin, A.: Instance migration in heterogeneous ontology environments. In: Aberer, K., Choi, K.-S., Noy, N., Allemang, D., Lee, K.-I., Nixon, L.J.B., Golbeck, J., Mika, P., Maynard, D., Mizoguchi, R., Schreiber, G., Cudré-Mauroux, P. (eds.) ASWC 2007 and ISWC 2007. LNCS, vol. 4825, pp. 452–465. Springer, Heidelberg (2007)
48. Shadbolt, N., et al.: The semantic web revisited. IEEE Intelligent Systems 21(3) (2006)
49. Sirin, E., et al.: Pellet: A practical OWL-DL reasoner. J. Web Sem. 5(2) (2007)
50. Thakkar, S., et al.: Composing, optimizing, and executing plans for bioinformatics web services. VLDB J. 14(3) (2005)
51. Uschold, M., Grüninger, M.: Ontologies and semantics for seamless connectivity. SIGMOD Record 33(4) (2004)
52. Yu, C., Popa, L.: Constraint-based XML query rewriting for data integration. In: SIGMOD Conference (2004)

F-STREAM: A Flexible Process for Deriving Architectures from Requirements Models

Jaelson Castro[1], João Pimentel[1,2], Márcia Lucena[3],
Emanuel Santos[1], and Diego Dermeval[1]

[1] Universidade Federal de Pernambuco – UFPE, Centro de Informática, Recife, Brazil
[2] Universitat Politècnica de Catalunya, Omega–122, CP: 08034, Barcelona, Spain
[3] Universidade Federal do Rio Grande do Norte – UFRN, DIMAp, Natal, Brazil
{jbc,jhcp,ebs,ddmcm}@cin.ufpe.br, marciaj@dimap.ufrn.br

Abstract. Some quality attributes are known to have an impact on the overall architecture of a system, requiring to be properly handled from the early stages of the software development. This led to the creation of different and unrelated approaches to handle specific attributes, such as security, performance, adaptability, etc. The challenge is to propose a flexible approach that could be configured to address multiple attributes of interest, promoting the reuse of best practices and reduction of development costs. We advocate the use of Software Product Line (SPL) principles to manage and customize variability in software processes targeted for the generation of architectural models from requirements models. Hence, in this paper we propose F-STREAM, a flexible and systematic process to derive architecture models from requirements. We define a common core process, its variation and extension points. The definition of this process was performed based on a survey of the existing approaches. As example, we instantiate a process for adaptive systems.

Keywords: Model-driven architectures; architecture derivation; non-functional requirements and architectures.

1 Introduction

It is well known that some kinds of systems present quality attributes, also called non-functional requirements (NFRs), that have an impact on the architecture of the system as a whole. These requirements must be elicited, analyzed and properly handled in the early requirements phase. Otherwise, it would compromise the software architectural design quality. Moreover, some NFRs demand specific approaches and mechanisms to enable their achievement. For instance, it is unlikely that an approach to develop mobile systems (portability) is also suitable to develop multi-server scalable systems (scalability).

The STREAM process [11] [13] allows a model-based systematic derivation of architectures—in Acme [8]—from requirements models—in i^* [19]. However, it does not properly address non-functional requirements (NFR). Instead of trying to define an entirely new process, we envision the integration of the original STREAM with already existing approaches for handling specific NFRs. With this purpose, in this paper we propose a Flexible Strategy for Transition between REquirements models and Architectural Models (F-STREAM). To provide such flexibility, we are going to use the concepts of variability management—i.e., define the common core (commonalities) and the variations (variabilities) of the process. Therefore, we are going to define a base process that can be extended through integration with already existing approaches that are tailored to handle specific NFRs—in contrast with other approaches that handle generic NFRs [2] [3] [4] [6]. The integration of F-STREAM with a specific approach is called an F-STREAM instance.

In order to identify the commonalities and variabilities for the F-STREAM process, we performed a survey on different goal-based approaches that address these specific NFRs. Table 1 gives a brief description of some of the analyzed approaches. Usually the approaches require the use of an extended goal model notation, to include information that is not present on the original goal model. Some of the approaches also provide reasoning algorithms, specific components or a reference architecture. These are the key characteristics that will be considered on our approach.

Table 1. Some of the surveyed *i**-based approaches that target specific NFRs

Approach	Description
For security [18]	Extends goal models by defining context annotations, preconditions and effects; Use anti-goal models; Provides a diagnostic component.
For adaptability [7]	Extends goal models with context annotations; Provides a self-configuring component.
For data warehouses [9]	Extends goal models by defining facts, attributes, dimensions and measures.
For software product lines [17][11]	Extends goal models to express cardinality; Provides heuristics to elicit variability information.

The remainder of this paper is organized as follows. Section 2 describes the common core of the process, whilst Section 3 presents how the process might vary to accommodate the specific approaches, in terms of variation points and extension points. As a case study, we instantiated the F-STREAM process by integrating it with an approach that tackle the adaptability NFR (Section 4). The final remarks and future works are presented in Section 5.

2 The F-STREAM Common Core Process

The common core of the F-STREAM process is the subset of the original STREAM process that is generic enough to be used with different complementary approaches, requiring at most minimal modifications. This common core is able to generate architectural models from requirements models, with an incremental and models-transformation based approach.

For expressing the requirements models and architectural models we use, respectively, *i** *(iStar)* [19] and Acme [8], since the original STREAM process also use these languages. Goal modeling is a an widespread approach in the academy to express requirements, such as in the Tropos method [14]. *i** defines goal-based models to describe both the system and its environment in terms of intentional dependencies among strategic actors [12] (*who*). There are two different diagrams, or views, of an *i** model: the Strategic Dependency (SD) view presents only the actors and the dependency links amongst them, whilst the Strategic Rationale (SR) view shows the internal details of each actor. Within a SR diagram is defined *why* each dependency exists and *how* they are going to be satisfied.

There is a variety of Architectural Description Languages (ADLs), each one with its set of tools and techniques. Acme ADL was proposed with the primary goal of providing an interchange format for tools and environments for architectural development. Therefore, it can be easily translated into an ADL of choice.

Based on the survey on specific goal-based approaches, we defined a core set of activities that may be carried out with any of the approaches. Fig. 1 presents the process diagram of this core set, which is the F-STREAM process common core. In the next sub-sections these activities will be further detailed.

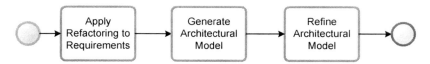

Fig. 1. Common core of the F-STREAM process

2.1 Apply Refactoring to Requirements

The aim of this activity is to modify the organization of the *i** diagram, splitting the responsibilities of the software actor into smaller actors. This allows the delegation of different issues of a problem, initially concentrated into a single actor, to new actors so that it is possible to deal with each of them separately. The decomposition of the main software actor into smaller actors has the objective of modularizing *i** models by delegating responsibilities of the software actor to other (new) software actors that are dedicated to a particular concern. The decomposition criterion is based on the separation and modularization of elements or concerns that are not strongly related to the application domain. Usual examples of this kind of domain independent elements are persistency, security, statistics, etc.

In order to assist the requirements engineer to identify the elements that can be extracted from the software actor, we use the following heuristics. H1: Search for internal elements in the software actor that are independent of the application domain. H2: Check whether these elements can be moved from the software actor to another software actor without compromising the behavior and the understandability of the internal details of the actor. H3: Verify whether these elements can be reused in different domains.

After the identification of the movable elements, they will be transferred to other actors, through horizontal transformation rules defined in previous work [13].

2.2 Generate Architectural Model

In this step, transformation rules will be used to translate the *i** requirements model onto an early architecture model in Acme. Since these transformations have different source and target languages, they are exogenous, or translation transformations. They are also vertical transformations, since the source and target models have different level of abstractions.

In summary, these transformations define the mapping from $i*$ actors to Acme components, and from $i*$ dependencies to Acme connectors and ports. A component in software architecture is a unit of computation or a data store having a set of interaction points (ports) to interact with external world. An actor in $i*$ is an active entity that carries out actions to achieve goals by exercising its knowhow. Thus, an actor representing the software establishes a correspondence with modules or components [10]. In addition, an actor may have as many interactions points as needed. Hence, an actor in $i*$ can be represented in terms of a component in Acme.

Thus, the first vertical transformation rule is a straightforward one, that maps $i*$ actors onto Acme components. Further details of this component will be added later during the mapping of $i*$ dependencies. In $i*$, a dependency describes an agreement between two actors playing the roles of depender and dependee, respectively [5]. In Acme, connectors mediate the communication and coordination activities among components. Thus, we can represent a dependency as an Acme connector. The complete transformation rules for mapping the $i*$ model to an Acme architecture are described in [11].

2.3 Refine Architectural Model

Having produced an early architectural design solution, we can now refine it. This activity relies on some commonly used architectural patterns, such as Model View Control (MVC), Layers and Client-Server. The components of early architectural model will be manually refined by the architect based on his/her expertise by applying these patterns. These patterns are analyzed to identify the similarity with the early architectural model. The refinement process follows three steps.

The first step is to analyze the components of the early architectural model and compare them with the elements of the pattern observing the similarities of their roles and responsibilities. The most similar architectural pattern can be used to structure the early architectural model. For instance, if the roles of the architectural model components are organized hierarchically they can be associated with the Layers pattern, then the components of a layer will communicate just with the components of the layer next to them. Thus, a new version of architectural model is generated. Since the components of architectural model have been related to components of an architectural pattern, also their connectors need be associated. Therefore, the second step is to analyze the connectors of the generated architectural model and compare them with the connectors of architectural. Applying the architectural patterns during the refinement can incorporate the qualities associated with the pattern to the refined model. However, if some component of the pattern is missing in the architectural model it needs to be included. The third step is to introduce new components to adjust the architectural model to the pattern, if any is missing. Since the architectural design can be iterative, components can be added anytime. Moreover, refining the architectural models with patterns to address system qualities (i.e., NFRs) is a common practice, existing several tactics to this end documented in the literature.

3 Variation and Extension Points of the F-STREAM Process

In this section we are going to present the Flexible STREAM process, which consists of the common core presented in Section 2 enriched with variability information. In a business process, a variation point is the place on which a variation occurs, and each possible alternative for a variation point is a variant [15]. In order to describe the variation points in the process without defining which are the variants themselves we are going to use the notation proposed by Schnieders and Puhlmann [16], which defines a set of stereotypes and association links for expressing variability in Business Process Modeling Notation (BPMN) diagrams.

The top of Fig. 2 shows the F-STREAM process. Its gray rectangle shows an instance of the process, which will be explained in Section 4. The variation points—*VarPoint* stereotype—are the activities that are already present on the F-STREAM common core. These activities are generic, but they still may be customized in order to better suit the approach being integrated. The extension points—*Null* stereotype—represent points of the process on which new activities may be inserted, in order to complement the process.

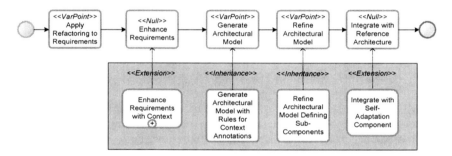

Fig. 2. The F-STREAM process with variability information. The gray rectangle shows modifications and extensions creating a process instance integrated with one approach to handle adaptability.

The process starts with the analysis of the requirements models to detect improvement possibilities. Then, the requirements are enhanced with more information followed by the generation of an initial architectural model. This early architectural model can be further refined and later integrated with a reference model.

The *Apply Refactoring to Requirements* activity consists of refactoring the goal models, based on a set of heuristics and transformation rules. This step is intended to improve the overall quality of the goal model and to turn its structure closer to the expected of an architectural model. Therefore, a modification of this activity would involve changing the heuristics to be used, changing the transformation rules or including new sub-activities.

However, some approaches require the model to be extended, for example with temporal, contextual annotations [7] or crosscutting concerns [1]. Furthermore, they may even require complementary models, such as data-entity models or contextual models. The activities to enrich the original goal models or to define new models may be inserted through the *Enhance Requirements* extension point. Some further requirements elicitation activity may be required in order to provide the information for these enhanced models.

The next activity is *Generate Architectural Model*. This activity consists of deriving an architectural model from the goal model using vertical transformation rules. The set of transformation rules may be modified to address the peculiarities of the approach being integrated in the process. This is the case when an extended version of goal models is used or when other kinds of models are used, requiring the creation of new rules in order to provide a more complete mapping. This is also the case when an architectural description language other than Acme is required. For the latter case, there are two possible approaches: modifying the current set of transformation rules to derive an architecture on the new target language, or defining new transformation rules for performing the mapping from the Acme language to the new target language.

The *Refine Architectural Model* activity concerns evolving the architectural model by applying architectural patterns. This activity can be simplified when the approach being integrated to the process requires the usage of a specific architectural pattern. Furthermore, new activities may be inserted to provide a more detailed architecture as well as intermediary steps towards integration of the current architecture with the reference architecture.

Lastly, the *Integrate with Reference Architecture* is an extension point to insert the activities that will close the gap between the refined architecture and the reference architecture of the approach that is being integrated with the process, if any. Basically, it consists of defining how to link the existing components to the components of the reference architecture. Nonetheless, further activities may be defined to conclude the architecture generation.

These variation and extension points are summarized in Table 2.

Table 2. A summary of the variability information of the F-STREAM process

Type of Variability	Activity	Variability description
Variation Points	Apply Refactoring to Requirements	Add, change and remove refactoring heuristics; Add, change and remove horizontal transformation rules; Add new sub-activities.
	Generate Architectural Model	Add, change and remove vertical transformation rules; Add new sub-activities.
	Refine Architectural Model	Add, change and remove architectural patterns to be considered; Add new sub-activities.
Extension Points	Enhance Requirements	Add new activities to handle goal model extensions or other kinds of models.
	Integrate with Reference Architecture	Add activities to integrate the derived architecture with the reference architecture of the approach being used.

4 Example of F-STREAM Instantiation for Adaptive Systems

In this section we instantiate the F-STREAM process to include activities for handling the development of adaptive systems. This particular instance is the result of integrating the F-STREAM process with an approach for developing adaptive systems, presented in

[7], which uses an extended version of *i** models to represent context information. This information will be used by a self-configuring component, which performs all the runtime reasoning related to adaptation. Its reference architecture is based on the definition of sensors and actuators, which interface with the system environment.

This process is depicted in Fig. 2. The first activity, *Apply Refactoring to Requirements*, was maintained as-is. On the other hand, the third activity—*Generate Architectural Model*—was modified, which is expressed by the *Inheritance* association link from the *Generate Architectural Model with Rules for Context Annotations* activity. Similarly, the *Refine Architectural Model Defining Sub-Components* activity modifies the *Refine Architectural Model* activity. Also, on this adaptability instance of the F-STREAM process, the *Enhance Requirements with Contexts* sub-process and the *Integrate with Self-Adaptation Component* were inserted on the extension points, which is expressed by the *Inheritance* association link.

In the following sub-sections we describe each activity of this instantiated process. To exemplify the use of these activities, we are going to use an adaptive smart-home system. In the specific domain of smart homes the adaptivity is a transverse issue. Even when we do not explicitly model a softgoal called Adaptivity, most of softgoals in the model will require adaptivity in some degree (e.g., reliability, customization).

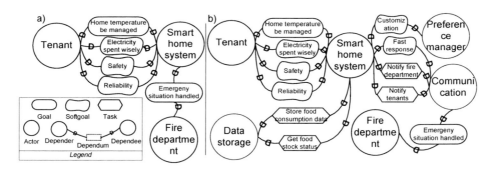

Fig. 3. a) Excerpt of the Strategic Dependencies model of the Smart home system b) Excerpt of the Strategic Dependencies model after refactoring, showing three new software actors.

4.1 Apply Refactoring to Requirements

No modification was required in this activity. Therefore, it can be performed as described in the common core. Fig. 3-a shows an excerpt of the Strategic Dependencies model of the *Smart home system*. A *Tenant*, who is the user of this system, depends on the *Smart home system* to have the house temperature managed, to have electricity spent wisely and to be safe. She also requires the system to be reliable. In order to fulfill these dependencies, the system also depends on other actors. For instance, it needs the *Fire department* to handle emergencies. After refactoring the Smart home system actor (see Section 2.1), three new actors were created: *Preference Manager*, *Communication* and *Data storage*. This is shown in Fig. 3-b. This refactoring is based on the content of the *Smart home system* actor, which is not presented here for the sake of space.

4.2 Enhance Requirements

In this extension point we inserted a sub-process concerned with context sensors and actuators, presented in Fig. 4. A context sensor is "any system providing up-to-date information about the context where the system is running", whilst a context actuator is "any actuator in the environment which can receive commands from the system to act on the environment context" [7]—i.e., a context sensor monitors the environment and a context actuator performs a change on the environment.

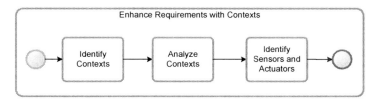

Fig. 4. Enhance Requirements with Contexts sub-process

The *Identify Contexts* activity defines the context information that has an impact on the system's behavior. This information is included in the goal model as context annotations. Fig. 5 shows an excerpt of the goal model of the Smart home system with context annotations. *Temperature be managed* is a goal of the system, but it is only required when the context C1 holds—i.e., when there is someone at home. To achieve this goal, the task *Control Heating Device* can be performed. This task is decomposed in *Turn on heating device*—when C2 holds—and *Turn off heating device*—when C3 holds. The system also has to perform the task *Manage lighting*, which is further decomposed.

The definition of these contexts is crucial for the proper specification of an adaptive behavior. In the *Analyze Contexts* activity these contexts are analyzed to provide the actual data entities that need to be monitored in order to define the context. This information will be used in the *Identify Sensors and Actuators* activity to discover the context sensors that the system will need. During this activity the context actuators

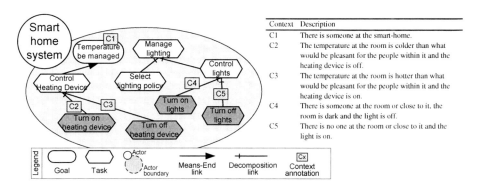

Fig. 5. Excerpt of the Smart home system goal model with context annotations

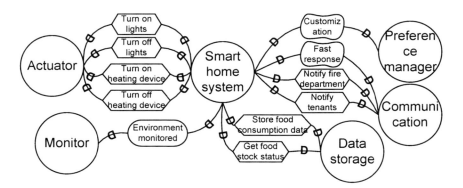

Fig. 6. Excerpt of the Strategic Dependencies model of the Smart home system after the *Identify Sensors and Actuators* activity. Non-software actors are omitted.

will also be identified, based on the tasks of the goal model. Both the sensor (monitor) and actuator for the Smart-home system are presented on the *i** excerpt of Fig. 6.

4.3 Generate Architectural Model

This variation is needed to add new transformation rules in order to consider the context annotations. Therefore, we defined a new activity that modifies the original activity by adding new rules: the *Generate Architectural Model with Rules for Context Annotations* activity. Fig. 7-a shows the resulting early architecture diagram of the Smart-home system—i.e., the mapping from the *i** model to an architecture in Acme. In summary, the actors are mapped to components and its dependencies are mapped to connectors. The context annotations are mapped as properties of the connectors, which are not explicit in the architecture diagram but are defined with the Acme textual notation.

4.4 Refine Architectural Model

Instead of applying the architectural patterns, at this point it is possible to define some sub-components of the components related to adaptability, using the information included in the goal models during the *Enhance Requirements with Contexts* activity. Therefore, we created a new activity named *Refine Architectural Model Defining Sub-Components*. This activity modifies the original *Refine Architectural Model* activity by including steps to define sub-components of the *Monitor* and *Actuator* components. This is achieved by analyzing the extra information added in the goal model during the *Enhance Requirements with Contexts* sub-process (Section 4.2). In Fig. 7-b we show the resulting sub-components of the *Monitor* and the *Actuator* components.

4.5 Integrate with Reference Architecture

Since the components of the architecture modeled so far need to be linked to the component defined in the reference architecture [7], in this extension point we defined the *Integrate with Self-Adaptation Component* activity. This component performs a

F-STREAM: A Flexible Process for Deriving Architectures from Requirements Models 351

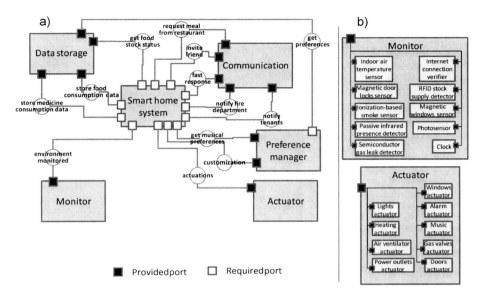

Fig. 7. a) Early architecture of the Smart-home system, after the *Generate Architectural Model with Rules for Context Annotations* activity. b) Sub-components of the *Monitor* and *Actuator* components, defined during the *Refine Architectural Model Defining Sub-Components* activity.

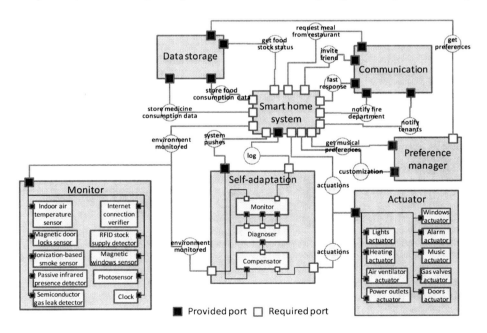

Fig. 8. Resulting architecture of the Smart home system, after the *Integrate with Self-Adaptation Component* activity

Monitor-Diagnose-Compensate (MDC) reasoning cycle, to check if the goals of the system are being achieved and, if not, what adaptations are required to achieve them. This is performed based on the context-annotated goal model and on the input of the context sensors. By encapsulating this reasoning, this component prevents the need of hard-coding the adaptation handling.

The *Self-adaptation* component will be linked to the main component of the system (in this example, the *Smart home system* component), to the *Monitor* component and to the *Actuator* component. The *Self-adaptation* component will receive a history of the system's execution from the main component (*log* connector) and the environmental data from the *Monitor* component (*environmentMonitored* connector). This data will be checked against the goal model of the system, and the required adaptations will be identified. Some of the adaptations will be required to be performed through the *Actuator* component (*actuations* connector), and others will be suggested to the main component (*system pushes* connector). The resulting architecture of the Smart-home system is presented in Fig. 8.

5 Conclusion and Future Work

In this paper we defined F-STREAM, a flexible, systematic and model-based process to derive architecture models from requirements. We faced the challenge of proposing an approach that could be configured to address multiple quality attributes of interest. Inspired by Software Product Line (SPL) principles we defined a set of common core, variation and extension points.

Our goal is to be able to deploy our generic approach to handle specific non-functional requirements, such as adaptability, security, reusability, etc, through integration with other existing approaches. Thus, all the support for NFR would come from these approaches, including NFR refinement and traceability. As a proof of concept, we described how F-STREAM could be applied to develop an adaptive Smart Home system.

As future work, we need to further validate our work with more case studies. We also intend to define a family of instances of the F-STREAM process, addressing some of works presented in Table 1. Additionally, we need to conduct further research to analyze how the different approaches may be weaved together to handle multiple and possibly conflicting NFR. There will be also a parallel effort to improve the STREAM process–for instance, by defining guidelines for its use.

Acknowledgments. This work has been partially supported by Erasmus Mundus External Cooperation Window - Lot 15 Brasil and the Brazilian institutions CAPES and CNPq.

References

1. Alencar, F., Castro, J., Moreira, A., Araújo, J., Silva, C., Ramos, R., Mylopoulos, J.: Integration of Aspects with i* Models. In: Kolp, M., Henderson-Sellers, B., Mouratidis, H., Garcia, A., Ghose, A.K., Bresciani, P. (eds.) AOIS 2006. LNCS (LNAI), vol. 4898, pp. 183–201. Springer, Heidelberg (2008)

2. Alencar, F., Marín, B., Giachetti, G., Pastor, O., Castro, J., Pimentel, J.: From i* Requirements Models to Conceptual Models of a Model Driven Development Process. In: Persson, A., Stirna, J. (eds.) PoEM 2009. Lecture Notes in Business Information Processing, vol. 39, pp. 99–114. Springer, Heidelberg (2009)
3. Ameller, D., Franch, X., Cabot, J.: Dealing with Non-Functional Requirements in Model-Driven Development. In: RE 2010, pp. 189–198 (2010)
4. Bastos, L., Castro, J.: From requirements to multi-agent architecture using organisational concepts. ACM SIGSOFT Software Engineering Notes 30, 1–7 (2005)
5. Castro, J., Silva, C., Mylopoulos, J.: Modeling Organizational Architectural Styles in UML. In: CAiSE 2003. LNCS, vol. 2681, pp. 111–126 (2003)
6. Chung, L., Gross, D., Yu, E.S.K.: Architectural Design to Meet Stakeholder Requirements. In: Proceedings of the TC2 First Working IFIP Conference on Software Architecture (WICSA1), pp. 545–564. Kluwer, B.V., Dordrecht (1999)
7. Dalpiaz, F., Giorgini, P., Mylopoulos, J.: An architecture for requirements-driven self-reconfiguration. In: van Eck, P., Gordijn, J., Wieringa, R. (eds.) CAiSE 2009. LNCS, vol. 5565, pp. 246–260. Springer, Heidelberg (2009)
8. Garlan, D., Monroe, R., Wile, D.: Acme: An Architecture Description Interchange Language. In: Proc. CASCON 1997, Toronto, Canada (1997)
9. Giorgini, P., Rizzi, S., Garzetti, M.: Goal-oriented requirement analysis for data warehouse design. In: Proceedings of the 8th ACM International Workshop on Data Warehousing and OLAP (DOLAP 2005), pp. 47–56. ACM, New York (2005)
10. Grau, G., Franch, X.: On the adequacy of i* models for representing and analyzing software architectures. In: Hainaut, J.-L., Rundensteiner, E.A., Kirchberg, M., Bertolotto, M., Brochhausen, M., Chen, Y.-P.P., Cherfi, S.S.-S., Doerr, M., Han, H., Hartmann, S., Parsons, J., Poels, G., Rolland, C., Trujillo, J., Yu, E., Zimányie, E. (eds.) ER Workshops 2007. LNCS, vol. 4802, pp. 296–305. Springer, Heidelberg (2007)
11. Lucena, M., Castro, J., Silva, C., Alencar, F., Santos, E., Pimentel, J.: A Model Transformation Approach to Derive Architectural Models from Goal-Oriented Requirements Models. In: Proc. the OMT Workshop IWSSA. LNCS, pp. 370–380. Springer, Heidelberg (2009)
12. Lucena, M., Santos, E., Silva, M., Silva, C., Alencar, F., Castro, J.: Towards a Unified Metamodel for i*. In: Proc. of RCIS 2008, pp. 237–246 (2008)
13. Lucena, M., Silva, C., Santos, E., Alencar, F., Castro, J.: Applying Transformation Rules to Improve i* Models. In: Proc. the 21st International Conference on Software Engineering and Knowledge Engineering (SEKE 2009), Boston, USA, pp. 43–48 (2009)
14. Mylopoulos, J., Castro, J., Kolp, M.: Tropos: Toward agent-oriented information systems engineering. In: Second International Bi-Conference Workshop on Agent-Oriented Information Systems, AOIS 2000 (2000)
15. Santos, E., Pimentel, J., Castro, J., Sanchez, J., Pastor, O.: Configuring the Variability of Business Process Models Using Non-Functional Requirements. In: Enterprise, Business-Process and Information Systems Modeling - LNBIP. vol. 50, part 2, pp. 274–286 (2010)
16. Schnieders, A., Puhlmann, F.: Variability Mechanisms in E-Business Process Families. Proc. of the 9th Int. Conference on Business Information Systems, BIS 2006 (2006)
17. Silva, C., Borba, C., Castro, J.: A Goal Oriented Approach to Identify and Configure Feature Models for Software Product Lines. In: Proc. of the 14th Workshop on Requirements Engineering (WER 2011), Rio de Janeiro, Brazil (2011)
18. Souza, V., Mylopoulos, J.: Monitoring and Diagnosing Malicious Attacks with Autonomic Software. In: Laender, A.H.F., Castano, S., Dayal, U., Casati, F., de Oliveira, J.P.M. (eds.) ER 2009. LNCS, vol. 5829, pp. 84–98. Springer, Heidelberg (2009)
19. Yu, E.: Modeling Strategic Relationships for Process Reengineering. PhD Thesis, Toronto University (1995)

Architecting Climate Change Data Infrastructure for Nevada

Michael J. McMahon Jr.[1], Sergiu M. Dascalu[1],
Frederick C. Harris Jr.[1], Scotty Strachan[2], and Franco Biondi[2]

[1] University of Nevada, Reno, Department of Computer Science & Engineering,
1664 N. Virginia St., Reno, NV, USA 89557
{mcmahon,dascalus,fredh} @cse.unr.edu
[2] University of Nevada, Reno, Department of Geography, DendroLab, MS 154,
1664 N. Virginia St., Reno, NV, USA 89557
scotty@dayhike.net, franco.biondi@gmail.com

Abstract. The NSF EPSCoR-funded Nevada Climate Change Project seeks to create a central, reusable, extensible infrastructure that can be used to collect geospatial climate data and information. Housing climate data for Nevada and its surrounding regions during the initial construction phases, the newly created system (with its central component: the Nevada Climate Change Portal) will ultimately be capable of storing any kind of geospatial data for multiple types of research, education and outreach activities. In order to meet the varied needs of the climate researchers, educators, students, and policy makers involved in the project, it was necessary to research and implement a new system architecture. The novelty of this architecture is that it addresses, in an extensible and robust manner, the end-to-end needs of all project stakeholders, implementing multiple sub-levels of architectural design that incorporate data acquisition from sensor networks, data storage using high-performance geospatially-enabled databases, asset tracking and management to improve data validation and verification, metadata collection and management, data curation, and advanced web-based data management and retrieval. The paper describes the proposed system architecture, discusses the major design challenges encountered, addresses some implementation points, and highlights the capabilities of the Nevada Climate Change Portal.

Keywords: Climate change, infrastructure, system architecture, web services, sensor network, climate research, education, public policy.

1 Introduction

Funded in 2008 by an NSF EPSCoR grant, the Nevada Climate Change Project (NCCP) seeks to address the topic of climate change with relation to Nevada while simultaneously building a reusable infrastructure for such research. Specifically, members of the project (organized into six components) interact to create a reusable, extensible infrastructure to gather geospatial climate data that is made available to researchers and interested entities. Simultaneously, other members will use that data and information to enable educational outreach, inform public policymakers, and fulfill the raw data requirements of climate modelers and scientists. In essence, the project involves the creation of a data infrastructure while answering key scientific questions.

The responsibility of meeting the computing infrastructure and data needs of other project components falls largely to the Cyberinfrastructure component. This group of individuals – in conjunction with key members of other components – has collaborated to research and architect an end-to-end system that connects climate measurements and information from field equipment and domain experts to interested members of the public and scientific community. Amongst other aspects that are unique to this architecture are: the ability to collect potentially high-frequency climate measurements over a high-speed communication network, the central maintenance and storage of measurements in a geospatial database, the selective retrieval and re-presentation (i.e. format) of data by/for consumers (i.e. researchers, modelers, external evaluators, etc.), and the incorporation of asset tracking and metadata to support long-term data management and curation. This architecture provides a high level of reliability, performance, and data validity and verification when compared to other climate-related data architectures and systems, such as those in Section 2. In lieu of a large number of implementation details, the current iteration of the system based upon this architecture is available at http://sensor.nevada.edu, though it may be password-protected until publicly released in 2011.

The remainder of this paper is dedicated to elaborating the architecture established for this project on multiple levels: overall, data collection, data processing and storage, and data availability. Section 2 provides background on the topic of climate research, the challenges of such activities, and similar attempts to create suitable solutions. In Section 3, the architectures (at various levels [1]) are described, with particular emphasis placed on the novelty and research involved in creating each optimized sub-architecture and its ultimate implementation. In Section 4, a discussion of challenges related to implementing each architecture is presented. Section 5 concludes with an outline of the future developments and enhancements that will be made to both the architectures and implementations of the system.

2 Background

Climate research is a broad and multi-faceted topic that frequently requires the talents of many individuals to produce both raw and interpreted data in a multitude of formats. In a typical scenario, field technicians install equipment – often consisting of power systems (e.g. solar panels), monitoring sensors (e.g. wind, radiation, rainfall, etc.), sensor processing equipment (e.g. data loggers), data storage (e.g. local and flash memory), and communication infrastructure (e.g. network protocols and interfaces, radios and cables, Internet connectivity and other telemetry services, etc.) – that climate scientists determine is necessary to answer specific research questions or monitor particular physical systems. The data collected by the sensor networks is then acquired and provided to the research scientists for analysis and evaluation.

This deceptively short description implies that climate research is a straightforward, simple process of data collection. However, upon closer inspection (or during implementation), numerous subtle and important requirements (domain, functional, and non-functional) and questions emerge. For example:

- What are the sources of data for the system (e.g. sensor networks, data repositories, files, etc.)? Further, how is that data acquired or accessed, and is that access mechanism reliable, fast, intermittent, and/or slow?
- How and where are data stored and organized? Storage and retrieval decisions affect efficiency, effectiveness, safety/security, data redundancy (i.e. backups), and long-term extensibility. Climate measurements may cover a variety of spatial and temporal ranges, influencing the storage mechanism.
- How can the system effectively address the dynamic long-term needs of data validation, curation, metadata management, many of which are "fast-moving targets?"
- How are data made available to consumers (i.e. researchers)? Security, reliability, verifiability, and performance are all influenced by the access mechanisms utilized by consumers. Data formats and access mechanisms (e.g. web services, FTP access, etc.) must meet the interoperability needs of data consumers to ensure quality results and maximize utility. Further, different research areas may not require the retrieval of all data, or may require the use of aggregates of data over specific intervals.

Clearly, the broad nature of climate research requires that the architecture of any system designed to support its efforts address these issues, as does this. Failing to take these and other issues into consideration introduces the potential to invalidate or nullify the value of the research being performed, or create a system that satisfies immediate needs but that is unable to adapt to long-term changes. While it is often sufficient to assume that researchers would not falsify data or that the original data is accurate, when dealing with more controversial issues such as anthropogenically-modified climate change, data must be clearly accurate and verifiable, and the process by which it was gathered transparent and reliable.

The remaining areas in this section summarize existing attempts to resolve these and other issues related to climate research, as well as the challenges encountered deriving suitable architectures (and their sub-architectures [2], as appropriate).

2.1 Related Work

Many different agencies across the United States and around the world have funded climate research projects in efforts to better understand the physical world. The approaches of these agencies differ significantly, often emphasizing the optimization of one particular feature while sacrificing another (e.g. multiple climate data sources being aggregated into one location at the expense of uniformity and documentation).

Table 1 provides a summary of features that some of these systems provide as a result of their architectural decisions. These metrics indicate the primary type of data each agency manages, whether they provide or manage metadata, whether they enforce data uniformity, and the level of data search functionality they have made available. Each of the example entities in this section has made advances in the field of climate research, addressing one or more of the common problems in the field.

Table 1. A summary of features from various example climate data systems and projects. Here, basic search features are simple date and site search options; advanced include at least date, time, location, and individual parameter selection.

	Type of Data	Metadata	Uniform Data	Search Features
WRCC [3]	Atmospheric	Partial	Yes	Basic
NOAA [4]	Various	No	No	Basic
NCDC [5]	Various	Partial	No	Basic
CUAHSI [6]	Hydrological	Yes	Yes	Advanced
RGIS [7]	Various	Yes	No	Advanced

2.2 Challenges

The architecture of the NCCP is unique: it addresses the end-to-end needs of researchers, educators, policy makers, and climate data consumers. Unlike other architectures that are focused on a narrow set of data, users, or climate research, this architecture addresses the entire climate research process from data to public information. This broad focus introduced a plethora of challenges and issues that needed to be resolved, many of them with the architecture itself.

A chief concern faced was the creation of an extensible, flexible, long-term infrastructure that could be used by the NCCP and future research projects. This required the architecture to specify enough structure and interaction to leverage emerging technologies (e.g. NEON and Internet2) to address current project needs, while remaining flexible enough to adapt to future (25+ year) innovations. A great deal of interviews with key personnel helped to determine the non-functional requirements, such as connectivity and reliability, maintenance, verifiability, resilience, data capacity, interoperability with other systems, and data integration that needed to be fulfilled by the architecture and resultant systems.

Climate measurements themselves present a host of complex issues that need to be resolved, ranging from representation to metadata management. Not only is it common for measurements to utilize different units (i.e. metric or Imperial) and scales, but many data sources store string representations of values (e.g. longitude, latitude, etc.) that can vary significantly. Future climate measurements will be highly-precise, both spatially and temporally, as technological advances are made. Metadata values (e.g. sensor depth below the soil surface) must be selected for storage and later use in data curation activities. Most importantly, the measurements themselves must be handled and stored such that, at any given time, their authenticity and accuracy can be evaluated.

Measurement collection from sensor networks (Figure 1) posed many unique challenges, largely requiring flexibility in the system architecture. Responsible for transforming sensor electrical information into usable numerical values and recording it, remote monitoring systems (often called "data loggers" or "loggers") are resource constrained, having limited power and (often intermittent) connectivity. Retrieving data from these loggers frequently requires the use of hardware-specific software, whose output varies with each manufacturer. The long-term storage and utility of any original files retrieved from these networks also vary, affecting data verifiability.

Even the needs of various end-users present an array of difficulties that affect the architecture. For instance, different scientific users need particular subsets of the collected data, not entire files. Further, the available search and selection functionality affects the data storage and retrieval mechanism. Flexible search and selection tools allow for innovative analysis methods to quickly explore large data collections. Per NCCP requirements, data and information collected by the various components was targeted at a public – not completely scientific – audience, making interface selection and design more difficult. The ability to support various output formats and units of measurement for end-users (especially scientists) is required to maximize the utility of the system, as is support of standards such as those of the OGC [8, 9, 10].

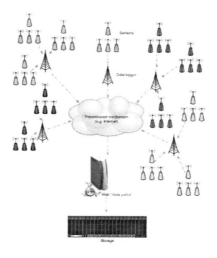

Fig. 1. A general representation of the data collection process involving sensor networks

Despite these challenges, the resultant architecture – as described in the next section – overcomes these hurdles, embodying a new, robust, extensible resource for climate research and, in effect, all fields that require reliable, verifiable geospatial data.

3 Architecture

After a great deal of research [1, 2, 11, 12, 13, 14, 15], the NCCP has been architected with a single, overarching architecture intended to facilitate the design and implementation of a robust, flexible, extensible infrastructure for climate research. In fact, this architecture is more broadly applicable to any kind of geospatial data system, not just climate research.

Similar to a tiered architecture or the TCP/IP model, the overarching architecture (Figure 2) addresses all the non-functional and domain requirements of climate research, creating a set of levels that communicate only with neighboring levels.

Fulfillment of many of functional requirements is delegated to an optimized sub-architecture, while the interaction between the levels is dictated by the larger architecture. The sub-architectures then perform their role in the systems, communicating with necessary external resources and other sub-architectures in structured, predictable ways that isolate changes and ensure future extensibility.

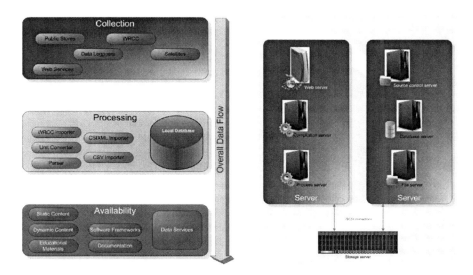

Fig. 2. Overall architecture and data flow (left) and server architecture (right)

This architecture – based upon the climate research process itself – organizes functionality into three layers, which are discussed next: Collection (Section 3.1), Processing (Section 3.2), and Availability (Section 3.3). Specifically, the typical climate data acquisition sequence follows the order: 1) collect data from sensors using sensor monitors, 2) transfer and integrate data from data repositories (i.e. sensor monitors) to central servers, and 3) distribute collected data to consumers. This mirrors the real-world process of collecting data, storing and processing it, and making it available for use.

3.1 Collection

This level encompasses all data sources – whether national repositories, sensor networks, data loggers, or files – that the system collects for centralized storage in the Processing level. The interaction between the Collection and Processing levels is not specific to any manufacturer or hardware, allowing any device or entity to provide data to the system, optimizing its own internal operation. Additionally, this allows the use of transparent network technologies, intermediate data services, and other similar features without explicit internal knowledge being passed to other levels. The only requirement is that data be *pulled* from that source by the Processing level.

The specification of a pull-interaction between levels addresses availability constraints common in sensor network deployments. Specifically, the fact that sensor networks may suffer from limited bandwidth and/or intermittent one- or two-way communication that result from environmental conditions or power constraints. This allows the Processing level to manage the retrieval process, handling disconnections or disruptions on its side. Although one-way communication (i.e. GOES satellite) is supported *within* this architecture, it must have an intermediate data service or layer that supports the pull (and, thus, two-way) interaction when providing data to the Processing level. Any implementation must ensure reliable transmission / transfer of data internally and to the Processing layer, eliminating transmission-induced data aberrations.

The compartmentalization of data loggers and general data sources into this layer has several advantages. Firstly, it allows the data source to optimize its internal operations accordingly. In the case of data loggers and sensor networks, this isolates the transparent details of network optimization and most aspects of logger programming to the remote installation, exposing only communication concerns with the Processing level. Secondly, this isolation ensures that the measurements and data are tamper-proof, insofar as they are not exposed to the public or researchers before storage. By removing the end-use (i.e. researcher) from the collection and processing interactions, the opportunity for data alteration (or accusations thereof) is eliminated, allowing later verification of any derivative results. Third, this allows multiple connection mechanisms between the Collection and Processing levels, depending on the specific availability constraints of the implemented hardware. Specifically, this allows manufacturer-specific or optimized software residing in the Processing level to pull data from sources in this level.

Also incorporated into this layer are user-provided data. This includes manual observations, metadata, asset management information, maintenance logs, and administrative logging information. While these are responsible for a comparatively small amount of information that is provided via the interfaces of the Availability level, they still represent an abstract data source whose data is collected by the Processing level. As such, they are a part of this level/sub-architecture.

3.2 Processing

The Processing level (or sub-architecture) is responsible for retrieving data from the Collection level and incorporating it into its data systems. After this data is incorporated, it is made accessible by the Availability level via query requests. To support the advanced, high-performance data retrieval and search needs of the Availability level, this layer specifies the use of a geospatially-capable database or other efficient mechanism.

This level involves the use of manufacturer-provided or customized data retrieval protocols, routines, and software to connect to data sources in the Collection level. Via whatever synchronization or heuristic mechanism they wish, the software obtains the original measurements and stores them in a non-modifiable location – these non-modifiable files provide a mechanism for detecting any potential data alteration during import into the database, as well as providing the ability to perform long-term data validation through comparison.

Once located in read-only storage, the retrieved data is imported into the database using whatever mechanisms the database, storage engine, or system supports. As this is a part of the internal architecture of this level, it ultimately has no bearing on any interaction with the Availability level. The import process requires the use of software or routines to take the read-only data and decompose it into an efficient, format-neutral structure used by the database. Because each data source may provide different data formats or representations, the import routines must losslessly transform the original data into this format, applying any unit conversion or format parsing necessary.

In this architecture (shown in Figure 3, using a database) a layered database schema has been developed to ensure long-term performance, maintainability, and extensibility [16, 17, 18]. This schema consists of a core set of tables that store scalar geospatial measurements. All import routines decompose vector or other composite measurements into scalar values, storing them in these core tables. The structure of these tables does not change, allowing the efficient, selective retrieval of individual measurements, categories, or other aggregations of data. Rather, as the system requirements or needs evolve, additional supplemental or support tables are added. For example, import routines may utilize information stored in some of these tables; when new import functionality is required, additional tables may be added without affecting the query functionality required by the Availability level. In this way, the core tables and related performance requirements are shielded from breaking changes while the ability to extend functionality to encompass any data source is retained.

This database schema organization, while independently developed, is similar in some ways to that of the CUAHSI system [19, 20, 21]. Although designed to handle hydrological data, some developments in the CUAHSI system were later integrated into the database schema – particularly, the use of "controlled vocabularies" to categorize and represent measurements.

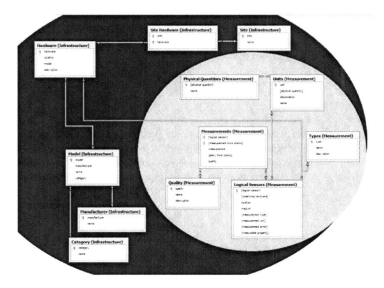

Fig. 3. Core database tables (gray) and extensibility-supporting buffer tables (blue)

Isolation of these operations to this architectural level has several advantages. First, direct access to the data sources is not allowed from the Availability level, securing the original data from tampering. Second, quality assurance and quality control operations are centralized within the data store, eliminating the need for complex interactions with other components. Third, the storage engine is free to be optimally configured (i.e. performance) without affecting the operations of any other level. Fourth, data management activities such as metadata management and data curation can be carried out within this level, isolated from any other operations. Fifth, asset tracking and management information stored in this level can be correlated to sensors and measurements, adding verifiability to the measurements. Finally, the mechanism by which data is retrieved from this level by the Availability level is left for implementation, allowing optimal communication mechanisms to be used. All that is required is for this level to provide the data retrieval and management functionality necessary for the Availability level.

3.3 Availability

The availability sub-architecture is responsible for retrieving data from the processing sub-architecture to satisfy the needs of data consumers (i.e. researchers, scientists, modelers, etc.). The communication mechanism between the processing and availability sub-architectures is implementation-specific, allowing database-specific features to be utilized optimally.

In large part, this layer exists to shield the processing layer from direct public access and to fulfill formatting and selection requests from end-users. Data selections are supported based upon the type of scalar value (i.e. solar radiation, soil moisture, etc.), the timeframe, geospatial region, physical property measured, originating project, monitoring station, and other features that implementers wish to support. This level also performs formatting (e.g. HTML, CSV, Excel, and XML) and conversion (i.e. units) operations when fulfilling data requests.

Data accessibility is also implemented in this level. Specifically, the transport and request protocols and communication mechanisms that support data selection and formatting requests located in this level. Any type of required industry-standard data access protocols/formats/methodologies are implemented as a part of this sub-architecture. This may include future and current access protocols such as REST or SOAP, or standards such as FGDC or OGC.

As with the other levels, organizing user activities in this level has many advantages. First, security and data access efforts are centralized, preventing direct access to the data store of the Processing level. Second, any data access technology can be implemented in this layer without affecting the Processing level – any format or protocol requirement can be fulfilled by using structured queries into the Processing level and transforming the results. This allows future data access standards to be implemented without requiring extensive system refactoring activities. Third, the isolation of user interfaces to this level allows the use of any technologies to meet the needs of users. For example, this level would house a web portal for public information, web services for climate modelers, FTP services for some researchers, and advanced search interfaces for other researchers. This layer is the primary point for public extensibility and system expansion.

4 Discussion

The derivation of an appropriate architecture to support climate monitoring activities is not a simple matter. While the general domain requirements seem relatively simple, the analysis of hardware feature variability and the limitations of supporting software quickly complicate the schema. Incorporating the varied needs of end-users (e.g. verifiability, specific research areas, etc.) and collaborating entities (i.e. data synchronization/sharing) present additional difficulties that necessitate the careful creation of an architecture that meets all requirements, yet avoids any specific implementation-level restriction to retain the greatest level of flexibility.

The architecture we have composed and implemented for the NCCP addresses these complex and diverse needs in a flexible, extensible, consistent manner. As described, the overall architecture effectively addresses the non-functional and domain requirements of the systems required to collect and disseminate data from a disparate collection of climate data sources to researchers and other data consumers. The division of functionality in this architecture allows each individual sub-architecture to optimize and arbitrarily extend its performance and features, communicating with adjacent sub-architectures in structured ways.

In implementing this architecture for the NCCP, several important, yet optional, decisions were made that improved system performance and extensibility. These decisions and their impact are discussed in Sections 4.1, 4.2, and 4.3.

4.1 Standards

As described in Section 3, the architecture defines the general interaction and functionality between different levels. While there is no restriction or requirement to use a particular standard at any level, the implementation of policies and standards within the NCCP has simplified implementation efforts and improved the verifiability of collected data. The policies responsible for these improvements target the Collection and Processing sub-architectures.

Chief amongst these policies is the decision to make all data stored in the database of the Processing level immutable. That is, it can only be removed by a system administrator, never altered by anyone. In cases of manual measurements, erroneous measurements must be deleted and re-entered; all modification is disallowed. Any corrective action undertaken by a system administrator is logged within the system.

Within the Collection sub-architecture, programming policies have ensured that the data loggers record data values using consistent units (i.e. metric values), simplifying import efforts. This standardization allows the data loggers to perform a single conversion to the sensor voltage readings they measure, removing the possibility of compounded calculation rounding. In addition, this ensures that the original data values retrieved from the loggers match those stored in the database, simplifying data verification and validation activities.

Further, the clocks of all data loggers are required to support synchronization to a central server to the greatest degree possible – for two-way communication, clocks are not allowed to drift by more than a few hundred milliseconds at any given time (less for highly-precise measurements or experiments). This policy ensures that the collected values can be correlated, allowing for highly-accurate and inter-related data analysis by researchers.

4.2 Performance

Critical to the performance of the overall system is the performance of the Processing sub-architecture, which is responsible for the long-term storage and retrieval of data. While the mechanism by which data is stored and retrieved is not dictated by the architecture directly, the optimization of the sub-architecture merited the use of a geospatially-aware relational database.

The relational database at the heart of the Processing sub-architecture uses a core schema that does not change. Rather, other support tables are added to facilitate parsing and import routines for any required external source. This decision optimizes the performance of searches on the core tables (which are indexed appropriately), eliminating the gradual changes that would otherwise occur to these tables. Such changes are generally required as new data sources are added and additional, import-specific information is required to import values. Not only does this preserve data retrieval and search performance, but also ensures system extensibility by isolating additions from existing information.

4.3 Public Interaction

To meet the requirements of the NCCP, a web portal was implemented to provide information to project members, researchers, and the public (http://sensor.nevada.edu). By creating a central, visible repository for project information, researchers and component members are able to make their efforts visible to the public, encouraging interest and attracting future funding opportunities.

5 Future Enhancements

The NCCP seeks to integrate and transform data from many disparate sources and integrate future projects that wish to utilize this infrastructure. In essence, this means that there is always room for enhancement and improvement – the system is designed for it.

One set of enhancements involves the incorporation of additional data sources into the system, beyond the data loggers deployed as a part of the NCCP. Depending on the data source (e.g. NOAA and NCDC), either data must be incorporated into the internal database or data queries be forwarded to the remote source and processed by appropriate routines when retrieved. Data access routines for the Western Regional Climate Center have already been developed; import routine development is underway. After this source is incorporated, others will be added depending on the priority given them by researchers and other data consumers.

The implementation of data synchronization routines with the collaborating entities of New Mexico and Idaho will be completed to allow the replication of collected data between the partners. Although these are also general data sources, the collaborative development efforts of the three institutions will yield a more cohesive, integrated data access system than with other data sources that have completed their development cycles.

Acknowledgements

The material presented in this paper is based upon work supported by the National Science Foundation under Grant No. 0814372.

References

1. Fowler, M.: Patterns of Enterprise Application Architecture. Addison-Wesley Professional, New york (2002)
2. Microsoft Patterns & Practices Team: Microsoft Application Architecture Guide, 2nd edn. Microsoft Press, Redmond (2010)
3. Western Regional Climate Center (2011), http://www.wrcc.dri.edu
4. National Oceanic and Atmospheric Administration (2011), http://www.noaa.gov
5. National Climatic Data Center (2011), http://www.ncdc.noaa.gov
6. Consortium of Universities for the Advancement of Hydrologic Science, Inc. (2011), http://www.cuahsi.org
7. New Mexico Resource Geographic Information System Program (2011), http://rgis.unm.edu
8. Open Geospatial Consortium: OGC Web Map Service Interface, Version 1.3.0 (2004), http://portal.opengeospatial.org/files/?artifact_id=4756
9. Open Geospatial Consortium: Web Feature Service Implementation Specification, Version 1.1.0 (2005), http://portal.opengeospatial.org/files/?artifact_id=8339
10. Open Geospatial Consortium: Web Coverage Service (WCS) Implementation Standard, Version 1.1.2 (2008), http://portal.opengeospatial.org/files/?artifact_id=27297
11. Jansen, A., Bosch, J.: Software Architecture as a Set of Architectural Design Decisions. In: Fifth Working IEEE/IFIP Conference on Software Architecture (WICSA 2005), pp. 109–120. IEEE Press, New York (2005)
12. Schmidt, M.-T., Hutchison, B., Lambros, P., Phippen, R.: The Enterprise Service Bus: Making service-oriented architecture real. IBM Systems Journal 44(4), 781–797 (2005)
13. Lu, X.: An Investigation on Service-Oriented Architecture for Constructing Distributed Web GIS Application. In: 2005 IEEE International Conference on Services Computing, vol. 1, pp. 191–197. IEEE Press, New York (2005)
14. Tsonis, A.A., Roebber, P.J.: The Architecture of the Climate Network. In: Physica A: Statistical and Theoretical Physics, vol. 333, pp. 497–504. Elsevier, Maryland Heights (2004)
15. Rew, R., Davis, G.: NetCDF: An Interface for Scientific Data Access. In: IEEE Computer Graphics and Applications, vol. 10(4), pp. 76–82. IEEE Press, New York (1990)
16. Delaney, K., Randal, P., Tripp, K., Cunningham, C., Machanic, A.: Microsoft SQL Server 2008 Internals. Microsoft Press, Redmond (2009)
17. Ben-Gan, I., Sarka, D., Wolter, R., Low, G., Katibah, E., Kunen, I.: Inside Microsoft SQL Server 2008: T-SQL Programming. Microsoft Press, Redmond (2009)
18. Aitchison, A.: Beginning Spatial with SQL Server 2008. Apress, New York (2009)
19. Piasecki, M., Ames, D., Goodall, J., Hooper, R., Horsburgh, J., Maidment, D., Tarboton, D., Zaslavsky, I.: Development of an Information System for the Hydrologic Community. In: 9th International Conference on Hydroinformatics, HIC 2010 (2010)
20. Ames, D.P., Horsburgh, J., Goodall, J., Whiteaker, T., Tarboton, D., Maidment, D.: Introducing the Open Source CUAHSI Hydrologic Information System Desktop Application (HIS Desktop). In: Anderssen, R.S., Braddock, R.D., Newham, L.T.H. (eds.) 18th World IMACS Congress and MODSIM 2009 International Congress on Modelling and Simulation Modelling and Simulation Society of Australia and New Zealand and International Association for Mathematics and Computers in Simulation, pp. 4353–4359 (July 2009)
21. Tarboton, D.G., Horsburgh, J.S., Maidment, D.R.: CUAHSI Community Observations Data Model (ODM), Version 1.1, Design Specifications (2008), http://his.cuahsi.org/documents/ODM1.1DesignSpecifications.pdf

A Coordination Space Architecture for Service Collaboration and Cooperation

Claus Pahl, Veronica Gacitua-Decar, MingXue Wang, and Kosala Yapa Bandara

Lero - The Irish Software Engineering Research Centre
School of Computing, Dublin City University
Dublin, Ireland
{cpahl,vgacitua,mwang,kyapa}@computing.dcu.ie

Abstract. With software services becoming a strategic capability for the software sector, service engineering needs to address integration problems based on support that helps services to collaborate and coordinate their activities. The increasing need to address dynamic and automated changes - caused by on-demand environments and changing requirements - shall be answered through a service coordination architecture based on event-based collaboration. The solution is based on a service coordination space architecture that acts as a passive infrastructure for event-based collaboration. We discuss the information architecture and the coordination principles of such a collaboration environment.

1 Introduction

Service-oriented architecture (SOA) as a methodological framework, using Web services as the platform technology, supports a range of integration problems. SOA aims at providing a service-based infrastructure for interoperable systems development and integration. However, trends such as on-demand and service outsourcing, which are supported by Web services as the platform technology, pose further challenges for software and systems engineering.

We introduce a platform for service collaboration that makes a significant step from static service architectures (based on Web service orchestration and choreography) to dynamic coordination and collaboration in open service communities [1]. Particularly scalability and dynamic flexibility are limitations of current orchestration techniques. WS-BPEL orchestrations require a static coupling of providers and users of services. Even if a mediator would manage WS-BPEL processes dynamically, this could create a bottleneck. The coordination solution based on a coordination space addresses the need to support dynamic collaborations. This solution enables the self-organisation of large service communities, thus addressing the scalability problem. In addition, the proposed platform can enable flexible dynamic composition of service architectures.

In contrast to existing registry and mediation solutions, where providers initially publish their services and where clients search for suitable services, here the approach is reversed - changing from a pull-mode for the client to a push-mode where the client posts requests (into the coordination space) that can be taken on by providers. We discuss the information models, the coordination principles and the architecture of the coordination space approach.

Different coordination models has been proposed, e.g. based on the Linda tuple space model [2,3,4]. More recently, domain- and application context-specific solutions [5,6,7] and approaches based on semantic extensions are investigated [8,9]. The latter ones have also been applied to service composition and mediation. We built up on these semantic mediation approaches by adding a process component and by linking this to a tuple coordination technique.

The next section discusses service collaboration using motivating scenarios and analysing current technologies. In Section 3, we describe technical aspects of the coordination space in terms of information models, coordination principles and the architectural issues. Section 4 discusses implementation and evaluation. We discuss related work in Section 5 before ending with some conclusions.

2 Service Collaboration

Our aim is to enable an integrated collaboration of service communities. These service-based applications often exhibit a dynamic nature of interaction, which requires novel techniques for identification of needs and behaviours and the adaptation of provided services to requested needs. The coordination of activities between communities of users and providers needs to be supported.

2.1 Motivating Scenarios

Two scenarios shall motivate our solution. Firstly, localisation is a multi-lingual Internet application scenario that involves distinct users and providers joined together through a common workflow process. With the emergence of multi-lingual knowledge exchange and social networking sites, localisation becomes an every-day activity that needs to be supported by coordination infrastructure.

- Sample objects are text documents (software manuals or legal documents) to be translated or translation memories to be used in the translation process.
- Sample activities that process the objects include translation (several different techniques may be supported), the creation of translation memory (e.g. crowd-source) as well as translation evaluation and correction.
- The activities can be combined into different localisation workflow processes.

For example, a software developer requires the translation of a software manual for a new market. The developer makes the document to be translated (object) together with a goal (the required language and quality of translation) available through the coordination space. Translators, represented by a provider service can accept available translation tasks, might even in turn request specific translation memories (e.g. through a direct retrieval request or crowd-sourced, both via the coordination space). After finishing the translation the translator makes the translated document available for further processing with an evaluation goal to validate the achieved quality. Another service provider takes on this task. While this process is ongoing, the infrastructure can incrementally identify the sequence of activities as being part of a standard localisation workflow pattern and can afterwards more closely guide and govern the process. At any stage, the infrastructure can also aid by mediating between service users and providers, e.g. converting between different data formats used.

Secondly, customer care is a classical Enterprise software scenario (layered on top of a full software system) that can be enhanced through distributed, on-demand collaboration infrastructure.

- Sample objects are software objects, problem descriptions and help files.
- Activities include explanations or activities to repair or adapt software.
- Two sample processes are a software help wizard that guides an end-user through a number of steps to rectify a problem and a customer care workflow that in a number of steps identifies a problem, decides on a resultion strategy and implements the latter.

Initially, a software user asks for help by posting a help request referring to the software component and the problem in question. An analysis service takes on the first task and determines whether explanation and guidance is sufficient or whether the software itself needs to be adapted. In both cases, new requests (objects and goals) are generated. In the first case, the discovery of suitable responses (e.g. by retrieving and/or assembling help files) is the aim. In the second case, software changes need to be implemented. Again, identifying the process pattern allows more targeted processing of the initial goal.

2.2 Discussion of Existing Technology

The current approach to service collaboration is to develop service processes that are orchestrations or choreographies of individual services. Service orchestrations are executable process specifications based on the invocation of individual services. WS-BPEL, the business process execution language, is the most prominent example, which has become a de-facto standard. A WS-BPEL process is executed through an execution engine. Choreographies, e.g. defined in terms of the choreography description language WS-CDL, are different from orchestration in that they describe assemblies of services as interactions between different partners from a global perspective. It is however similar in that predefined static process compositions are defined. While this has been successful for intra-organisational software integration, limitations can be observed:

- Inflexible nature: Common to both is the static nature of these assemblies, requiring them to be pre-defined and which can only be alleviated to some extent through dynamic adapter generation [10]. This makes the current dynamic nature of service architecture difficult to support. Orchestrations are based on a number of pre-defined partners, not providing sufficient flexibility for future Internet requirements. In traditional SOA, services are orchestrated centrally, assuming that what should be triggered is defined in a

predefined business process - which does not account for runtime events that occur elsewhere.
– Lack of scalability: Orchestrations and choreographies are simple process programs without abstraction mechanisms, thus restricting the possibility to define complex and manageable system specifications. Adding procedural abstraction mechanisms as in other programming languages would not suffice to deal with the aforementioned dynamic and flexibility problems.

A look at the two scenarios illustrates the identified limitations. Increasing flexibility of composition by allowing partners to dynamically join or leave the provider community is not possible using the classical approach. The localised requesting and providing of services (by asking for activities to be executed on objects to achieve a goal) avoids complex, pre-defined process definitions, thus making the coordination more scalable through self-organisation.

While Web service platform and service computing technologies exist, approaches that are suitable to support collaborative, dynamic applications are lacking and platform infrastructures are only beginning to mature. Particularly, scalability and dynamic flexibility, i.e. suitability for open and collaborative infrastructures and applications, are limited due to the restrictive nature of current service composition, collaboration and interaction techniques such as orchestration and choreography languages like WS-BPEL [11].

3 Service Coordination Space Architecture

The core concept of our solution to address flexibility and scalability of service collaboration is a coordination space. This coordination space acts as a passive infrastructure to allow communities of users and providers to collaborate through the coordination of requests and provided services, see Fig. 1. It is governed by coordination principles, which are event-driven at the core:

– tasks to perform an activity on an object occur in states
– services collaborate and coordinate their activities to execute these tasks
– advanced states are reached if the execution is permitted and successful

The central concepts of the coordination space solution are objects, goals (reflecting the outcomes of activies) and processes that are seen as goal-oriented assemblies of activities. Service requesters enter a typed object together with a goal that defines the processing request. Service and process providers can then select this processing task. The coordination space is a repository for requests that allows interaction between requesters and potential providers to be coordinated. The knowledge space provides platform functionality, e.g. the event coordination and request matching, following the platform-as-a-service idea. The Web service platform provides with UDDI a static mediator component that is not suitable to support dynamic collaboration. Our proposal is also different from UDDI in a more fundamental way. It changes the perspective of the client from a pull- to a push-approach. Instead of querying (pull) the repository for suitable entries that providers might have published before, the submit (push) requests here, which in turn are picked up by providers.

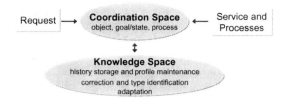

Fig. 1. Coordination and Knowledge Space Architecture

3.1 Information Architecture

Users are concerned with the processing of objects. In classical enterprise scenarios these objects are electronic documents passing through business processes, but within future Internet applications, the object notion will broaden, capturing any dynamic, evolving entity that is part of a process as an ongoing activity. The central concepts of the information architecture are objects, goals and processes:

- Objects play a central role. Changing, evolving objects are dynamic entities that represent an end-to-end view. This follows trends to focus on structured objects and documents as the central entities of processing, as proposed by ebXML and other business standards.
- Goals are declaratively specified, expressing the requested result of processed objects [12]. Essentially, the aim is to allow users and providers to refer to them declaratively, e.g. in the form of a goal-oriented user request (requesting object processing) and to enable semantic goal-based matching.
- The process notion refers to business and workflow processes. States of the process are points of variation for objects: data evolves as it passes through a process. Goals relating to objects are expressed in terms of states of the processes where a process state is considered at the level of individual object modifications. The link to objects is provided via states of processes. Process-centricity is still the central feature of service coordination, thus we retain the compositional principle of Web service technology. Common and successful patterns can be captured and reused [13].

For instance, service computing as an information processing and management infrastructure is becoming of significant importance that would benefit from requests being formulated in terms of the underlying information objects being processed, an abstract specification of goals and the process that the individual processing activities are embedded in.

We propose a semantically enriched information architecture here capturing object structure, object modification states and an object evolution process [14,15]. Ontologies with descriptive and operational layers through an encoding of dynamic logic in a description logic will provide the foundations for the object and process specification framework [16]. This allows us to include behavioural and temporal aspects into the core, static ontology framework capturing objects.

- Objects types are expected to be represented as concepts in a domain ontology. Objects in the form of XML data schemas represent the object type.

A composition relationship becomes a core generic relationship for our request ontology (in addition to the traditional subsumption-based taxonomic relationship). Structural nesting of XML elements is converted into ontological composition relationships.
– Goals are properties of the object concepts stemming from the ontology (covering domain-specific properties as well as software qualities). Goals are expressed in terms of ontology-based properties of objects (concepts), denoting states of an object reached through modification (processing).
– Processes are based on a service process ontology with specific service process composition operators (like sequencing ';', parallel composition '∥', choice '+' or iteration '!' – see [16] for details) as part of the ontology. Processes are specified based on input and output states linked to goals as properties.

This shall be illustrated using the second scenario used earlier on. A typical software component as an object in the context of the customer care and maintenance scenario has properties such as deployed, analysed, or redeveloped. A maintenance process could be expressed as a cyclic process *!(deployed; analysed; redeveloped)*, which defines an iteration of the 3-sequence of activities.

3.2 Coordination Principles

For goal-driven, event-based collaboration of services, coordination space functionality and event handling are important aspects. The functionality provided by the coordination space essentially follows established coordination approaches like tuple spaces [2,3,4] by providing deposit and retrieval function for the space elements - tuples which consist of object type, goal and supporting process. Specifically, one deposit and two retrieval functions are provided:

– deposit(object!, goal!, process!), where the parameters are defined as above in Section 3.1, is used by the client and deposits a copy of the tuple [object, goal, process] into the coordination space. The exclamation mark '!' indicates that values are deposited. The process element is optional; it can be determined later to guide individual processing activities. deposit returns the number of equal tuples already deposited (the tuple will be deposited nonetheless and internally a sequence number and an ID identifying the depositor is kept).
– meet(object?, goal?), with parameters as above, is used by a service provider and identifies a matching tuple in the coordination space. The question mark indicates that abstract patterns are provided that need to be matched by concrete deposited tuples. Ontological subsumption reasoning along the object concept hierarchy enhances the flexibility of retrieval by allowing subconcepts to be considered as suitable matches. A subconcept is defined as a subclass of the concept in terms of the domain ontology, but it also takes the composition properties (see explanation of structural composition in the previous section) into account, i.e. requires structural equality [16]. Operation meet does not block or remove the tuple; it does not have any side-effect. meet returns a boolean value indicating whether the match has been successful.

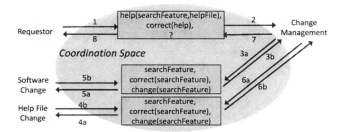

Fig. 2. Coordination Example

- fetch(object?, goal?), with parameters as above, is used by a service provider to identify a matching tuple. Ontological subsumption reasoning is used as above. fetch does remove the tuple, blocking any further access to the tuple. fetch also returns the number of matching tuples. The coordination space will select the tuple that is deemed to be the closest subsumption-based match, i.e. conceptually the closed on the ontological hierarchy.

meet is used to inspect the tuple space; fetch is used if a requested task is taken on and shall be interpreted as a commitment to achieve the specified goal.

The event handling complements the coordination space manipulation through the three functions: this includes registration mechanisms for requestors (in order to be allowed to deposit object processing requests) and service providers (in order to allow to discover, match and retrieve processing requests). The event handling provided by the infrastructure allows providers to register profiles, according to which notifications of matching request tuples are sent out.

In a concrete situation, a service requestor would deposit a request tuple, service providers able to fulfil the request (determined through meet) would compete to take on the task. The successful provider would block the request (using fetch) for others. He could, in turn, use the coordination space to request further internal tasks to be satisfied, as illustrated by the motivating scenarios. A sample scenario is illustrated in Fig. 2.

These coordination principles can be formalised and implemented using Event-Condition-Action (ECA) rules. These ECA rules govern the execution of the coordination space. For instance, with $E = deposit(...)$, $C = meet(...)$, $A = fetch(...)$, the reaction of a service provider (blocking retrieval of a matching tuple deposited by a requester) can be defined. In this simple form, the rules expresses synchronisation between requestor and provider and semantic matching. However, the rules can also be used to deal with SLAs, governance and compliance and competition aspects if additional parameters are taken into account during matching. In general, the rules allow constrained and controlled self-management of coordination.

In Fig. 2, a process is emerging from the sequence of events, indicated through the numbered coordination space operations. The processes can be automatically identified and used to guide and constrain further processing. The schematic example follows the second scenario (customer care) and abstracts its activities:

1. client deposits the help request (problem description object with guidance as the goal)
2. one service provider meets and fetches the request
3. provider creates and deposits two more requests - one to create an explanation of the problem, the other to determine whether the software needs to be modified (software entity as object and analysis request as goal)
4. these tuples are in turn fetched by other providers
5. these providers then deposit solutions
6. which are fetched by the initial provider
7. who in turn deposits an overall solution
8. which is finally used by the client.

The first provider might recognise, supported by the knowledge space, that a common process pattern can be applied [13] (we use the notion of a type to technically capture these patterns). The patterns can provide compliance with process regulations and guarantees of quality. A repository of common processes held in the knowledge space can be used to identify these and use the process to fill the optional process component of the tuple. In this case, the process will indicate a sequence of subactivities (some composed in parallel such as steps 3a and 3b), linked to subgoals, which decompose the original higher-level comprehensive rule - steps 3 to 6 in the example.

3.3 Architecture and Implementation

The functionality separation into basic coordination and advanced semantic analysis support is implemented by a joint architecture of two components - the coordination space and the knowledge space - which support the core coordination and analysis activities, respectively. This architecture is built on the software-as-a-service (SaaS) principle. The structure and functionality of these two spaces shall be described here.

- Coordination Space: The tuples entered consist of the object type, the goal and the process type - the latter identifies the process pattern and may not be available initially and could be determined by the knowledge component. An event model based on the ECA rules governs the operation of the coordination space. The event coordination model comprises rules on events such as deposit goal, identify type, accept task, etc. The functions of the coordination space include the storage of artefacts, the generation and handling of events, and the monitoring activities and collection of relevant information for storage.
- Knowledge Space: This repository for process types and ontologies defines the semantic structure for data objects and process behaviour. The functions of the knowledge space (provided as services) include: the matching support and the process type determination. In the localisation scenario, it can provide support to identify the workflow process to govern the overall execution.

The functionality of the coordination and knowledge spaces is implemented in the form of infrastructure services. The Coordination Engine implements the event model-based coordination functions that allow requests to be posted and tasks to be assigned. The Knowledge Services implement monitoring, collection and storage as core functions and the high-level analysis features. These services are based on Java implementations exposed as services. The coordination engine provides two APIs - a deposit API for requestors and a retrieval API for providers, see Fig. 2. The interaction with engines is based on classical service platform technology, i.e. services specified in WSDL and interaction through the SOAP protocol using the ActiveBPEL engine as the core platform component.

The coordination space idea is the central contributor to increased flexibility, as the coordination space, compared to static orchestrations, enables flexibility through de-coupling requester and provider and the possibility to compose services dynamically. The separate knowledge space provides scalability in terms of the infrastructure support as these services can be provided independent of core coordination functions. It follows what has made middleware successful.

4 Discussion and Evaluation

Part of the implementation and deployment aspects is the consideration of hosting scenarios. Beyond the technical implementation of the spaces as services, the question who hosts these needs to be answered as these are meant to act as intermediaries between requesters and providers. However, proposals exist for instance for hosting UDDI repositories as a static and more manually operated form of an intermediary or, more recently, for semantically enhanced mediators for semantic service matching and semantic spaces that demonstrate the viability of the hosting scenario. Once this infrastructure, involving a third part, is in place, value-added functions to coordination can easily be added to the knowledge space in the software-as-a-service spirit.

The two scenarios used to motivate the usefulness of the proposed approach have also been used by us to validate the conceptual architecture of coordination spaces, specifically demonstrating the benefits of the coordination principles and protocol aspects. Both scenarios are based on real-world applications. Traditionally implemented solutions for both exist as demonstrator applications within a research centre we participate in. The benefit of this evaluation setting in order to demonstrate the benefits of a novel platform technology is twofold:

- The demonstrator scenarios have been developed in close collaboration with industrial partners and represent state-of-the-art implementations.
- The existence of the technologically advanced solutions allows a comparison between the existing project demonstrators and their reimplementation based on the proposed infrastructure using the prototype discussed earlier.

While full applications have not been developed yet, we have focussed our evaluation on a systematic performance analysis of the scenarios with a larger number of clients and providers (> 20 for each), which allows us to conclude significant scalability benefits using the proposed collaboration approach as indicated in the discussions earlier. We have observed an acceptable performance overhead of around 10 % for coordination activities compared a hardwired WS-BPEL composition. In a traditional solution, either a significant number of WS-BPEL processes would have to be provided, or a mediator that explicitly executes provider selection would have to be added (which might create a bottleneck for larger service communities in contrast to the passive coordination space where some selection actitivies is carried out by providers).

Another key result is that decoupling through the coordination space provides more flexibility. The push-model allows for more dynamic composition as the example in Fig. 2 illustrates. The coordination primitives allow a localisation of collaboration activities, thus enhancing the scalability through local self-management. The semantic support infrastructure enhances flexibility through the matching techniques and allows for higher degrees of automation.

5 Related Work

The coordination paradigm applied here is a fundamental change to existing service discovery and matching approaches. Coordination models have been widely used to organise collaboration. The Linda tuple space coordination model [2] has influenced a wide range of variations including our on work on concurrent task coordination in programming languages [3], which in turn has influenced the solution here. More recently, domain- and application context-specific solutions and approaches based on semantic extensions have been investigated. However, the specifics of distributed on-demand environments has not yet been addressed. In particular over the past years, coordination has received much attention [5,6,7] due to the emergence of collaborative ICT-supported environments, ranging from workflow and collaborative work to technical platforms such as service collaboration. The latter ones have also been applied to service composition and mediation. Only recently, event handling has been considered in the SOA context in the form of event-driven SOA. In [17], an ontology-based collaboration approach is described that is similar to ours in that it advocates a push-style of coordination. We have added to semantic mediation approaches like [8,17,18] by including a process notion as a central components of request tuples [14], supported by a process-centric ontology languages. Through the goal/state link, this process context is linked to the request coordination technique focussing on objects are primary entities.

An important contributor to the overall success is backward compatibility. We can realise BPEL-style interaction as a collaboration in our coordination spaces. A request tuple can be automatically generated from a BPEL process by using the BPEL input parameters as the object and the BPEL process abstraction as the process element as the process type of the tuple. The goal would in this case be left unspecified, and provider matching would be individually carried out for each invocation in the BPEL process.

6 Conclusions

Integration and coordination of services is at the core of recent dynamic service architectures. However, their structural, inherent inflexibility makes changes and evolution difficult. Current service computing platforms suffer from flexibility and scalability problems, which can be overcome through the proposed coordination space. This coordination technologically significantly enhances the collaboration and also competition capabilities of the Web service platform, particularly in the context of dynamic applications.

The proposed coordination technology aims directly at the core challenges of service architecture, such as the lack of a flexible mechanism for service collaborations and the need for variability and flexibility in dynamic settings. Decoupling achieves flexibility. Scalability is achieved through a passive coordination architecture with reduced coordination support - which, however, necessitates the cooperation of providers to engage and pro-actively use the coordination space as a market place. The aims are to achieve cost reductions for service interoperation covering design and deployment; operation, maintenance and evolution, while still enabling flexibility for collaborating service architectures.

While we have defined the core coordination principles here, the range of supporting features through the knowledge space needs to be investigated further. Part of this are fault-tolerance features supporting self-management and semantic techniques deducing object and process types from possibly incomplete information [19]. Trust is a related aspects that needs to be addressed. We have occasionally indicated advanced functionality of the knowledge space, e.g. the automated identification of processes based on stored process history or the possibility to consider non-functional aspects reflected in profiles and context models during matching. This requires further investigation.

Acknowledgment

This work was supported by Science Foundation Ireland grant 03/CE2/I303_1 to Lero - the Irish Software Engineering Research Centre (www.lero.ie) and grant 07/RFP/CMSF429 CASCAR.

References

1. Rao, J., Su, X.: A Survey of Automated Web Service Composition Methods. In: Cardoso, J., Sheth, A.P. (eds.) SWSWPC 2004. LNCS, vol. 3387, pp. 43–54. Springer, Heidelberg (2005)
2. Gelernter, D.: Generative Communication in Linda. ACM Transactions on Programming Languages and Systems 7(1), 80–112 (1985)
3. Doberkat, E.-E., Hasselbring, W., Pahl, C.: Investigating Strategies for Cooperative Planning of Independent Agents through Prototype Evaluation. In: Hankin, C., Ciancarini, P. (eds.) COORDINATION 1996. LNCS, vol. 1061. Springer, Heidelberg (1996)

4. Doberkat, E.-E., Franke, W., Gutenbeil, U., Hasselbring, W., Lammers, U., Pahl, C.: PROSET - Prototyping with Sets, Language Definition. Software-Engineering Memo 15 (1992)
5. Johanson, B., Fox, A.: Extending Tuplespaces for Coordination in Interactive Workspaces. Journal of Systems and Software 69(3), 243–266 (2004)
6. Li, Z., Parashar, M.: Comet: A Scalable Coordination Space for Decentralized Distributed Environments. In: Proc. Intl. Workshop on Hot Topics in Peer-To-Peer Systems HOT-P2P, pp. 104–112. IEEE, Los Alamitos (2005)
7. Balzarotti, D., Costa, P., Picco, G.P.: The LighTS tuple space framework and its customization for context-aware applications. Web Intelligence and Agent Systems 5(2), 215–231 (2007)
8. Nixon, L., Antonechko, O., Tolksdorf, R.: Towards Semantic tuplespace computing: the Semantic web spaces system. In: Proceedings of the 2007 ACM Symposium on Applied Computing SAC 2007, pp. 360–365. ACM, New York (2007)
9. Pahl, C., Zhu, Y.: A Semantical Framework for the Orchestration and Choreography of Web Services. In: Proceedings of the International Workshop on Web Languages and Formal Methods (WLFM 2005). ENTCS, vol. 151(2), pp. 3–18 (2006)
10. Brogi, A., Popescu, R.: Automated Generation of BPEL Adapters. In: Dan, A., Lamersdorf, W. (eds.) ICSOC 2006. LNCS, vol. 4294, pp. 27–39. Springer, Heidelberg (2006)
11. Pahl, C.: A Conceptual Architecture for Semantic Web Services Development and Deployment. International Journal of Web and Grid Services 1(3/4), 287–304 (2005)
12. Andersson, B., Bider, I., Johannesson, P., Perjons, E.: Towards a formal definition of goal-oriented business process patterns. BPM Journal 11, 650–662 (2005)
13. Gacitua-Decar, V., Pahl, C.: Automatic Business Process Pattern Matching for Enterprise Services Design. In: 4th International Workshop on Service- and Process-Oriented Software Engineering (SOPOSE 2009). IEEE Press, Los Alamitos (2009)
14. Pahl, C.: A Formal Composition and Interaction Model for a Web Component Platform. In: ICALP 2002 Workshop on Formal Methods and Component Interaction. Elsevier Electronic Notes on Computer Science ENTCS, vol. 66(4), Malaga, Spain (2002)
15. Pahl, C.: A Pi-Calculus based Framework for the Composition and Replacement of Components. In: Proc. Conference on Object-Oriented Programming, Systems, Languages, and Applications OOPSLA 2001 - Workshop on Specification and Verification of Component-Based Systems. ACM Press, Tampa Bay (2001)
16. Pahl, C., Giesecke, S., Hasselbring, W.: Ontology-based Modelling of Architectural Styles. Information and Software Technology 1(12), 1739–1749 (2009)
17. Tsai, W.T., Xiao, B., Chen, Y., Paul, R.A.: Consumer-Centric Service-Oriented Architecture: A New Approach. In: Proc. Workshop on Software Technologies for Future Embedded and Ubiquitous Systems, pp. 175–180 (2006)
18. Pahl, C.: Layered Ontological Modelling for Web Service-oriented Model-Driven Architecture. In: Hartman, A., Kreische, D. (eds.) ECMDA-FA 2005. LNCS, vol. 3748, pp. 88–102. Springer, Heidelberg (2005)
19. Wang, M., Yapa Bandara, K., Pahl, C.: Integrated Constraint Violation Handling for Dynamic Service Composition. In: IEEE International Conference on Services Computing SCC 2009. IEEE, Los Alamitos (2009)

A Framework to Support the Development of Collaborative Components

Hien Le and Surya Bahadur Kathayat

Norwegian University of Science and Technology,
NO 7491 Trondheim, Norway
{hiennam,surya}@item.ntnu.no
www.item.ntnu.no

Abstract. In this paper, a framework to support the development of collaborative components is presented. The role of a collaborative component is to support the inter-working among components through their interfaces. By focusing on the behaviors of the collaborative components, the interaction between components can be independently verified and validated. The proposed framework includes: (1) the structural and architecture models of collaborative components; (2) the choreography models to specify the behaviors of the collaborative components; and (3) the orchestration models to specify the behaviors of component types that participate in the inter-working. The orchestration models are created by model transformations from the architecture and choreography models. The created components are placed in the repository so that they can be re-used and composed together.

Keywords: Collaborative components, model transformation.

1 Introduction

Components are commonly defined as reusable and composable software units having specified functionalities (i.e., local behaviors) and interfaces. Component composition is a process to build complex components from simpler or existing ones [1,7]. On one hand, new components can be rapidly developed by composing existing components together, and thus reducing the development costs. On the other hand, however, there are also many challenges which have not completely dealt with, for example, how to efficiently define and specify component interfaces so that components can be connected and deployed together, or how to specify the interactive and dependent behaviors of composite components [3,4].

We consider components which are collaborative and aiming to establish some desired goals among collaborating entities. Thus, the role of a collaborative component is to support the inter-working among components through their interfaces (also called semantic interfaces of components [2]). By focusing on the behaviors of the collaborative components, the interaction interfaces between components can be independently verified and validated. Once the interfaces of components are completed, the remaining work is to ensure that the local functionalities comply with the designed interfaces.

There works in the literature uses scenario-based approach using formalism such as Use Case Maps (UCM) describe system behavior consisting of large number of collaborating components. However, the problem with such approaches, as identified in [10], is that UCM do not have well-defined semantics for component interface specifications. Some approaches specify interactions and composition of components at the level of programming languages [12], however in this paper, we focus on high-level mechanisms with model-driven approach.

We specify the contracts, similar to conceptual contracts in [11], that specify essential aspects of integrating components. We present a framework to support the development of collaborative components by tackling two challenges: (1) how to model and design collaborative components in such a way they can be easily analyzed and re-used; and (2) how to support the compositions of existing components to create new components taking into account the dependent behavior among components.

The rest of the paper is as following. Section 2 discusses the overview of our collaboration component development framework. Section 3 addresses the issues of composition pattern to support the composition of components. Section 4 concludes the paper.

2 Collaborative Component Development Framework

Figure 1 shows the overview of the framework. The proposed framework includes two main layers: design layer and repository layer. The design layer includes: (1) the structural and architecture models of collaborative components; (2) the choreography models to specify the behaviors of the collaborative components; and (3) the orchestration models to specify the behaviors of component types that participate in the inter-working. The orchestration models are created by model transformations from the architecture and choreography models. The created components are placed in the repository layer so that they can be re-used and composed together.

The detail of each model and layer of the framework is discussed in the following sub-sections.

2.1 Component Structure and Architecture

We categories two types of components: elementary and composite components. Elementary components are the one which can not be decomposed further and composite components are composed from elementary components. UML collaboration composite structure are used to specify the structural (i.e., component roles and interactions) of elementary components and the architecture of composite components (i.e., how elementary component roles are combined together into composite roles), respectively. For example, Figure 2(a) shows an example of a LocationService component in which an elementary user role interacts with an elementary server role. When existing components (which can be either elementary or composite ones) are composed to form a new composite component, role of these components are bound to composite roles in the composite component. For example, in Figure 1, the roles *roleA* and *roleC* are bound to role *CroleA*.

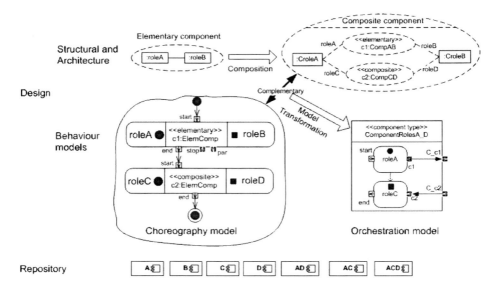

Fig. 1. Collaborative component development framework

2.2 Behavior Models of Collaborative Components

Choreography model describes the behavior of a collaborative component, i.e., how different component participants interact with each other [9,?]. In the case of elementary components, behavior models specify the interaction among participating roles in a component. Figure 2(b) illustrates the behaviors of the LocationService collaborative component.

An component can have all the different types of pins that UML allows, such as initiating, streaming and terminating pins. An initiating pin will start the component if it is not started yet. Terminating pins will terminate the called component. Streaming pins can pass tokens while the called component is active, i.e. a flow connected by streaming pins allows the called components to interact without being stopped.

In this particular example, the user part will take the initial role (i.e., denoted by a filled-circle) and the server part is the terminating role (i.e., denoted by a filled-square). The user periodically reads the geographic coordinate of the location of the user and sends to the server. This location information then can be forwarded to other components. The activities of LocationService component is ended when the server receives signal (via streaming pin stop). It is important to note that this behavior of the collaborative component is fully specified, however, it may not be composable due to the lack of connection points (explained later).

In the case of a composite component, global behavior is described by connecting (sub-) components together thereby specifying ordering and causality among them. In order to simplify the view of global collaborative behavior, an abstract representation of collaborative component will be used (as shown in

Figure 1). We have used choreography models with two different levels of details: flow-global choreography model and flow-localized model [9].

Flow-global choreography is used to define the intended collaborative behavior of composite collaborations on a high level of abstraction avoiding details of localization and resolution of coordination problems. The behavior is defined by an activity diagram connecting actions by flows (see Figure 4(a) for an example of flow-global in which the LocationService component is composed with the *InforService* component). From the flow-global choreography, by model transformation, a flow-localized choreography will be generated [9]. The flow-localized is used to refine the collaborative behavior in sufficient detail to allow extensive analysis and to automatically synthesize the behavior of component types providing orchestration (explained in Section 2.3).

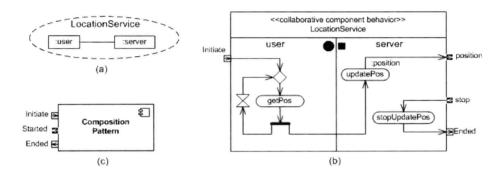

Fig. 2. Behavior of LocationService collaborative component

2.3 Orchestration Models to Specify the Behavior of Local Functionalities

From the global collaborative behavior models, one can synthesize component models, also called orchestration model [8,9]. Orchestration models describe local behavior (i.e., functionalities) of a component including the information about the collaborative components it participates in and their ordering. An orchestrator may have well defined interfaces and internal behavior. Orchestration models are created by model transformation mechanisms which are based on both collaboration architecture and choreography models. The architecture of components specify which roles (elementary or composite roles) should be placed within a component scope. While the choreography model instructs how should local components (e.g., related to user part) be connected together.

In Figure 1, the architecture specifies that the elementary role *roleA* and the composite role *roleC* will be placed in one component type. Information about the collaborations it participates in and the ordering imposed by external collaborative activities are retained in order to support automatic realization as well as compatibility checks during subsequent composition of components into working systems, detailed algorithm is given in [8,6].

3 Composition Pattern of Components

Components can be put into the library and composed later in order to make a complete system. Composition of components together is done by means of pins and collaborations as interfaces. However, in order to deal with the dependent behavior among components (either collaborative or non-collaborative components), collaborative components may need to be modified, for example, telling other components that the component has been initiated, started or ended.

In Figure 4, the InformationService will start when the location of the user is identified by the LocationService. This interactive behavior can be captured and specified by the choreography model. However, at orchestration level, this dependency property between *User_LocationService* and *User_InforService* components (which are composed within the scope of the User component) cannot be implemented. We have identified the following three possibilities:

- If a component is playing a initiating role in a collaboration, then it will retain *Initiate* pin indicating that it will start a component. In this case, a component may not have pins indicating when a component ends, for example user component in the *LocationService* component.
- If a component is playing a terminating role in a collaboration, then it will retain *Ended* pin indicating that component is terminated. In this case, a component may not have pin indicating when a component has been initiated, for example a server component in the *LocationService* component.
- If a component is playing participating role i.e., neither starting nor terminating, then component will not have any pins indicating start and end of a component.

In order to address these issues, we made adjustments by adding additional pins: *Initiate* to indicate that it starts a component, *Started* indicating that component has been started, and *Ended* indicating that component behavior terminated (see Figure 2c). The main novelty of this composition pattern is that, the pre-designed functional behavior of the collaborative component is unchanged with the additional coordination added in an enclosing activity indicated by dashed flows in Figure 3. Adjustments to the original behavior are done as following (and illustrated in Figure 3):

- In the initiating component type, add a fork after the Initiate pin and send signal indicating that all collaborative components have been initiated.
- In the terminating component type, add a fork before the Ended pin and send signal indicating that all collaborative components have been terminated.
- In the participating component type, capture the signal from other roles to indicate when it starts and when it ends.

Once we have the information about a component for example when it starts and when it ends, we can connect the components together by connecting these pins along the implied flow/ordering from choreography models. For example, Figure 4 shows the composition of inner-components in a User component. The

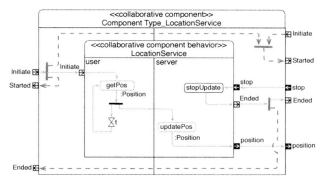

Fig. 3. Detailed design of LocationService collaborative component

user component plays roles in *LocationService* and *InforService*. Their ordering is such that once the LocationService component updates a position information then *InforService* component can be started, i.e., to be ready to receive information from the server components. Note that there is some implied concurrency between them due to the streaming pin. This means the user component of location service and user component of the information service may overlap. This is specified by a flow connecting *Started* pin of *User_LocationService* to *Initiate* pin of *User_InfoService* in Figure 4(b).

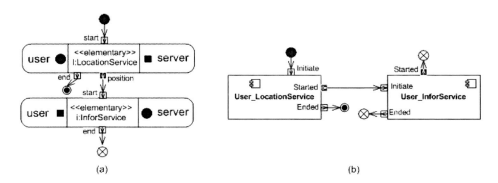

Fig. 4. Global component composition view (a) and Local composition of user composite components (b)

4 Concluding Remarks

A collaboration based framework to support the development of collaborative components is proposed. Structural and architectural model can be specified using UML collaboration structure and corresponding collaborative behavior, i.e. interaction among the participating components, is specified using UML activity diagrams. Elementary components can automatically be synthesized from choreography and orchestration models and put into a repository. Such components can later be reused and composed in making a complete system. We also discuss a general composition pattern which will be applied to modify the behavior of existing components which might not be composable due to lacking of connectivity points. In addition, the composition pattern can also capture both the sequential composition (i.e., via Ended pin) and parallel composition of components (i.e., via Started streaming pin).

Future work includes: (1) integrating the service-oriented architecture (SOA) paradigm into the structural and architecture of components in the framework so that existing components in the library, which are matched with the user requirements, can be quickly retrieved to be composed; (2) considering additional dependencies of components when they are composed (e.g., suspended or resumed); and (3) verifying and validating the semantic interfaces of composite components.

References

1. Szyperski, C.: Component Software: Beyond Object-Oriented Programming. Addison-Wesley Longman Publishing Co., Inc., Boston (2002)
2. Bræk, R., Floch, J.: ICT convergence: Modeling issues. In: 4th International SDL and MSC Workshop, System Analysis and Modeling, SAM (2004)
3. Crnkovic, I., Larsson, S., Chaudron, M.R.V.: Component-based Development Process and Component Lifecycle. CIT 13(4), 321–327 (2005)
4. Jisa, D.L.: Component based development methods: comparison. Computer Systems and Technologies, 1–6 (2004)
5. Kraemer, F.A., Kathayat, S.B., Bræk, R.: Unified modeling of service logic with user interfaces. In: Proceeding of the First International Workshop on Model Driven Service Engineering and Data Quality and Security, p. 3744. ACM, New York (2009)
6. Castejon, H.N., Bræk, R., Bochmann, G.V.: Realizability of collaboration-based service specifications. In: Proceedings of the 14th Asia-Pacific Software Engineering Conference, p. 7380. IEEE Computer Society, Los Alamitos (2007)
7. Lau, K., Wang, Z.: Software Component Models. IEEE Trans. Software Eng. 33(10), 709–724 (2007)
8. Kathayat, S.B., Bræk, R., Le, H.N.: Automatic derivation of components from choreographies - a case study. In: International Conference on Software Engineering, Phuket, Thailand (2010)
9. Kathayat, S.B., Bræk, R.: From flow-global choreography to component types. In: Kraemer, F.A. (ed.) SAM 2010. LNCS, vol. 6598, pp. 36–55. Springer, Heidelberg (2011)
10. Bruin, H.D.: Scenario-Based Analysis of Component Compositions. In: Proceedings of the Second Symposium on Generative and Component-Based Software Engineering, pp. 1–18. Springer, Heidelberg (2000)
11. Kiniry, J.R.: Semantic component composition. In: Proceedings of the Third International Workshop on Composition Languages, pp. 1–13. ACM, New York (2003)
12. Kristensen, B.B., May, D.C.: Component Composition and Interaction. In: Proceedings of International Conference on Technology of Object-Oriented Languages and Systems (TOOLS PACIFIC 1996) (1996)

Resource Allocation, Trading and Adaptation in Self-managing Systems

Guglielmo Lulli[1], Pasqualina Potena[2], and Claudia Raibulet[1]

[1] Università degli Studi di Milano-Bicocca, Dipartimento di Informatica,
Sistemistica e Comunicazione, Viale Sarca 336, U14, 20126 Milan, Italy
[2] Università degli Studi di Bergamo, Viale Marconi, 24024, Bergamo, Italy
{lulli,raibulet}@disco.unimib.it,
pasqualina.potena@unibg.it

Abstract. The allocation of a limited number of resources among multiple self-interested stakeholders is a challenging issue for many real life systems and applications. Resource management for this type of systems is a challenging task because of the different objectives of the owner of the resources and the stakeholders. The owner aims to an efficient usage of the resources, while stakeholders have self-interested objectives. This paper presents a software framework for resource management based on the integration of dynamic allocation, trading, and self-adaptation mechanisms. Resource allocation and adaptation are performed in a centralized manner, while resource trading is achieved through a decentralized approach. Furthermore, the paper presents the application of the proposed framework in two different domains: aeronautics and Internetware.

Keywords: Resource management, resource allocation, resource trading, self-adaptation, resource-constrained system, ATM, SOA.

1 Introduction

Many real life systems and applications concern the allocation of a limited number of resources among multiple self-interested stakeholders or agents [3, 7, 10, 21, 22]. The allocation of resources may be executed taking into account either the individual objectives of the stakeholders, the global efficiency of the overall system, or both. Often, for this class of systems, the stakeholders are reluctant to disclose their objectives that can also be in contrast with the efficiency of the overall system. This situation may lead to a trade-off between the system and the stakeholder objectives. In addition to the criteria used for the allocation of resources, the allocation has to satisfy a given set of constraints, which are both general purpose - e.g., it is not possible to allocate more than the available resources, a unit of resource cannot be assigned to more than one stakeholder or agent - and domain specific – e.g., a resource cannot be used by more than X stakeholders in a time interval.

The process of allocating resources can be either centralized or decentralized. In a centralized perspective, a central authority is in charge of the allocation process, while in a decentralized solution, stakeholders exchange, trade and/or barter resources to reach a final allocation. Selecting one solution or the other resolves the trade-off between the stakeholders' objectives and the efficiency of the overall system. Indeed, centralized solutions usually pose emphasis on the performances of the system, while in decentralized solutions stakeholders' objectives play a prominent role.

In this paper, we present a software solution for resource management, which is based on three main modules: allocation, trading, and self-adaptation. Specifically, we propose a modular framework which allows the allocation, the trading, the self-adaptation, or any combination of the three components (see Figure 1). In fact, there might be systems which combine all the three mentioned elements. Resource allocation [10, 22] represents the ability of a system to (re)-assign/distribute the resources to their stakeholders. Several criteria may be used to allocate resources (e.g., the types of stakeholder, the resource requests' priority, the time of the requests, objectives of the requests). Resource trading [5, 19, 20] is the process of the exchange of resources among the stakeholders to achieve their own objectives. Self-adaptation [6, 15] represents the ability of a system to perform changes by itself in the system itself at runtime as a consequence of changes occurred in the execution context of the system or inside the system.

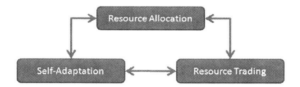

Fig. 1. Resource Management through Allocation, Trading and Self-Adaptation

This solution introduces a key innovative feature with respect to the state-of-the-art resource management systems because it proposes an integrated approach to resource management which may include all the modules described above and through which both global and individual objectives are addressed.

In the more general setting, we can imagine that our approach is both centralized and decentralized. The central authority performs a first allocation of resources and supervises the resource trading among the stakeholders, which is obviously a decentralized process. The result of the trading process is communicated to the central authority, which integrates all the partial results communicated by the stakeholders and it might either accept the new allocation, or try to adapt the system to the new allocation plan, when this new allocation plan is not appropriate from the centralized point of view/objectives. If the adaptation is possible, then the system adapts itself and accepts the new resource allocation plan. Otherwise, the system rejects the new allocation plan (indicating also which are the problems) and requires the stakeholders to resume the trading process. The resource management makes the right trade-off among the objectives of the stakeholders, which can be in conflict with each other (e.g., the service provider aims to maximize the resources utilization, whereas a user requires a certain level of system availability) or different (e.g., two users can require different quality attributes).

The scientific literature proposes a wide range of solutions for resource management in various application domains, which range from aeronautics [21] to telecommunications [5], from grid computing [10] to SOA [4, 17] and Web Services [3], from multimedia [18] to multi-agent systems. Typically, they focus on one or two functionalities offered by the framework proposed in this paper. For example, dynamic allocation and re-configuration (a facet of self-adaptation) of the resources based on the current controllers' workload in ATM are addressed in [21]. Self-adaptation in service-oriented application is discussed in [3, 4]. An example of resource trading in multi-agent systems is presented in [1].

The rest of the paper is organized as follows. Section 2 describes our framework for resource management based on resource allocation, trading and adaptation. Section 3 presents two application examples of our framework on two actual case studies. Conclusions and further work are dealt with in Section 4.

2 Resource Management: Allocation, Trading and Adaptation

Given a set of limited resources to be shared among a plurality of self-interested stakeholders, we propose a framework for resource management, which allows the allocation, trading, and self-adaptation. The resources are used by the stakeholders to achieve their own objectives. Their allocation, trading, and self-adaptation have to satisfy a set of constraints, which can be either general, domain specific, or both.

The proposed framework for resource management is shown in Figure 2. It considers an owner of the resources, which is also the manager (Resource Owner & Manager - ROM) and several stakeholders (Resource Stakeholders - RS), which are the users of the resources. RS may ask ROM for resources allocation and modifications in the resource allocation. ROM represents the centralized authority, while the stakeholders represent the decentralized part of the framework.

ROM allocates the available resources and accepts/rejects the requests of allocation changes received from the stakeholders. ROM holds a supervision role on the resource allocation process because it has knowledge on the resources (e.g., current number, availability) and on their constraints (e.g., time slot, safety/security). Moreover, it may be dictated by legal issues.

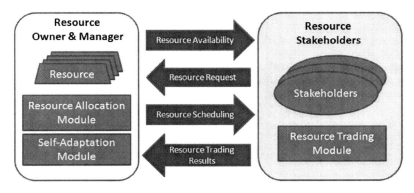

Fig. 2. The Main Elements of the Proposed Solution

2.1 The Resource Allocation Module

The Resource Allocation (RA) module assigns the available resources to the stakeholders based on global objectives (e.g., the efficient usage of the resources). To execute this task, RA has to know the pool of the resources to be allocated and the pool of stakeholders (see Figure 3). In addition to this information, RA receives in input the current resource allocation plan if any, and the application domain constraints. The RA module is equipped with a supervision capability on the use of resources thus guaranteeing a feasible and efficient allocation of resources. This functionality requires in input the results of the trading and the self-adaptation processes. To provide these functionalities, the RA uses assignment optimization models and methods [10, 11] suitably customized for the considered application domain.

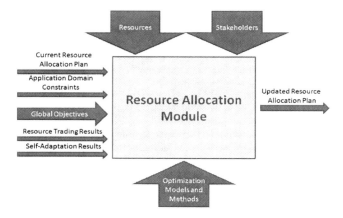

Fig. 3. The Resource Allocation Module

The described RA module is domain-independent and it can be used in different application domains.

2.2 The Resource Trading Module

The Resource Trading (RT) module, depicted in Figure 4, is used by the stakeholders to exchange resources with other stakeholders and to communicate with ROM. Each stakeholder has an RT module. The communication with ROM includes resource allocation/modification/usage/cancellation requests, which may or may not be a result of a trading process. The communication with the other stakeholders concern exchange requests, thus implying a trading process. Each RT receives in input the current resource allocation plan, if any, the application domain constrains, and the resource trading requests from other stakeholders. The stakeholder decides on an exchange of resources with other stakeholders based on its individual objectives and exploiting customized optimization models and methods. By customization of the optimization models we mean that the optimization models may consider specific constraints and objectives of the stakeholder, therefore different stakeholders may have different optimization models [14, 19].

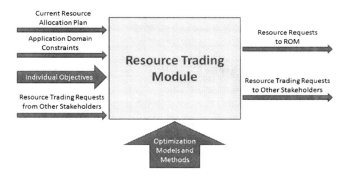

Fig. 4. The Resource Trading Module

The described RT module is domain-independent and it can be used in different application domains.

2.3 The Resource Self-adaptation Module

In the general vision of proposed framework, it may include a module for self-adaptation of the resources (see Figure 5). In this context self-adaptation is related to resources that may change over time in quantity and type according to some decision mechanisms. The self-adaption module, if implemented, belongs to the ROM.

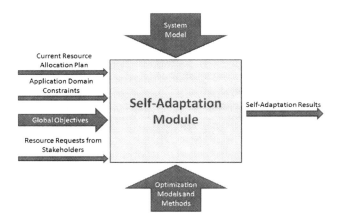

Fig. 5. The Self-Adaptation Module

The self-adaptation process is triggered by the stakeholders' resource requests (e.g., requests for new allocations or the results of the trading process). The Self-Adaptation (SA) module computes a distance measure (d) between the available resources (C) of the system and the new allocation resource plan (P) which would accommodate the stakeholders' requests. If this distance is lower than a given threshold $d(C,P)<\delta$ then the system tries to adapt itself and modifies the available resources (whenever this is possible) in order to accommodate the stakeholders' requests. If the distance *d* is greater than the given threshold, then the SA does not perform any adaptation. In any case, RA is notified of the SA results.

Also this module may exploit customized optimization models and methods [13].

The self-adaptation process is based on the MAPE (monitoring, analyzing, planning, and executing) feedback loop, which is exploited in the implementation of self-adaptive and self-management systems [6]. We address self-adaptation at the architectural level in an approach similar to the one proposed by Rainbow [9].

The described RT module is domain-independent and it can be used in different application domains.

2.4 The Interaction Workflow among the Modules for Resource Management

The workflow for the resource management framework is depicted in Figure 6. RA allocates the available resources to the stakeholders and notifies them the new resource allocation plan. The stakeholders may initiate a trading process with other stakeholders through their TR modules. This trading can be performed concurrently by the different stakeholders.

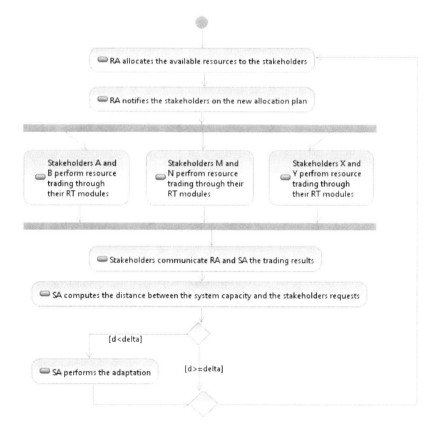

Fig. 6. The Interaction among the Modules of the Resource Management Framework

Once the trading process is over, the stakeholders communicate to the RA and the SA the results of the trading process consisting in variations of the previous resource allocation plan. SA computes the distance between the system capacity and the current requests of the stakeholders in order to decide whether adaptation would be effective or not. In the affirmative case, SA performs the adaptation of the resources.

If self-adaptation is performed, then the RA evaluates its results and updates the resource allocation plan based on these results. If no self-adaptation is performed, then the RA performs a re-allocation of resources trying to address as much as possible the stakeholders' requests (e.g., including the results of the trading process). The RA may require the stakeholders to resume the trading process by indicating also possible improvement hints in view of the global objective.

3 Application Examples

This section describes the application of our framework for resource management to two resource-constrained systems: the Air Traffic Management (ATM) and the Internetware Service-Oriented Architecture (ISOA) systems.

3.1 The ATM Example

An example of the application of our approach for resource management in resource-constrained systems is the Air Traffic Management (ATM) [8, 12, 20] system. In this application domain the resources are the capacity of the air traffic system elements, i.e., airports and airspace sectors. Capacity at airports is limited by the runway systems and the terminal airspace around them [14]. The capacity of en-route airspace sectors is limited by the maximum workload acceptable for air traffic controllers (measured as the average number of aircraft which are permitted to fly an en-route sector in a specific period of time) [12]. The main objective of the ATM system is safety, i.e., all flight operations have to be executed with no risk of collision. Due to the limited amount of capacity, imbalances between demand and capacity may occur at key times and points of the air transportation network. These local overloads create delays which propagate to other parts of the air network, amplifying congestion as increasing number of local capacity constraints come into play. Last year, more than 20% of US flights were delayed or cancelled (according to the US Bureau of Transportation Statistics). Similar statistics have been reported by European authorities. Airlines, which are the stakeholders of the ATM's resources, are very sensitive to a reduction of these delays and call for a wise use of the available resources. Specifically, they try to achieve their individual objective by gathering the required resources.

The proposed framework clearly fits to this application domain, and is consistent with the new decision paradigm of Collaborative Decision Making [20]. The ATM is ROM because it has the final decision on the resource allocation and has legal responsibility. The ATM receives as input information about the status of flights from the airlines, and tries to address airlines' requests. The main objective of airlines (besides the safety of the flights) is cost-effectiveness that is directly influenced by delays. However, the airline cost structure is sensitive information and is seldom disclosed outside.

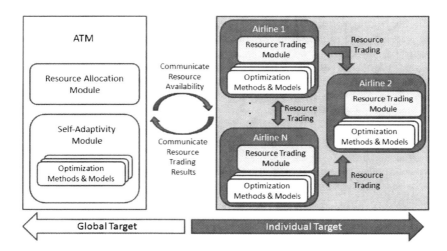

Fig. 7. The ATM Application Example

The three modules, described in Section 2, are used in this case study as shown in Figure 7. The RA and SA belong to the ATM, while the TA belongs to the airlines.

The instantiation of the inputs and outputs in each of three modules in the context of ATM are shown in Table 1.

3.2 The ISOA Example

A further example of an application domain which needs resource allocation, trading, and self-adaptation is represented by Internetware Service Oriented Architecture (ISOA), which is directly affected by the limitation of system resources [22]. The latter are considered for large-scale aggregation of distributed computing resources working together over the Internet, and should be able to dynamically adapt themselves (e.g., through reconfiguration mechanisms) in order to accommodate the requests for new allocations of servers' resources (e.g., CPU, memory and network bandwidth) to their services. Such new re-allocations could be triggered by several factors, e.g., dynamic changes of the runtime environment, current resources status, and/or variability of workload servers. A system should be able to predict its exact behavior, for example, as result of the impact of replacing one of its elementary services by analyzing what will be the impact to replace the service on the other services that will share its same resources (see, for example, [2], where it is remarked that more advanced and predictive models of adaptation are needed for systems that could fail to satisfy their requirements due to side-effects of change). If the system adaptation cannot be performed (e.g., for improving the efficiency of the resource allocation) we claim the cooperation between services (i.e. the resource trading mechanism). For example, a service provider could manage its high traffic load using additional resources provided by other providers and its unused resources could be offered to other providers (e.g., CPU-time and network bandwidth could be re-negotiated among the providers). Besides, for improving the efficiency of the resource trading, the providers, could also re-negotiate the service-level agreements with their users for example.

The instantiation of the inputs and outputs in each of three modules are shown in Table 2.

Table 1. Inputs and Outputs in the Three Modules Applied to the ATM Case Study

Input/Output	ATM Case Study Values
Resource Allocation	
Resources	System capacity (Time slots)
Stakeholders	Airlines
Current Resource Allocation Plan	Official airline guides and revisions
Global Objective	Safety and throughput
Trading Results	Time slots exchange
Self-Adaptation Results	Modification of sectors capacity
Optimization Models/Methods	Customized integer programs, Assignment programs [7, 8]
Updated Resource Allocation Plan	Current scheduling of flights
Resource Trading	
Current Resource Allocation Plan	Current scheduling of flights
Application Domain Constraints	See for example [7, 8, 19]
Individual Objectives	Airline's costs
Resource Trading Requests from Other Stakeholders	Time slots exchange
Optimization Methods and Models	See for example [12]
Resource Requests to ROM	Time slots
Resource Trading Requests to Other Stakeholders	Time slots exchange
Self-Adaptation	
Current Resource Allocation Plan	Current scheduling of flights
Application Domain Constraints	See for example [7, 8, 19]
Global Objectives	Efficient use of available resources
Resource Requests from Stakeholders	Requested capacity
Optimization Methods and Models	See for example [13]
System Model	Reifications of the resources, stakeholders, constraints representations [16]
Self-Adaptation Results	Modified capacity of the air traffic system

Table 2. Inputs and Outputs in the Three Modules Applied to the ISOA Case Study

Input/Output	ISOA Case Study Values
Resource Allocation	
Resources	CPU, memory, network bandwidth
Stakeholders	Service providers
Current Resource Allocation Plan	Resources current allocation
Global Objective	Maximize the throughput of the multiple service workflows running on a server
Trading Results	Resources negotiation results and/or Service Level Agreements
Self-Adaptation Results	Modifications of the pool of resources and/or the time allocated for their usage
Optimization Models/Methods	Resource-Allocation-Throughput model [22]
Updated Resource Allocation Plan	Resources updated allocation
Resource Trading	
Current Resource Allocation Plan	Resources current allocation
Application Domain Constraints	Context-awareness, users' preferences, different classes of service consumers, efficiency, scalability
Individual Objectives	Satisfy users' quality of services requirements
Resource Trading Requests from Other Stakeholders	Resources negotiation and/or Service Level Agreements
Optimization Methods and Models	Service negotiation and SLA optimization models [10, 13, 18]
Resource Requests to ROM	Resource allocation, modification, and/or cancellation requests
Resource Trading Requests to Other Stakeholders	Resources negotiation requests and/or Service Level Agreements
Self-Adaptation	
Current Resource Allocation Plan	Resources current allocation
Application Domain Constraints	Context-awareness, users' preferences, different classes of service consumers, efficiency, scalability
Global Objectives	Maximize the throughput of the multiple service workflows running on a server
Resource Requests from Stakeholders	Resource allocation, modification, and/or cancellation requests
Optimization Methods and Models	See for example [13]
System Model	Reifications of the resources and service providers, constraints representations [16]
Self-Adaptation Results	Modification of the pool of the resources

Note that there are application examples in which only two of the three modules are necessary (e.g., multi-agents, e-learning, telecommunications, robotics, multimedia).

4 Conclusions and Future Work

This paper has presented a framework for dynamic allocation, trading, and self-adaptation of resources. The proposed framework is remarkable for integrating all the described aspects of the resource management. The framework can be applied in various application domains. This paper has shown its application in two different domains: ATM and Internet SOA. Being a modular framework, its functionalities can be used together, separately, or in combination. For each of these functionality, there have been indicated the inputs which should be specified when exploiting the framework, and the outputs to be expected. The interaction among the three modules has been shown through an activity diagram.

Future work concerns the enhancement of the proposed framework with business intelligence mechanisms in order to allow the storage of the solutions adopted in various situations, and the application of these solutions in similar situations in order to avoid computation overheads (when possible). A prototype implementing our approach is currently under development. We aim to apply this prototype on realistic examples to validate and improve its functionalities, as well as to enhance it for achieving specific properties of various application domains. We plan to compare our prototype to existing resource management systems through the same case studies in order to better outline its novelties. We also intend to introduce evaluation criteria and metrics for the performance measurements.

Acknowledgments. This work is partially supported by the *Enhancing the European Air Transportation System* EATS research project funded by the Italian Government within the PRIN program.

References

1. Aldewereld, H., Buzing, P., Jonker, G.: Multi-Agent Plan Diagnosis and Negotiated Repair. In: Proceedings of the 7th International Joint Conference on Autonomous Agents and Multi-Agent Systems (2008)
2. Andersson, J., de Lemos, R., Malek, S., Weyns, D.: Modeling Dimensions of Self-Adaptive Software Systems. In: Cheng, B.H.C., de Lemos, R., Giese, H., Inverardi, P., Magee, J. (eds.) Software Engineering for Self-Adaptive Systems. LNCS, vol. 5525, pp. 27–47. Springer, Heidelberg (2009)
3. Boone, B., Hoecke, S.V., van Seghbroeck, G., Joncheere, N., Jonckers, V., Turck, F.D., Develder, C., Dhoedt, B.: Salsa: Qos-Aware Load Balancing for Autonomous Service Brokering. Journal of Systems and Software 83(3), 446–456 (2010)
4. Bucchiarone, A., Cappiello, C., Di Nitto, E., Kazhamiakin, R., Mazza, V., Pistore, M.: Design for Adaptation of Service-based Applications: Main Issues and Requirements. In: Dan, A., Gittler, F., Toumani, F. (eds.) ICSOC/ServiceWave 2009. LNCS, vol. 6275, pp. 467–476. Springer, Heidelberg (2010)

5. Burgkhardt, D., Cosovic, I., Jondral, F.: Dynamic Spectrum Allocation by Hierarchical Resource Trading. In: VTC Spring, pp. 1796–1800. IEEE Press, Los Alamitos (2008)
6. Cheng, B.H.C., de Lemos, R., Giese, H., Inverardi, P., Magee, J.: Software engineering for self-adaptive systems: A research roadmap. In: Software Engineering for Self-Adaptive Systems. LNCS, vol. 5525, pp. 1–26. Springer, Heidelberg (2009)
7. Dell'Olmo, P., Lulli, G.: A Dynamic Programming Approach for the Airport Capacity Allocation Problem. IMA Journal of Management Mathematics 14, 235–249 (2003)
8. Dell'Olmo, P., Lulli, G.: A New Hierarchical Architecture for Air Traffic Management: Optimisation of Airway's Capacity in a Free Flight Scenario. European Journal of Operational Research 144(1), 179–193 (2003)
9. Garlan, D., Cheng, S.-W., Huang, A.C., Schmerl, B., Steenkiste, P.: Rainbow: Architecture-based Self-Adaptation with Reusable Infrastructure. IEEE Computer 37(10), 46–54 (2004)
10. Li, C., Li, L.: Joint Optimization of Resource Allocation and User QoS Satisfaction Control for Efficient Grid Resource Management and Scheduling. IEEE Systems Journal 3(1), 65–77 (2009)
11. Luo, Z., Li, J.S.: A Web Service Provisioning Optimization Model in Web Services Community. In: Proceedings of the IEEE Conference on e-Business Engineering, pp. 689–696 (2005)
12. Majumdar, A.: Understanding En-RouteSector Capacity in Europe. In: European Air Traffic Management: Principles, Practice and Research, pp. 65–95. AJ Cook, Ashgate Publishing Limited, Hampshire (2007)
13. Mirandola, R., Potena, P.: Self-Adaptation of Service-based Systems on Cost-Quality Attributes Trade-Offs. In: Proceedings of the 1st Workshop on Software Services, co-located with the 12 th International Symposium on Symbolic and Numeric Algorithms for Scientific Computing, Timisoara, Romania (2010)
14. Hansman, R.J., Odoni, A.: Air Traffic Control. In: Belobaba, P., Odoni, A., Barnhart, C. (eds.) The Global Airline Industry, pp. 377–403. Wiley, Chichester (2009)
15. Raibulet, C.: Facets of Adaptivity. In: Morrison, R., Balasubramaniam, D., Falkner, K. (eds.) ECSA 2008. LNCS, vol. 5292, pp. 342–345. Springer, Heidelberg (2008)
16. Raibulet, C., Arcelli, F., Mussino, S., Riva, M., Tisato, F., Ubezio, L.: Components in an Adaptive and QoS-based Architecture. In: ICSE 2006 Workshop on Software Engineering for Adaptive and Self-Managing Systems, pp. 65–71. IEEE Press, Los Alamitos (2006)
17. Raibulet, C., Massarelli, M.: Managing Non-Functional Aspects in SOA through SLA. In: Proceedings of the First IEEE International Workshop on Engineering Non-Functional INformation for Emerging Systems, pp. 701–705 (2008)
18. Repantis, T., Drougas, Y., Kalogeraki, V.: Adaptive Component Composition and Load Balancing for Distributed Stream Processing Applications. Peer-to-Peer Networking and Applications 2(1), 60–74 (2009)
19. Vossen, T., Ball, M.O.: Slot Trading Opportunities in Collaborative Ground Delay Programs. Transportation Science 40(1), 29–43 (2006)
20. Wambsganss, M.C.: Collaborative Decision Making Through Dynamic Information Transfer. Air Traffic Control Quarterly 4, 107–123 (1996)
21. Webb, A., Sarkani, S., Mazzuchi, T.: Resource Allocation for Air Traffic Controllers using Dynamic Airspace Configuration. In: Proceedings of the World Congress on Engineering and Computer Science (2009)
22. Yau, S., An, H.: Adaptive Resource Allocation for Service-based Systems. International Journal of Software and Informatics 3(4), 483–499 (2009)

Preface ODISE 2011

Sergio de Cesare[1], Frederik Gailly[2], Grant Holland[3],
Mark Lycett[1], and Chris Partridge[4]

[1] Brunel University, Uxbridge, United Kingdom
{sergio.decesare,mark.lycett}@brunel.ac.uk
[2] Vrije Universiteit Brussel, Brussels, Belgium
frederik.gailly@vub.ac.be
[3] NuTech Solutions, U.S.A.
grant.holland.sf@gmail.com
[4] BORO Solutions, London, United Kingdom
partridgec@BOROGroup.co.uk

1 Introduction

Information systems (IS) Engineering has progressed considerably over the decades. Numerous advances, such as improved development methodologies, languages that enforce recognised software engineering principles and sophisticated CASE tools, have helped to increase the quality of IS. Regardless of such progress many IS Engineering projects remain unsuccessful (e.g., fail to meet stakeholder requirements, run excessively over budget and far beyond the deadlines initially scheduled). As the literature points out, most of these problems are due to (1) the difficulties of capturing and knowing the business requirements of a living organisational system, (2) realising such requirements in software designs and implementations and (3) maintaining an effective level of synchronicity between the needs of the living system and its information system. The causes underlying such problems are diverse and difficult to identify. Nonetheless it is plausible to assume that at the heart of such IS Engineering problems is the difficulty to conceptualise an organisational system and its real-world problem domain.

Ontologies are rapidly becoming mainstream within IS engineering as a means to create conceptual models of the real world that are both formalised and semantically accurate. Whilst ontologies have been in recent times widely researched by the Semantic Web and Artificial Intelligence communities, limited research has been conducted on how ontologies can help to shape and improve IS Engineering in terms of the development process, development techniques and tools, and the conceptual/physical artefacts produced. Ontologies have the potential to positively drive all phases of the IS lifecycle, from business modelling to implementation, and to improve over time the understanding that all stakeholders (business and technical) must share to more effectively evolve a technical solution (e.g., software) in sync with an organisation that grows.

This paper is intended as an introduction to the workshop on Ontology-Driven Information Systems Engineering (ODISE). This workshop is the third of a series that bears the acronym ODISE (pronounced odyssey). While the first two editions of the workshop were titled Ontology-Driven Software Engineering (and co-located at the Software Engineering conference OOPLSA/SPLASH in 2009 and 2010), this edition is being organised within the context of the Information Systems conference CAiSE 2011. At ODiSE 2010 it emerged that most of the problems that underlie systems development today are rooted in the difficulties inherent in producing accurate conceptualisations of the organisational problem space or domain. Focusing on Software Engineering rather than the wider context of IS Engineering was considered too restrictive as it was deemed to implicitly place greater emphasis on the solution space (program-centricity) rather than the problem space (domain-centricity). By broadening the scope of the workshop, the aim is to bring together researchers and practitioners of different fields and backgrounds (for example, from disciplines that span philosophy, organisational studies and computer science) so as to continue defining and shaping ODISE by identifying further areas of research and investigation.

Hence ODISE refers to the different ways in which ontologies can contribute to improving IS Engineering in all its aspects. These aspects broadly include the overlapping areas of methodological support, systems integration and interoperability, quality of software artefacts, model transformation, and alignment with changing organisational needs. The idea of adopting ontologies in the development, integration and evolution of software systems is not new (for example, see [1] and [2]), however much of the research to date is still heavily grounded in the use of Semantic Web technologies. While the Semantic Web has been a driving force in promoting ontologies, it must also be recognised that other research areas (such as conceptual modelling, philosophical ontologies and semiotics) have also contributed significantly toward demonstrating the benefits of adopting semantically rich and expressive modelling languages and approaches within an organisational IS context (for example, see [3] and [4]). This workshop wishes to encourage ODISE researchers and practitioners to discuss and research the challenging problems of IS Engineering not within stovepipe disciplines but by analysing such problems from a wide range of perspectives.

2 Accepted Papers

The workshop received 13 submissions of which 4 were accepted as research contributions and published in these proceedings. The acceptance rate was approximately 30%. The accepted papers present quality research in the specific areas of ontological design patterns for conceptual modelling, semantic-based case retrieval for service integration, and the integration and translation of the Web Ontology Language (OWL) with Java.

Guizzardi et al. in their paper titled *"Design patterns and Inductive Modeling Rules to Support the Construction of Ontologically Well-Founded Conceptual Models in OntoUML"* define a set of ontological design patterns to help conceptual modellers during the phase of domain analysis. The patterns are based on the metamodel of OntoUML, an ontologically well-founded conceptual modelling language. OntoUML represents an extension of the Unified Modelling Language (UML) that is grounded in the Unified Foundation Ontology (UFO). The authors exemplify the use of such patterns with three examples involving three ontological primitives: phases, roles and subkinds. The patterns are defined along with example usage execution scenarios in the form of a dialogue between the modeller and the interactive tool developed by the authors. In relation to ODISE this research emphasises the importance of producing models based on foundational ontologies and the use of conceptual design patterns to enforce the consistent adoption of the modelling primitives possibly not only by domain analysts but also by all those involved the development process (designers, architects, etc.).

Allgaier et al. in their paper titled "*Semantic-Based Case Retrieval of Service Integration Models in Extensible Enterprise Systems based on a Business Domain Ontology*" investigate the use of Case-Based Reasoning techniques to identify similar integration scenarios and reuse knowledge acquired from previous integration projects. As with the previous paper by Guizzardi et al., even here the authors' approach can be classified as pattern-based; the technique is aimed at identifying common and generic characteristics of integration cases so as to leverage (and not lose) in a cost-effective manner the corporate knowledge and experience acquired in the past. The approach adopts similarity measures to compare the unsolved integration problem with previous integration cases. The conceptualisation of such cases involves the use of a Business Domain Ontology aimed at mainly categorising the business functions of an organisation. The approach is evaluated via a developed prototype. This paper contributes to ODISE by emphasising the use of ontologies in systems integration. As it is widely known, most of the effort that organisations put into IS Engineering involve the integration and evolution of systems. While the use of patterns is quite common in software design and implementation, in other IS Engineering phases explicit reuse of previous experience is not widespread. As this paper and the previous demonstrate, ontologies can play a significant role in producing reusable patterns that are not confined only to the production of physical software artefacts.

Stevenson and Dobson in their paper titled "*Sapphire: Generating Java Runtime Artefacts from OWL Ontologies*" propose a mapping from OWL to Java that overcomes limitations of existing tool support. The problem of translating from an ontology development language (like OWL) to a programming language (like Java) is fundamental in the context of IS Engineering where the ultimate aim is to produce executable software that supports the business requirements of an organisation. OWL and Java serve different purposes but must work together in order to have enterprise software that benefits from the rich modelling constructs that OWL offers. The main challenge that such a translation imposes is the paradigm mismatch between the two languages. The authors describe the mapping proposed and present the Sapphire Runtime Library. The mapping defined in this paper is capable of overcoming significant limitations such as the lack of support for reification, the open-world assumption and the dynamic classification of individuals. The evaluation of Sapphire demonstrates how developers can write type safe code in a more concise way as compared with existing APIs. At the same time performance remains competitive.

Frenzel et al. in their paper titled "*Mooop – A Hybrid Integration of OWL and Java*" also investigate the general problem of integration between OWL and Java. Their approach uses hybrid objects. Hybrid integration represents a third type of approach to resolving this type of problem. Other approaches include: (1) direct integration which represents OWL classes and individuals as Java classes and objects respectively and (2) indirect integration which uses Java classes to represent the metaclasses of OWL and instances of these classes as Java objects. Hybrid integration instead integrates a few top-level concepts directly and specialised concepts indirectly. The authors propose Mooop which attempts to overcome the limitations of existing hybrid integration approaches. This goal is achieved by dividing the integration into three layers: OwlFrame as an indirect Java representation of ontological knowledge, the mapping as a customisable link between an OWL ontology and an OwlFrame, and the binding which defines the hybrid integration of the OwlFrame into the target Java application through hybrid classes. The approach is exemplified through a case study.

References

1. Tetlow, P., Pan, J., Oberle, D., Wallace, E., Uschold, M., Kendall, E. (eds.) W3C: Ontology Driven Architectures and Potential Uses of the Semantic Web in Software Engineering (2003), http://www.w3.org/2001/sw/BestPractices/SE/ODA/
2. Knublauch, H., Oberle, D., Tetlow, P., Wallace, E.(eds.): W3C: A Semantic Web Primer for Object-Oriented Software Developers (2006), http://www.w3.org/2001/sw/BestPractices/SE/ODSD/
3. Partridge, C.: Business Objects – Re-engineering for Re-use. Butterworth-Heinemann, Butterworths (1996)
4. West, M.: Developing High Quality Data Models. Morgan Kaufmann, San Francisco (2011)

Ontology Mining versus Ontology Speculation

Chris Partridge

BORO Solutions Limited, London, U.K.
Brunel University, Uxbridge, U.K.
`partridgec@borogroup.co.uk`

Abstract. When we embed the building of an ontology into an information system development or maintenance process, then the question arises as to how one should construct the content of the ontology. One of the choices is whether the construction process should focus on the mining of the ontology from existing resources or should be the result of speculation ('starting with a blank sheet of paper'). I present some arguments for choosing mining over speculation and then look at the implications this has for legacy modernisation.

Design Patterns and Inductive Modeling Rules to Support the Construction of Ontologically Well-Founded Conceptual Models in OntoUML

Giancarlo Guizzardi, Alex Pinheiro das Graças, and Renata S.S. Guizzardi

Ontology and Conceptual Modeling Research Group (NEMO)
Computer Science Department,
Federal University of Espírito Santo (UFES), Brazil
{gguizzardi,agracas,rguizzardi}@inf.ufes.br

Abstract. In recent years, there has a growing interest in the use of Ontologically Well-Founded Conceptual Modeling languages to support the domain analysis phase in Information Systems Engineering. OntoUML is an example of a conceptual modeling language whose metamodel has been designed to comply with the ontological distinctions and axiomatic theories put forth by a theoretically well-grounded Foundational Ontology. However, despite its growing adoption, OntoUML has been deemed to pose a significant complexity to novice modelers. This paper presents a number of theoretical and methodological contributions aimed at assisting these modelers. Firstly, the paper explores a number of design patterns which are derived from the ontological foundations of this language. Secondly, these patterns are then used to derive a number of model construction rule sets. The chained execution of these rule sets assists the modeler in the instantiation of these patterns, i.e., in the use of OntoUML as pattern-language. Thirdly, the article demonstrates how these rule sets can be materialized as a set of methodological guidelines which can be directly implemented in a tool support in the form of an automated dialogue with the novice modeler.

1 Introduction

In recent years, there has been a growing interest in the use of Ontologically Well-Founded Conceptual Modeling languages to support the domain analysis phase in Information Systems Engineering. OntoUML is an example of a conceptual modeling language whose metamodel has been designed to comply with the ontological distinctions and axiomatic theories put forth by a theoretically well-grounded Foundational Ontology [1]. This language has been successfully employed in a number of projects in several different domains, ranging from Petroleum and Gas [2] to Bioinformatics [3]. Moreover, the ontological distinctions underlying this language has been experimenting increasing adoption [4,5]. However, despite its growing popularity, OntoUML has been deemed to pose a significant complexity to novice modelers.

In order to assist these novice modelers, a number of efforts have been undertaken [6,7]. In particular, [6] proposes an automated model-checking editor that takes advantage of a well-behaved set of ontological constraints that govern the metamodel of this language. The editor constrains the users to only produce models which are consistent with these ontological constraints, i.e., if a user attempts to produce a model which does not adhere to these rules, the editor can automatically interfere in the process, identifying and explaining the model violation.

This editor, however, works in a *reactive* manner: in principle, the user can build any model using the primitives of the language; if the user attempts to build an ontologically inconsistent model, the editor prompts a proper action. In this paper, we pursue a different direction on providing tool support, i.e., we attempt to explore an *inductive* strategy in the construction of OntoUML models. As we illustrate in this paper, the ontological constraints underlying the language restrict its primitives to be combined in specific manners. To put it in a different way, in contrast with ontologically neutral languages such as UML, EER or OWL, OntoUML is a *Pattern Language*. When a model is built in OntoUML, the language induces the user to construct the resulting models via the combination of existing ontologically motivated design patterns. These patterns constitute modeling primitives of a higher granularity when compared to usual primitives of conceptual modeling such as *Class*, *Association*, *Specialization*, among others. Moreover, these higher-granularity modeling elements can only be combined to each other in a restricted set of ways. Thus, in each modeling step, the design space is reduced. The hypothesis of this work is that this strategy reduces the complexity of the modeling process for the novice modeler.

This paper, thus, presents a number of theoretical and methodological contributions aimed at assisting these novice modelers. In section 2, we briefly present the ontological foundations underlying a fragment of OntoUML. In section 3, we explore a number of design patterns which emerge from the ontological constraints underlying this language. After that, these patterns are used to derive a number of model construction rule sets. Furthermore, we illustrate how the chained execution of these rules assists the modeler in the instantiation of these patterns. Finally, we demonstrate how these rule sets can be materialized as a set of methodological guidelines which can be directly implemented in a tool support in the form of an automated dialogue with the novice modeler. Section 4 presents a brief discussion on how these ideas have been implemented in a Model-based OntoUML editor. To conclude the paper, section 5 elaborates on final considerations and directions for future work.

2 Background: OntoUML and Its Underlying Ontology

OntoUML has been proposed as an extension of UML that incorporates in the UML 2.0 original metamodel a number of ontological distinctions and axioms put forth by the Unified Foundation Ontology (UFO) [1]. In this work, we focus our discussion on a small fragment of this metamodel. This fragment discusses an extension of the *Class* meta-construct in UML to capture a number of ontological distinctions among the Object Types categories proposed in UFO. In fact, for the sake of space, we limit our discussion here to an even more focused fragment of the theory, namely, those categories of Object Types which extend the ontological notion of *Sortal types* [1]. The choice for this specific fragment for this particular paper is justified by the fact that this fragment comprises the ontological notions which are believed to be the more recurrent in the practice of conceptual modeling for information systems [4,5]. Besides incorporating modeling primitives that represent these ontological distinctions, the extended

OntoUML metamodel includes a number of logical constraints that govern how these primitives can be combined to form consistent conceptual models. In what follows, we briefly elaborate on the aforementioned distinctions and their related constraints for the fragment discussed in this article. For a fuller discussion and formal characterization of the language, the reader is referred to [1].

We start by making a basic distinction between categories of Object Types considering a formal meta-property named Rigidity [1]. In short, a type T is rigid iff for every instance x of that type, x is necessarily an instance of that type. In contrast, a type T' is anti-rigid iff for every instance y of T', there is always a possible world in which y is not instance of T'. In other words, it is possible for every instance y of T' to cease to be so without ceasing to exist (without losing its identity) [1]. A stereotypical example of this distinction can be found by contrasting the rigid type Person with the anti-rigid type Student.

Rigid types can be related in a chain of taxonomic relations. For instance, the rigid types Man and Person are related such that the former is a specialization of the latter. The type in the root of a chain of specializations among rigid types is termed a Kind (e.g., Person) and the remaining rigid types in this chain are named Subkinds (e.g., Man, Woman). As formally demonstrated in [1], we have the following constraints involving Kinds and Subkinds: (i) every object in a conceptual model must be an instance of exactly one Kind; (ii) as consequence, we have that for every object type T in OntoUML, T is either a Kind or it is the specialization of exactly one ultimate Kind; Subkinds of a Kind K typically appear in a construction named *Subkind Partition*. (iii) A Subkind Partition $\langle SK_1...SK_n \rangle$ defines an actual partition of type K, i.e., (iii.a) in every situation, every instance of SK_i is an instance of K; Moreover, (iii.b) in every situation, every instance of K is an instance of exactly one SK_i. In UML, and consequently also in OntoUML, partitions are represented by a disjoint and complete Generalization Set (see figure 1.a and 1.c).

Among the anti-rigid Sortal types, we have again two subcatetories: Phases and Roles. In both cases, we have cases of dynamic classification, i.e., the instances can move in and out of the extension of these types without any effect on their identity. However, while in the case of Phase these changes occur due to a change in the intrinsic properties of these instances, in the cases of Role, they occur due to a change in their relational properties. We contrast the types Child, Adolescent, Adult as phases of a Person with the Roles Student, Husband or Wife. In the former case, it is a change in the intrinsic property *age* of Person which causes an instance to move in and out of the extension of these phases. In contrast, a Student is a role that a Person plays when related to an Education Institution and it is the establishment (or termination) of this relation that alters the instantiation relation between an instance of Person and the type Student. Analogously, a Husband is a role played by a Person when married to (a Person playing the role of) Wife. Thus, besides being Anti-rigid, Role possesses another meta-property (absent in Phases) named Relational Dependence [1]. As a consequence, we have that the following constraints must apply to Roles: every Role in an OntoUML conceptual model must be connected to an association representing this relational dependence condition. Moreover, the association end connected to the depended type (e.g., Education Institution for the case of Student, Wife for the case of Husband) in this relation must have a minimum cardinality ≥ 1 [1].

Furthermore, as discussed in [1], Phases always occur in a so-called *Phase Partition* of a type T. For this reason, *mutatis mutandis*, constraints identical to (iii.a and iii.b) defined for Subkind Partitions are also defined for the case of Phase Partitions. However, for the case of Phase Partitions, we have an additional constraint: for every instance of type T and for every phase P_i in a Phase Partition specializing T, there is a possible world w in which x is not an instance of Pi. This implies that, in w, x is an instance of another Phase P_j in the same partition.

Finally, as formally proved in [1], rigid types cannot specialize anti-rigid types.

3 Ontological Design Patterns and Inductive Process Models

In this section, we present a number of Design Patterns which are derived from the ontological constraints underlying OntoUML as presented in the previous section. In other words, we limit ourselves here to the patterns which are related to the ontological constraints involving the three primitives previously discussed: Phases, Roles and Subkind. These patterns are depicted in figure 1 below.

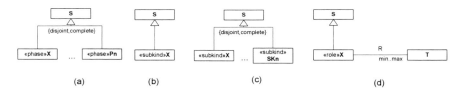

Fig. 1. Design Patterns emergent from the Ontological Constraints underlying OntoUML: (a) the Phase Pattern; (b-c) the Subkind Patterns, and (d) the Role Modeling Design Pattern

As a second objective of this section, we elaborate on a number of process models (representing inductive rule sets for model construction) which can be directly derived from these patterns. The hypothesis considered and illustrated here is the following: in each step of the modeling activity (i.e., each execution step of these process models), the solution space which characterizes the possible choices of modeling primitives to be adopted is reduced. This strategy, in turn, reduces the cognitive load of the modeler and, consequently, the complexity of model building using this language. Finally, this section demonstrates how these process models can be materialized through an interactive dialogue between the modeler and an automated tool running these rule sets. This idea is presented here via a running example and, in the following subsections, we will exemplify how the modeler may gradually build the ontology model of figure 5. For that, the design tool executes these process models and engages in dialogues with the user, guiding the development of the model from 5(1) to 5(11)

3.1 The Phase Design Pattern

Phases are always manifested as part of a Phase Partition (PP). In a PP, there is always one unique root common supertype which is necessarily a Sortal S. This pattern is depicted in figure 1.a above. By analyzing that pattern, we can describe a modeling rule set R_P which is to be executed every time a Phase P is instantiated in the model (an OntoUML class is stereotyped as phase). The rule set R_P is represented in the form of an UML activity diagram in figure 2 below. In the sequel, we exemplify the execution of this rule. In figure 2, the activities in grey represent the ones fired in this illustrative execution.

Example Execution: Let us suppose that the first type included by the user in the model is Child and that this type is stereotyped as ⟨⟨Phase⟩⟩. Thus, the rule set R_P (Child) is executed following the steps described in figure 2. Since there is no other modeling element in the model, a Phase Partition is created (step 1). Notice that, at this point, the following dialogue can be established with the user so that the supertype S of Child can be created (step 2) as well as the remaining subtypes of S complementary to Child (step 3). Each underlined term in the following dialogues can be automatically inferred in the execution of R_P:

1. **Modeling Tool:** Child is a phase for what kind of type?
2. **User:** Person
3. **Modeling Tool:** What should be the other phases of Person which are complementary to Child?
4. **User:** Teenager and Adult

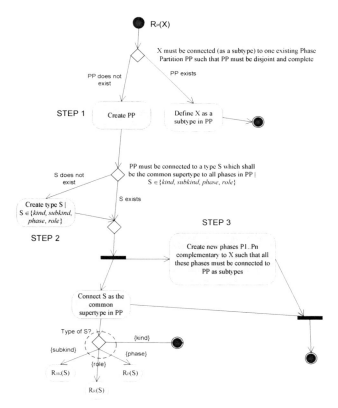

Fig. 2. Activity Diagram representing the Inductive Rule Set RP associated to the formation of an instance of the *Phase* Design pattern

At this point, the process execution is at the decision element circumscribed by the dashed oval. Once more, a dialogue with the user can be used here to determine whether Person is a kind (in which case the process reaches a final state) or not (in which case a subsequent rule is fired in a recursive manner).

1. **Modeling Tool:** Does exist another type which is a subtype of Person?
2. **User:** No

Thus, since in this example, Person must be kind, this execution of R_P (Child) reaches a final state. In figure 5, we illustrate the user's model after his choice of stereotyping Child as a Phase (figure 5.1) and the resulting design pattern which is configured by the execution of R_P(Child) (figure 5.2).

3.2 The Subkind Design Pattern

Subkinds can be manifested in two different manners: (i) as a specialization of a type S; (ii) as a part of a *generalization set* which has as a common superclass a type S. These two patterns are illustrated in figure 1.b and 1.c, respectively. The inductive formation rule set associated with the stereotype *subkind* is captured in figure 3. In the sequel, we exemplify the execution of this rule set.

Example Execution: Let us suppose that the next type included in the model is the type School which (in this example) is stereotyped as a subkind. The rule set R_{SK}(School) is then fired. The following dialogue can be used to discover whether School is a subkind of a type S already existent in the model. Since in this case, the answer is negative, the dialogue proceeds such that the proper supertype of School can be created (Step 1). Furthermore, after connecting Organization as a supertype of School, the tool dialogue attempts to uncover whether there are additional subkinds of Organization complementary to School forming a generalization set (DP1):

1. **Modeling Tool:** Is School a subkind of Person[1]?
2. **User:** No
3. **Modeling Tool:** Of which type is School a subkind then?
4. **User:** Organization
5. **Modeling Tool:** Is there another subkind of Organization complementary to School?
6. **User:** No

Finally, notice that in parallel (DP2), the tool attempts to discover whether Organization is itself a kind or a subkind (in which case the rule set R_{SK} (Organization)) should be recursively fired). Since, in this example, the former case obtains, then this execution of rule R_{SK} terminates. In fig. 5, we illustrate the user's model after his choice of stereotyping School as a subkind (fig. 5.3) and the resulting design pattern which is configured by the execution or R_{SK}(School) (fig. 5.4).

We can offer a second example execution which supposes that the next element included in the model of figure 5.5 is a type Woman, also stereotyped as subkind. The rule R_{SK}(Woman) is then fired and the step 1 of figure 4 is executed:

---

[1] If multiple kinds and subkinds already exist in a given model presenting themselves as alternatives for the supertype S, then the modeling tool's interface should present the user with such alternatives accordingly.

1. **Modeling Tool:** Is Woman a subkind of Person or Organization?
2. **User:** Person

In this case, the process goes straight to Step 2 and then once more to the decision point DP1. Since there is no other subkind of Person already in this model, the dialogue with the user is verbalized in the following manner:

1. **Modeling Tool:** Is there another subkind of Person complementary to Woman?
2. **User:** Man

We then have the execution of steps 3-5 in figure 3, resulting in the model of figure 5.6. Activities which are executed only in this second example execution of R_{SK}, are depicted in dark grey in figure 3.

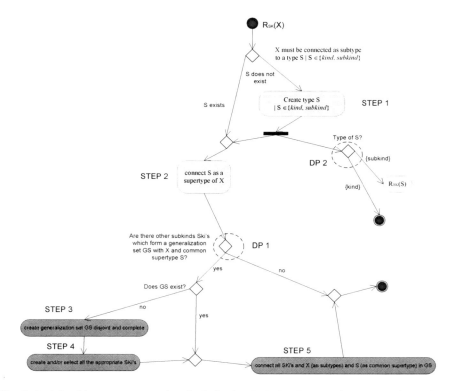

Fig. 3. Activity Diagram representing the Inductive Rule Set RP associated to the formation of instances of the *Subkind* Design patterns

3.3 The Role Design Pattern

Roles represent (possibly successive) specializations of a Kind by using a relational specialization condition. Figure 4 captures the modeling rules that induces the creation of the role design pattern depicted in figure 1.d. In the sequel, we present the dialogue the tool may engage with the reader, following this rule set.

Example Execution: Let us suppose that the next type included in the model of figure 5.7 is the type Student which (in this example) is stereotyped as a role. The rule R_R(Student) is then fired. The following dialogue can be used to discover whether Student is a subkind of a type S already existent in the model. Since in this case the answer is affirmative for Person, the dialogue proceeds to discover whether Student is a direct subtype of Person or of one of its subtypes (Child, Adolescent, Adult, Man, Woman). Since Student is a direct subtype of Person, step 1 in figure 4 is executed. Moreover, in decision point DP 1, a dialogue is established to discover if the type Student is *relationally dependent of* is already present in the model (line 5 in the dialogue below). Afterwards, in decision point 2 (DP2), since there is no relation connected to student, the tool enquires the user regarding the relation R representing the relational specialization condition for Student (line 7). After that, the *studies in* relation is created (step 2) and its cardinality constraints are assessed (step 3, see also lines 9-16 below). Finally, the *studies in* relation is connected to both Student and School. With the execution of R_R(Student) we then obtain the model of figure 5.8.

1. **Modeling Tool:** Is Student a subtype of Person or Organization?
2. **User:** Person
3. **Modeling Tool:** Is it a direct subtype of Person?
4. **User:** Yes
5. **Modeling Tool:** In relation to which type of entity does a Person plays the role of Student? School, Organization, Child, Adolescent, Adult, Man or Woman?
6. **User:** School
7. **Modeling Tool:** How would you name this relation between Student and School?
8. **User:** studies in
9. **Modeling Tool:** A Student is related to a minimum of how many different School(s) via the *studies in* relation?
10. **User:** 1
11. **Modeling Tool:** Is there a maximum?
12. **User:** No
13. **Modeling Tool:** A School is related to a minimum of how many different Student(s) via the *studies in* relation?
14. **User:** Zero
15. **Modeling Tool:** Is there a maximum?
16. **User:** No

Once more, we can offer a second example execution for the Role design pattern and its associated rule. This example supposes the next element included in the model of figure 5.9 to be the type Husband also stereotyped as Role. The rule R_R(Husband) is then fired and step 1 is executed. However, this time, as a subsequent step of decision point DP 1, step 5 of the process is executed instead (activity marked in dark grey in figure 5). This is due to the fact that (following lines 7 and 8 below), the type T to which Husband should be connected is absent in the model.

1. **Modeling Tool:** Is <u>Husband</u> a subtype of <u>Person</u> or <u>Organization</u>?
2. **User:** Person
3. **Modeling Tool:** Is it a direct subtype of <u>Person</u>?
4. **User:** No
5. **Modeling Tool:** Is Husband a direct subtype of <u>Man, Woman, Child, Teenager</u>, or <u>Adult</u>?
6. **User:** Man
7. **Modeling Tool:** In relation to which type of entity does a <u>Person</u> plays the role of <u>Husband</u>? <u>School, Organization, Child, Adolescent, Adult, Man</u> or <u>Student</u>?
8. **User:** None of these. The correct type is Wife

After this, steps 2-4 of figure 4 are executed and the relation *married to* between Husband and Wife is properly instantiated. The dialogue corresponding to these steps is omitted below for the sake of space economy. Finally, the recursive execution of rule R_R(Wife) is triggered (DP 3). This time the following steps of the process in figure 4 are executed: (i) Step 1 – in which the specialization between Wife and Woman is created; (ii) DP 1 – at this point since type T already exists (Husband), execution goes straight to DP 2; (ii) DP 2 - at this point since relation R already exists

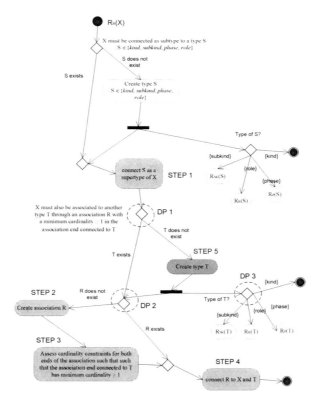

Fig. 4. Activity Diagram representing the Inductive Rule R_R associated to the formation of an instance of the *Role* Design pattern in OntoUML

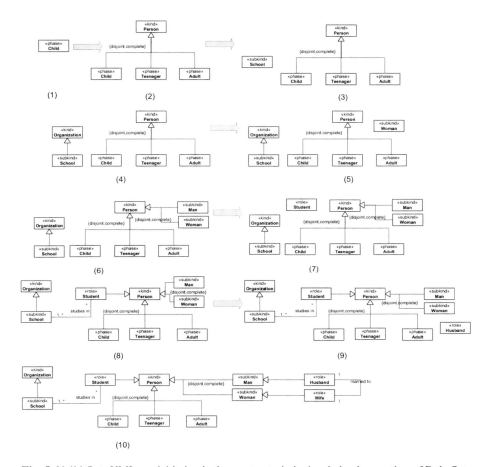

Fig. 5. Valid OntoUML model inductively constructed via the chained execution of Rule Sets

(*married to*), step 4 is executed and the process terminates. As a result, the final model of figure 5.10 is obtained.

4 Tool Support

This work applies some design patterns and its associated rule sets to create an interactive dialogue with the modeler to support model development in a kind of Model-Based Web Wizard for novice modelers. The architecture of this editor has been conceived to follow a Model Driven Approach. In particular, we have adopted the OMG MOF (Meta-Object Facility) metamodeling architecture with an explicit representation of the OntoUML metamodel. The rule sets presented here are implemented in a business logic layer which explicitly manipulates this metamodel. The interactive dialog with the modeler (which occurs via the execution of these rule sets) is implemented using a graphical interface as illustrated in figure 6 below.

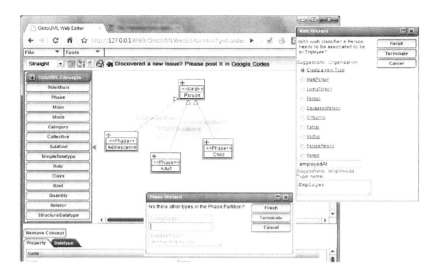

Fig. 6. Screeshots for the Web Implementation of an OntoUML editor using Design Patterns and Inductive Rule Sets

5 Final Considerations and Future Work

The work presented in this paper lies in the identification of Ontological Design Patterns underlying the OntoUML language. In [8], three major categories of Design Patterns for Ontology-Driven Conceptual Modeling are discussed, namely, *Modeling Patterns*, *Analysis Patterns* and *Transformation Patterns*. Design Patterns which are most frequently found in the Ontology Engineering literature fall in the third category. An example is the catalog of patterns proposed in [9] which aims at helping the user in codifying common modeling structures in the Semantic Web languages. Analysis Patterns in the sense mentioned in [8] differs from the most frequent use of the term in Conceptual Modeling [10]. While the latter refers to conceptual structures which are recurrent in different domain models, the former refers to patterns derived from ontological theories which can be use to analyze properties of conceptual models. The Analysis Patterns in the sense of [10] would actually be akin to the ones explored in this article, which fall in the category of Modeling Patterns [8]. However, while the former captures domain-level recurrent conceptual structures, the latter represents domain-independent modeling solutions originated from ontological theories.

In future works, the theoretical contributions presented here shall be expanded by exploring a complete set of patterns which contemplate the complete set of modeling primitives of OntoUML. Moreover, we intend to conduct some empirical research initiatives to verify the hypothesis underlying this article, namely: (i) that the inductive methodological strategy pursued here in fact contributes to diminish the complexity of the process of ontology-driven conceptual modeling; (ii) that it positively contributes to increase the quality of the resulting models when produced by novice modelers.

Our research agenda for the future also includes the investigation of how the tool can be augmented in terms of providing extra cognitive support [11] for conceptual model development using OntoUML. This includes issues related to the scalability of the models using the present tool. Suppose, for instance, that the model under development already has a hundred *kinds*. It would be quite cumbersome if the tool offered all of them as options to generalize a new *role* being created (see subsection 3.3). It is wise to consider, for instance, techniques for modularizing the model, so that the tool could reduce this set of possible *kinds*. Other visualization and navigation techniques could also be applied to provide further cognitive support on model creation [12].

The idea is also to advance with this work to enable the reuse of knowledge that was previously only tacit in the mind of the user when conceiving a model. In other words, we intend to provide support to capture the *design rationale* behind the development of a conceptual model in order to reuse these previous insights as hints for upcoming modelers, who can build new models on the basis of such knowledge. Particularly related to knowledge reuse, we could explore some intelligent support (e.g., recommendation techniques) to enable search within the tool knowledge base (i.e. previously designed models) as well as in external sources (e.g. other conceptual model repositories or even other types of general knowledge sources), seeking to find new contributions to model particular domains. Regarding the use of external sources, formal ontology excerpts could be adopted as fragments of a new conceptual model, based on similarity of concepts and concept patterns. And besides, the use of results extracted from unstructured content could be applied as input to suggest specific terms applied in connection to the concepts which are already part of the model under development.

Acknowledgments. This research has been partially supported by FAPES (Grant #45444080/09) and CNPq (Grant #481906/2009-6 and Productivity Grant #309382/2008).

References

1. Guizzardi, G.: Ontological Foundations for Structural Conceptual Models, pp. 1381–3617. Universal Press, Holanda (2005) ISBN 1381-3617
2. Guizzardi, G., Lopes, M., Baião, F., Falbo, R.: On the importance of truly ontological representation languages. In: IJISMD (2010) ISSN 1947–8186
3. Gonçalves, B., Guizzardi, G., Pereira Filho, J.G.: Using an ECG reference ontology for semantic interoperability of ECG data. Journal of Biomedical Informatics 43 (2010)
4. Bauman, B.T.: Prying Apart Semantics and Implementation: Generating XML Schemata directly from ontologically sound conceptual models. In: Balisage Markup Conf. (2009)
5. Halpin, T., Morgan, T.: Information Modeling and Relational Dababases. Morgan Kaufman, San Francisco (2008) ISBN 1558606726
6. Benevides, A.B., Guizzardi, G.: A Model-Based Tool for Conceptual Modeling and Domain Ontology Engineering in OntoUML. LNBPI, Vol. 24 (2009) ISSN 1865–1356
7. Castro, L., et al.: A Linguistic Approach to Conceptual Modeling with Semantic Types and OntoUML. In: Proceedings of the IEEE 5th VORTE/MOST 2010, Vitoria, Brazil (2010)
8. Guizzardi, G.: Theoretical Foundations and Engineering Tools for Building Ontologies as Reference Conceptual Models. Semantic Web Journal 1(1) (2010)
9. Ontology Design Patterns, http://ontologydesignpatterns.org/wiki/Main_Page
10. Fowler, M.: Analysis Patterns: Reusable Object Models. Addison-Wesley, London (1996)
11. Walenstein, A.: Cognitive support in software engineering tools: A distributed cognition framework. PhD thesis, Simon Fraser University, Vancouver, BC (2002)
12. Ernst, N.A., Storey, M., Allen, P.: Cognitive support for ontology modeling. International Journal of Human-Computer Studies 62(5), 553–577 (2005) ISSN: 1071-5819

Semantic-Based Case Retrieval of Service Integration Models in Extensible Enterprise Systems Based on a Business Domain Ontology

Matthias Allgaier[1], Markus Heller[1], Sven Overhage[2], and Klaus Turowski[2]

[1] SAP Research, Karlsruhe, Germany
{matthias.allgaier,markus.heller}@sap.com
[2] Business Informatics and Systems Engineering, University of Augsburg, Germany
{sven.overhage,klaus.turowski}@wiwi.uni-augsburg.de

Abstract. In spite of the advances in Service-Oriented Computing (SOC), the extension of standard enterprise systems with complementary services provided by third-party vendors still requires deep expert knowledge. However, valuable integration experience from similar problems already solved in the past is not systematically leveraged which leads to high integration costs. We tackle this problem by exploring Case-Based Reasoning techniques in this novel application context. A key challenge for the reuse of integration knowledge is to retrieve existing integration cases that have been developed in similar functional areas within the process space of standard enterprise systems. In this paper we present a Business Domain Ontology that provides a formal representation of reference processes in the domain of standard enterprise systems. In addition a case retrieval algorithm is proposed, that computes the similarity between two integration cases based on the semantic distance between concepts within the Business Domain Ontology.

Keywords: Case-Based Reasoning, Enterprise Systems, Enterprise Ontology, Extensibility, Service Integration, Knowledge-Based Systems.

1 Introduction

The extension of standard enterprise systems (ERP-, CRM-, SCM or SRM systems) with additional services provided by third-party vendors requires deep business domain as well as technical expert knowledge due to the wide and complex spectrum of supported processes and customizing options [4]. In most cases, extension or adaptation of the core enterprise system itself is required (e.g. by adding new UI elements to core UI components, adding new process steps to core process models or even extending business objects with additional fields). Today the integration of services is carried out in time- and cost-intensive projects. However, valuable experience from similar problems already solved in the past is not systematically leveraged that again leads to high integration costs. In order to provide a platform for the systematic reuse of integration knowledge we apply *Case-Based Reasoning* (CBR) in this novel application context of knowledge-based systems [1]. CBR is able to utilize the specific knowledge of previously experienced problem situations *(integration cases)*. Here, a new problem is solved by retrieving a similar past case, and reusing it in the new situation [2].

A key challenge for the reuse of integration knowledge is to retrieve existing integration cases that have been developed in similar functional areas within the complex process space of standard enterprise systems. In this paper we propose a *Business Domain Ontology (BDO)* that provides a formal representation of reference processes in the domain of standard enterprise systems. The BDO has been derived from a proven collection of cross-industry process reference models and allows the annotation of integration cases with machine-interpretable business semantics. As a second contribution this paper presents a *case retrieval algorithm* that computes the similarity between two integration cases based on the semantic distance between concepts within the BDO.

Our research is based on the design science paradigm [3], which defines a rigorous, iterative process for the creation of innovative artifacts to solve an identified problem. The remaining structure of the paper roughly follows this process and discusses the problem statement, solution concept, as well as the solution evaluation as major design steps. For a detailed discussion on the requirements for the solution proposed in this paper we refer the reader to our previous work [15]. To further motivate the problem that we address with our research, we present a service integration case study in section 2. Thereafter, we discuss the solution concept and introduce the novel Cased-Based Reasoning Framework for Service Integration (section 3.1) as well as the concept and structure of an integration case (section 3.2). In sections 3.3 and 3.4, we describe the developed Business Domain Ontology and establish various semantic distance algorithms along with examples. Section 4 covers the conducted evaluation and describes the prototype. After discussing related work in section 5, we conclude with an outlook on future research.

2   Background: Service Integration in Enterprise Systems

In this section we illustrate the integration of complementary services into enterprise systems with an example from the automotive industry.

A manufacturer of car seats has to react to legal changes in export guidelines that require him to certify for all of his products that the used materials comply with environmental laws. The company runs an enterprise system – in this case a Product-Lifecycle-Management System (PLM) – that supports its core business processes (Figure 1). The system does not support the required calculation of eco values for a given car seat in its core version. Such a service to compute the eco values for products including certification is offered by a third party service provider on a service marketplace. In the company, a product designer accesses the service marketplace from within his enterprise system and searches for services that match his needs. He selects the best fitting of the list of offered services for eco value computation, the "Eco-Calculator, and purchases it on the marketplace.

Afterwards the service has to be integrated into the PLM system. Thereby, the user interface of the PLM system has to be extended with (1) a new table column

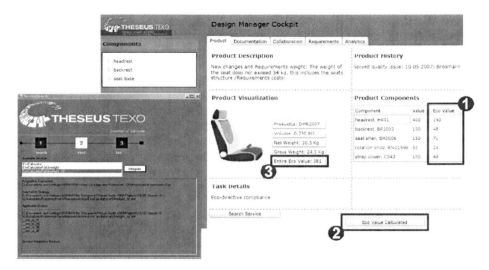

Fig. 1. PLM enterprise system extended with the complementary service

("Eco Value"), (2) a new button ("Calculate Eco Value") and (3) a new field to display the car seat's total eco value ("Entire Eco Value").

After the service is integrated, the service can be used. If the total eco value fulfills the legal requirements, a certificate is generated and passed to the PLM system.

3 Case Retrieval Solution Using Business Domain Ontology

In this section we present a *case retrieval solution* that allows the retrieval of existing integration scenarios based on their semantic similarity to the new integration problem. The presented case retrieval solution is embedded into a broader *Case-Based Reasoning Framework* that we will briefly introduce in the next section.

3.1 Case-Based Reasoning Framework for the Reuse of Integration Knowledge

The Case-Based Reasoning Framework for the systematic reuse of service integration knowledge in the context of extensible standard enterprise systems is comprised of five phases (Figure 2). This cycle has been derived from the generic CBR cycle [1] and adopted to the specific needs of our novel application domain of CBR techniques.

In the *first phase* the service integrator defines his integration problem by using a wizard-based questionnaire. As part of the problem description he defines the functional area of the enterprise system where the service should be integrated. In the *second phase* the Case-Based Reasoning Framework retrieves existing integration cases from the knowledge base that have similar problem descriptions. In the *third phase* the service integrator can select one of the suggested integration cases for reuse as the 'best fit template' that can then be further adapted with respect to the current integration problem. The problem solution part of the selected integration case is

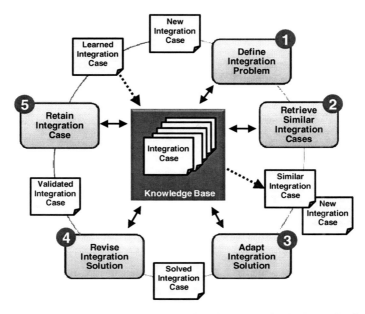

Fig. 2. Case-Based Reasoning Framework for Service Integration in Enterprise Systems

extracted and adapted to the new problem context. In the *fourth phase* the adapted integration case is validated whether it meets the defined integration requirements. In the *fifth phase* the validated integration case is stored in the knowledge base allowing an incremental, sustained learning of the new integration experience.

In this paper we particularly focus on the case retrieval step (second phase) and specifically present an ontology-based solution to measure the semantic integration context similarity between two integration problem descriptions.

3.2 Integration Case Structure and Case Similarity Assessment

Following the general principle of CBR [2], an integration case contains a problem description as well as a problem solution part. The *integration problem part* is defined by a structured or object-oriented case representation format that consists of attribute-value pairs, cf. [5]. The attributes of the integration problem description are divided into three groups: the *integration goal description* group contains attributes that define the general goal that should be reached by the integration solution (e.g. UI- or process extension flavors). The *integration context description* group contains attributes that define the functional area within the enterprise system where the service should be integrated. Finally the *integration requirements description group* contains attributes that define in detail the UI-, process-, business logic-, technical- as well as non-functional extension and integration requirements. The *integration solution part* is implemented using a pattern-based modeling approach, see [7].

In order to compute the similarity between a new integration problem *(query case)* and an existing integration case of the knowledge base both problem description parts are compared using the *local-global principle* shown in Figure 3.

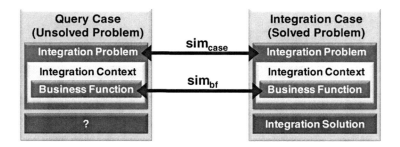

Fig. 3. Integration Case Structure and Similarity Assessment

The integration case similarity measure is calculated by the weighted average of the local similarity measures of each attribute, cf. [5]. For an integration case problem description consisting of n attributes, the similarity between a query case qc and an existing integration case ic is calculated as follows:

$$sim_{case}(qc, ic) = \frac{\sum_{i=1}^{n} w_i * sim_i(qc_i, ic_i)}{\sum_{i=1}^{n} w_i} \quad (1)$$

Here, sim_i and w_i denote the local similarity measure and the weight of attribute i, and sim_{case} represents the global similarity of an integration case.

A major challenge is to retrieve existing integration cases that have been developed in similar functional areas within the supported reference process space of a standard enterprise system. In order to tackle this problem the attribute *BusinessFunction* is introduced as part of the integration context description (Figure 3). This attribute defines the *business process* or *functional area* the integration case is related to and refers to concepts defined in the BDO. This allows implementing a local similarity function sim_{bf} that computes the similarity between two business functions.

3.3 Business Domain Ontology for Standard Enterprise Systems Categorization

In order to measure the integration context similarity of two integration cases we have developed a *Business Domain Ontology* (BDO) that models a rich taxonomy of business functions supported by a standard enterprise system. The BDO provides a functional view on the business process space of an organization, cf. [14].

Since the Case-Based Reasoning Framework addresses the reuse of integration knowledge in extensible enterprise systems we have decided to use *SAP Business Maps*[1], as an example process classification scheme of standard enterprise systems, as the main knowledge source of the BDO. SAP Business Maps provide a rich and extensively proven collection of cross-industry as well as industry-specific process reference models typically covered by standard enterprise systems. For the development of the BDO we have transformed part of the semi-formal cross-industry business maps into an expressive and machine-understandable ontological representation using OWL[2].

---

[1] SAP Business Maps, http://www.sap.com/solutions/businessmaps/index.epx
[2] Ontology Web Language, http://www.w3.org/TR/owl2-overview/

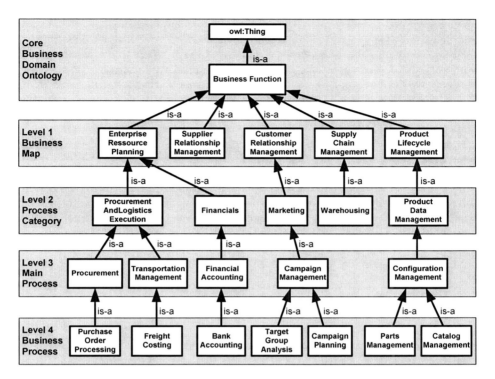

Fig. 4. Extract of the Business Domain Ontology derived from SAP Business Maps

Figure 4 shows an extract of the BDO that follows the categorization of business functions on four abstraction levels: *business maps (level 1)* define groups of processes that are supported by a specific type of enterprise system, e.g. *Enterprise ResourcePlanning*. Each business map consists of multiple *process categories (level 2)* that define a group of coarse-grained business functions, e.g. *Financials*. A process category is again refined into *main processes (level 3)* that define top-level business processes within an organization, e.g. *FinancialAccounting*. They are further decomposed into *business processes (level 4)*, e.g. *BankAccounting*.

The business map *EnterpriseResourcePlanning*, e.g., consists of 220 concepts. The concepts of the different levels are connected via *subClassOf* axioms. As a fundamental modeling assumption, the BDO has been designed in such a way that nodes on the same levels are defined as disjoint sets. We have decided on this restriction as the BDO is primarily used as a taxonomy of reference processes where a process instance can only refer to exactly one concept on each level. In general it is possible that a concept can have more than one super-concept. However this advanced modeling approach is currently not required by the outlined use case scenario of the BDO.

3.4 Semantic Distance Measurement for Integration Context Similarity

The BDO is designed as a taxonomy in which the nodes of the tree represent symbols that are used as attribute values to specify part of the integration context of a query and integration case (see section 3.1). Unlike flat case attributes, a taxonomy contains additional knowledge about the relationship between the symbols (concepts) through their position within the taxonomy-tree (ontology), cf. [5]. We exploit this knowledge within the ontological representation of the BDO in order to determine the similarity between two business functions based on their semantic or taxonomic distance within the ontology. It is possible to define query and integration cases with an integration context attribute referring to leaf nodes as well as to inner nodes of the BDO: an inner node of the BDO clusters more fine-granular business functions.

Various algorithms exist in literature to measure the semantic distance between two ontology concepts. The Case-Based Reasoning Framework is able to flexibly plug-in similarity algorithms. In [6] the authors propose four different similarity functions to compute concept-based similarity that are available in their open source software *jColibri*. As part of our prototype we have exemplarily adopted two of them to work with the BDO: similarity functions *fdeep* and *detail*. We have modified them to work with concepts as leaf nodes (instead of instances, cf. [6]).

The first similarity measure sim_{bf1} defines the similarity between two concepts representing business functions within the BDO as follows[3]:

$$sim_{bf1}(c_{qc}, c_{ic}) = \frac{max(depth(LCS(c_{qc}, c_{ic})))}{max(depth(c_{qc}), depth(c_{ic}))} \quad (2)$$

Here, c_{qc} represents the concept of the query case that defines the business function and c_{ic} represents the concept of the integration case that defines the business function. Furthermore $LCS(c_{qc}, c_{ic})$ is the set of the least common subsumer concepts of the two given concepts and $depth(c_i)$ is the depth of concept c_i in the BDO.

The second similarity measure sim_{bf2} measures the similarity between two concepts representing business functions within the BDO as follows[4]:

$$sim_{bf2}(c_{qc}, c_{ic}) = 1 - \frac{1}{2 * |super(c_{qc}, CN) \cap super(c_{ic}, CN)|} \quad (3)$$

Here, c_{qc} represents the concept of the query case that defines the business function and c_{ic} represents the concept of the integration case that defines the business function. CN is the set of all concepts in the BDO and $super(c_i, CN)$ defines the subset of concepts in CN that are super concepts of c_i. Note that $super(c_i, CN)$ does not include the root concept *owl:Thing*.

sim_{bf1} returns a decimal value between 0 *(lowest similarity)* and 1 *(highest similarity)* where sim_{bf2} returns a decimal value between 0,5 *(lowest similarity)* and 1 *(highest similarity)*. In Table 1 we have applied both similarity measures to sample concepts of the BDO shown in Figure 4.

For example the concept *PartsManagement* is compared to the concept *BankAccounting*. sim_{bf1} is computed as follows: the set of the least common subsumer concepts consists of the nodes *Business Function* and *owl:Thing* that leads to a maximum concept depth of 1. The maximum depth of both concepts within the ontology is 5

---

[3] Derived from the similarity function *fdeep* as part of the open source CBR system jColibri [6].
[4] Derived from the similarity function *detail* as part of the open source CBR system jColibri [6].

Table 1. Example integration context similarities between a query and an integration case

Query Case (Business Function)	Integration Case (Business Function)	sim_{bf1}	sim_{bf2}
PartsManagement	BankAccounting	0.200	0.500
PartsManagement	CatalogManagement	0.800	0.875
FreightCosting	PurchaseOrderProcessing	0.600	0.833
TransportationManagement	Procurement	0.750	0.833
FinancialAccounting	TransportationManagement	0.500	0.750

resulting in an overall similarity of 0.2. sim_{bf2} for this pair of concepts is computed as follows: the intersection size between the super concepts of both concepts is 1 due the common super concept *Business Function*[5]. This leads to an overall similarity value of 0.5.

4 Evaluation and Prototype

As a proof-of-concept we have instantiated the outlined Case-Based Reasoning Framework including the case similarity assessment within a prototype. The implemented prototype demonstrates how the framework can be realized as a software artifact. Regarding the chosen design science methodology, the prototype serves as a so-called *evaluation by instantiation* [3] which demonstrates the feasibility of our solution concept. In this section we will explain the usage of the introduced BDO including the proposed similarity measures within the case study introduced in section 2.

The service integrator has to integrate the eco-calculation service into the standard enterprise system. Instead of developing the solution from scratch he uses the Case-Based Reasoning System to search for similar integration projects already solved in the past. As outlined in section 3.1 he first defines the integration problem: he browses through the BDO taxonomy in order to select the business function of the core enterprise system where the service should be integrated. Figure 5 shows a part of the implemented Case-Based Reasoning Framework: The service integrator can select a business function of the BDO using a taxonomy browser containing the presented ontology (right hand side). He selects the business process *PartsManagement* as the core component that should be extended with the complementary service. This business process is part of the business map *ProductLifecycleManagement* (see Figure 4). In addition he defines further integration requirements.

Within the case retrieval step the Case-Based Reasoning Framework compares each integration case in the knowledge base with the query case by computing the global similarity measures (see section 3.2). As part of the overall integration case similarity assessment the local similarity measures for the business functions are determined using the similarity algorithms introduced in section 3.3. Following the example calculations introduced in Table 1 the service integrator finally selects the integration case in the second row for further reuse as the related business function

---

[5] Note that $super(c_i, CN)$ does not include the root concept *owl:Thing* within sim_{bf2}.

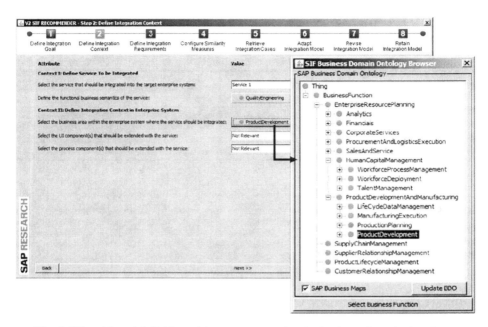

Fig. 5. Wizard-based definition of the query case using the Business Domain Ontology

CatalogManagement has the highest integration context similarity to the *PartsManagement* business function where the service should be integrated.

We have implemented the outlined approach as part of an overall Case-Based Reasoning Framework that supports the systematic reuse of integration knowledge as introduced in section 3.1. The ontology based similarity measures have been developed in Java. The reasoning service is implemented using the JENA Framework[6] including Pellet as an OWL DL reasoner.

5 Related Work

In recent years, there has been spent tremendous effort to formally describe the semantics that underlies application domains. In the business information systems domain, especially three kinds of approaches that use ontologies to capture domain semantics have gained importance. Among them, *enterprise ontologies* formally describe the structure of companies and their value nets [8, 9, 11, 12]. While such approaches rather describe the structure and goals of enterprises than providing a classification of business domains, they provide well-proven methodological general advice on how to create ontologies in the business application domain. We therefore took those guidelines into account when creating the presented BDO.

Reference models capture the semantics of individual business domains, e.g. to support communication, standardization, or the integration of information systems

---

[6] JENA, http://jena.sourceforge.net/

[10]. Compared to enterprise ontologies, such approaches usually have a significantly broader scope. However, they focus on individual application domains such as, e.g., Supply Chain Management [10]. While reference models therefore can deliver useful input for the description of functional information system properties, we have to have a formal structuring of business domains for our approach.

Approaches to provide a formal *business domain structuring* are still rare, though. Among the very few approaches, the Business Functions Ontology [13] describes various functional areas of enterprises. As the focus is on providing a standardized vocabulary for the specification of business processes, the ontology consists of a very large set of fine-granular business functions which would complicate the calculation of similar integration contexts in our approach, though. We therefore decided to design and implement the new Business Domain Ontology.

Different approaches exist that allow measuring the semantic distance between two ontological concepts, e.g. [17] or [18]. Our Case-Based Reasoning Framework is developed in such a way that is possible to flexibly plug-in in different algorithms. As outlined in the previous sections we have exemplarily adapted the algorithms suggested in [6].

6 Conclusion

In this paper we have presented a Business Domain Ontology that provides a formal representation of reference processes and business functions. It provides the foundation for a novel Case-Based retrieval algorithm to compute the similarity of business semantics within the context of two integration cases. With this ontology-based solution, we aim at providing a methodical support to facilitate the systematic reuse of existing extension and integration knowledge. With the rise of modular and reuse-based application building paradigms, the integration of third-party parts is becoming a critical success factor. Yet, systematic approaches to leverage existing knowledge gained during the extension of core parts in the past hardly exist. The results of our research have implications for academia and practice. For practice, they provide a systematic, tool-supported approach for sharing valuable integration or customizing experience, e.g. within consulting companies. For academia, our results indicate the need to build and test approaches for the systematic extension of standard enterprise systems with complementary services.

In future work, we will extend our prototype in order to support the adaptation, revision and retention phase of the Case-Based Reasoning cycle introduced in this paper. We plan to extend our Case-Based Reasoning Framework with a Rule-Based Reasoning (RBR) component that allows capturing general, case-independent knowledge in the domain of service integration and extensible enterprise systems. Based on this hybrid model of intelligent systems (cf. [16]) we particularly want to explore to what degree the adaptation of existing integration cases can be automated.

Acknowledgments. The work presented in this paper is partially embedded into THESEUS/TEXO which is funded by means of the German Federal Ministry of Economy and Technology under the promotional reference 01MQ07012. The authors take the responsibility of the contents.

References

1. Aamodt, A., Plaza, E.: Case-Based Reasoning: Foundational Issues, Methodological Variations, and System Approaches. AI Communications 7(1) (1994)
2. Leake, D.: Case-Based Reasoning: Experiences, Lessons and Future Directions. AAAI Press, Menlo Park (1996)
3. Hevner, A.R., et al.: Design Science in Information Systems Research. MIS Quarterly 28(1), 75–105 (2004)
4. Brehm, L., Heinzl, A., Markus, M.L.: Tailoring ERP systems: a spectrum of choices and their implications. In: Proc. 34th Hawaii Intl. Conf. System Sciences. IEEE, Hawaii (2001)
5. Bergmann, R.: On the Use of Taxonomies for Representing Case Features and Local Similarity Measures. In: Gierl, L., Lenz, M. (eds.) Proc. 6th German Workshop on Case-Based Reasoning (GWCBR 1998), pp. 23–32 (1998)
6. Recio-García, J.A., Díaz-Agudo, B., González-Calero, P.A., Sánchez-Ruiz, A.A.: Ontology based CBR with jCOLIBRI. In: Proc. Applications and Innovations in Intelligent Systems XIV (AI-2006), pp. 149–162. Springer, Heidelberg (2006)
7. Allgaier, M., Heller, M., Weidner, M.: Towards a Model-based Service Integration Framework for Extensible Enterprise Systems. In: Schumann, M., Kolbe, L.M., Breitner, M.H., Frerichs, A. (eds.) Tagungsband Multikonferenz Wirtschaftsinformatik, Göttingen, pp. 1523–1534 (2010)
8. Bertolazzi, P., Krusich, C., Missikoff, M.: An Approach to the Definition of a Core Enterprise Ontology – CEO. In: Proc. Intl. Workshop on Open Enterprise Solutions: Systems, Experiences, and Organizations (OES-SEO 2001), Rome, Italy (2001)
9. Fox, M.S.: The TOVE Project - A Common-sense Model of the Enterprise. In: Belli, F., Radermacher, F.J. (eds.) Proc. Industrial and Engineering Applications of Artificial Intelligence and Expert Systems. LNCS (LNAI), vol. 604. Springer, Heidelberg (1992)
10. Fox, M.S., Gruninger, M.: Ontologies for Enterprise Integration. In: Proc. 2nd Conf. on Cooperative Information Systems, Toronto, Canada (1994)
11. Geerts, G.: McCarthy. W. E.: The Ontological Foundation of REA Enterprise Information Systems. Working paper, Michigan State University (2000)
12. Uschold, M., King, M., Moralee, S., Zorgios, Y.: The Enterprise Ontology. The Knowledge Engineer Review 13(1) (1998)
13. Born, M., Filipowska, A., Kaczmarek, M., Markovic, I.: Business Functions Ontology and its Application in Semantic Business Process Modelling. In: Proc. 19th Australasian Conf. on Information Systems (2008)
14. Weske, M.: Business Process Management: Concepts, Languages, Architectures. Springer, Heidelberg (2007)
15. Allgaier, M.: Requirements for a Recommendation System Supporting Guided Service Integration Modelling in Extensible Enterprise Systems. In: Esswein, W., Juhrisch, M., Nüttgens, M., Turowski, K. (eds.) Proc. Modellierung betrieblicher Informationssysteme (MOBIS 2010), CEUR Online Proceedings, Germany. (2010)
16. Prentzas, J., Hatzilygeroudis, I.: Categorizing Approaches Combining Rule-Based and Case-Based Reasoning. Expert Systems 24(2), 97–122 (2007)
17. Stahl, A., Roth-Berghofer, T.R.: Rapid Prototyping of CBR Applications with the Open Source Tool myCBR. In: Althoff, K.-D., Bergmann, R., Minor, M., Hanft, A. (eds.) ECCBR 2008. LNCS (LNAI), vol. 5239, pp. 615–629. Springer, Heidelberg (2008)
18. Xia, S., Hu, Z., Niu, Q.: An Approach of Semantic Similarity Measure between Ontology Concepts Based on Multi Expression Programming. In: Proceedings of Sixth Web Information Systems and Applications Conference, pp. 184–188 (2009)

Sapphire: Generating Java Runtime Artefacts from OWL Ontologies

Graeme Stevenson and Simon Dobson

School of Computer Science,
University of St Andrews, UK
gs@cs.st-andrews.ac.uk

Abstract. The OWL ontology language is proving increasingly popular as a means of crafting formal, semantically-rich, models of information systems. One application of such models is the direct translation of a conceptual model to a set of executable artefacts. Current tool support for such translations lacks maturity and exhibits several limitations including a lack of support for reification, the open-world assumption, and dynamic classification of individuals as supported by OWL semantics. Building upon the state-of-the-art we present a mapping from OWL to Java that addresses these limitations, and its realisation in the form of a tool, *Sapphire*. We describe Sapphire's design and present a preliminary evaluation that illustrates how Sapphire supports the developer in writing concise, type safe code compared to standard approaches while maintaining competitive runtime performance with standard APIs.

Keywords: Information systems, OWL, Java, Ontology, Bytecode generation, Data binding.

1 Introduction

A goal of ontology-driven information systems engineering is the construction of real-world domain models with sufficient formality, expressiveness, and semantic-richness to allow information system software components to be automatically generated from the underlying ontological description [1].

Several commentators advocate mapping from ontologies to strongly-typed programming languages in order to eliminate a large class of typographic errors at compile time that might only be discovered at runtime or go undetected if a dynamic approach were taken [2,3]. Taking OWL as a specific example of an ontology language, tools that provide a mapping to strongly-typed languages exist [4,5], but exhibit limitations such as a lack of support for reification, the open-world assumption, and the dynamic classification of individuals as supported by OWL semantics. In this paper we address these limitations:

- We propose a novel mapping from OWL to Java that accounts for fundamental differences between ontological and object-oriented modelling. The mapping is realised by part of the *Sapphire* tool, which generates bytecode for a set of Java interfaces corresponding to a set of OWL ontologies (Section 2).

- We describe the design of runtime artefacts called *Sapphires* that conform to an OWL individual's type set and map method invocations to an underlying quad store. Type manipulation operations approximate the dynamic classification of OWL individuals within the statically-typed Java environment (Section 3).
- We present an initial evaluation that shows how Sapphire helps developers to write concise, type safe code while maintaining runtime performance competitive with standard APIs. We also show that our mapping approach improves upon state-of-the-art tool support for OWL's feature set (Section 4).

We conclude with an overview of related work (Section 5) and planned future work (Section 6).

2 OWL to Java: A Mapping Approach

Although ontological and object oriented models exhibit similarities that lend themselves to a mapping, the fit is not exact [2]. Here we explore some of the fundamental challenges that a mapping between OWL and Java presents before discussing our solution.

- Mapping OWL Classes to Java interfaces is an established technique for approximating OWL's multiple inheritance [4,5]. However, in generating implementation classes, schemes described in the literature provide no support for dynamic classification of OWL individuals.
- OWL properties are first class objects with rich descriptions. This includes domain restrictions identifying which classes may legally use them, range restrictions on the data types and data ranges they may take (e.g., the set of integers between 1 and 31), and relations with other properties (e.g., sub property, transitive, inverse). Java models do not capture such semantics naturally.
- OWL models make the open-world assumption, which states that the truth-value of a statement is independent of whether or not it is known by any single observer to be true. This is at odds with Java's boolean logic.
- In addition to direct naming, OWL classes may be defined as the union (member of any), intersection (member of all), or complement (not member) of other classes. They may also be defined as equivalent to (shared members) or disjoint with (no shared members) other classes, or as an enumerated set of individuals.

2.1 Realising the Mapping

To begin the mapping process we use the OWL API [6] to load a set of ontologies and create a representation of a Java package for each ontology namespace. Within each package we follow the established strategy of mapping OWL classes to Java interfaces. However, we take a novel approach of providing implementation logic via dynamic proxies that conform to an individual's class membership. This allows us to approximate the dynamic classification of objects (see Section 3.1). The root interface of the hierarchy, Thing, is constructed and added to the package corresponding to the OWL namespace, `org.w3.www._2002._07.owl`. Thereafter, each class in the ontology is mapped into the hierarchy according to its sub- and super-class relations.

The final manipulation of the interface hierarchy accommodates OWL union and intersection constructs, which map cleanly to Java subclass semantics [4]. The representations for equivalent, complement, and enumerated OWL classes do not affect the structure of the class hierarchy but are handled at runtime as we will later discuss.

In the next step, a representation for each property defined in the ontology set is constructed and mapped to the interface that corresponds to its domain, or `Thing` if its domain is undefined. Cardinality and range value restrictions are extracted from the ontology model. Object property ranges are mapped to the corresponding interface representation in the constructed hierarchy, while for datatype properties a registry provides mappings to Java classes for the range of OWL supported literal datatypes (Literal, XMLLiteral, XML Schema etc.).

Each datatype has a corresponding `DatatypeMapper` that marshals data between its OWL and Java forms, and by implementing and registering a `DatatypeMapper`, the datatype registry is straightforwardly extended. Additionally, developers may also define mappings between OWL classes (i.e., non-literals) and Java objects. This feature is useful in cases where complex ontological descriptions (perhaps spanning multiple individuals) are logically encapsulated by a single Java object. For example, a mapping between concepts in the OWL-Time ontology [7] and the Java Date and Time API. Where such a mapping is defined, the OWL class is omitted from the generated interface hierarchy.

Sapphire adopts closed-world logic by default, but provides an option whereby boolean return values are replaced by a three valued enumerated type to support open-world logic (`LogicValue {TRUE, FALSE, UNKNOWN}`). An `openEquals()` method that forms part of the `Thing` interface allows for the correct interpretation of `owl:sameAs`, `owl:differentFrom`, and `owl:AllDifferent` statements.

Once complete, the internal representation of the annotated Java interface hierarchy is realised using the ASM bytecode manipulation library [8]. Within each generated interface, the parameters and return values of generated *getter* and *setter* methods are typed according to property range and cardinality restrictions. Where appropriate, *add*, *remove*, *removeAll*, *contains*, *has*, *count*, and *reify* methods provide convenient data access. Generated interfaces are annotated with descriptions of their corresponding OWL class; this includes their URI, type, equivalent-, disjoint- and complement-classes, and instance URIs for enumerated types. Methods are similarly annotated with descriptions of their corresponding OWL property; this includes their URI, type, and cardinality and data rage information, which is used for runtime validation.

3 The Sapphire Runtime Library

Dynamically generated software artefacts called *Sapphires* provide the implementation logic for the generated interfaces. Factory methods: `get()`, `create()`, and `getMembers()`, illustrated in Listing 1, provide access individuals in the model. On creation, the Java Dynamic Proxy API is used to construct a Sapphire whose interfaces

Listing 1. Sapphire creation and access via factory methods.

```
// Fetching and Creating individuals
Person bob = Factory.get("urn:bob", Person.class);
Course course = Factory.create("urn:ont101", Course.class);
// To fetch all members of a class
Collection<Book> books = Factory.getMembers(Book.class);
```

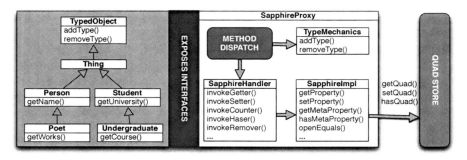

Fig. 1. An illustration of the internal structure of a Sapphire

conform to the set of OWL classes to which an individual belongs. A cache maintains a list of those recently accessed.

Figure 1 depicts the internal structure of a Sapphire, with the interfaces it exposes shown on the left hand side of the diagram. Listing 2 illustrates Sapphire's JavaBean style interaction model. When a method is invoked, the SapphireProxy dispatches the call to the appropriate handling method, such as those in the SapphireHandler and TypeMechanics classes shown.

The SapphireHandler class inspects interface annotations to check for potential cardinality or data range violations that operations may cause. If these checks pass, corresponding calls to the SapphireImpl class are made, which in turn map calls to primitive operations on the quad store[1]. As described in Section 2, data access and modification operations use a DatatypeMapper to marshall data between its OWL and Java forms.

Rather than translate OWL entailment rules to production code, we apply a reasoner to the underlying quad store. While this impacts performance, a hybrid approach yields several benefits: classifications that do not cleanly map to Java are handled by the reasoner, applications can be integrated seamlessly with legacy code operating over the same data, and certain types of schema evolution are supported without requiring that interfaces be regenerated.

---

[1] A standard triple store could be used in place of the quad store.

Listing 2. Sapphires support JavaBean style method invocation.

```
// Set Bob's name.
bob.setName("Bob Jones");
// Get Bob's date of birth
DateTime age = bob.getDateOfBirth();
// Get Bob's publications.
Collection<Publication> publications = bob.getPublications();
// Use reification to mark assertion time.
bob.reifyTeachingAssistantOf(course, Temporal.class).
    setAssertedAt(new DateTime());
// Clear Bob's teaching responsibilities.
bob.removeAllTeachingAssistantOf();
```

3.1 Type Mechanics

We approximate the OWL type system, supporting the addition and removal of types to and from an object, through the `addType()` and `removeType()` methods of the `TypedObject` interface, which map to the `TypeManipulator` component of the `SapphireProxy`.

When adding a type, the new type set supported by the object is calculated and used to generate a new proxy object that rewraps the internal components of the old proxy, updating the quad store in the background. The type removal process does likewise.

Casting of an object to its equivalent classes is supported by inspecting annotations describing class equivalence during the proxy construction process[2]. Similarly, the annotations describing disjoint classes are used to prevent violations in the type addition and removal processes.

The processes of adding and removing types may result in the implicit addition or removal of union, intersection, or complement class to an object's type set. This is handled automatically when the object's updated type set is calculated. Listing 3 illustrates this using an instance of the `Cat` class as defined by the Mindswap Pet Ontology [9]. To this instance, the `Pet` type is added, after which the object may be cast to the `PetCat` class — the intersection of the two. Removing the `Pet` type from the instance removes the intersection class from its type set.

There are several advantages of our approach to approximating OWL type semantics. In particular, we need not generate intersection classes to accommodate possible class combinations (which in the worst case would require the powerset $\mathbb{P}(n)$ generated classes for n classes in an ontology); Sapphires may assume multiple, unrelated types; and we preserve the semantics of the Java *equals*, *instanceof*, and *casting* operators.

One disadvantage of this approach is that old references to modified objects become out of date. As a result, problems might arise if a method is invoked on a type that an

---

[2] This results in a cleaner API than those produced by tools that create a composite interface for all equivalent classes.

Listing 3. Adding types to and removing types from a Sapphire

```
// Create a Cat and make it a Pet.
Cat tom = Factory.create("urn:ex:tom", Cat.class);
Pet tomAsPet = tom.addType(Pet.class);
// We may now cast between Cat, Pet, and PetCat classes.
PetCat tomAsPetCat = (PetCat) tomAsPet;
// Remove the Pet type from Tom (identifying return type).
tom = tomAsPetCat.removeType(Pet.class, Cat.class);
// New proxy interface prohibits access to old types, e.g.,
tomAsPetCat = (PetCat) tom; // ClassCastException thrown.
```

object no longer carries. To mitigate this, method calls are checked against a Sapphire's *graveyard type* set, to prevent such modifications.

4 Evaluation

We have undertaken a preliminary qualitative and quantitative evaluation of Sapphire. First, we illustrate the core benefits of Sapphire — brevity and safety — through a typical query example. We then compare Sapphire's capabilities to similar tools, and examine its impact on performance by comparing Sapphire with standard Java-based querying mechanisms.

This evaluation uses the Leigh University Benchmark (LUBM) [10], an ontology and data generator based on a university domain ontology.

4.1 Code Size and Error Prevention

Based on the example presented by Goldman [2], we construct a query using the LUBM ontology to find and print the name of the person whose email address is *FullProfessor7@Department0.University0.edu*. Listing 4 shows how this query is expressed using Sapphire, while Listing 5 expresses the same query using the Jena ontology API [11].

Listing 4. Sapphire query for a person with a given email address's name.

```
Collection<Person> people = a_factory.getMembers(Person.class
    );
for (Person person : people) {
  for (String emailAddress : person.getEmailAddress()) {
    if ("FullProfessor7@Department0.University0.edu".equals
        (emailAddress)) {
      System.out.printf("Name: %s", person.getName());
} } }
```

Listing 5. Jena query for a person with a given email address's name.

```
static final String U_URI = "http://www.lehigh.edu/~zhp2
    /2004/0401/univ-bench.owl#";
Literal emailAddress = ResourceFactory.createPlainLiteral("
    FullProfessor7@Department0.University0.edu");
OntClass personClass = model.getOntClass(U_URI + "Person");
OntProperty nameProperty = model.getOntProperty(U_URI + "name
    ");
OntProperty emailProperty = model.getOntProperty(U_URI + "
    emailAddress");
ExtendedIterator<Individual> instances = model.
    listIndividuals(personClass);
while (instances.hasNext()) {
    Individual resource = instances.next();
    if (resource.hasProperty(emailProperty, emailAddress)) {
        RDFNode nameValue = resource.getPropertyValue(
            nameProperty);
        Literal nameLiteral = (Literal) nameValue.as(Literal.
            class);
        String name = nameLiteral.getLexicalForm();
        System.out.printf("Name: %s", name);
    } }
```

It can be seen that the Sapphire representation of the query is as least half the size of the Jena representation. Representations of the same query using NG4J [12] and the Jena SPARQL API are similarly verbose. While the primary contributor to this brevity is the use of domain-typed objects and properties, this example illustrates how Sapphire prevents typographical errors affecting class and property names and does not require developers to cast values obtained from the model to an appropriate Java type.

4.2 Feature Comparison Matrix

Figure 2 provides a feature by feature comparison of Sapphire against four similar tools: RDFReactor [13], OntoJava [14], the work of Kalayanpur et al. [4], and Owl2Java [5], against the core features of the OWL specification. Two of these tools target RDF Schema and comparisons have therefore been drawn where appropriate.

Of the projects surveyed, Sapphire is the most feature complete. In particular, Sapphire is the only tool to support reification, open-world modelling, extension of OWL's supported datatypes, and dynamic re-classification of individuals. The hybrid schemes employed by both Owl2Java and Sapphire take advantage of reasoners to handle tasks that would otherwise be less straightforward for a complete Java conversion (e.g., computing the membership of complement classes). OWL versioning properties have no equivalent Java feature.

	Sapphire	RDFReactor	OntoJava	Kalyanpur et al.	OWL2Java
RDF/OWL	OWL	RDF	RDF	OWL	OWL
Approach	Hybrid	Hybrid	Standalone	Standalone	Hybrid
Mapping Technique	Interfaces + DynamicProxy	Implementation Classes	Interfaces + Implementation Classes	Interfaces + Implementation Classes	Interfaces + Implementation Classes
Preserves class hierarchy	Yes	No	Yes	Yes	Yes
Open-world assumption	Yes	No	No	No	No
Reification	Yes	No	No	No	No
Named Classes	Yes	Yes	Yes	Yes	Yes
Enumerated Classes	Yes	N/A	N/A	Yes	No
Property Restriction Classes	Yes	N/A	N/A	No	Yes
Intersection Classes	Yes	N/A	N/A	Yes	Yes
Union Classes	Yes	N/A	N/A	Yes	Yes
Complement Classes	Yes	N/A	N/A	No	Yes
Equivalent Classes	Yes	N/A	N/A	Yes	Yes
Disjoint Classes	Yes	N/A	N/A	Yes	Yes
Property Cardinality	Yes	Yes (OWL)	N/A	Yes	Yes
Intra-Property Relations (sub, super, inverse, equiv.)	Yes	Yes	Yes	Yes	Yes
Property Logic Characteristics (functional, transitive, etc.)	Yes	N/A	N/A	Yes	Yes
Individual Identity Relationships	Yes	N/A	N/A	No	No
Dynamic Individual Classification	Yes	No	No	No	No
Full Datatype Support	Yes	No	No	No	Yes
Extensible Datatype Support	Yes	No	No	No	No
Enumerated Data Ranges	Yes	N/A	N/A	Yes	No
RDF Container/Collections	Yes	List only	No	No	No
(Annotation) Imports	Yes	N/A	N/A	Yes	Yes
(Annotation) Versioning/ Compatibility	No	N/A	N/A	No	No
(Annotation) Deprecated Properties and Classes	Yes	N/A	N/A	No	No

Fig. 2. A comparison of support for features of the OWL specification within Sapphire and similar tools

4.3 Initial Performance Analysis

To evaluate Sapphire's overhead, we compare its performance with three alternative Java-based query models: the NG4J API, the Jena ontology model API, and the Jena SPARQL API.

We generated two data sets using LUMB: a small data set consisting of 8832 statements, and a larger data set consisting of 103,048 statements. Next we formulated queries to return the name of the professor identified by a specific URI (*Q1*), and to search for the name of the professor with the email address *FullProfessor7@Department0.University0.edu* (*Q2*) and ran them on each data set. The tests ran on an Intel Core i7 (2.66GHz) Macbook Pro with 4GB RAM. Each query was repeated 200,000 times and the mean duration taken to reduce the effect of external factors on the performance measurement. Figure 3 shows the results of this comparison. Note that execution times are shown on a logarithmic scale.

Evaluation of Sapphire's performance is best done in comparison to NG4J, upon which it is built. The data show that Sapphire introduces a small overhead to the baseline NG4J performance. For example, for Q2 on the large data set, we see that the primary cost comes from operations delegated to the NG4J library, while the remaining cost is due to the invocation of the `getName()` method on each `FullProfessor` instance in the data set. Examining the relative performance for both queries on each data set, we

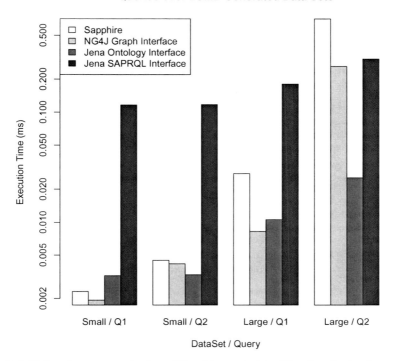

Fig. 3. Initial performance evaluation of Sapphire against traditional methods of querying OWL data using two queries over two data sets generated by LUMB

see that compared with NG4J, the Jena ontology API exhibits a superior performance ratio between queries that select single and multiple values from the model.

While further optimisations may reduce the overhead of the Sapphire library, we note that the execution time for Q2 on the larger data set remains under 1ms. This, we posit, is an acceptable overhead for the code brevity and type safety Sapphire provides. A more detailed evaluation of all of Sapphire's capabilities against data sets with different characteristics is planned for the future.

5 Related Work

Several approaches for working with RDF-based data models, that sit in a spectrum ranging from the ontology agnostic to the domain-specific, have been proposed. The most generic APIs (e.g., the model APIs of *Jena* [11] and *NG4J* [12]), provide operations that support manipulation of the data-graph (e.g., the addition and removal of triples or quads). *Tramp* [15] binds RDF nodes to Python dictionary structures, allowing indexing by property names, while *SETH* [16], supports dynamic schema extension through the writing of inline RDF/OWL snippets in Python code. Increasing the level of abstraction, *The OWL API* [6], and *O3L* [17] are libraries based on OWL concepts and semantics that provide reflection-like capabilities for indexing into a data model using classes such as `OWLClass` and `OWLProperty` and `OWLRestriction`.

Towards the domain-specific end of the spectrum sit tools that map from object-oriented representation to ontology-oriented representation and vice versa. The former category of tools, to which *Jenabean* [18], *Sommer* [19], *Spira* [20], and *Empire* [21] belong, operate through manual annotation of the fields of Java Bean style objects, from which ontological descriptions are then extracted or persisted to a back-end. While this approach removes the need for developers to construct ontologies natively, these tools realise only a small subset of the RDFS and OWL specifications. Of the latter category, *Sparta* [22] binds RDF nodes to domain-typed Python objects and RDF arcs to attributes of those objects, while *ActiveRDF* [23] provides RDF data inspection capabilities via a Ruby-based virtual API that intercepts method calls and dynamically maps them onto SPARQL queries against a data model. ActiveRDF does not use schema information as part of its mapping process, and while this allows for great flexibility in terms of the ability to easily manipulate schema and structure of individuals at runtime), this comes as a necessary trade off against the ability to verify application code both in terms of type correctness and typographical errors against an ontology.

The tools closest in spirit to Sapphire generate domain-specific APIs for strongly-typed programming languages directly from an ontology. *RDFReactor* [13] generates Java libraries for RDFS models that act as a proxy to a triple store back-end at runtime, while *Owl2Java* [5] gives OWL ontologies a similar treatment. *OntoJava* [14] and the work of Kalyanpur et al. [4] (on which Jastor [24] is based), perform the conversion of both ontology axioms and rules into executable code. As we presented in Section 4.2, Sapphire builds upon the strong foundational work of these tools to provide improved support for OWL's feature set. Sapphire also offers novel features in the form of an extensible type mapping system, support for reification, support for the open-world assumption, and support for the dynamics of multiply-classified individuals.

Puleston et al. [25] present a case study supporting an approach that conflates both domain-specific and ontology-agnostic aspects within a single API. Applications constructed using this technique are assumed to be structured around a static core that is accessed in a domain-specific manner, with highly dynamic concepts at its edges that are accessed via a generic API. The authors advocate this approach for application domains where parts of an ontology are frequently evolved, or a high number of concepts (e.g., tens of thousands) makes code generation impractical. We note that one limitation the authors found with existing domain-specific APIs was the inability to evolve the type of existing instances, an issue that Sapphire addresses.

Finally, Parreiras et al. [26] introduce a Domain Specific Language, *agogo*, that allows developers to describe a mapping between OWL and a conceptual API. Independently specified transformations between the DSL and programming languages allow the API to be realised in the developer's programming language of choice. The core novelty of this approach is support for *patterns* as first class objects in the DSL. This feature allows single calls in the generated API to be mapped to multiple operations on the underlying data store. Although Sapphire's extensible type registry can be thought of as providing similar functionality, the approach of Parreiras et al. lends itself to the generation of highly-customised APIs, something that we seek to investigate further.

6 Conclusion and Future Work

One goal of ontology-driven information systems engineering is to automatically generate software components from ontological descriptions. To this end, we presented a mapping from OWL to Java, and its realisation in the form of a tool, *Sapphire*. Building upon the state-of-the-art, our approach overcomes several limitations of existing tools by providing an extensible type mapping registry, supporting reification, accounting for the open-world assumption, and supporting the dynamic classification of OWL individuals in the Java model through a novel, dynamic-proxy-based solution. We demonstrated the primary benefits of Sapphire's API — code brevity and type safety — and quantified improvements to the state-of-the-art in the set of OWL's features supported. Through an initial performance evaluation, we showed that although Sapphire introduces an overhead compared with standard APIs, its performance remains competitive.

By profiling the codebase, we have observed that the main performance bottleneck comes from searches performed on the quad store. To mitigate this, we will devise data caching strategies to reduce such calls. Additionally, we are working towards fully supporting the feature set of OWL 2, and will investigate approaches to more closely integrate application logic with the generated artefacts.

Acknowledgements

This work has been supported by the EU-FP7-FET Proactive project SAPERE – Self-aware Pervasive Service Ecosystems, under contract no. 256873.

References

1. Uschold, M.: Ontology-driven information systems: Past, present and future. In: Proceedings of Formal Ontology in Information Systems, pp. 3–18. IOS Press, Amsterdam (2008)
2. Goldman, N.M.: Ontology-oriented programming: Static typing for the inconsistent programmer. In: Fensel, D., Sycara, K., Mylopoulos, J. (eds.) ISWC 2003. LNCS, vol. 2870, pp. 850–865. Springer, Heidelberg (2003)
3. Vanden Bossche, M., Ross, P., MacLarty, I., Van Nu??elen, B., Pelov, N.: Ontology driven software engineering for real life applications. In: Proceedings of the 3rd International Workshop on Semantic Web Enabled Software Engineering (2007)
4. Kalyanpur, A., Jimenez, D.: Automatic mapping of OWL ontologies into Java. In: Proceedings of Software Engineering and Knowledge Engineering (2004)
5. OWL2Java : A Java code generator for OWL. Website (2011), http://www.incunabulum.de/projects/it/owl2java
6. The OWL API. Website (2011), http://owlapi.sourceforge.net/
7. Hobbs, J.R., Pan, F.: An ontology of time for the semantic web, vol. 3, pp. 66–85 (March 2004)
8. Bruneton, E., Lenglet, R., Coupaye, T.: ASM: A code manipulation tool to implement adaptable systems. In: Proceedings of Adaptable and Extensible Component Systems (2002)

9. The Mindswap Pet Ontology. Website (2011), http://www.mindswap.org/2003/owl/pet
10. Guo, Y., Pan, Z., Heflin, J.: LUBM: A benchmark for OWL knowledge base systems. Journal of Web Semantics 3, 158–182 (2005)
11. Website of the Jena Semantic Web Framework. Website (2011), http://jena.sourceforge.net/
12. Bizer, C., Cyganiak, R., Watkins, E.R.: NG4J – Named Graphs API for Jena. In: Proceedings of the 2nd European Semantic Web Conference, Heraklion, Greece (2005)
13. Vökel, M.: RDFReactor – from ontologies to programmatic data access. In: The Jena Developer Conference, Bristol, UK (2006)
14. Eberhart, A.: Automatic generation of Java/SQL based inference engines from RDF Schema and RuleML. In: Proceedings of the First International Semantic Web Conference, Chia, Sardinia, Italy, pp. 102–116. Springer, Heidelberg (2002)
15. TRAMP: Makes RDF look like Python data structures. Website (2011), http://www.aaronsw.com/2002/tramp/
16. Babik, M., Hluchy, L.: Deep integration of Python with web ontology language. In: Proceedings of the 2nd Workshop on Scripting for the Semantic Web, Budva, Montenegro (2006)
17. Poggi, A.: Developing ontology based applications with O3L. WSEAS Transactions on Computers 8, 1286–1295 (2009)
18. Jenabean: A library for persisting Java Beans to RDF. Website (2011), http://code.google.com/p/jenabean/
19. Sommer: Semantic object (medata) mapper. Website (2011), http://sommer.dev.java.net/
20. Spira: A linked data ORM for Ruby. Website (2011), https://github.com/datagraph/spira
21. Empire: A JPA implementation for RDF. Website (2011), https://github.com/clarkparsia/Empire
22. Sparta: a simple API for RDF. Website (2011), https://github.com/mnot/sparta/
23. Oren, E., Delbru, R., Gerke, S., Haller, A., Decker, S.: ActiveRDF: object-oriented semantic web programming. In: Proceedings of the 16th International Conference on World Wide Web, pp. 817–824. ACM, New York (2007)
24. Jastor: Typesafe, ontology driven RDF access from Java. Website (2011), http://jastor.sourceforge.net/
25. Puleston, C., Parsia, B., Cunningham, J., Rector, A.: Integrating object-oriented and ontological representations: A case study in java and OWL. In: Sheth, A.P., Staab, S., Dean, M., Paolucci, M., Maynard, D., Finin, T., Thirunarayan, K. (eds.) ISWC 2008. LNCS, vol. 5318, pp. 130–145. Springer, Heidelberg (2008)
26. Parreiras, F.S., Saathoff, C., Walter, T., Franz, T., Staab, S.: APIs a gogo: Automatic generation of ontology APIs. International Conference on Semantic Computing, 342–348 (2009)

Mooop – A Hybrid Integration of OWL and Java

Christoph Frenzel[1], Bijan Parsia[2], Ulrike Sattler[2], and Bernhard Bauer[1]

[1] Institute of Computer Science, University of Augsburg, Germany
{christoph.frenzel,bernhard.bauer}@informatik.uni-augsburg.de
[2] School of Computer Science, The University of Manchester, UK
{bparsia,sattler}@cs.man.ac.uk

Abstract. Java is a widespread object-oriented programming language for implementing information systems because it provides means to express various domains of interest. Nevertheless, some fields like Health Care and Life Sciences are so complex that Java is not suited for their design. In comparison, the Web Ontology Language (OWL) provides various powerful modelling constructs and is used to formulate large, well-established ontologies of these domains. OWL cannot, however, be used alone to build applications. Therefore, an integration of both languages, which leverages the advantages of each, is desirable, yet not easy to accomplish. We present Mooop (Merging OWL and Object-Oriented Programming), an approach for the hybrid integration of OWL ontologies into Java systems. It introduces hybrid objects, which represent both an OWL and Java entity. We have developed a prototype of Mooop and evaluated it in a case study.

Keywords: Hybrid integration, Ontologies, OWL, Object-oriented programming, Java, Ontology-based applications.

1 Motivation

Object-oriented programming languages (OOPLs) like Java are a widely adopted technology for implementing ever bigger and more complex object-oriented (OO) information systems. They provide means for the expression of the structure, i.e., possible entities and their features, and the behaviour, i.e., possible modifications of the entities at run-time, of complex problem domains. Nevertheless, some problem fields, e.g., Health Care and Life Sciences, are so complex that OOPLs are not suited to design them. For instance, anatomical models are often characterised by a vast number of concepts with complex constraints and are laborious to express in Java. In comparison, the Web Ontology Language (OWL) provides expressive modelling constructs which have been used by domain experts to formulate large ontologies of these domains, e.g., GALEN[1] and SNOMED CT[2]. Additionally, OWL allows reasoning, i.e., the inference of implicit from explicit knowledge. However, OWL does not allow to implement dynamic behaviour and, thus, it alone cannot be used to build applications.

---
[1] http://www.opengalen.org/index.html
[2] http://www.ihtsdo.org/snomed-ct/

Ontology-based applications leverage the advantages of both paradigms by combining them. They are characterised by a complex OWL ontology and a sophisticated OOPL-expressed behaviour which regularly conducts reasoning in order to derive new knowledge form the ontology. Examples are the Patient Chronicle Model [13], and the context-aware application framework [15]. In comparison to typical semantic web applications like the FOAFMap [12], ontology-based applications require a tight integration of OWL and the OOPL. However, such integration is not easy to accomplish because differences in their semantics induce an impedance mismatch that needs to be taken into account [9].

This paper presents our novel approach for the integration of OWL ontologies into OO systems: Mooop (Merging OWL and Object-Oriented Programming). We introduce hybrid objects which are entities present in both the OWL ontology and the OO system. Additionally, we provide a flexible mechanism for linking both paradigms. In this way, Mooop creates a coherent hybrid model. This paper is based on [3] which provides more detailed information on Mooop.

Although the Mooop concept is not language specific, in this paper, we concentrate on the mainstream OOPL Java in order to exemplify the concepts. Furthermore, we use OWL 2 and the syntax introduced in [5].

2 Java and OWL

Java is a strongly typed, class-based OOPL [4]. Its basic elements are objects which exchange messages. Objects have a fixed and unique object identifier (OID), a structure defined by a collection of attributes and corresponding values, and a behaviour defined by a collection of methods. An object is created by instantiating a class which determines the structure and behaviour of the object. Java allows single inheritance, i.e., a class can inherit the structure and behaviour of at most one other class and, thus, can become a subclass. This allows the subclass to extend or overwrite the superclass. The type of an object is defined at compile-time and cannot change at run-time. Furthermore, it is forbidden to call an undefined method of an object. The methods are implemented in an imperative, Turing complete language. Java offers dynamic binding based on single dispatch which enables polymorphism.

OWL [16] is a modelling language based on Description Logic (DL) [1] for capturing knowledge in an ontology. It distinguishes between a concept level (TBox) and an instance level (ABox). The former defines OWL classes and OWL properties, and the latter OWL individuals. OWL allows the definition of atomic and complex classes. The latter are combinations of atomic classes and property restrictions. Both class types can be used in a subclass or equivalent class definition. A property is a first class citizen of an ontology and can be a subproperty or equivalent property of another property. OWL distinguishes between object properties and data properties. An OWL individual can have several explicit and implicit types, i.e., atomic or complex classes. In summary, OWL is very expressive concerning the structural features of a domain. In contrast to that, OWL cannot express any behaviour at all, and, thus, cannot be used alone to implement applications.

An important feature of OWL is reasoning, i.e., the inference of implicit knowledge from explicit knowledge, through reasoning services, e.g., consistency checking and classification. This enables post-coordination [6, p. 91]: not all concepts of the real world are modelled in the ontology as atomic classes, but the user of the system defines the concepts at run-time as anonymous complex classes. For instance, an OWL individual can have the types Allergy and $\exists$causedBy.Nuts simultaneously, thus, defining a not explicitly modelled nut allergy. In order to use post-coordination, the possibilities for defining complex classes at run-time should be restricted in a domain specific manner: it should only be possible to create reasonable concepts. This is called sanctioning [2].

3 Existing Integration Approaches

There are numerous existing approaches for integrating OWL into Java or similar OOPLs. Based on [13], we distinguish direct, indirect, and hybrid integration.

The direct integration represents OWL classes as Java classes and OWL individuals as Java objects. Hence, this approach offers the developers a domain-specific application programming interface (API) and type-safety which eases the application development. However, this comes at the price of limited reasoning capabilities: since Java classes cannot dynamically change their attributes at run-time, it is not possible to represent new, inferred OWL properties at run-time. Representatives of this category are So(m)mer [14] and Jastor [7].

The indirect integration utilises Java classes to represent the metaclasses of OWL, e.g., `OWLClass` or `OWLIndividual`. The OWL ontology is represented by instances of these Java classes, i.e., an object can represent, e.g., an OWL class, OWL property, or OWL individual. On the one hand, this provides run-time flexibility allowing a sophisticated reasoning. For instance, if a new OWL property instance is inferred then a new instance of the metaclass `OWLPropertyInstance` has to be created and linked with other objects. On the other hand, the development of complex software is complicated because of the generic, domain-neutral API. This approach is used by OWL API [10] and Jena [8].

The idea of the hybrid integration is to integrate a few top level concepts, i.e., very important core concepts, directly, and the vast number of specialised concepts indirectly [13]. Hence, a Java class can represent either an OWL metaclass or an OWL class, and a Java object can represent either an OWL class, an OWL property, or an OWL individual. In this way, it combines a domain-specific API and type-safety with great run-time flexibility. The disadvantage of the approach is a complexity overhead [13]. Representatives of this category are the Core Model-Builder [13] and TwoUse [11].

In order to exemplify the hybrid integration, Fig. 1 depicts a possible Java class model for a hybrid integration of the following ontology:

$$\text{Pizza} \sqsubseteq \exists\text{hasName.String} \sqcap \exists\text{hasTopping.Topping}$$
$$\text{Topping} \sqsubseteq \exists\text{hasName.String}$$
$$\text{PricedPizza} \sqsubseteq \text{Pizza} \sqcap \exists\text{hasPrice.Integer} \ .$$

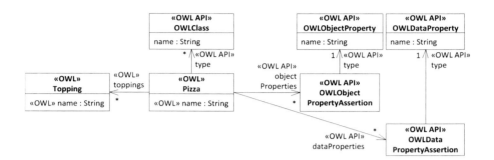

Fig. 1. Java class model for the hybrid integration of the example ontology

All directly integrated concepts are stereotyped with *OWL* and metaclasses for the indirect integration are stereotyped with *OWL API*.[3] Pizza and Topping are directly integrated top level OWL classes and have the directly integrated property name. Pizza has also indirect properties and types. The OWL class PricedPizza is integrated indirectly and, hence, is represented as an instance of OWLClass at run-time.

Hybrid integration is the most powerful integration approach [13]. Because of its numerous features, it is especially suited for the development of ontology-based applications. However, in order to match a wide range of requirements, the integration semantics has to be adaptable to the needs of a specific application. Integration semantics refers to the interpretation of the OWL model within Java. For example, it should be possible to implement a specific sanctioning mechanism which determines the structure of a Java object representing an OWL entity. Assume an OWL class Pizza with Pizza ⊑ ∃hasPrice.integer, then the sanctioning mechanism can define that a Java class representing the Pizza has a single-valued attribute price of type Integer. However, OWL would also allow Pizza individuals without an asserted price or with several prices. Obviously, such mechanisms are domain specific and difficult to generalise.

Current hybrid integration frameworks are limited in their applicability. TwoUse is actually a model-driven development framework allowing the design of a hybrid model. It allows only OWL classes to be integrated indirectly. Therefore, it is not possible to infer new properties of an OWL individual at run-time. The Core Model-Builder is, to the best of our knowledge, currently the most sophisticated framework for the hybrid integration of an OWL ontology into Java and offers a lot of features like hiding of OWL concepts, dynamic constraints on indirectly integrated attributes, and complex sanctioning. However, the adaptation of the integration is very complex since the integration semantics is spread all over the framework and, hence, numerous classes have to be changed.

---

[3] This convention will be used throughout this paper.

4 The Mooop Integration Approach

The Mooop integration approach was developed with the aim to create a powerful hybrid integration framework targeting ontology-based applications. Thereby, we focused on the ability to adapt the integration semantics to the requirements of a particular application. In this way, Mooop overcomes the shortcomings of current hybrid integration approaches. In order to accomplish these goals, Mooop splits the integration into the three layers shown in Fig. 2:

The OwlFrame indirectly integrates an OWL individual into Java for the domain neutral representation of knowledge from an OWL ontology.
The Mapping is an adaptable link between the OWL ontology and the OwlFrame and determines the integration semantics.
The Binding defines the hybrid integration of the OwlFrame into the target Java application. It enables the definition of hybrid classes, which represent OWL classes in Java, through Java annotations. Their instances, called hybrid objects, are present in both the OWL ontology and the Java model.

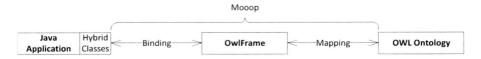

Fig. 2. The three conceptual layers of Mooop: OwlFrame, mapping, and binding

4.1 OwlFrame

Figure 3 depicts the OwlFrame as an indirectly integrated OWL individual. Notice that the association between OwlFrames and OWL individuals is injective. Since an OWL individual can have multiple types, an OwlFrame can also be associated to several type `OWLClass` objects, which indirectly integrate atomic and complex OWL classes. This enables complex post-coordination because it allows multiple typing using complex OWL classes. There are two different types of properties of an OwlFrame: `OwlObjectPropertyInstance` objects represent values for an OWL object property, i.e., OWL individuals, and `OwlDataPropertyInstance` objects represent values for an OWL data property, i.e., OWL literals.

Mooop distinguishes between asserted types and properties which express explicit knowledge about an OWL individual, and inferred types and properties which represent implicit knowledge. Thereby, the inferred information is read-only. The bound types of an OwlFrame are utilised by the mapping and binding for offering type safety (see Sect. 4.2). The method `classify()` triggers the classification of the assigned OWL individual by a reasoner. The classification result, i.e., inferred knowledge, will usually be represented as inferred types and properties.

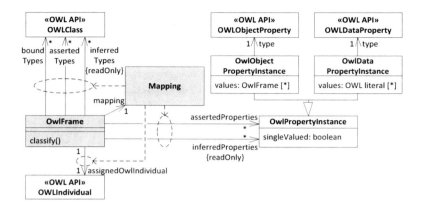

Fig. 3. The structure of the OwlFrame

In order to exemplify the OwlFrame's structure, Fig. 4 depicts a representation of an OWL individual pizza. Notice that this is just one possibility since the actual property values and types of an OwlFrame depend on the mapping. The pizza is defined by the following ontology:

$$pizza \in Pizza$$
$$mozzarella \in Mozzarella$$
$$tomato \in Tomato$$
$$\langle pizza, mozzarella \rangle \in hasTopping$$
$$\langle pizza, tomato \rangle \in hasTopping$$
$$PizzaMargherita = Pizza \sqcap \exists hasTopping.Mozzarella \sqcap \exists hasTopping.Tomato \ .$$

4.2 Mapping

The mapping links the OWL ontology and the OwlFrame, thereby determining the integration semantics. As shown in Fig. 3, an OwlFrame is associated with exactly one mapping which defines all structural features of an OwlFrame as well as their manipulations, e.g., the addition and deletion of types or property values. Furthermore, the mapping controls the reasoning process of an OwlFrame, and the life cycle of the assigned OWL individual, i.e., the creation, loading, and deletion. From a technical point of view, the mapping is the implementation of a specific interface, whose methods are called by the OwlFrame at run-time in order to access the ontology. The implementation, however, can be customised and, thus, adapted to the application's requirements.

The bound types can be seen as a set of special asserted types which offer type safety for hybrid objects. Thus, a special kind of type safety, strong type

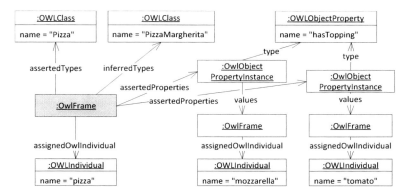

Fig. 4. The object model of an OwlFrame representing the OWL individual pizza

safety, can ensure that the asserted types of an OwlFrame are only subclasses or superclasses of the bound types. For instance, an OwlFrame o with the bound type Pizza cannot be asserted to be of type Vehicle if Vehicle is neither a subclass nor superclass of Pizza. In this way, it is guaranteed that an OwlFrame is specialised by its types in a reasonable manner. However, this logic can easily be changed as well.

The properties and property values of an OwlFrame are very likely to be customised, e.g., for implementing a specific sanctioning mechanism. For instance, assume the following OWL ontology:

$$\text{Pizza} \sqsubseteq \exists \text{hasTopping}.\top \sqcap \exists \text{hasBase}.\top$$
$$\text{pizza} \in \text{Pizza}$$
$$\langle \text{pizza}, \text{mozzarella} \rangle \in \text{hasTopping}\ .$$

The mapping can define that an OwlFrame representing pizza has an asserted property of type hasTopping with the value mozzarella, and an inferred property of type hasBase with the value null. Hence, the asserted and inferred properties together strictly conform to the definition of the OWL class Pizza.

4.3 Binding

The binding allows the definition of a hybrid integration by binding a Java class C to a specific OWL class O and attributes of C to information contained in an OwlFrame, e.g., the property values or the types of the OwlFrame. For instance, a Java class Pizza can be bound to the OWL class Pizza and the Java attribute price can be bound to the values of the OWL property hasPrice. The class C is a hybrid class and its instances are hybrid objects. Thereby, hybrid refers to their presence in both the OWL ontology and Java. Figure 5 depicts the relation between hybrid classes, which are stereotyped with *HybridClass*, and

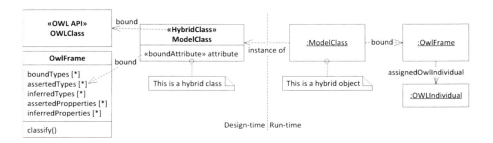

Fig. 5. A hybrid class is bound to an OWL class, its attributes are bound to features of the OwlFrame, and a hybrid object is bound to an OwlFrame object

hybrid objects. One can think of a hybrid class as the definition of a domain specific view on the information contained in an OwlFrame.

Upon instantiation of a hybrid class C which is bound to the OWL class O, the resulting hybrid object c is bound to an OwlFrame o. Thereby, O is added to the bound types of o. Furthermore, if C is a subclass of D which is bound to the OWL class P, then P is also added to the bound types of o. At run-time, several hybrid objects can be bound to the same OwlFrame object. For instance, assume an OwlFrame o that has the OWL classes O_1 and O_2 as types, and the Java classes C_1 and C_2 which are bound to O_1 and O_2, respectively. Then it is possible that a hybrid object of the Java class C_1 is bound to o while, at the same time, a hybrid object of the Java class C_2 is bound to o. As a result, both hybrid objects bound to the same OwlFrame share the same ontological information.

Mooop provides an OWL ontology-based dynamic method dispatch by annotating a method of a hybrid class to be overwritten by another method of that class if the bound OwlFrame has a specific type. For instance, assume the hybrid class Offer bound to the OWL class Offer. Offer has the method getPrice() which returns the value for the OWL property hasPrice. However, a SpecialOffer with SpecialOffer $\sqsubseteq$ Offer has an additional discount. Hence, Offer has a method getDiscountedPrice() which calculates a discounted price. Now, getPrice() is annotated to be overwritten by getDiscountedPrice() if the hybrid object has the type SpecialOffer.

The implementation of the binding in the Mooop framework is inspired by the Java Persistence API (JPA)[4]. It utilises Java annotations to allow a declarative definition of hybrid classes. The listing in Sec. 5 exemplifies this.

5 Case Study

We have developed a case study to show the feasibility of the Mooop approach: the pizza configurator which is inspired by The Manchester Pizza Finder[5]

---

[4] http://jcp.org/aboutJava/communityprocess/final/jsr317/index.html
[5] http://www.co-ode.org/downloads/pizzafinder

developed by Matthew Horridge. The pizza configurator offers the possibility to create a pizza at one's own option by adding desired pizza toppings to an initially empty pizza base. Thereby, the system has to ensure that there is at most one topping of each kind on the pizza. When the user has finished the customisation, the pizza is classified and its price is calculated: this can either be the sum of the prices of the selected toppings or, if it matches a predefined type of pizza, the price of that pizza type. For example, assume a pizza base is topped with mozzarella and tomatoes, then the system calculates the price of the pizza as the price of a pizza Margherita. Furthermore, the user can be presented additional information about the pizza like its spiciness. While the structure of this example has already been defined in the famous Pizza Ontology[6], the behaviour cannot be expressed with the means of OWL but has to be implemented in Java. Therefore, Mooop will be used to create a coherent hybrid model integrating both OWL and Java.

As with most hybrid integration approaches, the developer would start the implementation of the pizza configurator by picking several top level classes from the OWL ontology and creating hybrid classes for them. In our case the hybrid class `Pizza` is bound to the OWL class Pizza, and the hybrid class `Topping` to Topping. Afterwards the programmer defines the structure of the classes using bound attributes: the Java class `Pizza` gets the attributes `toppings` which is bound to the OWL property hasTopping, and `price` which is bound to hasPrice. Furthermore, an attribute `properties` is created in `Pizza` which contains additional properties of the bound OwlFrame, e.g., the origin of the pizza, and, thus, allows an indirect access to them.

The following listing shows an extract from the `Pizza` class. The method `calculatePrice()` sums up the prices of the toppings of a pizza. However, using the dynamic OWL ontology-based method dispatch, this method is overwritten by the method `getPrice()` if the pizza is a `PricedPizza`. Notice that the implementation of the annotated methods is ignored since the calls of these methods are intercepted and processed by the binding of Mooop.

```
@HybridClass("Pizza")
public class Pizza {
  @OwlProperty("hasTopping")
  public void addTopping(final Topping topping) { }
  @OwlProperty(value="hasTopping", valueType=Topping.class)
  public Set<Topping> getToppings() {
    return null;
  }
  @OwlDispatch({ @OwlDispatchEntry(owlType="PricedPizza",
    methodName="getPrice") })
  public Integer calculatePrice() {
    /* sum up prices ... */
  }
```

---

[6] http://www.co-ode.org/ontologies/pizza/pizza-latest.owl

```
    @Classify
    public void classify( ) { }
    @OwlProperty(value="hasPrice", valueType=Integer.class)
    protected Integer getPrice() {
      return null;
    }
    @OwlProperty()
    public Map<String, Set<Object>> getProperties() {
      return null;
    }
    ...
}
```

A custom mapping is employed to dynamically create a covering axiom for a pizza: assume the OwlFrame o with the type Pizza and the toppings Tomato and Mozzarella. In this case, the custom mapping adds an axiom stating that the assigned OWL individual of o has only the toppings Tomato and Mozzarella. This is necessary to enable the reasoner to infer the right type of pizza, here PizzaMargherita. The custom mapping is implemented by simply extending a default mapping class and overwriting the methods which define the properties.

The pizza configurator case study also shows the advantages of Mooop compared to other hybrid integration frameworks: TwoUse allows only a limited and inflexible integration, since only OWL classes can be integrated indirectly. Hence, it is not possible to define indirectly integrated OWL properties like the `properties` attribute in the class Pizza. Furthermore, it offers no means to change the integration semantics and, thus, the logic of the custom mapping of the pizza configurator would have to be mixed up with business logic. The integration features offered by the Core Model-Builder and Mooop are comparably. Accordingly, the Core Model-Builder allows defining indirectly integrated properties. However, the adaptation of the integration semantics is much more complicated since the logic is spread over a lot of classes. Thus, the custom mapping of the pizza configurator would have called for a complex adaptation of several classes in the Core Model-Builder framework.

6 Conclusion and Outlook

This paper presents Mooop, an approach for the hybrid integration of OWL into Java. Thereby, Mooop exploits the strengths of direct and indirect integration and, thus, is both powerful and easy to use. In contrast to other hybrid integration approaches, Mooop allows an easy customisation of the integration by introducing three layers: the OwlFrame is an indirect Java representation of ontological knowledge, the mapping is a customisable link between an OWL ontology and the OwlFrame, and the binding defines the hybrid integration of the OwlFrame into the target Java application through hybrid classes. Because of its flexibility, we think that Mooop can facilitate the broad application of OWL as a knowledge representation language for information systems. We have shown the advantages of Mooop in a case study.

In the future, the development of more sophisticated mappings and bindings is probably the most pressing issue. For instance, mappings for standard OWL modelling guidelines can extend the reuse immensely. Another subject which has not been investigated yet is the storage of the run-time model of a Mooop system which consists of OWL individuals and Java objects. Furthermore, a methodology for modelling hybrid models with Mooop is necessary.

The basic idea of Mooop, i.e., the division of the hybrid integration of OWL and Java into OwlFrame, mapping, and binding, can be generalised into a concept for a generic hybrid integration of any modelling approach, e.g., Topic Maps[7], into Java. It is an interesting future research topic to design, implement, and evaluate such a general concept.

References

1. Baader, F., Calvanese, D., McGuinness, D.L., Nardi, D., Patel-Schneider, P.F. (eds.): The Description Logic Handbook: Theory, Implementation and Applications. Cambridge University Press, New York (2003)
2. Bechhofer, S., Goble, C.A.: Using a Description Logic to Drive Query Interfaces. In: International Workshop on Description Logics (1997)
3. Frenzel, C.: Mooop – A Generic Integration of Object-Oriented and Ontological Models. Master's thesis, University of Augsburg (2010)
4. Gosling, J., Joy, B., Steele, G., Bracha, G.: The Java Language Specification, 3rd edn. Addison-Wesley, Boston (2005)
5. Horrocks, I., Patel-Schneider, P.F., van Harmelen, F.: From $\mathcal{SHIQ}$ and RDF to OWL: The Making of a Web Ontology Language. J. Web Sem. 1, 7–26 (2003)
6. International Health Terminology Standards Development Organisation: SNOMED Clinical Terms User Guide. Technical report (2010)
7. Jastor home page, http://jastor.sourceforge.net/
8. Jena Semantic Web Framework home page, http://jena.sourceforge.net/
9. Oren, E., Delbru, R., Gerke, S., Haller, A., Decker, S.: ActiveRDF: Object-Oriented Semantic Web Programming. In: 16th International Conference on World Wide Web, pp. 817–824. ACM, New York (2007)
10. OWL API home page, http://owlapi.sourceforge.net/
11. Parreiras, F.S., Staab, S.: Using Ontologies with UML Class-based Modeling: The TwoUse Approach. J. Data Knowl. Eng. 69, 1194–1207 (2010)
12. Passant, A.: FOAFMap: Web 2.0 meets the Semantic Web. In: 2nd Workshop on Scripting for the Semantic Web, pp. 67–68 (2006)
13. Puleston, C., Parsia, B., Cunningham, J., Rector, A.L.: Integrating Object-Oriented and Ontological Representations: A Case Study in Java and OWL. In: Sheth, A.P., Staab, S., Dean, M., Paolucci, M., Maynard, D., Finin, T.W., Thirunarayan, K. (eds.) ISWC 2008. LNCS, vol. 5318, pp. 130–145. Springer, Heidelberg (2008)
14. So(m)mer home page, http://java.net/projects/sommer
15. Springer, T., Turhan, A.Y.: Employing Description Logics in Ambient Intelligence for Modeling and Reasoning about Complex Situations. J. Ambient Intell. Smart Environ. 1, 235–259 (2009)
16. W3C OWL Working Group: OWL 2 Web Ontology Language Document Overview. W3C Recommendation (October 27, 2009)

---

[7] http://www.isotopicmaps.org/

Preface ONTOSE 2011

Following the aims and scope of ONTOSE to bring together researchers from different disciplines, ONTOSE 2011 covers a wide range of topics related to ontologies. As can be seen in the papers, ontologies have a big impact for supporting different applications (e.g., query expansion, dynamic composition of services, anti-pattern knowledge base in software project and entity retrieval). The first four papers presented in the ONTOSE section of these proceedings all are dedicated to this. In order to achieve such a support, this also implies that the ontology itself remains valid over time, that several ontologies can be integrated correctly for achieving an optimal support and that different views (e.g., intensional view and technical view) are aligned (as this is the case in a paper about Enterprise Architectures). The remainder of the ONTOSE section within these proceedings is related to these topics.

The following paragraphs give a brief overview of these two kinds of papers which can be found inside the proceedings.

Elisabetta Fersini and Fabio Sartori explain in the paper "*Improving the Effectiveness of Multimedia Summarization of Judicial Debates Through Ontological Query Expansion*" how query expansion based on an ontology can help to summarize the audio/video debates in courthouses in order to allow judicial actors to support fast navigation of the streams, efficient access to the information and effective representation of relevant contents.

The "Ontology-based Composition and Matching for Dynamic Service Coordination" by Claus Pahl, Veronica Gacitua-Decar, MingXue Wang and Kosala Yapa Bandara describes an improvement from static service architectures (i.e., Web Service composition) towards dynamic coordination of services at run time, based on ontology-based composition and matching techniques. Abstract specifications of data and behaviour, formalised as ontology-based models, are at the core. These models are processed to generate or control service execution.

Dimitrios Settas, Georgios Meditskos, Nick Bassiliades and Ioannis G. Stamelos continue work on ontologies as supporting knowledge in software projects ("Detecting Antipatterns Using a Web-based Collaborative Antipattern Ontology Knowledge Base"). Based on SPARSE, in which anti-patterns of Software projects are collected they propose that users in a web environment can simultaneously enrich the pattern catalogue. This strategy helps to improve the ontology allowing collaborative ontology editing as well as annotation and voting of both ontology components and ontology changes.

An ontology to cope with the acronyms, nicknames, roles and metaphoric expressions in the politics domain is presented in "*POWER- Politics Ontology for Web Entity Retrieval*" by Silvio Moreira, David Batista, Paula Carvalho, Francisco M. Couto and Mário J. Silva. The authors describe how POWER was designed for tracking such complex and dynamic setting, with the purpose of making it a key resource to analytics applications mining the media. This paper also discusses the question that knowledge will become invalid over time.

This problem is tackled in more detail in the paper "*An Error Correction Methodology for Time Dependent Ontologies*" written by Brett Drury, Jose Joao Almeida and Helena Morais. They propose to assign a lifespan to each relation between concepts. An evaluation of an ontology constructed with the proposed scheme revealed a gain in the total number of relations overtime without an increase in the number of the errors. The correction scheme removes: erroneous, "stale" or inconsequential information. The method also provides a procedure for resolving ambiguous relations via a "relation weight".

The paper "An Ontology-Based Integrated Approach to Situation Awareness for High-Level Information Fusion in C4ISR" written by María-Cruz Valiente, Rebeca Machín, Elena García-Barriocanal and Miguel-Ángel Sicilia is dedicated in the military domain. Particularly it focuses on the question how to combine and integrate a Situation Awareness Ontology supporting good decision making (i.e., SAW-CORE) into the Joint Consultation, Command and Control Information Exchange Data Model (JC3IEDM) expressed in OWL. Their proposal allows operators to approach situation awareness with reasoning capabilities from an ontological perspective in military or civil missions.

With their paper *"Socio-technic Dependency and Rationale Models for the Enterprise Architecture Management Function"*, Sabine Buckl, Florian Matthes and Christian M. Schweda close the gap between social dependency modelling (i.e., goals) and technical dependency modelling in context of Enterprise Architectures. The resulting model is helpful in linking the social and intensional dependencies in a management function to the structural and qualitative dependencies of the management subject.

These papers could be selected and presented since many people supported organization of this workshop. Therefore, finally, we would like to thank all the people who helped that the ONTOSE 2011 once again became a success. Namely, we thank all the authors who submitted the valuable contributions, the reviewers who helped that research quality standards were achieved and the CAiSE Workshop organizers (Óscar Pastor and Camille Salinesi) who actively supported us during all the process.

Improving the Effectiveness of Multimedia Summarization of Judicial Debates through Ontological Query Expansion

E. Fersini and F. Sartori

DISCo, Università degli Studi di Milano-Bicocca,
Viale Sarca, 336 - 20126 Milano, Italy
{fersini,sartori}@disco.unimib.it

Abstract. The growing amount of multimedia data acquired during courtroom debates makes information and knowledge management in judicial domain a real challenge. In this paper we tackle the problem of summarizing this large amount of multimedia data in order to support fast navigation of the streams, efficient access to the information and effective representation of relevant contents needed during the judicial process. In particular, we propose an ontology enhanced multimedia summarization environment able to derive a synthetic representation of audio/video contents by a limited loss of meaningful information while overcoming the information overload problem.

1 Introduction and Motivation

Recent technological advances in multimedia production, storage and distribution have moved to digitize the traditional analogical archives creating large digital libraries. This increases the need of tools for content analysis, information extraction and retrieval of multimedia objects in their native form in order to make easier both the access and the management of multimedia archives. These issues are strongly emphasized into the judicial domain: digital videos represent a fundamental informative source of events that occur during courtroom proceedings that should be stored, organized and retrieved in short time and with low cost. To this purpose multimedia summarization techniques, which analyze several informative sources comprises into a multimedia document with the aim of extracting a meaningful abstract, can support end users for browsing the stream, efficiently accessing to important information and effectively representing relevant contents.

By ananlyzing the state of the art of multimedia summarization, the most valuable contributions are mainly concerned with three research directions: (1) internal techniques, which exploit low level features of audio, video and text; (2) external techniques, which refer to the information typically associated with a viewing activity and interaction with the user; (3) hybrid techniques, which combine internal and external information. These techniques can be either domain specific, i.e. focused on typical characteristics of a given domain, or non-domain specific, that is focused on generic features associated with a generic context (no information a priori is known).

The state of the art on multimedia summarization comprises several valuable contributions belonging to the above mentioned categories. As far as is concerned with the internal techniques the main goal is to analyze low-level features derived from text, images and audio contents within a multimedia document. Interesting example can be found in [1,2,3]. In [1] the summarization of broadcast news is addressed by automatically transcribing the utterance of the speaker. In order to identify the most relevant phrases to be included into the summary, the prior and the generative probability of each sentence is combined for deriving its relevance. In [2] the scenes containing text in football videos are recognized using OCR techniques, for then a subsequent identification of key events through audio and video features. In [3] the identification of important video events is conceived through saliency models for the audio, video and textual information. In particular, audio saliency is assessed by quantifying waveform modulations, video saliency is measured through intensity, color and motion, while the text saliency is derived from part-of-speech tagging. At the end the saliency information are integrated in a single indicator for then deriving, through a bottom-up summarization algorithm, the final video skim.

In order to reduce the semantic gap between low level features and semantic concepts, research is moving towards the inclusion of external information that usually comprise knowledge about user-based information and the context in which a multimedia document evolves. The most recent investigations are focused on domain-specific [4] and non-domain specific contexts [5]. In particular, in [4] Fendri et al. present a video summarization approach able to generate a soccer video summary responding to the user profile. The summarization approach is based on semantic classified segments and textual information related to soccer video annotations. Oh the other side, in [5] Manzato et al. present an architecture that supports metadata extraction by exploring interaction mechanisms among users and contents. Relevant frames can be therefore distinguished by exploiting the annotation provided by users.

Although external summarisation techniques benefit by using high-level concepts during the summary generation, the minimization of the human effort is still a pending issue. An attempt that tries to combine the peculiarities of the previous approaches is represented by the hybrid techniques. Hybrid summarisation approaches combine the advantages provided by internal and external techniques by analyzing a combination of internal and external information. Some recent examples of hybrid technique can be found in [6] and [7]. In [6] Eldib at al. present a soccer video summarization engine, which is based on the detection of replay shots as interesting events. Video shots are identified through dominant color and histogram intersection methods. Replay shots are recognized by inducing a rule-based classifier able to exploit mid-level descriptors, as goalmouth and score board. In [7] video and textual information, through image and text processing techniques, are used for creating a classification model able to detect the four entities "who, what, where and when" occurring in a digital video. All the shots, classified with respect to the four entities, are then grouped into scenes according to a similarity measure.

As far as is concerned with the judicial debates, there is a very limited evidence about the multimedia summarization approaches [8] and in particular focused on semantic aspects. One of the main requirements of judicial users relates to the possibility of retrieving and viewing a meaningful representation of one (or more) debate(s) according to relevant events occurred during the celebration of the proceedings. This highlights two main requirements: (1) users entail to explicitly specify their needs through easy queries; (2) users want a system able to understand and augment their needs for then retrieving and presenting a limited set of relevant browseable contents. To this purpose we present a summarization environment, grounded both on machine learning and ontological query expansion techniques, for deriving a semantic-based storyboard of a courtroom proceedings recording.

The main outline of this paper is the following. In section 2 the key elements for deriving a semantic-based multimedia summary are presented. In section 3 an overview of the summarization process is given. In section 4 the core components, i.e. the ontological query expansion and the hierarchical clustering algorithm, are described. In section 5 a case study is presented, while in section 6 conclusions are briefly derived.

2 Multimedia Summarization: The Key Elements

In order to tackle the problem of generating a short and meaningful representation of a debate that is celebrated within a law courtroom, we propose a semantics-based multimedia summarization environment. The main objective is to generate a storyboard of a trial, by taking into account the semantics both beyond the user query and embedded into the courtroom recordings.

The main information sources exploited for creating a multimedia summary are represented by:

- *automatic speech transcriptions* that correspond to what is uttered by the actors involved into hearings/proceedings. Currently the speech transcriptions represent the main information source that can be semantically enriched for then supporting the multimedia summarization process. The automatic transcriptions are provided by the Automatic Speech Recognition (ASR) systems [9,10] trained on real judicial data coming from courtrooms. Since it is impossible to derive a deterministic formula able to create a link between the acoustic signal of an utterance and the related sequence of associated words, the ASR systems exploit a probabilistic formulations based on Hidden Markov Models [11]. In particular, a combination of two probabilistic models is used: an acoustic model able to represent phonetics, pronounce variability, time dynamics (co-utterance), and a language model able to represent the knowledge about the word sequences;
- *automatic audio annotations* coming from emotional states recognition. The affective state of the speakers represents a bit of knowledge embedded into

courtroom media streams that may be used to enrich the content available in judicial multimedia libraries. The emotional state annotations are derived through a framework based on a Multi-layer Support Vector Machine approach [12]. Given a set of sentences uttered by different speakers, a features extraction step is firstly performed in order to map the vocal signals into descriptive attributes (prosodic features, formant frequencies, energy, Mel Frequency Cepstral Coefficients, etc...). Then, these features are used to create a classification model able to infer emotional states of unlabelled speakers. In this work we modelled several affective states, among which *fear, neutral, anger, happy* and *boredom*, for introducing a first element of semantics associated to the "flat" automatic transcriptions;

– *automatic video annotations* that correspond to what happens during a debate. A further fundamental information source, for a semantic digital library into the trial management context, is concerned with the video stream. Recognizing relevant events that characterize judicial debates has great impact as well as emotional state identification. Relevant events happening during debates are "triggered" by meaningful gestures, which emphasize and anchor the words of witnesses, highlighting that a relevant concept has been explained. In order to achieve a reliable localization and tracking of people involved into the proceedings for then understanding "what is happening", the automatic video annotations are derived through a combination of video processing algorithms. To analyze the motions taking place in a video, and to track gestures or head movements of given subjects (typically the witnesses), the optical flow is extracted as the moving points. Then active pixels are separated from the static ones using a kurtosis-based method and finally through a wavelet based approach extracting relevant features. At this stage the link between low level features and a given set of relevant actions is performed through the induction of Bayesian learner. The semantics extracted through the approaches described in [13] and [14] consist of changes of witness posture, new witnesses' introduction, behavior of the actors, hand gestures and head movements;

– *user generated annotations* that correspond to free tags that judicial users assign to specific portions of the multimedia recordings of a given trial. Judicial users, i.e. judges, prosecutors and lawyers, usually tag manually some papers for highlighting and then remembering significant portions of the debate. This offers the possibility of personalizing contents according to the user preferences or working routines, providing then a better usability of multimedia contents. The possibility of digitally annotating relevant arguments discussed during a debate is particularly useful for future consultations and reasoning processes. For this reason, the user-generated annotations have been enclosed into the semantic-based summarization environment in order to organize and shortly represents the trials, according to the personal preferences.

All these information represent hidden knowledge that may be used to enrich the content available in multimedia digital libraries. The possibility for the end user to consult the transcriptions, also by considering the associated semantics, represents an important achievement that allow them to retrieve an enriched written sentence instead of a flat one. This achievement radically changes the consultation process: sentences can assume different meanings according to the events that are occurring at that time.

3 Multimedia Summarization: Overview of The Process

In this section we present an overview of the summarization process by outlining the main steps that need to be performed for extracting a semantic storyboard of recorded judicial debates (see figure 1 for a high-level workflow). In order to perform the multimedia summarization activity, all the recorded proceedings need to be represented and stored into a multimedia database that can be consequently searched through a retrieval engine. To this purpose, we represent a trial by a set of *semantic clips* that include transcriptions, audio annotations, video annotations and user generated tags. Each clip is a consecutive portion of a debate (transcription) in which there is one active speaker, i.e. there exists a sequence of words uttered by the same speaker without breaking due to others, enriched with the annotations extracted by audio and video processing and/or manually provided by the end users. Indeed, a clip comprises a textual transcription for each speaker period with the corresponding semantic tags.

Having a multimedia database that comprises all the recorded trials by their semantic clip representation, the summarization process can start by presenting to the end user a query form for specifying a set of key-words to be used to retrieve some relevant portions of a given debate (see figure 2). The user query

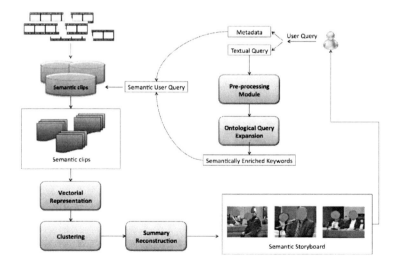

Fig. 1. Overview of the summarization process

Fig. 2. Query Form

can include both textual keywords and semantic annotations. In particular, the query may be composed by: (1) a *textual query* that will be used to match the transcription contents and user generated annotations, and (2) *metadata* that will be exploited to match the semantic tags provided by the automatic audio and video annotations.

Once the query has been specified by the end user, the textual part is submitted to the pre-processing module, which is aimed at reducing the size of vocabulary through stop words removal and stemming. Then, the reduced textual query is submitted to the ontological query expansion module for deriving a set of semantically enriched keywords. The augmented textual part, joint with the required semantic audio and video annotations, are provided to the search engine for retrieving those trials that match the required information.

Given the retrieved semantic clip, the next step is aimed at determining an appropriate representation of contents to be submitted to the clustering component that generates the browseable storyboard. To this purpose, we combine transcriptions, audio annotations, video annotations and user generated tags by using a vectorial representation of each retrieved semantic clip. A first set of coordinates are dedicated to the textual information, i.e. transcriptions and user tags, while a second set are appointed to the metadata, that is audio and video annotations. In particular the textual information are represented through TF-ISF coordinates, i.e. each term - belonging either to the speech transcription or to the user tags of a retrieved semantic clip - is represented through its TF-ISF weight [15]. On the other side, the metadata are represented through binary coordinates that denote the presence or absence of a specific audio/video annotation associated with the corresponding transcription or user tags.

As far as is concerned the TF-ISF representation, each term is weighted by considering its frequency into the semantic clip (TF) tuned by its inverse semantic clip frequency (ISF). Before computing the TF-ISF score of each term, the vectorial representation is refined. The original query terms specified by the user, joint with the expanded terms derived through the ontological query expansion, are used to bring the semantic gap that is still present into the vectorial representation. The relationships between the textual query terms and the corresponding ontological augmentation, i.e. synonyms and related terms, are exploited for tuning the TF scoring. The extracted synonyms and related terms - which have been originated starting from the user query and at the same time occur along the textual information of a given semantic clip - are removed from the vectorial representation, while their TF are added to the corresponding terms.

Now, having a refined vectorial representation of the semantic clip, the multimedia summarization module may start the extraction of the storyboard. In particular the refined vectorial representation is sumbitted to a clustering component, based on the Induced Bisecting K-means [16], for creating a hierarchical organization of the semantic clips according to their similarity. The last step relates to the summarization reconstruction, where the final storyboard is derived from the dichotomic tree structure produced by the Induced Bisecting K-means algorithm. Given the dichotomic tree, a pruning step is performed in order to choose only those clusters of semantic clips that satisfy a given intra-cluster similarity requirements [17]. Finally, only the first frames related to the representative semantic clip of each cluster are presented to the end user as pictures that could be clicked to start the corresponding audio-video portion.

4 Multimedia Summarization: The Core Components

4.1 The Semantic Component: Ontological Query Expansion

In order to enhance the precision and recall of user query, as briefly introduced in the previous section, a Query Expansion platform has been enclosed in our multimedia summarization environment.

There are two main approaches to accomplish the Query Expansion task [18]: probabilistic and ontological. The first is based on statistic data that indicates the frequency of terms in a collection of supposed relevant documents, or the frequency of co-occurence of terms. The second is based on knowledge models, in particular ontologies, in which the method search for the terms that have to be added to the query.

Although probabilistic query expansion is the dominant approach, it has shown limits in different fields and tasks: Carpineto et al. [19] highlight how this approach weights the terms on the basis of their relevance within the text rather than the real benefits for the user; moreover, it has been pointed out [20] [21] that probabilistic methods are very influenced by the corpus of documents and their relevance to the query.

On the contrary, ontological approaches are less developed and studied, but they virtually have a lot of undiscovered possibilities to semantically improve queries: being *corpus-independent*, they are more precise than probabilistic methods in the text disambiguation within a given domain. Moreover, they are particularly suitable to treat short queries. Anyway, as shown in [22] and [23], ontological methods have some important drawbacks: ontologies are typically difficult to create and maintain in order to guarantee the necessary level of precision to avoid the decrease of performance. The so called *query drift* (i.e. the choice of an expansion direction that is out of user scope) phenomenon is more probable with ontological approaches than probabilistic ones.

The query expansion module is a web service, realized with the JAX-WS 2 (Java API for XML Web Services) technology, which is part of the Java EE 5 platform. The chosen semantic framework is Jena , an open source Java framework for building Semantic Web applications grown out of work with the HP Semantic Web.

Currently, the adopted ontology is a *thesaurus* of legal terms, written both in *Italian* and in *Polish* : thesauri are structured vocabularies where relationships among terms are specified. They can be considered as a subclass of ontologies, since they represent only a part of the knowledge involved and their power of expression is limited [24]. Anyway, their main features are compatible with most of the ontological methods for QE available at the moment.

The ontological query expansion platform has been designed and implemented to support the execution of the hierarchical clustering algorithm for the retrieval of audio/video data in the judicial domain. This algorithm is the subject of the next section: further details about the design and implementation of the QE platform are out of paper scope and can be found in [25][26].

4.2 The Computational Component: Hierarchical Clustering

The approaches proposed in the literature for hierarchical clustering are characterized by good perfomance in terms of accuracy, but are also affected by high computational complexity. In order to take advantage of hierarchical approaches, but at the same time to reduce their time complexity, we introduced into the summarization system a novel approach based on Induced Bisecting k-Means [16]. It starts with a single cluster of multimedia clips and works in the following way:

The distance a_{ij} is computed as an averate linear combination of a cosine-based distance $1 - cos_T(m_i, m_j)$, for the TF-ISF coordinates concerned with transcriptions and user tags, and the jaccard distance $Jdist_B(m_i, m_j)$, for the binary coordinates concerned with audio/video annotations. The parameter α tunes the importance of each component, TF-ISF vs binary, during the distance computation. The same approach has been exploited for the similarity metric: its is an average linear combination of the cosine similarity $cos_T(m_i, m_j)$, for TF-ISF coordinates, and the jaccard similarity $Jsim_B(m_i, m_j)$, for the binary coordinates. Also in this case, the parameter α tunes the importance of each component, TF-ISF vs binary, during the similarity computation.

At the end of the summarization process, a dichotomic tree of semantic clips is generated. In order to derive the final storyboard we need to collapse the tree into

Algorithm 1. Induced Bisecting K-Means

1: Set the Intra Cluster Similarity (ICS) threshold parameter τ
2: Build a distance[1] matrix A whose elements a_{ij} represents distance between two semantic clips m_i and m_j, computed as

$$a_{ij} = \frac{\alpha \times (1 - cos_T(m_i, m_j)) + (1 - \alpha) \times Jdist_B(m_i, m_j)}{2} \quad (1)$$

3: Select, as centroids, the two semantic clips i and j s.t. $a_{ij} = \max_{l,m} A_{lm}$
4: Find 2 sub-clusters S1 and S2 using the basic k-Means algorithm[2]
5: Check the ICS of S_1 and S_2 as[2]

$$ICS(S_k) = \frac{1}{|S_k|^2} \sum_{m_x, m_y \in S_k} \frac{\alpha \times (1 - cos_T(m_i, m_j)) + (1 - \alpha) \times Jdist_B(m_i, m_j)}{2} \quad (2)$$

6: If the ICS value of a cluster is smaller than τ, then reapply the divisive process to this set, starting form step 3
7: If the ICS value of a cluster is over a given threshold, then stop. 6. The entire process will finish when there are no sub-clusters to divide.

Fig. 3. Storyboard of a sample judicial debate

"flat" clusters. To this purpose the dichotomic tree is visited in order to find those nodes (clusters) that respect a given intra-cluster similarity constraints, allowing us to select the most homogeneous groups of semantic clips. Now, suppose that the pruning activity after the Induced Bisecting K-means returns $C1, C2$ and $C3$ as the resulting clusters containing the semantic clips $1, \ldots, 9$. The presentation activity considers the most representative clip of each cluster (centroid) as the relevant element to be show into the summary, providing then a browseable storyboard as depicted in figure 3.

5 An Explicatory Judicial Case Study

5.1 Case Study

In order to understand the entire summarization process with respect to the judicial domain, we present a case study able to explain the impact that the ontological query expansion may have on real judicial multimedia summarization. As outlined in section 3, the entire process starts when the end user specifies a set of keywords for retrieving all the relevant debates related to his/her query. Now suppose that a judge is interested in viewing, through an interface that makes available the relevant browseable clips, those debates that are concerned with "white weapon".

In a traditional summarization system, where no ontological query augmentation is available, only those debates with clips that merely contain the terms "white weapon" are retrieved for the subsequent steps. Of course, this reduces the ability of the system to include a larger set of debates that do not explicitly contains the term "white weapon", but are strictly related to the corresponding concept. This means that the retrieval engine, and consequently the storyboard construction, will not take in consideration all the debates related to "knife", "blade" or "stab" (see Fig. 4).

In the proposed system, the multimedia summarization process has a different outcome. When the user provides the query "white weapon" the ontological query expansion component accomplishes its enhancement task by enriching the query term with the additional related concepts among which "knife", "blade" and "stab". After the retrieval phase, which is driven by the semantically enriched query terms, a greater set of debates than the ordinary may be available for the subsequent steps. Now, consider the representation step aimed at creating a suitable vectorial representation of the retrieved semantic clips. At this stage we can exploit the knowledge about the relationships that exist among "white weapon", "knife", "blade" and "stab" for tuning the TF-ISF representation. While in a fool-

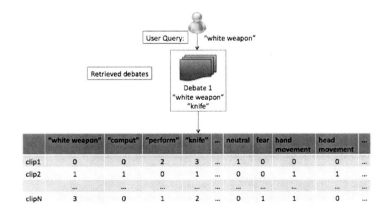

Fig. 4. Storyboard construction without QE

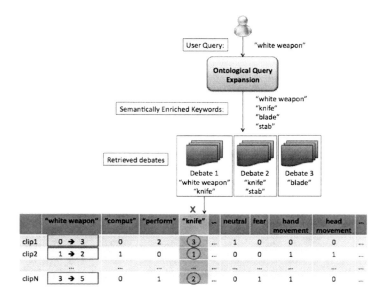

Fig. 5. Storyboard construction with QE

ish system the TF-ISF scoring is computed through a simple frequentist approach, where "white weapon", "knife", "blade" and "stab" belonging to a given semantic clip are considered as independent, in the proposed system their relationships strongly influence the TF-ISF representation. In particular, as highlighted in Fig. 5, the vectorial representation of the semantic clips is revised according to the knowledge about the augmented terms: the terms "knife", "blade" and "stab" of a given semantic clip are removed and their TF contribute to improve the TF of the "white weapon" term originally stated by the user. This improvement of TF, due to the semantic relationships among terms, implies an increasing relative importance that will have impact on the subsequent clustering phase.

5.2 Experimental Investigation

The semantic-based multimedia summarization environment has been validated by using real trials recorded at the Court of Naples. In particular, the validation was focused on 4 trials:

- Trial 1, composed of one session of 15 minutes
- Trial 2, composed by one session of 35 minutes
- Trial 3, composed by two sessions: Session One, with a 59 minutes duration, and Session Two, with a 3h 33min duration.
- Trial 4, composed of two sessions: Session One with a duration of 17 minutes and Session Two with a duration of 1h 15min.

For each trial, two different types of summarization have been constructed:

- Base summary: a basic summary with no ontological query expansion.

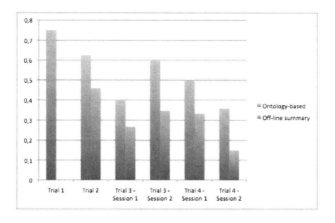

Fig. 6. Experimental Results

- Ontology summary: a summary created using, together with ASR transcriptions and audio/video annotations, a query for which the Query Expansion module has been invoked.

In particular, the following queries have been exploited:

- Trial 1: "coroner" and "defendant"
- Trial 2: "verdict" and "slaughter"
- Trial 3: "sequestration" and "preliminary investigation" for Session One; "ambush" and "gun" for Session Two.
- Trial 4: "homicide" for Session One; "homicide" and "eavesdropping" for Session Two.

Since the summarization process could be strongly affected by the number and the quality of the expanded query, only related terms with a relationship weight greater than 0.7 have been considered. A user opinion investigation has been performed on the produced summary. Each trial has been submitted to five users in order to discriminate relevant clips from the non-relevant ones. In particular, the whole collections of clips comprised in the considered trials have been evaluated and labelled with relevant and non-relevant labels. Starting from the results of the users opinions the accuracy of the derived summaries has been computed. A synthetic representation of the user perception of the generated storyboard is depicted in figure 6. The results show that the ontolgy-driven multimedia summarization approach outperforms the traditional approach. Interesting future comparisons could be related to Latent Semantic Analysis approaches, where the semantic gap that could exist among terms detected and managed by the Singular Value Decomposition technique.

6 Conclusions

In this paper a multimedia summarization environment based on semantic query expansion has been presented in order to allow judicial actors to browse multimedia documents related to judicial proceedings. In particular, by exploiting ontological query expansion and the representation of semantic clips of debates, the proposed system is able to derive a compressed and meaningful representation of what happens into a law courtroom. Our work is now focused on creating a testing environment for a quality assessment of the storyboard in order to verify the concrete applicability of the approach in Italian and Polish courtrooms, that is the final aim of the project.

Acknowledgment

This work has been partially supported by the European Community FP-7 under the JUMAS Project (ref.: 214306).

References

1. Chen, Y., Chen, B., Wang, H.: A Probabilistic Generative Framework for Extractive Broadcast News Speech Summarization. IEEE Transactions on Audio, Speech & Language Processing 17(1), 95–106 (2009)
2. Jiang, R.M., Sadka, A.H., Crookes, D.: Hierarchical Video Summarization in Reference Subspace. IEEE Transactions on Consumer Electronics 55(3), 1551–1557 (2009)
3. Evangelopoulos, G., Zlatintsi, A., Skoumas, G., Rapantzikos, K., Potamianos, A., Maragos, P., Avrithis, Y.: Video event detection and summarization using audio, visual and text saliency. In: Proc. of the 2009 IEEE International Conference on Acoustics Speech and Signal Processing (2009)
4. Fendri, E., Ben-Abdallah, H., Hamadou, A.B.: A Novel Approach for Soccer Video Summarization. In: Proc. of the Second International Conference on Multimedia and Information Technology (2010)
5. Manzato, M.G., Coimbra, D.B., Goularte, R.: Multimedia Content Personalization Based on Peer-Level Annotation. In: Proc. of the 7th European Conference on European Interactive Television Conference (2009)
6. Eldib, M.Y., Zaid, B., Zawbaa, H.M., El-Zahar, M., El-Saban, M.: Soccer video summarization using enhanced logo detection. In: Proc. of the 16th IEEE International Conference on Image Processing (2009)
7. Bo-Wei, C., Jia-Ching, W., Jhing-Fa, W.: A Novel Video Summarization Based on Mining the Story-Structure and Semantic Relations Among Concept Entities. IEEE Transactions on Multimedia 11(2), 295–312 (2009)
8. Fersini, E., Messina, E., Archetti, F.: Multimedia Summarization in Law Courts: A Clustering-based Environment for Browsing and Consulting Judicial Folders. In: Proc. of the 10th Industrial Conference on Data Mining (2010)
9. Lööf, J., Gollan, C., Ney, H.: Cross-language Bootstrapping for Unsupervised Acoustic Model Training: Rapid Development of a Polish Speech Recognition System. Interspeech, 88–91 (2009)
10. Falavigna, D., Giuliani, D., Gretter, R., Lööf, J., Gollan, C., Schlüter, R., Ney, H.: Automatic Transcription of Courtroom Recordings in the JUMAS project. In: Proc. of the 2nd International Conference on ICT Solutions for Justice (2009)
11. Rabiner, L.R.: A tutorial on Hidden Markov Models and selected applications in speech recognition. Proceedings of the IEEE 77(2), 257–286 (1989)

12. Fersini, E., Messina, E., Arosio, G., Archetti, F.: Audio-based Emotion Recognition in Judicial Domain: A Multilayer Support Vector Machines Approach. In: Proceedings of the 6th International Conference on Machine Learning and Data Mining in Pattern Recognition, pp. 594–602 (2009)
13. Avgerinakis, K., Briassouli, A., Kompatsiaris, I.: Video processing for judicial applications. In: Proc. of the 2nd International Conference on ICT Solutions for Justice (2009)
14. Kovács, L., Utasi, A., Szirányi, T.: Visret - a content based annotation, retrieval and visualization toolchain. In: Proc. of the 11th International Conference on Advanced Concepts for Intelligent Vision Systems (2009)
15. Larocca Neto, J., Santos, A.D., Kaestner, C.A.A., Freitas, A.A.: Document clustering and text summarization. In: Proc. 4th Int. Conf. Practical Applications of Knowledge Discovery and Data Mining, p. 4155 (2000)
16. Archetti, F., Fersini, E., Campanelli, P., Messina, E.: A Hierarchical Document Clustering Environment Based on the Induced Bisecting k-Means. In: Proc. of the Int. Conf. on Flexible Query Answering Systems (2006)
17. Kashyap, V., Ramakrishnan, C., Thomas, C., Bassu, D., Rindflesch, T.C., Sheth, A.: Taxaminer: An experiment framework for automated taxonomy bootstrapping. International Journal of Web and Grid Services 1(2), 240–266 (2005)
18. Tuominen, J., Kauppinen, T., Viljanen, K., Hyvnen, E.: Ontology-based query expansion widget for information retrieval. In: Proceedings of the 5th Workshop on Scripting and Development for the Semantic Web (SFSW 2009), 6th European Semantic Web Conference (ESWC 2009) (May 31-June 4) (2009)
19. Carpineto, C., de Mori, R., Romano, G., Bigi, B.: An information-theoretic approach to automatic query expansion. ACM Trans. Inf. Syst. 19(1), 1–27 (2001)
20. Voorhees, E.M.: Query expansion using lexical-semantic relations. In: SIGIR 1994: Proceedings of the 17th Annual International ACM SIGIR Conference on Research and Development in Information Retrieval, pp. 61–69. Springer-Verlag, New York Inc. (1994)
21. Ruthven, I., Tombros, A., Jose, J.M.: A study on the use of summaries and summary-based query expansion for a question-answering task (2001)
22. Navigli, R., Velardi, P.: An analysis of ontology-based query expansion strategies. In: Proc. of Workshop on Adaptive Text Extraction and Mining (ATEM 2003), in the 14th European Conference on Machine Learning (ECML 2003), September 22-26, pp. 42–49 (2003)
23. Durão, F.A., Vanderlei, T.A., Almeida, E.S., de L. Meira, S.R.: Applying a semantic layer in a source code search tool. In: SAC 2008: Proceedings of the 2008 ACM Symposium on Applied Computing, pp. 1151–1157. ACM, New York (2008)
24. Wielinga, B.J., Schreiber, A.T., Wielemaker, J., Sandberg, J.A.C.: From thesaurus to ontology. In: K-CAP 2001: Proceedings of the 1st International Conference on Knowledge Capture, pp. 194–201. ACM, New York (2001)
25. Sartori, F.: A Comparison of Methods and Techniques for Ontological Query Expansion. Communications in Computer and Information Science, Vol. 46, pp. 203–214 (2009)
26. Sartori, F., Palmonari, M.: Ontological Query Expansion for the Legal Domain: a Case Study from the Jumas Project. LNBIP, vol. 62 pp.107-122 (2010)

Ontology-Based Composition and Matching for Dynamic Service Coordination

Claus Pahl, Veronica Gacitua-Decar, MingXue Wang, and Kosala Yapa Bandara

Lero - The Irish Software Engineering Research Centre
School of Computing, Dublin City University, Dublin, Ireland
{cpahl,vgacitua,mwang,kyapa}@computing.dcu.ie

Abstract. Service engineering needs to address integration problems allowing services to collaborate and coordinate. The need to address dynamic automated changes - caused by on-demand environments and changing requirements - can be addressed through service coordination based on ontology-based composition and matching techniques. Our solution to composition and matching utilises a service coordination space that acts as a passive infrastructure for collaboration. We discuss the information models and the coordination principles of such a collaboration environment in terms of an ontology and its underlying description logics. We provide ontology-based solutions for structural composition of descriptions and matching between requested and provided services.

Keywords: Service coordination; Tuple space; Dynamic service composition; Service Ontology.

1 Introduction

Service-oriented architecture (SOA) as a methodological framework aims at providing a service-based infrastructure for interoperable development and integration [1]. However, recent trends such as on-demand and service outsourcing [2] pose challenges in terms of flexibility of composition and also scalability.

We introduce an ontology-based solution for service collaboration, focussing on its description logic foundations, that makes a step from static service architectures (based on Web service orchestration) to dynamic coordination [3]. The coordination solution based on a coordination space addresses the need to support dynamic collaboration through semantic matching of providers and requesters at runtime. It enables the self-organisation of service communities through flexible dynamic composition of service architectures. In contrast to existing mediation solutions, where providers initially publish their services and where clients search for suitable services, here the approach is reversed - changing from a pull-mode to a push-mode where the client posts requests that can be taken on by providers. Different coordination models have been proposed [4,5,6]. Domain- and application context-specific solutions [7,8,9] and approaches based on semantic extensions are investigated [10,11], which have also been applied to service composition and mediation. We built up on these semantic mediation approaches by adding a process perspective and by linking this to a coordination technique for requests of services [12]. We focus on the structural composition of objects and processes as part of service requests to support the coordination of requests and provided services. We use an ontology-based formalisation for description and subsumption-based matching. Our contribution is an ontology language for request coordination that adds a process view to existing service matching. We specifically investigate the structural composition of request elements within a dynamic coordination context.

The next section discusses the context of service collaboration. In Section 3, we address the description of requests and services in the coordination space in terms of ontology-based specification and composition techniques. In Section 4, the matching-based coordination is defined. Section 5 discusses evaluation aspects. We discuss related work in Section 6 before ending with some conclusions.

2 Service Collaboration and Coordination Spaces

Cloud and on-demand computing are emerging as new forms of providing and consuming software as services to enable an integrated collaboration of service communities. Applications often exhibit a more dynamic nature of interaction, which requires techniques for the identification of needs and behaviours and the association and customisation of provided services to requested needs [13,14].

A scenario shall motivate our solution. *Customer care* is a classical enterprise software scenario (layered on top of a full software system) that can be enhanced through distributed, on-demand collaboration infrastructure.

- Sample objects are software objects, problem descriptions and help files.
- Activities include explanations or activities to repair/adapt software.
- Two sample processes are a software help wizard that guides an end-user through a number of steps to rectify a problem and a customer care workflow that in a number of steps identifies a problem, decides on a resultion strategy and implements the latter (e.g. through adaptation/change of components).

Initially, a user asks for help by posting a request referring to a software component (e.g. a search feature) and a problem (help file not OK), Fig. 1. An analysis service takes on the task and determines whether explanation and guidance is sufficient or whether the software itself needs to be changed. In both cases, new requests (objects and goals) are generated. In the first case, the discovery of suitable responses (e.g. by correcting help files) is the aim. In the second case, software changes need to be implemented. Automatically identifying the ongoing process pattern allows a more targeted processing of the initial goal.

The current approach to service composition is to develop service processes that are orchestrations of individual services. Service orchestrations are executable process specifications based on the invocation of individual services, e.g. in WS-BPEL, the business process execution language. While this is successful for intra-organisational software integration, limitations exist. Firstly,

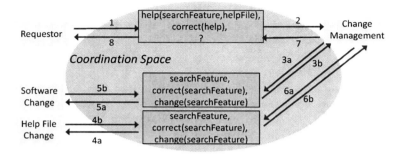

Fig. 1. Coordinated Process of Requests

the inflexible nature: common to both is the static nature of these assemblies, requiring them to be pre-defined and which can only be alleviated to some extent through dynamic adapter generation [15]. Secondly, the lack of scalability: orchestrations are simple process programs without abstraction mechanisms, thus restricting the possibility to define complex and manageable system specifications. Increasing flexibility of composition by allowing partners to dynamically join or leave the community is not possible using the classical approach. The dynamic requesting and providing of services (by asking for activities to be executed on objects to achieve a goal) avoids complex, pre-defined process definitions, thus making the coordination more scalable through self-organisation.

The solution to address flexibility and scalability of collaboration is a coordination space, which acts as a passive infrastructure to allow communities of users and providers to collaborate through matching of requests and provided services. It is governed by coordination principles:

- tasks to perform an activity on an object occur in states
- services collaborate and coordinate their activities to execute these tasks
- advanced states are reached if the execution is permitted by guards

The central concepts are objects and goals (reflecting outcomes of activities) provided together as services and processes that are seen as goal-oriented assemblies of services. Service requesters enter a typed object together with a goal that defines the processing request. Service and process providers can then select (match) this processing request.

3 Coordination Request Specification and Composition

Users are usually concerned with processing objects such as electronic documents passing through business processes. The central concepts of our *information model* are objects, goals and processes, which together form *requests*:

- Changing, evolving objects are dynamic entities. This follows trends to focus on structured objects and documents as the central entities of processing, as proposed by ebXML and other business standards.
 - Goals are declaratively specified, expressing the requested result of processed objects [16]. Essentially, the aim is to allow users and providers to refer to them declaratively, e.g. in the form of a goal-oriented user request (requesting object processing) and to enable semantic goal-based matching.
 - The process notion refers to business and workflow processes. States of the process are points of variation for objects: data evolves as it passes through a process. Goals relating to objects are expressed in terms of states of the processes where a process state is considered at the level of individual object modifications. The link to objects is provided via states of processes. Process-centricity is the central feature of service coordination here, thus we retain the compositional principle of Web services.

Cloud computing as an information processing and management infrastructure would benefit from requests being formulated in terms of the underlying information objects being processed, an abstract specification of goals and the process that the individual processing activities are embedded in. We will now formalise this information model in terms of a description logic-based ontology for specification and composition of requests.

3.1 Ontologies and Description Logic

Our solution is a description logic-based composition ontology to support matching between requests and provided services. Ontologies are a good candidate for semantic, goal-oriented specification of objects and processes [17]. We introduce the core of the description logic language $\mathcal{ALC}$ [18], which defines ontology languages like OWL-DL. $\mathcal{ALC}$ provides combinators and logical operators that suffice for our service composition ontology. It consists of three basic elements.

 - *Concepts* are the central entities. Concepts are classes of objects with the same properties. Concepts represent sets of objects.
 - *Roles* are relations between concepts. Roles define a concept through other concepts. We distinguish two role types: *descriptive* roles to define static properties and *transitional* roles to define activies (object state changes in processes).
 - *Individuals* are named objects.

A Tarski-style model semantics based on an interpretation I maps concepts and roles to corresponding sets and relations, and individuals to set elements. Properties are specified as *concept descriptions*:

 - *Basic concept descriptions* are formed as follows: A denotes an atomic concept; if C and D are (atomic or composite) concepts, then so are $\neg C$ (negation), $C \sqcap D$ (conjunction), $C \sqcup D$ (disjunction), and $C \rightarrow D$ (implication).

– Value restriction and existential quantification, based on roles, are concept descriptions that extend the set of basic concept descriptions. A *value restriction* $\forall R.C$ restricts the value of role R to elements that satisfy concept C. An *existential quantification* $\exists R.C$ requires the existence of a role value.

The combinators are defined using classical set-theoretic, i.e. extensional concept interpretations. Given a value set $\mathcal{S}$, we define the *semantics of concept descriptions* as

$$\top^I = \mathcal{S} \text{ and } \bot^I = \emptyset \text{ and } (\neg A)^I = \mathcal{S}\backslash A^I \text{ and } (C \sqcap D)^I = C^I \cap D^I$$
$$(\forall R.C)^I = \{a \in \mathcal{S} \mid \forall b \in \mathcal{S}.(a,b) \in R^I \to b \in C^I\}$$
$$(\exists R.C)^I = \{a \in \mathcal{S} \mid \exists b \in \mathcal{S}.(a,b) \in R^I \land b \in C^I\}$$

Combinators $\sqcap$ and $\to$ can be defined based on $\sqcup$ and $\neg$ as usual. An *individual* x defined by $C(x)$ is interpreted by $x^I \in \mathcal{S}$ with $x^I \in C^I$.

Structural subsumption $\sqsubseteq$, used for service component matching in Section 4, is a relationship defined by subset inclusions for concepts and roles.

3.2 Ontology-Based Specification of Requests

We semantically enrich an information model – a conceptualisation – capturing object structure, object modification states and an object evolution process [19,20]. Ontologies with descriptive and operational layers through an encoding of dynamic logic in a description logic provide the foundations for our object and process specification framework. This allows us include behavioural and temporal aspects into the core ontology framework capturing objects [21][1].

 – Objects types are expected to be represented as concepts in a domain ontology. Objects in the form of XML data schemas, embedded into an assumed domain ontology, represent the object type. A composition relationship becomes a core generic relationship for our request ontology (in addition to the traditional subsumption-based taxonomic relationship). Structural nesting of XML elements is converted into ontological composition relationships. Sample objects are a *searchFeature* and a *helpFile*, connected by a *help* role.
 – Goals are properties of the object concepts stemming from the ontology (covering domain-specific properties as well as software qualities). Goals are expressed in terms of ontology-based properties of objects (concept descriptions), denoting states of an object reached through processing.
 A sample goal is *correct(help)*, which might need to be resolved by modifying the respective role source and target.
 – Processes are based on a service process ontology with service process composition operators in the form of transitional roles (like sequencing ';', choice '+' or iteration '!' – see [21] for details) as part of the ontology. Processes are specified based on input and output states linked to goals as properties. A sample process is *analyse(help); (change(searchFeature) + change (helpFile))*.

---
[1] Transitional roles, which represent state changes and which link objects and their processing from state to state to processes, require a tailored semantics [21].

A sample object is a software component, the goal the request to change parameters. This would form a semantically annotated service goal specification

$$\exists change.typeOf(component, TypeA) \sqcup typeOf(component, TypeB)$$

here requesting the object to be changed such that the type of the component is one of the specified $TypeA$ or $TypeB$. $change$ is a transitional role here.

A software component as an object in the context of customer care has properties such as deployed, analysed, or changed. A maintenance process could be expressed as a cyclic process $!(deploy; analyse; change)$ which defines an iteration of the 3-sequence of activities. In terms of the ontology, this process specification is a composed role description that can be further specified, e.g.

$$\forall (deploy; analyse; change).equal(state, consistent)$$

saying that the sequence is expected to result in a consistent state. We call these roles *transitional* as they result in state transitions. A subprocess has been used above in the process part of the sample request triple.

The notions of a request specification and its semantics need to be made more precise. We assume a request to be a specification $request = \langle \Sigma, \Phi \rangle$ based on the elementary type ontology with a signature $\Sigma = \langle C, R \rangle$ consisting of concepts C and roles R and concept descriptions $\phi \in \Phi$ based on Σ which cover both goals and processes through descriptive and transitional roles. A $request$ is interpreted by a set of models M. The model notion refers to algebraic structures that satisfy all concept descriptions ϕ in Φ. The set M contains algebraic structures $m \in M$ with classes of elements C^I for each concept C, relations $R^I \subseteq C_i^I \times C_j^I$ for all roles $R : C_i \to C_j$ such that m satisfies the concept description. Satisfaction is defined inductively over the connectors of the description logic $\mathcal{ALC}$ as usual [18]. A signature Σ defines the request language vocabulary, e.g. consisting of domain-specific object *component*, activities *change* or *deploy*, and property *typeOf*.

3.3 Ontology-Based Object, Goal and Process Composition

Composition Principles. The core format for request specifications has been defined, which is built on the service process ontology from [21]. We add now support for the compositionality of the request elements, which extends approaches such as [17,22,23]. This faciliates the decomposition of requests into processing smaller objects through a composed process of individual object processing activities, as we already illustrated with the *help* decomposition into two smaller steps, see Fig. 1.

Subsumption is the central relationship in ontology languages, which allows concept taxonomies to be defined in terms of subtype or specialisation relationships. In conceptual modelling, composition is another fundamental relationship that focuses on the part-whole relationship. In ontology languages, composition is less used [18]. The notion of composition can be applied in different ways:

- *Structural composition.* Structural hierarchies of architectural elements define the core of architectures. It can be applied to objects here.

- *Sequential (and behavioural) composition.* Dynamic elements can be composed to represent sequential behaviour. Sequential composition can be extended by adding behavioural composition operators like choice or iteration.

We use the symbol "$\triangleright$" to express the composition relationship. It is syntactically used in the same way as subsumption "$\sqsubseteq$" to relate concept descriptions.

- *Composition object hierarchies* shall consist of unordered subcomponents, expressed using the component composition operator "$\triangleright$". An example is $ProblemDescr \triangleright FaultCause$, i.e. a $ProblemDescr$ consists of $FaultCause$ as a part. Composed objects are interpreted by unordered multisets.
- *Processes* can be *sequences* or *complex behaviours* that consist of ordered process elements, again expressed using the composition operator "$\triangleright$". An example is $maintenance \triangleright analysis$, meaning that $maintenance$ is actually a composite process, which contains for instance an $analysis$ activity. A more complex decomposed subprocess is $maintenance \triangleright analysis; change; deployment$. We see composite process implementations as being interpreted as ordered tuples providing a notion of sequence. For more complex behavioural compositions, graphs serve as models to interpret this behaviour.

Request Composition. We introduce two basic syntactic composition constructs for object and process composition[2], before looking at behavioural composition as an extension of sequential composition:

- The *structural composition* between C and D is defined through $C \triangleright \{D\}$, i.e. C is structurally composed of D if $type(C) = type(D) = Object$.
- The *sequential composition* between C and D is defined through $C \triangleright [D]$, i.e. C is sequentially composed of D if $type(C) = type(D) = Process$.

Note, that the composition operators are specific to the respective request element. This basic format that distinguishes between the two composition types shall be complemented by a variant that allows several parts to be associated to an element in one expression.

- The structural composition $C \triangleright \{D_1, \ldots, D_n\}$ is defined by $C \triangleright \{D_1\} \sqcap \ldots \sqcap C \triangleright \{D_n\}$. The parts $D_i, i = (1, .., n)$ are not assumed to be ordered.
- The sequential composition $C \triangleright [D_1, \ldots, D_n]$ is defined by $C \triangleright [D_1] \sqcap \ldots \sqcap C \triangleright [D_n]$. The parts D_i with $i = (1, .., n)$ are assumed to be ordered with $D_1 \leq \ldots \leq D_i \leq \ldots \leq D_n$ prescribing an execution ordering $\leq$ on the D_i.

The latter allows us to write $maintenance \triangleright [deploy, analyse, redevelop]$ as a composed behavioural specification, which gives semantics to the expression $deploy; analyse; redevelop$.

The semantics of the two composition operators shall now be formalised. So far, models $m \in M$ are algebraic structures consisting of sets of elements C^I for each concept C in the service object signature and relations $R^I \subseteq C^I \times C^I$ for roles R. We now consider elements to be composite:

---

[2] Goals are logical expressions, i.e. structural/behavioural composition is not applicable.

- Structurally composite concepts $C \triangleright \{D_1, \ldots, D_n\}$ are interpreted as multisets $C^I = \{\{D_1^{I^1}, \ldots, D_1^{I^k}, \ldots, D_n^{I^1}, \ldots, D_n^{I^l}\}\}$. We allow multiple occurrences for each concept $D_i, (i = 1, .., n)$. With $c \in C^I$ we denote set membership.
- Sequentially composite concepts $C \triangleright [D_1, \ldots, D_n]$ are interpreted as tuples $C^I = [D_1^I, \ldots, D_n^I]$. Tuples are ordered collections of sequenced elements. Apart from membership, we assume index-based access to the tuples in the form $C^I(i) = D_i^I, (i = 1, .., n)$, selecting the i-th element in the tuple.

While subsumption as a relationship is defined through subset inclusion, composition relationships are defined through membership in collections (multisets for structural composition and ordered tuples for sequential composition).

Behavioural specification is based on the process composition operators. These operators allow us to refine a process and specify detailed behaviour. While a basic form of behaviour (sequencing) has been defined, we extend it to a more comprehensive approach that requires a more complex model semantics (graphs). This has reasoning implications, as we will discuss at the end of Section 4. We define a process P through a behavioural specification: $P \triangleright [B]$ where B is a behavioural expression consisting of a basic process P or

- a unary operator '!' applied to a behavioural expression $!B$ (*iteration*), or
- a binary operator '+' applied to two behavioural expressions $B_1 + B_2$, expressing *non-deterministic choice*, or
- a binary operator ';' applied to two behavioural expressions B_1 ; B_2, expressing the previously introduced *sequencing*.

In line with the basic forms of composition, the iteration $P \triangleright [!B]$ is defined by $P \triangleright [B, \ldots, B]$, the choice $P \triangleright [B_1 + B_2]$ is defined by $P \triangleright [B_1] \sqcup C \triangleright [B_2]$, and the sequence $C \triangleright [B_1 ; B_2]$ is defined as above in Section 3.3.

We extend the semantics by interpreting behaviourally composite processes through graphs (N, E) where processes are represented by edges $e \in E$ and nodes $n \in N$ represent connection points for sequence, choice and iteration. The three operators are defined through simple graphs.

4 Coordination Principles

The coordination functionality follows established coordination approaches like tuple spaces [4,5] by providing deposit and retrieval functions for the space elements – tuples which consist of object type, goal and supporting process. Specifically, one deposit and two retrieval functions for the ontology-defined requests from the previous section are provided:

- deposit(object!, goal!, process!), where the parameters are defined as above in Section 3, is used by the client who deposits a copy of the tuple [object, goal, process] into the coordination space. The exclamation mark '!' indicates that values are deposited. The process element is optional; it can be determined later to guide individual processing activities.

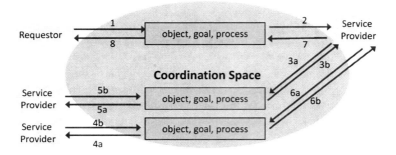

Fig. 2. Abstract Coordinated Process of Requests

- meet(object?, goal?), with parameters as above, is used by a service provider and identifies a matching tuple in the coordination space. The question mark indicates that abstract patterns are provided that need to be matched by concrete deposited tuples. Ontological subsumption reasoning along the object concept hierarchy enhances the flexibility of retrieval by allowing subconcepts to be considered as suitable matches. A subconcept is here defined as a subclass of the concept in terms of the domain ontology, but it also takes the composition properties (see structural composition in the previous section) into account, i.e. requires structural equality.
- fetch(object?, goal?) is used as meet, but it does remove the tuple, blocking further access to the tuple. The coordination space will select the tuple that is deemed to be the closest subsumption-based match, i.e. conceptually the closest in the ontological hierarchy of a given central domain ontology.

meet is used to inspect the tuple space; fetch is used if a requested task is taken on and is taken as a commitment to achieve the goal. We assume for simplicity here that provider results are directly communicated to the requester.

Matching in the meet and fetch operations is the critical activity here and shall be defined in terms of the ontological framework. Subsumption is a relationship defined by subset inclusions for concepts and roles:

- *Subsumption* $C_1 \sqsubseteq C_2$ between two concepts C_1 and C_2 is defined through set inclusion for the interpretations $C_1^I \subseteq C_2^I$.
- *Subsumption* $R_1 \sqsubseteq R_2$ between two roles R_1 and R_2 holds, if $R_1^I \subseteq R_2^I$.

Subsumption is not implication. Structural subsumption (subclass) is weaker than logical subsumption (implication), see [18]. $C_1 \sqcap C_2 \sqsubseteq C_1$ or $C_2 \to C_1$ implies $C_2 \sqsubseteq C_1$. We use subsumption to reason about matching of two request descriptions based on transitional roles.

In Fig. 2, a process emerges from the sequence of events, indicated through numbered coordination operations. If this process is initially not given by the requester, then a process mining tool might identify one to guide and constrain further processing, but that is beyond the scope here. The schematic example follows the customer care scenario and abstracts its activities that we outlined in Section 2: 1) client deposits the help request (problem description object with guidance as the goal), 2) one service provider meets and fetches the request, 3) provider creates and deposits two more requests - one to create a suitable help file for the problem, the other to determine whether the software needs to be modified (software entity as object and analysis request as goal) 4) these tuples are in turn fetched by other providers, 5) these providers then deposit solutions, 6) which are fetched by the initial provider, 7) who in turn deposits an overall solution, 8) which is finally used by the requester.

While description and reasoning capabilitiues of our ontology solution have been illustrated, the tractability of reasoning is a central issue in the dynamic context here. While the richness of our description logic with complex roles that represent processes has some potentially negative implications for the complexity of reasoning, the complexity can be reduced here. We can restrict roles to functional roles. Another beneficial factor is that for roles negation is not required [18]. Then, decidability is achieved, which is critical for dynamic reasoning.

5 Evaluation

Our key concern here was the definition of an ontology-based language for dynamic request coordination. We have already discussed the theoretical limitations of the language in terms of e.g. decidability earlier on. The sample illustrate the need for the novel components of our approach - the process aspect and the request composition mechanisms, which allow complex taks to be broken up and managed by a specific process. Now, we briefly address the concrete implementation to demonstrate the feasibility of the implementation, which also looks at tractability and performance concerns. The functionality of the coordination and knowledge spaces is currently implemented in the form of infrastructure services. These services are based on Java implementations exposed as services. We represent dynamic requests as constraints, which need to be validated at runtime. Our environment facilitates constraints generation. We express constraints as CLiX (Constraint Language in XML, http://clixml.sourceforge.net/) rules and use the Xlinkit validator engine (http://www.messageautomation.com/) to validate them dynamically. This architecture demonstrates the feasibility of ontology-based processing at runtime.

Full behavioural composition is currently not supported. This technology platform has already been used for dynamic service compositions [24], but our approach differs in that it refers to OWL-DL-based ontology request specifications. It uses an analogy between description logics and predicate logics to rewrite the ontology specifications as first-order predicates that are checked by Xlinkit. Our results todate show an acceptable performance overhead of around normally not more than 10 % for coordination activities (dynamic matching) compared a traditional hardwired WS-BPEL composition of service. The required flexibility gain is achieved (in comparison to a WS-BPEL solution) by enabling dynamic composition.

Another issue is scalability. However, this remains to be investigated further using on-demand systems. We currently have automated process graph generation techniques in place. These shall be used to test the coordination space, firstly, with more complex processes and, secondly, with more processes in parallel. A central success criterion is here the ability to deal with (i.e. match) requests in adequate time (assuming suitable providers).

6 Related Work

The coordination paradigm applied here is a fundamental change to existing service discovery and matching approaches. Coordination models have been widely used to organise collaboration. The Linda tuple space coordination model [4] has influenced a wide range of variations including our on work on concurrent task coordination in programming languages [5], which in turn has influenced the solution here. More recently, domain- and application context-specific solutions and approaches based on semantic extensions have been investigated [10]. However, dynamic environments have not yet been addressed. Over the past years, coordination has received much attention [7,8,9] due to the emergence of collaborative ICT-supported environments, ranging from workflow and collaborative work to technical platforms such as service collaboration. The latter ones have also been applied to service composition and mediation. In [25], an ontology-based collaboration approach is described that is similar to our in that it advocates a push-service object of coordination. We have added to semantic mediation approaches like [10,25] by including a process notion as a central component of request tuples [19], supported by a process-centric ontology language. Through the goal/state link, this process context is linked to the request coordination technique focussing on objects are primary entities.

WSMO [17] is an example of a service ontology that provides composition and matching support. Service ontologies are ontologies to describe Web services, aiming to support their semantics-based discovery in Web service registries. WSMO is not an ontology, as OWL-S is, but rather a framework in which ontologies can be created. The Web Service Process Ontology WSPO [21,26,27] is also a service ontology, but its focus is the support of description and reasoning about service composition and service-based architectural configuration. An important development is the Semantic Web Services Framework (SWSF), consisting of a language and an underlying ontology [28], which takes OWL-S work [29] further and is also linked to convergence efforts in relation to WSMO. The FLOWS ontology in SWSF comprise process modelling and it equally suited to support semantic modelling within the MDA context. We combine here a process-centric ontology with composition and deploy this in a dynamic composition environment.

7 Conclusions

Manually designed service architectures support software systems in classical sectors such as finance and telecommunications. However, their structural inflexibility makes changes and evolution difficult. Current service computing platforms suffer also from scalability problems. Our coordination space techniques enhances collaboration capabilities in the context of dynamic applications. Decoupling requesters from providers through the space achieves flexibility. Scalability can be achieved through a passive coordination architecture with reduced coordination support - which, however, necessitates the cooperation of providers to engage and pro-actively use the coordination space as a market place.

Our focus here has been on an ontology language for service request composition and matching. Based on a description logic formalisation, it provides composition-oriented description operators and a subsumption-based matching construct. We have specifically looked at tractability problems, which are important for dynamic environments. The main contribution is an ontology-based matching solution that is based on structured, composed requests and the customisation of this framework for a dynamic composition environment. Abstract specifications of data and behaviour, formalised as ontology-based models, are at the core. These models are processed to generate or control service execution.

While we have defined the core coordination principles here, the range of supporting features needs to be investigated further. Part of this are fault-tolerance features supporting self-management and semantic techniques deducing object and process types from possibly incomplete information [30]. Trust is a related aspect that needs to be addressed. We have occasionally indicated advanced functionality; this could further include the automated identification of processes based on stored process history or the possibility to consider non-functional aspects reflected in profiles and context models during matching.

Acknowledgment

This research work was supported, in part, by Science Foundation Ireland grant 03/CE2/I303_1 to Lero - the Irish Software Engineering Research Centre (www.lero.ie) and grant 07/RFP/CMSF429 CASCAR.

References

1. Alonso, G., Casati, F., Kuno, H., Machiraju, V.: Web Services - Concepts, Architectures and Applications. Springer, Heidelberg (2004)
2. Hayes, B.: Cloud computing. Communications of the ACM 51(7), 9–11 (2008)
3. Rao, J., Su, X.: A Survey of Automated Web Service Composition Methods. In: Cardoso, J., Sheth, A.P. (eds.) SWSWPC 2004. LNCS, vol. 3387, pp. 43–54. Springer, Heidelberg (2005)
4. Gelernter, D.: Generative Communication in Linda. ACM Transactions on Programming Languages and Systems 7(1), 80–112 (1985)
5. Doberkat, E.-E., Hasselbring, W., Pahl, C.: Investigating Strategies for Cooperative Planning of Independent Agents through Prototype Evaluation. In: Ciancarini, P. (ed.) Proc. First International Conference on Coordination Models and Languages, Cesena, Italy. LNCS, vol. 1061. Springer, Heidelberg (1996)

6. Doberkat, E.-E., Franke, W., Gutenbeil, U., Hasselbring, W., Lammers, U., Pahl, C.: PROSET - Prototyping with Sets, Language Definition. Software-Engineering Memo 15 (1992)
7. Johanson, B., Fox, A.: Extending Tuplespaces for Coordination in Interactive Workspaces. Journal of Systems and Software 69(3), 243–266 (2004)
8. Li, Z., Parashar, M.: Comet: A Scalable Coordination Space for Decentralized Distributed Environments. In: Proceedings of the Second International Workshop on Hot Topics in Peer-To-Peer Systems HOT-P2P, pp. 104–112. IEEE, Los Alamitos (2005)
9. Balzarotti, D., Costa, P., Picco, G.P.: The LighTS tuple space framework and its customization for context-aware applications. Web Intelligence and Agent Systems 5(2), 215–231 (2007)
10. Nixon, L., Antonechko, O., Tolksdorf, R.: Towards Semantic tuplespace computing: the Semantic web spaces system. In: Proceedings of the 2007 ACM Symposium on Applied Computing SAC 2007. ACM, New York (2007)
11. NIST. Process Specification Language (PSL) Ontology - Current Theories and Extensions. National Institute of Standards and Technology, USA (2007), http://www.mel.nist.gov/psl/ontology.html
12. Pahl, C.: Dynamic adaptive service architecture – towards coordinated service composition. In: Babar, M.A., Gorton, I. (eds.) ECSA 2010. LNCS, vol. 6285, pp. 472–475. Springer, Heidelberg (2010)
13. Pahl, C., Zhu, Y.: A Semantical Framework for the Orchestration and Choreography of Web Services. In: Proceedings of the International Workshop on Web Languages and Formal Methods (WLFM 2005). Electronic Notes in Theoretical Computer Science, vol. 151(2), pp. 3–18 (2006)
14. Gacitua-Decar, V., Pahl, C.: Automatic Business Process Pattern Matching for Enterprise Services Design. In: 4th International Workshop on Service- and Process-Oriented Software Engineering (SOPOSE 2009). IEEE Press, Los Alamitos (2009)
15. Brogi, A., Popescu, R.: Automated Generation of BPEL Adapters. In: Dan, A., Lamersdorf, W. (eds.) ICSOC 2006. LNCS, vol. 4294, pp. 27–39. Springer, Heidelberg (2006)
16. Andersson, B., Bider, I., Johannesson, P., Perjons, E.: Towards a formal definition of goal-oriented business process patterns. BPM Journal 11, 650–662 (2005)
17. Lara, R., Stollberg, M., Polleres, A., Feier, C., Bussler, C., Fensel, D.: Web Service Modeling Ontology. Applied Ontology 1(1), 77–106 (2005)
18. Baader, F., McGuiness, D., Nardi, D., Schneider, P.P. (eds.): The Description Logic Handbook. Cambridge University Press, Cambridge (2003)
19. Pahl, C.: A Pi-Calculus based Framework for the Composition and Replacement of Components. In: Proc. Conference on Object-Oriented Programming, Systems Languages, and Applications OOPSLA 2001 - Workshop on Specification and Verification of Component-Based Systems, Tampa Bay. ACM Press (2001)
20. Pahl, C.: A Formal Composition and Interaction Model for a Web Component Platform. In: ICALP 2002 Workshop on Formal Methods and Component Interaction. Elsevier Electronic Notes on Computer Science ENTCS, Malaga,Spain. vol. 66(4) (2002)
21. Pahl, C.: An Ontology for Software Component Description and Matching. International Journal on Software Tools for Technology Transfer - Special Edition on Foundations of Software Engineering 9(2), 169–178 (2007)
22. Arroyo, A., Sicilia, M.-A.: SOPHIE: Use case and evaluation. Inf. Softw. Technol. Journal 50(12), 1266–1280 (2008)

23. Pahl, C., Giesecke, S., Hasselbring, W.: Ontology-based Modelling of Architectural Styles. Information and Software Technology 12(1), 1739–1749 (2009)
24. Dingwall-Smith, A., Finkelstein, A.: Checking Complex Compositions of Web Services Against Policy Constraints. In: 5th International Workshop on Modelling, Simulation, Verification and Validation of Enterprise Information Systems (2007)
25. Tsai, W.T., Xiao, B., Chen, Y., Paul, R.A.: Consumer-Centric Service-Oriented Architecture: A New Approach. In: Proceedings IEEE Workshop on Software Technologies for Future Embedded and Ubiquitous Systems, and Workshop on Collaborative Computing, Integration, and Assurance, pp. 175–180 (2006)
26. Pahl, C.: A Conceptual Architecture for Semantic Web Services Development and Deployment. International Journal of Web and Grid Services 1(3/4), 287–304 (2005)
27. Pahl, C.: Layered Ontological Modelling for Web Service-Oriented Model-Driven Architecture. In: Hartman, A., Kreische, D. (eds.) ECMDA-FA 2005. LNCS, vol. 3748, pp. 88–102. Springer, Heidelberg (2005)
28. Semantic Web Services Language (SWSL) Committee. Semantic Web Services Framework, SWSF (2006), http://www.daml.org/services/swsf/1.0/
29. Ankolekar, A., Burstein, M., Hobbs, J.R., Lassila, O., Martin, D., McDermott, D., McIlraith, S.A., Narayanan, S., Paolucci, M., Payne, T.R., Sycara, K.: DAML-S: Web service description for the semantic web. In: Horrocks, I., Hendler, J. (eds.) ISWC 2002. LNCS, vol. 2342, pp. 279–348. Springer, Heidelberg (2002)
30. Wang, M., Yapa Bandara, K., Pahl, C.: Integrated Constraint Violation Handling for Dynamic Service Composition. In: IEEE International Conference on Services Computing SCC 2009. IEEE, Los Alamitos (2009)

Detecting Antipatterns Using a Web-Based Collaborative Antipattern Ontology Knowledge Base

Dimitrios Settas[1], Georgios Meditskos[2],
Nick Bassiliades[2], and Ioannis G. Stamelos[2]

[1] United Nations University, International Institute for Software Technology,
Macau, SAR, China
settdimi@iist.unu.edu
[2] Department of Informatics, Aristotle University, 54124, Thessaloniki, Greece

Abstract. The enrichment of the antipattern ontology that acts as the lexicon of terms to communicate antipatterns between people and software tools, is a labor intensive task. Existing work has implemented SPARSE, an ontology based intelligent system that uses a symptom based approach in order to semantically detect and retrieve inter-related antipatterns that exist in a software project. In this paper, we propose a Web-based environment that uses the Protege platform, in order to allow collaborative ontology editing as well as annotation and voting of both ontology components and ontology changes. This technology allows multiple users to edit and enrich the antipattern ontology simultaneously. Preliminary results on SPARSE show the effectiveness of the antipattern detection process during the research and development of a software project.

Keywords: Collaborative Ontology Development, Collaborative software engineering, Antipatterns.

1 Introduction

Ontology has become become a widespread mechanism for representing and managing almost any kind of data, information and knowledge in various domains. However, ontology-based software engineering is still at an early stage of gestation due to not only the problems regarding the technology of ontologies but mainly due to the nature of software engineering itself. In software engineering an action, process or structure that may appear to be beneficial, can prove problematic and produce more bad consequences than benefits. These repeated bad practices are referred to as antipatterns [1],[2]. By documenting antipatterns, a software project can be architected, developed and managed more effectively by having insight into the causes, symptoms and consequences of the negative solutions and by providing successful refactored solutions, which make antipatterns beneficial.

The number of antipatterns that appears documented in literature and the Web is constantly increasing. As a result a software developer, architect or manager who wishes to use antipatterns requires expertise in memorizing and identifying a specific antipattern. Furthermore, the different available official antipattern templates [1], [2] impose further difficulties on documenting antipatterns. As a result, most antipatterns appear documented in an unstructured and unofficial manner. To further add to these issues, antipatterns are usually related to other antipatterns and do not appear in isolation [1]. This requires expertise in order to understand how antipatterns are related through their cause, symptoms and consequences.

Antipattern literature is mainly concerned with the documentation of new antipatterns and as far as we are aware, SPARSE (A Symptom-based Antipattern Retrieval Knowledge based System Using Semantic Web Technologies) [3] is the first software tool to support project management antipattern detection. SPARSE uses semantic web technology to bring the software project managers' attention to focus on antipatterns that are specifically suitable to a specific software project. The OWL (Web Ontology Language) ontology knowledge base offers an extensible framework and accommodates software development, architecture and management antipatterns. Hence, a software developer, architect project or manager who wishes to detect antipatterns shall not require expertise to determine which antipattern is most likely to appear at a given moment.

However, SPARSE assumes that the users of the system are adequately motivated to not only search for already documented antipatterns by browsing the OWL ontology but also to enrich the ontology itself. This is time-consuming process that requires managers to install an OWL editor such as Protege as a desktop application, familiarize themselves with OWL language and read through the existing roles of the ontology. For example the description of an antipattern, it's causes, symptoms and consequences. As a result, the main challenge faced by the tool is how to allow users to effectively contribute and share new antipatterns in a central OWL ontology file. In order for a worldwide community of users to develop, SPARSE needs a web-based environment that supports effective ontology editing. Furthermore, antipattern contributors will need to be able to reach consensus and agree on ontology changes. With multiple contributors to the ontology, user management is required to document the activities of users and access control must limit the data entry and editing to specific parts of the antipattern ontology. Finally, synchronous access to the ontology is required to ensure that all users that edit the ontology simultaneously will have changes seen as soon as they are entered.

There is a wide variety of ontology editors offering different functionality. Protege is one of the most widely used open source ontology editors which supports collaborative ontology development process with the Collaborative Protege [4] extension. We tackle the challenge of providing a web-based environment by using WebProtege[1] [5], which is a web-client for Collaborative Protege.

---

[1] http://protegewiki.stanford.edu/wiki/WebProtege

2 Related Work

The research direction proposed in this paper builds upon the area of ontologies in software engineering [6] and the antipattern ontology [7], [8]. The fields of collaborative software engineering [9], [10] and collaborative ontology development [4] are also relevant. The antipattern ontology offers a solid theoretical and also practical formalism that allowed the encoding of antipattern knowledge from a knowledge representation level using UML [7] to the analysis of ontology similarity using semantic social networks [8] and more recently to the development of SPARSE [3]. Antipatterns are the latest generation of design pattern research and an antipattern might be the result of the misuse of a design pattern. As a result, the proposed system is also relevant to design pattern based expert systems [11], [12]. Moynihan et al [12] has developed a prototype expert system for the selection of design patterns that are used in object-oriented software. In [11], the authors have used OWL to formally define design patterns and presented a prototype of a Java client that accesses the pattern definitions and detects patterns in Java software. However, such tools cannot be applied in the area of antipatterns due to their fundamental differences in their structure, documentation and due to the fact that design patterns can not be applied in software project management.

3 Antipattern Detection in a Nutshell

A complete description of SPARSE [3] is outside the scope of this paper. However, it is important to present the underlying operation of the tool in order to understand the need and the benefits of achieving web-based collaborative ontology editing. There are three underlying technologies involved in SPARSE: (a) ontologies, through the use of the OWL ontology language, (b) DL reasoners, through the use of the Pellet DL reasoner and (c) production rule engines, through the use of the CLIPS production rule engine.

The OWL antipattern ontology documents antipatterns as ontology instances and defines the relationships with other antipattern attributes (i.e. causes, symptoms or consequences) through OWL properties. The semantic relationships that derive from the antipattern definitions are determined using the Pellet DL (Description Logic) reasoner [13]. The knowledge base of this reasoner is then transformed into the COOL object-oriented language of the CLIPS production rule engine [14]. This transformation is carried out in order to create a compact representation of the antipattern knowledge, enabling a set of object-oriented CLIPS production rules to run and retrieve antipatterns relevant to some initial symptoms. By using a combination of rules and ontologies, we are able to express richer semantic relationships that exist among antipatterns, in a more declarative manner and SPARSE is able to incorporate logical consequences expressed as SWRL rules that are handled by the underlying Pellet DL reasoner. Finally, the Pellet DL reasoner ensures the semantic consistency of the ontology-based antipatterns and is the reasoning infrastructure that derives implicit knowledge from the antipattern definitions. For example it ensures that for each created antipattern there is at least one associated primary cause, symptom and consequence.

By defining a top level ontology for describing antipatterns, we have the following advantages.

1. Collaborative definition of antipatterns, allowing software project managers to create antipatterns using new ontology instances of causes, symptoms and consequences or using any such attributes that have already been documented. The standard-based and open-world nature of OWL ontologies allow their extension, reuse and merge, creating an antipattern knowledge base that encapsulates different perspectives, according to the project they appear in.
2. Semantic processing of antipatterns, based on DL algorithms (DL reasoners). DL reasoners ensure the semantic consistency of the ontology-based antipatterns, as well as the derivation of any implicit (hidden) knowledge that derives from the antipattern definitions. In SPARSE we have used the Pellet DL reasoner [13] as the underlying reasoning infrastructure.
3. Exploitation of the research that has been done on the combination of rules and ontologies. In that way, we are able to express richer semantic relationships among antipatterns, in a more declarative way. SPARSE is able to incorporate logical consequences expressed as SWRL rules [15] that are handled by the underlying Pellet DL reasoner.

In SPARSE we make a distinction between the ontology inference rules and the domain rules that are used for deriving conclusions over the ontological knowledge (CLIPS production rules). The former are used at the ontology reasoning level and they are embedded into the DL reasoning procedure in order to infer the appropriate semantic relationships among antipatterns. The latter are used for defining the rule-based applications over the OO model of the extensional ontological knowledge, without altering the ontology itself. In that way we give the opportunity to use an efficient and well-known production rule engine in order to develop the rule-based application of SPARSE over a shared ontology in a hybrid manner.

OWL is built upon RDF and RDFS and has the same syntax, the XML-based RDF syntax [16]. A more machine processable syntax is the N-Triples format [17], that is a textual format for RDF graphs which stems directly from the RDF/XML syntax. More specifically, N-Triples is a line-oriented format where each triple must be written on a separate line, and consists of a subject, a predicate and an object.

A common way of representing the asserted and inferred OWL ontology axioms in a rule engine is to store the ontology triples in the form of facts. The limitation of the triple-based representation is that it is not able to exploit any form of semantics that could potentially exist in the environment where the mapping will take place. In that way, all the triples should be explicitly stated, following a brute force approach with increased space requirements. We argue

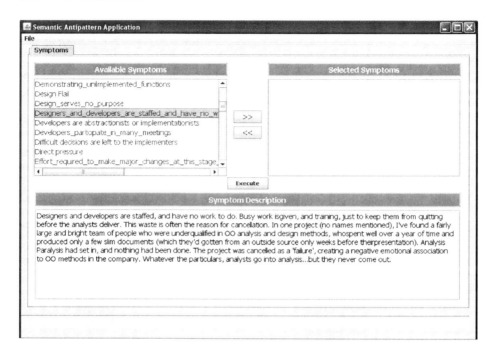

Fig. 1. Selecting antipattern symptoms using SPARSE

that the semantics of an OO environment can be effectively used in order to represent the instance-related DL reasoner axioms in an OO model that embeds the notion of class subsumption transitivity. In SPARSE, instead of defining the CLIPS rule-based application directly over the ontology triples that derive from DL reasoning, we perform a transformation of the derived ontological knowledge of Pellet into the COOL OO language of CLIPS. The purpose of this transformation is twofold:

1. The generated OO knowledge base is more compact than the corresponding triple-based model. This happens since the OO model exploits the environmental class and property semantics, such as class and property inheritance, in contrast to the triple-based model that needs to state explicitly all the relevant relationships. In that way, we are able to group the related information about an antipattern instance in a single resource represented as an object and we can have direct access to all of its properties and values by exploiting the message passing mechanism of CLIPS.
2. The rule-based application of SPARSE consists of OO production rules that match objects and not triple-based facts. We consider the utilization of domain rules as a more intuitive rule programming paradigm than of the triple-based rules, using OO notations and semantics that are well established.

The main functionality of SPARSE is to detect and propose antipatterns based on a set of symptoms that users select from the antipattern ontology (Figure 1). The antipatterns that are returned can be classified into two categories:

- Symptom-based matched antipatterns. These are the antipatterns that contain one or more user-selected symptoms. The matching of antipatterns is performed by a set of production rules that traverse the antipattern objects of the COOL KB and select the ones that satisfy one or more user-selected symptoms.
- Relevant antipatterns. SPARSE proposes also a set of antipatterns that might be relevant to the symptom-based returned antipatterns, examining their causes and consequences. More specifically, the algorithm finds antipatterns that have common causes and/or consequences with one or more symptom-based matched antipatterns.

Finally, an explanation mechanism presents to users in textual description the relationships that resulted in the inclusion of a specific antipattern in the result set. In the case of a symptom-based matched antipattern, SPARSE presents the user-selected symptoms that the antipattern satisfies, along with their category. In the case of a relevant antipattern to one or more symptom-based matched antipatterns, SPARSE presents all the relationships that the antipattern shares with the symptom-based matched antipatterns, along with their category.

4 Web-Based Collaborative Ontology Editing

Using the Protege environment, either as a desktop application or using WebProtege online users can create new instances of antipatterns, causes, symptoms and consequences in order to define new antipatterns and their attributes. Furthermore, users can add further attributes to existing antipatterns or remove and edit other attributes. OWL roles and properties that define antipattern attribute relationships can then be added, edited or removed. For example, Figure 2 illustrates how WebProtege can be used to define a "CauseToSymptom" relationship. This relationship indicates that a specific cause of an antipattern is related with a specific symptom of another antipattern.

WebProtege is important step towards achieving collaboration using ontology (Fig. 3)[5]. SPARSE offers an extensible antipattern ontology knowledge base that combined with the support of web-based collaborative ontology editing currently allows us to:

- Achieve multi-user simultaneous access to a single antipattern ontology knowledge base. At the moment the OWL antipattern ontology can be edited using Protege either as a stand-alone application or using WebProtege. A user can install Protege as a desktop application and download the antipattern OWL ontology file. This is the mode of operation that the prototype tool was designed for in its early stages. However, a user can also launch a desktop installation and connect to the server remotely to edit the ontology. This

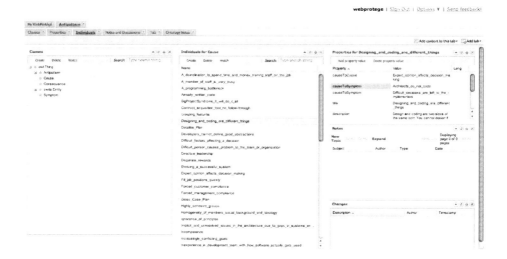

Fig. 2. Example of editing the antipattern ontology using WebProtege

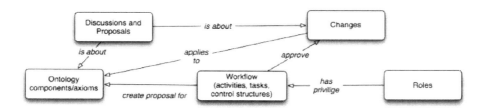

Fig. 3. Collaborative ontology editing using WebProtege

option allows the user to use Collaborative Protege in a client-server mode. Finally, WebProtege server can be accessed by any user to access the antipattern ontology online. Users can add,edit,delete instances and add notes and user roles can be defined to control access to the ontology.

– Broadcast up-to-date ontology changes and data to all ontology instances either on Collaborative Protege stand-alone installations or Web Protege. Using synchronous access to the shared antipattern ontology, when a change is made in a stand alone installation of Protege that is connected to the WebProtege server, the change is immediately seen by all online users as well. This ensures that all antipattern contributors are provided with up-to-date ontology data.

– Control and limit user access to specific parts of the ontology. During ontology development, it is important for users to identify which users makes a change or votes for a change and which other users vote in favor of or against it. The search function of Collaborative Protege allows a user to find

all changes made by a specific user or browse the latest changes. Access control allows the owner of the ontology to restrict access to certain parts of the ontology. It is possible to allow certain users only to propose a change but not make the actual change.
- Document and manage discussions and annotations in ontology development. Antipatterns authors might not always have the same opinion on a particular antipattern, attribute or property. In this case, a discussion needs to be made in order to reach consensus. Both WebProtege and Collaborative Protege incorporate discussions and notes during ontology development. Other advantages of this functionality is that users are able to understand why a change was made, track changes and consider alternatives. Furthermore, the ontology concepts, instances or roles being discussed can be easily examined since these discussions are being carried out during ontology development.
- Make proposal for changes, review and approve changes with a voting mechanism. A user create a new proposal for a change in the ontology. Other users can then vote whether they agree or disagree with this proposal.
- Communicate with other antipattern users using chat and discussions. Since many users can connect to the same server, they can communicate using chat and carry out discussions in threads.

5 Tool Information and Preliminary Results

Implementation. SPARSE has been implemented in Java over the last two years as part of a Ph.D. It is evolving towards an entirely web-based application.

Tool Availability. The stand-alone SPARSE application together with the antipattern OWL ontology can be obtained at http://sweng.csd.auth.gr/∼dset/SPARSE/ and the WebProtege server installation can be accessed at http://192.203.232.39:8080/webprotege_2011.05.13/

Experience. SPARSE has been used as a standalone application during the research and development of a geographically dispersed software development project involving academy and industry. At the moment, the knowledge base of the software tool does not support the Web-based version of the ontology. However, the OWL ontology that is distributed with SPARSE contains the same antipatterns with the Web-based version of the ontology. Therefore, the evaluation of the knowledge that is contained in the antipatterns of the ontology can be carried out using the existing stand alone version of the tool.

The manager of a project team consisting of 11 members, provided real world feedback on how the proposed framework can be used in detecting and resolving antipatterns in an effective order. The real case study used, provided valuable feedback regarding the benefits and applicability of the tool in the context of a multi-partner software development project. Figure 4 illustrates the process that was used to assess SPARSE. An important outcome of the assessment process was that feedback from the manager on detected antipatterns and on the

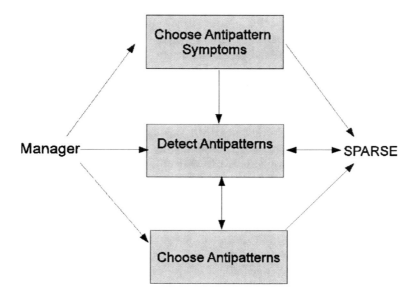

Fig. 4. The SPARSE assessment process

symptoms presented by SPARSE, was used in order to make appropriate corrections to the SPARSE ontology. This feedback process is illustrated in Fig. 4.

During the first interview, the first step of the assessment aimed to detect which antipattern symptoms exist in the software project. From the total 206 antipattern symptoms contained in the antipattern ontology, the manager chose 22 antipattern symptoms that actually existed in the project used for the assessment. SPARSE was then executed for the selected symptoms and the application retrieved 31 symptom based antipatterns. In the next step of the assessment, the manager was asked to read through the explanation of each of the 31 possible antipatterns and decide which ones actually exist in the software project. Out of the 31 antipatterns, four antipatterns were decided that actually existed in the software project:

- Project Manager who writes specs
- Absentee Manager
- Ultimate Weapon
- Mr. Nice Guy

In the interview that followed, SPARSE was executed for the four detected symptom-based antipatterns in order to retrieve semantically-related antipatterns through their causes and consequences. 44 antipatterns were detected that are related to the 4 symptom-based antipatterns through causes and consequences attributes. During this second interview with the manager, out of those antipatterns, 43 antipatterns were rejected and it was decided that only one antipattern "The Emperor's new clothes" existed at that time of the software project. The manager read the proposed refactored solution and decided to use the recommended coaching practices in order to resolve the antipattern. Out of the 43 rejected antipatterns, the manager mentioned that there was indication of the possible existence of the antipattern "Train the trainer" but was not convinced that the antipattern actually existed. The manager also mentioned that detecting a large number of antipatterns is not reasonable as it is an indication of a project that will most likely fail. The antipatterns "Batteries not Included" and "Wherefore art though architecture" interested the manager, who thought that these might appear in the future and took notice of them.

A total of five software project management antipatterns were detected in the software project used for the assessment. The manager mentioned that the symptoms of one of the four antipatterns ("Project Manager who writes specs") that were detected in the initial interview, were significantly reduced by applying the refactored solution proposed by SPARSE. Regarding the "Absentee Manager" antipattern, the manager noticed that none of the refactored solutions proposed by SPARSE were applicable. Instead, the manager proposed his own refactored solution which aimed to increase communication with the manager. This solution was added in the OWL antipattern ontology used by SPARSE. The manager adopted the refactored solution of the "Ultimate Weapon" antipattern entirely as it was proposed by SPARSE and took under consideration the refactored solution of the "Mr. Nice Guy" antipattern.

The interview highlighted the need to allow effective ontology editing as the antipattern detection process proved to be an iterative task that required modification to the antipattern OWL ontology knowledge base. Using WebProtege managers are able to collaborate with other antipattern users and contributors and are hopefully more motivated in contributing by being part of a community and by being able to communicate with other users through the ontology editing environment.

6 Concluding Remarks

Effective ontology enrichment and editing is an essential requirement for any software tool that uses an ontology knowledge base. In this paper, SPARSE has been provided with a collaborative ontology editing platform that allows synchronization of up-to-date ontological information across stand-alone Collaborative Protege, Protege and WebProtege. The proposed technology is a social platform for developing the antipattern ontology and leverages collaborative ontology editing techniques, such as annotations, user management, discussions and voting mechanisms to populate the antipattern ontology in an effective manner.

Although the results so far have been encouraging, further work is required in order to encapsulate SPARSE and WebProtege in a single Web-based environment that will encourage software developers to use the proposed system and host the antipattern user community.

References

1. Brown, W., Malveau, R., McCormick, H., Mowbray, T.: AntiPatterns: Refactoring Software, Architectures, and Projects in Crisis. Wiley Computer publishing, Chichester (1998)
2. Laplante, P., Neil, C.: Antipatterns: Identification, Refactoring and Management. Taylor & Francis, Abington (2006)
3. Settas, D.L., Meditskos, G., Stamelos, I.G., Bassiliades, N.: Sparse: A symptom-based antipattern retrieval knowledge-based system using semantic web technologies. In: Expert Systems with Applications, vol. 38, pp. 7633–7646. Elsevier, Amsterdam (June 2011)
4. Tudorache, T., Natalya, F., Noy, T.S., Musen, A.M.: Supporting collaborative ontology development in protégé. In: Sheth, A.P., Staab, S., Dean, M., Paolucci, M., Maynard, D., Finin, T., Thirunarayan, K. (eds.) ISWC 2008. LNCS, vol. 5318, pp. 17–32. Springer, Heidelberg (2008)
5. Tudorache, T., Vendetti, J., Noy, F.N.: Web-protege: A lightweight owl ontology editor for the web. In: Proceedings of the fourth workshop in the The OWL: Experiences and Direction, OWLED (2008)
6. Happel, H.J., Seedorf, S.: Applications of ontologies in software engineering. In: Proceedings of the 2nd International Workshop on Semantic Web Enabled 12 Dimitrios Settas et al. Software Engineering (SWESE 2006), Held at the 5th International Semantic Web Conference (ISWC 2006), pp. 1–14 (2006)
7. Settas, D., Stamelos, I.: Using ontologies to represent software project management antipatterns. In: Proceedings of the Sofware Engineering Knowledge Engineering Conference (SEKE 2007), pp. 604–609 (2007)
8. Settas, D., Sowe, S., Stamelos, I.: Addressing software project management antipattern ontology similarity using semantic social networks. The Knowledge Engineering Review 24(3), 287–308 (2009)
9. Whitehead, J.: Collaboration in software engineering: A roadmap. In: Proceedings of the Future of Software Engineering(FOSE 2007), pp. 214–225. IEEE, Los Alamitos (2007)
10. Hattori, L., Michele, L.: Syde: a tool for collaborative software development. In: Proceedings of the 32nd International Conference on Software Engineering (ICSE 2010), pp. 235–238. ACM/IEEE (2010)
11. Dietrich, J., Elgar, C.: Towards a web of patterns. In: SWESE 2005. Web Semantics: Science, Services and Agents on the World Wide Web Archive, vol. 5, pp. 108–116 (2007)
12. Moynihan, G.P., Suki, Abhijit, Fonseca, Daniel, J.: An expert system for the selection of software design patterns. Expert Systems 23, 39–52 (2006)
13. Sirin, E., Parsia, B., Grau, B.C., Kalyanpur, A., Katz, Y.: Pellet: A practical owl-dl reasoner. J. Web Sem. 5(2), 51–53 (2007)
14. Meditskos, G., Bassiliades, N.: HOOPO: A hybrid object-oriented integration of production rules owl ontologies. In: 18th European Conference on Artificial Intelligence (ECAI), pp. 729–730 (2008)
15. Horrocks, I., Patel-Schneider, P.F., Boley, H., Tabet, S., Grosof, B., Dean, M.: SWRL: A Semantic Web Rule Language Combining OWL and RuleML, tech. rep., W3C Member Submission (2004)
16. Beckett, D.: RDF/XML syntax specification (revised), W3C recommendation, W3C (February 2004)
17. Grant, J., Beckett, D.: RDF Test Cases, W3C recommendation (2004)

POWER - Politics Ontology for Web Entity Retrieval

Silvio Moreira, David Batista, Paula Carvalho, Francisco M. Couto, and Mário J. Silva

University of Lisbon, Faculty of Sciences, Portugal

Abstract. POWER is an ontology of political processes. It is designed for tracking politicians, political organisations and elections, both in mainstream and social media. In social media, these entities (particularly humans) are frequently named by emergent abbreviations, non-standardized acronyms, nicknames, metaphoric expressions and neologisms. Politicians are also frequently mentioned in texts by their roles in the political scene, which may change rapidly over time. This paper describes how POWER was designed for tracking such complex and dynamic setting, with the purpose of making it a key resource to analytics applications mining the media.

Keywords: social systems, natural language, politics, ontology.

1 Introduction

The intensive use of the web as a media channel and the democratisation of publishing tools is leading to a paradigm shift in media production and distribution. On one hand, the line between producers and consumers of news content is fading and, on the other hand, the abundance of content dictates the need for technologies that effectively monitor, gather, analyse and integrate news.

Politics is one the most relevant and prolific topics in the media, but representing and describing this domain pose different challenges on advanced Information Systems. In this context, names are mostly unambiguous, which may suggest that such types of entities would be adequately represented in simple knowledge bases, such as specialized dictionaries. However, political actors and their roles in the political scene change quickly over time, being crucial to create a resource capable of modelling this type of dynamic information. For example, *José Sócrates* is the incumbent Prime Minister of Portugal and the General-Secretary of the Portuguese Socialist Party, since 2005, but he was also the Environment Minister, an ergonym often used in texts to refer this politician. Politicians can also be mentioned by a multiplicity of other forms, which poses additional challenges to their modelling and recognition. For example, they are often mentioned by means of *nicknames* (e.g. *Pinócrates*, instead of *Sócrates*) and non-standardized *acronyms* (e.g. *MFL; FL*, instead of *Manuela Ferreira Leite*).

Identifying all these mentions in text and mapping them to a unique real-world referent requires up-to-date knowledge of the world and society, robustness to "noise" introduced by metaphorical mentions, neologisms, abbreviations and nicknames, and the capability of performing co-reference resolution.

In this paper, we present POWER, an ontology that formalises the dynamic domain knowledge defining the political landscape, i.e. the political actors (politicians and political organisations), their roles in the political scene, and the relationships and interactions that can be observed among these entities.

Currently, the ontology only covers the Portuguese political environment, but it was designed to describe the different electoral systems at multiple levels, from local to national and supranational . The ontology contains information about the possible forms of mention (birth name, media name(s), ergonym(s), acronym(s) and nickname(s)), enabling their recognition both in mainstream and social media.

The remainder of the paper is organized as follows. Section 2 describes related work. Section 3 presents the conceptual model, identifying the concepts and the relationships used to describe the political landscape. The development and deployment of the ontology are described in Section 4. Section 5 describes the approaches used to populate POWER and provides statistics on the created individuals. The paper concludes by highlighting the future research steps, namely concerning the ontology expansion, enrichment and alignment with other public datasets.

2 Related Work

The success of most natural language applications depends on the adequate recognition of named entities and their normalisation, i.e. identifying the different named-entity mentions in text and mapping them to a unique real-world referent.

Wikipedia has been promoting the creation of large-scale knowledge bases, which can support named entity recognition and normalisation tasks, such as DBpedia [1], YAGO [2], YAGO2 [3]. Typically, these knowledge resources describe a vast immensity of named entities, which are classified into relatively flexible semantic classes, and identify the possible relationships between them.

DBpedia describes more than 1.67 million entities (including 364,000 persons, 462,000 places and 148,000 organisations) and over 672 million RDF triples, extracted from Wikipedia. YAGO's first version comprises more than 1.7 million entities and 15 million facts. These have been automatically extracted from the category system and from the infoboxes of Wikipedia, and have been combined with taxonomic relations from WordNet [4]. YAGO2 also uses GeoNames [5]. Currently, it describes more than 10 million entities (including 882,534 people, 240,047 organisations and 695,712 locations) and more than 80 million facts about these entities. In YAGO2, the basic triple model was extended to include time and location. The temporal and spatial data were derived from Wikipedia and assigned to semantically meaningful facts.

Freebase[6] is a collaboratively created database of general, structured information intended for public use. It differs from typical ontologies as it does not define a controlled vocabulary; instead, it follows a folksonomy approach allowing the users to create new types to express new relations and properties. This model allows the fast evolution of the knowledge base, but it raises questions about the quality and authority of the data.

Despite of being extremely valuable, these resources do not contain information about a huge number of media personalities, such as most of the Portuguese politicians at local level, mainly because these entities do not have (yet) an article in Wikipedia. Additionally, such type of resources do not systematically represent the multiplicity of forms that each human noun can take in text. As shown by Carvalho et al. [7], proper names only cover 36% of the mentions to human targets, in a collection of comments posted by the readers of a daily newspaper to a set of news articles covering the 2009 Portuguese parliament election debates.

The POWER ontology is being developed to support the recognition of media named entities, particularly politicians, appearing in different genres and types of text, ranging from well structured journalistic articles to highly unstructured and spontaneous opinionated text from user generated content in social media. The development of this ontology follows some of the vocabularies and principles used in GeoNet-PT [8], a geospatial ontology of Portugal, such as the separation between entities and their names.

3 Domain Conceptualisation and Scope

As in any other realm of knowledge, the political reality can be described from countless perspectives. Therefore, the first step in defining this knowledge base was delimiting its scope. The domain of the ontology is politics (using Portuguese post-1974 politics as case-study). In order to define the scope and validate it, we began the conceptualisation phase by posing questions that POWER should be able to answer, such as:

- How is José Sócrates referred to in the media?
- Who is known as 'Pinócrates' ?
- In which mandates has served Cavaco Silva?
- Who were the general secretaries in the government in 2000?
- Who were the head members of the main political parties in 1995?
- Who are the members of the list endorsed by the Socialist Party (Partido Socialista) for the last legislative elections?

Then, keeping in mind the target and range of applications intended for the ontology we have defined "political landscape" as a set of relationships between the concepts of:

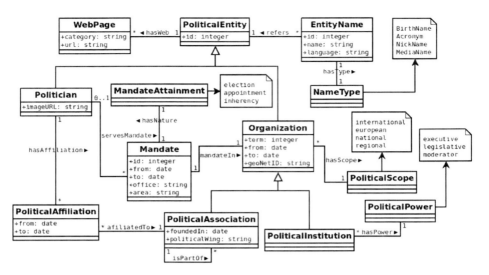

Fig. 1a. Conceptual Model

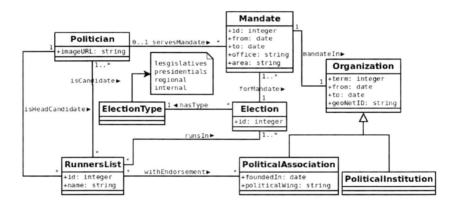

Fig. 1b. Conceptual Model (Elections)

- Politician (*Mário Soares, Cavaco Silva, Jerónimo de Sousa,...*)
- Political Association (*Partido Socialista, Partido Comunista Português, CDS-Partido Popular,...*)
- Political Institution (*Parliament, government, the president,...*)
- Election (*Legislative, Presidential, Regional,...*)
- Mandate (*Minister of defense in 2001, general secretary of foreign affairs in 2010, ...*)

With these concepts we are able to capture knowledge about: i) **political structure**, the institutions that represent the different political powers (legislative, executive and moderator) at any level of intervention (international, national or local) and the respective geographic scope; ii) **relationships between politicians, political organisations and institutions**, such as offices held in institutions and organisations (mandates), political affiliations and endorsements; iii) **elections**, the process by which politicians attain mandates in a political institution. Depending on the type of election, politicians can run individually for a specific mandate, like the mandate for president of the republic, or run in lists. Elections based on lists of runners define mandates either directly, which means that each list must have candidates for all the offices in the political institution, or with the notion of list proportional representation. In a list proportional representation system each list gets a number of mandates proportional to the number of received votes. Runners for mandates can have party endorsements or run independently and the results of an election determine one or several mandates. Some mandates can be attained by inherency or by appointment from the head of the executive.

One of the main motivations to build POWER was the necessity of a knowledge base to support the tasks of recognizing and resolving named entities in the media. As a result, the ontology model separates the entities (*PoliticalEntity*) from the way(s) they are mentioned (*EntityName*). These may include the full name, acronym or media name (the name by which an entity is normally mentioned in the media).

Figure 1a shows the proposed model represented as UML class diagram depicting political individuals and organisations and Figure 1b shows the additional concepts required for representing electoral processes. These concepts and relations are detailed in Appendix A.

4 Architecture and Deployment

This section details some of the key aspects of the ontology development, namely, the choice of vocabularies for the definition of terms (classes, relations and properties), data flow, deployment and linking of the dataset.

POWER adopts *OWL2* [9], *DCMI* [10] and *SKOS*[11] vocabularies and defines additional, domain specific, terms (see Figure 3 and Table 2). None of the terms has a range or domain defined, to promote their reusability. The definition of all the classes and properties, known as *T-Box* (terms), was generated using *Protegé 4.1.0* [12]. The instances, known as *A-Boxes* (assertions), are collected using several information extraction tools, organised under a common framework providing reusable functions. The tools process data from selected databases and websites (see Section 5). The ontology is serialized in the RDF/XML format and deployed under a *Virtuoso* tripletstore [13] . The organisation of the ontology production software enables the enrichment and expansion of the ontology by simply adding new files to the triplestore. The dataset is available via a *SPARQL* endpoint and a web user interface is planned. This data flow is illustrated in Figure 2.

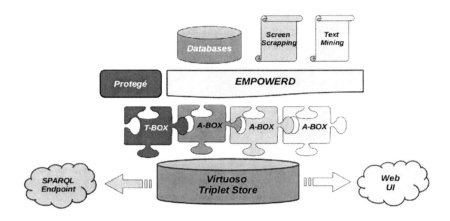

Fig. 2. Data Flow

4.1 Linked Data and Provenance

POWER is publicly available, following the linked data principles outlined in [14], allowing it to serve several purposes and applications. In the linked data vision of the web, a knowledge base is as valuable as the links it provides to additional data. POWER accomplishes this principle in several ways: i) providing links to homepages, Wikipedia articles or other relevant websites trough the relation `power:hasWeb` between political entities and their webpages (`power:WebPage`); ii) mapping the geographical scope of a political institution to a location in the GeoNet-PT ontology[1] using the property `power:geoNetID`; iii) using `skos:extactMatch`, `skos:closeMatch` and `owl:sameAs` relations for the enrichment of POWER individuals and connection to individuals in other datasets.

Another important aspect of the ontology design is the assertion of its data provenance [15]. Providing lineage information allows its consumers to ascertain the authority of the claimed facts and decide whether or not, and to what degree, they should be considered. The provenance metadata for each statement describes its *source*, *creator* (script, tool or person) and *creation date*. These annotations are implemented with terms from the *DCMI* vocabulary using RDF reification [16] (see Figure 4).

5 Populating POWER

For the population of POWER we have developed *EMPOWERD (Enrichment Manager for POWER Dataset)*, a framework that wraps the details of extracting information from various sources and generating RDF statements that assert knowledge about the political domain expressed using the POWER vocabulary.

---

[1] This ontology also defines formal mappings to the Yahoo!Planet geographic dataset.

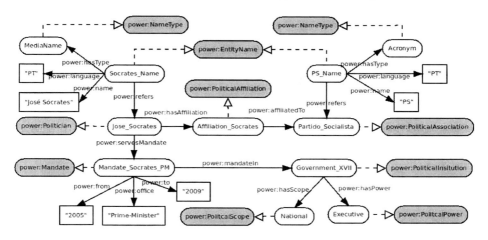

Fig. 3. Political Actors and Mandates

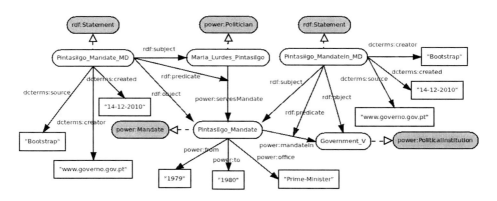

Fig. 4. Provenance Metadata (Reification)

This process follows a two-step approach: i) a **bootstrap phase** that creates instances semi-automatically trough a set of scripts that harvest data from selected sources, and ii) an **enrichment phase**, which adds new individuals and their properties using text mining methods and other tools for the extraction of data from relevant sources.

5.1 Bootstrap

The bootstrap step consisted in the development of a set of scripts that *scrap* data from authoritative sources and generate statements about instances of each of the POWER classes. The generated code is then merged into a *bootstrap script* that deploys the ontology with an initial set of assertions.

We have bootstrapped POWER with data from the Portuguese Government [17] and National Elections Commite[18] websites. Using the EMPOWERD framework, we have generated statements about Portuguese parties, politicians, their affiliations and their mandates in the constitutional governments, parliament and presidency of the republic since 1976. Considering that these instances constitute the *backbone* of the ontology, against which new concepts and individuals will be attached in the future, we have selected highly authoritative sources for populating it in this phase. We also manually inspected each of the added instances as an additional normalisation and validation step. However, the obtained dataset at the end of this phase is not rich enough for our purpose. For instance, it does contain the full names of all elected politicians, but not their short names used in the (traditional) media or nicknames used in social media.

5.2 Enrichment

The EMPOWERD framework handles the enrichment of the ontology by providing methods to: i) create new individuals in POWER; ii) add new facts (properties or relations) to an existing individual. The extraction of relevant individual names, properties and facts is based on text mining tools.

Tools and scripts developed for the enrichment of POWER rely on this framework to generate new *A-Box* files augmenting the knowledge base with newly collected facts extracted after scanning the media. Individuals identified in different runs of distinct text mining tools may have similar or identical names, but having similar or identical names may not necessarily imply that they may refer to the same individual. We therefore handle them as distinct, but relate these individuals through SKOS mapping properties, such as `skos:exactMatch` and `skos:closeMatch`.

Initial enrichment of POWER with Portuguese politics personalities was done with the Voxx tool at Sapo, a Portuguese media portal [19]. Voxx provides web services for obtaining the list of mentioned personalities in the media (together with mentioning dates and frequencies). For each personality, Voxx also provides webservices for querying the list of ergonyms associated to each personality over time. We run an EMPOWERD script periodically that scans these personality names and matches them against the POWER personality names loaded in the bootstrap. We assert SKOS matches between POWER entities and Voxx-collected media names through a statistical learning model that takes as features the Jaccard similarity coefficient [20] between the POWER entity full name and the media name, and a set of common heuristics for inferring these associactions. Among others, matching first names, matching last names, two matching family names (common in Portugal).

5.3 Statistics

Following the approach presented in the previous sections we were able to deploy the *backbone* of POWER, with data extracted from authoritative sources, describing:

- 3590 Politicians
- 3043 terms of office in Political Institutions
- 74 Political Associations (18 of them are in fact coalitions)
- 5959 Mandates

This first version of the dataset is publicly available for download as RDF file and may be queried at a SPARQL endpoint [21].

In terms of evaluation, all the political entities were manually validated. We will be assessing the coverage and quality of the POWER ontology based on the performance of the the entity tracking tools using it.

6 Conclusions and Future Work

The work described in this article represents the inception phase of POWER, an ontology for the political domain tailored to aid in the tasks of named entity recognition and resolution. It represents the complexity and dynamic nature of relations between political agents (politicians, political associations and political institutions) over time. This knowledge base is specially useful to support entity tracking, expert finding and question-answer systems. It ensures the recognition of entities referred by several types of mention, such as birth name, acronym or ergonym. We believe it is a valuable resource and could be useful in other contexts like political science, sociology and academic research, thus it is published as a public resource following the guidelines of linked data and can be accessed via SPARQL endpoint [21].

To further expand the value and scope of this resource we will enhance it in two separate, but complementary, directions:

i) **enrichment**, using text mining tools to scan and extract facts from traditional media (newspapers and articles) and from informal and social media (blogs, microblogs, forums and social networks). Defining formal mappings to other public knowledge bases and datasets, such as DBPedia, YAGO, FOAF [22] and Freebase will also increment the knowledge base and allow the inference of new properties and relations of previously "known" individuals.

ii) **expansion**, by refining and extending the presented model to accommodate other types of media personalities such as sportsmen, actors, influent businessmen or other relevant personalities of the society.

Following these lines of development we hope to achieve a rich dataset capable of describing common knowledge about our society, enabling reasoning and discovery of unknown patterns and relations among social organisations, personalities and events. The development of POWER takes place within the REACTION project [23], an iniative for developing a computational journalism [24] platform for automatic analysis of content (news, blogs, micro-blogs, comments) and implicit and explicit networks in social media.

Acknowledgments

We thank João Ramalho for his assistance in the development of the POWER software. This work was partially supported by FCT (Portuguese research funding agency) under grant UTA-Est/MAI/0006/2009 (REACTION project), and scholarships SFRH/BPD/45416/2008 and SFRH/BD/70478/2010. We also thank FCT for its LASIGE multi-annual support.

References

1. DBpedia, http://wiki.dbpedia.org/About
2. Suchanek, F., Kasneci, G., Weikum, G.: YAGO: A Core of Semantic Knowledge Unifying WordNet and Wikipedia. In: Proceedings of the 16th International Conference on World Wide Web, pp. 697–706 (2007)
3. Hoffart, J., Suchanek, F., Berberich, K., Weiku, G.: YAGO2: A Spatially and Temporally Enhanced Knowledge Base from Wikipedia. Research Paper (2010)
4. WordNet: A lexical database for English, http://wordnet.princeton.edu/
5. Geonames Ontology, http://www.geonames.org/ontology/documentation.html
6. Freebase: An entity graph of people, places and things, http://www.freebase.com
7. Carvalho, P., Sarmento, L., Teixeira, J., Silva, M.: Liars and Saviors in a Sentiment Annotated Corpus of Comments to Political Debates. In: 49th Annual Meeting of the Association for Computational Linguistics: Human Language Technologies, Portland, Oregon, USA, June 19-24 (2011)(submitted)
8. Lopez-Pellicer, F., Chaves, M., Rodrigues, C., Silva, M.: Geographic Ontologies Production in GREASE-II Technical Report (2009)
9. OWL2 Vocabulary, http://www.w3.org/TR/owl2-overview
10. Dublin Core Metadata Iniative Vocabulary, http://www.dublincore.org/documents/dcmi-terms/
11. SKOS Vocabulary, http://www.w3.org/TR/skos-reference/skos.html
12. Protegé Ontology Editor, http://protege.stanford.edu
13. Virtuoso Triplet Store, http://virtuoso.openlinksw.com
14. Linked Data Design Principles, http://www.w3.org/DesignIssues/LinkedData
15. Buneman, P., Khanna, S., Tan, W.: Data Provenance: Some Basic Issues. In: Foundations of Software Technology and Theoretical Computer Science (2000)
16. RDF Semantics, http://www.w3.org/TR/rdf-mt
17. Portuguese Government, http://www.governo.gov.pt
18. Portuguese Election Committee, http://www.cne.pt/
19. Voxx website, http://voxx.sapo.pt/
20. Tan, P., Steinbach, M., Kumar, V.: Introduction to Data Mining. Addison-Wesley, London (2005)
21. POWER SPARQL Endpoint, http://xldb.di.fc.ul.pt/wiki/POWER-PT_01_SPARQL_endpoint
22. FOAF Vocabulary, http://www.foaf-project.org
23. Reaction Project, http://xldb.di.fc.ul.pt/wiki/Reaction
24. Hamilton, J., Turner, F.: Accountability Through Algorithm: Developing the Field of Computational Journalism. Report, Center for Advanced Study in the Behavioral Sciences at Stanford University and the DeWitt Wallace Center for Media and Democracy (2009)

A Summary of Classes, Relations and Terms

Table 1. POWER classes and relations

Classes	EntityName	implements the separation between names and concepts allowing the reference of a concept trough different types of mention
	PoliticalEntity	political individual (politician) or organization
	Politician	a politician
	Organization	an organization that can be a political association or institution. An organization has a political scope to represent organizations in different levels (international, national or local)
	PoliticalAssociation	a political association such as a political party or non-governmental organization
	WebPage	a political entity's web page
	PoliticalAfilliation	affiliation of an individual in a political association
	PoliticalInstitution	institutions that represent the political powers such as the parliament or the government
	Mandate	an office held by an individual in an organization for a period of time
	RunnersList	group of candidates that run together in an election. A group can have endorsements from political associations.
	Election	an election can be legislative, executive, regional or internal
Relations	refers	a political entity is referred by an entity name
	hasWeb	a political entity has a webpage
	hasType	an entity name has a type (acronym, birth name, ...)
	hasScope	a political organization has a scope (regional, national, ...)
	hasPower	a political institution has a type of political power (executive, legislative, ...)
	hasNature	the nature of a mandate attainment (election, appointment, ...)
	isPartOf	a political association can be part of coalition
	hasAffiliation	an individual has a political affiliation
	affiliatedTo	an individual is affiliated to a political association
	servesMandate	an individual serves a mandate
	mandateIn	the mandate is served in an political organization
	isCandidate	an individual is candidate in a list
	isHeadCandidate	an individual is head candidate of a list
	runsIn	a candidate list runs for election
	hasType	an election has a type (legislatives, presidentials, ...)
	withEndorsementOf	a candidate list has endorsement of political association
	forMandate	an election is for mandate(s)

Table 2. Power terms

Type	Term	Specializes
Class	power:EntityName	-
	power:NameType	-
	power:PoliticalEntity	-
	power:WebPage	-
	power:Politician	power:PoliticalEntity
	power:Organization	power:PoliticalEntity
	power:PoliticalAssociation	power:Organization
	power:PoliticalInstitution	power:Organization
	power:PoliticalAfilliation	-
	power:PoliticalScope	-
	power:PoliticalPower	-
	power:Mandate	-
	power:MandateAttainment	-
Object Property	power:refers	-
	power:hasType	-
	power:hasWeb	-
	power:hasScope	-
	power:hasPower	-
	power:isPartOf	-
	power:hasAffiliation	-
	power:affiliatedTo	-
	power:servesMandate	-
	power:mandateIn	-
	power:hasNature	-
	power:isCandidate	-
	power:isHeadCandidate	-
	power:forMandate	-
	power:withEndorsementOf	-
	power:runsIn	-
	dc:source	-
	dc:creator	-
	dc:created	-
	skos:closeMatch	-
	skos:exactMatch	-
DataType Property	power:language	-
	power:id	-
	power:category	-
	power:url	-
	power:term	-
	power:from	-
	power:to	-
	power:geoNetID	-
	power:foundedIn	-
	power:politicalWing	-
	power:office	-
	power:area	-
	power:imageURL	-

An Error Correction Methodology for Time Dependent Ontologies

Brett Drury, J.J. Almeida, and M.H.M. Morais

[1] LIAAD-INESC
[2] University of Minho
[3] Department of Physics, I3N, University of Aveiro

Abstract. An increasing number of applications have become dependent upon information described in ontologies. Information may be correct for a limited period of time, for example, the assertion: "Barack Obama is the current president of the USA" will be incorrect in 2017. A presidential lifespan can be measured in years, however in a more dynamic domain, assertions may have lifespans of: months, weeks or days. In addition, erroneous relations may be introduced into an Ontology through mistakes in the information source or construction methodology. Ontologies which contain a large number of errors may impair the effectiveness of applications which depend on it. This paper describes an error correction methodology for ontologies automatically generated from news stories. The information contained in news stories can have a very limited lifespan, consequently constructing an Ontology by an addition of assertions will overtime accumulate errors. The proposed method avoids this problem through an assignment of a lifespan to each relation. A relation's lifespan is dependent upon: frequency of assertion, relation volatility and domain volatility. Once a relation's lifespan has elapsed the relation is either deleted or archived as a temporal "snapshot" of the domain. Individuals with 0 relations are also removed or archived. An evaluation of an Ontology constructed with the proposed scheme revealed a gain in the total number of relations overtime without an increase in the number of the errors. A comparison with an Ontology constructed with an accumulative addition of relations over an eight week period revealed that the proposed method reduced the error count by 81%.

Keywords: Business News, Temporal Ontologies, Ontology Management.

1 Introduction

An increasing number of applications have become dependent upon information described in ontologies, for example news recommendation [1] and question answering [2]. Ontologies which contain errors, ambiguous or "stale" information may impair the effectiveness of the applications which depend upon it. This problem is exacerbated by volatile domains because information changes quickly and consequently Ontologies which represent this area can quickly accumulate a large number of errors [3].

The proposed method is an error correction methodology for Ontologies generated from news stories. News stories can provide a detailed and timely description of a specific area, however the information published in news is limited, either by the free market [4] or by public interest [5]. For example, an appointment of a new CEO may be published where as his retirement may not be newsworthy. The fallible nature of news ensures that ontologies generated from news information will contain errors [3] and current correction techniques [3] may not be optimal. The proposed method is predicated upon the redundancy of news information. The news publication process ensures that facts are repeated in multiple information sources and at regular intervals over time. The method assigns: 1. a nominal value (weight) to each relation, 2. a constant to represent the relation's volatility, 3. the last assertion date, 4. a counter which represents the frequency of assertion. The nominal value is reduced overtime until a predefined value when the relation is deleted or archived. The relation's nominal value is refreshed with each new repetition and the decay of the nominal value is restarted. The speed of the decay of a relation's weight (lifespan) depends upon the following: 1. relation volatility, 2. domain volatility and 3. frequency of assertion. The combination of these factors ensures that a relation's lifespan may range from a single day to a number of years. The remainder of this paper will consider the following: 1. initial Ontology construction, 2. adaptation of Ontology , 3. evaluation.

2 Initial Ontology Construction

2.1 Centred Domain Ontology

The central aim of this work is to construct a Centred Domain Ontology. A Centred Domain Ontology for the purposes of this paper is an Ontology constructed around an individual (an Ontology element). This research concentrated on economic actors: Companies, Government Institutions, Financial Markets as the central individual. The motivation was to represent in detail the domain of the economic actor. News was a natural medium because it contains up-to-date and detailed information about economic actors. The following section will describe an Ontology construction methodology which was used to construct an Ontology from news information [3] over a period of 53 days. The Ontology will be evaluated and it's failings will be illustrated.

2.2 Ontology Construction

The Ontology was constructed with the methodology described by Drury [3]. The construction process was separated into three parts: corpus construction, Ontology bootstrapping and enrichment.

Corpus construction. consisted of harvesting stories from free sources on the Internet. A crawler harvested these stories at the same time each day. The stories were published by the content providers in Really Simple Syndication (RSS) format. The crawler recorded Headline, Description, Story Text, HTML, Published Date and Harvested Date information. The content providers embedded links in the stories between related stories and background information. This information was recorded. Story text was extracted from the HTML and stored. The story text was sent to the Open Calais web service [6]. The Open Calais web service provided meta-data for each story. This meta-data included relation extraction for the identified named entities in the story text.

Bootstrapping. the Ontology construction process involved identifying a highly relevant "seed set of news stories" from which relations can be extracted. The "seed set" was selected by searching the headlines for keywords. These stories were highly relevant because if a headline contained a keyword then the following story text would be relevant [7] to the aforementioned keyword. The relations were extracted from the Open Calais meta-data to construct the initial Ontology.

Ontology enrichment. was achieved by the expansion of the initial keywords with similar terms from the Ontology. The similar terms were identified by the OWL predicate "SameAS" [8] in the meta-data. This predicate referred to keywords which were the same as the initial keyword. In addition further information was gathered from Linked Data. The Linked Data was identified by following a unique URI provided by Open Calais for each named entity. The URI pointed to a "landing page" [1] on the Open Calais website. The "landing page" contained a "redirect" to the Linked Data web page from which extra relations can be extracted. The URI's which were redirected to the same Linked Data web page were considered to be instances of the same entity, consequently the URI provided a form of disambiguation. The construction and enrichment process is fully described in Algorithm 1. A simplified view of the Ontology generated with this method is demonstrated in Figure 2.2.

Algorithm 1. Ontology Construction

Input: Keywords: List of topic search words
Input: Corpus: Set of news stories
Output: Ontology: Domain Centred Ontology
$Ontology \leftarrow ()$;
repeat
$\quad newstories \leftarrow searchforstories(Keywords, Corpus)$;
$\quad$**forall** $story \in newstories$ **do**
$\quad\quad MD \leftarrow MetaData(story)$;
$\quad\quad$**forall** $relation \in MD$ **do**
$\quad\quad\quad push(Ontology, relation)$;
$\quad\quad\quad LD \leftarrow LinkedData(relation)$;
$\quad\quad\quad$**forall** $linkedrelation \in LD$ **do**
$\quad\quad\quad\quad push(Ontology, linkedrelation)$;

$\quad Keywords \leftarrow expandkeywords(Ontology, Keywords)$;
until *No new keywords obtained* ;
$return(Ontology)$;

---

[1] An example of a landing page can be found at: http://goo.gl/p5Clj

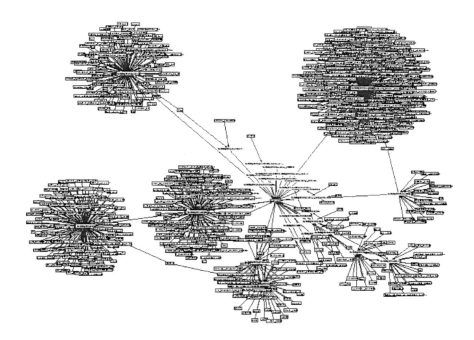

Fig. 1. Ontology viewed with Growl [3]

2.3 Validation of Initial Ontology

As previously described, an Ontology was generated from news stories over a period 53 days with the accumulative relation addition methodology [3]. This Ontology was to provide a baseline for comparison with the proposed method. The Ontology described the "Microsoft Domain". The Microsoft Domain was chosen to simplify the validation task because it was assumed that the main assertions should be "well known" or "easy" to verify. The Ontology validation was with Vrandecic's [9] tests. The Ontology was validated for: Accuracy, Adaptability, Clarity, Completeness, Computational efficiency, Conciseness, Consistency, and Organizational fitness. The validation was conducted manually by a domain expert. The Ontology was too large to validate in it's entirety, consequently the individual with the most relations was chosen for the validation tasks. The evaluation methodology obliged the evaluator to positively validate errors, consequently a relation was assumed to be "correct" if it could not be verified as incorrect. There was limited time to verify relations and consequently it was necessary to restrict the effort spent on verification. A positive error identification ensured that the manual verification task could be completed in the allocated time.

Accuracy: The individual with the most relations was the Microsoft individual. The Microsoft individual contained 436 relations. 61 relations were positively verified as incorrect.

Clarity: The number of assertions were large, in-excess of 11,000. There were 10 class types and 20 relation types. Each class and relation type conformed to Vrandecic's [9] tests of understandability and transparency.

Completeness: The Microsoft individual relations were verified for completeness. There were a number of unverifiable relations, for example "Microsoft employs the Governor of California", however the verifiable relations provided a rich description of the domain. The assertions exceeded the experts knowledge and ability to locate all valid relations.

Conciseness: The Ontology contained a number of irrelevant axioms, for example "Microsoft employs current CEO"

Consistency: There were a number of axioms where were inconsistent, for example the Ontology asserted that both Microsoft and Adobe produced Acrobat Reader.

The initial Ontology failed three of Vrandecic's [9] validation tasks: conciseness, consistency and accuracy. A comparison of an Ontology generated with one day's information with one generated on day 53 indicated that the number of irrelevant and inconsistent axioms increased with time as did the correctly asserted axioms.

3 Adaptation of Ontology

The initial validation of the Ontology constructed with an accumulative relation addition methodology [3] indicated there were a significant number of positively verified errors. The errors could be categorized as: factual errors in the story text, errors in Open Calais meta-data, outdated information or irrelevant information in the story text. An absence of some form of error correction would imply that these errors would accumulate in numbers over time.

Drury [3] has attempted to use two error correction approaches to resolve this problem: 1. "contrary information",2. regular Ontology regeneration. "Contrary information" identifies contradictory relations. A relation which is not reasserted after the creation of the new contradictory relation is assumed to be false. Drury [3] provided the example of Jerry Yang and Carol Bartz, both were asserted to be the CEO of Yahoo!. After a certain period of time there were no reassertions for Jerry Yang as being the CEO of Yahoo!, but there were reassertions for Carol Bartz holding this position. Carol Bartz was correctly assumed to be the CEO of Yahoo. "Contrary information" is not a general error correction scheme, and requires manual tuning to identify the relations which can be corrected by this method. "Contrary information" also may be a non-optimal solution in the news domain because of the economics of news publication [4]. The news publication process limits the amount of information published and consequently contradictory information may not be published. Regular regeneration of the Ontology may expel accumulated errors, but it will also remove correct relations.

The proposed method seeks to avoid the disadvantages of the previously described error correction methodologies. As described earlier the proposed method is predicated upon the redundancy of news where "true" assertions are repeated in multiple locations and at regular intervals. The redundancy of information is created by the dynamics of news publication; the initial story is published by an agency [10](Reuters,AP, UPI, AFP) and then is repeated by other news publishers. For example, the story concerning an appointment of a Microsoft executive to Nokia was repeated in our corpus by several information sources with slight differences in the headlines. The central assertion of the story was that "Stephen Elop is the CEO of Nokia", was repeated multiple times in each story and separately by multiple information sources [11][12].

3.1 Adaptation Measures

The proposed decay of an assertion of a relation is influenced by three factors: 1. domain volatility, 2. relation volatility and 3. assertion frequency. The domain volatility, for the purposes of this paper, is the frequency of relation addition and repetition. The assumption is that the faster the addition and repetition of information the higher the rate of change of the information contained in the Ontology. A uniform relation decay rate may have ensured a too rapid relation deletion rate in static domains and a too slow deletion rate in dynamic domains. The domain volatility was calculated by counting the number of relevant stories over a fixed period of time. The relevant stories were selected by identifying domain keywords in the story headline. The assumption was that if a headline contained a domain keyword then the following story would be strongly relevant [7]. The relation volatility was a constant assigned by a domain expert. The assertion frequency was a count of the repetition of a relation assertion. The formulas are fully described below and the function which decays the relation weight is described in Algorithm 2.

$$DomVolatility = \frac{NumberOfStories}{Constant} \quad (1)$$

$$TotalVolatility = DomVolatility \times \frac{RelationVolatilityConstant}{NumberOfAssertions} \quad (2)$$

$$TotalLife = \frac{MaximumLifeConstant}{TotalVolatility} \quad (3)$$

$$DecayRate = 1 - \frac{DaysElapsed}{TotalLife} \quad (4)$$

3.2 Decay Rate Characteristics

There were three factors which directly influenced a lifespan of a relation: domain volatility, relation volatility and frequency of assertion. In addition the distribution of the reassertions over time, a property of the "frequency of assertion", also exerted an influence on the relation lifespan. This section will describe the

Algorithm 2. Function Decay of the Relation Weight

Input: maxlifeconstant
- An arbitrary assigned maximum relation constant
Input: domainvolatility
- The volatility of a domain is directly related to the number of stories published in the last month
begin

    forall $newRel \in newRelations$ **do**
        insert newRel in $allRelations$
    forall $relation \in allRelations$ **do**
        $noassertions \leftarrow relation.noassertions$;
        $dayselapsed \leftarrow currentdate - relation.noassertions$;
        $relationweight \leftarrow currentdate - relation.relationweight$;
        $relationvolatility \leftarrow relation.relationvolatility$;
        $lvol \leftarrow domainvolatility \div noassertions$;
        $tvol \leftarrow lvol \times relationvolatility$;
        $totallife \leftarrow maxlifeconstant \div tvol$;
        if $dayselapsed \geq totallife$ **then**
            $DeleteRelation(relation)$
        $decayratio \leftarrow 1 - dayselapased \div totallife$;
        $newweight \leftarrow relationweight \times decayratio$;
        $UpdateRelationWeight(relation, newweight)$;

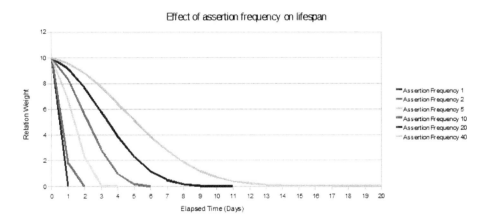

Fig. 2. Decay graph for relation with varying frequencies

effects of these factors on the decay rate on a relation of a fixed volatility. The influence of relation volatility has been excluded because of space considerations.

Assertion frequency: the influence on the decay rate is illustrated in figure 2. The data series, Assertion Frequency 1, is a relation which has been asserted once and consequently has a short lifespan which was 1 day. The data series,

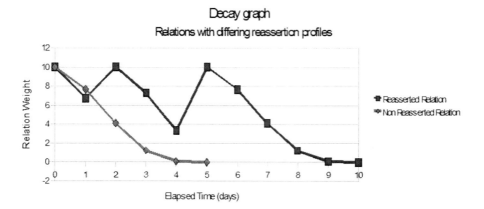

Fig. 3. Decay graphs for assertions with differing reassertions over time

Assertion Frequency 40, is a relation which has been asserted forty times and consequently has a longer lifespan which was 20 days.

Distribution of assertion frequency over time: has a direct effect on the relation's lifespan. The graph illustrated in Figure 3 demonstrates the effect of assertions over time. Each relation has an equal number of total assertions, however the data series: Reasserted relation, is reasserted at day 2 and day 5. The reasserted relation has a longer lifespan than the non reasserted relation although both series have an equal number of total reassertions.

Domain volatility: has direct effect on a relation lifespan. The graph described in figure 4 illustrates the effect of lowering the domain volatility on a relation life. The data series, "domain volatility (standard)" has the domain volatility of the aforementioned Microsoft domain. The remaining data series represent a gradual decline in domain volatility from 80% of the Microsoft domain to 40%. The decline of the volatility is represented by the labels "domain volatility (standard) -2" to "domain volatility (standard) -6". Each label represents a decline in domain volatility of 20%. The graph represents a clear increase in a relation's life as domain volatility declines.

3.3 Decay Rate Proof

This subsection is a brief discussion of the mathematical properties of the relation decay. It has been shown experimentally that the lifespan of a relation expands or contracts depending upon two factors (frequency of assertion and domain volatility). The larger the frequency of assertion and the smaller the domain volatility, the shallower the slope and consequently the larger life of the relation. The remainder of this section will show a mathematical proof that the characteristics shown on the graphs: Figure 2 and Figure 4 will continue for other values.

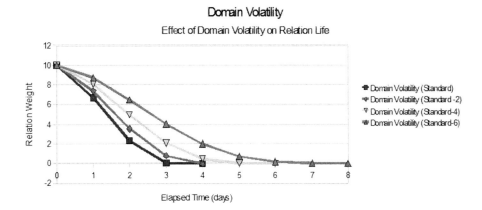

Fig. 4. Decay graphs for assertions with differing domain volatilities

Gaussian Distribution Decay Proof

The relation decay scheme (Figure 2 and Figure 4) follows approximately a Gaussian curve i.e. $y = y_0\, e^{-x^2/2\sigma^2}$. Therefore, the slope of the graph is shallower for larger standard deviation and this quantity can also provide a measure of the relation lifespan (when $x = 3\sigma$ we have $y = y_0/e^{4.5} \approx 0.01\, y_0$ i.e. at time 3σ the relation weight decreased to about 1% of the original value).

If $y = y_0\, e^{-x^2/2\sigma^2}$ then by the standard properties of the exponential and logarithm functions we have $\sqrt{-\ln(y/y_0)} = x/(\sqrt{2}\sigma)$. The values of $\sqrt{-\ln(y/y_0)}$ were plotted for each x and we saw that the data fits straight lines with slope $1/(\sqrt{2}\sigma)$. The values of the slopes and respective error bars obtained from the fits to the data in Figure 2 are 0.267 ± 0.007 (data set with Assertion Frequency 20) and 0.148 ± 0.002 (data set with Assertion Frequency 40). These values imply standard deviations $\sigma = 2.65$ and $\sigma = 4.77$, respectively, which as shown above, provide estimates of the relation lifespan. Therefore, it is possible to conclude that the relation decay scheme, when the assertion frequency is reasonably large, follows approximately a Gaussian curve. This implies that the larger the assertion frequency the longer the lifespan of the relation.

4 Evaluation

As described earlier, an Ontology was generated with the accumulation of relations from news methodology. This Ontology will be known as the "Original Ontology". For the evaluation, an Ontology which was generated with the proposed method will be known as the "Modified Ontology". The evaluation of the proposed methodology was by a comparison of the Modified Ontology with the Original Ontology. The Ontologies were generated from news gathered from a period of 53 days. Intermediate Ontologies were archived on a daily basis. A

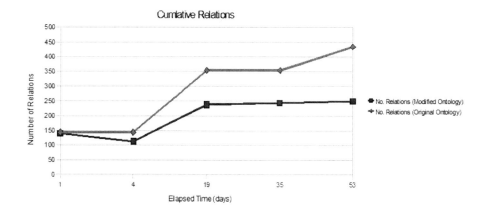

Fig. 5. Cumulative number of relations

random selection of the intermediate Ontologies were evaluated. The manual evaluation used the same methodology as the initial validation: 1. the individual with most relations was evaluated, 2. errors had to be positively identified and 3. relations which were not positively validated as false were assumed to be correct.

Results. The cumulative number of errors is presented in Figure 6. As expected, the Original Ontology gains errors overtime, where as the Modified Ontology has an initial reduction in the total number of errors and thereafter the number of errors is almost constant over time. The total number of relations for both Ontologies is described in Figure 5. The Original Ontology gained more relations than the Modified Ontology, but the error rate is significantly less for the Modified Ontology. The figures for total number of errors and the error rate are presented in the following table.

Days Elapsed	Error Rate (M.O.)	Error Rate (O.O.)	No. Errors (M.O.)	No. Errors (O.O.)
1	11%	13%	15	18
4	4%	13%	5	18
19	4%	10%	10	37
35	6%	10%	14	37
53	5%	14%	12	63

Comparison of error rates and number of relations

O.O. = Original Ontology, M.O. = Modified Ontology

4.1 Discussion of Results

The evaluation criteria underplayed the effectiveness the proposed methodology because: 1. errors had to be "positively" identified, 2. the "quality" of the

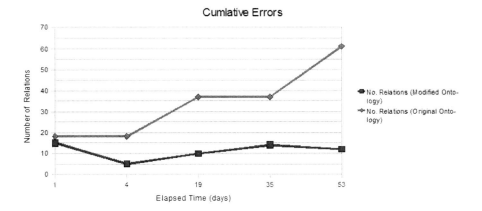

Fig. 6. Cumulative number of errors

relations were not considered. There were a larger number of "unverifiable relations" in the Original Ontology than the Modified Ontology. The "unverifiable relations" were not "obviously wrong", however it was not clear if they were part of the domain. The "unverifiable relations" accounted for the significant part of the difference in total relations between the Modified and Original Ontology.

The evaluation criteria did not consider the ability of the Modified Ontology to resolve ambiguous relations, for example at day 19 both Ontologies asserted that Microsoft and Adobe produced Acrobat Reader. In the Modified Ontology there was a measure of "confidence" for both relations in a form of a "relation weight". The "relation weight" for the assertion "Adobe produces Acrobat Reader" was higher than the weight for the assertion "Microsoft produces Acrobat Reader". It was possible to identify the "true" relation by accepting the relation with the highest weight.

It was not possible to evaluate the "completeness" of the Ontology as it was not feasible to generate a "Gold Standard" of all of the relations and individuals in the domain, however the Modified Ontology contained a number of stable relations which described the commonly known "facts" of the domain. The stable relations did not exit the Ontology at the points the intermediate ontologies were manually evaluated.

5 Conclusion and Future Work

The proposed methodology provides a basis for an automatic construction of a "timely" Ontology from news sources. The correction scheme removes: erroneous and "stale" or inconsequential information. The method also provides a procedure for resolving ambiguous relations via a "relation weight". The Modified Ontology formed the basis of a "breaking financial news" recommender system which ranked news stories in order of "importance" to a domain. An evaluation of the recommender system demonstrated a clear advantage for the system which used this methodology [13].

There were some weaknesses in the proposed technique. A number of values in the decay formulas were arbitrary. It was assumed that the relationships of these values were correct, but the relationships may be non-optimal. The future work will be to discover the optimal rates for these values. It may be possible to use machine learning (ml) to discover the optimal relationship between relation addition and expulsion. As stated earlier, it was not possible to produce a "Gold Standard" of domain relations, however it is possible to produce a "Gold Standard" of "breaking news stories". The relative performance of competing Ontologies can measured by the "distance" between the news stories recommended by a news recommender which relies upon the Ontology. A learner may be able to identify optimal values for the decay formulas.

References

1. Flavius, F., Borsje, J., Levering, L., Embregts, H., Frasincar, F.: Hermes: an ontology-based news personalization portal (2007)
2. Lopez, V., Uren, V., Motta, E., Pasin, M.: Aqualog: An ontology-driven question answering system as an interface to the semantic web. Journal of Web Semantics 5(2), 72–105 (2007)
3. Drury, B., Almeida, J.J.: Construction of a local domain ontology from news stories. In: Lopes, L.S., Lau, N., Mariano, P., Rocha, L.M. (eds.) EPIA 2009. LNCS, vol. 5816, pp. 400–410. Springer, Heidelberg (2009)
4. McManus, J.: An economic theory of news selection. In: Annual Meeting for Education in Journalism and Mass Communication (1988)
5. Rosengren, K.E.: International news: Methods, data and theory. Journal of Peace Research 11(2), 145–156 (1974)
6. Reuters. Calais web service, http://opencalais.com/ (consulted in 2009)
7. Blake, C.: Andrew. Media-generated shortcuts: Do newspaper headlines present another roadblock for low-information rationality? The Harvard International Journal of Press/Politics 12(2), 24–43 (2007)
8. McGuinness, D.L., van Harmelen, F., et al.: OWL Web Ontology Language Overview. W3C Recommendation 10, 2004–2003 (2004)
9. Ontology Evaluation. In: Staab, S., Studer, R. (eds.) Handbook on Ontologies. International Handbooks on Information Systems, pp. 293–313. Springer, Heidelberg (2004)
10. Bell, A.: The Language of News Media. Language in Society, Blackwell (1991)
11. BBC. Nokia appoints microsoft executive as new head, http://www.bbc.co.uk/news/business-11257069 (consulted September 2010)
12. Yahoo. Nokia replaces ceo with microsoft exec in smart phone war, http://finance.yahoo.com/news/Nokia-Replaces-CEO-With-ibd-4210132396.html?x=0&.v=1 (consulted September 2010)
13. Drury, B., Almeida, J.J.: Magellan: An adaptive ontology driven "breaking financial news" recommender. In: CISTI Proceedings (2011)

An Ontology-Based Integrated Approach to Situation Awareness for High-Level Information Fusion in C4ISR

María-Cruz Valiente[1], Rebeca Machín[2], Elena García-Barriocanal[1], and Miguel-Ángel Sicilia[1]

[1] Computer Science Department, University of Alcalá,
Ctra. Barcelona km. 33.6 – 28871 Alcalá de Henares (Madrid), Spain
{maricruz.valiente,elena.garciab,msicilia}@uah.es
[2] AMPER Programas,
Ctra. de Andalucía, km 12.700, 28906 Getafe (Madrid), Spain
rmachin@amper.es

Abstract. Sharing of situation awareness is considered a fundamental capability for C4ISR systems, including decision support systems. However, the current evolution of information and communication technology stress this need even further, because of the fast changing environment and the need to perceive, analyse and understand a huge amount of data. The adoption of adequate tools and technologies to increase proper situation awareness is required. The SAW-CORE Ontology formalizes the knowledge associated to situation awareness enabling operators to increase good decision-making and good performance. On the other hand, the JC3IEDM is a data model aimed at providing interoperability among heterogeneous C2 systems. In this context, this paper presents the integration of the SAW-CORE Ontology and the JC3IEDM OWL Ontology using mappings in order to provide high-level information fusion for situation awareness in C4ISR systems. This allows us to approach C4ISR situation awareness with reasoning capabilities from an ontological perspective in military missions. For this purpose, SAW-CORE constructs are integrated into the JC3IEDM ontological constructs.

Keywords: C4ISR, Situation Awareness, Ontology, JC3IEDM, OWL, SRWL.

1 Introduction

The ever changing environment of the *Command, Control, Communications, Computers, Intelligence, Surveillance and Reconnaissance* (C4ISR) domain, in particular, military missions specially in coalition operations, requires operators to adopt new technologies so they can successfully face the rapid changes that take place and make correct decisions. Therefore, shared relevant situation awareness information is considered to be a critical issue in C4ISR decision-making. Situation awareness entails a broad range of information about objects and items, and their relationships, so the monitoring and management of associated knowledge for successful mission execution is of major importance. Furthermore, situation awareness is represented at Level 2 (*Situation Assessment*) of information fusion in the *Joint Directors of Laboratory*

(JDL) data fusion model (Fig. 1). Since military missions have to deal with information originated from various independent origins, data fusion is a critical task in their systems. Steinberg et al. [1] define situation assessment as "estimation and prediction of relations among entities, to include force structure and cross force relations, communications and perceptual influences, physical context, etc."

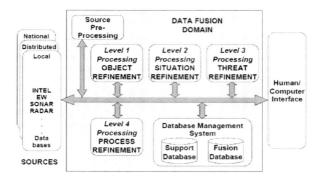

Fig. 1. JDL data fusion model [1]

In the C4ISR domain, the *Joint Consultation, Command and Control Information Exchange Data Model* (JC3IEDM) [2] is broadly used as an information exchange data model for C4ISR systems. In short, the JC3IEDM specifies the minimum data set required for interoperability between *Command and Control Information Systems* (C2ISs) and the information exchange mechanism. A C2IS is a way by which military organizations implement command and control.

In another direction, the Situation Awareness Core Ontology (hereinafter, the SAW-CORE Ontology) [3] formalizes the main concepts of situation awareness using a language that can be processed and supported by computer tools. In this sense, the SAW-CORE Ontology is an approach to capture the knowledge associated with situation awareness that supports high-level reasoning. That is, the SAW-CORE Ontology represents a unifying theory of situation awareness compatible with current thinking about situation awareness in military scenarios.

In this paper, we propose an ontology-based situation awareness model that integrates the concepts of the SAW-CORE Ontology into the elements of the JC3IEDM OWL Ontology described by Matheus and Ulicny [4] using mappings.

The rest of this paper is structured as follows. Section 2 covers the background of situation awareness in the C4ISR domain, including a brief explanation of the JC3IEDM model. Section 3 briefly introduces the SAW-CORE Ontology, describing the main elements of the ontology, whereas situation awareness in the JC3IEDM OWL Ontology is described in Section 4. In Section 5, it is explained in detail how SAW-CORE constructs can be integrated into the JC3IEDM OWL constructs in order to provide situation awareness improvement for high-level information fusion in C4ISR systems. Finally, we conclude in Section 6 with some final remarks and future work.

2 Background

2.1 Situation Awareness for C4ISR

Key to efficient and safe cooperation is to share a jointly maintained, accessible and reliable situation awareness picture. The operational approach to build requires for each party involved to provide its local situational data, have fusion of them and dissemination of the consolidated result to the parties involved in the area. The information involved can be either the outcome of human field observations or sensor data.

In the recent years, situation awareness has started facing the challenge of shifting the research focus from Level 1 to Level 2 in the JDL data fusion model [1]. In a broad sense, situation awareness can be defined "as the perception of the elements in the environment within a volume of time and space, the comprehension of their meaning and the projection of their status in the near future" [5]. The statement "within a volume of time and space" contained in the definition of situation awareness pertains to the fact that operators constrain the parts of a situation that are of interest to them, based on not only space (i.e., how far away an specific element is), but also how soon that element will have an impact on the operator's goals and tasks. Perception of time and the temporal dynamics associated with events play represents key components of situation awareness in several domains [6].

Although the concepts related to situation awareness vary widely depending on the domain, situation awareness principles and the mechanisms used for achieving situation awareness can be described generically [6]. For example, three levels of situation awareness have been identified in [6]: (i) *Level 1- Perception*: this level represent the perception of relevant information to form correct pictures of the situation under study; (ii) *Level 2 – Comprehension*: this level represents the integration of multiple pieces of information and a determination of their relevance to the operator's goal; and (iii) *Level 3 – Projection*: this level represents the ability to forecast future situation events and dynamics. This ability to project from current events and dynamics to anticipate future events (and their implications) allow for timely decision-making. The dynamic nature of situations dictates that as the situation is always changing, so the operator's situation awareness must constantly change or be rendered out-dated and thus inaccurate.

2.2 The JC3IEDM

Although the JC3IEDM is intended first and foremost for the exchange of command, control and communication information between information systems, it nowadays serves more and more as the basis for the general data models that underlie C2ISs. Its evolution has been governed by formal statements of operational information exchange requirements supplemented by the knowledge of domain experts. In this evolution of the model, the information structure is defined in terms of a data model that specifies the basic elements to obtain interoperability between C2ISs. The JC3IEDM does not impose any restriction and, therefore, each organization can adapt it to their own specific circumstances.

The *Multilateral Interoperability Programme* (MIP)[1] in conjunction with the *North Atlantic Treaty Organization* (NATO)[2] is the configuration manager of JC3IEDM specifications. The JC3IEDM is included into NATO STANAG 5525. Fig. 2 illustrates the common core of data to be exchanged when using the JC3IEDM information exchange data model [7].

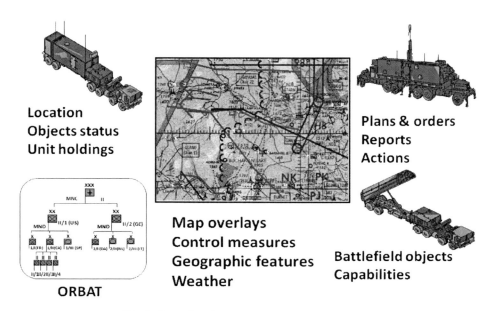

Fig. 2. Operational awareness as depicted in [7]

The JC3IEM specification is a relational schema that was developed using the IDEF1X[3] notation and it makes also a UML[4] notation version available by conversion of IDEF1X. IDEF1X represents a method for designing relational databases with a syntax designed to support the semantic constructs necessary to develop a conceptual schema.

The JC3IEDM model is aimed at monitoring activities with some objective to meet. In the JC3IEDM model, situation awareness is the basis for planning the use of the available resources in activities that lead to the achievement of objectives. Once the missions are planned, they are turned into orders for execution. Execution needs to be monitored to determine the effects achieved. This, in turn, modifies the current situation on which the next mission planning cycle is based. For this purpose, the first requirement to define is the objects that will be managed. The five basic categories of objects include facilities, features, materiel, organisations and persons. Once the

---

[1] https://mipsite.lsec.dnd.ca/
[2] http://www.nato.int/
[3] http://www.idef.com/
[4] http://www.omg.org/

objects of interest are defined, then their location, state and relationships between them can be specified [7].

Situation awareness in the JC3IEDM model provides information relating to objects and may encompass many kinds of information. For example, knowledge derived from relevant events, recorded in the data model, is part of the situation awareness. The main objective is to capture all time-dependent or dynamic properties of interest (for example, the operational status of the positioned units or their current spatial and temporal localization) with the exception of planned activities which are separated from situation awareness. Although events are described structurally in the same way as plans and orders (i.e., planned activities), they are separated because events belong conceptually to situation awareness [7].

There are five independent entities in the JC3IEDM model that could be used for situation awareness, as shown in Fig. 3.

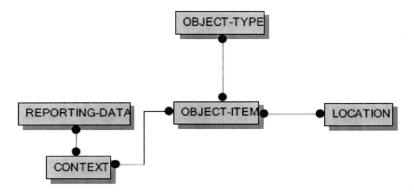

Fig. 3. JC3IEDM entities for Situation Awareness (adapted from [8])

3 The SAW-CORE Ontology

In the work presented in [3], Matheus et al. proposed the SAW-CORE Ontology for modelling situation awareness. the SAW-CORE Ontology is a formal approach, encoded in OWL [9], for reasoning about situations, which represents objects, relationships and their evolution over time. The main elements of the SAW-CORE Ontology has demonstrated its capability to support situation modelling. The main elements of the SAW-CORE Ontology are depicted in Fig. 4.

The *Situation* class defines a situation as a collection of *Goals*, *SituationObjects* and *Relations*. The *SituationObject* class represents entities in a situation (physical and abstract) that can have characteristics (i.e., *Attributes*) and can participate in relationships (i.e., *Relations*). The *Attribute* class defines values of specific object characteristics, such as weight or colour. The *PhysicalObject* class is a special type of *SituationObject* that defines the *Volume*, *Position* and *Velocity* of a specific object. The *Relation* class define the relationships between ordered sets of *SituationObjects*. Each relation may be defined according to a set of rules (using the *Rule* class) involving situation awareness. That is, relations combine pairs of situation objects with truth values defined over time by the firing of *Rules* that define the *Relation*s. For example, as described by Matheus et al. [10], a part at a facility is classified as 'critical' if the current demand at the facility exceeds the current local supply, and it is classified as 'marginal' if the total 'resuppliable rate' for the part at the facility is below a required-surplus threshold.

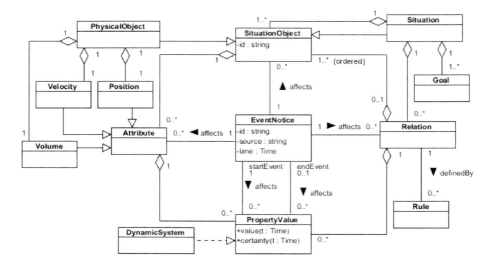

Fig. 4. UML class diagram representing the SAW-CORE ontology (adapted from [3])

An important aspect of *Attributes* and *Relations* is that they need to be associated with values that can change over time. To do so, *Attributes/Relations* are associated with zero or more *PropertyValues* each of which defines two time-dependant functions, one for the actual value and the other for the certainty assigned to that value. A new *PropertyValue* is created for an *Attribute/Relation* whenever an *EventNotice* arrives that *affects* that *Attribute/Relation*. The value of an *Attribute/Relation* at a particular point in time (current, past or future) can be determined by accessing the value function of the *PropertyValue* instance that is in effect at the prescribed time. The *EventNotice* class contain information about events in the real-world situation observed by a sensory source at a specific time that affects a specific *Relation* or *Attribute* (of a specific *SituationObject*) by defining or constraining its *PropertyValue*. These are the entities that indicate change in the situation and thus are the vehicles by which changes are affected in the *Attributes* and *Relations* of the situation representation. The ontology permits a *PropertyValue* to be implemented as a *DynamicSystem*. What this means is the value and certainty functions are dynamically modelled and therefore they cause the *PropertyValue* to change even in the absence of new *EventNotices*. For example, it is reasonable to assume that an object continues to move with its last reported speed and direction until informed otherwise. To be able to make such projections in the absence of explicit sensory information predictive models are required. It is for this reason that the SAW-CORE Ontology shows *DynamicSystems* as a way of implementing *PropertyValues*. Certain attributes, such as *Position*, would be modelled by dynamic systems that might themselves generate internal *EventNotices* to update the attribute values, with some lesser degree of certainty, until new external sensory information arrives.

4 The JC3IEDM OWL Ontology for Situation Awareness

VIStology[5] developed a JC3IEDM OWL Ontology that comprises over 7900 elements (OWL classes, properties and their instances) from the JC3IEDM ERWIN specification [4]. The JC3IEDM OWL Ontology can act as the basis for providing situation awareness in C4ISR systems.

Five named element groups classify all of the elements of interest [4]: (i) *Entity_Group*: this group includes specific entities that will become OWL classes along with their corresponding *Attribute_Group*; (ii) *Attribute_Group*: this group contains the specific attributes (OWL object properties or OWL datatype properties) for the corresponding entities; (iii) *Relationship_Group*: this group includes the relationships that can occur between entities, each of which will be turned into OWL object properties; (iv) *Domain_Group*; and (v) *Validation_Rule_Group*. The *Domain_Group* in conjunction with the *Validation_Rules_Group* contains the allowed values for the domains and ranges of the attributes. Many of the attributes in the JC3IEDM range over values that are codes having corresponding text descriptions of their meanings. These codes are organized into domains that have associated validation rules to define the set of valid values. Codes are captured within enumeration classes within OWL.

Many of the entities exist as sub-classes of at most one other entity. However, not all entities are defined as OWL classes, only those that have additional attributes or relations appear as OWL classes. All others are represented by values of *category-codes*. A *category-code* value is a string that is used to identify a sub-class of a specific OWL class. OWL classes that have sub-classes defined in this way will have an OWL object property whose name is the class name in lowercase with the string 'category-code' added to it. For example, the OWL object property *reporting-data-category-code* for the class *REPORTING-DATA* (domain of the property). Furthermore, there will be a range for this OWL object property with the same name. For example, the OWL class *ReportingDataCategoryCode* is the range of the OWL object property *reporting-data-category-code* with the next values: 'ASS' (Assumed), 'ERR' (Erroneous), 'INFER' (Inferred), 'PLAN-6' (Planned), 'PRDCTD' (Predicted) and 'REP-1' (Reported). Fig. 5 shows an excerpt of the JC3IEDM OWL Ontology involving situation awareness.

The *CONTEXT* class is defined as a collection of information that provides in its entirety the circumstances, conditions, environment, or perspective for a situation in a particular mission (operation). Operators can use the context information to judge the merits of an operational plan, and make changes in order to respond to a changing operational situation. The *CONTEXT* class can also be used to record the history of an evolving operation, capture a situation, as it existed at some time in the past, or portray a situation, as it is expected to exist at a future date [2]. The *CONTEXT-ELEMENT* class is part of a *CONTEXT* and contains information about all *REPORTING-DATA*s that are

---

[5] http://vistology.com/

part of a specific operation. The *REPORTING-DATA* class is the specification of source, quality and timing that applies to reported data [2]. The *CONTEXT-ELEMENT-STATUS* class keeps track of the inclusion status and its timing. This technique preserves data integrity while allowing the data content to change for any instance of CONTEXT [2].

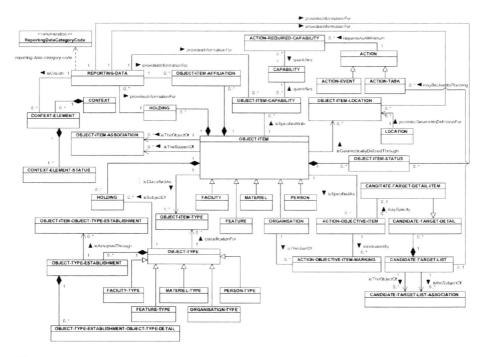

Fig. 5. UML class diagram representing an excerpt of the JC3IEDM OWL Ontology for situation awareness

The objectives of an operation are captured by the *ACTION-OBJECTIVE-ITEM-MARKING* and *CANDIDATE-TARGET-LIST* classes. The *ACTION-OBJECTIVE-ITEM-MARKING* class represents the technique of indicating the position of an *ACTION-OBJECTIVE-ITEM* at a given time for the benefit of a using *ORGANISATION*. This class is used to specify requirements, plans, and results of marking an *ACTION-OBJECTIVE-ITEM* position or an associated reference position [2]. The *ACTION-OBJECTIVE-ITEM-MARKING* class provides an opportunity to add coordinating details for the user of the marking services. On the other hand, the *CANDIDATE-TARGET-LIST* class represents a list of selected battlespace objects or types that have potential value for destruction or exploitation, for consideration in planning battlespace activities. That is, the *CANDIDATE-TARGET-LIST* class is aimed at enabling the maintenance of target lists for consideration during planning processes [7]. A CANDIDATE-TARGET-LIST is composed of CANDIDATE-TARGET-DETAILs that itemise candidate targets individually. The CANDIDATE-TARGET-DETAIL-ITEM class is a CANDIDATE-TARGET-DETAIL that may be specified as an ACTION-OBJECTIVE-ITEM. Since target lists are often likely to be related to each other, such as battalion and brigade-nominated lists with division lists, the model includes the *CANDIDATE-TARGET-LIST-ASSOCIATION* class.

In the JC3IEDM OWL Ontology, a full characterization of an individual thing includes both item and type attribution. Where the attributes are placed is a design decision [7]. In this way, *FACILITY-TYPE, FEATURE-TYPE, MATERIEL-TYPE, ORGANISATION–TYPE* and *PERSON-TYPE* are the classes that represent the *OBJECT-TYPE*s in the JC3IEDM OWL Ontology (that is, classes of objects that have military or civilian significance for situation awareness), whereas *FACILITY, FEATURE, MATERIEL, ORGANISATION* and *PERSON* are the classes that represent *OBJECT-ITEM*s (that is, individually identified objects that has military or civilian significance for situation awareness). The OBJECT-ITEM-TYPE class represents the assignment type classification to an OBJECT-ITEM (i.e., an *OBJECT-ITEM* is classified as one or more *OBJECT-ITEM-TYPE*s using the *OBJECT-ITEM-TYPE* class).

Another important aspect of situational awareness in the JC3IEDM OWL Ontology is the relationship between items and types that are part of an operation. The *OBJECT-ITEM-ASSOCIATION* class associates *OBJECT-ITEM*s with other *OBJECT*-ITEMs in the sense of belonging, using, controlling, being constrained by, occupying, etc. For example, a division has full command of three brigades, or full command of two and operational control of the third [7]. The *HOLDING* class specifies what an *OBJECT-ITEM* actually has or is estimated to have at a particular time. The *HOLDING* class associates a specific object with a class of objects where the general notion of inclusion has the sense of ownership, possession, assignment, or control, that is who has what at which time. This is an accounting of available assets. One of the purposes of *HOLDING* is to provide operators with a dynamic update of changes to information on stockpiles of equipment personnel and consumable held by forces [7]. Establishments are specifications that associate, under specified conditions for a given instance of a type of object, a number of instances of other object types as its constituent elements. Essentially, it is a statement of composition of a type of object [7]. The *OBJECT-TYPE-ESTABLISHMENT* class collects all the components that make up the composition through the detail entity. An instance of *OBJECT-TYPE* has zero, one or more *OBJECT-TYPE-ESTABLISHMENT*s each of which consists of a number of instances of other *jc3:OBJECT-TYPE*s that are listed as instances of *jc3:OBJECT-TYPE-ESTABLISHMENT-OBJECT-TYPE-DETAIL*. Furthermore, instances of establishments are assigned to instances of *OBJECT-ITEM* by means of the *OBJECT-ITEM-OBJECT-TYPE-ESTABLISHMENT* class.

Finally, *OBJECT-ITEM-AFFILIATION, OBJECT-ITEM-CAPABILITY, OBJECT-ITEM-LOCATION* and *OBJECT-ITEM-STATUS* are other OWL classes that we use in our context of situation awareness in C4ISR.

The *OBJECT-ITEM-AFFILIATION* class is refers to geopolitical, ethnic, religious, or functional preferences of a specific *OBJECT-ITEM*. Geopolitical affiliation is often referred to as nationality. Functional affiliation may refer to anyone of multinational, political, terrorist, exercise, or other user-defined categories [7].

The OBJECT-ITEM-CAPABILITY class holds the perceived value of a specific *CAPABILITY* of an *OBJECT-ITEM*. A *CAPABILITY* defines or specifies a diverse range of potential abilities to do work, perform a function or mission, achieve an objective, or provide a service, such as maximum speed or maximum storage capacity. *CAPABILITY* is associated with the *ACTION-REQUIRED-CAPABILITY* class in order to state the required capability of *OBJECT-ITEM*s when they are needed as resources for carrying out *ACTION*s [2]. The *ACTION* class represents an activity, or the occurrence of an activity that may use resources and may be focused against an objective. *ACTION-EVENT* and *ACTION-TASK* are the subclasses of *ACTION*. The *ACTION-EVENT* class is intended to capture *ACTION*s that simply occur and need to be noted for which planning is not known. For example, a unit may report its current activity as an event, or an observer in the field could use the *ACTION-EVENT* class to report his/her sightings. The *ACTION-TASK* class are *ACTION*s for which control can be exercised or are predicted, such as friendly operations, and those enemy activities that are being anticipated as a result of intelligence assessment. The *ACTION-TASK* specification supports plans, orders, and requests.

The *OBJECT-ITEM-LOCATION* class links an instance of *OBJECT-ITEM* to a specific *LOCATION*. The *LOCATION* class represents the specification of position and geometry with respect to a specified horizontal frame of reference and a vertical distance measured from a specified datum. Examples of *LOCATION*s are point, sequence of points, polygonal line, circle, rectangle, ellipse, fan area, polygonal area, sphere, block of space, and cone. The *LOCATION* specifies both location and dimensionality [2].

The *OBJECT-ITEM-STATUS* class represents the perceived condition of a specific *OBJECT-ITEM* as determined by the reporting organisation, indicating whether a specific *OBJECT-ITEM* has been booby-trapped (Yes, No or Unknown), and the emission control status of a specific *OBJECT-ITEM* (Electronic silence, Radio silence and Normal operations) [7]. Situation awareness require knowledge of the status of various objects (past, present, or predicted) to capture administrative, medical, physical, and procedural states or conditions [2].

5 Analysis of the Integration

The summarized results of the integration between JC3IEDM OWL constructs and SAW-CORE constructs in our context of situation awareness in C4ISR systems, which we cannot discuss in detail for reason of space, are provided in Table 1.

Context in Situation Awareness

First, the elementary and core concept in the integration model is a situation. As mentioned earlier, the *jc3:CONTEXT-ELEMENT*[6] construct, which is part of *jc3:CONTEXT*, contains information about all *jc3:REPORTING-DATA*s that are part of a specific operation or mission. Therefore, the *saw:Situation* maps to the *jc3:CONTEXT-ELEMENT* construct enabling operators to obtain a complete integration model for situation awareness. In this context, the *saw:DynamicSystem* construct represents the part of the C4ISR system responsible of implementing the *jc3:REPORTING-DATA* construct and the related information.

---

[6] From here on, constructs from the JC3IEDM OWL ontology are prefixed with 'jc3:', and constructs from the SAW-CORE ontology are prefixed with 'saw:'

Table 1. Representation mapping analysis of the JC3IEDM OWL and SAW-CORE integration model

SAW-CORE Construct	JC3IEDM OWL Construct
Situation	CONTEXT-ELEMENT
Goal	ACTION-OBJECTIVE-ITEM-MARKING, CANDIDATE-TARGET-LIST and CANDIDATE-TARGET-LIST-ASSOCIATION
Relation	OBJECT-ITEM-ASSOCIATION, HOLDING, OBJECT-ITEM-OBJECT-TYPE-ESTABLISHMENT and OBJECT-TYPE-ESTABLISMENT
Rule	Business rules
RelationSymbol	No direct mapping
SituationObject	OBJECT-ITEM
PhysicalObject	FACILITY-TYPE, FEATURE-TYPE, MATERIEL-TYPE, ORGANISATION-TYPE, PERSON-TYPE, FACILITY, FEATURE, MATERIEL, ORGANISATION, PERSON
Attribute	OBJECT-ITEM-AFFILIATION, OBJECT-ITEM-CAPABILITY, OBJECT-ITEM-LOCATION and OBJECT-ITEM-STATUS
Volume	Included in the LOCATION specification
Velocity	Included in the LOCATION specification
Position	Included in the LOCATION specification
AttributeSymbol	No direct mapping
PropertyValue	No direct mapping
EventNotice	ACTION-EVENT
DynamicSystem	No direct mapping

Objects in Situation Awareness

The *saw:PhysicalObject* maps to a number of JC3IEDM OWL constructs: *jc3:FACILITY-TYPE*, *jc3:FEATURE-TYPE*, *jc3:MATERIEL-TYPE*, *jc3:ORGANISATION–TYPE* and *jc3:PERSON-TYPE*. Since each object has a location in the JC3IEMD-OWL Ontology, we consider all the JC3IEDM objects as physical objects (i.e., according to the SAW-CORE Ontology, objects that defines the volume, position and velocity of a specific object). In this way, *saw:PhysicalObject*s can take advantage of the instance information associated with *jc3:OBJECT-TYPE*s, such as *jc3:OBJECT-ITEM-LOCATION* and *jc3:OBJECT-ITEM-CAPABILITY*, increasing good decision-making.

The *saw:Attribute* construct maps to the next JC3IEDM OWL constructs: *jc3:OBJECT-ITEM-AFFILIATION*, *jc3:OBJECT-ITEM-CAPABILITY*, *jc3:OBJECT-ITEM-LOCATION* and *jc3:OBJECT-ITEM-STATUS*. These are the attributes that we use in our context of situation awareness in C4ISR, which provide a complete and a valid view of a specific situation.

Properties in Situation Awareness

The *saw:PropertyValue* construct although it does not have a direct mapping to any JC3IEDM OWL construct, it is related to the next values from *jc3: ReportingDataCategoryCode*: 'PLAN-6' (Planned), 'PRDCTD' (Predicted) and 'REP-1' (Reported). Therefore, *saw:PropertyValue* could be integrated into the *jc3:REPORTING-DATA* construct in order to obtain additional information about attributes and events related to the situation under study.

Objectives in Situation Awareness

The *saw:Goal* maps to two JC3IEDM OWL constructs: *jc3:ACTION-OBJECTIVE-ITEM-MARKING* and *jc3:CANDIDATE-TARGET-LIST*. Recall that the situational awareness is the basis for planning processes in operations that lead to the achievement of objectives.

Relationships in Situation Awareness

The *saw:Relation* maps to four JC3IEDM OWL constructs that represent relationships: *jc3:OBJECT-ITEM-ASSOCIATION*, *jc3:HOLDING*, *jc3:OBJECT-ITEM-OBJECT-TYPE-ESTABLISHMENT* and *jc3:OBJECT-TYPE-ESTABLISHMENT*. These complementary relations enrich situation awareness with additional information of objects and instances involved in a specific situation. As described earlier, the *saw:Relation* construct is defined by *saw:Rule* constructs. The *saw:Rule* construct maps to the JC3IEDM business rules that are included in [11], and which can be modelled using the Semantic Web Rule Language (SWRL) [12]. For example, the next rule shows how the system can suggest the assignment of resources to actions that have to be performed by a specific situation:

```
jc3:CAPABILITY(?cap) ∧ ACTION(?act) ∧
ACTION-REQUIRED-CAPABILITY(?act,?cap) ∧
OBJECT-ITEM-CAPABILITY(?cap,?object)
-> Suggest(?act,?object)
```

Events in Situation Awareness

The *saw:EventNotice* construct maps to the *jc3:ACTION-EVENT* construct. The *jc3:ACTION-EVENT*s may trigger *jc3:ACTION-TASK*s. For example, depending on the *jc3:OBJECT-ITEM-HOSTILITY-STATUS* of a target, a set of alarms will be triggered in order to manage a specific situation. In the JC3IEDM model, candidate target lists and individual candidate targets can be associated with ACTION-TASKs at the entire list level and at an individual item or type that is being nominated for consideration in the operational planning process.

6 Conclusions and Outlook

In this paper, a fusion of the SAW-CORE Ontology and the JC3IEDM OWL Ontology is proposed as a mechanism for improved the generation and sharing of situation awareness in C4ISR systems. Using the mapping results summarized in Table 1, the high-level information fusion and enhanced Situation Awareness as well as increase operator performance can be exploited in C4ISR systems including decision making systems. In addition, the ontology-based integration enables operators to elaborate perceptual and cognitive tasks that enhance their decision-making capabilities. The lack of mapping of a SAW-CORE construct to a JC3IEDM OWL construct is not relevant to the integration between these two ontologies, since SAW-CORE constructs could be easily added to the JC3IEDM OWL domain by defining relations to the JC3IEDM OWL constructs that have been mapped.

It is important to note that the most relevant information for building the situation and awareness is covered as for instance the information exchanged by means of the *jc3:REPORTING-DATA* construct. Considerable amount of information about an operational situation consists of reports by persons or organisations. These generally refer to dynamic data, such as location, status, holdings, associations, and classification, regardless of whether the information refers to friendly, neutral, or hostile elements. It is also important to know for each report the source, the effective and reporting datetimes, and the degree of validity of information. If information is provided without an indication of the source, the validity, and the applicable times, it raises questions as to the source (Who says so?), the quality (Is this information verified?), and timing (When did it happen and when was this reported?). The model can capture both types of information: the substantive information is represented in numerous entities and the amplifying reporting information in the *jc3:REPORTING-DATA* structure. The *jc3:REPORTING-DATA* structure provides a mechanism for maintaining a time record that applies not only to the historical past and the immediate present, but also to the future.

Interoperability is also a very important issue for C4ISR systems. On the operational level, interoperability is the ability of a technical system, agency, or person to share information via voice and data signals to another system, agency, or person on demand, in real time, when needed, and as authorized. Regarding interoperability, one of the main achievements of this proposal is to achieve vertical interoperability to ensure situational awareness knowledge spread. Vertical interoperability it is assured by means of a MIP solution, which involves the use of JC3IEDM OWL Ontology since the JC3IEDM is an accepted and established military standard with large support from different nations. Adopting this solution implies that, through this proposal, command and control systems could exchange information among them and among systems based on the SAW-CORE Ontology.

In addition, it is worth noting the duality of the approach since the fusion of these two ontologies could also be applied to civil scenarios, such as *Emergency Management Systems* (EMS), where the key to efficient and safe cooperation among security forces is to share a jointly maintained, accessible and reliable situation awareness. However, our approach has some limitations:

- In the JC3IEDM OWL Ontology there are two high-level object classes, *jc3:OBJECT-TYPE* and *jc3:OBJECT-ITEM*, which are not considered in the SAW-CORE Ontology. The *jc3:OBJECT-TYPE* construct is derived from an OBJECT-TYPE of the JC3IEDM where is defined as "An individually identified class of objects that has military or civilian significance." It is a generalisation of

five other object classes that are treated in the data model as subtypes of OBJECT-TYPE (Facility, Feature, Person, Materiel and Equipment). It is used for more generic information associated with a specific class of objects, whereas the *jc3:OBJECT-ITEM* construct is used to capture information specific to individuals (e.g., height, length, width, major building type...). However, the representation of instances as classes in the JC3IEDM OWL Ontology can difficult the definition of rules and specific class constraints in the fusion ontology.
- On the other hand, the SAW-CORE Ontology lacks of spatio-temporal relation types, which can be solved with the fusion of the two ontologies. In this sense, the SAW-CORE Ontology can be considered as a good starting point in order to extent the information of situation awareness ontologies.

In our future work, we intend to integrate other foremost ontologies to the JC3IEDM OWL Ontology at different levels of the JCL data fusion model in order to improve different C4ISR systems functionalities. Other possible future work that could be tackled is to study a possible extension of the SAW-CORE Ontology and its fusion with the JC3IEDM OWL Ontology to cover new concepts for improving situation awareness.

Acknowledgements

This work is funded by AMPER Programas through Integra project (CDTI, Spanish Ministry of Science and Innovation).

References

1. Steinberg, A.N., Bowman, F.L., White, F.E.: Revisions to the JDL Data Fusion Model. In: Joint NATO/IRIS Conference Proceedings, and in Sensor Fusion: Architectures, Algorithms, and Applications. Proceedings of the SPIE, vol. 3719, pp. 330–441 (1999)
2. MIP: The Joint C3 Information Exchange Data Model Overview. Version 3.0.2 (2009), https://mipsite.lsec.dnd.ca
3. Matheus, C.J., Kokar, M.M., Baclawski, K.: A Core Ontology for Situation Awareness. In: Proceedings of the Sixth International Conference on Information Fusion, pp. 545–552 (2003)
4. Matheus, C., Ulicny, B.: On the Automatic Generation of an OWL Ontology Based on the Joint C3 Information Exchange Data Model. In: 12th International Command and Control Research and Technology Symposium (2007)
5. Endsley, M.R.: Design and evaluation for situation awareness enhancement. In: Proceedings of the Human Factors Society 32nd Annual Meeting, pp. 97–101 (1988)
6. Endsley, M.R.: Theoretical underpinnings of situation awareness: a critical review. In: Situation Awareness Analysis and Measurement. Lawrence Erlbaum Associates, Mahawah (2000)
7. Simiatis, E.: Joint C3 Information Exchange Data Model (JC3IEDM) Training Presentation. Part I – General Introduction. Institute for Defense Analyses: Draft Final, IDA Document D-3532 (2007), http://mda.ida.org/CIO-G-6-Deliverables/d-3532/d-3532.document.pdf

8. MIP: Joint C3 Information Exchange Data Model (JC3IEDM) 3.1d edn., Unclassified (2008)
9. Smith, M.K., Welty, C., McGuinness, D.L.: OWL Web Ontology Language Guide. W3C Recommendation (2004), http://www.w3.org/TR/owl-guide/
10. Matheus, C.J., Baclawski, K., Kokar, M.M., Letkowski, J.J.: Using SWRL and OWL to Capture Domain Knowledge for a Situation Awareness Application Applied to a Supply Logistics Scenario. In: Adi, A., Stoutenburg, S., Tabet, S. (eds.) RuleML 2005. LNCS, vol. 3791, pp. 130–144. Springer, Heidelberg (2005)
11. Annex G2, I.D.A.: Compendium Of Coded Business Rules. MIP Support, Online Documentation, US Army JC3IEDM 3.0.2, http://mda.ida.org/US-JC3IEDM_302/index.html
12. Horrocks, I., Patel-Schneider, P.F., Boley, H., Tabet, S., Grosof, B., Dean, M.: SWRL: A Semantic Web Rule Language Combining OWL and RuleML. W3C Member Submission (2004), http://www.w3.org/Submission/SWRL/

Socio-technic Dependency and Rationale Models for the Enterprise Architecture Management Function

Sabine Buckl, Florian Matthes, and Christian M. Schweda

Technische Universität München (TUM)
Chair for Informatics 19 (sebis)
Boltzmannstr. 3, 85748 Garching bei München, Germany
{sabine.buckl,matthes,christian.m.schweda}@mytum.de

Abstract. Enterprises are complex socio-technical system, whose management can be considered a challenging task. Especially against the background of intricate relationships, dependencies, and contributions that link social actors and technical components, the design of an effective enterprise architecture (EA) management function is not easy to accomplish. While for modeling social dependencies on the one hand and for modeling technical dependencies in the context of an EA on the other hand, well established approaches exist, yet no attempt has been undertaken to bring together the disciplines of modeling. Regarding such an embracing modeling approach as a valuable contribution for designing organization-specific EA management functions, this paper closes the aforementioned gap by combining facilities for intensional and technical dependency modeling. The integrated model is thereby devised along an anonymized practice case.

Keywords: enterprise architecture, i* models, EA management governance.

1 Introduction

Enterprises present themselves as complex socio-technical systems, in which information technology (IT) plays a crucial role in delivering business services to both internal and external customers. In the light of an ever changing economic as well as regulatory environment, the mutual alignment between business and IT has become an increasingly important goal for modern enterprises. First discussions on this topic date back to the early works of Henderson and Venkatraman in 1993 [14]. Not least the enduring need for guidance on how to align business and IT has recently promoted the development of a new management discipline, namely the discipline of enterprise architecture (EA) management. Central to this discipline is a comprehensive understanding of the enterprise as a system, whose architecture deserves mindful management. Architecture thereby is defines as the "fundamental organization of a system embodied in its components, their relationships to each other, and to the environment, as well as the principles guiding its design and evolution" [16]. The enterprise architecture (EA) covers manifold different facets of the enterprise ranging from business-related aspects to more IT-related ones, see Figure 1. Complementing this static understanding of the enterprise as system of interrelated social and technical constituents, different cross-cutting aspects exert influence or realize the design of the architecture, namely *standards*, *goals*, and *projects*. Especially the latter two cross-cutting aspects play a crucial role in evolving the architecture: goals describe the desired result of the evolution, whereas projects are the implementors'' of architectural change. Between these two concepts a delicate relationship exists in a way that projects can be analyzed in respect to their goal contribution. This analysis pertains to the underlying *means-end*-relationship connecting projects and goals, respectively. While this relationship may be regarded a cornerstone of governing the evolution of the EA, it has yet not been subjected to in-depth research. This is especially surprising against the background of goals as well as projects being objects of research in EA management and EA modeling for several years now (see the work of Aier et al. [1], Buckl et al. [3,9], or Frank et al. [12]).

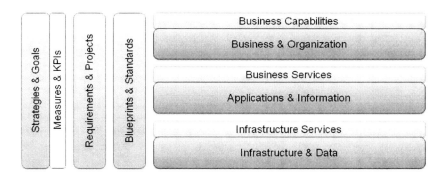

Fig. 1. Conceptual structure of an EA

This paper contributes to the field of EA management, especially in the area of EA evolution governance, by making the relationships between EA-related goals on the one hand and EA-relevant projects on the other hand explicit. By doing so the paper promotes a systemic view on the activity of EA management centered around a conceptual model covering the inner nature of this activity. This model can build on different relevant prefabricates from distinct discipline, among other the *i*-model* of Yu [19], the *goal-question-metric*-approach of Basili et al. [2] as well as related approaches, and the conceptualization of EA change projects presented by Buckl et al. in [3]. Each of these foundational theories and works is shortly introduced in Section 2, preparing the exposition of the interlinking EA governance model in Section 3. Complementing this exposition, the section further delivers some insights into the application of the method at a financial service provider. This application example is anonymized due to confidentiality reasons. Section 4 shows how the presented approach compares to related approaches in the field of EA management and the development of ultra-large scale systems. Final Section 5 critically reflects the contribution of the paper and gives an outlook on future research topics in the field.

2 Foundations and prefabricates

A model for governing the evolution of the EA, i.e. a model targeting the function of EA management, has to bring together three largely different perspectives. Firstly, it has to account for the *intensional* perspective in which *dependers* and *dependees*, i.e. different actors, make explicit the *dependa*, as goals or resources, via which they influence and relate to each other. Secondly, a model for the EA management function must incorporate a more mechanistic and computational perspective on EA-related goals, which are operationalized via *questions* to concrete architectural *metrics*. Thirdly and finally, such EA management model must account for the transformational nature of EA-relevant projects by providing mechanisms to reflect the changes made by a project in the according model of the EA. In the following three Sections 2.1 to 2.3 prominent models and theories covering one or another of the aforementioned aspects are introduced. Together these models form the basis for the comprehensive EA management model introduced in Section 3.

2.1 i* Model

The i* model, initially developed by Yu (cf. [19]) and ever since applied and furthered in manifold publications not at least from an own workshop series, is a model that aims at making explicit the intensional relationships between different actors of a complex system. In its current form the i* model is comprised of two submodels, namely the *strategic dependency* and the *strategic rationale* model. The former model describes the dependencies between two actors in terms of *depender*, *dependee*, and *dependum* which can be a (soft) goal, a task, or a resource, respectively. These dependencies are explained in the strategic rationale model, especially detailing on the intentionally desired elements for the corresponding actors. Put in other words, the dependency model provides an abstract black-box perspective on actors and their relationships, whereas the rationale model explains dependencies via a white-box perspective on actors and their intentions. Figure 2 exemplifies a strategic dependency model, also providing an example for the notion of the one-side dependency. In such dependencies, only depender and dependum or dependee and dependum are known, leaving the opposite actor unknown.

A final remark on the different types of dependa in i* strategic dependency models should be added. Two actors can depend via

goals where the depender needs the dependee to get the (measurable) goal fulfilled (as shown in Figure 2),
tasks where the depender relies on the dependee for getting a task executed,

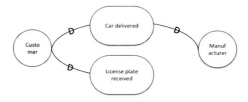

Fig. 2. Modelling dependers, dependa, and dependees with i*

resources where the depender needs the dependee to provide a certain artifact, or
softgoals where the dependee can satisfy a not-measurable goal of the depender.

For the context of EA management especially goal-mediated dependencies may be of interest. Using the mechanisms of the strategic rationale model such goals may further be operationalized via tasks necessary to accomplish these goals and resources necessary to perform the task. We shall revisit these decomposition or means-end-links in Section 3 in more detail.

2.2 Goal-Question-Metric Approach

In [2], Basili et al. present the goal-question-metric (GQM) approach as a way to define measurements in a top-down fashion, focused on goals and based on models. With this way they seek to address a challenge from the field of software development, where many observable characteristics of the design product exist, but a concise interpretation of according metrics is not easily at hand. Central to the approach is a trifecta of steps starting with "goal specification", proceeding over "goal anchoring" to "interpreting measurements". These steps are reflected in the measurement model of the GQM approach, which employs three distinct levels:

Conceptual level defining goals that target specific objects of analysis from perspectives reflecting certain characteristics or models of quality.
Operational level defining a set of questions characterizing the way of assessing the achievement of the according goal. The questions thereby characterize the object of measurement.
Quantitative level defining concrete metrics used to answer the according questions in a quantitative way.

The levels of GQM allow a differentiation between three aspects, which are colloquially subsumed under the term "goal". Thereby, GQM especially facilitates discussions on the abstract nature of a goal and its anchoring in a concrete model of the artifact, on which the goal should be specified. In [9], Buckl et al. make use of this understanding and differentiation to discuss on the role of goals in EA management and modeling. They specifically delineate that goals are *cross-cutting aspects* of EA modeling (cf. Section 1). Further, they show how *dispersive* types, so called *mixins*, may be used to incorporate goals – more precisely their corresponding questions – into structure-oriented models of an EA. Figure 3 shows the basic idea of modeling the relationship between goals, questions (as mixin types), and metrics (as attributes of questions) and gives an application example from the context of EA modeling.

Fig. 3. Modelling goals and questions in the EA context

2.3 Project Dependency Model

Projects, i.e. the facilitators of organizational change, make up an important cross-cutting aspect of EA models. This has manifold reasons, of which two prominent ones as discussed by Buckl et al. in [4,3] as well as Ernst and Schneider in [11] should be shortly stated here. Firstly, projects are used during EA planning to describe different possible ways to evolve the EA or parts thereof. Where this understanding of projects focuses on the change perspective associated to a project, secondly they are also modeled to control the EA evolution process itself. In the latter sense, the relationships between projects and EA elements are explored to identify architecture-mediated project dependencies that may aggravate the implementation of specific project portfolios. Both aforementioned scenarios critically rely on an understanding on how projects and elements in the EA are interlinked, although the first scenario presents a more intricate set of relationships. Before delving into the very details thereof, we briefly revisit the term project to highlight a distinction between two types of projects: *run projects* and *change projects*. Projects of both types actually change the enterprise in some way, but only projects of the latter type perform adaptations on a level that is "visible" in the corresponding EA model. An appropriate modeling – using mixins to designate the architecture concepts subject to change – is shown in Figure 4. This model introduces a general relationship "change" to reflect run projects. Specialized relationships, as "introduces" or "retires", may be used designate transformations performed by a change project. These relationships may further be used to supply a *period of validity* to an architecture element in a way that no such element may be regarded valid prior to the completion of its introducing project. Complementing, an architecture element ceases to be valid at that point in time, when its retiring project is completed.

Concluding the exposition of the prefabricates of this paper's approach a minor remark has to be added concerning the relationship between "projects"

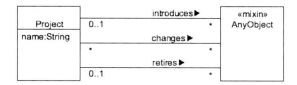

Fig. 4. Modeling run and change projects in the EA context

and "activities" as covered by the i* approach. Whereas Buckl et al. (cf. [3]) do not explicitly account for ongoing maintenance activities in an enterprise, their understanding of "run projects" may also apply on these activities, although statements on "startDate" and "endDate" should not be used in this context. Conversely, every project in the sense of Buckl et al. may be understood as activity in the i* approach. With neither the temporal planning for projects nor the distinction between run and change projects being of central importance for our subsequent considerations, we will identify "projects" and "activities" in the following, hence allowing a uniform treatment of both types.

3 Socio-technic Dependency and Rationale Models for the EA Management Function

In this section, we devise a model bringing together intensional dependency modeling from the i* method with goal and project dependency modeling from typical EA models. In order to facilitate a good understanding of this model, we explain the steps of model creation along a practice case.

EA management is performed by the bank SBM in order to achieve distinct EA-related goals, as increased disaster tolerance or reduced operating cost. These EA-related goals are raised by different *stakeholders* in SBM, i.e. by different individuals or groups that have certain interests in respect to the system enterprise [16]. As part of EA management or more precisely the setup of EA management, SBM concretizes the abstract goal statements by anchoring them in the architecture elements, which they are to be realized at (cf. Buckl et al. in [8]). This leads to the following concrete goal: "increased disaster tolerance in business process execution", stating that the first abstract statement is anchored in the concept of the business process. The corresponding stakeholder of this goal is a business unit of the organization, which depends on the execution of the corresponding business processes. Understanding this dependency in terms of an i* model, we may identify it with a one-sided dependency, where the dependee is yet not made explicit.

Further detailing "disaster tolerance of business processes" the GQM approach is applied to derive a question suitable for operationalizing the according goal. In the case of SBM the notion of disaster tolerance is reflected in a question of availability on business processes. The goal building on the notion can in this sense be put in more operational terms by stating that availability and disaster tolerance are positively related. Put in other words, this means that an increased availability implies an increased disaster tolerance. With the operationalization via a question on the one hand and an explicit understanding of the relationship quality on the other hand, the dependum of the business unit's one-sided dependency is directly linked to a corresponding concept from the architecture, namely the business process. Using a notation combining notational elements of i* on the one hand and of the UML on the other hand as language to describe EA information models, the afore described situation can be visualized as shown in Figure 5.

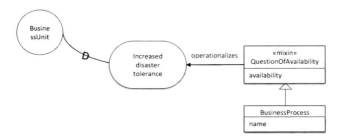

Fig. 5. Partial strategic dependency model enhanced with EA management information

At this point SBM explores the remainder of its EA information model, especially traversing the conceptual relationships starting and ending in the concept of the business process. Domain experts thereby diagnose that the attribute of availability in the business process may be affected by the availability of the supporting business applications. This conversely means that the question of availability also applies to the business application, whereas a feature dependency relationship mechanisms as described by Buckl et al. in [5] may be used to relate business process and business application availability. With this modeling the goal dependency of the business unit is traced down to an operational quality characteristic of an architecture element, namely the business applications supporting the business process under consideration.

Utilizing the mechanisms of EA modeling, SBM is able to describe that maintenance projects executed by the IT department exert influence on the business applications and may hence also influence the relevant property of availability. Identifying a project with a task of the strategic dependency model, SBM can establish a link back to the IT department as dependee, i.e. as responsible actor for this task. Figure 6 illustrates the complete set of dependencies as devised by the EA management team of SBM.

The EA-enhanced strategic dependency model allows SBM to discover the relationship between availability-relevant maintenance activities of the IT department and the goal "increased disaster tolerance in business process execution" on which the business unit critically depends. Having uncovered this relationship, the EA management team of SBM decides to adapt the EA management

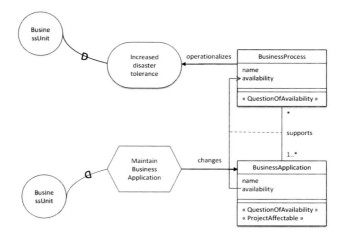

Fig. 6. Enhanced strategic dependency model in the EA management context

function to better pursue the business relevant goal. In particular, an artificial goal "increased business application availability" is introduced and linked to the question of availability as already incorporated in the corresponding architectural concept. Further assuming that the IT department pursues a softgoal of "increased reputation", the EA management team decides to establish a contribution from the availability goal on business applications to the unit's reputation. For doing so the EA management team creates a dashboard on application availability values and makes this dashboard available in the corporate intranet. Thereby, the control loop is closed as a high availability makes a positive contribution to the subjective reputation of the corresponding IT unit.

Above we presented how i* models can be combined with project dependency modeling and the GQM approach in order to comprehensively cover both the intensional and technical dependencies behind an EA management function. What has been modeled in an intuitive manner above, is subsequently grounded in a formal conceptual model based on a revisited understanding of the foundational approaches. Figure 7 presents the conceptual meta-model backing the strategic dependency modeling as utilized by our approach. The terms and conception of this model is rooted in the basics of the i* model as described by Yu in [19]. In this meta-model, we apply the notion of the mixin (cf. Section 2) to form a *dispersive* type "dependum" to reflect the different kinds of concepts that may mediate dependencies between different actors. The thereby supplied modeling facility largely corresponds to the facility provided in Yu's original work.

Further detailing on the nature of the dependencies and their underlying rationales, we present a conceptual meta-model for strategic rational modeling as shown in Figure 8. Central to this model is the linkage between projects and tasks, more precisely a specialization relationship identifying any project with a task. On the contrary, goals are concretized via questions which are complementary operationalized via metrics. These metrics – attributes of the corresponding

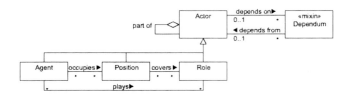

Fig. 7. Conceptual meta-model for strategic dependency modeling

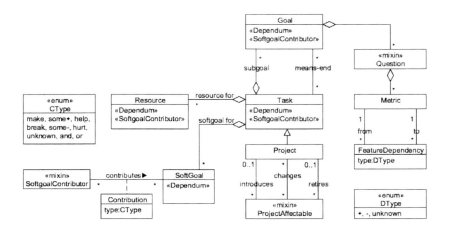

Fig. 8. Conceptual meta-model for strategic rationale modeling

type in the sense of an object-oriented model – may finally be linked via feature dependencies describing in which way one property exerts influence on another.

In line with the understanding of Buckl et al., who in [7,9] discuss different cross-cutting aspects of the EA, the meta-model presented above may be regarded as EA information model building block covering the cross-cutting aspects of projects and goals (cf. Figure 1) in conjunction. By doing so, this building block delineates relationships that back the EA management activity. These relationships can be subjected to further investigations, when the overall performance of the EA management function should be assessed. Further, the dependencies are subject to configuration and adaptation in case the EA management function does not perform as expected. Especially the introduction of additional contribution relationship, i.e. the organizational implementation of feedback mechanisms, may help to respond to unexpected management behaviors.

4 Related Work

In [18], Pulkkinen discusses the difficulties of rationalizing architectural decisions in EA management against the background of a layered understanding of the EA. This understanding, while deemed advisable for controlling the complexity of the overall architecture, hampers an integrated perspective on the causal and intensional relationships that interlink the architectural elements and actors. Pulkkinen illustrates this with a typical decision making process, where requirements decided on one layer, e.g. the business architecture layer, are handed over e.g. to the application architecture layer for implementation. This reflects a separation of concerns between the different facets of the enterprise, but may result in a kind of "waterfallian" way of management, that Pulkkinen seeks to counter with a bottom-up information supply. In this sense the hierarchical management system is complemented with cycles that feed relevant architectural information to higher layers. This well aligns with the approach presented in Section 3, although the ideas presented by Pulkkinen in [18] are more general in their claim, while being less detailed in the realization guidance. Put in other words, the model of Pulkkinen does not concentrate on specific bottom-up relationships, but embraces feedback in a highly general manner. Nevertheless, exact statements on how to model and implement such feedback mechanisms in an enterprise are not provided.

The social and managerial dimension of adaptation is also recognized and picked up as a relevant theme in the field of *ultra-large-scale (ULS) systems*. In [17], the author team emphasize on the importance of the "human element" in ULS system. By this they mean not only that quality attributes apply to technical and social components, but also that correlations between human behavior and system quality attributes will become more prominent. Further detailing this conception, the work describes that interactions between people have to be modeled and accounted for in order to understand and control the behavior of the socio-technical ULS systems. Complementing this, the author team of [17] delineates that human and system quality attributes have to be "blended" illustrating this with typical questions that target ULS systems as socio-technical holons. An exemplary question taken from the work asks, what the human part of a system was to do, when the technical part fell below certain thresholds. The model and approach presented in Section 3 of our paper may in this sense be regarded as a contribution to a riposte on the challenges presented in [17]. Moreover, the model allowing to conjointly reason on technical and intensional dependencies linking the actors in an enterprise may provide a valuable ground on which game-theoretic methods prospected in the ULS systems environment can be based on.

Strong emphasis on the social dimension of enterprises is made by the *enterprise ontology* approach presented by Dietz [10]. Central to the ontological approach is an understanding of the enterprise as a system of interlinked commitments. These commitments relating different social actors in the EA are modeled from a *language-action*-perspective, which allows an enterprise ontology to abstract from, what Dietz calls "implementation details". The perspective's underlying Ψ-theory defines four axioms that are used to understand the activities of an enterprise performed as part of their business activities. Against the background of this limitation on business activities not accounting for transformation activities, the approach presented in this paper may be regarded as a continuation of Dietz' Ψ-theory to the level of the management processes concerned with developing and evolving enterprises.

Hoogervost discusses in [15] aspects of governance on the levels of the IT, the corporation, and the enterprise in total. Central to these discussions is a new understanding of governance seeking to bring together what Hoogervost calls the "western and eastern ways of management", respectively. The two ways are distinguished as "mechanistic" and "holistic", of which the former falls short of accounting for the human or social perspective on the enterprise. Put in other words, Hoogervost criticizes prevalent management methods of "western" style to be not open enough for covering the social interdependencies in an appropriate way. As an example for this, the notion of *uncertainty* is presented. Uncertainty is, according to [15], not well accounted for in traditional management and governance models, leading to not-optimal governance and dependency structures. The approach presented by us in Section 3 may be helpful to address the aforementioned issue and close the gap between mechanistic and human-centric management models. More precisely, the relationship between tangible and measurable questions, and informal as well as intensional dependency structures allows analyses covering both relevant management aspects. Furthermore, the both dependency models – namely the one relating different quality characteristics as well as the one expressing dependencies and intensional relationships – may well be augmented to cover uncertainty in respect to the strength of the dependencies.

5 Critical Reflection and Outlook

The approach and model presented in Section 3 is helpful in linking the social and intensional dependencies in a management function to the structural and qualitative dependencies of the management subject. The simplified practice example allows to get first insights into the applicability of the approach, whereas its grounding in well-established techniques and research results from related fields as described in Section 2 may be regarded as further indication towards the soundness of the approach. Nevertheless, a singular case in addition to a consequent derivation from literature may not completely replace more in-depth investigations covering different applications in distinct practical settings. More evaluation would be needed to show both the utility of the model as well as its practical applicability in different enterprise environments.

Further streams of research originate from the findings presented in this paper. The model for relating stakeholders, goals, and projects in an interlinked web may be helpful for designing and adapting the processes and methods of an EA management function. As such function is always performed to satisfy the goals raised by its stakeholders, an understanding of the dependencies of goal satisfaction can be beneficially in revising the management structures for this field. In this vein, both model and approach provide a contribution to the field of *EA management governance* (cf. Buckl et al. in [6] and Harmsen et al. in [13]), i.e. to the field of establishing, maintaining, and evolving the appropriate structures for managing the EA. This well aligns with another perspective on this subject, namely a systemic perspective on the EA management function itself. In such perspective the social and technical relationships may be aggregated to relatively abstract models, e.g. as *causal loop diagrams*. While it would – against the background of the importance of soft-goals in this model – not be sensible to make quantitative analyses of the causal dependencies, it may nevertheless be possible to derive qualitative statements on the overall behavior of the management system. Especially statements on oscillating management behavior as well as unintended control trends may be discovered qualitatively.

Finally, the model and approach as presented in Section 3 albeit targeting the topic of EA management do not rely on specific assumptions rooted in this management field. In this sense, one may reasonably assume that the model can be applied to other management functions targeting socio-technical management subjects as well. The field of IT service management seems to be a valuable candidate in this respect, especially when incidents and their technical reasons are interlinked. Future research may target the applicability of our model and approach on this or other management functions.

References

1. Aier, S., Kurpjuweit, S., Saat, J., Winter, R.: Enterprise Architecture Design as an Engineering Discipline. AIS Transactions on Enterprise Systems 1, 36–43 (2009)
2. Basili, V.R., Caldiera, G., Rombach, H.D.: The Goal Question Metric Approach. Wiley, New York (1994)
3. Buckl, S., Ernst, A.M., Matthes, F., Schweda, C.M.: An information model for managed application landscape evolution. Journal of Enterprise Architecture (JEA) 5(1), 12–26 (2009)
4. Buckl, S., Ernst, A.M., Matthes, F., Schweda, C.M.: Visual roadmaps for enterprise architecture evolution. In: The 1st International Workshop on Enterprise Architecture Challenges and Responses, Korea (2009)
5. Buckl, S., Franke, U., Holschke, O., Matthes, F., Schweda, C.M., Sommestad, T., Ullberg, J.: A pattern-based approach to quantitative enterprise architecture analysis. In: 15th Americas Conference on Information Systems (AMCIS), San Francisco, CA, USA (2009)
6. Buckl, S., Matthes, F., Schweda, C.M.: A viable system perspective on enterprise architecture management. In: Proceedings of the IEEE International Conference on Systems, Man and Cybernetics, San Antonio, TX, USA, 2009, October 11-14, pp. 1483–1488. IEEE, Los Alamitos (2009)
7. Buckl, S., Matthes, F., Schweda, C.M.: Conceptual models for cross-cutting aspects in enterprise architecture modeling. In: 5th International Workshop on Vocabularies, Ontologies, and Rules for the Enterprise, VORTE 2010 (2010)
8. Buckl, S., Matthes, F., Schweda, C.M.: A design theory nexus for situational enterprise architecture management – approach and application example. In: 14th IEEE International EDOC Conference (EDOC 2010), Vitoria, Brazil (2010)
9. Buckl, S., Matthes, F., Schweda, C.M.: A technique for annotating EA information models with goals. In: Barjis, J. (ed.) EOMAS 2010. Lecture Notes in Business Information Processing, vol. 63, pp. 113–127. Springer, Heidelberg (2010)
10. Dietz, J.L.: Enterprise Ontology. Springer, Heidelberg (2006)

11. Ernst, A.M., Schneider, A.W.: Roadmaps for enterprise architecture evolution. In: Engels, G., Luckey, M., Pretschner, A., Reussner, R. (eds.) 2nd European Workshop on Patterns for Enterprise Architecture Management (PEAM 2010), Paderborn, Germany, pp. 253–266 (2010)
12. Frank, U., Heise, D., Kattenstroth, H., Schauer, H.: Designing and utilising business indicator systems within enterprise models – outline of a method. In: Modellierung betrieblicher Informationssysteme (MobIS 2008) – Modellierung zwischen SOA und Compliance Management 2008, Saarbrücken, Germany, November 27.-28 (2008)
13. Harmsen, A.F., Proper, E.H., Kok, N.: Informed governance of enterprise transformations. In: Proper, H.E., Harmsen, F., Dietz, J.L. (eds.) Advances in Enterprise Engineering II, pp. 155–180. Springer, Heidelberg (2009)
14. Henderson, J.C., Venkatraman, N.: Strategic alignment: leveraging information technology for transforming organizations. IBM Systems Journal 32(1), 472–484 (1993)
15. Hoogervorst, J.A.P.: Enterprise Governance and Enterprise Engineering, 1st edn (The Enterprise Engineering Series). Springer, Heidelberg (2009)
16. International Organization for Standardization. ISO/IEC 42010:2007 Systems and software engineering – Recommended practice for architectural description of software-intensive systems (2007)
17. Pollak, B.: Ultra-Large-Scale Systems – The Software Challenge of the Future. In: Carnegie Mellon University, Pittsburgh, PA, USA (2006)
18. Pulkkinen, M.: Systemic management of architectural decisions in enterprise architecture planning. four dimensions and three abstraction levels. In: 39th Hawaii International Conference on System Sciences (HICSS 2006), vol. 8, p. 179c (2006)
19. Yu, E.S.K.: Modelling strategic relationships for process reengineering. PhD thesis, University of Toronto, Toronto, Ont., Canada (1996)

Preface SSW 2011

Paolo Cappellari[1], Roberto De Virgilio[2], and Mark Roantree[1]

[1] Dublin City University, Dublin, Ireland
{pcappellari,mark}@computing.dcu.ie
[2] Universitá Roma Tre, Rome, Italy
dvr@dia.uniroma3.it

We are witnessing a smooth evolution of the Web from a worldwide information space of linked documents to a global knowledge base, composed of semantically interconnected resources. To date, the correlated and semantically annotated data available on the web amounts to 25 billion RDF triples, interlinked by roughly 395 million RDF links. The continuous publishing and the integration of semantic datasets from companies, government and public sector projects is leading to the creation of the so-called Web of Knowledge. Each semantic dataset contributes to extend the global knowledge and increases its reasoning capabilities. Researchers are now looking with growing interest to semantic issues in this huge amount of correlated data available on the Web. Many progresses have been made in the field of semantic technologies, from formal models to repositories and reasoning engines. While many practitioners focus on exploiting semantic information to contribute to IR problems from a document centric point of view, we believe that such a vast, and constantly growing, amount of semantic data raises data management issues that must be faced in a dynamic, highly distributed and heterogeneous environment such as the Web.

The SSW workshop was organized by researchers at Universitá Roma Tre and Dublin City University to provide a forum for discussion and advancement of data management in searching the web, and in relationships with semantic web technologies that propose new models, languages and applications. The workshop has four full research papers and one poster paper. Ferre et al. introduce semantic faceted search, a combination of an expressive query language and faceted search to improve the query process for end users. Schuller and Weinzierl offer semantic reasoning in the area of multi-context systems with a top-down approach with no imposition on the context of either logic or syntax. A collaborative framework for annotating images in semantic search is presented in the paper by Hong and Reiff-Marganiec. Tian et al. address the issue of homonym search, developing a new interface for an ontology-supported web search. In the short poster paper, McGinnes presents a semantic strategy to exploit ontologies for image retrieval in conceptual modeling.

We wish to express special thanks to the Program Committee members for helping us prepare an interesting program and express our appreciation to the authors of the papers for sharing their work with us. We thank the CAiSE 2011 organizers for their help and organizational support. Finally, we would like to extend many thanks to Universitá Roma Tre and to Dublin City University for their support in organizing the workshop.

April 2011

Paolo Cappellari
Roberto De Virgilio
Mark Roantree

Organization

Program Committee Chairs

Paolo Cappellari	Dublin City University, Ireland
Mark Roantree	Dublin City University, Ireland
Roberto De Virgilio	Universitá Roma Tre, Italy

Program Committee

François Bry	University of Munich, Germany
Paolo Cappellari	Dublin City University, Ireland
Vassilis Christophides	University of Crete, Greece
Simona Colucci	Technical University of Bari, Italy
Roberto De Virgilio	Universitá Roma Tre, Rome, Italy
Beniamino Di Martino	Second University of Naples, Italy
Tommaso Di Noia	Technical University of Bari, Italy
Bettina Fazzinga	University of Calabria, Italy
Flavius Frasincar	Erasmus University Rotterdam, Netherlands
Tim Furche	University of Munich, Munich, Germany
James Geller	New Jersey Institute of Technology, U.S.A.
Laura Hollink	Delft University of Technology, Netherlands
Clemens Ley	Oxford University, U.K.
Dimitris Plexousakis	University of Crete, Greece
Mark Roantree	Dublin City University, Ireland
Michele Ruta	Technical University of Bari, Italy
Michael Schmidt	University of Freiburg, Germany
Luciano Serafini	FBK-IRST, Italy
Eufemia Tinelli	Technical University of Bari, Italy
Kees Van Der Sluijs	Technische Universiteit Eindhoven, Netherlands
Antonius Weinzierl	Vienna University of Technology, Austria

Enhancing the Interface for Ontology-Supported Homonym Search

Tian Tian[1], James Geller[1], and Soon Ae Chun[2]

[1] New Jersey Institute of Technology,
Newark, NJ, USA
{tt25,geller}@njit.edu
[2] CSI, City University of New York,
Staten Island, NY, USA
soon.chun@csi.cuny.edu

Abstract. Keyword-based search engines face a complication when a search term is a homonym, that is, a word with multiple meanings. In a pervious study, we have built an Ontology-Supported Web Search system to categorize the homonymous terms and display their *suggested completions* separately. The suggestions of the homonyms are extracted from an ontology developed in this research. In this paper, we present new ways of displaying homonymous search results. To help the user better understand and differentiate the homonymous terms, we display snippets of search results belonging to the suggested completions separately as follows. For every homonymous sense, the snippets are in a separate pane, and panes are tiled horizontally, i.e., are next to each other. In addition, we present an improvement of Google's instant feature, in that snippets are refreshed as soon as a user hovers with the mouse on a suggested completion for more than a certain period, e.g. two seconds.

Keywords: Ontology, Ontology-supported Web search, Homonyms, Web search with homonyms, Improvement of search experience, Suggested completions.

1 Introduction

In what is shaping up to be the "Century of the Web" a computer literate person with an information need is likely to eschew traditional sources of information such as libraries, yellow pages and newspapers and turn immediately to a Web search engine. Such information needs define the work sphere ("from where can I source this industrial part that I need") as much as private life ("where is a nice, affordable restaurant near my home") and everything in between ("I need a cheap flight for a job/private trip"). Thus, the quality of the *search experience* of a user has become of major importance. A user wants an answer, and she wants it **now**, and she wants it many times a day. Search engines are expected to provide correct results quickly, and with a minimal amount of user interaction.

To satisfy this expectation of an agreeable search experience, major efforts have gone into improving both the backends and frontends of common search engines. For example, Google has switched from making users type in complete search terms and hitting return (or clicking a button) to suggesting to the user what she is mostly likely to ask for. Such suggested completions [1] have also been introduced by other search engines. Figure 1 shows Google's suggested completions for the query term "Barack Obama." Google has access to the search terms entered by its millions of users, which makes it easy for them to propose crowd-based suggested completions.

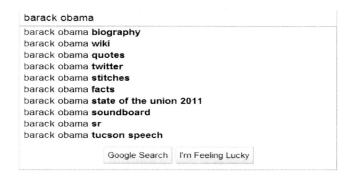

Fig. 1. Google's suggested completions for search term "Barack Obama"

Changes to the backend are harder to discern for the user, but search results are often long lists of snippets referring to a few relevant links among many irrelevant results [2] [3]. Previous research has focused on refining the search terms and on filtering the results, to improve the precision of the returned snippets [2] [4] [5].

Search engines also suffer from three common problems in Natural Language Processing, the synonym problem, the homonym problem, and the wrong granularity problem. The synonym problem appears in the form that the user might send a different term to the search engine than what is contained in a document that would provide a relevant answer. Thus, a query term "43rd president of the US" might miss documents with George Bush, even though these two terms are synonymous.

The wrong granularity problem would appear when a user performs a search with a general or wide term, and a relevant document contains only a more specific or narrow term (or vice versa). Thus, a search for "government officials having been impeached" might not bring up President Clinton, who was indeed impeached.

The third problem in this category occurs when a search term is a homonym [6] [7] [8] (a term with multiple meanings or multiple referents) and the user does not know that. For example, when using the search term "President George Bush" without any further qualification, it might refer to George W. Bush or his father George H. W. Bush, the 43rd and 41st president of the United States, respectively. If the user wants information about the former, she would get results about both of them with this search term, which is an unintended and misleading result.

Thus, when using a search engine to find information about a homonymous term, two kinds of difficulties might arise. There might be an overwhelming number of responses about the more popular homonym, while the second homonym with a less popular meaning that she is really interested in is hidden in a snippet on a much later page of hits. This situation will occur for a user with an untypical information need.

For example, the singer "Tony Bennett" appears to be more popular than the basketball coach of the same name, and/or more information about the singer is available in the public domain. Hence many more returned snippets are about the singer. In this situation, the user is at least aware that the results she is getting are not about the basketball coach that she has been looking for. At this point, she needs to wade through many hits for the wrong Tony Bennett or append terms to her query that will exclude the unwanted homonym and repeat the search.

If the user does not know that the search term is a homonym with two referents, she might not even notice if all snippets that appear on the first few pages of hits are to the "wrong" referent. For example, a user who types "Congo" into Google will see a large number of references to the Democratic Republic of the Congo and a few references to the Republic of the Congo. These two countries are located in Central Africa, bordering each other. The returned information about the two different countries is mingled together in the search results. Typing "Congo" into the Google search box leads to suggested completions such as river, bars, movie, war, etc. There is no hint to a user that there are two different countries called Congo in Africa.

The goal of this research is to develop and implement a Web search mechanism that combines support for homonymous search terms with an improved search experience for the user that minimizes the necessity for input actions. In Section 2 we present background material about Ontology-Supported Web Search and the Instant Feature. Section 3.1 reviews the principles of an Ontology-Supported Web Search system (OSWS). In Section 3.2 we illustrate the "vertical view" mechanism. Then, in Section 3.3, we discuss the new instant feature incorporated into the OSWS system. Section 4 concludes the paper and describes future research directions.

2 Background

Semantic search on the Web, which aims at enabling more intelligent Web searches, has become one of the hottest Semantic Web research topics [9]. Keyboard-based approaches have been studied by many researchers in the field to improve the search process [9]. For example, [10] improves the traditional search method by augmenting the search results with relevant data aggregated from the Semantic Web. Falcons is a keyword-based search engine for concepts and objects on the Semantic Web [11]. SWSE [12] and Sig.Ma [13] allow users to locate RDF entities via keyword search [9]. Some of the mentioned studies have also addressed the problem of query disambiguation, considering user preferences or heuristics [9].

In a previous study, we have built a prototype of an Ontology-Supported Web Search (OSWS) system with an ontology-based mechanism for generating suggested search completions [6]. The Ontology-Supported Web Search system is an extension of work by Y. An [14][15][16] on making the Web search process "ontology-aware."

A special-purpose search engine (also known as vertical search engine) limits its coverage in order to tailor the search results to one well-defined application domain [17]. There are many special-purpose search engines on the Web, e.g., Google Image Search, Yahoo Video Search, Twitter Search, Technorati, etc. Our goal is to build a special-purpose search engine for the domain of famous people. The OSWS ontology contains information about 8000 celebrities in the areas of music and sports. We are currently extending the ontology by adding 5000 famous people from other domains.

The knowledge necessary to generate the suggested completions is extracted from the "famous people" ontology developed in this research. The OSWS system separates between suggested completions for up to four homonymous concepts that fit the search terms that a user has already typed in [6]. The suggested search term completions are visually categorized and separated to make it clear to the user that homonymous concepts exist for her search term. Differentiating visually between too many senses in the limited space of a browser window would likely be difficult and overwhelming, or too little information about each sense would be displayed, thus the limitation to four homonyms.

Google has rolled out the new instant feature (Google Instant) in September 2010 [18]. As the user starts to type the first few letters of her search term, Google Instant automatically shows snippets of results for the most popular search term (the first suggested completion) that begins with those letters. The snippets appear below the box with suggested completions. As the user keeps typing, the snippets are dynamically updated. The user does not need to press enter or click the search button.

Google Instant helps the user to get better search results faster. Most importantly, seeing results as the user types her input helps her formulate a better search term by providing her with instant feedback [12]. However, Google Instant only displays result snippets for the first suggested completion in the drop-down suggestion box, even if the user moves the mouse over other suggestions. There are cases in which the user may be interested in making a choice between two suggested completions below the first one, but she cannot get instant feedback about them by using Google Instant. Rather she has to "make a commitment" to one of the suggested completions by clicking on it, which defeats the purpose of the instant feature, which is to minimize the number of user actions necessary to obtain a satisfactory result.

3 Improving the Web Search Experience When Using Ontology-Supported Web Search

3.1 Principles of Ontology-Supported Web Search

The OSWS System provides search suggestions based on the user's input, every time she types a new character. After the user completes the search term "Adam," the system finds all the people in the knowledge base with "Adam" as the first name. (Figure 2; the display is updated after every single letter.) Additional information about all the Adams in the ontology is extracted for the purpose of generating suggested completions, which make the user aware of the fact that he is dealing with a homonym. In this example, the singers Adam Lambert, Adam Sandler, Adam Bomb and the Basketball player Adam Morrison are found. From the information stored about these four people in the ontology, the suggested completions are generated and displayed in the dropdown box.

The processing is done as follows. For each concept of a famous person that is found in the ontology and has a name that matches the search term, all immediate neighbors along with their connecting relationships are retrieved. The current ontology in the OSWS system contains information about over 5000 musicians, more than 3000 basketball players and a selection of athletes from other kinds of sports. In the

OSWS system, the first proposed suggestion about a famous person is always based on the class (modeling the occupation) of the person, which defines the name of the professional domain that the person belongs to.

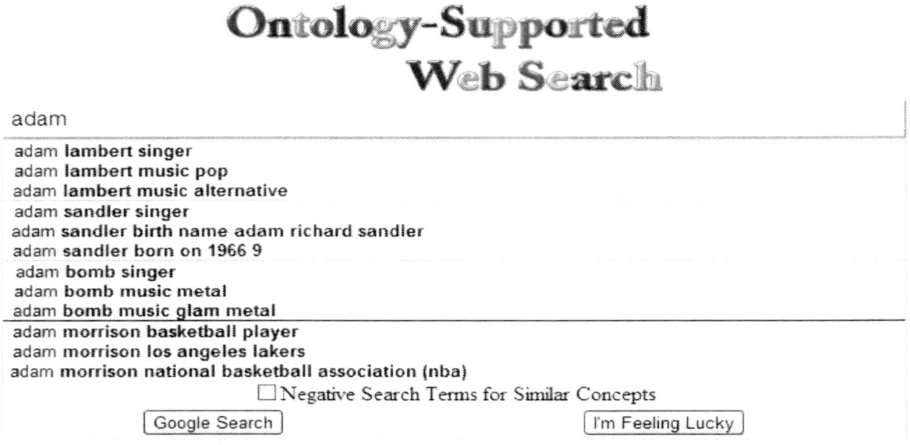

Ontology-Supported Web Search

```
adam
  adam lambert singer
  adam lambert music pop
  adam lambert music alternative
  adam sandler singer
  adam sandler birth name adam richard sandler
  adam sandler born on 1966 9
  adam bomb singer
  adam bomb music metal
  adam bomb music glam metal
  adam morrison basketball player
  adam morrison los angeles lakers
  adam morrison national basketball association (nba)
           ☐ Negative Search Terms for Similar Concepts
  [ Google Search ]                              [ I'm Feeling Lucky ]
```

Fig. 2. Interface of the OSWS System for search term "Adam"

The remaining suggested completions are constructed based on other knowledge in the ontology. They may include background information about a person, like the date of birth and the place of birth, and sometimes the birth name. Besides, for musicians, the ontology stores the genres of music the artist performs. For sportsmen, the league and the team he or she belongs to are represented in the ontology.

Figure 3 shows the representation[1] of four homonymous "example Adams" in the ontology. Note that the OSWS processing happens in real time, whenever a new letter is added to the search term. Thus, when the user finishes the word "Adam," these four Adams in the ontology are candidates for completion. They should be viewed as "homonymous according to the input currently made available to the search engine."

In the OSWS interface, different senses of a homonymous term are visually separated by two mechanisms, horizontal lines of two different widths and different background colors. This separation clearly expresses the fact that there are different conceptual distances among the homonyms expressed by different sets of suggested completions. This makes it easier for the user to learn or remember that she is dealing with a homonym. Current search engines do not support such a separation. For example, the visual display in Figure 2 expresses the fact that Adam Lambert is conceptually closer to Adam Sandler and Adam Bomb (all of them are singers) than to Adam Morrison (the Basketball player) by separating the singers by thin lines from each other, and by separating them with a heavy line from the basketball player.

---

[1] Classes in the figure are represented as boxes. Instances are shown as ellipses. IS-A links are drawn as arrows from the child class to the parent class. Dashed arrows connect instances to the classes that they are instances of. Finally, lines terminated by little black circles indicate semantic relationships other than IS-A and instance of relationships.

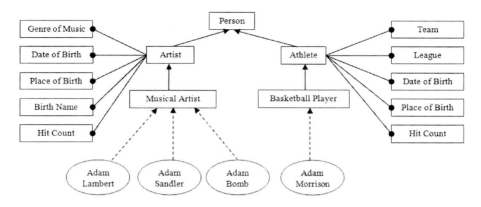

Fig. 3. Excerpt from the "famous people" knowledge base with homonym example "Adam"

Similarly, the background color of the suggested completions also distinguishes famous people from different domains. In Figure 2, the suggestions for the three singers are generated by the system with a common background color, in contrast to the suggested completions of the Basketball player that are displayed with a different background. To avoid cognitive overload of the user, at most four homonyms are used for generating suggested completions. Thus, at most four background colors are needed. Furthermore, to stay close to the Google look and feel of the interface that many Web users are comfortable with, we designed the OSWS system to show at most 12 suggested completions in total, independent of how many homonyms are displayed. This implies that not all knowledge in the ontology can be used for generating suggested completions. We have assigned priority weights to the relationships to decide on the ranking of the suggestions. Up to four homonyms are displayed, considering the degree of connectivity of the entity in the ontology or its hit count information. The detailed selection mechanism is explained in [6].

After the user chooses the suggestion that best fits her search needs and clicks the "Google Search" button, a result page will be generated, using the Google AJAX API. In this example, when the user types "Adam S" the visible choices switch to "Adam Sandler," "Adam Sherburne," and "Adam Schmitt," based on the people known in the ontology. As noted before, there are cases where complete names are still homonymous (e.g., Tony Bennett, George Bush, etc.).

In the following subsections we discuss methods for combining Ontology-Supported Web Search with techniques for providing the user with an improved search experience. First, to help the user choose the desired homonym, we split the result screen vertically and show result page snippets for the different homonymous terms next to each other. This gives the user more detailed information about different categories to help her decide what results best fit her interests. This display method gives the different homonymous concepts the same visibility "in the first row" and thus does not have a vertical bias towards one of the senses of the user's search term.

Secondly, the system shows the result page snippets for one specific homonym every time the user hovers with the mouse on top of a suggested completion for a selectable time period, currently set to two seconds or longer. This helps the user to acquire a deeper and clearer understanding of the suggested term without having to make a choice. Google, at this point in time, does not automatically change the displayed snippets when the mouse is moved down to a lower suggested completion.

3.2 Improving the OSWS System with Parallel Result Display for Homonyms

One innovative feature we have implemented into the OSWS System is the "vertical view" of the returned search results. As we categorize the suggestions for the different homonyms of a search term, such as singers, sports players, politicians, etc., we also divide the display screen below the suggested completions box into a few (two to four) vertical panels with result snippets for the different homonyms, so that the panels are displayed next to each other. Every vertical panel contains the Google results for the first suggested completion of a different homonym. In this way, none of the homonyms is given the privileged position of being displayed in the first row.

As seen in Figure 4, after the user types "Adam," four homonymous famous "Adams," the singers Adam Lambert, Adam Sandler, Adam Bomb and the Basketball player Adam Morrison are found in our ontology and suggested to the user. Before she decides which Adam fits her interest or moves her mouse to a lower suggested completion, the system instantly shows the result snippets for the first suggestion of each of the four different Adams. The display screen is tiled into four vertical panels, which are respectively the results for the search terms "Adam Lambert singer," "Adam Sandler singer," "Adam Bomb singer" and "Adam Morrison basketball player." Thus, the top down order in the suggested completions is reflected in the left-to-right order of the tiled windows containing result snippets.

As mentioned before, due to the structure of the ontology, the first suggested completion of each homonym is in most cases the occupation of the famous person. The returned snippets give the user richer and more detailed information about different homonyms to help her decide what result best fits her interests.

The OSWS system shows the parallel results for all the homonyms only at the beginning of the search. During the time that the user types letters into the search box, we feature the vertical view of the returned results to help the user make a choice among the homonyms. Once the user moves the mouse down, the display is changed to the instant feature view that we are about to introduce in Section 3.3.

3.3 Improving the OSWS System with Instant Visual Feedback

In this section we describe an improved implementation of the instant feature [12]. As mentioned in Section 3.2, as soon as the user types letters into the search box, the system will automatically display the result snippets for the first suggested completion of each of the homonyms, if there are any, next to each other. Once the user moves the mouse to another suggestion in the drop-down menu and hovers over it, the OSWS System changes the display from horizontally parallel panels to one single panel, which contains the returned snippets of the suggested completion the user is apparently interested in because he is hovering on top of it.

Enhancing the Interface for Ontology-Supported Homonym Search 551

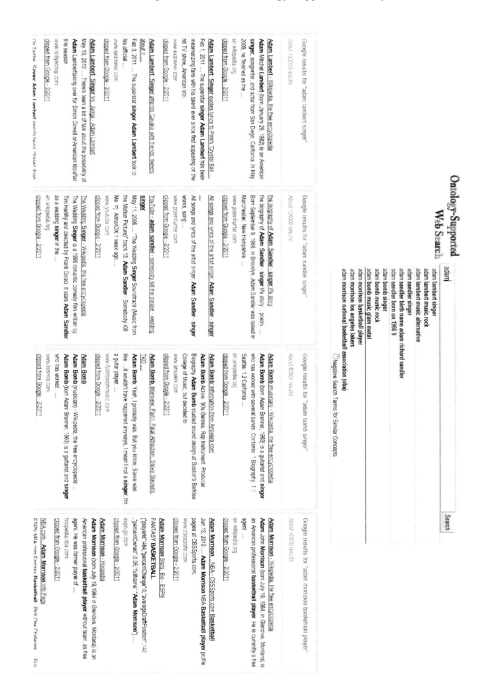

Fig. 4. Interface of the OSWS System with the parallel result display for search term "Adam"

As opposed to Google, not only the snippets of the first suggestion will be displayed, but if the user moves down to any other suggested completion, the snippet display is dynamically refreshed and updated. Thus, the user will instantly see results elaborating the suggested completions, to help her acquire a deeper and clearer understanding of the meaning of the suggested completion she is on. This helps her improve her searches significantly and efficiently. Google currently only shows instant results for the first suggested completion.

To avoid an overload of the server and to better react to the user's interests, we have defined a criterion for the minimum time required to be spent by the user hovering over a selected completion. Thus, only if the user stays for a while on one suggested completion (without clicking), the corresponding result snippets are displayed. The hover time is currently set to two seconds, but this is a user-adjustable parameter. To make it possible for the user to move back and forth between different suggested completions, snippets are cached locally and do not have to be reloaded from the server.

Once the user clicks on one of the suggested completions, the display will be changed. The selected suggestion will be shown in its entirety in the search box. By clicking the search button next to it, the user will be led to the regular Google result page of the selected search term. For the extraction of the Web information we are using the Google AJAX API.

4 Conclusions and Future Work

In order to improve the search experience of Web users while discriminating between different senses of a homonymous term, we have developed a new interface for the OSWS System improving it in two ways. In the first stage, we divide the snippet display into vertical panels to visually separate the results for the different homonyms. When the user moves the mouse down to one of the suggested completions and hovers there, the processing enters the second stage. For every suggested completion the user points to, the system instantly shows the result snippets of the suggestion he is hovering over. This improves the Google Instant feature. Currently Google shows instant results only for the first suggested completion. These two new features help the user acquire a deeper understanding of the suggested terms and to enjoy a better search experience than provided by today's search engines, while minimizing the number of actions she has to perform.

Our current and future work is focused on improving the backend ontology. We are in the process of preparing a new ontology with famous people from many more domains, by mining information about them from different structured Web sources such as DBpedia and YAGO. Our current ontology is queried using special-purpose Java code. We are considering using SPARQL in the future, as the ontology grows in size and complexity. We are also planning to collect user feedback and to perform a formal evaluation study of the new features, e.g. using a tool such as Morae™.

Acknowledgments. We thank our students Yuwen Sun and Christopher Ochs for their work on the implementation of the new OSWS system and Shrutee Shah, who has contributed to the original OSWS program. David Kaufman has introduced us to Morae™.

References

1. Google Query Suggestion, http://www.google.com/support/websearch/bin/answer.py?hl=en&answer=106230
2. Radev, D.R., Fan, W., Zhang, Z.: WebInEssence: A Personalized Web-Based Multi-Document Summarization and Recommendation System. In: NAACL Workshop on Automatic Summarization, Pittsburgh, PA (2001)
3. Al-Masri, E., Mahmoud, Q.H.: Discovering Web Services in Search Engines. IEEE Internet Computing 3, 74–77 (2008)
4. Lawrence, S.R.: Personalization of Web Search Results Using Term, Category, and Link-Based User Profiles. United States Patent Appl. 20100228715, Kind Code: A1 (2010)
5. Tian, T., Geller, J., Chun, S.A.: Predicting Web Search Hit Counts. In: 2010 IEEE/WIC/ACM International Conference on Web Intelligence and Intelligent Agent Technology, Toronto, Canada, pp. 162–166 (2010)
6. Tian, T., Geller, J., Chun, S.A.: Improving Web Search Results for Homonyms by Suggesting Completions from an Ontology. In: 2nd International Workshop on Semantic Web Information Management (SWIM). LNCS, Vienna, Austria, pp. 175–186 (2010)
7. Radlinski, F., Szummer, M., Craswell, N.: Inferring Query Intent from Reformulations and Clicks. In: WWW 2010, Raleigh, North Carolina, USA (2010)
8. Henzinger, M.: Search Technologies for the Internet. Science 317(5837), 468–471 (2007)
9. Fazzinga, B., Lukasiewicz, T.: Semantic Search on the Web. In: Semantic Web – Interoperability, Usability, Applicability, vol. 1, pp. 1–7 (2010)
10. Guha, R.V., McCool, R., Miller, E.: Semantic Search. In: WWW 2003, Budapest, Hungary, pp. 700-709 (2003)
11. Cheng, G., Ge, W., Qu, Y.: Falcons: Searching and Browsing Entities on the Semantic Web. In: WWW 2008, Beijing, China, pp. 1101-1102 (2008)
12. Harth, A., Hogan, A., Delbru, R., Umbrich, J., O'Riain, S., Decker, S.: SWSE: Answer before Links! In: Proceedings of Semantic Web Challenge, CEUR Workshop 2007 (2007)
13. Tummarello, G., Cyganiak, R., Ctasta, M., Danielczyk, S., Delbru, R., Decker, S.: Sig.Ma: Live Views on the web of Data. In: WWW 2010, Raleigh, NC, USA, pp.1301–1304 (2010)
14. An, Y., Chun, S., Huang, K., Geller, J.: Enriching Ontology for Deep Web Search. In: Bhowmick, S.S., Küng, J., Wagner, R. (eds.) DEXA 2008. LNCS, vol. 5181, pp. 73–80. Springer, Heidelberg (2008)
15. An, Y., Geller, J., Wu, Y., Chun, S.: Semantic Deep Web: Automatic Attribute Extraction from the Deep Web Data Sources. In: Proceedings of the 2007 ACM Symposium on Applied Computing, ACM-SAC, Seoul, Korea, pp. 1667–1672 (2007)
16. An, Y., Chun, S., Huang, K., Geller, J.: Assessment for Ontology-Supported Deep Web Search. In: 2008 10th IEEE Conference on E-Commerce Technology and the Fifth IEEE Conference on Enterprise Computing, E-Commerce and E-Services, pp. 382–388. IEEE Computer Society, Los Alamitos (2008)
17. Ke, Y., Deng, L., Ng, W., Lee, D.: Web Dynamics and their Ramifications for the Development of Web Search Engines. Computer Networks: The International Journal of Computer and Telecommunications Networking – Web Dynamics 50(10), 1430–1447 (2006)
18. Google Instant, http://www.google.com/instant/

Combining Faceted Search and Query Languages for the Semantic Web

Sébastien Ferré[1], Alice Hermann[2], and Mireille Ducassé[2]

[1] IRISA/Université de Rennes 1, Campus de Beaulieu, 35042 Rennes cedex, France
ferre@irisa.fr
[2] IRISA/INSA de Rennes, Campus de Beaulieu, 35708 Rennes cedex 7, France
{alice.hermann,ducasse}@irisa.fr

Abstract. Faceted search and querying are the two main paradigms to search the Semantic Web. Querying languages, such as SPARQL, offer expressive means for searching knowledge bases, but they are difficult to use. Query assistants help users to write well-formed queries, but they do not prevent empty results. Faceted search supports exploratory search, i.e., guided navigation that returns rich feedbacks to users, and prevents them to fall in dead-ends (empty results). However, faceted search systems do not offer the same expressiveness as query languages. We introduce *semantic faceted search*, the combination of an expressive query language and faceted search to reconcile the two paradigms. The query language is basically SPARQL, but with a syntax that better fits in a faceted search interface. A prototype, Camelis 2, has been implemented, and a usability evaluation demonstrated that semantic faceted search retains the ease-of-use of faceted search, and enables users to build complex queries with little training.

1 Introduction

With the growing amount of available resources in the Semantic Web (SW), it is a key issue to provide an easy and effective access to them, not only to specialists, but also to casual users. The challenge is not only to allow users to retrieve particular resources (e.g., flights), but to support them in the exploration of a knowledge base (e.g., which are the destinations? Which are the most frequent flights? With which companies and at which price?). We call the first mode *retrieval search*, and, following Marchionini [Mar06], the second mode *exploratory search*. Exploratory search is often associated to *faceted search* [HEE+02, ST09], but it is also at the core of Logical Information Systems [Fer09], and Dynamic Taxonomies [Sac00]. Exploratory search allows users to find information without *a priori* knowledge about either the data or its schema. Faceted search works by suggesting restriction values, i.e., selectors for subsets of the current selection of items. Restriction values are organized into facets, and only those that share items with the current selection are suggested. This has the advantage to remove the need to write queries, and to prevent dead-end queries, i.e., queries with no answer. Therefore, faceted search is *easy* and *safe*: *easy* because users only have to choose among the suggested restriction values, and *safe* because, whatever the choice made by users, the resulting selection is not empty. The selections that can be reached by navigation correspond to queries that are generally limited to conjunctions of restriction values, possibly with restricted negation and disjunction. This is far from the expressiveness of query languages for the semantic web, such as SPARQL[1]. SlashFacet [HvOH06] and BrowseRDF [ODD06] are faceted search systems for RDF data that extend the expressiveness of reachable queries, but still to a small fragment of SPARQL. For instance, both of them allow for neither cycles in graph patterns, nor unions of graph patterns (disjunction).

Querying languages for the semantic web, such as SPARQL [AG08], OWL-QL [FHH04], or SPARQL-DL [SP07], are quite expressive but are difficult to use, even for specialists. They do not return enough feedback to offer exploratory search, and nothing prevents users to write a query that has no answer. Indeed, even if users have a perfect knowledge of the syntax and semantics of the query language, they may be ignorant about the data schema, i.e., the *ontology*. If they also master the ontology or if they use a query assistant (e.g., Protégé[2]) or an auto-completion system (e.g., Ginseng [BKK05]), the query will be syntactically correct and semantically consistent w.r.t. the ontology but it can still produce no answer.

The contribution of this paper is to extend faceted search to the Semantic Web, so as to offer an exploratory search that is (1) easy to use, (2) safe, and (3) expressive. Ease-of-use and safeness are retained from existing faceted search systems by keeping their general principles, as well as the visual aspect of their interface. Expressiveness is obtained by representing the current selection by a *query* rather than by a set of items, and by representing navigation links by *query transformations* rather than by set operations (e.g., intersection). In this way, the expressiveness of faceted search is determined by the expressiveness of the query language, rather than by the combinatorics of user interface controls. In this paper, the query language is based on SPARQL graph patterns, but with a syntax that better fits in a faceted search interface: LISQL.

The use of queries for representing selections in faceted search has other benefits than navigation expressiveness. The current query is an intensional description of the current selection that complements its extensional description (listing of items). It informs users in a precise and concise way about their exact position in the navigation space. It can easily be copied and pasted, stored and retrieved later. Finally, it allows expert users to modify the query by hand at any stage of the navigation process, without loosing the ability to proceed by navigation.

The paper is organized as follows. Section 2 presents *semantic faceted search*, and illustrates it with our prototype implementation Camelis 2. Section 3 reports about a user study that demonstrates the usability of our approach. Our approach is also compared in Section 4 to other work in faceted search for the Semantic Web. Section 5 concludes this paper.

---

[1] see http://www.w3.org/TR/rdf-sparql-query/
[2] See http://protege.stanford.edu/

2 Semantic Faceted Search

The principle of our approach, *Semantic Faceted Search* (SFS), is to reconcile querying and navigation. Navigation can be defined as moving from place to place through navigation links. In faceted search, a navigation place is a set of items, and a navigation link is the choice of a restriction value. In SFS, a navigation place is defined by a query, whose answers form the current set of items; and a navigation link is defined as a query transformation. The set of possible query transformations is designed to make it possible to build arbitrary queries. However, the set of navigation links is restricted to those query transformations that do not lead to empty results, like in standard faceted search. In the following, SFS is illustrated on genealogical datasets converted from GED files[3].

2.1 Queries and Query Transformations

The reference query language for the Semantic Web is SPARQL. While its semantics is adequate to our needs, we find that its syntax is not best-suited to SFS. First, it makes it difficult to define query transformations, because it is not regular and compositional enough. Second, it tends to be verbose, and exhibits relational algebra operators, and a number of symbols that are alien to most people: e.g., UNION, &&.

We propose an alternative syntax, LISQL, for a large fragment of SPARQL. This fragment corresponds to unary queries, i.e., queries with only one variable in the SELECT clause. This restriction is not due to LISQL, but to the very definition of faceted search, where a navigation place is a set and not a relation. For reasons of space, we present LISQL and its query transformations through examples only. Full definitions can be found in a research report [FHD11].

As an illustrating example covering all aspects of LISQL, we consider the task of retrieving, in the genealogy of George Washington, "every person that was born in 1601 or 1649 at some place in England, and some child of which was not born at the same place". In SPARQL, this query can be expressed as follows.

```
SELECT DISTINCT ?p
WHERE {
   ?p a person.
   ?p birth ?b.
      ?b year ?y FILTER (?y=1601 || ?y=1649).
      ?b place ?X. ?X in England.
   ?c father ?p.
      ?c birth ?bc.
         ?bc place ?pc FILTER ?pc != ?X }
```

The same query can be expressed in LISQL as:

> a person and birth : (year : (1601 or 1649) and place : (?X
> and in England)) and father of birth : place : not ?X.

---
[3] http://jay.askren.net/Projects/SemWeb/

A LISQL query is a LISQL expression, where some subexpression, the *query focus*, is underlined. LISQL expressions denote sets of items (RDF resources), and can be coordinated by Boolean operators that correspond to set operations: **and** for intersection, **or** for union, and **not** for complement. Atomic expressions can be individuals (e.g., `1601`, `England`) that denote themselves as singleton sets, or classes (e.g., `person`) that denote their set of instances. The subexpression `year : (1601 or 1649)` is a *restriction*, made of the property `year` and of the subexpression, `(1601 or 1649)`, and here denotes the set of events whose year is 1601 or 1649. The keyword (`of`) is used instead of (`:`) for the inverse reading of a property. The variable `?X` is here used to refer to the birthplace of the father, whatever it is. A LISQL expression translates to a SPARQL graph pattern, using a variable for each entity. The *query focus* determines which of those variables is put in the SELECT clause. Therefore, the query `a woman and father : ?` denotes the women's fathers, and is equivalent to `father of a woman`. A focus is never ambiguous; however, two different foci can be equivalent, i.e., put the same variable in the SELECT clause, if they are conjunctively coordinated or associated to a same LISQL variable. LISQL variables therefore allow for cycles in the graph patterns.

We present the different kinds of query transformations through a possible scenario for building the above query. Table 1 gives for each step the query transformations, and the resulting intermediate query. Most transformations apply to the query focus, letting the rest of the query unchanged. Transformation *Reset* resets the whole query to the most general query `?`. Transformation *And* appends a given subexpression to the focus, connecting the two with **and** (`?` is a neutral element for **and**). When the focus is on the whole expression, this transformation corresponds to faceted search selection. Transformation *Focus on* moves the focus on a given subexpression. Transformation *Cross* is an abbreviation for a common navigation idiom: the *And* of a restriction followed by a *Focus on* the subexpression of the restriction. Transformation *Name* does the same as a *And*, but for a freshly generated variable. The *And* of the same variable at a later stage allows for the formation of cycles. Transformation *Or* introduces an alternative to the focus with the connector **or**. Transformation *Not* applies the connector **not** to the focus.

Only transformation *And* requires a LISQL expression to be passed. A set of expressions is suggested to the user so as to avoid dead-ends, and to allow for arbitrarily complex queries. It is sufficient to suggest individuals, variables already in the query, classes, and unqualified restrictions (e.g., `father of ?`) [FHD11].

2.2 Faceted User Interface and Interaction

SFS has been implemented as a prototype, Camelis 2[4]. Figure 1 shows a screenshot of Camelis 2. From top to bottom, and from left to right, it is composed of a menu bar (M), a toolbar (T), a query box (Q), query controls (QC), feature controls (FC), an answer list or extension box (E), a facet hierarchy (F), and

---

[4] downloadable at http://www.irisa.fr/LIS/ferre/camelis/camelis2.html

Table 1. A navigation scenario in Camelis 2 on the genealogy of George Washington

0	Reset ?
1	*And* a person a person
2	*And* birth : year : 1601 a person and birth : year : 1601
3	*Focus on* year : 1601 a person and birth : year : 1601
4	*Cross* place : ? + *Name* a person and birth : (year : 1601 and place : <u>?X</u>)
5	*And* in England a person and birth : (year : 1601 and place : (?X and <u>in England</u>))
6	*Focus on* 1601 + *Or* a person and birth : (year : (<u>1601</u> or ?) and place : (?X and in England))
7	*And* 1649 a person and birth : (year : (1601 or <u>1649</u>) and place : (?X and in England))
8	*Focus on* a person + *Cross*.father of birth : place : ? a person and birth : (year : (1601 or 1649) and place : (?X and in England)) and father of birth : place : <u>?</u>
9	*Not* a person and birth : (year : (1601 or 1649) and place : (?X and in England)) and father of birth : place : not <u>?</u>
10	*And* ?X + *Focus on* a person a person and birth : (year : (1601 or 1649) and place : (<u>?X</u> and in England)) and father of birth : place : not ?X

a set of value boxes (V). A query engine can be derived from Camelis 2 by retaining only the components Q and E. A standard faceted search system can be derived by retaining only the components E, F, and V.

Navigation links, i.e., suggested query transformations, are available on all components. Whenever a navigation control is triggered, the corresponding query transformation is applied, and components (Q,E,F,V) are refreshed accordingly. The toolbar (T) has a button for *Reset*. The query box (Q) is clickable for setting the focus on any subexpression. Query controls (QC) provide buttons for *Name*, *Or*, *Not* (and a few others). Every element of components (E,F,V) can be used as an argument for *And*, with the guarantee that the resulting query does have answers; *And* is replaced by *Cross* for unqualified restrictions. The contents of components (E,F,V) play the role of restriction values in standard faceted search, and are here dispatched in the three components according to their type. The facet hierarchy (F) contains variables of the current query (e.g., ?X, classes (e.g., a person), and *unqualified* restrictions (e.g., father of ?, birth : year : ?). Value boxes (V) contain *qualified* restrictions with individuals as subexpressions

Combining Faceted Search and Query Languages for the Semantic Web

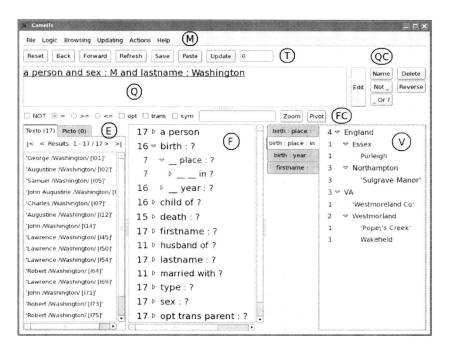

Fig. 1. A screenshot of the user interface of Camelis 2. It shows the selection of male persons whose lastname is Washington.

(e.g., `father of 'George Washington'`, `birth : year : 1601`), grouped by property path. The extension box (E) contains individuals (e.g., `England`). The hierarchical organization of facets in (F) is based on RDFS class and property hierarchies. A value box (V) is hierarchically organized according to the last property of its property path, if it is transitive (e.g, `in`).

3 Usability Evaluation

This section reports on the evaluation of Semantic Faceted Search in terms of usability[5]. we have measured the ability of users to answer questions of various complexities, as well as their response times. Results are strongly positive and demonstrate that semantic faceted search offers expressiveness and ease-of-use at the same time.

Methodology. The subjects consisted of 20 graduate students in computer science. They had prior knowledge of relational databases but neither of Camelis 2, nor of faceted search, nor of semantic web. None was familiar with the dataset used in the evaluation. The evaluation was conducted in three phases. First, the

---
[5] Details can be found on http://www.irisa.fr/LIS/alice.hermann/camelis2.html

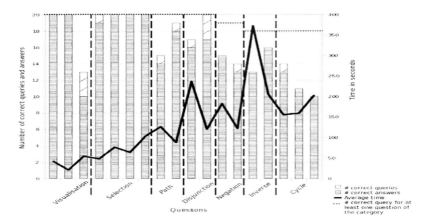

Fig. 2. Average time and number of correct queries and answers for each question

subjects learned how to use Camelis 2 through a 20min tutorial, and had 10 more minutes for free use and questions. Second, subjects were asked to answer a set of questions, using Camelis 2. We recorded their answers, the queries they built, and the time spent on each question.

The test was composed of 18 questions, with smoothly increasing difficulty. The questions can be grouped in 7 categories: the first 2 categories are covered by standard faceted search, while the 5 other categories are not in general. The first category, *Visualization*, did not require the creation of a query. The exploration of the facet hierarchy was sufficient: e.g., "How many men are there?". In the second category, *Selection*, we asked to count or list items that have a particular feature: e.g., "How many women are named Mary?". In the third category, *Path*, subjects had to follow a path of properties: e.g., "Which man is married with a woman born in 1708?". The fourth category, *Disjunction*, required to use disjunction: e.g., "Which women have for mother Jane Butler or Mary Ball?". The fifth category, *Negation*, required to use negation: e.g., "How many women have a mother whose death's place is not Warner Hall?". The sixth category, *Inverse*, required to use the inverse of a property: e.g., "Who was born in the same place as Robert Washington?". In the seventh category, *Cycle*, required the use of variables: e.g., "How many persons have the same firstname as one of their parent?".

Results. Figure 2 shows the number of correct queries and answers, the average time spent on each question and the number of participants who had a correct query for at least one question of each category. For example, in category "Visualization", the first two questions had 20 correct answers and queries; the third question had 10 correct answers and 13 correct queries; all the 20 participants had a correct query for at least one question of the category; the average response times were respectively 43, 21, and 55 seconds. The difference between the number of correct queries and correct answers is explained by the fact that some subjects forgot to set the focus on the whole query after building the query.

All subjects but one had correct answers to more than half of the questions. Half of the subjects had the correct answers to at least 15 questions out of 18. Two subjects answered correctly to 17 questions, their unique error was on a disjunction question for one and on a negation question for the other. All subjects had the correct query for at least 11 questions. For each question, there is at least 50 percent of success. The subjects spent an average time of 40 minutes on the test, the quickest one spent 21 minutes and the slowest one 58 minutes.

The first 2 categories corresponding to standard faceted search, visualization and selection, had a high success rate (between 94 and 100) except for the third question. The most likely explanation for the latter is that the previous question was so simple (`a man`) that subjects forgot to reset the query between the questions 2 and 3. All questions of the first two categories were answered in less than 1 minute and 43 seconds on average. Those results indicate that the more complex user interface of semantic faceted search does not entail a loss of usability compared to standard faceted search for the same tasks.

For other categories, all subjects but two managed to answer correctly at least one question of each category. Within each category, we observed that response times decreased, except for the *Cycle* category. At the same time, for *Path*, *Disjunction* and *Inverse*, the number of correct answers and queries increased. Those results suggest a quick learning process of the subjects. The decrease in category *Negation* is explained by a design flaw in the interface. For category *Cycle*, we conjecture some lassitude at the end of the test. Nevertheless, all but two subjects answered correctly to at least one of *Cycle* questions. The peak of response time in category *Inverse* is explained by the lack of inverse property examples in the tutorial. It is noticeable that subjects, nevertheless, managed to solve the *Inverse* questions with a reasonable success rate, and a decreasing response time.

4 Related Work

As faceted search is becoming widespread, a number of proposals have been made to apply it on the Semantic Web (SW). They all have in common to assume that data is represented in a SW format, either RDF(S) or OWL. Most of them, such as Ontogator [MHS06], mSpace[6], and Longwell[7], do not claim for a contribution in terms of expressiveness, and contribute either to the design of better interfaces and visualizations, or to methods for the rapid or user-centric configuration of faceted views [SVH07]. Therefore, their contributions are somewhat orthogonal to ours, and could certainly complement ours. Other approaches, such as Slash-Facet [HvOH06], BrowseRDF [ODD06], and SOR [LMZ+07], extend faceted search towards a more expressive navigation.

The most essential ingredient for an expressive and flexible semantic search in RDF graphs is *focus change*. It allows to change the perspective without changing the underlying graph pattern. To the best of our knowledge, no faceted search

---

[6] see http://mspace.fm/
[7] see http://simile.mit.edu/wiki/Longwell

system offers this in a general way. SlashFacet and SOR have the *crossing* operation that selects the images of the items in the current selection through a property. Crossing includes a focus change, but crossing back a property is not equivalent to a focus change, because it introduces an additional restriction: starting from a query Q and crossing p : ? and then p of ? leads to p : p of Q instead of Q and p : ? (they are not equivalent). Other systems allow to focus on different types of items, but this focus cannot be changed in the course of a search. For example, in a dataset about publications, a choice has to be made between authors and documents.

It is generally considered that the query should be hidden from the interface. In fact, in most faceted search systems, the query *is* displayed as the list of the restriction values users have already selected in the course of their search. This is important so that users do not feel lost, and can easily reverse previous selections. When expressiveness is raised to SPARQL with graph patterns, disjunction, and negation, it becomes necessary to introduce syntax. While, in Camelis 2, the query is simply rendered as a sentence following some grammar, nothing prevents to render syntax through graphical widgets (e.g., lists for conjunction, trees for restrictions, tab panels for disjunction).

Disjunction and negation are either absent or strongly limited in existing approaches. Disjunction is restricted to build sets of values or sets of items, e.g., in SlashFacet. Negation is restricted to restriction values, and also applies to unqualified restrictions (not father of ?) in BrowseRDF. No other system allows to form cycles as we do with variables.

5 Conclusion

We have introduced *Semantic Faceted Search* (SFS) as a search paradigm for Semantic Web knowledge bases, in particular RDF graphs. It combines the expressiveness of the SPARQL query language, and the benefits of exploratory search and faceted search. The user interface of semantic faceted search includes the user interface of other faceted search systems, and can be used as such. It adds a query box to tell users where they are in their search, and to allow them to change the focus or to remove query parts. It also adds a few controls for applying some query transformations such as insertion/deletion of disjunction, negation, and variables. We have introduced a new query syntax, LISQL, to better fit with a faceted interface and query transformations. Beside the list of selected items, the user interface has a hierarchy of facets organizing classes and properties by subsumption.

SFS has been implemented as a prototype, Camelis 2. Its usability has been demonstrated through a user study, where, after a short training, all subjects were able to answer simple questions, and most of them were able to answer complex questions involving disjunction, negation, or cycles. This means semantic faceted search retains the ease-of-use of other faceted search systems, and gets close to the expressiveness of query languages such as SPARQL.

Acknowledgments. We would like to thank the 20 students, from the University of Rennes 1 and the INSA engineering school, for their volunteer participation to the usability evaluation.

References

[AG08] Angles, R., Gutierrez, C.: The expressive power of SPARQL. In: Sheth, A.P., Staab, S., Dean, M., Paolucci, M., Maynard, D., Finin, T., Thirunarayan, K. (eds.) ISWC 2008. LNCS, vol. 5318, pp. 114–129. Springer, Heidelberg (2008)

[BKK05] Bernstein, A., Kaufmann, E., Kaiser, C.: Querying the semantic web with Ginseng: A guided input natural language search engine. In: Work. Information Technology and Systems (WITS) (2005)

[Fer09] Ferré, S.: Camelis: a logical information system to organize and browse a collection of documents. Int. J. General Systems 38(4) (2009)

[FHD11] Ferré, S., Hermann, A., Ducassé, M.: Semantic faceted search: Safe and expressive navigation in rdf graphs. Research report (2011)

[FHH04] Fikes, R., Hayes, P.J., Horrocks, I.: OWL-QL - a language for deductive query answering on the semantic web. J. Web Semantic 2(1), 19–29 (2004)

[HEE+02] Hearst, M., Elliott, A., English, J., Sinha, R., Swearingen, K., Yee, K.-P.: Finding the flow in web site search. Communications of the ACM 45(9), 42–49 (2002)

[HvOH06] Hildebrand, M., van Ossenbruggen, J., Hardman, L.: /facet: A browser for heterogeneous semantic web repositories. In: Cruz, I., Decker, S., Allemang, D., Preist, C., Schwabe, D., Mika, P., Uschold, M., Aroyo, L.M. (eds.) ISWC 2006. LNCS, vol. 4273, pp. 272–285. Springer, Heidelberg (2006)

[LMZ+07] Lu, J., Ma, L., Zhang, L., Brunner, J.S., Wang, C., Pan, Y., Yu, Y.: SOR: A practical system for ontology storage, reasoning and search (demo). In: Int. Conf. Very Large Databases (VLDB), VLDB Endowment, pp. 1402–1405. ACM, New York (2007)

[Mar06] Marchionini, G.: Exploratory search: from finding to understanding. Communications of the ACM 49(4), 41–46 (2006)

[MHS06] Mäkelä, E., Hyvönen, E., Saarela, S.: Ontogator — A semantic view-based search engine service for web applications. In: Cruz, I., Decker, S., Allemang, D., Preist, C., Schwabe, D., Mika, P., Uschold, M., Aroyo, L.M. (eds.) ISWC 2006. LNCS, vol. 4273, pp. 847–860. Springer, Heidelberg (2006)

[ODD06] Oren, E., Delbru, R., Decker, S.: Extending faceted navigation for RDF data. In: Cruz, I., Decker, S., Allemang, D., Preist, C., Schwabe, D., Mika, P., Uschold, M., Aroyo, L.M. (eds.) ISWC 2006. LNCS, vol. 4273, pp. 559–572. Springer, Heidelberg (2006)

[Sac00] Sacco, G.M.: Dynamic taxonomies: A model for large information bases. IEEE Transactions Knowledge and Data Engineering 12(3), 468–479 (2000)

[SP07] Sirin, E., Parsia, B.: SPARQL-DL: SPARQL query for OWL-DL. In: Golbreich, C., Kalyanpur, A., Parsia, B. (eds.) Work. OWL Experiences and Directions (OWLED). CEUR-WS, vol. 258 (2007)

[ST09] Sacco, G.M., Tzitzikas, Y. (eds.): Dynamic taxonomies and faceted search. The information retrieval series. Springer, Heidelberg (2009)

[SVH07] Suominen, O., Viljanen, K., HyvÃnen, E.: User-centric faceted search for semantic portals. In: Franconi, E., Kifer, M., May, W. (eds.) ESWC 2007. LNCS, vol. 4519, pp. 356–370. Springer, Heidelberg (2007)

Towards a Collaborative Framework for Image Annotation and Search

Yi Hong* and Stephan Reiff-Marganiec

Department of Computer Science
University of Leicester, UK, LE1 7RH

Abstract. Users tag images with plain text information, which is then used as the basis for search. For the large amount of digital images available on the web this becomes challenging because the tags are abstract concepts whose relationship is undefined. For effective search which requires reasoning on concepts and their relations one requires richer data structures for tagging and one needs to take into account the confidence and credibility of the tagging user. In this paper, we introduce a novel collaborative framework for image annotation, which allows users to create tags that are based on a concept repository which provides a hierarchical context for them as well as allowing to define relationships among said concepts. It also provides a new and systematic way to establish user credibility as well as to compute the truthfulness or reliability of a particular statement, which are used for ranking search results. A prototype has been implemented using this approach and we will show some examples to explain our methodology in detail.

1 Introduction

In recent years the number of images available online has increased significantly leading to a problem of "information overload" in the sense that finding what one is looking for becomes hard. Tagging or annotating has become a popular way of adding searchable information to images, especially in shared environments such as social networking websites. An image tag is a small piece of plain text or some keywords attached to a specific area of an image. It helps users in organising and searching image content. However, it raises a challenging question about how to structure metadata to enable users to describe, extract and search information based on images in a more accurate and efficient way.

Currently there are a number of tagging approaches available. Generally these are based on keywords, but there have also been some efforts centered around ontologies. We will now highlight some problems of the keyword-based tagging approaches and some known issues existing in semantic-oriented tagging frameworks [8]. Keyword-based tagging approaches have the following drawbacks:

---

* This work was partially supported by Leverhulme Trust Funded "Tracing Networks" Programme.

Ambiguous semantics. In traditional image tagging system, a tag is normally a freely-chosen, non-hierarchical keyword or term. The tag in several pictures can be identical but the meaning maybe ambiguous. For example, plain text "date" tagged on an image might have different interpretation. It may refer to a day on the calendar, a fruit or the image is showing someone out on a date. Because the word has several meanings and the context of its use is not mentioned it is unclear what is meant. Similarly, a system is unable to tell whether the picture with tag "mouse" is referring to a computing device or an animal, something totally different.

Inadequate support for describing relationships. Current tagging systems are focused on labelling elements in the picture rather than the relationships among them, but in the real world specifying relationships between entities is as important as identifying the entities themselves. For example, a user can select two tagging areas on the image and annotates them with "cat" and "mouse", but most annotation systems do not provide enough support to describe the relationship between them in a formal way e.g. "the cat is chasing the mouse" (but not "the mouse is chasing the cat", or even "the cat is sleeping near a [computer] mouse").

Ability to perform automatic reasoning. Unstructured plain text tags do not allow to perform any reasoning tasks along with the search. For example, given a query "display all images with two animals on it", the system will not be able to answer this question because it does not have sufficient knowledge to reason about the facts, such as e.g. cats and mice being in fact animals. Due to the previous point there can also not be any reasoning for searching for pictures where for example "mice are chasing cats".

To overcome the limitation of traditional tagging approaches, semantic tagging applications have been developed e.g. [11]. These are also not perfect:

Maintaining domain-specific ontology without domain experts. Many of these systems are developed specifically for a particular domain (e.g. Medicine, Bioinformatics etc.) and are normally implemented on the basis of a domain-specific ontology. Although these ontologies provide a formal knowledge representation as a set of concepts and relationships within this particular domain which fits and works quite well, the ontologies need to be maintained by domain experts in collaboration with ontology developers. Long-term maintenance may become an issue.

Describing truthfulness and reliability of a statement. Current semantic tagging applications do not have the functionality to say how truthful or reliable user's statement is. The system does not support statements such as "I have strong evidence to believe that there is a cat in the tagging area" or "It is probably a cat in the picture, but I am not sure about it", nor a way to express these in any other form.

Measuring user credibility in collaborative environment. Most collaborative image tagging applications do not take into account the trustworthiness of a statement and the reputation of a user based on their expertise. E.g. Alex is a zoologist and she believes the animal in the picture is a house cat without a doubt while a 5 year old child tagged it as a lion. The trustworthiness of the opinion or statement should be determined by both the credibility of a user in a certain field along with how certain they are in making the judgement.

In this paper, we introduce a novel collaborative framework for image annotation, which allows users to create tags that are based on a concept repository which provides a hierarchical context for them as well as allowing to define relationships among said concepts. It also provides a new and systematic way to establish user credibility as well as to compute the truthfulness or reliability of a particular statement, which are used for ranking search results.

The next section will introduce the framework, section 3 will look at the implementation and evaluation. Section 4 shows related work and section 5 completes the paper with conclusions and an outlook to future work.

2 Collaborative Image Annotation and Search Framework

We propose a framework for image annotation and search in collaborative working environments to address the problems listed above. The framework is built on the basis of an *Image Annotation Ontology*, which functions as an abstract data model for organising and storing tagging data. It provides the infrastructure for annotators to link a tag to the predefined concept within a conceptual-semantic lexical database. This forms our knowledge base, therefore a reasoner can be used to exploit implicit knowledge as the tagging data are structured in a machine readable and understandable way. The tagging framework also allows users to define the degree of uncertainty of a statement. This is called certainty factor and will subsequently be used in conjunction with user credibility to compute the truthfulness of statements. This additional user context will greatly improve the efficiency and accuracy of a query. We will illustrate the main components and steps with a few examples in the following sections.

2.1 Data Model

To allow for reasoning and structuring the tagging information an underlying structure is needed. The basic structure of the Image Annotation Ontology is shown in Fig. 1. This structure allows to store information about a tagging area from the image and the relevant annotations as in conventional image tagging system. In addition to that, assumptions concerning a subject-predicate-object triple or a link between tagged area and resources can be stored. Every assumption is associated with an original certainty factor given by the annotator. Each individual user is assigned a set of credibility values for the different domains in which they annotate according to their expertise and reputation in that domain.

Resources are a group of synonyms defined in the WordNet lexical database, organised into hierarchies by hypernym (or hyponyms). A hypernym is referred as an "is a" relationship, for example the phrase *airplane is a craft* can be used to

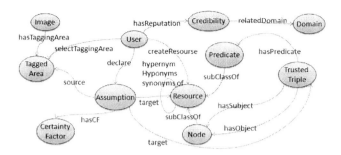

Fig. 1. Image Annotation Ontology Overview

Table 1. hypernym, hypernyms and synonyms of "aircraft" in WordNet

```
airplane, aeroplane, plane
 heavier-than-air_craft
   aircraft
     craft
       vehicle
         conveyance, transport
           instrumentality, instrumentation
             artifact, artefact
                .........
```

describe the hyponymic relationship between airplane and craft. The WordNet hierarchy for the word "aircraft" [16] is shown in Table 1.

While linking a tagging area to a term defined within WordNet, the definition of the term as well as the whole branch of the hypernym tree describing the semantic relations between these nodes, will be added to the triple store to populate the knowledge base. A user is free to create new terms by adding a new branch to the tree. A new term is fully defined as long as all leaf nodes in its branch are linked to already predefined terms.

Using WordNet provides us with an ontology that is not domain specific, but rather generic and that is maintained in a collaborative fashion. In addition it is not specific to our application and hence maintenance becomes a property somewhat distant from our immediate concerns.

2.2 Uncertainty in Trusted-Triple Graph

The subject-predicate-object relation mentioned in the previous section is common to ontologies and the usual structure used for storage is a Triple Graph. We are proposing an extension to Triple graphs to include a certainty factor (cF)[10] which is a number from -1.0 to 1.0 indicating how accurate or certain a user is about an assumption. Positive certainty means the user basically believes the assumption is a true statement, but he or she is possibly not 100% certain. Negative certainty means a disagreement with a given assumption, but might

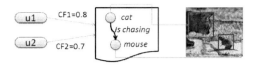

Fig. 2. An example of user's opinion on a statement

not rule out the possibility. For example, a statement such as "The blonde girl wearing the blue T-shirt is Alice" might be given a number such as 0.95 from a friend of hers; who would be reasonably certain of the fact. But if you had never met Alice, but heard that she is an Asian girl then you will probably give a negative certainty number, say -0.7 as generally Asians are not blonde. Assume $cF(u, s)$ is the original certainty factor given by a user u for assumption s. To combine the certainty factor and user reputation we define the concept of a composite user certainty-credibility factor $CF(u, s, r_d)$ applying to an assumption s made by a user u with reputation r in a domain d. CF is defined as follows:

$$CF(u, s, r_d) = r_d \cdot CF(u, s) \quad (1)$$

where s is a subject-predicate-object triple or an assumption about the relationship between tagging area and a predefined concept, $CF(u, s)$ is the certainty factor given by user u on s, and r_d is the user's reputation r in domain d.

We will come back in section 2.3 to explain how r_d is calculated. To compute the overall certainty-credibility factor CF_s based on all available judgements of all users (e.g. $u1, u2$) over the same statement s, we combine $CF_1 = CF(u_1, s, r_{d_1})$ and $CF_2 = CF(u_2, s, r_{d_2})$ using the parallel function [10] in (2):

$$CF_s = \begin{cases} CF_1 + CF_2(1\text{-}CF_1), & \text{if } CF_1, CF_2 \geq 0, \\ CF_1 + CF_2(1 + CF_1), & \text{if } CF_1, CF_2 < 0 \\ \dfrac{CF_1 + CF_2}{1 - min(|CF_1|, |CF_2|)}, & \text{other} \end{cases} \quad (2)$$

For example, consider the statement "a cat is chasing a mouse" shown in Figure 1. For $CF_1 = 0.8$ and $CF_2 = 0.7$, we have $CF = 0.8 + 0.7 \cdot (1 - 0.8) = 0.94$.

In this case, the overall composite user certainty-credibility factor is 0.94, significantly above the average of the individual users' claims, which might come as a surprise. There is a certain sense in this: if many user's tend to claim the same thing with reasonable confidence then one can overall be more confident in it actually being true and the effect of people being 'shy' in claiming certainty becomes reduced. However, it also stops us from arguing that the a statement is 'twice as true' as another just because it has double the score.

2.3 User Credibility Extraction

We need to obtain the reputation [9] r of a user to calculate the user certainty-credibility factor. The expertise factor [7] defines the degree of a user's competency to provide an accurate prediction in a particular field. In our case, the reputation r of a user u in a domain d, it is defined by (3)

$$r(u,d) = \beta(u,d) \left(1 - \frac{\Sigma_{s \in D(s)} \Sigma_{a \in U(s)} |CF(u,s) - CF(a,s)|}{|D(s)|}\right) \quad (3)$$

where $CF(u,s)$ is the original certainty factor given by user u on s, $U(s)$ is a set of users who commented on statement s (excluding user u), $D(s)$ is the statement set in the domain of target statements s, and $\beta(u,c)$ is the activity weighting and is defined as $1 - (1/n)$ (n is the number of comments within this category), meaning that a user will be assigned a higher value of expertise if making more comments for more statements within a particular category[1].

Note that we refer to $r(u,d)$ as r_d if it is clear which user is concerned.

As can be seen in formula (3), the reputation of an annotator is determined by several aspects. In general, (a) the more statements in the same category a user commented the more likely are they to have specific expertise in the field and this will increase their reputation in this category, but only if (b) the opinions the user provided reflect the truthfulness of the actual statement as measured by the similarity between their judgement and judgements made by other users.

For example, our zoologist Alex commented on a lot of pictures regarding wildlife and her judgement is quite accurate in most cases, so normally her opinion in this domain does not differ much from the general public including other zoologists. Also, the annotations she created about wildlife were generally accepted by the community. In this case, Alex should have a hight reputation in the wildlife domain. While (say) a computer scientist called Tom also made lots of comments on wildlife, but his opinions received negative feedback; therefore he is less credible than Alex in this domain.

2.4 Query and Reasoning

So far we have presented how image information is enhanced with semantic data and other aspects. This is the preparation for successful searches. The Annotation Ontology model we used for structuring the tagging data and user context makes it possible for the system to run intelligent queries in conjunction with a reasoning component. Queries can be defined by graph patterns rather than simple keywords. It allows for more flexible ways of obtaining answers for queries. A modified version of our example in the introduction could be:

"Display all images with two animals in them, along with what is happening between them"

A specific variant of that query might be 'find all pictures where mice are chasing cats'. This query is concerned with entities and their relationships in the picture. Our trusted-triple repository, which is built on top of the Image Annotation Ontology, contains the information about the tagged areas and their

---

[1] Bear with us! We are not claiming that just because someone makes lots of comments they are more qualified to do so.

relationships. It also contains the hypernym hierarchy (e.g. the fact that a cat is an animal) derived from the WordNet database. In other words, the background knowledge we need to answer this query is already captured by the data model. Apart from this, we will need a set of inferencing rules to perform the reasoning. To formulate the questions in a formal way, we rewrite it as listed below.

```
Ask for: ?a1 ?relation ?a2
Image(?i),appearsOn(?a1,?i),appearsOn(?a2,?i)
Animal(?a1),Animal(?a2),?relation(?a1,?a2)
```

This query will have to be run together with several deductive reasoning rules (rules of the form "antecedents → consequent"), to get the search results. Examples of these are:

```
Mouse(?a),hyponymOf(Mouse, Animal)-> Animal(?a)
Cat(?a),hyponymOf(Cat, Animal)-> Animal(?a)
```

Clearly if one had to specify all of these this would not be sensible. However, the reasoning rules can be rewritten in a more generic and reusable form. The relation "hyponymOf" is a transitive property and the second rule will compute the transitive closure over the relation "hyponymOf".

```
Concept(?c1),Concept(?c2),?c1(?x),hyponymOf(?c1, ?c2)-> ?c2(?x)
hyponymOf(?c1,?c2),hyponymOf(?c2,?c3)->hyponymOf(?c1,?c3)
```

The query and inference rules are in fact graph patterns and they can be translated to SPARQL [2] queries and SWRL [3] rules. Though unbounded predicate support (such as *?relation*) is currently not available in many rule-based query languages such as SQWRL [13], we can still translate it to SPARQL-DL.

In addition to this, as we are using a trusted triple graph, we can also carry the information on uncertainty through the reasoning by attaching a certainty factor to each custom reasoning rule as suggested in [10].

2.5 Ranking

Once the search results are obtained they are ranked by the degree of truthfulness. This is calculated for every sub graph in the result set that matched the pattern. The weight of the subgraph is defined by the function:

$$W_G = \prod_{s \in T} CF_s \qquad (4)$$

where G is a trusted subgraph matching the search pattern, T contains all triples in G, and CF_s is the overall composite certainty-credibility factor of triple s.

W_G will then be used in the ORDER BY clause of the concrete query implementation providing a result set with the most trusted results at the top.

3 Implementation and Evaluation

A web-based prototype application has been implemented in Java. Figure 4 illustrates the architecture of the system, which consists of several parts. A web-based annotation interface allows users to annotate the image. An annotator can describe concepts and relationships in the image by constructing a set of trusted triple statements, with help of an extendable WordNet lexical database and a remote OpenCalais[1] service. WordNet groups the synonymous words, provides precise definition of terms and defines the semantic relation between these synonym sets. It works in conjunction with the OpenCalais service to help user identify the possible topics (category or domain) of an image. Besides, an annotator can also specify the degree of certainty about an assumption. A screenshot of the interface is shown in Fig. 3. For every triple statement, the overall user certainty and credibility factor will be computed by a certainty calculator and a user credibility calculator respectively; these will then be combined into the composite user certainty-credibility factor used for ranking search results. The query engine retrieves annotation data from the trusted triple repository by means of SPARQL queries and a native OWL API. The system also utilises both description logics (DL) and deductive rule-based reasoning for inferencing. The search screen is currently simply a textbox that allows entry of a query and the results show a ranked list of images that match the given query – both not very exciting to look at in a screenshot.

We are evaluating our approach with users from the archaeology community. "Tracing Networks: Craft Traditions in the Ancient Mediterranean and Beyond"

Fig. 3. Screenshow of the prototype implementation

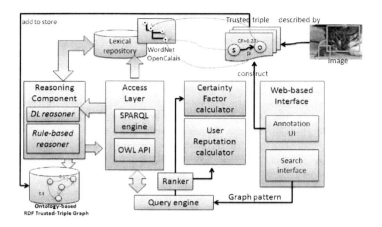

Fig. 4. System architecture overview

[4] is a joint archaeological research programme, which involves archaeologists and Computer Science researchers. This research programme investigates the network of contacts across and beyond the Mediterranean region, between the late Bronze Age and the late classical period (1500-200 BCE). Researchers in different sub-projects have already gathered massive amounts of image resources and cross-team knowledge sharing and analysis are vital – and being able to retrieve the right pictures is essential. The intention is to apply the presented approach to enhance the collaboration of teams and enable future research by others.

4 Related Work

Various approaches and techniques for tagging have been proposed by different research groups in the last few years, especially to identifying the vocabulary such as folksonomies [15]. A survey of approaches for various semantic annotation techniques is presented in [14]. We have already in the introduction summarised the shortcoming of these works. Many other existing collaborative semantic tagging systems such as SemKey make use of external resources such as WordNet in their approaches [12,6]. However, most available systems and frameworks are more focused on metadata modelling, concept identification and relationship extraction instead of representing uncertainty, user credibility and taking into account all these factors for reasoning and searching. The closest effort on uncertainty is the W3C Uncertainty Reasoning for the World Wide Web Incubator Group (URW3-XG), which proposed an Uncertainty Ontology in their report in 2008 [5]; however their focus is more defining the data structure to hold uncertainty information than on its calculation and use.

5 Conclusion and Future Plan

In this paper, we identified problems and limitations of available tagging systems and proposed a framework for image annotation and search in a collaborative environment. We developed an ontology-based data model for identifying concepts, relationships and storing context regarding users. The WordNet lexical database, which describes the semantic relations betweens different terms is used to disambiguate the keywords and populate the knowledge base. We also introduced a systematic way to represent uncertainty of a statement as well as user credibility measurement; these two factors are combined into a composite uncertainty-credibility factor, which is used for ranking the search results. We explained with examples how rule-based reasoning can be used in conjunction with graph patterns to help us answer advanced queries. Finally, we presented a prototype implementation that illustrates our methodology.

We are currently looking into several areas of future work, such as (1) evaluating the approach with a variety of users from different communities, (2) considering a more complex user context to provide a more context-aware search and (3) an evaluation of how these factors affect search results and ranking.

References

1. Calais: Connect. Everything, http://www.opencalais.com/
2. SPARQL Query Language for RDF , http://www.w3.org/TR/rdf-sparql-query
3. SWRL: A Semantic Web Rule Language Combining OWL and RuleMl, http://www.w3.org/Submission/SWRL/
4. Tracing Networks: Craft Traditions in the Ancient Mediterranean and Beyond, www.tracingnetworks.ac.uk
5. Uncertainty Reasoning for the World Wide Web (March 2008), http://www.w3.org/2005/Incubator/urw3/XGR-urw3-20080331/
6. Cernea, D.A., Del Moral, E., Labra Gayo, J.E.: SOAF: Semantic Indexing System Based on Collaborative Tagging. Interdisciplinary Journal of E-Learning and Learning Objects 4, 137–149 (2008)
7. Cho, J., Kwon, K., Park, Y.: Q-rater: A collaborative reputation system based on source credibility theory. Expert Systems with Applications 36(2, Part 2), 3751–3760 (2009)
8. Fu, W.-T., Kannampallil, T., Kang, R., He, J.: Semantic imitation in social tagging. ACM Trans. Comput.-Hum. Interact. 17, 12:1–12:37 (2010)
9. Gutowska, A., Buckley, K.: A computational distributed reputation model for b2c e-commerce. In: Proceedings of the 2008 IEEE/WIC/ACM International Conference on Web Intelligence and Intelligent Agent Technology, vol. 03, pp. 72–76. IEEE Computer Society, Washington, DC, USA (2008)
10. Heckerman, D.E., Shortliffe, E.H.: From certainty factors to belief networks. Artificial Intelligence in Medicine 4(1), 35–52 (1992)
11. Kim, H.-L., Scerri, S., Breslin, J., Decker, S., Kim, H.-G.: The State of the Art in Tag Ontologies: A Semantic Model for Tagging and Folksonomies. In: International Conference on Dublin Core and Metadata Applications, Berlin, Germany (2008)

12. Marchetti, A., Tesconi, M., Ronzano, F., Rosella, M., Minutoli, S.: Semkey: A semantic collaborative tagging system. In: Proc. WWW 2007 Workshop on Tagging and Metadata for Social Information Organization, Banff, Canada (May 2007)
13. O'Connor, M.J., Das, A.K.: SQWRL: a Query Language for OWL. In: OWL: Experiences and Directions (OWLED), Fifth International Workshop (2009)
14. Reeve, L.: Survey of semantic annotation platforms. In: Proceedings of the 2005 ACM Symposium on Applied Computing, pp. 1634–1638. ACM Press, New York (2005)
15. Smith, G.: Folksonomy: social classification, Atomiq (August 2004)
16. Michael, M.: Stark and Richard F. Riesenfeld. Wordnet: An electronic lexical database. In: Proceedings of 11th Eurographics Workshop on Rendering. MIT Press, Cambridge (1998)

Semantic Reasoning with SPARQL in Heterogeneous Multi-context Systems*

Peter Schüller and Antonius Weinzierl

Institut für Informationssysteme, Technische Universität Wien
Favoritenstraße 9-11, A-1040 Vienna, Austria
{schueller,weinzierl}@kr.tuwien.ac.at

Abstract. Multi-Context Systems (MCSs) are an expressive framework for interlinking heterogeneous knowledge systems, called contexts. Possible contexts are ontologies, relational databases, logic programs, RDF triplestores, etc. MCSs contain bridge rules to specify knowledge exchange between contexts. We extend the MCS formalism and propose SPARQL-MCS where knowledge exchange is specified in the style of SPARQL CONSTRUCT queries. Different from previous approaches to variables in MCSs, we do not impose any restrictions on contexts. To achieve this, we introduce a general approach for variable substitutions in heterogeneous systems. We define syntax and semantics of SPARQL-MCS and investigate fixpoint evaluation of monotonic MCSs.

1 Introduction

Multi-Context Systems (MCSs) [4] are the result of a successful line of research [9,12,5] to describe interlinking of heterogeneous knowledge bases (called contexts) using (possibly nonmonotonic) bridge rules.

Intuitively, a bridge rule $1:u \leftarrow (2:v), not(3:w)$ at context C_1 adds *formula* u to the knowledge base of C_1 whenever *belief* v is *accepted* by context C_2 and w is *not accepted* by C_3. However, MCS bridge rules are not designed to contain variables, which limits the applicability of the formalism in practice.

In this paper we extend MCS and introduce SPARQL-MCS, where information flow is specified using SPARQL queries with variables. We propose SPARQL-MCS, where knowledge exchange is specified by SPARQL bridges of the form

CONSTRUCT $2:\{$?Person $\langle \#needsMed \rangle$?Med. $\}$
  WHERE $\{$ $(1:person(?Person, ?Id))$ AND $(3:require(?Id, ?Med))$ $\}$

which intuitively states that an RDF-triple[1] ?Person $\langle \#needsMed \rangle$?Med is added to context C_2 if context C_1 believes an atom *person* and context C_3

---

* This research has been supported by the Vienna Science and Technology Fund (WWTF) project ICT08-020.
[1] RDF is a semantic web framework for storing information as graphs, encoded in (subject predicate object) triples.

believes an atom *require* such that their join (over contexts) yields a mapping of variables *?Person* and *?Med* that can be substituted into the RDF-triple.

While this example looks quite simple, it already demonstrates a difficulty arising from the combination of variables and heterogeneous contexts, namely that values must be converted between formalisms. For example a person *sue* must be represented as an IRI in an RDF-triple, while a database might require a format different from ⟨#*sue*⟩. Furthermore, substituting variables into formulas and beliefs requires knowledge about the inner structure of these objects: replacing variable *?X* in formula *p*("*foo?X*", *?X*) is not a matter of simple search-and-replace, depending on the application scenario, one or both occurances of *?X* might be a target for variable substitution.

Both issues are likely to arise in the heterogeneous setting of MCSs where different formalisms are interlinked. These issues are not addressed in a satisfactory way by existing proposals to add variables to MCSs: in [7], variables are seen as schematic variables only, i.e., a bridge rule is only a short notation for the set of instantiated (thus variable-free) bridge rules. In [8], bridge rules with variables require that the contexts of the MCS adhere to a given syntax for predicates; and similar in [13] where only first order languages are considered. The first solution is infeasible for large numbers of instantiations, while the second and third cannot capture formalisms that do not use predicate syntax, e.g., RDF stores.

In this work, we propose a uniform solution for combining heterogeneous logics with variables, thereby solving both issues, and apply that solution in the SPARQL-MCS formalism. Our main contributions are as follows.

- We introduce the syntax of SPARQL-MCS where information flow is specified using SPARQL queries. To that end we extend the core fragment of SPARQL (cf. [2]) to query arbitrary data sources, without restricting to first-order theories.
- To handle variables and variable substitutions in heterogeneous systems, we propose a framework for variable substitutions. The framework uses a global set of (abstract) entities that can be substituted for variables, and consists of two functions for

  - applying variable substitutions to expressions, and for
  - matching an expression with beliefs of a context to obtain variable substitutions.

  This framework allows us to view expressions with variables as objects without inner structure, therefore we are able to introduce variables without adding restrictions on contexts. Furthermore, our approach captures conversion between entities in different logics.

- We give a declarative characterization of the semantics of SPARQL-MCS.
- For the special case of monotonic SPARQL-MCS, we give a fixed-point characterization of its semantics.

2 Preliminaries

A heterogeneous nonmonotonic MCS [4] consists of *contexts*, each composed of a knowledge base with an underlying *logic*, and a set of *bridge rules* which control the information flow between contexts. A logic $L = (\mathbf{KB}_L, \mathbf{BS}_L, \mathbf{ACC}_L)$ is an abstraction, which allows to capture many monotonic and nonmonotonic logics, e.g., classical logic, description logics, default logics. It consists of the following components; the first two intuitively describe syntax, the third semantics:

- $\mathbf{KB}_L$ is the set of well-formed knowledge bases of L. We assume each element of $\mathbf{KB}_L$ is a set of "formulas".
- $\mathbf{BS}_L$ is the set of possible belief sets, where a belief set is a set of "beliefs".
- $\mathbf{ACC}_L : \mathbf{KB}_L \to 2^{\mathbf{BS}_L}$ is a function describing the semantics of the logic by assigning to each knowledge base a set of acceptable belief sets.

Each context has its own logic, which allows to model heterogeneous systems.

Example 1. All kinds of logics can be captured with this definition. In the following we present specific logics, which we use in later examples in this paper.

i) For quantifier- and function-free, predicate logic over language Σ, the logic $L_{CL} = (\mathbf{KB}_{CL}, \mathbf{BS}_{CL}, \mathbf{ACC}_{CL})$ is such that $\mathbf{KB}_{CL}$ is the set of well-formed Σ-formulas (using predicates, and variables, but no function symbols or quantifiers), $\mathbf{BS}_{CL}$ is the set of sets of atoms wrt. Σ, and for each $kb \in \mathbf{KB}_{CL}$ is $N \in \mathbf{ACC}_{CL}(kb)$ iff N is a model of kb under the closed-world assumption.

ii) For an RDF triplestore [2], the logic $L_{RDF} = (\mathbf{KB}_{RDF}, \mathbf{BS}_{RDF}, \mathbf{ACC}_{RDF})$ is such that $\mathbf{KB}_{RDF}$ consists of all valid RDF-triplestore contents, including syntax like '⟨#foo⟩ ⟨#bar⟩ 1 ; ⟨#baz⟩ 'abc' .'. $\mathbf{BS}_{RDF}$ contains all valid RDF graphs, i.e., sets of RDF triples (without shortcut syntax). $\mathbf{ACC}_{RDF}$ accepts for each element in $\mathbf{KB}_{RDF}$ the corresponding RDF graph from $\mathbf{BS}_{RDF}$.

iii) For an $\mathcal{AL}$ description logic [3] the logic $L_{\mathcal{AL}}$ is such that $\mathbf{KB}_{\mathcal{AL}}$ is the set of well-formed theories in $\mathcal{AL}$, $\mathbf{BS}_{\mathcal{AL}}$ is the powerset of the set of well-formed assertions $C(o)$ with C a concept name and o an individual name of $\mathcal{AL}$, and $\mathbf{ACC}_{\mathcal{AL}}(kb)$ returns the set of concept assertions entailed by kb. □

Ordinary MCSs (in the sense of [4]) model information flow between contexts using *bridge rules* without variables: a bridge rule can add information to a context, depending on the belief sets accepted at other contexts [4]. Let $\mathcal{L} = (L_1, \ldots, L_n)$ be a tuple of logics. An L_k-*bridge rule* r over $\mathcal{L}$ is of the form $(k:s) \leftarrow (c_1:p_1), \ldots, (c_j:p_j), \mathbf{not}\ (c_{j+1}:p_{j+1}), \ldots, \mathbf{not}\ (c_m:p_m)$ where $1 \leq c_i \leq n$, p_i is an element of some belief set of L_{c_i}, and k refers to the context receiving formula s. We denote by $h_b(r)$ the formula s in the head of r.

An *MCS* [4] $M = (C_1, \ldots, C_n)$ is a collection of contexts $C_i = (L_i, kb_i, br_i)$, $1 \leq i \leq n$, where $L_i = (\mathbf{KB}_i, \mathbf{BS}_i, \mathbf{ACC}_i)$ is a logic, $kb_i \in \mathbf{KB}_i$ a knowledge base, and br_i is a set of L_i-bridge rules over $(L_1, \ldots, L_n)$.

Example 2. Let $M = (C_1, C_2)$ be an MCS where C_1 is an RDF triplestore about persons and their social security numbers while C_2 is a propositional logic checking the completeness of C_1; the respective logics are as in Example 1; knowledge bases are $kb_1 = \{\langle \#reg\rangle\ \langle \#person\rangle\ sue.\ \langle \#sue\rangle\ \langle \#ssn\rangle\ 123.\}$ and $kb_2 = \{sue \wedge has\_ssn \to data\_complete\}$. The information flow is given by two bridge rules of C_2 which are $(2 : sue) \leftarrow (1 : \langle \#reg\rangle\ \langle \#person\rangle\ sue.)$ and $(2 : has\_ssn) \leftarrow (1 : \langle \#sue\rangle\ \langle \#ssn\rangle\ 123.)$ □

Let $M = (C_1, \ldots, C_n)$ be an MCS, a sequence $S = (S_1, \ldots, S_n)$ with $S_i \in \mathbf{BS}_i$ is called a *belief state* of M. Semantics of MCSs is defined in terms of *equilibria*, intuitively, a belief state S which is acceptable at every context given the information exchange of applicable bridge rules. A bridge rule r of context C_k is *applicable* in S if its positive (negative) body literals are present (absent) at their respective context's belief states, i.e., for a L_k bridge rule (over $\mathcal{L}$ as before) we write $r \in app(br_i, S)$ iff $p_\ell \in S_{c_\ell}$ for $1 \le \ell \le j$ and $p_\ell \notin S_{c_\ell}$ for $j < \ell \le n$.

A belief state $S = (S_1, \ldots, S_n)$ of M is an *equilibrium* [4] iff, for $1 \le i \le n$, the following condition holds: $S_i \in \mathbf{ACC}_i(kb_i \cup \{hd(r) \mid r \in app(br_i, S)\})$.

Example 3. In Example 2 there is one equilibrium $S = (S_1, S_2)$ with $S_1 = kb_1$ and $S_2 = \{sue, has\_ssn, data\_complete\}$. Both bridge rules are applicable in S. □

3 SPARQL-Based Multi-context Systems

SPARQL-MCS use the same formalism as ordinary MCSs for abstracting from contexts, but they use SPARQL queries to specify information flow and they allow the use of variables without imposing any restrictions on contexts. Note that, for simplicity, we do not consider blank nodes or value invention in our SPARQL-MCS. We proceed with a concrete example of a SPARQL-MCS and later on present all technical details for variable substitution, syntax and semantics of SPARQL-MCS.

Example 4. Our running example is a hospital information system M consisting of the following contexts: a patient data RDF triplestores $C_{patients}$, a laboratory test triplestore C_{lab}, a disease description logic ontology C_{onto}, and a (classical logic) decision support system C_{dss} which suggests proper treatments for patients. For brevity, we only consider patient 'Sue'. The knowledge bases are as follows:

$$\begin{aligned}
kb_{patients} &= \{\langle \#sue\rangle\ \langle \#ssn\rangle\ 123\ ;\ \langle \#allergy\rangle\ ab\_s\ .\ \}, \\
kb_{lab} &= \{\langle \#sue\rangle\ \langle \#xray\rangle\ pneumonia\ .\ \}, \\
kb_{onto} &= \{Pneumonia \sqcap Marker1 \sqsubseteq AtypPneumonia\}, \\
kb_{dss} &= \{need(Id, ab) \to (give(Id, ab\_s) \vee give(Id, ab2)), \\
&\quad \neg(\ give(Id, ab\_s) \wedge give(Id, ab2)\ ), \\
&\quad \neg(\ forbid(Id, Drug) \wedge give(Id, Drug)\ )\ \}.
\end{aligned}$$

$C_{patients}$ and C_{lab} are RDF triplestores using L_{RDF} (see Ex. 1). $C_{patients}$ stores Sue's social security number and an allergy to antibiotic 'ab_s'. C_{lab} stores blood and X-ray examinations results: '$pneumonia$' was detected in Sue's X-ray. C_{onto} uses $L_{\mathcal{AL}}$ and specifies that presence of a blood marker in combination with pneumonia indicates atypical pneumonia. C_{dss} uses L_{CL} and suggests medications using $give$, e.g., adding $\{need(sue, ab)\}$ to kb_{dss} causes C_{dss} to accept belief sets $\{need(sue, ab), give(sue, ab\_s)\}$ and $\{need(sue, ab), give(sue, ab2)\}$.

We have the following knowledge interlinking between contexts: C_{onto} imports X-ray and blood test results from $C_{patients}$, we indicate a need for antibiotic medication in C_{dss} whenever C_{onto} classifies a patient as having pneumonia, and we specifically require ab_s for atypical pneumonia. Furthermore, in C_{dss} we forbid administration of all drugs where an allergy is stored in $C_{patients}$.

Knowledge exchange is formulated with SPARQL-bridges as follows:

$$r_1 = \text{CONSTRUCT}\ onto: \{\ ?Test(?Id)\ \}$$
$$\text{WHERE}\ \{\ lab: ?Id\ ?T\ ?Test\ .$$
$$\text{FILTER}\ (?T = \textbf{xray} \vee ?T = \textbf{blood})\ \}$$
$$r_2 = \text{CONSTRUCT}\ dss: \{\ need(?Id, ab), forbid(?Id, ?Drug)\ \}$$
$$\text{WHERE}\ \{\ onto: Pneumonia(?Id)\ .$$
$$\text{OPT}\ \{\ patients: ?Id\ \langle \#allergy \rangle\ ?Drug\ \}\ \}$$
$$r_3 = \text{CONSTRUCT}\ dss: \{\ give(?Id, ab\_s)\ \}$$
$$\text{WHERE}\ \{\ onto: AtypPneumonia(?Id)\ \}$$

Bridge r_1 imports xray and blood test results from patients into the ontology. Bridge r_2 links pneumonia with a medication requirements (antibiotics) and optionally forbids drugs if an allergy is known. Bridge r_3 triggers administration of antibiotic 'ab_s' for atypical (severe form of) pneumonia. □

We next introduce the formalism that tackles the core challenge of variables in knowledge interlinking, then we formally introduce SPARQL-MCS syntax and semantics.

3.1 Abstract Variable Substitution

One of the strengths of MCSs is the abstract view on heterogeneous systems, where formulas and beliefs are unstructured objects. However, our SPARQL bridges use variables, therefore we need to establish a way how those variables interact with (probably variable-free) beliefs of contexts and formulas in knowledge bases.

Given an MCS M, we assume a set of variable symbols V which is common to all contexts; wlog. we assume $V = \{?X, ?Y, ?Z, \ldots\}$. With respect to a logic $L = (\mathbf{KB}_L, \mathbf{BS}_L, \mathbf{ACC}_L)$, there are two kinds of expressions containing variables: (a) $\mathcal{F}$-expressions $VE^{\mathbf{KB}_L}$, which are knowledge base formulas containing variables, and (b) $\mathcal{B}$-expressions $VE^{\mathbf{BS}_L}$, which are beliefs containing variables. Intuitively, an expression is a formula or a belief of L containing variables of V.

Substituting all variables in an $\mathcal{F}$-expression ($\mathcal{B}$-expression) yields a knowledge base formula $s \in \bigcup \mathbf{KB}_L$ (a belief $b \in \bigcup \mathbf{BS}_L$). Given expression e we denote by $vars(e)$ the set of all variables that occur in e.

Example 5 (ctd). For $C_{patients}$ which uses L_{RDF}, '$?X\ \langle \#allergy \rangle\ ?Y$' in $VE^{\mathbf{BS}_{RDF}}$ is used to query allergies of patients, while '$?X\ ?Y\ ?Z$' in $VE^{\mathbf{KB}_{RDF}}$ could be used to add arbitrary triples to $C_{patients}$.

For C_{onto}, '$Pneumonia(?Id)$' in $VE^{\mathbf{BS}_{\mathcal{AL}}}$ allows to query patients in the concept $Pneumonia$, and '$?Test(?Id)$' in $VE^{\mathbf{KB}_{\mathcal{AL}}}$ allows to assert membership of an individual $?Id$ in some concept $?Test$ in the ontology. □

As the shape of an object substituted for a variable depends on the specifics of the logic at hand, we introduce a finite, *abstract universe* U containing a context-independent representation of all individuals that can be substituted for variables in the system. A *variable mapping* (for short, mapping) $\mu : V \to U$ is a partial function mapping variables to individuals of the abstract universe. Such μ then is used to substitute variables in an expression with their context-dependent representation. Abusing notation, we also write μ for a mapping of multiple distinct variables and denote its signature by $V \to U$.

Example 6 (ctd). We represent patient Sue as $\mathbf{sue} \in U$. Intuitively, applying mapping $\mu_{ex} = \{?X \mapsto \mathbf{sue}\}$ to an RDF-triplestore expression '$?X \langle \#ssn \rangle \, 123$' maps object $\mathbf{sue}$ into an IRI and yields '$\langle \#sue \rangle \langle \#ssn \rangle \, 123$'. Applying μ_{ex} to $\mathcal{AL}$ expression '$Pneumonia(?X)$' maps object $\mathbf{sue}$ into individual constant 'sue' and yields '$Pneumonia(sue)$'. □

In the following we introduce an abstraction for (i) applying a mapping to a $\mathcal{F}$-expression, which yields a formula without variables, and for (ii) matching a $\mathcal{B}$-expression with a belief set of a certain context, which yields all matching variable mappings.

Definition 1. *Given sets V, U, and $VE^{\mathbf{KB}_L}$ as described above, a variable substitution $subst_L$ is a function $subst_L : VE^{\mathbf{KB}_L} \times (V \to U) \to \bigcup \mathbf{KB}_L$ such that $subst_L(e, \mu) = e'$ iff applying μ to e yields e' and $e' \in \bigcup \mathbf{KB}_L$.*

Intuitively, $subst_L$ applies the mapping μ to a given $\mathcal{F}$-expression e and yields a knowledge base formula e'. Defining $subst_L$ for a logic L has the effect of defining what '*applying substitution μ to expression e*' means for formulas of L.

Example 7 (ctd). Reusing μ_{ex}, $subst_{RDF}(?X \langle \#allergy \rangle \, ab1, \mu_{ex}) =$ '$\langle \#sue \rangle \langle \#allergy \rangle \, ab1$' and $subst_{\mathcal{AL}}(Pneumonia(?X), \mu_{ex}) =$ '$Pneumonia(sue)$'. Therefore, in L_{RDF} entities are substituted as IRIs, in $L_{\mathcal{AL}}$ as individual symbols. □

Definition 2. *Given sets V, U, and $VE^{\mathbf{BS}_L}$ as described above, a variable matching $match_L$ is a function $match_L : VE^{\mathbf{BS}_L} \times \mathbf{BS}_L \to 2^{V \to U}$ such that $match_L(e, bs) = \{\mu \mid applying\ \mu : V \to U\ to\ e\ yields\ some\ e' \in bs\}$.*

Intuitively, $match_L$ takes a $\mathcal{B}$-expression e and returns all mappings that, applied to e, yield a belief of bs. Similarly as above, $match_L$ captures what '*applying μ to e*' means for $\mathcal{B}$-expressions of L.

Example 8. Given belief set $bs = \{\langle \#sue \rangle \langle \#allergy \rangle \, ab1\} \in \mathbf{BS}_{RDF}$, we have $match_{RDF}(?X \langle \#allergy \rangle \, ab1,\ bs) = \{\mu_{ex}\}$ with μ_{ex} the only mapping. □

3.2 SPARQL-MCS Syntax

We modify SPARQL's CONSTRUCT$\{H\}$ WHERE$\{B\}$ queries to establish knowledge exchange between contexts. Instead of graph templates H we permit sets of $\mathcal{F}$-expressions that yield formulas which are compatible with the context which receives information from the query. Similarly, we extend the concept of graph pattern expressions B and SPARQL built-in conditions by allowing $\mathcal{B}$-expressions and elements of the universe U as basic building blocks. E.g., if a context is a propositional logic, then the pattern expression of our bridge allows to query that context with any propositional formula occuring at those positions where in ordinary SPARQL queries an RDF triple occurs.

Definition 3. *A graph pattern expression (gpe) wrt. logics $L_1, \ldots, L_n$ is recursively defined as follows:*
- *if p is a belief of logic L_i (there is a $bs \in \mathbf{BS}_i$ with $p \in bs$) then $(i : p)$ is a gpe,*
- *if $p \in VE^{\mathbf{BS}_{L_i}}$ is a $\mathcal{B}$-expression of L_i, then $(i : p)$ is a gpe,*
- *if P_1 and P_2 are gpes then so are $(P_1 \text{ AND } P_2)$, $(P_1 \text{ OPT } P_2)$, and $(P_1 \text{ UNION } P_2)$,*
- *if P is a gpe and R is a built-in condition (bic), then $(P \text{ FILTER } R)$ is a gpe.*

A bic is constructed using variables from V, objects from U, logical connectives $(\neg, \wedge, \vee)$, equality $(=)$, and the unary predicate 'bound':
- *if $?X, ?Y \in V$ and $o \in U$, then $\text{bound}(?X)$, $?X = o$, and $?X = ?Y$ are bics, and*
- *if R_1 and R_2 are bics, then $(\neg R_1)$, $(R_1 \vee R_2)$, and $(R_1 \wedge R_2)$ are bics.*

Definition 4. *An L_k-SPARQL bridge over logics $\mathcal{L} = (L_1, \ldots, L_n)$ is of the form*

$$\text{CONSTRUCT } k : \{H\} \text{ WHERE } \{P\}, \tag{1}$$

where $H \subseteq VE^{\mathbf{KB}_{L_k}}$, P is a gpe, and $1 \leq k \leq n$.

Definition 5. *A SPARQL-MCS $M = (C_1, \ldots, C_n)$ is a collection of contexts $C_i = (L_i, kb_i, sbr_i)$, $1 \leq i \leq n$, where $L_i = (\mathbf{KB}_i, \mathbf{BS}_i, \mathbf{ACC}_i)$ is a logic, $kb_i \in \mathbf{KB}_i$ a knowledge base, and sbr_i is a set of L_i-SPARQL bridges over $(L_1, \ldots, L_n)$.*

3.3 SPARQL-MCS Semantics

Semantics of SPARQL-MCS are defined in terms of equilibria, as for ordinary MCS, with the difference being in the notion of applicable bridges. Therefore we define semantics of SPARQL bridges, gearing the definitions to the SPARQL semantics in [2].

Analogous to applicable rules in ordinary MCSs, we first define how variable mappings are obtained from a SPARQL bridge and a belief state. We then describe how these variable mappings instantiate a set of CONSTRUCT templates in a SPARQL bridge. This set is then added to the respective knowledge bases and corresponds to the set of heads of applicable bridge rules in ordinary MCS.

For variable mappings the following operations are used: $dom(\mu)$ denotes the subset of V where the partial mapping μ is defined, furthermore we call two mappings μ_1 and μ_2 *compatible* iff for all $x \in dom(\mu_1) \cap dom(\mu_2)$ it holds that $\mu_1(x) = \mu_2(x)$.

We next define the semantics $[[\cdot]]_S$ of a gpe wrt. a belief state S in an MCS M. Note that the main difference to existing semantics of SPARQL are the first two cases.

Definition 6. *Let $S = (S_1, \ldots, S_n)$ be a belief state, $p \in \bigcup \mathbf{BS}_i$ a belief, $e \in VE^{\mathbf{BS}_i}$ a $\mathcal{B}$-expression, $1 \leq i \leq n$, P_1, P_2 gpes, and R a built-in condition (bic). Then $[[\cdot]]_S$ is recursively defined as follows:*

- $[[(i:p)]]_S = \{\emptyset\}$ *if* $p \in S_i$, $\emptyset$ *otherwise*,
- $[[(i:e)]]_S = match_{L_i}(e, S_i)$,
- $[[P_1 \text{ AND } P_2]]_S = \{\mu_1 \cup \mu_2 \mid \mu_1 \in [[P_1]]_S \text{ and } \mu_2 \in [[P_2]]_S \text{ are compatible}\}$,
- $[[P_1 \text{ OPT } P_2]]_S = \{\mu \mid \mu \in [[P_1 \text{ AND } P_2]]_S \text{ or } \mu \in \Omega\}$ *where*
  $\Omega = \{\mu \in [[P_1]]_S \mid \text{ for all } \mu' \in [[P_2]]_S, \mu \text{ and } \mu' \text{ are not compatible}\}$,
- $[[P_1 \text{ UNION } P_2]]_S = \{\mu \mid \mu \in [[P_2]]_S \text{ or } \mu \in [[P_2]]_S\}$, *and*
- $[[P_1 \text{ FILTER } R]]_S = \{\mu \in [[P_1]]_S \mid \mu \models R\}$.

where $\mu \models R$ holds (for variables $?X, ?Y \in V$, constant $o \in U$, and bics R', R_1, R_2) if R is of form

- *bound($?X$) and $?X \in dom(\mu)$*,
- *$?X = o$, $?X \in dom(\mu)$ and $\mu(?X) = o$*,
- *$?X = ?Y$, $?X \in dom(\mu), ?Y \in dom(\mu)$ and $\mu(?X) = \mu(?Y)$*,
- *$\neg(R')$ and $\mu \models R'$ does not hold*,
- *$(R_1 \vee R_2)$ and at least one of $\mu \models R_1$ and $\mu \models R_2$ holds*,
- *$(R_1 \wedge R_2)$ and $\mu \models R_1$ and $\mu \models R_2$*.

For a bridge r of form (1), and a belief state S, the set of constructed formulas $constr_k(r, S) = \{e \mid e = subst_{L_k}(h, \mu), \mu \in [[P]]_S, h \in H\}$ contains all knowledge base formulas resulting from substituting a head $h \in H$ with a variable mapping obtained from evaluating P wrt. S.[2] Finally, the set of formulas constructed at context C_k wrt. a belief state S is defined as $app_k(S) = \{constr_k(r, S) \mid r \in sbr_k\}$.

Example 9 (ctd). Consider bridge r_2 of our running example, its query expressions evaluated against belief state S with $S_{patients} = \{\langle\#sue\rangle \langle\#allergy\rangle \text{ ab\_s.}\}$ and $S_{onto} = \{Pneumonia(sue)\}$ yields a mapping $\mu = \{?Id \mapsto sue, ?Drug \mapsto ab\_s\}$. Similarly, for S' with $S'_{patients} = \emptyset$ and $S'_{onto} = S_{onto}$, mapping μ' is $\{?Id \mapsto sue\}$.

Now we have all necessary notions to define semantics of the whole system.

Definition 7. *A belief state $S = (S_1, \ldots, S_n)$ of an SPARQL-MCS M is an equilibrium iff for all $1 \leq i \leq n$ holds $S_i \in ACC_i(kb_i \cup app_i(S))$.*

Example 10 (ctd). Our running example has one equilibrium $S = (kb_{patients}, kb_{lab}, \{Pneumonia(sue)\}, \{need(sue, ab), forbid(sue, ab\_s), give(sue, ab2)\})$. □

---

[2] Note, that invalid formulas or formulas where not all variables were substituted, are simply ignored; furthermore if $[[P]]_S = \emptyset$, then $constr_k(r, S) = \emptyset$.

4 Monotonicity and Minimal Equilibria

Minimal equilibria are of special interest as they precisely capture that knowledge which necessarily follows from a given SPARQL-MCS with no superfluous information being present in such an equilibrium. Such a unique minimal equilibrium can be computed using the least fixed-point of an immediate-consequences operator.

This, however, only applies to monotonic SPARQL-MCS where all contexts and SPARQL bridges are *monotonic*. For SPARQL bridges, several options exist; e.g., if the OPT is disregard, the resulting bridges are monotonic. For a context C_i, it is monotonic iff i) for all belief states S holds that the semantics gives a unique result, i.e., $\mathbf{ACC}_i(kb_i \cup app_i(S)) = \{N\}$, and ii) this result is monotonic in S, i.e., for all belief states $S \subseteq S'$ with $\mathbf{ACC}_i(kb_i \cup app_i(S)) = \{N\}$ and $\mathbf{ACC}_i(kb_i \cup app_i(S)) = \{N'\}$ holds $N \subseteq N'$ where $S \subseteq S'$ holds if $S = (S_1, \ldots, S_n), S' = (S'_1, \ldots, S'_n)$ and for all $1 \leq i \leq n$ holds $S_i \subseteq S'_i$.

We give the immediate-consequences operator on monotonic SPARQL-MCS:

Definition 8. *Let M be an MCS and $\mathbf{S}$ the set of all belief states of M, the immediate-consequences operator $T_M : \mathbf{S} \to \mathbf{S}$ is defined as $T_M(S) = (S'_1, \ldots, S'_n)$ where for all $1 \leq i \leq n$ we have $ACC_i(kb_i \cup app_i(S)) = \{S'_i\}$.*

One can show that the following holds:

Proposition 1. *Let M be a monotonic SPARQL-MCS and T_M the respective immediate-consequences operator, then T_M is monotonic and continous.*

Using the Knaster-Tarski theorem we therefore conclude that the minimal equilibrium S_m of M equals the least-fixed point of T_M, i.e.,

$$S_m = \mathit{lfp}(T_M) = T_M(T_M(\ldots T_M((\emptyset_1, \ldots, \emptyset_n))\ldots)).$$

As our abstract universe U and the set of bridge queries are finite, it follows that each set of constructed formulas, $app_i(S)$, for any belief state S and context C_i is finite. Therefore the least-fixed point of T_M is reached after finitely many steps.

For non-monotonic SPARQL-MCS (by non-monotonic contexts or unrestricted SPARQL bridges), the problem of finding an equilibrium becomes harder as recursive negation comes into play (see also [11]) as there is a significant increase in computational complexity even for bridge rules without variables (cf. [4]).

5 Related and Future Work

An existing proposal to support reasoning with variables in bridge rules of ordinary MCSs extends logics in a bottom-up way to 'relational logics' [8] by adding an extra set of predicate symbols and variables that can be used in bridge rules. Different from that, our approach is top-down as we introduce an intermediate variable mapping layer, which does not impose any restrictions on a context's logic or syntax. We also extend bridge rules, allowing for more powerful queries via the OPT and FILTER conditions.

Note that the extension of [8] closely follows the way variables are treated in logic programming where the task of instantiating (grounding) a logic program with its universe of constants is a problem that is very relevant for the performance of current solver engines. In this work, we disregard this issue and focus on the formalism of substitution itself. Nevertheless, grounding strategies, e.g., [10], are highly relevant for implementing SPARQL-MCS.

The MWeb approach [1] also is related to this work. It links heterogeneous knowledge-based systems with rules that may contain variables. Different from this approach, MWeb restricts context logics (there called constituent rule bases) and does not consider converting between constants in different constituent rule bases.

Another approach for extending RDF and SPARQL with a notion of context is the N-Quads [6] proposal. For provenance, RDF triples are extended to quadruples containing an additional identifier marking the origin of the RDF triple. The N-Quads proposal does not consider heterogeneous knowledge sources, but the SPARQL-MCS framework is general enough to support contexts and SPARQL bridges using such N-Quads.

For future work we plan to investigate the complexity of SPARQL-MCS and optimised evaluation algorithms for SPARQL bridges. We also aim for supporting value invention across heterogeneous knowledge sources to allow blank nodes in construct templates.

References

1. Analyti, A., Antoniou, G., Damasio, C.V.: MWeb: A principled framework for modular web rule bases and its semantics. ACM Trans. Comput. Logic 12(2) (2011)
2. Arenas, M., Gutierrez, C., Pérez, J.: Foundations of RDF Databases, pp. 158–204. Springer, Heidelberg (2009)
3. Baader, F., Calvanese, D., McGuinness, D., Nardi, D., Patel-Schneider, P. (eds.): The Description Logic Handbook: Theory, Implementation and Applications. Cambridge University Press, Cambridge (2003)
4. Brewka, G., Eiter, T.: Equilibria in heterogeneous nonmonotonic multi-context systems. In: AAAI, pp. 385–390 (2007)
5. Brewka, G., Roelofsen, F., Serafini, L.: Contextual default reasoning. In: IJCAI, pp. 268–273 (2007)
6. Cyganiak, R., Harth, A., Hogan, A.: N-Quads: Extending N-Triples with Context (2009), http://sw.deri.org/2008/07/n-quads/
7. Eiter, T., Fink, M., Weinzierl, A.: Preference-based inconsistency assessment in multi-context systems. In: Janhunen, T., Niemelä, I. (eds.) JELIA 2010. LNCS, vol. 6341, pp. 143–155. Springer, Heidelberg (2010)
8. Fink, M., Ghionna, L., Weinzierl, A.: Relational information exchange and aggregation in multi-context systems. In: Delgrande, J.P., Faber, W. (eds.) LPNMR 2011. LNCS, vol. 6645, pp. 120–133. Springer, Heidelberg (2011)
9. Giunchiglia, F., Serafini, L.: Multilanguage hierarchical logics, or: How we can do without modal logics. Artificial Intelligence 65(1), 29–70 (1994)

10. Leone, N., Perri, S., Scarcello, F.: Improving ASP instantiators by join-ordering methods. In: Eiter, T., Faber, W., Truszczyński, M. (eds.) LPNMR 2001. LNCS (LNAI), vol. 2173, pp. 280–294. Springer, Heidelberg (2001)
11. Polleres, A.: From sparql to rules (and back). In: Williamson, C.L., Zurko, M.E., Patel-Schneider, P.F., Shenoy, P.J. (eds.) WWW, pp. 787–796. ACM, New York (2007)
12. Roelofsen, F., Serafini, L.: Minimal and absent information in contexts. In: IJCAI, pp. 558–563 (2005)
13. Serafini, L., Giunchiglia, F., Mylopoulos, J., Bernstein, P.A.: Local relational model: A logical formalization of database coordination. In: Blackburn, P., Ghidini, C., Turner, R.M., Giunchiglia, F. (eds.) CONTEXT 2003. LNCS, vol. 2680, pp. 286–299. Springer, Heidelberg (2003)

Semantic Ontology-Based Strategy for Image Retrieval in Conceptual Modelling

Simon McGinnes

School of Computer Science and Statistics, Trinity College Dublin, Ireland
Simon.McGinnes@tcd.ie

Abstract. A strategy is described which integrates the use of keyword matching, thesaurus and a simple ontology to retrieve images. The strategy was developed to support a conceptual modelling technique that depicts concepts using images, in which searching must integrate tightly into the modelling process without interrupting the train of thought. Suggested by cognitive mechanisms, the strategy varies semantic constraints over time to tune results. It exploits commonalities between modelling and searching tasks to minimise cognitive task-switching penalties and to maintain momentum in modelling sessions. Aside from its use in modelling, the strategy has potential applications in semantic search and information retrieval more broadly, where identification of underlying concepts may help to increase the relevance of search results.

Keywords: Semantic search; semantic retrieval; image search; conceptual modelling; ontologies; database design.

1 Introduction

Conceptual modelling (CM) is an expert task, and conceptual models can be hard to understand. One way of making models more understandable is to use images (Fig. 1.); this practice facilitates recognition, reducing the need for slow and cognitively-intensive interpretation and searching. Well-chosen symbols convey meaning effortlessly, by triggering mental associations. Most CM techniques use "box-and-line" notations. UML, for example, depicts classes as rectangles, regardless of what they represent. But this makes it harder to differentiate between items, so a valuable channel for conveying meaning is lost. The BCM technique [1] instead depicts each entity type with its own image, which the modeller may choose using a suitable search facility. In this context, image search must be fast and require little interaction, to maintain a free flow of ideas; task-switching incurs a heavy cognitive penalty. Relevant results should be returned earliest and distractions should be avoided. Every image found for a given entity type should correspond to its related mental concept.

Image search techniques that rely on text matching alone can be overly sensitive to choice of search terms, synonyms, homonyms and so on. The lack of semantic context creates a gap between the coding of images and the searcher's intentions. Various ways of adding semantics to image search have been tested. For example, one technique places images in n-dimensional semantic space and maps them onto specified context planes [2]; as in many techniques, the images must be tagged in advance, which can be onerous. Machine interpretation of images would facilitate rapid tagging but remains insufficiently reliable, in the general case. Certain semantics can be inferred, however. Some techniques use hyperlinks as a proxy for semantic associations; others tag images according to similarity to exemplar images, or try to infer the searcher's domain of reference [3-4].

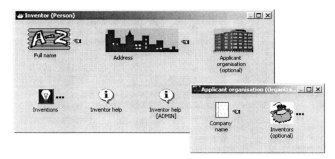

Fig. 1. A BCM model fragment. Each image symbolises an entity type (mental concept); the presence of an image in a window represents a relationship between entity types

2 Search Strategy

Our search strategy is loosely inspired by aspects of cognition. We apply a simple single-level ontology of *archetypal categories*, reflecting innate concepts such as people, places and activities, and pitched at an "everyday" level to minimise cognitive effort [5-6]. *Associative recall* is emulated with keyword matching and *memory* with a bank of images, each linked to an archetypal category and search terms. *Lateral thinking*, where one idea leads to another, is invaluable in CM; we emulate it using a thesaurus containing linked terms. We use *segregated processing and competition;* different search steps are handled by separate threads and the outputs are combined.

The search function is invoked when a user adds a new entity type to a model. In BCM, each entity type is named and corresponds to a particular domain concept. It is also associated with an archetypal category from the list *people, places, documents, organisations, activities, physical objects, conceptual objects, systems* and *categories*. Although it is very simple, when used in CM this single-level ontology has been found to reduce modellers' skill requirements and improve model quality [1]. The search function is therefore supplied with two values: (a) an initial search term, which is the name of an entity type, and (b) the associated archetypal category. The aim is to use search term and category to find one or more relevant images.

The process is progressive (Table 1). In steps 1 and 2, exact or near-exact matches are sought for the search term and category. For common or very general concepts, such as *customer*, this will typically retrieve a variety of images (Fig. 2). However, for unusual concepts (e.g. *inventor*) exact matches are less likely. The search proceeds in steps 3 and 4 to find images that match the search term but *not* the category. The purpose is to find images that do not represent the concept itself, but may nonetheless symbolise it. In Fig. 1., *applicant organisation* is depicted as a building; obviously, an organisation is not a building, but the building can represent an organisation because the ideas are closely linked. For the same reason the abstract concept *bank account* could be depicted with the image of an ATM card. The term "analogy" is used in Table 1 as shorthand for this type of relationship between image and concept.

Table 1. Example of search algorithm for entity type *customer rep* (category *person*)

Step	Category	Terms sought	Images returned
1.	people	*customer rep*	Exact matches only
2.		*customer* or *rep*	Near-exact matches
3.	not *people*	*customer rep*	Close analogies/related ideas
4.		*customer* or *rep*	Near analogies/related ideas
5.	*people*	Thesaurus terms matching *customer*	Synonyms, closely-related concepts and their analogies
6.	not *people*	*rep*, *customer* or *rep*	
7.	*people*	Repeated recursively using the terms from thesaurus matching those from 5.	Successively less-closely-related concepts & analogies
8.	not *people*		
9.	*people*	Any	Loose matches (any people)

In Steps 5 and 6, images are sought for thesaurus terms linked to the search term; each linked term may represent a synonym or a related idea. The process continues asynchronously in steps 7 and 8, traversing links recursively. The result is akin to *spreading activation* and produces a progressively widening set of results. Relevance gradually decreases as the semantic net widens. Competition is achieved by giving preference to images retrieved most often and via the shortest semantic paths.

Concurrently (step 9), the search displays any other images matching the category. Even if no suitable images were previously found, some broadly-relevant images will

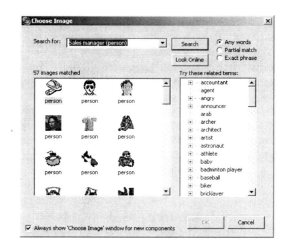

Fig. 2. Prototype image search facility

now be displayed; this is particularly helpful for unusual concepts. The algorithm continues until termination criteria are met or the user interrupts the search. The strategy is not designed to find optimal results; instead, potential solutions are offered and the user exercises subjective judgment, as in *satisficing*. The modeller benefits since each image is related to the original concept, if only tenuously, and the mind is adept at identifying links. For example, in Fig. 1. *inventions* is depicted as a light bulb (which was found because it is linked with *idea*, which in turn is linked to *invention*).

The search strategy was implemented in a tool supporting BCM and tested in group sessions [1]. Designed to exploit synergies between modelling and searching, the tool performed well enough to integrate seamlessly into the modelling process. As anticipated, the most relevant images were displayed earliest and (crucially) looser matches were provided as well. This allowed the modeller to proceed even if he/she intended to search later for a better image. As hoped, synonyms were found automatically and homonyms were less of a problem than with pure keyword search, because the archetypal category automatically disambiguated ambiguous terms.

3 Conclusion and Further Work

This research suggests that benefits might be obtained in ontology-based search by giving preference to certain basic-level categories. It also demonstrates the effects of relaxing semantic constraints during search. The ontology was a simple one, but any more complex ontology could be used, and experimentation with a more complex ontology might permit more sophisticated tuning. In the context of CM, the strategy could go further. For example, the content of the conceptual model might beneficially be used in a similar way to the thesaurus. For the strategy to be useful in more general semantic search, large-scale tagging of content would be required; while automated tagging remains a challenge, one possible solution might be to crowdsource the task.

References

1. McGinnes, S., Amos, J.: Accelerated Business Concept Modeling: Combining User Interface Design with Object Modeling. In: Harmelen, M.V., Wilson, S. (eds.) Object Modeling and User Interface Design: Designing Interactive Systems, pp. 3–36. Addison Wesley, London (2001)
2. Kawamoto, M., Kiyoki, Y., Yoshida, N., Fujishima, S., Aiso, S.: An Implementation of a Semantic Associative Search Space for Medical Document Databases. In: SAINT 2004 Workshops, International Symposium on Applications and the Internet, pp. 488–493. IEEE Computer Society, Tokyo (January 26-30, 2004)
3. Xu, X., Lee, D.J., Antani, S., Long, L.R.: A Hybrid Approach for Online Spine X-ray Image Retrieval Based on CBIR and Relevance Feedback. IEEE Transactions on Information Technology in Biomedicine, 1–10 (2005)
4. Zhuge, H.: Retrieve images by understanding semantic links and clustering image fragments. The Journal of Systems and Software 73, 455–466 (2004)
5. Moore, C.J., Price, C.J.: A Functional Neuroimaging Study of the Variables that Generate Category-Specific Object Processing Differences. Brain 122, 943–962 (1999)
6. Pansky, A., Koriat, A.: The Basic-Level Convergence Effect in Memory Distortions. Psychological Science 15, 52–59 (2004)

Preface WISSE 2011

Information systems security problems are currently a widespread and growing concern that covers most of the areas of society, such as business, domestic, financial, government, healthcare, and so on. The scientific community is beginning to realize the importance of aligning information systems engineering and security engineering in order to develop more secure information systems.

The First International Workshop on Information Systems Security Engineering (WISSE) expands the vision of the information system engineering from a perspective of security. It aims to identify current research on methods, models, and tools for IS security and to bring together researchers and practitioners who want to discuss key issues in IS security engineering.

This workshop, held in London (United Kingdom) on June 21th, 2011, was organized in conjunction with the 23rd International Conference on Advanced Information Systems Engineering (CAiSE'11).

In order to ensure a high quality workshop, among 12 received papers, the Program Committee selected 4 papers as full papers, thus coming up with an acceptance rate of 33%. The proceedings also includes 2 short papers. The selected research papers for presentation address the following topics:

- Methodologies and models for evaluating IS security aspects,
- Security Architectures and Patterns for Information Systems,
- Secure Information Systems development methodologies,
- Models and approaches for the verification of security properties,
- Ontologies for IS security,
- Integrating functional and security requirements,
- Access and Usage control models,
- Formal methods for modelling security.

Besides these papers, a keynote address deals with modelling and reasoning about security and privacy and how they should be treated under one unified framework. The keynote speaker, Dr. Haris Mouratidis, is widely known for his expertise on this subject and we gratefully acknowledge his contribution.

We wish to thank all the contributors to WISSE'2011, in particular the authors who submitted papers and the members of the Program Committee who carefully reviewed them. Special thanks to Dr. Haris Mouratidis who will honour us by offering the Keynote Speech which we hope you find motivating. We express our gratitude to the CAiSE'11 Workshop Chairs, Oscar Pastor and Camille Salinesi, for their helpful support in preparing the workshop. Finally, we thank our colleagues from the Steering Committee, Nora Cuppens, Jan Jürjens and Luis Enrique Sánchez, for initiating the workshop and contributing to its organization.

June 2011

Nadira Lammari
David G. Rosado

WISSE'2011 Organization

Workshop co-chairs:

Nadira Lammari	CEDRIC, CNAM, France
David G. Rosado	University of Castilla-La Mancha, Spain

Steering committee

Nora Cuppens	LUSSI/SERES Telecom-Bretagne, France
Jan Jürjens	Technical University of Dortmund, Germany
Luis Enrique Sánchez	University of Castilla-La Mancha, Spain

Program Committee

Jacky Akoka	CEDRIC, CNAM, France
Yudis Asnar	Università di Trento, Italy
Isabelle Comyn-Wattiau	CEDRIC, CNAM, France
Frédéric Cuppens	Telecom Bretagne, France
Ernesto Damiani	Università degli Studi di Milano, Italy
Sabrina De Capitani di Vimercati	degli Studi di Milano, Italy
Eduardo B. Fernández	Florida Atlantic University, USA
Eduardo Fernández-Medina	University of Castilla-La Mancha, Spain
Marc Frappier	University of Sherbrooke, Québec
Paolo Giorgini	University of Trento, Italy
Régine Laleau	LACL, University of Paris-Est, France
Jaejoon Lee	Lancaster University, UK
Yves Ledru	LIG, University of Grenoble, France
Javier López	University of Málaga, Spain
Antonio Maña	University of Malaga, Spain
Jérémy Milhau	LACL, University of Paris-Est, France
Haralambos Mouratidis	University of East London, UK
Brajendra Panda	University of Arkansas, USA
Kouichi Sakurai	Kyushu University, Japan
Duminda Wijesekera	University George Mason, USA
Louise Yngström	Stockholm University, Sweden

Auxiliary Reviewers

Christos Kalloniatis	University of the Aegean. Greece
Satoshi Hada	IBM Research, Japan
Shareeful Islam	Technical University of Munich, Germany
Carlos Blanco	University of Cantabria, Spain
Wook Shin	KDDI R&D Laboratories, Inc., Japan

Taking into Account Functional Models in the Validation of IS Security Policies

Yves Ledru[1], Akram Idani[1], Jérémy Milhau[2,3], Nafees Qamar[1],
Régine Laleau[2], Jean-Luc Richier[1], and Mohamed-Amine Labiadh[1,*]

[1] UJF-Grenoble 1/Grenoble-INP/UPMF-Grenoble2/CNRS, Laboratoire
d'Informatique de Grenoble UMR 5217, F-38041, Grenoble, France
`Yves.Ledru@imag.fr`
[2] Université Paris-Est, LACL, IUT Sénart Fontainebleau,
Fontainebleau, France
`laleau@u-pec.fr`
[3] GRIL, Département Informatique, Université de Sherbrooke,
Québec, Canada
`Jeremy.Milhau@USherbrooke.ca`

Abstract. Designing a security policy for an information system (IS) is a non-trivial task. Variants of the RBAC model can be used to express such policies as access-control rules associated to constraints. In this paper, we advocate that currently available tools do not take sufficiently into account the functional description of the application and its impact on authorisation constraints and dynamic aspects of security. We suggest to translate both security and functional models into a formal language, such as B, whose analysis and animation tools will help validate a larger set of security scenarios. We show how various kinds of constraints can be expressed and animated in this context.

Keywords: RBAC, authorisation constraints, validation.

1 Introduction

The design of today's information systems (IS) must not only take into account the expected functionalities of the system, but also various kinds of non-functional requirements. Security is one of these non-functional requirements. Security policies are designed to fulfill requirements such as confidentiality, integrity and availability. Security policies are usually expressed as abstract access control rules, independently of target technologies. In the past, various access control models have been proposed. In this paper, we focus on role-based access control models (RBAC) [1], including evolutions such as SecureUML [2]. An important feature of such models is the notion of role: permissions are granted to roles which represent functions in an institution. Each role corresponds to several users and users may play several roles with respect to the secure system.

---

[*] This work was partly supported by the ANR-08-SEGI-018 Selkis and ANR-09-SEGI-014 TASCCC projects.

Advanced RBAC models allow to express constraints such as Separation of Duty (SoD) properties [3], and other properties on roles (e.g. precedence, see Sect. 2). For information systems, contextual information may also be taken into account when granting permissions. This contextual information may correspond to the current state of the information system, or to the history of interactions with the system. This reveals the need to link the security model of the application to the functional model of the information system, often expressed as UML diagrams. Therefore, SecureUML [2] groups UML diagrams of the application with security information describing the access control rules. In the remainder, we will refer to the UML diagrams of the application as the *functional model*. The term *security model* will refer to the access control model. Other approaches have integrated security concerns in UML diagrams. Fernandez [4] proposes to address security concerns through the whole software development and builds on UML and patterns to structure his approach. UMLSec [5] is another UML profile that focuses on secrecy and cryptographic protocols.

Contextual constraints give flexibility to describe security policies, but the resulting models are more complex to validate. Validation checks that the policy corresponds to the user's requirements. Animation of the model can play a significant role in this validation activity, playing scenarios or answering questions about the consequences of the model. Animation also brings a limited level of verification: traces demonstrate that constraints are not contradictory.

When systems become complex, separation of concerns is often perceived as a good strategy to master complexity. In our context, this means that functional and security models should be validated separately. This explains why most existing works are mainly interested by the security part. Although it is definitely useful to first analyse both models in isolation, interactions between these models must also be taken into account. Such interactions result from the fact that constraints expressed in the security model also refer to information of the functional model. Hence, evolutions of the functional state will influence the security behaviour. Conversely, security constraints can impact the functional behaviour. For example, it is important to consider both security and functional models in order to check liveness properties on the information system. Indeed, it can be the case that security constraints are too strict and block the system.

In this paper we review several tools aimed at the validation of RBAC security properties, and state that most of them focus on the security model without taking into account the functional model. We will then propose an approach, based on the B method [6], which allows to express contextual and history based constraints, and to validate these models using animation tools.

In Sect. 2, we review several tools representative of the current state of the art. In Sect. 3, we present an example whose validation requires to take into account dynamic aspects of the functional model. Such aspects cannot be investigated with current tools. Sect. 4 proposes solutions based on the B formal method to address these issues. Finally Sect. 5 draws the conclusions of this work.

2 Tools for V&V of Role-Based Authorisation Constraints

2.1 Validation Tools Based on OCL

OCL [7] (Object Constraint Language) is part of UML and allows to express invariant constraints on a class diagram as well as pre- and postconditions on the methods. The USE tool (UML-based Specification Environment) [8] takes as input an object diagram and an OCL constraint. It checks whether the constraint holds on the given object diagram. The tool also allows to program a random generator for object diagrams, and to program sequences of object diagrams, where pre- and post-conditions can be checked.

Sohr et al [9] have adapted this tool for the analysis of security policies. Their work focuses on the security model, i.e. users, roles, sessions and permissions, constrained by OCL assertions. This allows to express properties such as the cardinality of a given role, the precedence between roles (e.g. only members of role r_1 may be assigned role r_2), or SoD (i.e. conflicting roles). Their work also takes into account a limited amount of functional information by adding some attributes to the users. For example, if a constraint states that the doctor accessing medical information about a patient must be linked to the hospital of the patient, some attribute *currentHospital* should be added to the users. Unfortunately such extensions of the security model don't really scale up, and duplicate information already included in the functional model.

Sohr et al [9] report on two kinds of validation activities. An object diagram can be given to the tool, and the tool will check which constraints are violated. The object diagram can be user-defined, randomly generated, or member of a programmed sequence. This allows to detect unsatisfiable constraints, i.e. constraints which are always false. They have also developed a tool named authorisation editor, which implements the administrative, system and review functions of the RBAC standard. The tool is connected to the API of USE so that the constraints of the security policy are checked after each operation. This allows to detect erroneous dynamic behaviour of the security policy. For example, if two roles are constrained both by a precedence and a conflict relations, it will always be impossible to find a sequence of RBAC administrative and system operations which leads to create the second role.

Other works have addressed the validation of security policies using UML and OCL. They focus on SoD properties in the security model. Ahn and Hu [10] stated an approach using UML class diagrams, a language dedicated to the specification of role-based authorization constraints (RCL2000), and OCL to validate SoD constraints. In that approach, it is checked whether a current state is violated by the authorization constraints. A snapshot based on object diagram is created in order to determine violated constraints. Ray et al. [11] also discuss SoD constraints by using object diagrams and try to alleviate the complexity of OCL. The RBAC constraints that are checked are SoD, prerequisite constraints and cardinality constraints that help imposing a maximum number of role assignments to a user.

2.2 RBAC Constraints and Alloy

Alloy Analyzer [12] emerged as a powerful and rigorous semantic based tool that can be used for precise specification and modeling of a system. Using first order logic, it offers a static structure of the models. Based on specified entities, the set of instances generated by the Alloy analyzer are then checked against the established constraints. The constructs of Alloy are similar to OCL and compatible with it.

To our interest, Alloy should be used for behavioral or dynamic modeling in terms of operations execution. Simulating a system using Alloy involves individual transitions or properties of sequences of transitions. However, use of Alloy for dynamic modeling of security policies has been a scant subject so far. Most of the proposed approaches merely focus on the static analysis where Alloy is used for generating counterexamples against specifications. As an added advantage of Alloy over other languages (e.g., OCL and UML), it is reported [13] as more amenable to automatic analysis. Alloy offers two kinds of automated analysis i.e., *simulation* and *checking*. In simulation, operations are interpreted to compute resulting states, and check that they conform to invariant properties. In checking, Alloy attempts to generate instances of a data structure up to a given (small) maximum size, and can identify counterexamples which don't satisfy a given property. The types of answers that Alloy provides are: *"this property always holds for problems up to size X"* or *"this property does not always hold, and here is a counter example'*.

Regarding the analysis of security models, especially RBAC with constraints, significant amount of work has been carried out using Alloy, mainly based on SoD constraints. Zao [14] has proposed a technique to verify algebraic characteristics of RBAC schema using Alloy. Alloy is used as a constraint analyzer to check inconsistencies among policies. The authors focus on static properties of the security model and don't take into account evolutions of its state. Schaad et al., [15] and Ahn et al. [10] have discussed SoD constraints from RBAC. [15] advocates the suitability of Alloy, and deeply discusses decentralized administration of RBAC and arbitrary changes to a initially stated model that may result in conflicting policies over time w.r.t, SoD constraints. They argue that SoD constraints may introduce implicit security policies flaws because of role hierarchies. Several counterexamples are generated to examine the policy which they are interested in. Yu et al. [16] propose scenarios in terms of state transitions to uncover violations in security policies. Such approaches and Alloy analyzer (unlike model checkers) have advantages over model checking tools since model checking merely considers closed-world view of systems [16]; that means no inputs are taken from external resources. In their approach, all operation calls take the form of scenarios and a system state is a configuration of objects. Based on a generated tree (limited depth, limited number of objects, and small domain) of various invocations, scenarios are generated. Using this technique, one can analyze role activation constraints and SoD constraints.

In [17], functional and security models are merged into a single UML model which is translated into Alloy. Alloy can then be used to find a state which

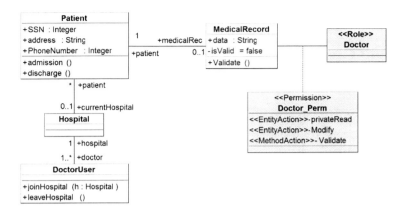

Fig. 1. Functional model enriched by security information (grey shaded classes)

breaks a given property. The properties described in [17] are mainly of static nature, i.e. they focus on the search for a state which breaks a property, and don't search for sequences of actions leading to such a state. Nevertheless, Alloy can take into account the behaviour of the actions of the model, and we believe it has the potential to perform such dynamic analyses.

2.3 SecureMova

The tools presented so far, based on OCL and Alloy, only address the validation of security models, e.g. addressing SoD properties. Most of them don't consider constraints which involve elements of the functional model, and hence don't consider evolutions of the state of the functional model.

In [18], Basin et al report on SecureMova, a tool which supports SecureUML+ComponentUML. The tool allows to create a functional diagram, i.e. a class diagram, and to relate it to permission rules. Constraints can be attached to permissions and may refer to the elements of the functional diagram.

For example, this allows to express the property that doctors may modify a medical record if and only if they are employed by the hospital of the patient. A class *Hospital* may be defined in the functional model (Fig. 1) and relations drawn between *Hospital* and *Patient*, and between *Hospital* and *DoctorUser*. In Sect. 4.2, we will associate an OCL constraint to the permission to access a medical record. This constraint navigates through the functional model to retrieve the *Patient* associated to the medical record, and his/her current *Hospital*. It also retrieves the *DoctorUser* corresponding to the user asking to access the medical record and retrieves his/her associated *Hospital*. Finally, the constraint compares these two hospitals.

With SecureMOVA it is possible to ask questions about a current state, i.e. a given object diagram. Such queries return the actions authorized for a given role, or a given user. They also allow to investigate on overlapping permissions, i.e. permissions which have a common set of associated actions. The tool provides an extensive set of queries over a given model, possibly associated with a given initial state. All reported examples [18] are of static nature, i.e. they don't allow to sequence actions (either administrative or functional) and check that a given sequence is permitted by the combination of the security and functional models. In the next sections, we will see that a thorough validation of a security policy which includes contextual constraints must also take into account evolutions of the state of the functional model.

3 Motivating Example

Our motivating example is based on the constraint stated above: "If a doctor wants to modify the medical record of a given patient, he must belong to the same hospital as the patient". Let us now consider a malicious doctor, who wants to modify the information of a patient in another hospital. Since the patient and the doctor belong to different hospitals, the doctor will not be permitted to access this information. In order to validate the rules of the security policy, one may try several typical situations and query about the permitted/forbidden actions. Using a tool such as SecureMova, one would provide an object diagram od_1 with one doctor and one patient linked to two different hospitals, and query if the doctor may perform action $setData$ on the patient's medical record. The tool would answer that the doctor is not authorized to perform this action.

Further validation of this security policy should explore dynamic aspects of the policy. For example, is it possible for this malicious doctor to eventually modify the patient's information? Using only static tools, one can check that, given an object diagram od_2 where the malicious doctor belongs to the same hospital as the patient, he will be granted this access. The next question to investigate is: does there exist a sequence of actions which leads a malicious doctor to belong to the same hospital as the patient? This requires to animate a sequence of actions which leads from od_1 to od_2. Such a sequence will presumably call an intermediate operation $joinHospital$ which will link the malicious doctor to the hospital of the patient. Here the dynamic analysis will allow to identify these intermediate actions and check which role has permission to perform these actions.

Another way to group the malicious doctor and the patient in the same hospital is to transfer the patient in the hospital of the doctor. In this second sequence, one should investigate who has the permission to perform such a transfer.

This simple example shows that the validation of a security policy may require dynamic analyses to identify sequences of actions leading to an unwanted state. Moreover, these sequences of actions are not restricted to the standard RBAC functions and may refer to operations defined in the functional model. This is actually the case when constraints referring to the functional model are expressed on permissions. Current tools, such as the ones presented in Sect. 2, which focus on static queries or on the dynamic execution of the sole RBAC functions are not sufficient to perform such dynamic investigations.

4 Using Testing and Verification Techniques

The example of Sect. 3 shows that there is a need for dynamic analyses involving both functional and security models when designing a security policy. Moreover, when the security policy refers to the functional model through the use of constraints, the dynamic analysis should not only cover the RBAC standard functions, but also take into account the behaviour of the functional model.

Dynamic analyses can take two forms: tests and verifications. Tests correspond to the execution of a sequence of actions on the security and functional models, or on their implementations. The test sequence is either defined by the security policy designer, possibly on the basis of use cases, or it may be the output of a test generation tool on the basis of some coverage of the models. Test can contribute to both validation and verification activities. Tests based on use cases correspond to the validation activity because they contribute to show that the security policy meets the users/customers needs. Tests based on model coverage contribute to verification. They can check that the covered behaviours of the model will respect some global properties of the security policy like SoD. Tests also contribute to detect unsatisfiable constraints because such constraints may forbid any state different from the empty state.

Tests can only check a limited number of behaviours. When absolute guarantees are needed, such as ensuring that all threats are handled, verification techniques should be considered. Verification techniques include model-checking and symbolic proof techniques. Both techniques are of interest in the verification of a security policy. Proof techniques can show the existence of some state, and hence prove that constraints are satisfiable, or establish that some property, like SoD, is an invariant of the model. Model-checking is based on model exploration, and can be used to find a sequence of actions leading to a given state or property. In our motivating example, model-checking tools should be experimented to find a path between od_1 and od_2.

4.1 Some Solutions to Explore

Testing techniques require the availability of executable models or implementations. Security policies based on RBAC can easily be made executable, as demonstrated by Sohr in his authorisation editor [9]. Executability of a functional model can be achieved in two ways: either by providing an implementation of the model which can interface with the contextual constraints of the security model, or by providing an executable model. Providing an implementation makes sense in a context where the functional system is designed first, without considering security aspects, and where a security policy must be designed later for this application. It also makes sense during a maintenance phase where a given implemented security policy must evolve. Some prototypes of RBAC can be coupled with an existing implementation. For example, the MotOrBAC tool provides an API between its security engine and the application [19].

The other way is to get an executable functional model. In the case of USE or SecureMova, the model is expressed as a class diagram combined with OCL

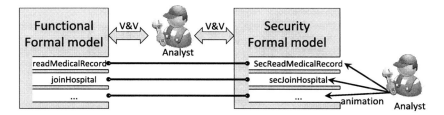

Fig. 2. Analysis of the functional and security models

predicates. In order to turn UML methods into executable ones, one needs to provide an implementation of the methods. Actually, USE allows to define a body for each method using an imperative language based on OCL. It seems that this feature was not explored in [9] and might be interesting to investigate. Another way is to animate the methods based on their pre- and post-conditions. We don't know of tools which support this approach for OCL, but they exist for formal languages such as B[6].

4.2 Using the B Formal Method

The B language actually appears as an interesting option. Several tools have been defined to translate UML models into B specifications; they show at least the feasibility of such translations [20,21]. Regarding the security model, Sohr[9] has already shown that it can be specified in UML+OCL. Since the B language is based on the same principles as OCL (first order predicate logic and set theory), it is possible to propose a similar translation of the security model into B specifications. The B specifications produced from both security and functional models (Fig. 2) can then be analysed using either animation tools such as ProB [22] or proof tools such as Atelier-B[1]. ProB also includes model-checking facilities which can be of interest to search for malicious sequences of operations.

Fig. 2 illustrates the proposed translation of a functional model enriched by an access control policy such as the one of Fig. 1. The functional B specification in the left hand side of Fig. 2 is widely inspired by existing UML to B translation approaches [20,21]. We developed a model driven platform [23] in order to be able to combine and adapt rules proposed by these approaches. The right hand side of Fig. 2 represents the formal specification produced from the security model and which is intended to control the use of the functional B operations. Playing scenarios is done by animating the secured operations (*e.g.* secReadMedicalRecord, secJoinHospital) which give access uniquely to the authorized functional operations. This approach allows to validate the functional model as well as the security policy. In fact, animation of an authorized operation evolves the state of the functional model and hence allows the analyst to validate both models.

---
[1] http://www.atelierb.eu

Terms "*shallow embedding*" and "*deep embedding*" [24] are often used to describe a mapping between formalisms. The first notion means a direct translation from a source model into a target model, while the second notion means that the mapping leads to structures that represent data types. In the proposed approach we adopt a *shallow embedding* approach when translating the functional model, and a *deep embedding* approach for the security model. In the following we give an overview of the translation principles.

Translation of the Functional Model. As proposed by the existing approaches which transform a UML model into a B specification [20,21] concepts of a UML class diagram lead to sets, variables and relations in the B specification. For example, class *MedicalRecord* of Fig. 1 leads to an abstract set MEDICALRECORD and a variable MedicalRecord representing respectively the set of possible instances and the set of existing instances of class *MedicalRecord*.

```
MACHINE
    Functional_Model
SETS
    MEDICALRECORD, PATIENT, ...
VARIABLES
    MedicalRecord, Patient, isValid, ...
INVARIANT
    MedicalRecord ⊆ MEDICALRECORD ∧
    isValid ∈ MedicalRecord → bool
    ...
INITIALISATION
    MedicalRecord := ∅
    ...
```

Basic operations such as constructors, destructors, getters, setters..., are automatically produced in order to allow state evolution of the functional formal model. We developed a tool which generates all these basic operations and takes into account some basic structural invariants related to mandatory and/or unique attributes, inheritance, composition, multiplicities... The resulting B specification can be enriched in order to take into account less obvious functional constraints and also to add manually other functional operations such as operation *Validate* of Fig. 1. Proof and animation tools can then be used in order to analyse the correctness of the functional model independently from security aspects. Let us consider for example a functional OCL constraint which indicates that a patient can't leave an hospital if his medical record is not validated:

```
context MedicalRecord inv MR_Validation:
    self.isValid = FALSE
    implies self.Patient.currentHospital -> notEmpty()
```

In other words, this constraint considers that if attribute *isValid* of a medical record is false then the patient of this medical record must be linked to some hospital. This can be translated in B as follows:

$$\forall p \cdot (p \in Patient \;\land\; isValid(PatientMedicalRecordRel^{-1}(p)) = FALSE$$
$$\Rightarrow PatientHospitalRel[\{p\}] \neq \emptyset$$

Relations *PatientMedicalRecordRel* and *PatientHospitalRel* are issued respectively from the association between class *Patient* and class *MedicalRecord* and the association which links class *Patient* to class *Hospital*. Taking into account this invariant leads to improvements of the functional model. For example, operation *setData*, which is a basic setter, modifies attribute *data* of a *MedicalRecord*, and also turns the attribute *isValid* into false. Hence, precondition of operation *setData* must be enforced in order to avoid a violation of the previous invariant when trying to modify data of a medical record of a patient who is not admitted in any hospital.

```
setData(mr, dd) ≙
  PRE
    mr ∈ MedicalRecord ∧ dd ∈ TheData
    ∧ PatientMedicalRecordRel(mr) ∈ dom(PatientHospitalRel)
  THEN
    isValid(mr) := FALSE ||
    data(mr) := dd
  END;
```

Such validations are done using the AtelierB tool which allows to prove the functional model consistency with its invariants.

Translation of the Security Model. Translation of the security model follows a *deep embedding* approach. Indeed, we propose a B formalization of a variant of the secureUML meta-model [2]. Elements of a security model are then directly injected in this B specification. The access to the operational part of the functional formal model is controlled by the B specification issued from the security model. As shown in Fig. 2, we associate to each functional operation a secured operation in the security formal model which verifies that a user has permission to call a functional operation. For example, operation *secure_setData* is intended to verify accesses to operation *setData* above.

```
secure_setData(mr, data) ≙
  PRE
    mr ∈ MedicalRecord ∧ data ∈ TheData
  THEN
    SELECT
      MedicalRecord_setData ∈ isPermitted[currentRole]
    THEN
      setData(mr, data)
    END
  END;
```

Variable *currentRole* contains the set of roles activated by a user in a session. Set *isPermitted* computes for each role the set of authorized functional operations. Then, the guard *MedicalRecord_setData* ∈ *isPermitted*[*currentRole*] verifies whether *setData* is allowed to the connected user using his active roles. Fig. 1 grants to doctors the permission to call modify operations such as *setData*. Hence, animation of *secure_setData* shows that every doctor may modify medical records. In Sect. 2.3, we considered an additional constraint saying that in order to modify a medical record, the doctor must be employed by the current hospital of the patient. This constraint can be expressed in OCL as follows:

```
context Doctor_Perm::Modify inv :
    session.user.isTypeOf(DoctorUser) implies
    session.user.Hospital = self.medicalRecord.Patient.currentHospital
```

As this constraint is expressed in the context of a modification permission (*i.e. Doctor_Perm*), then we take it into account in our formal specifications by strengthening the guard of *secure_setData* as follows:

$$MedicalRecord\_setData \in isPermitted[currentRole] \land$$
$$(currentUser \in DoctorUser$$
$$\Rightarrow HospitalDoctorRel(currentUser)$$
$$= PatientHospitalRel(PatientMedicalRecordRel(mr)))$$

Now, animation of *secure_setData* will fail if the doctor and the patient are linked to different hospitals. This constraint shows the impact of the functional model on the security model because the guard of the secured operation navigates through the functional model state in order to retrieve and compare the hospital in which the patient is admitted and the hospital of the connected doctor.

4.3 Support of History-Based Constraints

The constraints expressed in OCL only refer to a given instant of time. When expressing history-based constraints, it is necessary to refer to several distinct instants of time. For example, consider the following rule: "If a patient has left the hospital, all doctors belonging to the hospital during the patient's stay will keep read access to his medical record.". If we want to express this rule as a read permission associated to an OCL constraint, we need to extend the functional model with information about past states, and this information is for security's sake only. This goes against separation of concerns.

In [9], Sohr suggests the use of TOCL, an extension of OCL with temporal operators. Although this provides a way to express history based constraints, it appears that no tool is currently available to support the use of this formalism.

In the sequel, we address history-based constraints using process algebra and the B method. Process algebra can be used to model workflows of actions and all ordering and security constraints related to a dynamic security policy.

4.4 The ASTD Notation

In order to specify information systems, the EB[3] [25] method was developed. It features a process algebra similar to CSP [26] with some IS-oriented additions such as quantifications. However, it lacks a graphical representation that can help during the modeling process and that is one of the advantages of UML statecharts. The ASTD notation [27] is a graphical representation linked to a formal semantics created to specify systems such as IS. An ASTD (e.g. Fig. 3) defines a set of traces of actions accepted by the system. ASTD was introduced as an extension of Harel's Statecharts [28] and is based on operators from EB[3]. An ASTD is built from transitions, denoting action labels (i.e. method calls) and parameters, and places that can be elementary (as states in automata theory) or

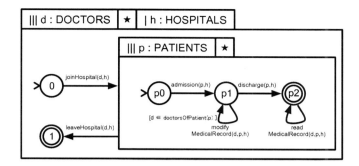

Fig. 3. An ASTD rule expressing ordering constraints in an hospital IS

ASTD themselves. Each ASTD has a type associated to a formal semantics. One of the main features of ASTD is to allow parameterized instances and quantifications, aspects missing in original statecharts. This means that ASTD can describe not only the behavior of one instance but also the behavior of sets of entities and relationships of a system. A formal description of the ASTD notation is given in [29].

In the example of the hospital IS, ASTD can help modeling properties such as "If a patient has left the hospital, all doctors belonging to the hospital during the patient's stay will keep read access to his medical record". The ASTD of Fig. 3 expresses that for all doctors (||| d : DOCTORS), at a given time there is a unique hospital where the doctor is affected (| h : HOSPITALS). This hospital can change during the doctor career (thanks to the * operator). Once the doctor d joined an hospital h, he can modify medical records of patient p if p was admitted in hospital h and if he is one of his/her doctors. If p leaves the hospital, d can still read his/her medical records, unless d leaves the hospital. At any time, d can leave the hospital, loosing its reading rights over medical records.

4.5 Using ASTD to Validate a Policy

ASTD models are executable using the iASTD [30], an interpreter for ASTD. iASTD efficiently determines if actions can be executed by the model and computes the ASTD state after the execution. iASTD accepts as inputs 2 files. The first one is a description of the topology of the ASTD model to validate and the second one is a trace of actions with their parameters to be executed. After parsing both files, iASTD computes the initial state of the ASTD and then tries to execute the first action of the trace. If the execution succeeds, iASTD computes the new state of the ASTD and goes on to the next action of the trace to be executed. If the execution is not allowed, iASTD does not modify the current state of the ASTD and warns the user of refusal of the action. iASTD then tries to execute the next action in the trace. Validation of an ASTD is thus performed by providing scenarios (traces) that should be accepted and others that should be rejected. Such scenarios can be generated in order to check usual access-control policy properties or requirements.

In the example presented in Fig. 3, we would like to grant doctors linked a given hospital the right to read medical records of patients only if they were linked to this hospital during the patient stay. We can validate our policy by executing some scenarios over the model. Executing the trace { joinHospital($Alex, H1$) ; admission($Bob, H1$) ; discharge($Bob, H1$) ; readMR($Alex, Bob, H1$) } will check that a doctor linked to hospital $H1$ can read the record of a patient linked to the same hospital in the same time interval. With another scenario such as { joinHospital($Alex, H1$) ; admission($Bob, H1$) ; discharge($Bob, H1$) ; leaveHospital($Alex, H1$) ; readMR($Alex, Bob, H1$) }, the interpreter will reject the last action because $Alex$ is not linked to the hospital at the time he attempts to read the medical record. However the scenario { admission($Bob, H1$) ; joinHospital($Alex, H1$) ; discharge($Bob, H1$) ; readMR($Alex, Bob, H1$) } should be accepted by our policy, but will be rejected by iASTD since $Alex$ joined the hospital after the admission of Bob. Our security policy is hence too strict and should be adapted in order to accept this scenario. This example shows how to use iASTD and use case scenarios in order to validate ASTD specifications which define history-based constraints on security policies.

4.6 Putting It All Together

In Sect. 4.2, we propose a set of rules to produce B specifications from both the functional part of the system and the static access control model. Translation rules from ASTD models into event-B have also been defined in [31]. Hence, the proposed methodology for modeling IS security starts from a set of graphical models: (i) a class diagram for the functional model, (ii) a static security policy linked to the class diagram and (iii) ASTD models describing a set of allowed traces of actions. These graphical models are used for specifying, visualizing, understanding and documenting a security policy. In order to rigorously check their correctness, a formal B specification can be derived. Thus, a functional model and its associated access control policy, including both static and dynamic aspects, are specified using the same formal notation. We extensively use the inclusion mechanism of B to link secured operations with functional operations. This allows the consistency of the whole system to be formally checked, activity that can be assisted by the tools associated to the B method.

5 Conclusion

This paper has addressed the validation of security policies which include contextual constraints referring to the functional model of an information system. These are essential activities when designing or modifying a security policy. Separation of concerns suggests to treat the functional and security models in isolation. Unfortunately, when constraints establish a link between these models, validation activities must consider both security and functional models, because changes in the state of the latter may grant or deny permissions in the former. In Sect. 2, we have stated that most tools focus on the validation of the security model and can't take into account constraints which link it to the functional model. Only a few tools, like SecureMova, take both models into account, but their analyses are of static nature, and don't support evolutions of the state of the functional model. In Sect. 3, a motivating example has illustrated the need for dynamic analyses which take into account both models. Our example includes properties whose context is either the current functional state, or the history of this state.

We have proposed an approach, based on the B method and ASTD, where such contextual constraints may be expressed, and included in a formal model. This model can be animated with user defined scenarios and the constraints are evaluated during this animation. The scenarios are defined during requirements analysis, and can be shown to the customer, contributing to the validation of both functional and security models. Playing these scenarios may reveal that the security policy is too strict and forbids normal behaviours. Scenarios may also correspond to potential attacks, and help evaluate the capabilities of the security policy to detect and prevent such attacks.

Our current work implements the tools associated to this approach and studies the interactions between state-based and history-based constraints. This toolset will then be evaluated on case studies of the ANR Selkis Project[2].

References

1. Ferraiolo, D.F., Kuhn, D.R., Chandramouli, R.: Role-Based Access Control. Computer Security Series. Artech House, Boston (2003)
2. Basin, D.A., Doser, J., Lodderstedt, T.: Model driven security: From UML models to access control infrastructures. ACM Transaction of Software Engineering Methodology 15(1), 39–91 (2006)
3. Clark, D.D., Wilson, D.R.: A comparison of commercial and military computer security policies. In: IEEE Symposium on Security and Privacy, pp. 184–195 (1987)
4. Fernández, E.B.: A methodology for secure software design. In: Proc. of the Int. Conf. on Software Engineering Research and Practice, SERP 2004, pp. 130–136. CSREA Press (2004)
5. Jürjens, J.: Secure Systems Development with UML. Springer, Heidelberg (2004)
6. Abrial, J.: The B-Book. Cambridge University Press, Cambridge (1996)
7. Warmer, J.B., Kleppe, A.G.: The Object Constraint Language: Precise Modeling With UML. Addison-Wesley, London (1998)
8. Gogolla, M., Büttner, F., Richters, M.: USE: A UML-based specification environment for validating UML and OCL. Sci. Comput. Program. 69(1-3), 27–34 (2007)
9. Sohr, K., Drouineaud, M., Ahn, G.J., Gogolla, M.: Analyzing and managing role-based access control policies. IEEE Trans. Knowl. Data Eng. 20(7), 924–939 (2008)
10. Ahn, G., Hu, H.: Towards realizing a formal RBAC model in real systems. In: 12th ACM Symp. on Access Control Models and Technologies. ACM Press, New York (2007)
11. Ray, I., Li, N., France, R.: Using UML to visualize role-based access-control constraints. In: Proceedings of the 9th ACM Symposium on Access Control Models and Technologies, pp. 115–124. ACM Press, New York (2004)
12. Jackson, D.: Alloy: A Lightweight Object Modelling Notation. ACM Trans. Softw. Eng. Methodol. 11(2), 256–290 (2002)

---

[2] http://lacl.univ-paris12.fr/selkis/

13. Power, D., Slaymaker, M., Simpson, A.: On the modelling and analysis of amazon web services access policies. In: Frappier, M., Glässer, U., Khurshid, S., Laleau, R., Reeves, S. (eds.) ABZ 2010. LNCS, vol. 5977, pp. 394–394. Springer, Heidelberg (2010)
14. Zao, J., Wee, H., Chu, J., Jackson, D.: RBAC Schema Verification Using Lightweight Formal Model and Constraint Analysis. In: Proceedings of 8th ACM Symposium on Access Control Models and Technologies (2003)
15. Schaad, A., Moffett, J.D.: A lightweight approach to specification and analysis of role-based access control extensions. In: Proc. of 7th SACMAT. ACM Press, New York (2002)
16. Yu, L., France, R., Ray, I., Ghosh, S.: A Rigorous Approach to Uncovering Security Policy Violations in UML Designs. In: Int. Conf. on Engineering Complex Computer Systems. IEEE, Los Alamitos (2009)
17. Toahchoodee, M., Ray, I., Anastasakis, K., Georg, G., Bordbar, B.: Ensuring spatio-temporal access control for real-world applications. In: 14th ACM Symp. on Access Control Models and Technologies, SACMAT 2009. ACM, New York (2009)
18. Basin, D.A., Clavel, M., Doser, J., Egea, M.: Automated analysis of security-design models. Information & Software Technology 51(5), 815–831 (2009)
19. Autrel, F., Cuppens, F., Cuppens-Boulahia, N., Coma-Brebel, C.: MotOrBAC 2: a security policy tool. In: SARSSI 2008: 3e Conf. sur la Sécurité des Architectures Réseaux et des Systèmes d'Information, (Télécom Bretagne) (2008)
20. Mammar, A., Laleau, R.: From a B formal specification to an executable code: application to the relational database domain. Inf. Softw. Technol. 48, 253–279 (2006)
21. Snook, C., Butler, M.: UML-B: Formal modeling and design aided by UML. ACM Transactions on Software Engineering Methodology 15(1), 92–122 (2006)
22. Leuschel, M., Butler, M.J.: ProB: an automated analysis toolset for the B method. STTT 10(2), 185–203 (2008)
23. Idani, A., Labiadh, M.A., Ledru, Y.: Infrastructure dirigée par les modèles pour une intégration adaptable et évolutive de UML et B. Ingénierie des Systèmes d'Information 15(3), 87–112 (2010)
24. Wildmoser, M., Nipkow, T.: Certifying Machine Code Safety: Shallow versus Deep Embedding. In: Slind, K., Bunker, A., Gopalakrishnan, G. (eds.) TPHOLs 2004. LNCS, vol. 3223, pp. 305–320. Springer, Heidelberg (2004)
25. Frappier, M., St-Denis, R.: EB^3: an entity-based black-box specification method for information systems. Software and Systems Modeling 2(2), 134–149 (2003)
26. Hoare, C.A.R.: CSP–Communicating Sequential Processes. Prentice Hall, Englewood Cliffs (1985)
27. Frappier, M., Gervais, F., Laleau, R., Fraikin, B., St-Denis, R.: Extending statecharts with process algebra operators. Innovations in Systems and Software Engineering 4(3), 285–292 (2008)
28. Harel, D.: Statecharts: A visual formalism for complex systems. Science of Computer Programming 8(3), 231–274 (1987)
29. Frappier, M., Gervais, F., Laleau, R., Fraikin, B.: Algebraic state transition diagrams. Technical Report 24, Université de Sherbrooke, Département d'informatique, Sherbrooke, Québec, Canada (June 2008)
30. Salabert, K., Milhau, J., et al.: iASTD: un interpréteur pour les ASTD. In: AFADL 2010, Poitiers, France (2010)
31. Milhau, J., Frappier, M., Gervais, F., Laleau, R.: Systematic translation rules from ASTD to event-B. In: Méry, D., Merz, S. (eds.) IFM 2010. LNCS, vol. 6396, pp. 245–259. Springer, Heidelberg (2010)

Expressing Access Control Policies with an Event-Based Approach

Pierre Konopacki[1,2], Marc Frappier[1], and Régine Laleau[2]

[1] GRIL, Département d'informatique, Université de Sherbrooke, Canada
[2] Université Paris-Est, LACL, IUT Sénart Fontainebleau, Fontainebleau, France
{pierre.konopacki,marc.frappier}@usherbrooke.ca, laleau@u-pec.fr

Abstract. Information systems are widely used and help in the management of huge quantities of data. Generally, these data are valuable or sensitive, their access must be restricted to granted users. Security is a mandatory requirement for information systems. Several methods already exist to express access control policies, but few of them support all kinds of constraints that can be defined in access control policies. In this paper, we present EB^3SEC, a language used to formally model and interpret access control policies in information systems. Permissions, prohibitions and static separation of duty are specified by a class diagram. As EB^3SEC includes a process algebra, dynamic access control constraints such as obligations and dynamic separation of duty can be easily expressed. Finally, we present the architecture of the tool used to interpret EB^3SEC models.

Keywords: formal method, access control, security.

1 Introduction

Information Systems (IS) are widely used in various economical and social areas. They contain private and valuable data for their owners. In IS, security is enforced by different mechanisms, such as secured protocols between clients and servers or between servers in a distributed architecture. One common purpose of these tools is to enforce an access control (AC) policy. An AC policy is part of a security policy that deals with authorizations granted to users. An AC policy badly defined can lead to major issues for the company that uses the IS: for example we can cite banks that lost billions since a trader used more authorizations that he should have been granted [1]. After these scandals, governments of different nations decided to create new laws to protect information by regulating their access. In the financial domain, we can cite the Mer law in France [2] and Sarbanes-Oxley law in USA [3]. To comply with these laws, companies have to precisely define their AC policies.

Generally, AC constraints are classified into four categories: i) Permissions allowing the execution of an action, ii) Prohibitions forbidding the execution of an action, iii) Obligations linking two actions: if a person performed one of them, he must execute the second action [4], iv) Separation of duty (SoD) linking two actions: once a person performed one of them, he is not allowed to perform the second action.

We can also differentiate them according to their static or dynamic feature. Static constraints can be considered as invariants on the system state. They are always true whatever the state. Permissions, prohibitions and static SoD are static constraints. A static SoD constraint means that if a user is assigned to one role, he is prohibited from being a member of a second role [5]. Dynamic constraints require to take into account the history of the system, that is the set of actions already performed on a system. Obligations and dynamic SoD are dynamic constraints. With dynamic SoD, users may be authorized for roles that may conflict, but limitations are imposed while the user is actively logged onto the system.

In this article we propose a new formal specification language, called EB^3SEC, which aims to model AC policies. The main objectives of the language are: i) to enable the definition of the four categories of AC constraints, ii) to be supported by tools such as formal verifiers or interpreters. EB^3SEC is based on the EB^3 language, a process algebra language. This kind of languages is more suitable to express event ordering constraints, compared to state-based languages like B or Z [6]. The paper describes first how the four kinds of AC constraints can be expressed in EB^3SEC and then presents the associated interpreter which is an extension of the EB^3 interpreter. EB^3SEC is currently used in projects led with companies from financial domain[1] and healthcare domain[2].

Section 2 presents the EB^3 method and a case study, inspired from a real case study provided by our industrial partner; it has been simplified for illustrative purposes. Section 3 presents how we can model AC policies with the EB^3SEC method. Section 4 describes the EB^3SEC interpreter. Section 5 compares EB^3SEC to other similar languages. Finally, we conclude in Section 6, outlining future work.

2 Background

2.1 An Overview of EB^3

EB^3 [7] (entity-based black box) is a formal language for the specification of IS. An EB^3 specification contains four parts. A requirements class diagram describes classes and associations of the IS. A process expression (PE), denoted by **main(,)** describes valid input traces that must be accepted by the IS. A trace is a sequence of events. An event corresponds to an instanciation of an action of the IS. The other parts are omitted in this paper since they are not needed to understand the presentation of EB^3SEC. The EB^3 process algebra is similar to several other process algebras like CSP, CCS, ACP and Lotos. We shall briefly introduce it here; the reader is referred to [7] for a complete description.

Complex EB^3 process expressions (PE) are constructed from elementary process expressions (actions) using the following operators:

- The Kleene closure written $*$ is used to iterate a process expression an arbitrary number of time.
- The choice which is denoted by $|$ and expresses that one of two process expressions can be executed.

---

[1] http://pages.usherbrooke.ca/eb3sec/
[2] http://lacl.univ-paris12.fr/selkis/

- The quantified choice is a variant of the previous operator. When a process expression depends on the value of a free variable, a quantified choice can be used to express the fact we can execute this process expression for a specific value of the free variable. It is denoted by: $|x \in ens : \mathbf{a}(x)$, and it means that $\mathbf{a}(x)$ is executed with a specific value of x taken in the set ens.
- The wildcard _ is a syntax shortcut used instead of a quantified choice. For example, $a(\_)$ means $|x \in ens : \mathbf{a}(x)$
- The guard denoted by $p \Longrightarrow a$ where p is a first order logic predicate and a is a process expression, allows one to execute a only if the predicate p holds. If p does not hold, the process expression waits (blocking behavior) until p becomes true.
- The sequence denoted by $\mathbf{a \cdot b}$ allows one to execute the process expression $\mathbf{b}$ after the execution of the process expression $\mathbf{a}$.
- The parallel denoted by $\mathbf{a} \parallel \mathbf{b}$ allows one to execute the process expression $\mathbf{a}$ and the expression $\mathbf{b}$ in parallel with synchronization on common actions.
- The interleaving denoted by $\mathbf{a} \interleave \mathbf{b}$ allows process expressions $\mathbf{a}$ and $\mathbf{b}$ to be executed in parallel without any synchronization, even if they have common actions.
- The quantified interleaving is denoted by $\interleave p \in ens : \mathbf{exp}(p)$. It corresponds to the interleaving of process expressions $\mathbf{exp}(p)$ for all values of p contained in the set ens.

The main differences between EB^3 and CSP are: i) EB^3 allows one to use a single state variable, the system trace, in predicates of guard statements (as we shall see below); ii) EB^3 uses a single operator, concatenation (as in regular expressions), instead of prefixing and sequential composition, which makes specifications easier to read and write.

EB^3 is implemented in a platform called APIS that allows its interpretation. Section 4 will described more precisely this platform.

2.2 The Running Example

The example used to illustrate the article deals with a check deposit process in a bank. A bank client wants to deposit a check on his account. To start the check deposit procedure, the client has to bring the check to his bank branch where a bank employee starts the procedure. The check is first entered in the system and then registered to the client. The check is then validated or cancelled. If the check is validated the account of the client is credited, otherwise the client's account is not credited.

To prevent frauds, actions of a check deposit procedure must be delegated to different persons. We provide below a typical natural description of security rules that can be found in a bank.

- **rule 1:** Only clerks and bankers are allowed to make check deposit effective.
- **rule 2:** Only bankers and directors of branch are allowed to cancel or validate a check deposit.
- **rule 3:** Only clerks and bankers are allowed to modify the amount of a bank account.
- **rule 4:** The validation or the cancellation of a deposit cannot be done by the same person that did the check deposit.

- **rule 5:** If the value of a check deposit exceeds a given amount, the check deposit must be validated by two different persons including the director of branch. In Quebec this amount is equal to 10 000 $ whereas in Ontario this amount is equal to 8 000 $.
- **rule 6:** The modification of the bank account of the client must be done by the same employee that did the check deposit effective, with the same role (clerk or banker) in the same branch.

In this example, four different actions are used: deposit, cancel, validate credit. These actions have three arguments, which refer to the client, the identifier of the check and the value of the check deposit. In this example, a person can play different roles: *clerk*, *banker* and *branch − director*. We also assume that we have at least two bank branches one in Montreal, QC and the other in Toronto, ON.

3 Modeling Access Control Policies

3.1 EB^{3}SEC

The EB^{3}SEC language uses the EB^3 operators to specify valid input traces of *secure* events. A secure event is composed of an EB^3 event enhanced with security parameters representing persons, roles, organizations... The originality of EB^{3}SEC versus other AC languages is that the number and the type of security parameters can be adapted to the IS. Thus EB^{3}SEC allows the designer to define his own AC model. It can be existing models such as Bell and LaPadula [8], RBAC [9] or OrBAC [10]... or extensions of them in order to capture specific AC requirements of the IS. The AC model defined for the running example is derived from the RBAC model. Moreover, as we need to represent the different branches of a bank, we also used the concept of organization presented in OrBAC. We could represent this concept in RBAC thanks to the role concept. However it would duplicate the number of roles because, in our case, roles are the same in any branches. Security parameters chosen for the running example are: person, role, branch and time. Thus, a secure event is represented by a 5-tuple:

$\langle p, r, o, t, evt \rangle$ where $p \in Person, r \in Role, o \in Branch, t \in Timestamp,$
$label(evt) \in Action$

Function *label* returns the label of an event (*e.g. label*(deposit(...)) = deposit).

In EB^{3}SEC, the following kinds of AC constraints can be expressed:

- **Permission** allows the execution of an action.
- **Prohibition** forbids the execution of an action.
- **Obligation** links two actions. Once a person performed one of them, he must execute the second action.
- **Separation of duty (static and dynamic)** links two actions. Once a person performed one of them, he is not allowed to perform the second action.

The class diagram of an EB^3SEC specification is used to express static AC constraints. Process expressions are used to express dynamic AC constraints. Thus, static and dynamic AC constraints can be expressed in the same language. Furthermore, another advantage is that consistency of EB^3SEC models can be verified with model checking tools.

3.2 Permission and Prohibition

In comparison with other AC modeling languages, EB^3SEC allows permissions and prohibitions to be expressed with the same level of expressiveness as [11,10,12].

The class diagram presented in figure 1 describes permissions and prohibitions of the running example. The class *Person* lists the different persons of the IS. The class *Role* represents the roles that can be played in the IS. In the example, they are: *clerk*, *banker*, *branch-director*. The class *Branch* encompasses all branches of the IS (*i.e.*, *Montreal*, *Toronto*). The association *Play* linking these three classes depicts roles played by persons in the different branches. The class *Action* contains all actions that can be executed in the IS. The associations *Permission* and *Prohibition* associate a subset of actions of the class *Action* to a role in a branch. For *Permission* (resp. *Prohibition*) it gives the actions that a role is allowed (resp. not allowed) to execute.

Note that, even if it is not considered in the running example, EB^3SEC allows inheritance of roles or hierarchies of organizations to be defined in the security class diagram.

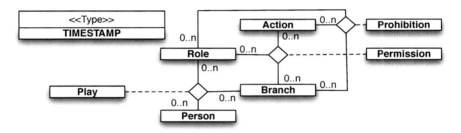

Fig. 1. Security class diagram for the running example

In our case study, the rules **Rule 1**, **Rule 2** and **Rule 3** concern permissions. Figure 2 gives an instanciation of the association *Permission* for **Rule 1**.

The security class diagram must be supplemented with a predicate that determines how an event (i.e., an action executed by a user) satisfies the permissions and prohibitions described in the security class diagram. The static predicate $sp(\langle p,r,o,t,evt \rangle)$ is built using the parameters of the security event and the classes and associations of the security class diagram. For the bank example, this predicate is the following:

$$sp(\langle p,r,o,t,evt \rangle) \triangleq \langle p,r,o \rangle \in play \wedge \\ \langle r,o,label(evt) \rangle \in permission \wedge \\ \langle r,o,label(evt) \rangle \notin prohibition \wedge \\ t \in TIMESTAMP$$

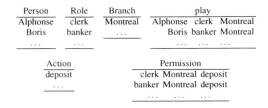

Fig. 2. Instantiation of the security class diagram for the running example

This predicate states that a security event of the form $\langle p,r,o,t,evt \rangle$ (from the signature above) holds iff the triple $\langle p,r,o \rangle$ is an instance of association Play, the triple $\langle r,o,label(evt) \rangle$ is an instance of association Permission and the triple $\langle r,o,label(evt) \rangle$ is not an instance of association Prohibition.

We omit here the EB^3SEC syntax for defining predicate sp. It is similar to the syntax used for predicates in attribute definitions and guards in EB^3. Essentially, the predicate sp can refer to any class and association attributes. Usual logical connectors and quantifiers are supported: $\wedge, \vee, \neg, \Rightarrow, \Leftrightarrow, \forall, \exists$. Transitive closure on recursive associations is also supported, in order to deal with inheritance and hierarchical data (*e.g.* hierarchical roles, hierarchical group of actions, hierarchical organizations).

EB^3SEC is an AC modeling language that allows one to specify both permissions and prohibitions. This feature is very useful but can be very dangerous too. Indeed, it can lead to permissions and prohibitions that contradict each other. Model checking tools can be used to verify the consistency of the model, but it is strongly advised to use permissions or prohibitions only.

Permissions and prohibitions used in the running example do not contain any constraints. EB^3SEC can also be used to model AC policy containing permissions and prohibitions with constraints. Examples of such AC rules can be found in [13].

3.3 Obligation

Contrary to permissions and prohibitions, the concept of obligation is not precisely defined in the literature. Roughly speaking, each AC language gives its own definition. In XACML [12], an obligation is always associated to a permission. If the obligation cannot be fulfilled, the permission is denied. In [10,9,4], it refers to an organizational constraint that obliges the user to perform another action after, before or while executing another one. For instance, we can express an obligation for a person to execute an action of acknowledgement after performing an action. Typically, it is the kind of constraints expressed in the sixth rule.

Basically, an obligation generally involves an ordering constraint between a number of security events, linked by the value of at least one security parameter (*i.e.*, the person ...). Thus it can be expressed in EB^3SEC by a process expression.

For example, **Rule 6** is specified by:

1. $\text{Rule6}(\,) \triangleq$
2. $\quad ||| \, c \in Customer : \ ||| \, d \in int : \ ||| \, m \in int :$

3. $\mid p \in Person : \mid r \in Role : \mid o \in Branch :$
4. $(\quad \langle p,r,o,\_,\mathsf{deposit}(c,d,m)\rangle$
5. $\bullet\quad \langle p,r,o,\_,\mathsf{credit}(c,d,m)\rangle)^*$

The second line contains the quantifications over functional parameters, in other words, it can be translated by: *For each customer c, for each check deposit with the number d and the amount m*. The third line contains quantifications related to the security class diagram and can be translated by: *there exist a person p, a role r and a branch o*. 5-tuples of the fourth and fifth lines stipulate that this person p can play the role r in the branch o and that, for this role and branch, actions deposit and credit are permitted and not prohibited. Furthermore, the sequence expresses that the deposit and the credit must be done by the same person playing the same role in the same branch. Suppose that the security event $\langle adrian, clerk, Montreal, \mathsf{deposit}(zoe,1,23)\rangle$ has already been executed. Thus, a security event corresponding to the event $\mathsf{credit}(zoe,1,23)$ can be performed only by *adrian* playing the role *clerk* in the branch of *Montreal*.

The process expression only expresses that the two actions have to be done by the same person with the same role in the same branch. However the system cannot physically force the person to perform the second action after executing the first one. We propose two methods that can be acceptable solutions for this problem.

A first method to enforce the obligation is to forbid any action, other than the second action, for the person after he executed the first one. It is modeled by the following PE.

1. **Rule6bis( )** $\triangleq$
2. $\mid\mid\mid c \in Customer : \mid\mid\mid d \in int : \mid\mid\mid m \in int :$
3. $\mid p \in Person : \mid r \in Role : \mid o \in Branch :$
4. $(\quad \langle p,r,o,\_,\mathsf{deposit}(c,d,m)\rangle$
5. $\bullet\quad (\quad \langle p,r,o,\_,\mathsf{credit}(c,d,m)\rangle$
6. $\mid FALSE \Longrightarrow$
7. $\langle p,r,o,\_,\_,\mathsf{deposit}(\_,\_,\_)\rangle$
8. $\mid FALSE \Longrightarrow$
9. $\langle p,r,o,\_,\_,\mathsf{cancel}(\_,\_,\_)\rangle$
10. $\mid FALSE \Longrightarrow$
11. $\langle p,r,o,\_,\_,\mathsf{validate}(\_,\_,\_)\rangle))^*$

In this PE, after performing the action deposit, the person has the choice between four actions. Three of these four actions are blocked by a guard that will never hold. Thus, the person can perform only the action deposit for the check deposit he performed.

The second approach used in [10], consists in adding sanctions to enforce obligations. In other words, the second action of the obligation is guarded by a constraint (generally temporal). While the guard holds, the person can execute the second action, but once it does not hold any more the sanction is executed. In **Rule6ter**, a second version of **Rule 6** called **Rule 6 ter** is given. **Rule 6 ter** adds to the sixth rule a temporal constraint: the modification has to be executed at least one hour after the deposit.

1. **Rule6ter( )** $\triangleq$
2. $\mid\mid\mid c \in Customer : \mid\mid\mid d \in int : \mid\mid\mid m \in int :$

3. $|p \in Person :\ |r \in Role :\ |o \in Branch :$
4. $|t \in TIMESTAMP :\ |t' \in TIMESTAMP :$
5. $(\quad \langle p,r,o,t, \mathsf{deposit}(c,d,m) \rangle$
6. $\cdot\ (\quad t'-t \leq 1\ h \Longrightarrow \langle p,r,o,t', \mathsf{credit}(c,d,m) \rangle$
7. $|\quad t'-t > 1\ h \Longrightarrow \langle \_,\_,\_,t', \mathsf{sanction}(p) \rangle))^*$

Once the person performed the action **deposit**, there is a choice between two guarded actions. The two guards partition the state space. Only during the hour following the deposit, the user can execute **credit**. After that, the only action that can be performed is **sanction**(p).

3.4 Separation of Duty

SoD (Separation of duty) is a security requirement that divides a task into subtasks and dispatches the execution of these subtasks to different persons [5]. Thus, the security of the process has fewer chances to be corrupted by a single person who could execute all the subtasks by himself. To express this kind of constraints, two methods can be used.

Static separation of duty
A first way to address the problem of SoD is called *static*. This method is used in [14,15] and consists in avoiding a person to play two different roles that are involved in the same SoD. To adapt this method to $\mathrm{EB}^3\mathrm{SEC}$, one has to perform a static analysis on the instantiated class diagram and check that the association *Play* respects this property.

In the running example, we want to express that Person *alphonse* cannot play the role *branch − director* both in branches *Montreal* and *Toronto*. This means that the two triples $\langle alphonse, branch - director, Montreal \rangle$ and $\langle alphonse, branch - director, Toronto \rangle$ cannot be present together in the association *Play*.

Dynamic separation of duty
For two actions, dynamic SoD forbids the user to execute the second action, once the first action has been executed. To achieve dynamic SoD, a history of tasks already performed needs to be registered. Methods [16,17] use this solution to implement dynamic SoD.

The fourth and fifth rules deal with dynamic SoD constraints. **Rule 4** can be expressed by the following PE.

1.   **Rule 4( )** $\triangleq$
2. $|||c \in Customer :\ |||d \in int :\ |||m \in int :$
3. $|p \in Person :\ |p' \in Person :$
4. $(\ \langle p,\_,\_,\_, \mathsf{deposit}(c,d,m) \rangle$
5. $\cdot\ p \neq p' \Longrightarrow$
6. $(\langle p',\_,\_,\_, \mathsf{validate}(c,d,m) \rangle\ |\ \langle p',\_,\_,\_, \mathsf{cancel}(c,d,m) \rangle))^*$

The second line is a quantification over functional attributes, and means that the process expression holds for all check deposits. The third line is a quantification over security attributes that stipulates that we can find two persons. One of them has to perform the action **deposit** (line 4), whereas the other has to perform either the action cancel or the action validate (line 6). The guard (line 5) specifies that the two persons are different.

In EB^{3}SEC, dynamic SoD constraints are defined at a workflow process level. For example, a person making the deposit of a check can still do other deposit but won't be able to make the validate or the cancel for the check he deposited. We illustrate this by the following sequences of events that can be received. The two first sequences can be accepted by PE **Rule 4**:

$\langle adrian, clerk, Montreal, 1234, \text{deposit}(zoe, 1, 123) \rangle \cdot$
$\langle jenny, clerk, Montreal, 4235, \text{validate}(zoe, 1, 123) \rangle$

and

$\langle adrian, clerk, Montreal, 1234, \text{deposit}(zoe, 1, 123) \rangle \cdot$
$\langle jenny, clerk, Montreal, 4235, \text{deposit}(arthur, 7, 51) \rangle \cdot$
$\langle adrian, clerk, Montreal, 8410, \text{validate}(arthur, 7, 51) \rangle \cdot$
$\langle jenny, clerk, Montreal, 4235, \text{cancel}(zoe, 1, 123) \rangle$

whereas the third one is not admissible by PE **Rule 4**:

$\langle adrian, clerk, Montreal, 1234, \text{deposit}(zoe, 1, 123) \rangle \cdot$
$\langle adrian, clerk, Montreal, 1234, \text{validate}(zoe, 1, 123) \rangle$

Rule 5 can be expressed by the following PE.

1. **Rule 5**( ) $\triangleq$
2. $\ \ \ |||\, c \in Customer : \ |||\, d \in int : \ |||\, m \in int :$
3. $\ \ \ \ \ \ |\, p \in Person : \ |\, o \in Branch :$
4. $\ \ \ \ \ \ |\, p' \in Person : \ |\, p'' \in Person :$
5. $\ \ \ \ \ \ \ \ \ (\langle p, \_, o, \_, \text{deposit}(c, d, m) \rangle \cdot$
6. $\ \ \ \ \ \ \ \ \ ((m > Branch.limit(o) \Longrightarrow$
7. $\ \ \ \ \ \ \ \ \ \ \ \ p \neq p' \wedge p \neq p'' \wedge p' \neq p'' \Longrightarrow$
8. $\ \ \ \ \ \ \ \ \ \ \ \ (\langle p', \_, o, \_, \text{validate}(c, d, m) \rangle$
9. $\ \ \ \ \ \ \ \ \ \ \ \ \|\, \langle p'', branch-director, o, \_, \text{validate}(c, d, m) \rangle))$
10. $\ \ \ \ \ \ \ \ \ |\, (m \leq Branch.limit(o) \Longrightarrow$
11. $\ \ \ \ \ \ \ \ \ \ \ \ p \neq p' \Longrightarrow \langle p', \_, o, \_, \text{validate}(c, d, m) \rangle))$
12. $\ \ \ \ )^*$

For checks with a value greater than the branch limit, two validate must be executed by two different persons. Otherwise there is only one validate to execute. In the example, the constraint on the check value is modeled in the PE by the expression $m > Branch.limit(o)$ used in a guard, *limit* being an attribute of the class *Branch*.

3.5 Combining AC Rules

AC rules are expressed in different PE involving common actions. It remains to state, in the following PE **main**, how these rules are combined.

$$\mathbf{main}(\,) \triangleq$$
$$\quad \mathbf{Rule\ 6}(\,)$$
$$\|$$
$$\quad \mathbf{Rule\ 4}(\,)$$
$$\|$$
$$\quad \mathbf{Rule\ 5}(\,)$$

To enforce the AC policy, we must be sure that all rules are satisfied. We use the parallel composition operator $\|$ to represent the conjunction of all the ordering constraints specified in the rules. For an event to be accepted, it must satisfy each rule where it is mentioned. This is exactly what the parallel operator expresses: its operands must synchronize on common events.

Only rules corresponding to obligations and SoD are involved in the PE **main**. Permissions and prohibitions are enforced by the static predicate, which is checked for each secure event received.

3.6 Discussion about EB^3SEC

Different approaches can be considered to specify AC rules in EB^3SEC. In this paper we advocate to distinguish rules according to the type of constraints which they refer to: *permissions*, *prohibitions*, *obligations* or *separation of duty*. However it could be difficult to classify rules given by users into one of these categories since a rule can involve more than one category. Another approach consists in defining one process expression for each user rule. This will promote traceability between user requirements and the EB^3SEC model.

Once an EB^3SEC model is defined, some verifications can be carried out. For instance, liveness or correctness of models can be checked.

A first step of these verifications is to check that all instances of the security class diagram are useful. In our running example, the designers can check that all instances of *Role* could at least be activated to execute an action. This usability of all instances of *Role* are generalizable to all classes and associations of the diagram. With these verifications, the designer can be sure that all permissions described in the diagram could finally be used. On the opposite, he could check that all prohibitions described in the diagram are really enforced. These steps of verification ensure the correctness of the model. Furthermore, the designer can also check liveness properties over the model. Once the model is validated, it can be used as a specification to implement the part of the IS which enforces AC policy. This implementation step can be automated, by using some controller synthesis techniques or could be implemented by hands.

4 Interpreting EB^3SEC Models

EB^3SEC is based on the same process algebra as EB^3 but extended with security environments. EB^3 is implemented in a platform called APIS [18] that allows its interpretation. Components of this platform can be reused to create a Policy Decision Point (PDP), which enforces an AC policy. Figure 3 illustrates the architecture of the PDP.

EB^3PAI [19] is an interpreter for EB^3 process expressions. It can be used to run EB^3SEC process expressions by translating secure events into EB^3 events:

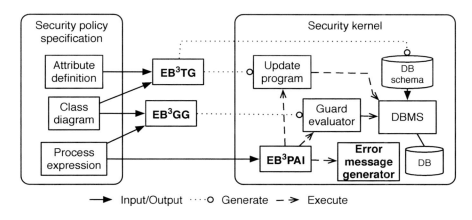

Fig. 3. Architecture of the PDP

$$\langle p,r,o,t,\mathsf{evt}(a_1,\ldots,a_n)\rangle \triangleq sp(\langle p,r,o,t,\mathsf{evt}\rangle) \implies \mathsf{evt'}(a_1,\ldots,a_n,p,r,o,t)$$

Process expressions can contain predicates referring to attributes of the requirements class diagram and the security class diagram. The requirements class diagram deals with functional requirements: all classes and associations used by the IS without considering security issues. We suppose that each class diagram is implemented in its own relational database. To implement the security class diagram, EB^3TG generates a relational database schema and update programs to implement attribute definitions. Update programs are used by EB^3PAI to maintain the database in a consistent state while secure events are executed. The module EB^3GG generates a *guard evaluator* program which contains procedures that are used by EB^3PAI to determine if a guard holds. It generates SQL queries on the database to obtain attribute values of objects. These procedures can refer to both security and requirements class diagrams. If an event is rejected by EB^3PAI, the *error message generator* generates an adapted error message. SQL code to evaluate predicate sp on a relational database implementing the security class diagram can also be generated.

EB^3PAI can execute arbitrary process expressions and the state of process expressions is stored in a database. It can efficiently execute quantified expressions over arbitrary large sets (both choice and interleave) thanks to optimization techniques [19]. Its main weaknesses are that its OODB is rather slow and its execution cannot be easily distributed over several processors. For high throughput banking applications, this is not sufficient. Hence, we are currently working on a new process algebra interpreter which will be restricted to deterministic and optimizable process expressions. These process expressions can be translated into an algebraic state transition diagram (ASTD) [20]. The execution of an ASTD is easier to distribute over several processors, thereby exploiting parallelism in the processing of events. The state of an ASTD is more compact than the one in EB^3PAI and can be easily stored into a relational database.

5 Related Work

Many methods deal with modeling access control policies. A first point will be to find comparison criteria. The article [21] proposes a framework that provides a set of comparison points. As EB^{3}SEC is mainly an AC policy modeling language, only comparison points called *model specification*, *policy expressiveness* and *policy language* are relevant. The first point deals with the abstraction level of models (*i.e.*, from implementation to requirements). The second point compares modeling methods by listing all concepts that can be expressed in the language. The last point compares languages on their syntax and formalisms.

EB^{3}SEC allows AC policies to be modeled at an abstract level and deals with AC requirements. Many other languages, such as [10,9,22,12,23], also deals with requirements as input. Generally these languages have a fix metamodel. In other words, if the requirements do not comply with this metamodel, it could be tricky to achieve the modeling. OrBAC [10] has a new notion of *organization* but has also a fix metamodel. EB^{3}SEC offers a flexible model to fit security requirements. Thereby, one can use a basic RBAC model in EB^{3}SEC but extensions can be defined by modifying the security class diagram.

Once the metamodel is defined, concepts that can be used are also a criteria of comparison. Permission is a basic concept included in all AC policy modeling languages but only few of them propose the concept of prohibition [24,25,26]. Permissions and prohibitions can have constraints to restrict their application domain [27,12]. Static SoD is integrated in the RBAC model [9,15], thus all languages based on RBAC can also be used to express static SoD. Dynamic SoD is considered in [17,22]. In [28], mechanisms to define dynamic SoD in XACML are lightly described. The Soda language [29] is an AC policy modeling language that exclusively focuses on modeling SoD with algebra. The concept of obligation is defined in languages such as [4]. EB^{3}SEC can express permissions, prohibitions, both of them can have additional constraints, static and dynamic SoD and obligations.

Another relevant characteristic of AC policy modeling languages is their formal or semi-formal feature. Formal languages own a precise semantics and allow different kinds of analyses, such as theorem proving, model-checking or animation, to be carried out. This indubitably improves the quality of the resulting models. Methods based only on metamodels [30,10] are semi-formal by nature. The work of [31] aims at formalizing XACML, or a subset of, in order to achieve some verifications. Generally, existing formal methods adopt a state-based approach [17,32,33]. In other words, expressing dynamic AC constraints implies to define additional data necessary to memorize previous states of the system. Other formal methods [29,34,35] are based on process algebra, Petri nets or temporal logic but focuses on dynamic SoD constraints. EB^{3}SEC is a formal language based on a process algebra that can express all kinds of AC constraints. EB^{3}SEC specifications can be simulated by an interpreter (see section 4) and verification tools are under construction.

Most languages previously cited have an implementation. [16] describes how to transform a Soda model into a CSP specification to implement a monitor. XACML has two implementations [3,4] which are used in industrial contexts to enforce AC policies. MotOrBAC [36] is an implementation of OrBAC. We are currently working on an implementation of EB^3SEC in a SOA architecture.

6 Conclusion and Future Work

This paper presents EB^3SEC, a formal language to express permissions, prohibitions, obligations and SoD constraints. Thanks to its high level of expressiveness, it allows the modeling of access control constraints at the workflow level in a unique framework. Another originality of EB^3SEC is that the AC model is not fixed and can be adapted to the requirements of the IS. For instance, in the paper, we have chosen an OrBAC model extended with the concept of time. EB^3SEC is currently tested in projects led with industrial partners from financial and healthcare domains. EB^3SEC access control policies can be efficiently interpreted, by reusing components from the APIS platform supporting the EB^3 method from which EB^3SEC originates.

As a formal method, EB^3SEC will allow one to use formal verification tools to verify a security policy. The next step in our work will be to develop a model-checker. As EB^3SEC is derived from EB^3, we plan to reuse results and tools developed for EB^3. Alloy [37] will surely be the tool we will consider. The first step will be to transform EB^3SEC models into Alloy models. To achieve this, the static part of an EB^3SEC model (i.e.: the security class diagram) has to be transformed into an Alloy model. At this step we will be able to verify the consistency between permissions rules and prohibition rules. Then, we will need to transform the dynamic part (i.e.: obligations, SoD and more generally all PEs) in an Alloy model. Thus, we will be able to verify that dynamic and static parts are consistent.

Moreover, if a formal method is used to specify the functional part of an information system, especially EB^3, it is also possible to verify the combination of the functional specification and the security rules. We also advocate a clear separation between the information system and its associated security policy, in order to have the ability to modify a security policy without having to modify the information system.

References

1. Société-Générale: Note explicative concernant la la fraude exceptionnelle (2008), http://www.communiques-presse.net/Banque/societe-generale-note-explicative-concernant-fraude-exceptionnel.html
2. Mer, F.: loi de sécurité financière. Journal Officiel (177) (January 2003)
3. Sarbanes, P., Oxley, M.: Sarbanes-oxley act. Public Law (116), 107–204 (2002)
4. Ni, Q., Bertino, E., Lobo, J.: An obligation model bridging access control policies and privacy policies. In: Proceedings of the 13th ACM Symposium on Access Control Models and Technologies. SACMAT 2008, pp. 133–142. ACM, New York (2008)
5. Ferraiolo, D.F., Kuhn, D.R., Chandramouli, R.: Role-Based Access Control. Artech House, Inc., Norwood (2003)

---

[3] http://code.google.com/p/enterprise-java-xacml/
[4] http://sunxacml.sourceforge.net/

6. Fraikin, B., Frappier, M., Laleau, R.: State-based versus event-based specifications for information systems: a comparison of B and EB^3. Software and Systems Modeling 4(3), 236–257 (2005)
7. Frappier, M., St-Denis, R.: EB^3: an entity-based black-box specification method for information systems. Software and System Modeling 2(2), 134–149 (2003)
8. Bell, D.E., LaPadula, L.J.: Secure computer systems: Mathematical foundations and model. The MITRE Corporation Bedford MA Technical Report M74244 May 1(M74-244), 42 (1973)
9. International Committee for Information Technology Standards (INCITS) American National Standard for Information Technology (ANSI): Role-Based Access Control. 359-2004 edn (February 2004)
10. Kalam, A.A.E., Benferhat, S., Miège, A., Baida, R.E., Cuppens, F., Saurel, C., Balbiani, P., Deswarte, Y., Trouessin, G.: Organization based access control. In: Proceedings of the 4th IEEE International Workshop on Policies for Distributed Systems and Networks. POLICY 2003, IEEE Computer Society, Washington, DC, USA (2003)
11. Sandhu, R.S., Coyne, E.J., Feinstein, H.L., Youman, C.E.: Role-based access control models. IEEE Computer 29(2), 38–47 (1996)
12. Moses, T.: eXtensible Access Control Markup Langage (XACML) Version 2.0. OASIS Standard (2005)
13. Konopacki, P., Frappier, M., Laleau, R.: Expressing access control policies with an event-based approach. Technical Report TR-LACL-2010-6, LACL (Laboratory of Algorithms, Complexity and Logic), University of Paris-Est, Paris 12 (2010), http://lacl.univ-paris12.fr/Rapports/TR/TR-LACL-2010-6.pdf
14. Anderson, A.: XACML Profile for Role Based Access Control (RBAC). OASIS Standard (2004)
15. Xin, J.: Applying model driven architecture approach to model role based access control system. Master's thesis, University of Ottawa (2006)
16. Basin, D., Burri, S.J., Karjoth, G.: Dynamic enforcement of abstract separation of duty constraints. In: Backes, M., Ning, P. (eds.) ESORICS 2009. LNCS, vol. 5789, pp. 250–267. Springer, Heidelberg (2009)
17. Miège, A.: Définition d'un environnement formel d'expression de politiques de sécurité. Modèle Or-BAC et extensions. PhD thesis, Paristech, ENST (September 2005)
18. Frappier, M., Fraikin, B., Gervais, F., Laleau, R., Richard, M.: Synthesizing information systems: the apis project. In: Rolland, C., Pastor, O., Cavarero, J.L. (eds.) RCIS, pp. 73–84 (2007)
19. Fraikin, B., Frappier, M.: Efficient symbolic computation of process expressions. Science of Computer Programming 74(9), 723–753 (2009)
20. Frappier, M., Gervais, F., Laleau, R., Fraikin, B., St-Denis, R.: Extending statecharts with process algebra operators. In: Innovations in Systems and Software Engineering, pp. 285–292. Springer, London (August 2008)
21. Alm, C., Drouineaud, M., Faltin, U., Sohr, K., Wolf, R.: A classification framework designed for advanced role-based access control models and mechanisms. Technical report, Technologie-Zentrum Informatik Bremen University (2009)
22. Wainer, J., Barthelmess, P., Kumar, A.: W-rbac a workflow security model incorporating controlled overriding of constraints. International Journal of Cooperative Information Systems 12(4), 455–486 (2003)
23. Basin, D., Doser, J., Lodderstedt, T.: Model driven security: From uml models to access control infrastructures. ACM Trans. Softw. Eng. Methodol. 15(1), 39–91 (2006)
24. Bertino, E., Catania, B., Ferrari, E., Perlasca, P.: A logical framework for reasoning about access control models. In: Proceedings of the Sixth ACM Symposium on Access Control Models and Technologies. SACMAT 2001, ACM, New York (2001)

25. Cholvy, L., Cuppens, F.: nalyzing consistency of security policies. In: Proceedings IEEE Symposium on Security and Privacy, pp. 103–112 (May 1997)
26. Jajodia, S., Samarati, P., Sapino, M.L., Subrahmanian, V.S.: Flexible support for multiple access control policies. ACM Trans. Database Syst. 26, 214–260 (2001)
27. Bertino, E., Bonatti, P.A., Ferrari, E.: Trbac: A temporal role-based access control model. ACM Trans. Inf. Syst. Secur. 4, 191–233 (2001)
28. Crampton, J., Khambhammettu, H.: Xacml and role-based access control. In: Presentation at DIMACS Workshop on Security of Web Services and e-Commerce, p. 174. Springer, Heidelberg (2005)
29. Li, N., Wang, Q.: Beyond separation of duty: An algebra for specifying high-level security policies. J. ACM 55(3), 1–46 (2008)
30. Lodderstedt, T., Basin, D.A., Doser, J.: Secureuml: A uml-based modeling language for model-driven security. In: Proceedings of the 5th International Conference on The Unified Modeling Language. UML 002, London, UK, pp. 426–441. Springer, Heidelberg (2002)
31. Kolovski, V., Hendler, J., Parsia, B.: Analyzing web access control policies. In: WWW 2007: Proceedings of the 16th International Conference on World Wide Web, pp. 677–686. ACM, New York (2007)
32. Sohr, K., Drouineaud, M., Ahn, G.J., Gogolla, M.: Analyzing and managing role-based access control policies. IEEE Trans. on Knowl. and Data Eng. 20, 924–939 (2008)
33. Basin, D., Clavel, M., Doser, J., Egea, M.: Automated analysis of security-design models. Inf. Softw. Technol. 51, 815–831 (2009)
34. Ayed, S., Cuppens-Boulahia, N., Cuppens, F.: Deploying access control in distributed workflow. In: Proceedings of the Sixth Australasian Conference on Information Security, Darlinghurst, Australia. AISC 2008, vol. 81, pp. 9–17. Australian Computer Society, Inc. (2008)
35. Kallel, S., Charfi, A., Mezini, M., Jmaiel, M., Klose, K.: From formal access control policies to runtime enforcement aspects. In: Massacci, F., Redwine Jr., S.T., Zannone, N. (eds.) ESSoS 2009. LNCS, vol. 5429, pp. 16–31. Springer, Heidelberg (2009)
36. Cuppens, F., Cuppens-Boulahia, N., Coma, C.: MotOrBAC: un outil d'administration et de simulation de politiques de sécurité. In: Security in Network Architectures (SAR) and Security of Information Systems (SSI), First Joint Conference, June 6-9 (2006)
37. Jackson, D.: Software Abstractions: Logic, Language, and Analysis. The MIT Press, Cambridge (2006)

An Extended Ontology for Security Requirements

Fabio Massacci[1], John Mylopoulos[1], Federica Paci[1],
Thein Thun Tun[2], and Yijun Yu[2]

[1] Department of Information Engineering and Computer Science,
University of Trento, Italy
[2] Department of Computing, The Open University, UK
{fabio.massacci,mylopoulos,paci}@disi.unitn.it, {t.t.tun,y.yu}@open.ac.uk

Abstract. Security concerns for physical, software and virtual worlds have captured the attention of researchers and the general public, thanks to a series of dramatic events during the past decade. Unsurprisingly, this has resulted in increased research activity on topics that relate to security requirements. At the very core of this activity lies the problem of determining a suitable set of concepts (aka ontology) for modeling security requirements. Many proposals for such ontologies exist in the literature. The main objective of this paper is to amalgamate and extend the security ontologies proposed in [1] and [2]. The amalgamation includes a careful comparison of primitive concepts in Problem Frames and Secure Tropos, but also offers a novel account for rather nebulous security concepts, such as those of vulnerability and threat. The new concepts are justified and related to the literature. Moreover, the paper offers a number of security requirements adopted from industrial case studies, along with their respective representation in terms of the proposed ontology.

1 Introduction

Security concerns for physical, software and virtual worlds have captured the attention of researchers and general public, thanks to a series of dramatic events during the past decade. Unsurprisingly, this has resulted in increased research activity on topics that relate to security requirements. At the very core of this activity lies the problem of determining a suitable set of concepts (aka ontology) for security requirements. In other words, the problem consists of selecting a suitable set of primitives through which security requirements can be conceptualised [3] for purposes of modeling, analysis and communication. The problem is clearly articulated in [4], where more than a dozen recent proposals for such security ontologies are reviewed and compared.

Massaccci et al. [1] presents one such proposal for an ontology, based largely on the PhD thesis of Nicola Zannone [5], and founded on the modeling framework of i* and Tropos. In parallel, Haley et al. [2] proposed Abuse Frames to take advantages of the analytical capability of Problem Frames [6]. Both proposals have their advantages: with goal-oriented security requirements analysis, malicious intentions of attackers can be identified through explicit characterization of social dependencies among actors; with problem-oriented security requirements analysis, valuable assets that lie within or beyond the system boundary can be identified through explicit traceability of shared phenomena among physical domains and the machine itself. There are also other proposals to address security requirements, such as misuse cases, obstacle analysis of anti-goals, information flow analysis of attack scenarios, etc. Each one of these has unique features that others do not. Having seen the advantages of alternative proposals, we would like to have a unified ontology to reach a shared understanding of the domain of security requirements, and also take advantage of multiple analysis techniques. The main objective of this paper is to amalgamate the security ontologies of SI* [1] and Abuse Frames [2], and also to account for rather nebulous security concepts, such as those of vulnerability and threat. A secondary objective is to develop techniques for using the amalgamated framework in order to model and analyze security requirements.

The research reported in this paper is conducted within the context of the SecureChange EU project [7]. The project has generated a number of realistic case studies including one from the Air-Traffic Management (ATM) domain. A first evaluation of our proposed security ontology is offered in the paper by applying it to a fragment of the ATM case study.

The rest of the paper is structured as follows. Section 2 briefly illustrates the baseline concepts from Secure i*/Tropos (SI*) and Problem Frames, and highlights the analysis facilities of each methodology to analyse security requirements. Section 3 presents the unified ontology, while Section 4 illustrates the application of the ontology to the ATM case study. Section 5 presents related work and Section 6 concludes the paper and highlights future directions.

2 Baseline

Tropos [8] is a development methodology for agent-oriented software, founded on i*. i* [9] is a modeling framework for early requirements. Through it, one can model the stakeholders for a given project, their goals and their social interdependencies. Both frameworks are grounded on the concepts of actor. An actor is an entity that wants (goals) and acts (by carrying out tasks) in order to fulfill its goals. Actors can be agents, roles or positions. Agents are materialized (as organizational or human agents, also systems). A role has goals and can carry out tasks, but only once it has an agent who plays the role. Positions are aggregates of roles. In order to fulfill their goals, actors depend on other actors to fulfill goals, carry out tasks or deliver resources. Such dependencies (aka dodependencies) constitute a basic form of relationship in modeling and analyzing social settings.

SI* [1] adopts and extends this framework. Firstly, actors not only want goals, but also own resources, tasks and goals. The meaning of owning a task or resource is an extension of the concept of owning a resource. There are tasks such as "Take a seat on flight AC847" that cannot be carried out by an actor (e.g., Paolo), unless another actor (e.g., Airline AC) who "owns" the task gives permission. Likewise, the University of Trento (UniTN) owns the goal "earn degree from UniTN", and another actor is not allowed to fulfill it unless she has permission from the owner. Given that services (i.e., goals, tasks and resources) can be owned, SI* also proposes permission dependencies (also known as can-dependencies) to indicate that one actor has given permission to another to use a given service. SI* also includes trust dependencies between actors and a service to represent a situation where actor A trusts actor B for a given service C, i.e., A trusts B to fulfill/carry out/deliver C.

There are at least two types of security analysis supported by SI*: [1] proposes an analysis where an SI* model is checked to confirm that all actors who have been delegated services (i.e., they are responsible for delivering some service) actually have permission to do so. In earlier work, Liu et al [10] proposed a complementary type of analysis which involves checking the consequences if an actor within a network of actors and delegations actually behaves like an attacker.

Problem Frames [6] (PF) is an intellectual tool to explore the typical contextual relationship between the machine domains to be specified and the related physical domains in the world. The behaviour of each domain is described by a number of phenomena. At the interfaces between these domains, phenomena are shared: some domains control the phenomena whilst other domains observe them. Having the knowledge of these physical domain expressed, requirements are modelled as constraints on the referred phenomena. In the security area, two problem-oriented approaches are interesting. Abuse Frames [11] analyses anti-requirements and their satisfaction arguments. The analysis of the anti-requirements and assoicated problem structure reveals typical situations where security requirements are violated. The intentions of stakeholders behind these anti-requirements are further treated as anti-goals [12]. Another one is the security argumentation framework [2, 13], which challenges the trust assumptions on all phenomena included or excluded in the problem structure, in the context of whether they may cause harm to the assets identified with value to the stakeholders.

Not all phenomena are referred by the requirements, and not all are related to the requirements problem. Therefore two kinds of analysis in Problem Frames methodology are fundamental to the requirements analysts. One analysis is to establish the satisfaction argument semantics between the indicative phenomena in the world domains W and the optative properties of the machine domain to specify S and the constraints in requirements, denoted by $W, S \vdash R$ [14].

The other analysis explores the relationships of phenomena at the boundaries between the system and the context. A phenomena in the knowledge may be excluded from the argument, therefore hidden from the problem analysis. Hidden Domains or Hidden Phenomena are methodological concepts in PF. It helps one focus on the relevant information to analyse a problem, and also helps one consider the relationship between decomposition and composition of problems, reflecting the widsom "Divide and conqueor, unite and rule". The term Frames refers to typical structural relationships between certain types of behaviour domains (e.g., Causal, Biddable or Lexical), in order to reason about the associated typical concerns such as interaction and initialisation using Event Calculus [15].

3 The Extended Ontology

A bird's eye view of our proposal has as follows. The very top of the taxonomy is adopted from DOLCE [16], a foundational ontology intended to account for basic concepts that underlie natural language and human cognition. Lower levels of the taxonomy include concepts from i*, problem frames and argumentation frameworks, with security concepts occupying the lowest strata of the taxonomy. Key among the concepts we introduce is the concept of Proposition, with instances such as "Want for customers for our business" and "Paolo is married". The other key concept is that of Situation, representing a partial state of the world, e.g., "High oil prices", or "Many unhappy customers".

The most general concept is *Thing*, which has as instances all the things that can exist in the world.

An object is a thing that persists (endurant in [16]). An event, instead, is an instantaneous happening (perdurant) that changes some objects. Specializations of the concept Object include *Proposition, Situation, Entity* and *Relationship*.

A proposition is an object representing a true/false statement. A situation is a partial world described by a proposition (its description)[17]. Arbitrary propositions are true/false/ undefined in a situation, given its partial world status. The status of the world is expressed by a predicate over the entities involved[1]. Situations can have structure consisting of relationships and things standing in those relationships. Some entities and relationships according to the common sense always satisfy certain predicates, making them strong beliefs or trust assumptions. Therefore we consider predicates in the logical world on every entity and relationship to question even their absense/existence. This makes a security argumentation more powerful.

An entity is an object that has a distinct, separate existence from all other things, though that existence need not be material. Thus, Santa Claus, my cancelled trip, a square circle are entities. A relationship, on the other hand, is an object that participates in a certain situation along with other objects (its relata); the existence of a relationship depends on that of its relata.

Entities. *Entity* is specialized into *Actor, Action, Process, Resource,* and *Asset*, all concepts adopted from Goal-Oriented Requirements Engineering (GORE) approaches. An actor is an entity that can act and intend to want or desire. *Stakeholder* and *Attacker* are two important specializations of *Actor* for the domain of security requirements. A stakeholder is an actor who has a stake in the system-to-be, while an attacker wants to prevent the fulfillment of the requirements for the system-to-be. An action is an entity performed by an actor, which can generate events, and can have preconditions and post-conditions. A Process

---

[1] Note that predicates are a special form of propositions, and through reification they can be grounded into sentences of propositions.

is an entity that generates events and changes objects. *Activity* is a specialization of *Process*, consisting of actions. *Attack* specializes *Activity*, and is always carried out by an Attacker. We distinguish between Process and Activity in our ontology because we want to allow for processes that do not involve any actions, e.g., a fire burning, or an earthquake. A resource is an entity without intention or behaviour. An asset is an entity of value that can be owned and used. For example, an asset can be an passenger (actor) whose life needs to be protected, can be an engine (process) whose behaviour has a value to the protector, or can be an aircraft (resource) whose value are tangible for other actors. A relationship such as the organization chart of the air traffic management organisation is also an asset as long as its value need to be protected.

Relationships. Specializations of *Relationship* include *do-dependency*, *can-dependency* and *trust-dependency* adopted from SI*. These are all ternary relationships between two actors and an asset. In addition, there are many binary relationships that characterize other concepts in our ontology. For example, actors are entities who *want* goals and *carries out* actions. *composes*, *contributes*, *uses*, and *provides* are some of the other relationships included in the ontology. AND/OR refinement is a relationship between a goal and two or more other goals that indicates that a goal can be refined into subgoals. contributes relates two goals and indicates that one goal has a positive or negative impact on the satisfaction of the other. provides is a relationship from an actor to resource, which specifies that an actor provides a certain resource. uses is a Relationship from a process to a resource denoting that the process generates or consumes the resource. fulfills relates an entity to a goal that the entity fulfills.

For the sake of security requirement analysis, the ontology includes also the following specializations of Relationship: *damages*, *exploits*, *protects*, and *denies*. damages is a relationship between an attack and an asset, where the attack causes harm to the asset. exploits is a relationship between attack and vulnerability. protects relates a security goal to an asset. Finally, denies relates an anti-goal to a requirement. A complete list of all the possible relationships is found in Figure 1.

Propositions. Proposition is specialized into *Fact*, *Claim*, *Argument*, *Domain Assumption*, *Quality Proposition*, and *Goal*, depending on the different types of proposition modalities. A fact is a true proposition. A claim is a proposition claimed to be true by an actor. An argument is a proposition consisting of a set of claims. A domain assumption is a proposition about the domain assumed to be true by an actor. A quality proposition is a proposition about the quality of the system-to-be. A goal is a concept found in GORE approaches, and represents a proposition an actor wants to make true. For security analysis purposes, Goal is specialized into *Requirement, Security Goal,* and *Anti-Goal*. A requirement is a goal wanted by a stakeholder. A security goal prevents harm to an asset through the violation of confidentiality, integrity, and availability [2]. An anti-goal is a goal an attacker wants which denies the fulfillment of a requirement of the system-to-be.

```
Thing   :: = Event | Object | ...
Object  :: = Situation | Proposition | Entity | Relationship
Situation :: = Domain | Context | Vulnerability | Threat | Specification
Context :: = Domain
Proposition :: = Argument | Predicate| Claim |Domain Assumption|
Quality  Proposition |Goal
Argument :: = {Claim}
Goal :: = Requirement | Security Goal | Anti Goal
Entity :: = Action | Process | Actor | Resource | Asset
Activity :: = {Action}
Attack :: = Activity
Actor :: = Stakeholder | Attacker
Specification :: = {Domain Assumption} {Quality Proposition} {Action}
Relationship :: = fulfills | exploits | protects | denies | damages |
 wants |carries out | uses | provides | trust-dependency | do-dependency |
 can-dependency | composes | contributes| ...
```

Fig. 1. Ontology Representation in EBNF

Situations. The *Context* and *Domain* concepts coming from Problem Frames are specializations of Situation. These concepts are useful to define the situation of system boundaries, to allow one place focus on analysis while hide the unnecessary details. For the analysis of every problem or subproblem, a different situation may be selected from the physical world. Thus the context is a situation in which the system-to-be will operate; and a domain is a situation that is part of the context. In Problem Frames, domains can be classified as biddable, causal, and lexical. By biddable, a domain's behaviour is not fully predicable or controllable, usually represented by human actors or natural processes. By causal, a domain's behaviour is predicable or controllable, usually represented by activities. By *lexical*, a domain's behaviour is predefined, usually by a resource.

Another concept adopted from Problem Frames is *Specification*. A specification is an entity consisting of actions, quality propositions, and domain assumptions. Thus, is a collection of indicative propositions about the entities in the system-to-be.

Vulnerability is a specialization of Situation and is adopted from the Security domain. A vulnerability is a situation where some actions that are part of an attack can be carried out (i.e., their preconditions are satisfied). A threat, on the other hand, consists of a situation that includes an attacker and one or more vulnerabilities.

Figure 1 summarizes the elements of our ontology in Extended Backus-Naur Format (EBNF)[2]. A EBNF rule of the form A ::= B | C | ... indicates that concept A has concepts B and C (and possibly others) as specializations. A rule

---

[2] When ... abbreviation is used in the production rule, its semantics is to rewrite all the previous rules of the same LHS by extension [18].

of the form A ::= {C} indicates that each instance of A consists of (has parts) zero or more instances of C. [] is similar to { } but allows for zero or one instance.

4 ADS-B - A Case Study

Air traffic control management systems are changing. They are moving from systems that rely on radar technology to systems that use precise location data from the global satellite network. Automatic Dependent Surveillance-Broadcast (ADS-B) technology is enabling such evolution. ADS-B-equipped aircrafts determine their own position using a global navigation satellite system, and periodically broadcast their position, identity and other relevant information such as speed, and height to the ground stations and other aircrafts with ADS-B equipment. With ADS-B, both pilots and controllers will see on their displays (the controller working position) highly accurate traffic data from satellites. Thus, ADS-B provides accurate information and frequent updates to airspace users and controllers, and hence supports improved use of airspace, reduced ceiling/visibility restrictions, improved surface surveillance, and enhanced safety.

If on one side, ADS-B has several benefits for air traffic management, on the other side, it arises several security concerns, because ADS-B transmissions can be easily corrupted. A concrete example of corruption of ADS-B transmissions is the spoofing of the GPS Satellite that provides the GPS signal to aircrafts equipped with ADS-B to allow them to determine their position. Such an attack can be easily accomplished using a GPS satellite simulator. To conduct the spoofing attack, an adversary broadcasts a fake GPS signal with a higher signal strength than the true signal. The GPS receiver believes that the fake signal is actually the true GPS signal from space and ignores true signal. The receiver then proceeds to calculate erroneous position or time information based on this false signal.

We now illustrate how Problem Frames and Goal-Oriented approaches, and the security ontology we have proposed here allow one to model a security requirement problem domain at different levels of abstraction.

4.1 Modeling the ADS-B Example in Problem Frames

Using the Problem Frames approach (including Abuse Frames), we first describe the problem context, which include the following problem world domains (Figure 2):

GPS satellite broadcasts position signals
Aircraft (i) receives GPS signals, (ii) calculates their positions, (iii) broadcasts the position and identity information over ADS-B, (iv) follow instructions from the ATC operator, and they need to be routed safely and securely
ADS-B Ground Receivers receive ADS-B broadcasts and reports to the central processor
Central Processor (i) validates the position and identity information, (ii) produces tracking reports for the operator, (ii) sends the instructions from the the ATC operator to the aircrafts.

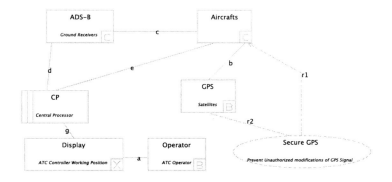

Fig. 2. ADS-B: Problem World Domains

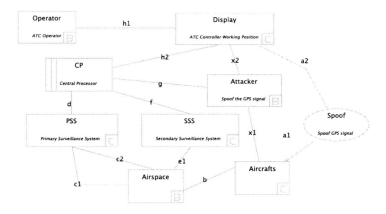

Fig. 3. ADS-B: Problem World Domains from an Attacker's Perspective

Display shows the tracking reports of the controller working position and receives the operator instructions

ATC Operator checks tracking reports and send routing instructions

Figure 2 shows the basic structure of the problem, which includes three types of nodes (Requirements as ellipses, Physical Domains as rectangles, and Machine Domains as rectangles marked by strips). The relationship between them are viewed as three types of links (Interface Phenomena as solid lines, Reference Phenomena as dashed lines and Constraint Phenomena as dashed arrows).

We consider as main security requirement to prevent unauthorized modifications of the aircraft position. In the above context, we can make a tentative argument that the behavior of the problem world domain ensures that the requirement is satisfied.

For the security analysis, we need to introduce into the problem context an attacker with its own requirement: that is, an attacker who wishes to harm an

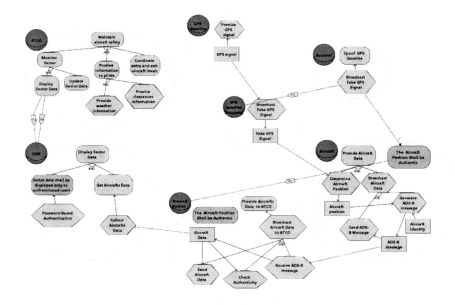

Fig. 4. The ADS-B Example modeled in Secure Tropos

asset protected by the system. Such a requirement of an attacker could be to spoof the GPS signal broadcasted by GPS Satellite to compromise the aircrafts position (as shown in Figure 3). In that case, the asset is the aircraft position.

We can construct a tentative argument showing that the ATM system will satisfy the "Prevent Unauthorized Modifications of Aircraft Positions" requirement, thus preventing the attacker from achieving his/her requirement. However, our analysis has to recognise the attacker is likely to modify parts of the problem world domain by exploiting vulnerabilities, using which the attacker will have his/her requirement satisfied by the ATM system. These vulnerabilities are rebuttals to the tentative arguments.

In the problem context shown in Figure 3, several vulnerabilities could be exploited by an attacker. An attacker could produce fake GPS signals in order to force aircrafts to produce incorrect position information, thus potentially allowing aircrafts to follow flight paths desired by the attacker.

Although Problem Frames concepts help explore the functional requirements that concerns the interfaces at the system boundary, they do not express the intentions behind the actors for both stakeholders and attackers.

4.2 Modeling the ADS-B Example in Secure Tropos

Using Secure Tropos concepts, one would model the physical domains by detailing the rationale ("why") behind them. Note that not all the rationale of physical domains can be modelled as intentions (goals desired by actors), thus the notion of tasks and resources are used to represent the physical domains interacting with the actors. The goals represent the requirements of the actor, the tasks represent the processes by which the goals are fulfilled, and the resources represent the shared phenomena that are observed or controlled by an actor or a process.

In the following (Figure 4), we present all the domains as actors: the ovals model goals, the rectangles represent resources, and the exagons model the tasks.

ATCO. The main goal of the ATCO is to "Maintain aircraft safety" that is AND-decomposed into three subgoals:"Monitor Sector", "Provide Information to Pilots", and "Coordinate entry and exit aircraft levels". The "Monitor Sector" goal can be further AND-decomposed into the subgoals "Display Sector Data " and "Update Sector Data ". The fulfillment of the goal "Display Sector Data " is delegated by the ATCO to the CWP.

CWP. The "Display Sector Data" goal is AND-decomposed into the goal "Sector Data shall be displayed only to authenticated users" and in the goal of "Display Aircraft Data". Note that the former subgoal is in fact a constraint on the latter in order to protect the confidentiality of the valuable assets, users. Furthermore, the latter is fulfilled by the task "Password Based Authentication"; the former is fulfilled by the task "Display Aircraft Data" that takes in input the resource "Aircraft Data". The "Aircraft Data" resource is provided to the CWP by the Ground Station.

Ground Station. The main goal of Ground Station actor is "Provide Aircraft Data to ATCO". This goal is fulfilled by the task "Broadcast Aircraft Data " which is decomposed into the tasks "Receive ADS-B message", "Check Authenticity", and "Send Aircraft Data". "Check Authenticity" realises the security goal of protecting the confidentiality of data, therefore it is regarded as a security requirement that constraints the other tasks that fulfils the functional requirements.

GPS Satellite. The main goal of GPS Satellite is "Provide GPS Signal" that is fulfilled by the task "Broadcast GPS Signal" that produces the GPS Signal resource.

Attacker. The main goal of the Attacker actor is "Spoof GPS Satellite" whose satisfaction is delegated to the GPS Satellite Simulator actor.

GPS Satellite Simulator. The GPS Satellite Simulator fulfills the goal "Spoof GPS Satellite" of the Attacker by providing the task "Broadcast Fake GPS Signal" that produces the "Fake GPS Signal" resource.

Aircraft. The Aircraft actor has two goals: "Provide Aircraft Data", and the security goal "Aircraft Position shall be Authentic". "Provide Aircraft Data" is fulfilled by the tasks "Determine Aircraft Position", and "Broadcast Aircraft Data". In absence of Attacker, "Determine Aircraft Position" should process the GPS signal resource provided by GPS Satellite and produce the resource "Aircraft Position". Due to the presence of Attacker, "Determine Aircraft Position" identify the aircraft position on the basis of the "Fake GPS Signal" transmitted by the task "Broadcast Fake GPS Signal" of the GPS Satellite Simulator under control of the Attacker. "Broadcast Fake GPS Signal" fulfills Attacker's goal "Spoof GPS Signal" but has a negative impact on the fulfillment of Aircraft's Security Goal "Aircraft Position shall be Authentic". The satisfaction of "Aircraft Position shall be Authentic" is delegated to the Ground Station actor which fulfills it with the task "Check Authenticity". "Broadcast Aircraft Data" task is decomposed in two tasks, "Generate ADS-B Message", and "Send ADS-B Message".

4.3 Modeling the ADS-B Example Using the Extended Ontology

In this section we show how using the concepts of the security ontology, we are able to model the ADS-B example at a more detailed abstraction level than both PF and SI* approaches and reason about the security argumentations that would not be possible using just PF or just SI*. Figure 5 sketches the spoofing of the GPS Satellite threat scenario, and the impact that it has on the assets and on the satisfaction of the security requirements of the ABS-B-based surveillance system. Due to the lack of space, we model only the domains involved in the threat that is, the Aircraft, Attacker, GPS Satellite Simulator, and the Ground Station. The requirements of each actor are modeled using the notion of goals, and the relationship wants between the actor and the goal the actor desires to achieve.

The threat scenario is represented by the threat "Spoofing GPS Signal" that consists of two attackers "Adversary" and "GPS Satellite Simulator", the vulnerability "Aircraft receiver is not able to distinguish a Fake GPS Signal from a Fake one", and the attack "Broadcast Fake GPS Signal". Thus, the "Adversary" attacker wants the anti goal "Spoof GPS Satellite" to cause harm to the asset "Aircraft Position" of the Aircraft actor. To fullfill the anti-goal, the "Adversary" attacker carries the attack "Broadcast Fake GPS Signal" which exploits the vulnerability "Aircraft receiver is not able to distinguish a Fake GPS Signal from a Fake one". If the attack is successful, the anti goal is satisfied denying the satisfaction of the the security goal "Aircraft Position shall be Authentic" wanted by the Aircraft actor, which aims to protect the "Aircraft Position" asset from.

5 Related Work

The need of the security community to have a common ontology to promote knowledge sharing and understanding of the security domain has been widely recognized [19] as a branch of research. Several ontologies for security [20, 21, 22, 23, 24, 25, 1, 26] have been proposed but they fall short in completeness and generality. We can classify the existing proposals about security ontologies in two main categories: ontologies that includes only security specific concepts such as those coming from threat analysis, and ontologies that includes security related

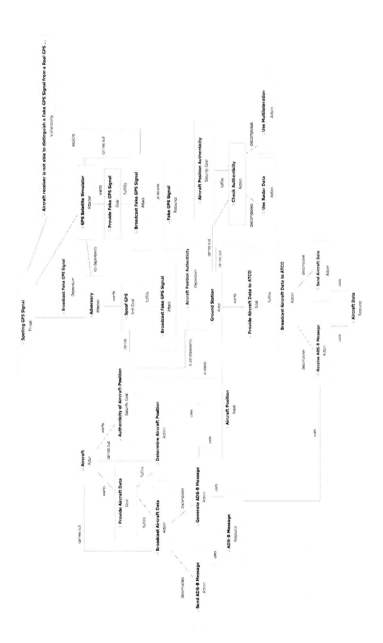

Fig. 5. The ADS-B Example modeled using the security ontology concepts

concepts, concepts for modeling requirements, and the dependencies between them. The ontologies proposed by Denker et al. [20], Kim et al.[25], Fenz et al. [22], Karyda et al. [24] , and Undercoffer et al. [26] belong to the first category; instead the proposals by Firesmith et al. [23], Dobson et al. [21], and Massacci et al. [1] fell in the the second category.

Denker et al. [20] propose an ontology to augment web service and agents descriptions with security annotations: the ontology consists of two subontologies that captures respectively security mechanism and credentials. Similarly to Denker et al. ontology, the security ontology proposed by Kim et al.[25] consists of seven ontologies that include concepts related to security mechanisms, protocols, algorithms, and credentials. In our security ontology we do not include explicitly the concepts of security mechanism and credentials but they can be included in our ontology as a specialization of process and the resource concepts. Fenz et al. [22] and Karyda et al. [24] propose two ontologies including concept used in threat analysis. Fenz et al. ontology consists of five ontologies to model threats, countermeasures, affected infrastructures, the impact of threat, the enterprise being threaten, and the persons involved. Similarly, Karyda et al. ontology includes the concepts of assets, countermeasures, persons, and threats. Undercoffer et al. [26] have defined an ontology to specify computer attacks. Our ontology is not less expressive than the above security ontologies because in our ontology we are able to model the threat that can harm the system-to-be, that is a situation that involves one or more attackers that carries out an attack which exploits a vulnerability. We are, also, able to model which is the asset that is damaged by the attack and the possible countermeasures can be modeled using the action concepts.

Firesmith et al. [23] defined an ontology for safety related requirements which models how the derivation of safety requirements depends on threat analysis. Instead, Dobson et al. [21] have defined an ontology for dependability requirements that includes security issues such as dependability, reliability, availability, integrity, confidentiality, and safety. In our ontology we do not focus on a specific type of requirements but we are able to model both functional and non functional requirements such as security requirements and how these requirements will be fulfilled by the system-to-be. Moreover,we are able to capture the dependencies between the security requirements of the system-to-be and the assets that need to be protected by security requirements, and the threats that can deny the satisfaction of those requirements.

Massacci et al. [1] has proposed a security ontology which extends the i* ontology [9] to model security at an organizational level that is based on the concepts of ownership, trust and delegation dependencies between actors.

Our ontology unifies the concepts from Massacci et al. ontology and the concepts from Problem Frames and Abuse Frames approaches to model requirements, and other security relevant concepts such as threat, attack, attack, vulnerability. Thus, our ontology is the first attempt to define a complete ontology that helps understanding the security problem domain.

6 Conclusions

This paper presents an ontology for security requirements that unifies existing concepts from the Problem Frames and Secure i* methodologies, and security concepts such as asset and threat. The propopsed extended ontology brings together these concepts to facilitate a security argumentation that was not feasible in each method due to the missing constructs. We have illustrated the expressiveness of the proposed ontology with respect to PF and SI* by modelling the security requirements of a case study from the Air Traffic Management domain. The ontology we show here has the potential to be further extended to accommodate more concepts in the area of security requirements by incorporating other methodologies such as misuse cases.

Acknowledgement

This work has been partially funded by EU-SecureChange project, and the EU-NESSoS NoE.

References

1. Massacci, F., Mylopoulos, J., Zannone, N.: Computer-aided support for secure tropos. Automated Software Engg. 14(3), 341–364 (2007)
2. Haley, C.B., Laney, R.C., Moffett, J.D., Nuseibeh, B.: Security requirements engineering: A framework for representation and analysis. IEEE Trans. Software Eng. 34(1), 133–153 (2008)
3. Gruber, T.R.: Toward principles for the design of ontologies used for knowledge sharing. Int. J. Hum.-Comput. Stud. 43(5-6), 907–928 (1995)
4. Blanco, C., Lasheras, J., Valencia-García, R., Fernández-Medina, E., Toval, A., Piattini, M.: A systematic review and comparison of security ontologies. In: ARES 2008: Proceedings of the 2008 Third International Conference on Availability, Reliability and Security, pp. 813–820. IEEE Computer Society Press, Washington, DC, USA (2008)
5. Zannone, N.: A requirements engineering methodology for trust, security, and privacy (2006)
6. Jackson, M.: Problem frames: analyzing and structuring software development problems. Addison-Wesley Longman Publishing Co., Inc., Boston (2001)
7. Secure change project
8. Bresciani, P., Perini, A., Giorgini, P., Giunchiglia, F., Mylopoulos, J.: Tropos: An agent-oriented software development methodology. Autonomous Agents and Multi-Agent Systems 8, 203–236 (2004)
9. Yu, E.S.K.: Modelling strategic relationships for process reengineering. PhD thesis, Toronto, Ont., Canada, Canada, Adviser-Mylopoulos, John (1995)
10. Liu, L., Yu, E.S.K., Mylopoulos, J.: Security and privacy requirements analysis within a social setting. In: [27], pp. 151–161 (2003)
11. Lin, L., Nuseibeh, B., Ince, D.C., Jackson, M., Moffett, J.D.: Introducing abuse frames for analysing security requirements. In: [27], pp. 371–372 (2003)

12. van Lamsweerde, A.: Elaborating security requirements by construction of intentional anti-models. In: ICSE, pp. 148–157. IEEE Computer Society, Los Alamitos (2004)
13. Nuseibeh, B., Haley, C.B., Foster, C.: Securing the skies: In requirements we trust. IEEE Computer 42(9), 64–72 (2009)
14. Hall, J.G., Rapanotti, L., Jackson, M.: Problem frame semantics for software development. Software and System Modeling 4(2), 189–198 (2005)
15. Laney, R.C., Tun, T.T., Jackson, M., Nuseibeh, B.: Composing features by managing inconsistent requirements. In: du Bousquet, L., Richier, J.L. (eds.) ICFI, pp. 129–144. IOS Press, Amsterdam (2007)
16. Gangemi, A., Guarino, N., Masolo, C., Oltramari, A., Schneider, L.: Sweetening ontologies with DOLCE. Knowledge Engineering and Knowledge Management: Ontologies and the Semantic Web, 223–233 (2002)
17. Gangemi, A., Presutti, V.: Ontology Design Patterns. In: Handbook of Ontologies, 2nd edn., Springer, Berlin (pres)
18. Cordy, J.R.: Txl - a language for programming language tools and applications. Electron. Notes Theor. Comput. Sci. 110, 3–31 (2004)
19. Blanco, C., Lasheras, J., Garcia, R.V., Fernandez-Medina, E.: A systematic review and comparison of security ontologies (2008)
20. Denker, G., Kagal, L., Finin, T., Sycara, K., Paoucci, M.: Security for daml web services: Annotation and matchmaking. In: Second International Semantic Web Conference (2003)
21. Dobson, G., Sawyer, P.: Revisiting ontology-based requirements engineering in the age of semantic web. International Seminar on Dependable Requirements Engineering of computerised Systems at NPPs (2006)
22. Fenz, S., Weippl, E.: Ontology based it-security planning. In: Twelve Pacific Rim International Symposium on Dependable Computing (2006)
23. Firesmith, D.: Engineering safety related requirements for software intensive systems. In: 27th International Conference on Software Engineering (2005)
24. Karyda, M., Balopoulos, T., Gymnopoulos, L., Kokolakis, S., Lambrinoudakis, C., Gritzalis, S., Dritsas, S.: An ontology for secure e-government applications. In: International Conference on Availability, Reliability and Security (2006)
25. Kim, A., Luo, J., Kang, M.: Securit ontology for annotating resources. In: 4th International Conference on Ontologies, Databases, and Applications of Semantics (2005)
26. Undercoffer, J., Joshi, A., Pinkston, J.: Modeling computer attacks: An ontology for intrusion detection. In: 6th International Symposium on Recent Advances in Intrusion Detection, pp. 113–135. Springer, Heidelberg (2003)
27. In: RE 11th IEEE International Conference on Requirements Engineering (RE 2003), September 8-12. IEEE Computer Society, Los Alamitos (2003)

A Pattern Based Approach for Secure Database Design

Jenny Abramov[2], Arnon Sturm[1], and Peretz Shoval[1]

[1] Department of Information Systems Engineering
[2] Deutsche Telekom Laboratories (T-Labs)
Ben-Gurion University of the Negev
Beer Sheva 84105, Israel
{jennyab,sturm,shoval}@bgu.ac.il

Abstract. Security in general and database protection from unauthorized access in particular, are crucial for organizations. Although it has long been accepted that system requirements should be considered from the early stages of the development, non-functional requirements, such security, tend to be neglected or dealt-with only at the end of the development process. Various methods have been proposed, however, none of them provide a complete framework to guide, enforce and verify the correct implementation of security policies within a system design, and generate source code from it. In this paper, we present a novel approach that guides database designers, to design a database schema that complies with the organizational security policies related to authorization. First, organizational policies are defined in the form of security patterns. Then, during the application development, the patterns guide the implementation of the security requirements and the correct application of the patterns is verified. Finally, the secure database schema is automatically generated.

Keywords: Secure software engineering, database design, authorization.

1 Introduction

Data is the most valuable asset for an organization as its survival depends on the correct management, security, and confidentiality of the data [5]. In order to protect the data, organizations must secure data processing, transmission, and storage. Nowadays, organizational systems are developed with minor emphasis on security aspects; system developers tend to neglect security requirements or deal with them only at the end of the development process.

Various efforts to promote the security aspect at the early stages of the software development life cycle have been made. These include the development of modeling methods such as UMLsec [11] and SecureUML [2,13] and methodologies for designing secure databases, such as [7]. Nevertheless, such methods primarily provide guidelines of how to incorporate security within a certain stage of the software development process, or address a specific aspect in the development of secure applications. In addition, these methods do not refer to the organizational security policies. We are not aware of existing methods that provide a complete framework to both guide and enforce particular organizational security policies on a system design, and finally transform the design to code. Since most organizational data are stored and managed using databases, this research focuses on protecting databases against unauthorized access and use.

In this paper, we propose a comprehensive approach that addresses the aforementioned gaps. The approach deals with both the organizational level and the application level. At the organizational level, organizational security policies are defined by security officers and domain experts in the form of security patterns. These patterns capture expert knowledge about a recurring problem and provide a well-proven solution to it [8]. As the patterns are independent of specific application, they can be used in the development of many applications. At the application level, the designers create a conceptual data model. This model is refined to include the security requirements, and then it is verified compared to the organizational security policies (the patterns). Finally, the secure database schema is automatically generated.

The rest of this paper is structured as follows: section 2 provides a review of related studies. Section 3 elaborates on the approach, and section 4 concludes and set plans for future research.

2 Related Work

Since it has been recognized that security must be treated throughout all stages of the software development life cycle, it is the task of the designer to ensure that all required security requirements are included in the specifications, and that adequate mechanisms are implemented to address those specifications. Over the years, many techniques and methods have been suggested in order to incorporate security within the development process. In the following we review major approaches for secure software development, with an emphasis on Model Driven Development (MDD) [22].

Several specification techniques for representing different security policies in a MDD process have been proposed. For example, UMLsec [11] is a UML extension that enables specifying security concerns in the functional model. It uses the standard UML extension mechanisms, stereotypes with tagged values to formulate the security requirements, and constraints to check whether the security requirements hold in the presence of particular types of attacks. In the context of access control, UMLsec provides a notation to represent only Role-Based Access Control (RBAC) policies; nonetheless it does not support specification of fine grained constraints (i.e., specification at the property or the instance levels). Furthermore, UMLsec does not provide generation or transformation from the application model to code.

Another example is the SecureUML [2, 13], which is a modeling language based on RBAC that is used to formalize role based access control requirements and to integrate them into application models. It is basically a RBAC language (where the concrete syntax is based on UML) with authorization constraints that are expressed in OCL [16]. SecureUML supports automatic generation of access control specification for particular technologies. Basin et al. [1] extended SecureUML and showed how OCL expressions can be used to formalize and check security properties of application models. Although it provides rich facilities for specifying role based authorization, SecureUML does not support enforcements of security constraints, and it is suitable only for role based authorization models.

Koch and Parisi-Presicce [12] present another approach to integrate specifications of access control policies into UML. The models are specified in three levels: the access control metamodel, the application information model and the instance of the access control model in a specific application. In addition, they present a verification mechanism of the model with respect to consistency properties. However, this method does not support the transformation of the models into database schemata.

Secure Tropos [14] is a security extension to the Goal-Driven Requirements Engineering methodology, which enables to model security concerns of agent-based systems. The most notable limitation of Secure Tropos is that it mainly focuses on the requirements analysis phase, and therefore does not provide adequate support to the design of security policies. To overcome this, Mouratidis and Jurjens [15] combined Secure Tropos and UMLsec to create a structured methodology for software development, which supports most of the software development phases. In the context of our work, the limitations of the combined approach derived from those of UMLsec.

Another approach for security specification is security patterns, which are based on the classic idea of design patterns introduced by Gamma et al. [8]. Security patterns were proposed to assist developers to handle security concerns and provide guidelines to be used from the early stages of the development lifecycle [21]. To successfully utilize a security pattern, there must be systematic guidelines supporting its application throughout the entire software development lifecycle. Such a methodology to build secure systems using patterns is presented by Fernandez et al. [6]. The methodology integrates security patterns into each one of the software development stages, where each stage can be tested for compliance with the principles presented by the patterns. A catalog of security patterns can help in defining the security mechanisms at each architectural level and at each development stage. This method mainly provides guidelines about which security related procedural patterns could be useful in the various development stages, but no verification algorithm is proposed in order to verify the implementation of the design patterns in the application, and no concrete way to transform the application into code is provided.

Other methodologies present the use of the aspect-oriented software design to model security as separate aspects which would later become weaved into the functional model. For example, Ray et al. [18] propose to deal with access control requirements while utilizing UML diagrams. Access control patterns are modeled as aspects in template forms of UML diagrams, while other functional design concerns are addressed in the primary model. Then, the aspect models are woven into the primary functional model, creating an application model that addresses access control concerns. Yet, this method does not address verification of the application, nor transformations in any way. Another example is the framework proposed by Pavlich-Mariscal et al. [17], which enable to model access control policies with the use of built-in UML extensions and transform them into code. Additionally, a set of composable access control features, i.e., components that realize specific capabilities of RBAC, Mandatory Access Control (MAC), and Discretionary Access Control (DAC), are proposed in a set of access control diagrams. Although the presented extensions allow specifying a fairly broad range of requirements, there are still access control capabilities that are not included in the framework, such as the ability to specify time constraints indicating when subjects can access to the protected resources.

Several studies deal with secure database design, such Fernández-Medina and Piattini [7], who propose a methodology to design multilevel databases based on MAC policies. The methodology allows creating conceptual and logical models of multilevel databases, and implements the models by using Oracle Label Security [4]. The resultant database imposes that access of a user to a particular row is allowed only if (1) that user is authorized to do so by the DBMS; (2) that user has the necessary privileges; and (3) the label of the user dominates the label of the row. Following that methodology, the authors provide a way for transforming specification artifacts into code. However, they do not provide tools for verifying the application against security policies.

Information security is crucial to many organizations, and it is necessary to assure that the security policies of a database are not neglected during the development process. However, existing methods do not provide means to enforce particular organizational security policies on a database design. The aforementioned approaches mainly provide guidelines regarding how security can be handled within certain stages of the software development process, or address specific aspects in developing secure applications. Although some of the methods provide means for checking models, they do not support the ability to verify the correct application of the organizationl security policies. Our study specifically addresses these gaps by introducing a comprehensive approach for developing secure database schemata, and enables the organization to enforce its security policies within the developed systems.

3 The Pattern-Based Approach

The proposed approach aims at guiding, enforcing and verifying the correct usage of security patterns and utilizing the knowledge encapsulated in these patterns for generating secure database schemata. It is a part of a comprehensive methodology that supports the core phases of the development lifecycle of secured (authorization wise) database schemata. The approach was developed to enable its integration into an existing development process. Thus, the techniques and tools that are used are kept as similar as possible to the standard ones. For example, we adopt the modeling language UML along with OCL.

We use the Application-based Domain Modeling (ADOM) [19] framework as an infrastructure to the proposed approach. ADOM is rooted in the domain engineering discipline, which is concerned with building reusable assets on the one hand, and representing and managing knowledge in specific domains on the other hand. ADOM supports the representation of reference (domain) models, construction of enterprise-specific models, and verification of the enterprise-specific models against the relevant reference models. Before application developed can be started, the security patterns to be enforced during the database development are defined within ADOM's domain layer (i.e., organizational level), along with their transformation rules which depict on how to transform the logical model (that is based on the pattern) into a database schema. These security patterns meant to reflect general access control policies within the organization. They are reusable and may be applied to numerous applications. During the development process of an application, the patterns are employed in the application layer (of ADOM). The designer is guided and compelled to apply the patterns that are defined in the organizational layer. After the application is verified against the patterns, the transformation rules are used to generate a secure database schema. As this work refers to database specifications, i.e., structural models, class diagrams are used for in both the organizational and the application layers.

3.1 Pattern Specification

The patterns are specified according to the ADOM approach within the domain layer. These patterns serve as a guideline for application developers as well as a verification template, and they provide infrastructure for the transformation process. Similarly to the classical pattern approach, security patterns are specified in a structured form. The standard template aids designers who are not security experts to identify and understand security problems and solve them efficiently. In order to specify the patterns, we use a common template that was introduced by Schumacher [20]. The template consists of five main sections: name, context, problem, solution, and consequence (due to space limitations, we discuss only the solution section as other sections are similar to those found in the literature). The solution section describes a generic solution to the problem. In the proposed approach, it consists of a UML class diagram that specifies the static structure of the solution and OCL constraints that are used to specify additional requirements that ought to be verified in the application model. In case that finer grained solution is required than the one provided by the diagrams, OCL rules in the form of general templates can be defined. These general OCL templates are specified using the specific elements and language that were already defined by the class diagrams specifying the structure of the pattern. The designer should use these templates to specify fine grained access control policies.

As RBAC patterns are commonly used for database authorization, in the following example we show a simple RBAC pattern that is adjusted to some specific organizational policies. Other access control patterns can be specified in a similar way. Figure 1 presents our RBAC pattern based on the proposed approach.

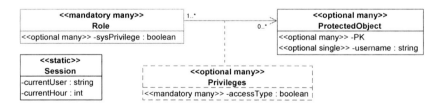

Fig. 1. The RBAC security pattern residing within the domain layer

In the described pattern, *Role* is akin to an external group of entities or users playing a specific role that needs to access the database. While applying or implementing this RBAC pattern, it is obligatory to define at least one *Role* as it is defined as a <<*mandatory*>> element. In addition, one can specify the system privileges assigned to some *Role* by using the *sysPrivilege* classification. *ProtectedObject* is akin to a database table, where the *PK* classification is used to indicate the primary keys of the table. Additionally, when a *ProtectedObject* is also classified as a *Role*, one can specify the user related to the object (or row in a table) by using the *username* classification. *Privileges* association class determines the schema object privileges of a *Role* with respect to a specific *ProtectedObject*. A class that is classified as *Privileges* must include at least one object privilege - *accessType*.

In addition to the pattern structure, OCL rules that further constraint and clarify the pattern can be specified. These OCL rules are evaluated in the application layer during the verification stage, rather than in the domain layer where they are defined. For example, the following constraint limits object privileges to SELECT, INSERT, UPDATE and DELETE:

```
context Privileges inv:
 Set{'SELECT','INSERT','UPDATE','DELETE'}->
  includesAll(self.accessType->collect(name))
```

Another example is the constraint that limits system privileges to CREATE SESSION, CREATE VIEW and SYSDBA:

```
context Role inv:
 Set{'CREATE SESSION', 'CREATE VIEW', 'SYSDBA'}->
  includesAll(self.sysPrivilege -> collect(name))
```

Additionally, the following constraint ensures that roles that have the system privilege SYSDBA do not have access to any object:

```
context Role inv:
 if self.protectedObject->size() > 0 then
   self.sysPrivilege->collect(name)->excludes('SYSDBA')
 endif
```

In general RBAC models define privileges for objects as one unit; however sometimes finer-grained access control is required. Access control on the objects' properties and instances (i.e., columns and rows in database tables, respectively) enable preservation of security principles such as the minimal privilege principle. In order to support fine-grained access control specifications, OCL templates are defined in the domain model so that the designer could use them to create property and instance access control rules in the application model. These templates are defined using the various elements that specify the structure of the pattern, such as the *Role*, and the *accessType* in our example. The OCL templates are used for two purposes: guiding the developer on fine-grained constraints; and defining transformation rules.

Text templates [24] are essentially exemplars of the desired output code with "blanks" that should be filled in with a value of an attribute or with an output code from a nested template. These "blanks" contain meta-code and are delimited between "< >". For example, the following OCL expression defines a simple OCL template:

```
context <class name> inv <constraint name>:
 <simple OCL expression>
```

For every OCL template, we define a corresponding SQL template, with the same set of "blank" elements. The corresponding template in SQL is defined as:

```
ALTER TABLE <class name> ADD CONSTRAINT <constraint name>
  CHECK (<simple OCL expression>)
```

After the missing values are inserted, a template engine is used to create the output code. The processing of the inserted elements can be a simple replacement of a variable with its value, or a more complex transformation. Following the template example above, let's assume we would like to constraint an *Enrollment* class so that the property *grade* is limited to values between 0 and 100. The missing values for `<class name>`, `<constraint name>`, and `<simple OCL expression>` are Enrollment, grade_in_range, and grade>=0 and grade<=100, respectively. After processing, the OCL output code is as follows:

```
context Enrollment inv grade_in_range:
  grade>=0 and grade<=100
```

The corresponding SQL output code is as follows:

```
ALTER TABLE Enrollment ADD CONSTRAINT grade_in_range
  CHECK (grade>=0 and grade<=100)
```

As in the target language (SQL and Oracle VPD) the approach for handling object privileges is to first grant the privilege to the table and then to limit the access by some condition; in this RBAC pattern we apply the same approach. First, the privileges are given to the role (in the model) and then the access can be limited to some of the instances or properties by OCL constraints.

In order to incorporate **property (column or cell) level** access control constraints, an extension of OCL is required. The Boolean operation isAuthorized is used to restrict a role from performing an action on an element, depending on the result of the condition: `role.isAuthorized(action, element, guard): Boolean`, where `role` is the activating role, `action` is the operation (e.g., select, insert, update, or delete) to be performed on the `element`, `element` is an object or a property of an object that needs to be protected, and `guard` is the condition that has to be fulfilled in order to allow the role to perform the action on the `element`. For each property within a class that requires different restrictions on its access than its class, the following **property (column) level** OCL template can be used:

```
context <Privileges> inv:
  self.<Role>.isAuthorized(self.<accessType>,
    self.<ProtectedObject>.<property>,
    <guard>)
```

This OCL template means that in the context of a class that is classified as <<*Privileges*>>, a privilege of type <<*accessType*>> of a <<*Role*>> to a *property* of the <<*ProtectedObject*>> is limited by the *guard*.

To provide support for **instance (row) level** access control, the following OCL template could be applied on application models:

```
context <Privileges> inv:
  [self.<constrained-type :accessType> implies]
  Session.currentUser = <ProtectedObject>.<username>
  and <ProtectedObject>.[<navigate-between-the-
  ProtectedObject-and-the-Role>].<Role>->includes(<Role>)
```

This OCL means that in the context of some <<Privileges>>, the user of the application (indicated by Session.currentUser) may have the access only to objects related to this user. In addition, the user has to have a <<Role>> that is part of the collection related to the <<ProtectedObject>>. This template is meaningful only if the <<ProtectedObject>> is additionally classifies as a <<Role>>. Note that this template enables the designer to specify constraints on a specific <<accessType>> (line 2) or all the <<accessTypes>> within a <<Privileges>>.

Additional templates can be specified to include other requirements, such as policies that restrict access based on time.

3.2 Transformation Rules Specification

Model transformation plays an important role in MDD approaches. As models become first class artifacts that drive the whole development process, software engineers should be supported during the development process by mature MDD tools and techniques in the same way that IDEs, compilers, and debuggers support them in traditional programming paradigms. Thus, in order to complete the process, the transformation rules of a pattern need to define how application elements should be transformed into a database schema. To transform the UML class diagram into SQL code, a "model to code" transformation tools have to be provided. This type of transformation can use technologies such as the ATLAS Transformation Language (ATL) [10] to first transform the application model into an SQL application model, and then to translate it to SQL code. The following example specifies the rule to transform application object privileges - *accessType*:

```
rule Permission {
  from element :
    ADOM!"Model::RBAC::Role::Privilege::accessType"
  to permission : SQL!Permission (
    roles <- element.getParent().getSource(),
    object <- element.getParent().getTarget(),
    operation <- element.getName()
  )}
```

This rule iterates over all elements stereotyped as *accessType* and assigns the specified permission (specified by the attribute name) to the connected roles (specified by the association class *Privilege* end - source) on the objects (specified by the association class *Privilege* end - target).

The transformation of OCL templates to SQL or PL/SQL code can combine text templates such as StringTemplate [24], with more SQL oriented transformation techniques such as the Dresden OCL Toolkit [9]. The following template example is for the specific case where the privileges refer to a class that is classified both as *Role* and as *ProtectedObject*; this template is a short version of the *instance level template*:

```
-- From: OCL
context <Privileges> inv:
  [self.<constrained-type:accessType> implies]
  Session.currentUser = <ProtectedObject>.<username>
```

```
-- To: Oracle VPD function and policy
CREATE FUNCTION <Privileges>[_<accessType>]
  (SCHEMAV VARCHAR2, OBJ VARCHAR2) RETURN VARCHAR2 AS
BEGIN
  IF (NOT DBMS_SESSION.IS_ROLE_ENABLED('<Role>')) THEN
    RETURN NULL;
  END IF;
  RETURN '<username> = ' ||
          SYS_CONTEXT('USERENV', 'SESSION_USER');
END;
BEGIN DBMS_RLS.add_policy(
  object_schema => '<application-class-diagram-name>',
  object_name   => '<ProtectedObject>',
  policy_name   => '<Privileges>[_<accessType>]',
  policy_function => '<Privileges>[_<accessType>]',
  statement_type => '<constrained-type: accessType |
                     {Privileges.accessType*}>'
  <if {INSERT, UPDATE, DELETE} •
       <constrained-type:accessType |
         {Privileges.accessType*}> != ∅>
  , update_check => TRUE
  <endif>
);
END;
```

This VPD function first checks if the activating *Role* is relevant to the constraint, if not it returns Null (i.e., no constraint) otherwise, it returns a filtering string with the current user's username. The VPD policy registered to the stated object, specifies when the function should be activated by stating the relevant *accessType*s. This template contains both simple values substitution and nested template (lines 22-26).

To summarize, the outcome of the two tasks at the organizational level are: a) the specification of security patterns that will guide developers and compel them to specify security requirements as determined by the security policies, and b) the definition of transformation rules from application models into database schemata. The security patterns are defined using UML and OCL, and the transformation rules are expressed in ATL and templates.

3.3 Application Development

Before elaborating on application development phases, we present a simple example that will be used to demonstrate the various tasks and the resulting artifacts. The example deals with a university application that manages lecturers, course, students, and their enrollments and grades. Each department offers some courses, and each course offering is given by a lecturer. Most of the information about departments, lecturers, courses and course offerings is public and therefore all users may view their details. However, the information about students enrolled to certain course offerings may be visible only to the lecturers of those courses. A lecturer's phone number may be visible only to students who are enrolled to one of the lecturer's courses; other lecturers and secretaries may view this data unconditionally. Secretaries may add new courses to the system and update course's level or credits. Secretaries may also add or delete course offerings and assign lecturers to them; however the secretaries may not read or modify the students enrolled to course offerings. Lecturers may update all of the information related to their assigned course offerings, except the students enrolled. In addition, lecturers may see the students enrolled in each of their course offerings (i.e., access their IDs and names), but they may not see to which other courses their students are enrolled. Lecturers are only allowed to give (add) grades to their students. Lecturers may update their personal information, excluding the department they belong to and their assignments to course offerings. Students may read and modify their own personal information and enrolled courses, and they may see their grades. Secretaries may add or delete students and lecturers from the system.

During the design stage at the application level, the designer formalizes the data model and the privilege specifications into a unified class diagram. Meaning that the authorization rules are weaved into the class diagram as specified by the patterns; the relevant elements are classified, via stereotypes, according to the predefined patterns. Figure 2 presents a class diagram of the university system along with the security specification as determined by the RBAC pattern, specified at the organizational level (see section 3.1). The various elements that are relevant for the RBAC pattern are classified (by stereotypes) with the pattern elements: *Role*, *ProtectedObject*, and *Privileges*. Note that *accessType* and *sysPrivilege* elements are presented only if their assigned value is true. For example, the *Student* role has a system privilege of {CREATE SESSION} and the following schema object privileges: {SELECT} to *Department*, *Lecturer*, *Course* and *CourseOffering*, {SELECT, INSERT, and DELETE} to *Enrollment*, and {SELECT and UPDATE} to *Student*.

As explained before, the expressiveness of class diagrams is limited in representing fine grained access control privileges. For example, in the case of the university system as presented in figure 2, a student can enroll other students to courses and update their personal information. Thus, working under the RBAC pattern defined in section 3.1, the designer should constrain this by using the predefined OCL templates. The following OCL example illustrates the use of the *instance* level template that limits students to read, insert, or delete an enrollment only for them:

context Student-Enrollment **inv**:
 Session.currentUser = self.student.username
 and self.enrollment.student -> includes(self.student)

Another example is of a *property* level constraint, in which students may see a lecturer's phone number only if they are enrolled to one of the lecturers' courses:

context Student-Lecturer **inv**:
 self.student.isAuthorized(self.SELECT,
  self.lecturer.phone,
  Session.currentUser = self.student.usermane
  and self.lecturer.courseOffering.enrolled ->
     includes(self.student))

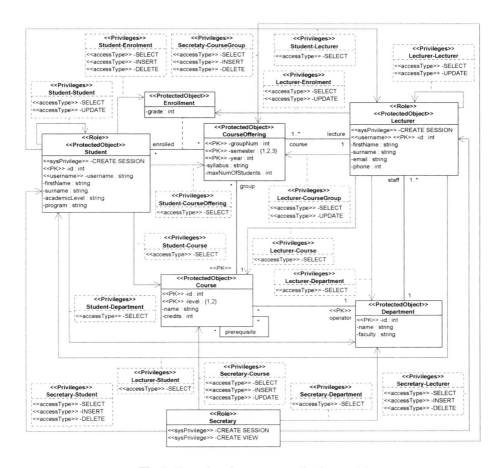

Fig. 2. The university system application model

3.4 Data Model Verification

Having created a refined data model, we need to check if it adheres to the organizational security policies as defined by the patterns. In the following we define a pattern-based verification which is based on the ADOM validation algorithm [19] for checking the adherence of application models with the domain model. The application is verified in several facets: (a) multiplicity, (b) OCL, (c) language, and (d) cardinality.

Multiplicity verification checks that the application adheres with the patterns (which reside within the domain layer) with respect to elements multiplicity. It is performed in three phases as defined in ADOM's validation algorithm: element reduction, element unification, and model matching. In the *element reduction step*, elements that are not stereotyped by elements of the security pattern are disregarded. During the *element unification step*, elements having the same domain stereotype are unified, leaving only one element instantiating the same type in the resultant model. The multiplicity of that element denotes the number of distinct elements in the application model having the same stereotype. In the *model matching step*, the resultant model of the previous step is matched against the pattern (the domain model) in order to verify the multiplicity of the elements, and the application model structure with respect to the pattern (the domain model). In the university example there are no unclassified classes, thus the reduction step of the multiplicity verification is redundant. The resultant model after performing the unification step consists of three classes: *Role* with multiplicity 3, *sysPrivilege* with multiplicity <<1..2>, *ProtectedObject* with multiplicity 6, *PK* with multiplicity <<0..3>>, *username* with multiplicity <<0..2>>, *Privileges* with multiplicity <<2..5>>, and *accessType* with multiplicity <<1..3>>. Thus, the matching step finds no violation. An example to a possible violation would have been in case that there were association classes that are classified as *Privileges* with no relevant *accessType*s specified.

OCL verification checks that the OCL rules defined in the pattern hold in the application. This verification iterates over all pattern elements. For each such element, it extracts its OCL rules, and retrieves its logical instantiations from the application. For each logical instantiation, the verification checks that the extracted OCL rules hold. In the university example, all of the OCL constraints defined in the pattern are evaluated to true. An example for a violation would have been if one or more of the roles would have some object privilege and the SYSDBA system privilege, or one of the *Role*s would have object privileges different from the ones defined, i.e., SELECT, INSERT, UPDATE and DELETE.

Language verification confirms that logical instantiations in the application have the same types and modifiers as their classifying element in the pattern. Specifically, all attributes in the application model that instantiate domain attributes must have the same type, or a subtype thereof. For instance, in the RBAC pattern defined in figure 1, the *username* attribute in the *Role* class is defined as string, that means that all attributes that are classified as *username* in the application have to be of type string. However, for attributes such as the *PK* in the *ProtectedObject* class, that were defined as object (or do not define the type), classified attributes can be of any type.

Cardinality verification confirms that the cardinality defined on association ends in the pattern hold. The number of logical instantiation of associations must be within the cardinality bounds defined on the classifying association in the pattern (the domain). For instance, the cardinality defined on the *Privilege* association class states that at least one *Role* must be connected to every *ProtectedObject*, yet not vice versa.

3.5 Data Model Transformation

In this stage the developer has a verified data model enhanced with security constraints that need to be transformed into a database schema. The transformation of the class diagram to the relational tables can be done according to existing algorithms, such as Blaha et al. [3] and Shoval [23]. This and pattern related transformations are done by following the transformation rules and templates which were defined at the organizational level, and the application specification created in the design phase. The generated SQL commands for the *Student* role and a sample of the SQL fine-grained code for the university application are as follows:

```
-- Role creation
CREATE ROLE STUDENT;
-- Granting privileges to Student
GRANT CREATE SESSION TO STUDENT;
GRANT SELECT ON DEPARTMENT TO STUDENT;
GRANT SELECT ON LECTURER TO STUDENT;
GRANT SELECT ON COURSE_OFFERING TO STUDENT;
GRANT SELECT ON COURSE TO STUDENT;
GRANT SELECT ON PREREQUISITE TO STUDENT;
GRANT SELECT, INSERT, DELETE ON ENROLLMENT TO STUDENT;
GRANT SELECT, UPDATE ON STUDENT TO STUDENT;
-- Instance level template transformation
-- Students can update only their personal information:
CREATE FUNCTION STUDENT_STUDENT_UPDATE
   (SCHEMAV VARCHAR2, OBJ VARCHAR2) RETURN VARCHAR2 AS
BEGIN
  IF (NOT DBMS_SESSION.IS_ROLE_ENABLED('STUDENT')) THEN
     RETURN NULL;
  END IF;
  RETURN 'username = ' ||
         SYS_CONTEXT('USERENV', 'SESSION_USER');
END;
BEGIN DBMS_RLS.add_policy(
   object_schema    => 'UNIVERSITY',
   object_name      => 'STUDENT',
   policy_name      => 'STUDENT_STUDENT_UPDATE ',
   policy_function  => 'STUDENT_STUDENT_UPDATE ',
   statement_types  => 'UPDATE',
   update_check     => TRUE);
END;
```

4 Summary

In this paper we have presented a novel approach that utilizes organizational security patterns for enforcing security in database application design. The approach guides developers on how to incorporate security aspects, in particular authorization, within the development process. It handles the specification and implementation of the authorization aspect from the early stages of the development process to implementation, leading to a more secure system design. The proposed method addresses the limitations of existing studies by providing a coherent framework that facilitates the enforcement of security organizational patterns on applications development.

So far we have used the approach in a few small cases. Yet, it should be further tested and evaluated in terms of applicability and usage. We already have conducted an experiment to verify that the use of the proposed approach indeed ease the developer efforts and increase specifications correctness. In that experiment we examine whether the abstraction achieved by the patterns proposed within the approach helped undergraduate students to achieve better security specification than directly coding in SQL. In that experiment, the students received a requirement document that explicitly lists all of the security requirements. They were required to add the security constraints over an existing database schema using the patterns

(Group A) and using SQL (Group B). The experiment results showed that the group that used the patterns achieved statistically significant better results than the other in terms of security specification related to table/object, column/property, and row/instance levels. Yet, the results still requires further inspection and analysis.

Despite providing many advantages, the Pattern Based Approach may suffer from several drawbacks. Pattern specification is not a straightforward task. In order to provide the necessary support to database designers, the security expert specifying the pattern has to have a lot of knowledge regarding general access control mechanisms, and different technologies that can be utilized for the generation of the secure database schema. The security expert must also be able to express organizational policies in the general access control patterns. In addition, at the application level, the designer may have difficulties related to exploiting the OCL templates, or in specifying complex requirements in an object oriented model for relational database.

Future research may include the evaluation of the proposed approach using real-world case studies and actual development and manipulation of databases, so as to enable comparisons of the alternative approaches in close to real conditions. Additionally, as specifying a pattern and its transformation rules is not an easy task; in order to fully understand this process, further investigation is required. In addition, the Pattern Based Approach presented in this study used access control patterns; however, the approach can be extended to deal with broader areas of security concerns in databases and secure application design, using other types of security design patterns. This is important, as working with a variety of approaches and standards on different security aspects is not sufficient and requires a lot of efforts in combining the artifacts. Therefore, a common infrastructure that will allow the smooth integration of the various security aspects is a necessity.

Acknowledgment. This work was partially funded by Deutsche Telekom Laboratories at Ben-Gurion University of the Negev.

References

1. Basin, D., Clavel, M., Doser, J., Egea, M.: Automated Analysis of Security-Design Models. Information and Software Technology 51(5), 815–831 (2009)
2. Basin, D., Doser, J., Lodderstedt, T.: Model Driven Security: From UML Models to Access Control Infrastructures. ACM Transactions on Software Engineering and Methodology 15(1), 39–91 (2006)
3. Blaha, M., Premerlani, W., Shen, H.: Converting OO Models into RDBMS Schema. IEEE Software 11, 28–39 (1994)
4. Czuprynski, J.: Oracle Label Security. The Database Journal (2003), http://www.databasejournal.com
5. Dhillon, G.: Information Security Management: Global Challenges in the New Millennium. IGI Publishing, Hershey (2001)
6. Fernandez, E.B., Larrondo-Petrie, M.M., Sorgente, T., VanHilst, M.: A Methodology to Develop Secure Systems Using Patterns. In: Integrating Security and Software Engineering: Advances and Future Vision, ch. 5, pp. 107–126. IDEA Press (2006)
7. Fernández-Medina, E., Piattini, M.: Designing Secure Databases. Information and Software Technology 47(7), 463–477 (2005)

8. Gamma, E., Helm, R., Johnson, R., Vlissides, J.M.: Design Patterns: Elements of Reusable Object-Oriented Software. Addison-Wesley, Boston (1994)
9. Heidenreich, F., Wende, C., Demuth, B.: A Framework for Generating Query Language Code from OCL Invariants. In: Akehurst, D.H., Gogolla, M., Zschaler, S. (eds.) Proceedings of the 7th OCL Workshop at the UML/MoDELS Conference, Ocl4All - Modelling Systems with OCL. ECEASST, vol. 9 (2008)
10. Jouault, F., Allilaire, F., Bézivin, J., Kurtev, I.: ATL: A Model Transformation Tool. Science of Computer Programming 72(1-2), 31–39 (2008)
11. Jürjens, J.: Secure Systems Development with UML. Springer, Heidelberg (2004)
12. Koch, M., Parisi-Presicce, F.: UML Specification of Access Control Policies and their Formal Verification. Software and System Modeling 5(4), 429–447 (2006)
13. Lodderstedt, T., Basin, D.A., Doser, J.: SecureUML: A UML-Based Modeling Language for Model-Driven Security. In: Jézéquel, J.-M., Hussmann, H., Cook, S. (eds.) UML 2002. LNCS, vol. 2460, pp. 426–441. Springer, Heidelberg (2002)
14. Mouratidis, H., Giorgini, P.: Secure Tropos: A Security-Oriented Extension of the Tropos Methodology. International Journal of Software Engineering and Knowledge Engineering 27(2), 285–309 (2007)
15. Mouratidis, H., Jurjens, J.: From Goal Driven Security Requirements Engineering to Secure Design. International Journal of Intelligent Systems 25(8), 813–840 (2010)
16. Object Constraint Language. OMG Specification, Version 2.2, http://www.omg.org/spec/OCL/2.2/
17. Pavlich-Mariscal, J.A., Demurjian, S.A., Michel, L.D.: A Framework of Composable Access Control Features: Preserving Separation of Access Control Concerns from Models to Code. Computers & Security 29(3), 350–379 (2010)
18. Ray, I., France, R.B., Li, N., Georg, G.: An Aspect-Based Approach to Modeling Access Control Concerns. Information and Software Technology 46(9), 575–587 (2004)
19. Reinhartz-Berger, I., Sturm, A.: Utilizing Domain Models for Application Design and Validation. Information & Software Technology 51(8), 1275–1289 (2009)
20. Schumacher, M.: Security Engineering with Patterns: Origins, Theoretical Models, and New Applications. Springer-Verlag New York, Inc., Secaucus (2003)
21. Schumacher, M., Fernandez, E.B., Hybertson, D., Buschmann, F., Sommerlad, P.: Security Patterns: Integrating Security and Systems Engineering. John Wiley & Sons, Chichester (2006)
22. Selic, B.: The Pragmatics of Model-Driven Development. IEEE Software 20(5), 19–25 (2003)
23. Shoval, P.: Functional and Object-Oriented Analysis and Design - An Integrated Methodology. IGI Publishing, Hershey (2007)
24. String Template (2010), http://www.stringtemplate.org

Analysis of Application of Security Patterns to Build Secure Systems

Roberto Ortiz[1], Javier Garzás[2], and Eduardo Fernández-Medina[3]

[1] S21SecLabs-SOC. Group S21Sec Gestión S.A., Valgrande, 10, 28108. Madrid, Spain
r.ortizpl@gmail.com
[2] Kybele Group. Dep. of Computer Languages and Systems II. University Rey Juan Carlos, Tulipán. s/n, 28933. Madrid, Spain
javier.garzas@urjc.es
[3] GSyA Research Group. Dep. of Information Technologies and Systems. University of Castilla-La Mancha. Paseo de la Universidad, 4. Ciudad Real, Spain
Eduardo.FdezMedina@uclm.es

Abstract. Both new technology business models and the new tendencies in the field of computing are forcing organizations to undergo a constant evolution in order to maintain their competitiveness in markets. This evolution has led to a continuous remodeling of companies 'systems to enable them to adapt to the new needs. These changes increase these systems' complexity, making them more vulnerable. Computer attacks against organizations are therefore increasing considerably. If this is to be avoided, information security engineers need reliable and validated solutions with which to confront security problems, along with agile solutions to confront the new technological necessities in an optimal manner. Security patterns are good mechanisms with which to perform this task since they provide documented, validated and tested solutions to recurring problems. In this paper we carry out an analysis of those proposals that use security patterns to build secure systems when this task is performed in the information systems of a real organization, with the objective of detecting any shortcomings and new needs.

Keywords: Security patterns, secure systems, information security, security.

1 Introduction

One of the most important problems in the field of information systems in the last few years has been that of security, principally owing to the emergence of new vulnerabilities caused by the increased complexity of these systems and by the fact that organizations have opened their databases on the internet [1]. The number of attacks has therefore significantly increased and the advantages obtained by attackers are greater and greater [2].

Information security is therefore one of the main concerns of IT organizations, and these organizations' security engineers consequently find it necessary to incorporate security requirements into their systems, whilst always bearing mind business needs in order to, on the one hand, safeguard their assets and, on the other, minimize the number of attacks against their systems and reduce these attacks' effectiveness [3].

To optimize the task of incorporating security into the existing systems in an agile and optimal manner, it is necessary that engineers have reliable, validated and tested solutions at their disposal. It is also important for these engineers to offer homogeneous solutions to similar problems with the purpose of maintaining a defense strategy that is aligned within the corporation in which they work.

Security patterns are a good tool to satisfy the aforementioned necessities since they encapsulate experts' knowledge and experience regarding a recurring problem in a particular security discipline [4]. In other words, a pattern solves a specific problem in a determined context and can be adapted to different situations [5].

Information security engineers can therefore use security patterns to build secure information systems since they are a good tool for systematizing the process of solving recurring problems, and provide guidelines for the construction and evaluation of secure systems [6]. However, when information security engineers perform this task within the systems of a real and complex organization, they must take into account a set of considerations related to certain important parameters of the system or of the organization, such as compatibility, performance, cost, time spent, type of asset to be protected, organizational rules, etc.

In this paper we have therefore carried out an in-depth analysis of a set of some of the most important proposals, extracted from a previously performed systematic review, which use security patterns to build secure systems. This has allowed us to obtain conclusions concerning the current use of security patterns in information systems, along with the factors or parameters that should currently be considered when applying these patterns to an organization's real and complex systems. A discussion of the results obtained is then provided.

The remainder of this paper is organized as follows: in Section 2, we present the analysis of the selected proposals and the results. Section 3 provides a discussion of this and other related works. The paper ends with some conclusions in Section 4.

2 Analysis of Proposals

This section shows the analysis performed and discusses the results obtained from some of the most relevant proposals which use security patterns in specific contexts in order to build secure systems [7-17]. Both the analysis and the discussion are focused on analyzing whether these works take into account a set of the considerations that are necessary when the patterns are used to develop secure systems within a real and complex organization. Finally, the detected shortcomings and the current needs in this field are analyzed, and a series of suggestions to improve these deficiencies is proposed in order for this type of solutions to be optimally implemented in real organizations.

This task has been carried out by using Table 1, in which the selected initiatives that are compared are presented. This comparative study has been made with the use of an analytical framework (partially based on [18]). This framework contains a series of technical applicability criteria based on the considerations put forward by Kienzle et al. [19], which are detailed as follows. Each of these criteria are considerations that must be taken into account by security engineers when building a real secure system, since they are related to highly important parameters such as performance, cost, time spent, effectiveness and learning. In order to provide details of certain consequences of disregarding some of these considerations and thus facilitate the reader's understanding, we give brief, clear and real examples to explain each necessity.

- **Impact on other components** *in the system*: in this criterion, we shall analyze whether the proposals consider the pattern's compatibility with the other components in the system, along with any possible consequences of its use. The following example is presented to enable the reader to understand this criterion. An organization decides to use the security strategy of carrying out a centralized identity management in order that the people in charge of security in the organization have from a unique point the control of, for example, the digital certificates needed for systems to perform authentication and establish trust relationships with other organizations' systems. One possible solution is to use a single centralized cryptographic store that is independent of the product or system that requires it. In this case, if compatibilities between the elements existing in the system and the solution implemented by the security pattern are not considered, problems such as the unfeasibility of the solution could arise if, for example, certain Microsoft products such as Outlook are used. Since this product does not permit integration with any cryptographic stores that are external to its local store, it is necessary to perform an ad-hoc development to be able to implement the pattern in the organization's systems.
- **Impact on the system**: In this criterion, we shall analyze whether the proposals consider the possible increases in the system involved with regard to the need for storage, an increase in the memory consumed, patching frequency, process capacity, bandwidth, etc. We shall attempt to clarify the meaning of this criterion through the following example. An organization wishes to implement an access control system in its information systems. As an alternative, it decides to use RBAC [4] which is based on authenticating and authorizing access depending on the role of each user/subsystem within the organization. It is therefore necessary to consider the aforementioned parameters owing to the fact that the technical features may be affected, depending on the amount of system users, the frequency of their accesses and the different combinations needed to grant access to a resource. If, for example, the amount of users is not correctly estimated, it is probable that the system performance, the process capacity, the bandwidth, and the consumed memory will be affected, which could cause the solution to fail.
- **Solution cost**: We shall analyze whether the cost of installing or implementing the solution in the systems of an organization is considered. An example of this will be presented together with the that of following criterion.
- **Used time**: We shall verify, without going into great detail, whether the proposals estimate the time needed to implement or use a pattern in an organization's systems. The two aforementioned criteria can be analyzed from a common perspective, and are also dependent on the other criteria. This is owing to the fact that if any of the criteria shown in this section are not considered, these two criteria will be affected and this will also affect the final solution. When criteria that may affect the final solution are disregarded, these parameters might be affected because, for example a later cost increase with regard to the dimension of the problem may occur, thus leading to an increase in the time needed to solve the problem with the solution proposed by the pattern.

- *Presentation of **real examples***: We shall verify whether the proposals are accompanied by a real implementation example that backs the validation of the solution. It is evident that if the application of the security pattern includes a real example in its description, this will signify that, on the one hand, it has been implemented in a real system and, on the other, it has been tested by verifying its behavior as solution.
- *Evaluation of the **criticality of the asset** to protect*: We shall analyze whether the proposals catalog the criticality of the asset to be protected. Not all assets have the same importance within an organization, and if they are all treated in the same way, this may significantly affect the solution. Let us take the case of the protection of a web application as an example. To do so, the use of a sequence of security patterns to ensure authentication, authorization, role-based access control along with a data ciphering in databases to ensure data confidentiality is suggested. If accessible information is of a public nature and the service availability is not critical, then the majority of controls will not be necessary, since the installation of a perimeter control such as the Firewall [4] pattern will be sufficient to avoid problems of denial of service attacks . However, if the information accessed is of a special nature and its spreading would compromise the organization, then it would perhaps be necessary to increase controls. That is to say, we should introduce security patterns such as Securepipe [4] and additional security measures to cipher the data. The generalization of solutions for apparently similar problems without considering the criticality of the assets to be protected may cause inefficiency or the failure of the solution.
- *Fulfillment of **rules and regulations***: We shall verify whether the proposals consider that the different legislation of the countries in which the solution will be implemented may condition this solution, or whether changes to the organization's rules are considered. The example is as follows: Let us suppose that an organization has different subsidiary enterprises in several countries and that it intends to unify the access system in order to optimize the access control to the systems of the whole organization. A new central repository in which the credentials of all the organization's system users throughout the world are located is therefore proposed. Depending on each country's regulations, this common repository will have some characteristics or others. More specifically, if the repository is located in countries such as Argentina, Venezuela or USA, then these countries' regulations oblige their enterprises to store these data in a determined manner that does not apply to other countries. It might also occur that these countries do not allow the output of determined information concerning their local users to be shared with the organization's other subsidiary enterprises, with the exception of the main headquarters.

Having presented the criteria to be analyzed, we shall now verify whether each of the analyzed proposals completely fulfils each of the applicability technical criterion evaluated (Y), whether it refers briefly to this criterion (P), or whether it neither mentions nor considers the criterion (N). In Table 1 the vertical columns show the references to the papers analyzed and the rows show the aforementioned criteria.

As can be observed in Table 1, most of the proposals principally lack: An evaluation of the compatibilities and possible consequences with regard to the other components in the system when using a pattern. This lack may cause incompatibilities with

Table 1. Analysis of Proposals

Proposals		Applicability technical criteria						
		Impact on other components	Impact on the system	Solution cost	Used time	Real examples	Criticality of the asset	Rules and Regulations
	[7]	P	Y	N	N	Y	N	Y
	[8]	N	N	N	N	P	N	N
	[9]	N	P	N	N	N	Y	N
	[10]	N	P	N	N	N	Y	Y
	[11]	N	P	N	N	Y	N	N
	[12]	N	P	N	N	P	N	N
	[13]	Y	Y	Y	N	N	N	N
	[14]	N	N	N	N	Y	N	N
	[15]	N	N	N	N	P	N	N
	[16]	N	N	N	N	P	N	N
	[17]	N	N	N	N	N	N	N

some of the elements in the system that were not detected a priori to arise, thus causing the solution to fail; A detailed evaluation of the impact that the pattern might have on the system into which it is introduced in terms of storage, the memory consumed, patching frequency, processing capacity, bandwidth, etc. A failure to analyze these critical parameters could compromise the service's availability; A specific classification of the criticality of the assets to be protected by the pattern. If this parameter is not analyzed, the risk of not appropriately measuring the security measures to be provided exists, thus leading to excessive investments or, in their absence, leaving the system vulnerable to any attack not considered earlier; A general presentation of the impact on the cost and time necessary to implement the pattern. This lack may cause an organization to discard the solution because it is not able to assume the related costs or because it is unable to plan a business strategy for the organization since the time needed is not available; Specific considerations in relation to the limitations that may be imposed by the rules and regulations in different countries. This aspect is as critical as the others, but directly affects international organizations. When an organization's business depends on, among other factors, the regulations of the country in which its systems are located, it is necessary to include this criterion as a variable in the equation since it can condition the solution at all times. All these parameters are critical, and should therefore be decisive when using security patterns in the organization's real systems. Neglecting to analyze them may frequently cause the solution to fail.

3 Discussion and Related Works

In spite of the analysis results, security patterns are, in our opinion, a good tool with which to homogenize security solutions to similar problems confronted by different engineers, along with providing agile, proved, validated and secure solutions to recurring security problems. For this reason and for all the considerations presented in the previous section, we believe that it is necessary for current security patterns to evolve to reflect each of the aforementioned considerations in order to permit their easy application in real systems. We also believe that the creation of a security pattern use methodology is necessary to help information security engineers to build secure systems in real organizations through a systematic process. This type of guided process will facilitate the process of considering all of the aforementioned aspects, since each of the considerations that may affect an organization's systems will be analyzed when implementing solutions in the form of security patterns.

Various works which are focused on the application of patterns in security systems through a systematic process are attempting to cover this need. In [20] the author puts forward a general methodology for developing secure-critical software. He uses UMLsec to extend UML to model security properties in informatics systems. This proposal has recently been extended in order to use patterns to support the modeling and verification of formal aspects of security. In [21, 22] the authors apply security patterns through the use of a secure system development method based on hierarchical architectures whose levels define the scope of each security mechanism. These works are all evolutions of the same approach, and one of their main advantages are the guidelines offered in each stage to assist the user to discover where to apply and how to select the security pattern which is most appropriate to satisfy the functional requirements or restrictions in each stage. In [23] the authors propose a systematic method with which to integrate security patterns into a software engineering process. This proposal assists experts to close the gap between the abstract solution described in the pattern and the implementation proposed in the application.

4 Conclusions

The principal purpose of this paper has been to perform an analysis of proposals which use security patterns to build secure systems. This analysis is focused on the way in which these patterns are used, in order to verify whether these proposals take into account a set of considerations that are necessary when solutions are introduced into real systems. A discussion of the results in which the principal shortcomings and research needs in this field were detected is then presented.

The main conclusion of this research is that the current proposals that use security patterns to build secure systems do not take into account considerations that may condition the solution, and are therefore critical considerations when the solution is implemented in an organization's real and complex information systems. That is to say, they do not consider the impact that the pattern could have on the system or on some of its components; they do not perform a classification of the criticality of the assets to be protected, generalizing solutions inefficiently. Furthermore, they do not consider the different rules and regulations that exist in different countries. The lack of analysis of these and the other considerations presented in the paper may cause a drastic increase in terms of cost and time when confronting the security problem and the solution may sometimes fail.

We are currently working on the definition of a methodology for security pattern use that will guide the security engineer, in an agile and efficient manner, at the time of developing a secure system within a real and complex organization. This methodology uses a new template that can be found in [24], in which all the parameters considered in the previous analysis are reflected.

Acknowledgments

This research has been carried out in the framework of the following projects: MODEL-CAOS (TIN2008-03582/TIN) financed by the Spanish Ministry of Education and Science, SISTEMAS (PII2I09-0150-3135) and SERENIDAD (PEII11-0327-7035) financed by the "Viceconsejería de Ciencia y Tecnología de la Junta de Comunidades de Castilla-La Mancha" and FEDER, and BUSINESS project (PET2008-0136) financed by the "Ministerio de Ciencia e Innovación", Spain.

References

1. Fernandez, E.B., Pan, R.: A pattern language for security models PLoP 13 (2001)
2. Internet Crime Complaint Center. IC3, http://www.ic3.gov
3. Stoneburner, G., Goguen, A., Feringa, A.: Risk Management Guide for Information Technology Systems, pp. 800–830. NIST Special Publication (2002)
4. Schumacher, M., Fernandez, E.B., Hybertson, D., Buschmann, F., Sommerlad, P.: Security Patterns: Integrating Security and Systems Engineering (2006)
5. Gamma, E., et al.: Design Patterns: Elements of Reusable Object Oriented Software. Addison Wesley, London (1995)
6. Ortiz, R., Moral-García, S., Moral-Rubio, S., Vela, B., Garzás, J., Fernández-Medina, E.: Applicability of security patterns. In: Meersman, R., Dillon, T.S., Herrero, P. (eds.) IS 2010 – OTM 2010. LNCS, vol. 6426, pp. 672–684. Springer, Heidelberg (2010)
7. Busnel, P., El Khoury, P., Li, K., Saidane, A., Zannone, N.: S&D Pattern Deployment at Organizational Level: A Prototype for Remote Healthcare System. ENTCS, vol. 244, pp. 27–39 (2009)
8. Brown, S.G., Yip, F.: Integrating Pattern Concepts & Network Security Architecture. In: NOMS 2006: 10th IEEE/IFIP Network Operations and Management Symposium, pp. 1–4 (2006)
9. Fernandez, E.B., Wu, J., Larrondo-Petrie, M.M., Shao, Y.: On building secure SCADA systems using security patterns. In: CSIIRW 2009: Proceedings of the 5th Annual Workshop on Cyber Security and Information Intelligence Research, pp. 1–4. ACM Press, NY (2009)
10. Fernandez, E., et.al.: M.M.: Designing Secure SCADA Systems Using Security Patterns. In: 43rd Hawaii International Conference on System Sciences (HICSS), p. 8 (2010)
11. Bellebia, D., Douin, J.M.: Applying patterns to build a lightweight middleware for embedded systems. In: Proceedings of the 2006 Conference on Pattern Languages of Programs, ACM, Portland (2006)
12. Fernandez, E.B., Pelaez, J.C., Larrondo-Petrie, M.M.: Security Patterns for Voice over IP Networks. In: ICCGI 2007, International Multi-Conference on Computing in the Global Information Technology, pp. 33–33 (2007)

13. Xiangli, Q., Xuejun, Y., Jingwei, Z., Xuefeng, L.: Integration Patterns of Grid Security Service. In: Proceedings of the Sixth International Conference on Parallel and Distributed Computing Applications and Technologies, IEEE Computer Society, Los Alamitos (2005)
14. Lirong, D., Kendra, C.: Using FDAF to bridge the gap between enterprise and software architectures for security. Sci. Comput. Program. 66, 87–102 (2007)
15. Schnjakin, M., Menzel, M., Meinel, C.: A pattern-driven security advisor for service-oriented architectures. In: Proceedings of the 2009 ACM Workshop on Secure Web Services. ACM, Chicago (2009)
16. Michael, M., Robert, W., Christoph, M.: A Pattern-Driven Generation of Security Policies for Service-Oriented Architectures. In: Proceedings of the 2010 IEEE International Conference on Web Services, IEEE Computer Society, Los Alamitos (2010)
17. Delessy, N., Fernandez, E.B., Larrondo-Petrie, M.M.: A Pattern Language for Identity Management. In: ICCGI 2007, International Multi-Conference on Computing in the Global Information Technology. pp.31-31(2007)
18. Khawaja, A., Urban, J.: A synthesis of evaluation criteria for software specifications and specifications techniques. International Journal of Software Engineering and Knowledge Engineering 12, 581–599
19. Kienzle, D.M., Elder, M.C., Tyree, D.S., Edwards-Hewitt, J.: Security patterns template and tutorial (2002)
20. Jürjens, J.: Secure Systems Development with UML. Springer, Heidelberg (2004)
21. Fernandez, E.B.: Security Patterns and A Methodology to Apply them. Security and Dependability for Ambient Intelligence, 37–46 (2009)
22. Fernandez, E.B., Larrondo-Petrie, M.M., Sorgente, T., VanHilst, M.: A methodology to develop secure systems using patterns. In: Integrating Security and Software Engineering, Advances and Future Vision, ch.5, pp. 107–126. IDEA Press (2006)
23. Sanchez-Cid, F., Maña, A.: SERENITY Pattern-Based Software Development Life-Cycle. In: Bhowmick, S.S., Küng, J., Wagner, R. (eds.) DEXA 2008. LNCS, vol. 5181, pp. 305–309. Springer, Heidelberg (2008)
24. Moral-García, S., Ortiz, R., Moral-Rubio, S., Vela, B., Garzás, J., Fernández-Medina, E.: A New Pattern Template to Support the Design of Security Architectures. In: The Second International Conferences of Pervasive Patterns and Applications, Lisbon, Portugal (2010)

Modeling Support for Delegating Roles, Tasks, and Duties in a Process-Related RBAC Context

Sigrid Schefer and Mark Strembeck

Institute for Information Systems and New Media
Vienna University of Economics and Business (WU Vienna), Austria
{firstname.lastname}@wu.ac.at

Abstract. The definition of access control concepts at the modeling level is an important prerequisite for the thorough implementation and enforcement of corresponding policies and constraints in a software system. In this paper, we present an approach to provide modeling support for the delegation of roles, tasks, and duties in the context of process-related RBAC models. The delegation model elements are integrated into a software engineering and business process context by providing UML2 modeling support for role-, task-, and duty-level delegation. The semantics of our UML extension are formally specified via OCL constraints.

Keywords: Access Control, Delegation, RBAC, UML.

1 Introduction

In recent years, role-based access control (RBAC) [8,12] has developed into a de facto standard for access control. In the area of workflow modeling, roles are also used as an abstract concept for delegation [6,17] or for the assignment of duties defined via obligations [13,15,21]. Delegation provides a mechanism to increase flexibility in security management. In essence, one subject can delegate its permissions and duties to another subject [13]. Subsequently, the subject receiving the delegation will act on behalf of the delegator. In order to model the delegation of roles, tasks, and duties in a process-related context, we need an approach that integrates the different concepts in a modeling language. However, standard process modeling languages, such as BPMN or UML Activity diagrams [11], do not provide native language constructs to model RBAC elements. Due to missing modeling support for process-related delegation of roles, tasks, and duties, organizations often try to specify delegation processes via informal textual comments. However, such work-arounds easily result in significant problems regarding consistency between process descriptions and actual process executions [18], and they make it difficult to translate the respective modeling-level concepts to actual software systems.

In this paper, we present an approach for the integrated modeling of business processes and the delegation of roles, tasks, and duties. For this purpose, we present a UML metamodel extension to model the delegation of roles, tasks, and duties via extended UML2 Activity diagrams. Moreover, we formally define the semantics of our newly introduced UML elements via OCL constraints. The remainder of this paper is structured as follows. Section 2 introduces our extension for UML Activity diagrams which allows for the process-related modeling of the proposed delegation model elements. Subsequently, Section 3 presents an example business process model including delegation. Section 4 discusses our approach in comparison to related work and Section 5 concludes the paper.

2 UML Extension for Modeling Delegation

An organization's business processes and software systems are often modeled via graphical modeling languages. The Unified Modeling Language (UML) [11] offers a comprehensive and well-defined modeling framework and is the de facto standard for modeling and specifying information systems. Providing modeling support for delegation of roles, tasks, and duties in business processes via a standard notation like UML can bridge the communication gap between software engineers, security experts, and non-technical stakeholders (see, e.g., [9]).

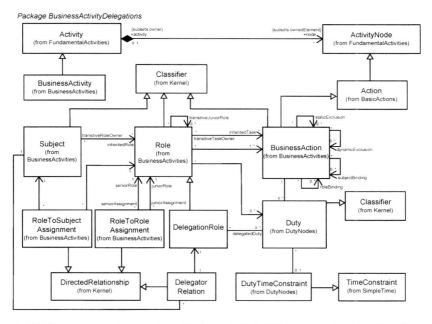

Fig. 1. UML metamodel extension *BusinessActivityDelegations* for Activity diagrams

To achieve the above, we model the delegation of roles, tasks, and duties via *extended UML2 Activity diagrams*. UML2 Activity models provide a process modeling language that allows to model the control and object flows between different actions (for details on UML2 Activity models, see [11]). We introduce a UML metamodel extension *BusinessActivityDelegations* for modeling delegation of roles, tasks, and duties (see Figure 1). Moreover, we use OCL invariants [10] to define the semantics by encoding delegation-specific constraints.

A *BusinessActivity* is a special UML Activity (see Figure 1). It can include all elements available for ordinary UML Activities in addition to our newly introduced elements. A *BusinessAction* corresponds to a task and comprises all necessary permissions to perform the task (see [16] for further details on BusinessActivities and BusinessActions). A *Duty* is a special UML Classifier (see Figure 1) and is used to model that an action must be performed by a certain Subject [14]. The link between Duties and BusinessActions assures that a Subject being assigned to a Duty also receives all necessary permissions to perform these Duties. *Roles* and *Subjects* are specialised UML Classifiers [16] which are linked to BusinessActions and Duties (see Figure 1). Furthermore, a Duty may be linked to a *DutyTimeConstraint* which is a specialised UML TimeConstraint (from the SimpleTime package, see [11]). If a DutyTimeConstraint has expired, a *Compensation Action* is triggered which is defined as stereotype of the Action metaclass (see [14] for further details).

A *DelegationRole* is a special type of Role which is assigned to a set of delegated Roles, BusinessActions, and/or Duties (see Figure 1). A *DelegatorRelation* is a special UML DirectedRelationship (from the Kernel package, see [11]) and indicates that a certain Subject acts as a delegator for a special DelegationRole. Only delegators may delegate Roles, BusinessActions, or Duties to Delegation-Roles (see OCL constraint 1). DelegationRoles are assigned to delegatees which thereby are authorized to perform the respective BusinessActions and Duties (see OCL constraint 2). A delegator can *delegate a Role* by defining this Role as junior role of one of his or her DelegationRoles. All BusinessActions and Duties assigned to this Role need to be delegatable (see below). Note, DelegationRoles must not have senior regular Roles to avoid invalid permission inheritance (see OCL constraint 3). For *delegating a BusinessAction*, the delegator assigns the BusinessAction to the respective DelegationRole. Only if a BusinessAction is delegatable, it can be delegated to a DelegationRole (see OCL constraints 4 and 6). To realize *delegation of Duties* in UML models, a Duty also needs to be defined as being delegatable (see OCL constraints 5, 7, and 9). After assigning a delegatee, the delegator loses his obligation to perform this Duty. Yet, a review duty can be defined [13] which obliges the delegator to control the proper enforcement of his delegated Duties (see OCL constraints 8 and 9).

OCL Constraint 1. *The delegator of a Duty, a BusinessAction, or a Role needs to be the Subject who is directly assigned to the respective delegation unit:*

```
context Subject
inv: self.delegatorRelation.delegationRole.delegatedDuty.role->exists(r |
        r.roleToSubjectAssignment->exists(rsa |
            rsa.subject.name = self.name ))
inv: self.delegatorRelation.delegationRole.businessaction.role->exists(r |
        r.roleToSubjectAssignment->exists(rsa |
            rsa.subject.name = self.name ))
inv: self.delegatorRelation.delegationRole.juniorAssignment.role->exists((r |
        r.roleToSubjectAssignment->exists(rsa |
            rsa.subject.name = self.name ))
```

OCL Constraint 2. *Each DelegationRole defines an attribute called "delegatee". The delegatee is the responsibleSubject for the delegated BusinessActions and Duties:*

```
context DelegationRole inv:
self.instanceSpecification->forAll(i |
  self.businessAction.instanceSpecification->forall(b |
    self.delegatedDuty.instanceSpecification->forall(d |
      i.slot->select(s | s.definingFeature.name = delegatee
        b.slot->select(rsb | rsb.definingFeature.name = responsibleSubject
          d.slot->select(rsd | rsd.definingFeature.name = responsibleSubject
            s.value = rsb.value and
            s.value = rsd.value ))))))
```

OCL Constraint 3. *A DelegationRole is only allowed to have senior-assignments to other DelegationRoles (see [20]):*

```
context DelegationRole
inv: self.seniorAssignment->forAll(sa | sa.seniorrole.oclIsKindOf(DelegationRole))
```

OCL Constraint 4. *Each BusinessAction defines an attribute called "delegatable" stating if a special BusinessAction may be delegated or not:*

```
context BusinessAction inv:
self.instanceSpecification->forAll(i | i.slot->exists(s | s.definingFeature.name = delegatable))
```

OCL Constraint 5. *Each Duty defines an attribute called "delegatable":*

```
context Duty inv:
self.instanceSpecification->forAll(i | i.slot->exists(s | s.definingFeature.name = delegatable))
```

OCL Constraint 6. *Each BusinessAction defines an attribute called "isDelegated" stating if a special BusinessAction has already been delegated or not. If it has already been delegated, it cannot be delegated further (single-step delegation, see [3]):*

```
context BusinessAction inv:
self.instanceSpecification->forAll(i |
  i.slot->exists(s | s.definingFeature.name = isDelegated and
    if s.value = true then
      i.slot->exists(d | d.definingFeature.name = delegateable and
        d.value = false)
    else true endif ))
```

OCL Constraint 7. *Duties define an attribute "isDelegated" (single-step delegation):*

```
context Duty inv:
self.instanceSpecification->forAll(i |
  i.slot->exists(s | s.definingFeature.name = isDelegated and
    if s.value = true then
      i.slot->exists(d | d.definingFeature.name = delegateable and
        d.value = false )
    else true endif ))
```

OCL Constraint 8. *Each Duty defines an attribute called "isReviewDuty" [13]:*

```
context Duty inv:
self.instanceSpecification->forAll(i |
  i.slot->exists(s | s.definingFeature.name = isReviewDuty ))
```

OCL Constraint 9. *If a Duty is delegatable, it cannot be a reviewDuty. If a Duty is a reviewDuty, it is not delegatable. Furthermore, if a Duty is a reviewDuty, it must not have been delegated [13]:*

```
context Duty inv:
  self.instanceSpecification->forAll(i |
    i.slot->select(d | d.definingFeature.name = delegatable
      i.slot->select(r | r.definingFeature.name = isReviewDuty
        i.slot->selelct(si |
          si.definingFeature.name = isDelegated and
          d.delegatable.value <> r.isReviewDuty.value and
          r.isReviewDuty.value <> si.isDelegated.value ))))
```

To consider the aspect of permanence in delegation [3], our DelegationRoles can either be defined for *temporary* or for *permanent* delegation, i.e. for one or for all instances of a business process (see OCL constraints 10 and 11). Furthermore, we support *single-* and *multi-step delegation* for BusinessActions and Duties. Single-step delegation means that a delegated BusinessAction or Duty can not be delegated further by the delegatee [3]. This is achieved by defining an attribute called *isDelegated* for each BusinessAction and for each Duty. The isDelegated attribute is set to true as soon as the respective BusinessAction or Duty has been delegated. If a BusinessAction's or a Duty's isDelegated-attribute is set to true, its *delegatable*-attribute is set to false (see OCL constraints 6 and 7). Multi-step delegation can easily be activated by using OCL constraints 12 and 13.

OCL Constraint 10. *Each DelegationRole defines an attribute called "isTemporary" indicating if a DelegationRole is intended for temporary or for permanent delegation:*

```
context DelegationRole inv:
self.instanceSpecification->forAll(i |
   i.slot->select(si | si.definingFeature.name = isTemporary ))
```

OCL Constraint 11. *If a DelegationRole is intended for temporary delegation only (isTemporary=true), it defines an attribute called "relatedProcessInstance" to ensure that the respective DelegationRole can only be used in the defined process instance:*

```
context DelegationRole inv:
self.instanceSpecification->forAll(i |
   self.businessAction.activity.instanceSpecification->exists(a |
      i.slot->select(si | si.definingFeature.name = isTemporary
         if si.value = true then
            i.slot->select(so | so.definingFeature.name = relatedProcessInstance
               a.slot->select(sa | sa.definingFeature.name = processID and
                  so.value = sa.value ))
         else true endif )))
```

OCL Constraint 12. *To allow for multi-step delegation of BusinessActions, use the following OCL constraint instead of OCL constraint 6:*

```
context BusinessAction inv:
self.instanceSpecification->forAll(i | i.slot->exists(s | s.definingFeature.name = isDelegated)
```

OCL Constraint 13. *To allow for multi-step delegation of Duties, use the following OCL constraint instead of OCL constraint 7:*

```
context Duty inv:
self.instanceSpecification->forAll(i | i.slot->exists(s | s.definingFeature.name = isDelegated)
```

3 Example Process with Delegation

In Figure 2, a standard UML2 credit application process is extended by including the new modeling constructs introduced in Section 2. However, note, that the visualization presented here primarily serves as a presentation option to graphically illustrate the relations between the modeling elements. As each UML model needs to conform to its OCL constraints (see Section 2), the formally defined relations exist independent of their actual graphical representation (see [10,11]).

The process in Figure 2a) includes five actions, three of which are defined as BusinessActions. The BusinessActions are associated with Duties. In addition, the Compensation Action *Reassign Duty* is triggered if the Duty *Check applicant rating* is not discharged in time. Figure 2b) presents the Duty *Check applicant*

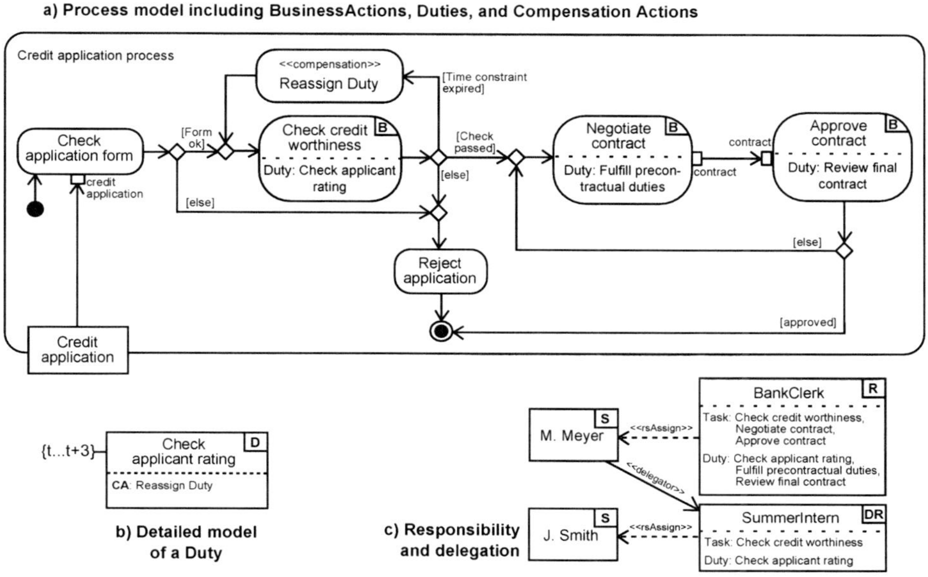

Fig. 2. Extended credit application process

rating which is connected to the BusinessAction *Check credit worthiness*. It is associated with a DutyTimeConstraint and a Compensation Action. The DutyTimeConstraint expresses that the Duty *Check applicant rating* needs to be completed within three time units (e.g. days) after the corresponding BusinessAction has been started. Otherwise, the Compensation Action *Reassign Duty* is executed.

The responsibility for the Duties is illustrated in Figure 2c) showing the Role BankClerk which is assigned to the three BusinessActions and the associated Duties defined in the credit application process. Thus, a Subject assigned to the BankClerk role is responsible for performing these Duties and related BusinessActions. In this example, the Subject *M. Meyer* is assigned to the BankClerk role and therefore also needs to discharge the associated Duties. M. Meyer decides to delegate her Duty *Check applicant rating* to her summer intern *J. Smith*. For this purpose, she creates a permanent DelegationRole *SummerIntern* and assigns the Duty to the DelegationRole. Subsequently, she assigns the Subject *J. Smith* to her DelegationRole *SummerIntern*. J. Smith is now authorized and responsible for discharging the Duty *Check applicant rating* when performing the BusinessAction *Check credit worthiness*, until either the Duty is revoked from the DelegationRole or he loses his assignment to the DelegationRole.

4 Related Work

To the best of our knowledge, this work represents the first attempt to address delegation of duties from a business process modeling context. Other approaches usually concentrate on the modeling of authorization constraints. As each duty holder also needs sufficient authority to perform the assigned duties [13,15], our approach complements existing approaches. In recent years, there has been much work on various aspects of delegation (see, e.g., [2,19,20]), especially in a business process context. In [1], the notion of delegation is extended to allow for conditional delegation. Different types of constraints, such as authorization constraints, are addressed in the context of delegation. The effects of some delegation operations on three workflow execution models are described in [7]. In [5], the satisfiability problem of workflows while supporting user delegation mechanisms is addressed. Moreover, duties/obligations may also be subject to delegation. However, the delegation of duties has received little attention in literature so far, although it has been identified as important phenomenon, e.g., in [4], where different ways of delegating obligations are discussed. In [13], some issues for delegation of obligations are considered, mainly addressing the reasons for delegating obligations and the balance between authorizations and obligations.

5 Conclusion

Our UML2 extension can help organizations to integrate the specification of processes and related access control, obligation, and delegation policies. An integrated modeling approach yields a number of advantages, such as supporting a proper mapping of models to software systems, facilitating communication between different stakeholders, making responsibility for tasks and duties explicit, and detecting task- or duty-related conflicts. Moreover, it allows for tracing policy rules to the (regulatory) reasons they exist and to trace them to the software components that have to ensure their monitoring and enforcement. This facilitates the reporting on a company's fulfillment of compliance requirements. We chose to define an extension to the UML2 standard to enable a complete and correct mapping between policies, models, and the respective software system. This mapping assures consistency between modeling-level specifications and the software system enforcing respective policies and process instances.

References

1. Atluri, V., Warner, J.: Supporting conditional delegation in secure workflow management systems. In: Proceedings of the Tenth ACM Symposium on Access Control Models and Technologies (SACMAT), pp. 49–58 (2005)
2. Barka, E., Sandhu, R.: A Role-Based Delegation Model and Some Extensions. In: Proceedings of the 23rd National Information Systems Security Conference, NISSEC (2000)
3. Barka, E., Sandhu, R.: Framework for Role-Based Delegation Models. In: Proceedings of the 16th Annual Computer Security Applications Conference (2000)
4. Cole, J., Derrick, J., Milosevic, Z., Raymond, K.: Author obliged to submit paper before 4 july: Policies in an enterprise specification. In: Sloman, M., Lobo, J., Lupu, E.C. (eds.) POLICY 2001. LNCS, vol. 1995, pp. 1–17. Springer, Heidelberg (2001)

5. Crampton, J., Khambhammettu, H.: Delegation and Satisfiability in Workflow Systems. In: Proceedings of the 13th ACM Symposium on Access Control Models and Technologies (SACMAT), pp. 31–40 (2008)
6. Crampton, J., Khambhammettu, H.: Delegation in role-based access control. International Journal of Information Security 7(2), 123–136 (2008)
7. Crampton, J., Khambhammettu, H.: On Delegation and Workflow Execution Models. In: Proceedings of the 2008 ACM symposium on Applied computing, SAC (2008)
8. Ferraiolo, D.F., Kuhn, D.R., Chandramouli, R.: Role-Based Access Control, 2nd edn. Artech House (2007)
9. Mouratidis, H., Jürjens, J.: From Goal-Driven Security Requirements Engineering to Secure Design. International Journal of Intelligent Systems 25(8), 813 (2010)
10. OMG. Object Constraint Language Specification. available at: technology documents formal o cl.htm, Version 2.2, formal/2010-02-01, The Object Management Group (February 2010), http://www.omg.org
11. OMG. Unified Modeling Language (OMG UML): Superstructure. available at: http://www.omg.org technology documents formalu ml.htm, May 2010. Version 2.3, formal/2010-05-05, The Object Management Group.
12. Sandhu, R., Coyne, E., Feinstein, H., Youman, C.: Role-Based Access Control Models. IEEE Computer 29(2) (1996)
13. Schaad, A., Moffett, J.D.: Delegation of Obligations. In: Proceedings of the 3rd International Workshop on Policies for Distributed Systems and Networks, POLICY (2002)
14. Schefer, S., Strembeck, M.: Modeling Process-Related Duties with Extended UML Activity and Interaction Diagrams. Proc. of the International Workshop on Flexible Workflows in Distributed Systems, Workshops der Wissenschaftlichen Konferenz Kommunikationin Verteilten Systemen (WowKiVS), Electronic Communications of the EASST 37 (2011)
15. Strembeck, M.: Embedding Policy Rules for Software-Based Systems in a Requirements Context. In: Proceedings of the 6th IEEE International Workshop on Policies for Distributed Systems and Networks, POLICY (2005)
16. Strembeck, M., Mendling, J.: Modeling Process-related RBAC Models with Extended UML Activity Models. Information and Software Technology 53(5) (2010), doi:10.1016/j.infsof.2010.11.015
17. Wainer, J., Kumar, A., Barthelmess, P.: DW-RBAC: A formal security model of delegation and revocation in workflow systems. Information Systems 32(3), 365–384 (2007)
18. Wolter, C., Menzel, M., Schaad, A., Miseldine, P., Meinel, C.: Model-driven business process security requirement specification. Journal of Systems Architecture 55(4), 211–223 (2009)
19. Zhang, L., Ahn, G.-J., Chu, B.-T.: A Rule-Based Framework for Role-Based Delegation and Revocation. ACM Transations on Information System Security (TISSEC) 6(3), 404–441 (2003)
20. Zhang, X., Oh, S., Sandhu, R.: PBDM: A Flexible Delegation Model in RBAC. In: Proceedings of the Eighth ACM Symposium on Access Control Models and Technologies (SACMAT), pp. 149–157 (2003)
21. Zhao, G., Chadwick, D., Otenko, S.: Obligations for Role Based Access Control. In: Proceedings of the 21st International Conference on Advanced Information Networking and Applications Workshops, vol. 01, pp. 424–431 (2007)

Author Index

Abdullah, Norris Syed   249
Abramov, Jenny   637
Agt, Henning   149
Akkermans, Hans   81
Allgaier, Matthias   414
Almeida, J.J.   501
Ameller, David   296
Amyot, Daniel   228
An, Yuan   119
Andersson, Birger   1, 45
Asplund, Fredrik   270

Bassiliades, Nick   478
Batista, David   489
Bauer, Bernhard   197, 437
Bauhoff, Gregor   149
Bernaert, Maxime   29
Bettin, Jorn   29, 164
Berwing, Carolin   208
Bharosa, Nitesh   238
Biehl, Matthias   270
Biondi, Franco   354
Bonazzi, Riccardo   57
Bos, Rik   259
Buckl, Sabine   528

Cabanillas, Cristina   218
Cappellari, Paolo   541
Carvalho, Paula   489
Castro, Jaelson   342
Ceccaroli, Charlotte   57
Challenger, Moharram   177
Chen, David   69
Christiaanse, Rob   238
Chun, Soon Ae   544
Chung, Lawrence   294
Claes, Jan   282
Clark, Tony   164
Cohen, Sholom   29
Corchuelo, Rafael   330
Couto, Francisco M.   489

Dascalu, Sergiu M.   354
das Graças, Alex Pinheiro   402

de Cesare, Sergio   397
De Leenheer, Pieter   81
Demirkol, Sebla   177
Dermeval, Diego   342
De Virgilio, Roberto   541
Dobson, Simon   425
Drury, Brett   501
Ducassé, Mireille   554

El-Khoury, Jad   270

Fatemi, Hassan   41
Favre, Julien   93
Fernández-Medina, Eduardo   652
Ferré, Sébastien   554
Fersini, E.   450
Fill, Hans-Georg   134
Foorthuis, Ralph   259
Franch, Xavier   102, 296
Frappier, Marc   607
Frenzel, Christoph   437
Fritscher, Boris   4
Fuentes, Lidia   318

Gabdulkhakova, Aygul   249
Gacitua-Decar, Veronica   366, 464
Gailly, Frederik   397
García-Barriocanal, Elena   513
Garzás, Javier   652
Geller, James   544
Getir, Sinem   177
Giannoulis, Constantinos   16
Gordijn, Jaap   81
Guédria, Wided   69
Guizzardi, Giancarlo   402
Guizzardi, Renata S.S.   402

Hadar, Ethan   302
Hadar, Irit   302
Harris Jr., Frederick C.   354
Harrison Jr, John J.   302
Haugen, Øystein   166
Hayek, Erich   93
Heller, Markus   414

Hermann, Alice 554
Hernández, Inma 330
Holland, Grant 397
Hong, Yi 564
Hulstijn, Joris 238

Idani, Akram 592
Indulska, Marta 207

Janke, Thomas 167
Janssen, Marijn 238

Karagiannis, Dimitris 102
Kardas, Geylani 177
Kathayat, Surya Bahadur 378
König-Ries, Birgitta 249
Konopacki, Pierre 607
Krcmar, Helmut 208
Kühn, Harald 104
Kutsche, Ralf-D. 149

Labiadh, Mohamed-Amine 592
Laleau, Régine 592, 607
Lammari, Nadira 590
Le, Hien 378
Ledru, Yves 592
Lucena, Márcia 342
Lulli, Guglielmo 385
Lycett, Mark 397

Machín, Rebeca 513
Massacci, Fabio 622
Matthes, Florian 528
McGinnes, Simon 586
McMahon Jr., Michael J. 354
Meditskos, Georgios 478
Miksa, Krzysztof 104
Milanovic, Nikola 149
Milhau, Jérémy 592
Missonier, Stéphanie 57
Morais, M.H.M. 501
Moreira, Silvio 489
Mylopoulos, John 622

Naudet, Yannick 69

Ortiz, Roberto 652
Overbeek, Sietse 207
Overhage, Sven 414

Paci, Federica 622
Pahl, Claus 366, 464
Palomares, Noelia 45
Parsia, Bijan 437
Partridge, Chris 397, 401
Pascual, Gustavo G. 318
Petit, Michaël 16
Pigneur, Yves 4
Pimentel, João 342
Pinto, Mónica 318
Poels, Geert 29, 282
Potena, Pasqualina 385
Pourshahid, Alireza 228

Qamar, Nafees 592

Raibulet, Claudia 385
Razo-Zapata, Iván S. 81
Regev, Gil 93
Reiff-Marganiec, Stephan 564
Reinhartz-Berger, Iris 164
Resinas, Manuel 218
Richier, Jean-Luc 592
Rivero, Carlos R. 330
Roantree, Mark 541
Romeikat, Raphael 197
Rosado, David G. 590
Ruiz, David 330
Ruiz-Cortés, Antonio 218
Rychkova, Irina 1

Sadiq, Shazia 207
Santos, Emanuel 342
Sartori, F. 450
Sattler, Ulrike 437
Schefer, Sigrid 660
Schermann, Michael 208
Schmid, Friso 238
Schüller, Peter 575
Schweda, Christian M. 528
Settas, Dimitrios 478
Shamsaei, Azalia 228
Sherman, Sofia 302
Shoval, Peretz 637
Sicilia, Miguel-Ángel 513
Silva, Mário J. 489
Song, Il-Yeol 119
Stamelos, Ioannis G. 478
Stevenson, Graeme 425

Strachan, Scotty 354
Strembeck, Mark 660
Sturm, Arnon 164, 637
Subramanian, Nary 294, 308

Tan, Yao-Hua 238
Thonggoom, Ornsiri 119
Tian, Tian 544
Törngren, Martin 270
Tun, Thein Thun 622
Turowski, Klaus 414

Valiente, María-Cruz 513
van Sinderen, Marten 41
van Wijk, Remco 238
Viscusi, Gianluigi 1

Wand, Yair 164
Wang, MingXue 366, 464
Wegmann, Alain 93
Weinzierl, Antonius 575
Wieringa, Roel 41
Wiesche, Manuel 208
Wilson, Paul 93

Yapa Bandara, Kosala 366, 464
Yu, Yijun 622

Zdravkovic, Jelena 16
Zivkovic, Srdjan 104
zur Muehlen, Michael 207
Zwanziger, André 187